Teach Yourself VISUALLY™ iLife® '04

by Michael E. Cohen and Dennis R. Cohen

Visual™

From
maranGraphics®
&
WILEY
Wiley Publishing, Inc.

Teach Yourself VISUALLY™ iLife® '04

Published by
Wiley Publishing, Inc.
111 River Street
Hoboken, NJ 07030-5774

Published simultaneously in Canada

Copyright © 2004 by Wiley Publishing, Inc., Indianapolis, Indiana

Certain designs and illustrations Copyright © 1992-2004 maranGraphics, Inc., used with maranGraphics' permission.

maranGraphics, Inc.
5755 Coopers Avenue
Mississauga, Ontario, Canada
L4Z 1R9

No part of this publication may be reproduced, stored in a retrieval system, or transmitted in any form or by any means, electronic, mechanical, photocopying, recording, scanning, or otherwise, except as permitted under Section 107 or 108 of the 1976 United States Copyright Act, without either the prior written permission of the Publisher, or authorization through payment of the appropriate per-copy fee to the Copyright Clearance Center, 222 Rosewood Drive, Danvers, MA 01923, 978-750-8400, fax 978-646-8600, or on the web at www.copyright.com. You can contact the Publisher directly for permission by email at permcoordinator@wiley.com or on the web at www.wiley.com/about/permission.

Library of Congress Control Number: 2003116994

ISBN: 0-7645-4466-7

Manufactured in the United States of America
10 9 8 7 6 5 4 3 2 1

1K/QT/QV/QU/IN

Trademark Acknowledgments

Wiley, the Wiley Publishing logo, Visual, the Visual logo, Read Less - Learn More and related trade dress are trademarks or registered trademarks of John Wiley & Sons, Inc. and/or its affiliates. The maranGraphics logo is a trademark or registered trademark of maranGraphics, Inc. iLife is a registered trademark of Apple Computer, Inc. All other trademarks are the property of their respective owners. Wiley Publishing, Inc. and maranGraphics, Inc. are not associated with any product or vendor mentioned in this book.

FOR PURPOSES OF ILLUSTRATING THE CONCEPTS AND TECHNIQUES DESCRIBED IN THIS BOOK, THE AUTHOR HAS CREATED VARIOUS NAMES, COMPANY NAMES, MAILING, E-MAIL AND INTERNET ADDRESSES, PHONE AND FAX NUMBERS AND SIMILAR INFORMATION, ALL OF WHICH ARE FICTITIOUS. ANY RESEMBLANCE OF THESE FICTITIOUS NAMES, ADDRESSES, PHONE AND FAX NUMBERS AND SIMILAR INFORMATION TO ANY ACTUAL PERSON, COMPANY AND/OR ORGANIZATION IS UNINTENTIONAL AND PURELY COINCIDENTAL.

Important Numbers

For U.S. corporate orders, please call maranGraphics at 800-469-6616 or fax 905-890-9434.

For general information on our other products and services or to obtain technical support please contact our Customer Care Department within the U.S. at 800-762-2974, outside the U.S. at 317-572-3993 or fax 317-572-4002.

Permissions

maranGraphics
Certain text and Illustrations by maranGraphics, Inc., used with maranGraphics' permission.

LIMIT OF LIABILITY/DISCLAIMER OF WARRANTY: THE PUBLISHER AND THE AUTHOR MAKE NO REPRESENTATIONS OR WARRANTIES WITH RESPECT TO THE ACCURACY OR COMPLETENESS OF THE CONTENTS OF THIS WORK AND SPECIFICALLY DISCLAIM ALL WARRANTIES, INCLUDING WITHOUT LIMITATION WARRANTIES OF FITNESS FOR A PARTICULAR PURPOSE. NO WARRANTY MAY BE CREATED OR EXTENDED BY SALES OR PROMOTIONAL MATERIALS. THE ADVICE AND STRATEGIES CONTAINED HEREIN MAY NOT BE SUITABLE FOR EVERY SITUATION. THIS WORK IS SOLD WITH THE UNDERSTANDING THAT THE PUBLISHER IS NOT ENGAGED IN RENDERING LEGAL, ACCOUNTING, OR OTHER PROFESSIONAL SERVICES. IF PROFESSIONAL ASSISTANCE IS REQUIRED, THE SERVICES OF A COMPETENT PROFESSIONAL PERSON SHOULD BE SOUGHT. NEITHER THE PUBLISHER NOR THE AUTHOR SHALL BE LIABLE FOR DAMAGES ARISING HEREFROM. THE FACT THAT AN ORGANIZATION OR WEBSITE IS REFERRED TO IN THIS WORK AS A CITATION AND/OR A POTENTIAL SOURCE OF FURTHER INFORMATION DOES NOT MEAN THAT THE AUTHOR OR THE PUBLISHER ENDORSES THE INFORMATION THE ORGANIZATION OR WEBSITE MAY PROVIDE OR RECOMMENDATIONS IT MAY MAKE. FURTHER, READERS SHOULD BE AWARE THAT INTERNET WEBSITES LISTED IN THIS WORK MAY HAVE CHANGED OR DISAPPEARED BETWEEN WHEN THIS WORK WAS WRITTEN AND WHEN IT IS READ.

Wiley Publishing, Inc.

U.S. Corporate Sales
Contact maranGraphics
at (800) 469-6616 or
fax (905) 890-9434.

U.S. Trade Sales
Contact Wiley
at (800) 762-2974 or
fax (317) 572-4002.

Some comments from our readers...

"I have to praise you and your company on the fine products you turn out. I have twelve of the *Teach Yourself VISUALLY* and *Simplified* books in my house. They were instrumental in helping me pass a difficult computer course. Thank you for creating books that are easy to follow."
— Gordon Justin (Brielle, NJ)

"I commend your efforts and your success. I teach in an outreach program for the Dr. Eugene Clark Library in Lockhart, TX. Your *Teach Yourself VISUALLY* books are incredible, and I use them in my computer classes. All my students love them!"
— Michele Schalin (Lockhart, TX)

"Like a lot of other people, I understand things best when I see them visually. Your books really make learning easy and life more fun."
— John T. Frey (Cadillac, MI)

"I have quite a few of your Visual books and have been very pleased with all of them. I love the way the lessons are presented!"
— Mary Jane Newman (Yorba Linda, CA)

"I write to extend my thanks and appreciation for your books. They are clear, easy to follow, and straight to the point. Keep up the good work!"
— Seward Kollie (Dakar, Senegal)

"I am an avid fan of your Visual books. If I need to learn anything, I just buy one of your books and learn the topic in no time. Wonders! I have even trained my friends to give me Visual books as gifts."
— Illona Bergstrom (Aventura, FL)

"Thank you for making it so clear. I appreciate it. I will buy many more Visual books."
— J.P. Sangdong (North York, Ontario, Canada)

"I was introduced to maranGraphics about four years ago and YOU ARE THE GREATEST THING THAT EVER HAPPENED TO INTRODUCTORY COMPUTER BOOKS!"
— Glenn Nettleton (Huntsville, AL)

"Compliments to the chef!! Your books are extraordinary! Or, simply put, extra-ordinary, meaning way above the rest! THANK YOU THANK YOU THANK YOU! for creating these."
— Christine J. Manfrin (Castle Rock, CO)

"I just purchased my third Visual book (my first two are dog-eared now!) and, once again, your product has surpassed my expectations. The expertise, thought, and effort that go into each book are obvious, and I sincerely appreciate your efforts. Keep up the wonderful work!"
— Tracey Moore (Memphis, TN)

"Thank you, thank you, thank you...for making it so easy for me to break into this high-tech world. I now own four of your books. I recommend them to anyone who is a beginner like myself. Now...if you could just do one for programming VCR's, it would make my day!"
— Gay O'Donnell (Calgary, Alberta, Canada)

"You're marvelous! I am greatly in your debt."
— Patrick Baird (Lacey, WA)

maranGraphics is a family-run business
located near Toronto, Canada.

At **maranGraphics**, we believe in producing great computer books — one book at a time.

maranGraphics has been producing high-technology products for over 25 years, which enables us to offer the computer book community a unique communication process.

Our computer books use an integrated communication process, which is very different from the approach used in other computer books. Each spread is, in essence, a flow chart — the text and screen shots are totally incorporated into the layout of the spread.

Introductory text and helpful tips complete the learning experience.

maranGraphics' approach encourages the left and right sides of the brain to work together — resulting in faster orientation and greater memory retention.

Above all, we are very proud of the handcrafted nature of our books. Our carefully-chosen writers are experts in their fields, and spend countless hours researching and organizing the content for each topic. Our artists rebuild every screen shot to provide the best

clarity possible, making our screen shots the most precise and easiest to read in the industry. We strive for perfection, and believe that the time spent handcrafting each element results in the best computer books money can buy.

Thank you for purchasing this book. We hope you enjoy it!

Sincerely,

Robert Maran
President
maranGraphics
Rob@maran.com
www.maran.com

CREDITS

Project Editor
Maureen Spears

Acquisitions Editor
Tom Heine

Product Development Manager
Lindsay Sandman

Copy Editors
Kim Heusel
Marylouise Wiack

Technical Editor
Lisa Spangenberg

Editorial Manager
Robyn Siesky

Senior Permissions Editor
Carmen Krikorian

Manufacturing
Allan Conley
Linda Cook
Paul Gilchrist
Jennifer Guynn

Illustrators
Karl Brandt
Ronda David-Burroughs
David E. Gregory
Sean Johanessen
Russ Marini
Steven Schaerer
Mary Gillot Virgin

Book Design
maranGraphics®

Production Coordinators
Maridee Ennis
Courtney MacIntyre

Layout
LeAndra Hosier
Kristin McMullan

Screen Artist
Jill A. Proll

Proofreader
Laura L. Bowman

Quality Control
John Greenough
Susan Moritz

Indexer
Joan Griffitts

Special Help
John Tyler Connoley
Kim Heusel
Adrienne Porter

Vice President and Executive Group Publisher
Richard Swadley

Vice President and Publisher
Barry Pruett

Composition Director
Debbie Stailey

ABOUT THE AUTHORS

Michael E. Cohen has been straddling the Great Divide between the humanities and the sciences for almost thirty years. He is a pioneer developer of instructional writing software and electronic books, a co-founder of a major university's humanities computing center, and a three-time contributing editor to the *Macintosh Bible*. He lives in Santa Monica, CA, with his wife, Lisa, and a closet full of delightfully obsolete computers and peripherals.

Dennis R. Cohen is the author, or co-author of, the *iLife Bible*, *Mac Digital Photography*, and a half-dozen other titles, as well as a contributor to, or the technical editor of, a wide variety of other Macintosh and cross-platform books. As a software developer of over 20 years, and a Mac developer since Mac's release in 1984, Dennis has vast experience not only with the Mac, but also with other platforms, including Unix. He lives in Sunnyvale, CA, with his Boston Terrier, Spenser.

AUTHORS' ACKNOWLEDGMENTS

We'd like to express our thanks to Bruce Kijewski for the loan of some equipment as well as for his cameo appearance, Dr. Tom Beghin for the use of his performance videos, and a certain hummingbird for uncharacteristic cooperation. Special thanks go to our project editor for guiding us along the VISUALLY path and keeping us out of the thickets along the way.

Michael's Dedication:
To a most beloved Digital
Medievalist, my muse in geek's clothing.

Dennis' Dedication:
To Michael, who made this book a reality,
and to Spenser, who gets me out in all sorts of weather.

TABLE OF CONTENTS

GETTING STARTED WITH ILIFE

1) Getting Started with iLife

Introducing the iLife Programs 4
Understanding iTunes 6
Understanding iPhoto 8
Understanding iMovie 10
Understanding iDVD 12
Understanding GarageBand 14
Explore the Macintosh Dock 16
Start and Quit an iLife Application 17
Explore the Finder 18
Open and Save Files 20

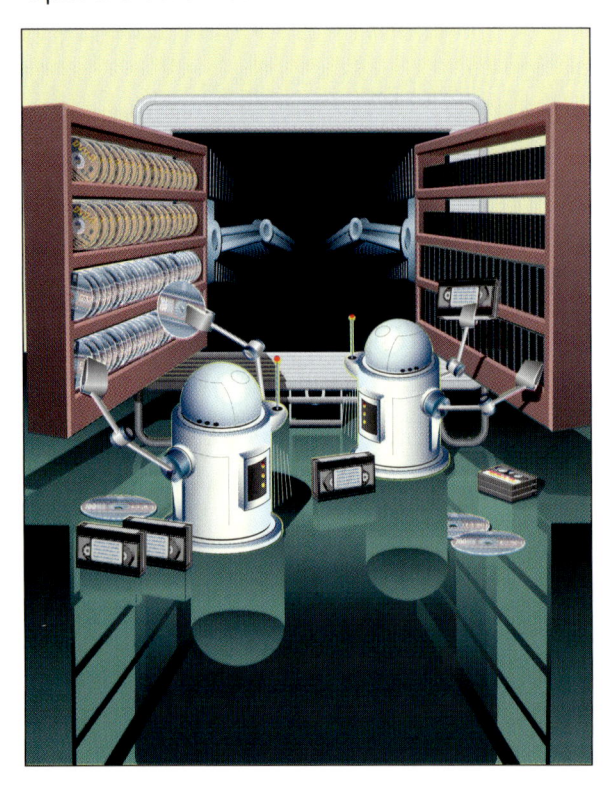

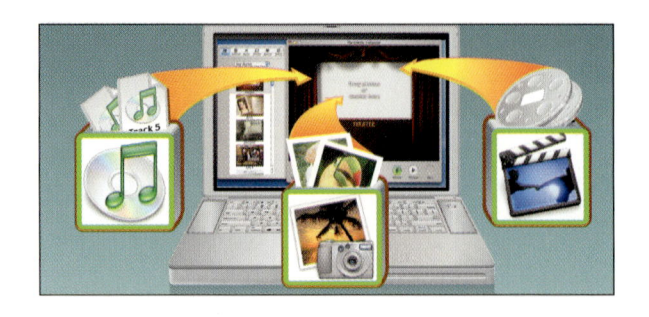

WORKING WITH ITUNES

2) iTunes Basics

Set Up iTunes 24
Play a CD 28
Rip a Music CD 30
Search the Music Library 32
Browse the Music Library 34
Remove a Song from the Music Library 36
Rate a Song 38
Play Internet Radio 40
Add an Internet Radio Station 42
Share Music over a Network 44

3) Creating Playlists and Burning Disks with iTunes

Create a Playlist 46
Rearrange a Playlist 48
Burn a Standard Audio CD 50
Burn an MP3 CD .52
Burn an Archive CD or DVD 53
Create a Simple Smart Playlist 54
Create an Advanced Smart Playlist 56

4) Using the iTunes Music Store

Sign Into and Out of the iTunes Music Store 58
Search the iTunes Music Store 60
Purchase Music with 1-Click Shopping 62
Purchase Music with the Shopping Cart 64
Deauthorize a Computer to Play
    Purchased Music 66

5) Using Advanced iTunes Features

Using the Equalizer 68
View and Add Album Artwork 70
Change the Import Format 72
Convert a Song's Format 74
Set a Song's Tag Information 76
Change an Album's Tag Information 78
Adjust a Song's Start and End Times 80
Using the Visualizer .82
Update Songs on an iPod 84
Copy Songs to and Delete Songs from
    an iPod 86

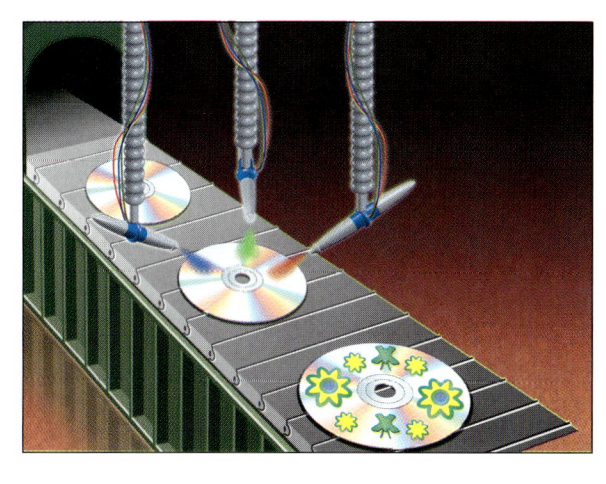

WORKING WITH IPHOTO

6) iPhoto Basics

Set Up iPhoto 90
Import Images from a Camera 92
Import Images from a Card Reader 94
Import Images from Files 96
Organize the iPhoto Library by Film Roll 98
Set Photo Titles and Descriptions 100
Assign Keywords to Photos 102
Organize the iPhoto Library by Date, Title,
    or Rating 104
View Photo Information 106
Rotate a Photo 108
Delete Photos from the iPhoto Library 110
Create an Album 112
Organize an Album 114
Share Photos on a Network 116
Create a Smart Album 118

TABLE OF CONTENTS

7) Editing Photos with iPhoto

Adjust the Edit View	120
Select and Crop a Photo	122
Enhance a Photo's Color	124
Change a Photo to Black and White, or Sepia	125
Eliminate Red Eye	126
Retouch a Photo	128
Adjust Brightness and Contrast	130
Using a Separate iPhoto Editing Window	132
Customize a Separate iPhoto Editing Window	134
Using a Separate Picture Editing Program in iPhoto	136

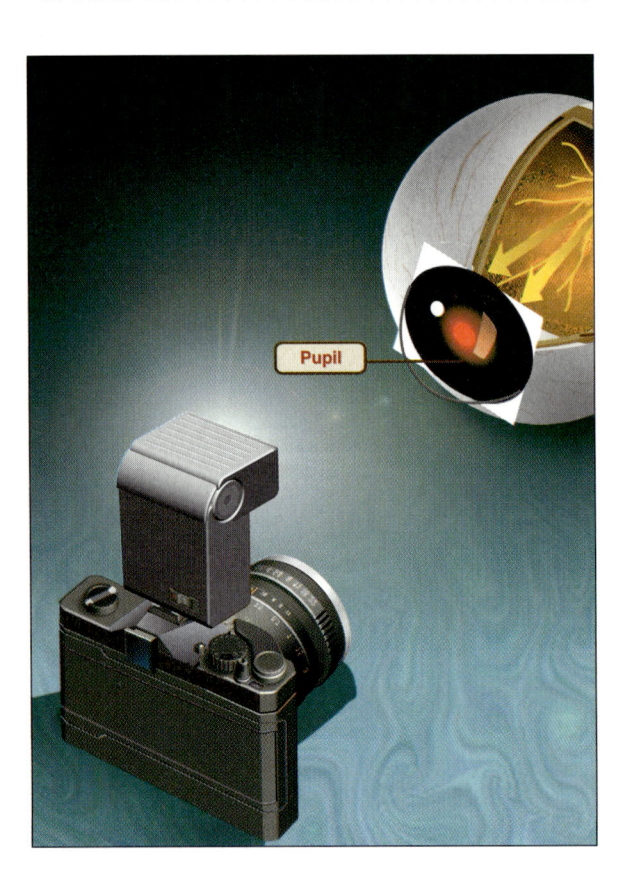

8) Using Photos with iPhoto

E-mail a Photo	138
Print a Photo	140
Create a Slideshow	142
Save a Slideshow as a QuickTime Movie	144
Make a Slideshow DVD	146
Set Up an iPhoto Account with Apple	148
Order Prints from Apple	150
Make a Photo Book	152
Arrange a Photo Book's Pages	154
Add and Change a Photo Book's Captions	156
Preview and Order a Photo Book	158
Create a .Mac Web Page	160
Export Web Pages	162
Publish a Slideshow on .Mac	164
Using a Photo as a Desktop Picture	166
Export Photos to a Hard Disk	168
Create a CD or DVD Archive	170
Using an Archive CD or DVD	172

WORKING WITH IMOVIE

9) iMovie Basics

Set Up iMovie	176
Connect a Digital Camcorder	180
Import Video from a Digital Camcorder	182
Import Video Clips from Disk	184
Insert and Arrange Clips in a Movie	186
Make a Clip from a Still Image	188
Create a Still Frame from a Clip	189
Create a Clip from an iPhoto Picture	190
Adjust the Ken Burns Effect	192

11) Using Advanced iMovie Features

Work with the Timeline 216
Separate Audio from Video 220
Adjust Audio Volume 222
Add iTunes Audio to a Movie 224
Add iMovie Sound Effects 226
Record Narration 228
Record from iSight .230
Change a Clip's Speed 232
Reverse a Clip's Direction 233
Paste Over at Playhead 234
Add Chapters for iDVD 236
Export to Camera 238
Share a Movie 240

WORKING WITH IDVD

12) iDVD Basics

Set Up iDVD 244
Select a Picture Theme 248
Change a Theme's Audio 250
Select a Motion Theme 252
Change a Motion Theme Movie 254
Select a Drop Zone Theme 256
Add Media to a Drop Zone Theme 258
Save a Modified Theme as a Favorite 260

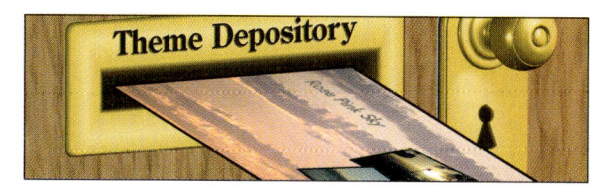

10) Editing with iMovie

Crop a Clip 194
Split a Clip 196
Using the Trash 197
Apply a Transition to a Single Clip 198
Apply a Transition Between Two Clips 200
Apply a Visual Effect to a Clip 202
Modify a Visual Effect 204
Add Single Titles 206
Add Multiple Titles .208
Add Subtitles 210
Adjust Title Animation 212
Modify Title Font and Color 214

TABLE OF CONTENTS

13) Creating DVD Menus with iDVD

Change a Menu Title's Format 262
Create a Movie Menu Button 264
Change a Menu Button's Shape 265
Change a Menu Button's Text Format 266
Add a Custom Button Image or Movie 268
Arrange Menu Buttons 270
Change a Motion Menu Button's Start Frame . . .272
Change the Motion Menu Buttons' Duration . . .273
Create a Submenu 274
Create a Scene Submenu from iMovie 278
Using the Map 280

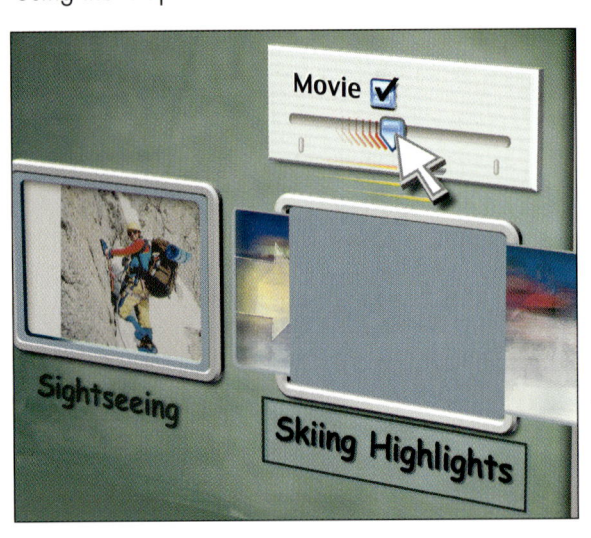

14) Using Advanced iDVD Features

Create and Add Photos to a Slideshow 282
Arrange Pictures in a Slideshow 286
Change a Slideshow's Duration 288
Change a Slideshow Button's Image 289
Add Audio to a Slideshow 290
Check an iDVD Project's Status 292
Check the TV Safe Area 293
Preview a DVD .294
Add Data Files to a DVD 296
Burn a DVD 298

WORKING WITH GARAGEBAND

15) GarageBand Basics

Set Up GarageBand 302
Create a Software Instrument Track 306
Create a Real Instrument Track 307
Browse Loops 308
Add a Loop 310
Edit a Software Loop 312

16) Make Music with GarageBand

Using the On-screen Keyboard 314
Record a Software Loop 316
Edit a Software Loop's Notes 318
Adjust Track Volume 320
Change a Software Instrument Track's
  Settings 322
Record a Real Instrument 324
Edit a Real Instrument Loop 326
Change a Real Instrument Track's Settings 328
Export a Song to iTunes 330

HOW TO USE THIS BOOK

Teach Yourself VISUALLY iLife '04 contains straightforward sections, which you can use to learn the basics of using the five iLife applications — iTunes, iPhoto, iMovie, iDVD, and GarageBand. This book is designed to help a reader receive quick access to any area of question. You can simply look up a subject within the Table of Contents or Index and go immediately to the section of concern. A *section* is a set of self-contained units that walks you through a computer operation step-by-step. That is, with rare exception, all the information you need regarding an area of interest is contained within a section.

The General Organization of This Book

The first chapter of this book richly illustrates the entire iLife suite, showing you how the various applications work together, and points out the major parts of the iLife interface. The rest of the book devotes several chapters each to the individual iLife applications — iTunes, iPhoto, iMovie, iDVD, and GarageBand. Every chapter contains a series of sections, most of which are two pages long. The top half of each two-page section contains an introduction, and a tip area. The bottom half contains screen illustrations that provide step-by-step instructions for performing that section's tasks. The introduction explains why you would want to perform the task, definitions and terms, and cross references to other areas of interest in the book. The tip area gives you additional information and alternative ways to perform a task.

The Organization of Each Chapter

Teach Yourself VISUALLY iLife '04 has sixteen chapters. Chapter 1 explores the iLife applications, shows you how to navigate with the Dock and Finder, and how to manage files. Chapters 2 through 5 discuss iTunes, and show how to use playlists, the Music Library, the Music Store, and the iPod. Chapters 6 through 8 detail the inner workings of iPhoto including how to import, manipulate, and distribute your favorite pictures. iMovie is covered in Chapters 9 through 11, which explain how to import, manipulate, and add effects to your movie clips. You also learn how to export your movies and organize your clips into chapters for iDVD. In Chapters 12 through 14, you discover important iDVD features, including how to create DVD menu themes, on-screen menu buttons, and slideshows, as well as how to create and burn a DVD. Chapters 15 and 16 introduce you to music composition with GarageBand, and show you how to combine your own music with GarageBand's built-in loops to create songs that you can save in your iTunes Library.

Who This Book Is For

This book is highly recommended for the visual learner who wants to learn the basics of iLife, and who may or may not have prior experience with a computer.

What You Need to Use This Book

To perform the tasks in this book, you need a Macintosh computer with a PowerPC G3, G4, or G5 processor installed: 600MHz G3 or faster required for GarageBand; G4 required for GarageBand software instruments; 733MHz G4 required for iDVD. In addition, the iLife programs require:

- 256MB of physical RAM
- Mac OS X 10.2.6 or later (Mac OS X 10.2.8 or later recommended)
- Monitor capable of displaying 1024x768 pixels
- 4.3GB of free disk space (250MB if iDVD is not installed)
- DVD drive required for installing GarageBand and iDVD (Apple SuperDrive required for producing DVDs with iDVD).

Conventions When Using the Mouse

This book uses the following conventions to describe the actions you perform when using the mouse. Note that the standard Macintosh mouse has one button; if your mouse has more than one button, use the left button unless otherwise directed:

Click

Press and release the mouse button. You use a click to select an item on the screen.

Double-click

Quickly press and release the mouse button twice. You double-click to open a document or start a program.

`Control` **+click**

Press the `Control` key on your keyboard while clicking. You use a `Control` +click to display a shortcut menu, a list of commands specifically related to the selected item.

Right-click

Press and release the right mouse button on a two or more button mouse. Right-click performs the same function as `Control` +click.

Click and Drag, and Release the Mouse

Position the mouse pointer over an item on the screen and then press and hold down the mouse button. Still holding down the button, move the mouse to where you want to place the item and then release the button. Clicking and dragging makes it easy to move an item to a new location.

`Shift` **+click**

To select consecutive items, press the `Shift` key on your computer while clicking the items you want to select.

`⌘` **+click**

To select non-consecutive items, press the `⌘` key on your computer while clicking the items you want to select.

The Conventions in This Book

A number of typographic and layout styles have been used throughout *Teach Yourself VISUALLY iLife '04* to distinguish different types of information.

Bold

Indicates text, or text buttons, that you must click in a menu or dialog box to complete a task.

Italics

Indicates a new term being introduced.

Numbered Steps

Indicate that you must perform these steps in order to successfully perform the task.

Bulleted Steps

Give you alternative methods, explain various options, or present what a program will do in response to the numbered steps.

Notes

Give you additional information to help you complete a task. The purpose of a note, which appears in italics, is three-fold: It can explain special conditions that may occur during the course of the task, warn you of potentially dangerous situations, or refer you to tasks in the same or a different chapter. References to tasks within the chapter are indicated by the phrase "*See the section...*" followed by the name of the section. References to other chapters are indicated by "*See Chapter...*" followed by the chapter number.

Icons

Icons in the steps indicate a button that you must click to continue to the next step.

Operating System Difference

There are minor differences in the appearance and operation of Finder windows, Open and Save dialogs, and System Preferences between Mac OS X 10.2 ("Jaguar") and Mac OS X 10.3 ("Panther"). This book uses Mac OS X 10.3 screens; consult your particular Mac's Help files and other documentation for details.

Reproducing Copyright Materials

The iLife programs allow you to make copies of audio and visual works for your own use. Keep in mind that copying and distributing works for which you do not have permission from the copyright holders may be a violation of copyright law and is unfair to the artists who produced them.

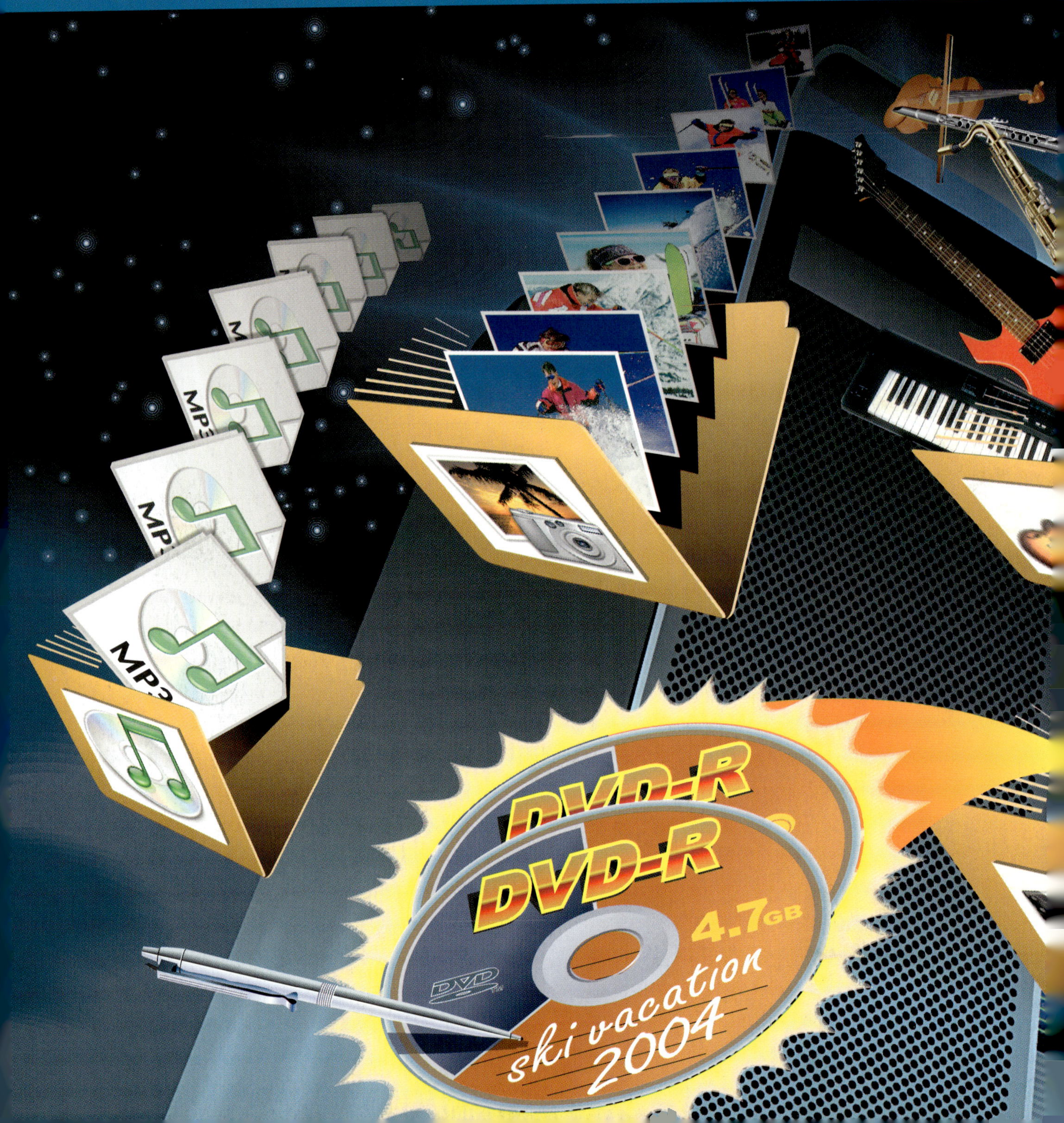
DVD-R
DVD-R
4.7GB
ski vacation
2004

PART 1

Getting Started with iLife

Apple's iLife programs are all about helping you make and manage your memories and dreams. The five iLife programs — iTunes, iPhoto, iMovie, iDVD, and GarageBand — work together to let you organize and enjoy your photo and music collections, edit and score your home videos, and share them all with your friends and family.

1 Getting Started with iLife
Pages 4–21

INTRODUCING THE iLIFE PROGRAMS

The iLife programs — GarageBand, iTunes, iPhoto, iMovie, and iDVD — let you use your Macintosh to make and manage your music, organize your photos, edit your home videos, and record them on DVDs.

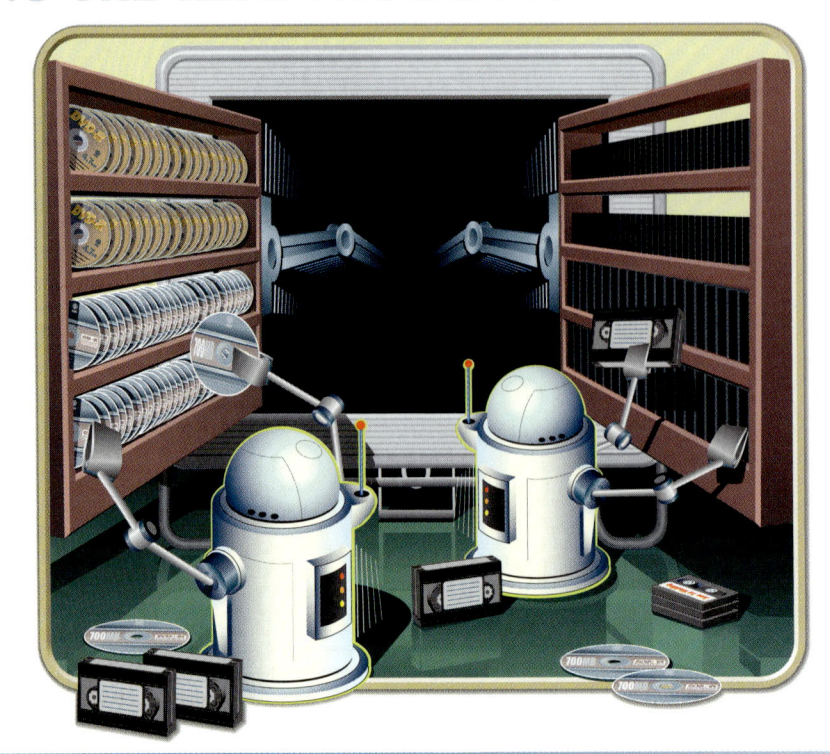

Obtaining iLife

The five iLife programs are preinstalled on all current Macintosh computers. If you have an older Mac, you can purchase the complete iLife package on a two-disc CD and DVD-ROM set from Apple for less than $50.

About iTunes

iTunes is the iLife program that you use to manage your digital music library. With it, you can play digital music, import music into your Mac from CDs, build playlists, burn CDs, store your GarageBand creations, listen to your favorite Internet radio stations, copy music to a portable digital music player — such as an iPod — and purchase digital music from Apple's iTunes Music Store. For more on iTunes, see Chapters 2 to 5.

1 Getting Started with iLife

GETTING STARTED WITH ILIFE

About iPhoto

You can use iPhoto to copy photos into your Mac from most digital cameras. iPhoto lets you arrange your photos into albums, retouch, crop, and enhance them, and print them. You can also use your photos to produce slideshows that include musical accompaniment from your iTunes music library. With iPhoto and an Internet connection, you can create an iPhoto account with Apple and order professional prints and cloth-bound photo books from within the iPhoto program. For more about the various features of iPhoto, see Chapters 6 to 8.

About iMovie

You can connect your digital camcorder to your Mac with a FireWire cable and use iMovie to import and edit your digital video. iMovie provides transitions, animated titles and subtitles, special visual effects, sound effects, and a simple but powerful clip and soundtrack editor. You can add still photos from your iPhoto Library to your movies, as well as music from your iTunes music library. When you finish, you can record your movie back to your camcorder. For more information on iMovie and its features, see Chapters 9 to 11.

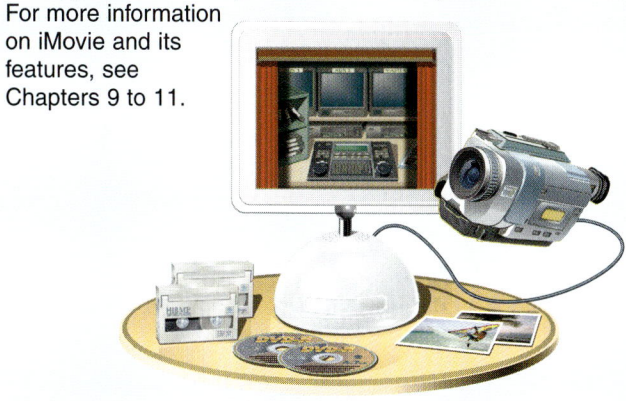

About iDVD

You can use iDVD to burn a DVD containing movies you have made with iMovie, and slideshows containing photos from your iPhoto Library, accompanied by music from your iTunes music library. iDVD comes with an assortment of professionally designed themes you can use for creating your DVD's on-screen menus. You can customize iDVD's menu themes and save them to use again. For more on iDVD, see Chapters 12 to 14.

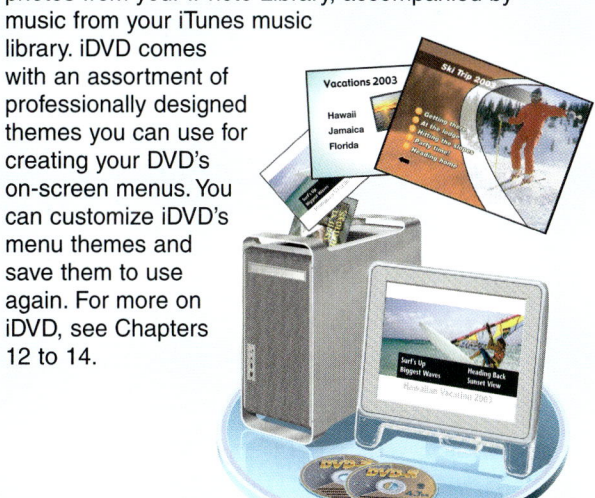

About GarageBand

GarageBand lets you create your own songs by turning your Mac into a simple yet powerful music recording and editing studio. The program comes with over 1,000 royalty-free music loops that you can use as the basis for your own compositions, and it provides 50 software instruments you can play on-screen — or you can hook up your own guitar and keyboard and start jamming! You can save your songs in your iTunes library and use them in the slideshows and movies that you make with iPhoto, iMovie, and iDVD.

5

UNDERSTANDING ITUNES

With iTunes you can copy and store music from your entire CD collection, make special CD mixes of your favorite songs, enjoy your GarageBand compositions, and add more music from the iTunes Music Store. For more on iTunes, see Chapters 2 to 5.

Import Music

You can import music from your CD collection and store it compactly in your iTunes library. It usually takes only a few minutes for iTunes to import an entire CD's worth of music. If you have an Internet connection, iTunes searches the online CD database to retrieve the CD's album and song titles so you do not have to type them yourself.

Browse Your Library

You can quickly find any song in your music library using the iTunes browse and search features. You can browse your library by genre, artist, and album title, or simply type a few letters from a song's title or artist's name to find the music for which you are looking.

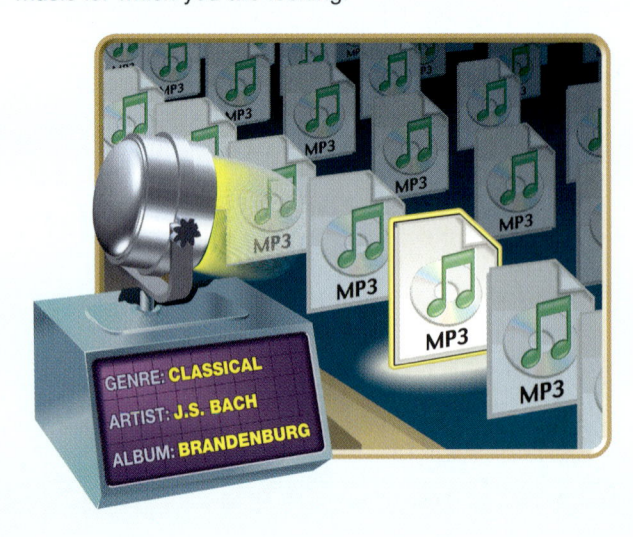

1 Getting Started with iLife

GETTING STARTED WITH ILIFE

Make Playlists

You can make playlists of the songs you want to hear in the order you want to play them. You can also make Smart Playlists that automatically contain songs based upon criteria that you specify. iTunes updates your Smart Playlists whenever you change your music library.

Make CDs

You can copy the songs in your playlists to recordable CDs, letting you keep your CD collection at home while you play your custom CDs in the car or at work. If you have an MP3 CD player, you can also make special MP3 CDs, which hold many more songs than a regular CD.

Shop for Music

Apple has created an online iTunes Music Store that offers hundreds of thousands of songs from both the major and the independent music labels, most of which cost less than a dollar. You can establish an Apple Account, download music legally from the iTunes Music Store, send music gift certificates to other iTunes users, set up music purchase allowances for your kids, and burn your purchased music onto CDs.

Do Not Steal Music

iTunes is designed to let you easily play and share your music legally with very few technical restrictions. Keep in mind that copying and distributing music that you did not purchase violates copyright law and is unfair to the artists who produce the music. Enjoy your music; do not steal it.

7

UNDERSTANDING IPHOTO

iPhoto takes the confusion out of sorting and storing your photo collection and lets you order professional prints right from your Mac. For more about the various features of iPhoto, see Chapters 6 to 8.

Import Photos

When you connect a digital camera to your Mac, iPhoto can import all the photos on the camera and add them to your digital photo library. iPhoto can also import and organize pictures from files you already have on your Mac. iPhoto keeps track of each group of imported photos as a virtual film roll; you can rename both the rolls and their individual photos. You can also sort your photos in various ways.

Make Albums

You can create albums in iPhoto to keep related photos together, even if they were taken months apart or with different cameras. Albums also form the basis of the books and slideshows that you can create with iPhoto.

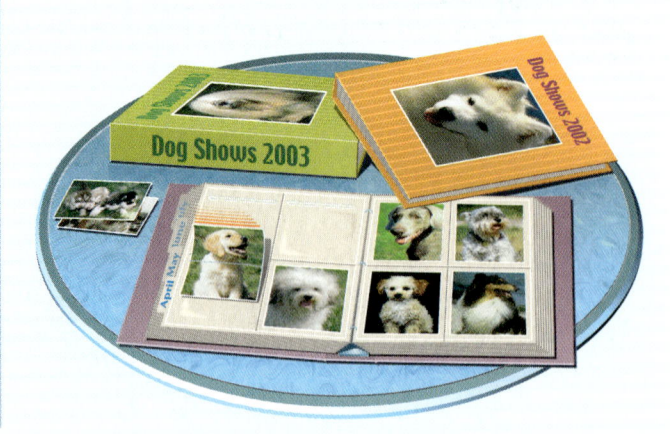

1 Getting Started with iLife

GETTING STARTED WITH ILIFE

Retouch Your Photos

iPhoto offers you simple tools to retouch and crop your photos. You can eliminate the Red Eye effect caused by the camera's flash, sharpen and enhance colors, adjust brightness and contrast, and convert your photos to black-and-white or sepia tones. iPhoto can link to more powerful picture editing software as well.

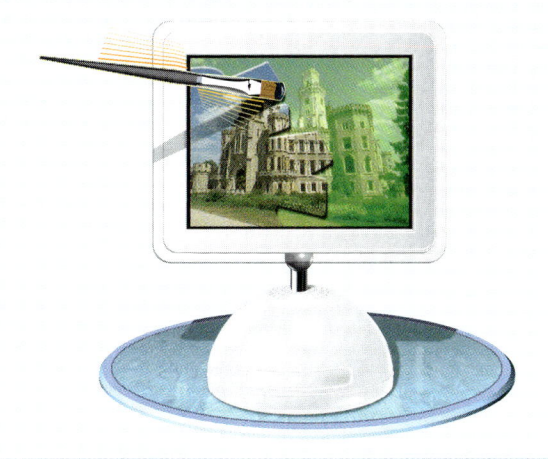

Share Photos

You can share your photo collection over your home network for your family to enjoy. If you have an Apple .Mac account, you can use iPhoto to caption and publish your photos on the Web using professionally designed Web page templates. Even if you do not have a .Mac account, iPhoto can produce Web page files that you can upload to any Web site to which you have access.

Design a Book

iPhoto provides templates you can use to create several kinds of photo books, including yearbooks, catalogs, and story books. You can print these books on your own printer or order a professionally printed cloth-bound book from Apple using your Internet connection.

Order Prints

Using your Apple Account from within iPhoto, you can order prints on high-quality photo paper in a variety of sizes from Kodak's Print Service. Prints are usually shipped to you within two working days.

9

UNDERSTANDING iMOVIE

With iMovie and a digital camcorder, you can edit your home, school, or business videos into polished productions. To learn more about iMovie and its various features, see Chapters 9 to 11.

Import and Export Video

iMovie can import digital video from most digital camcorders. When you finish your editing work, just place a fresh tape in your camera and iMovie can export your movie back to tape. iMovie can also export your movie to QuickTime or make it ready for use in iDVD. If you have an Apple iSight camera, you can record directly into iMovie with it.

Arrange Clips

You can split your video into separate clips, label them, and arrange them as you work. iMovie can also split your video into separate clips when it imports your video, using the invisible time codes that many digital camcorders add to your recording.

1 Getting Started with iLife

GETTING STARTED WITH ILIFE

Assemble Movies

iMovie provides a simple but powerful clip editor. You can drag your clips into whatever order you like, crop them, and add transitions between them. If you need finer control, you can switch to iMovie's Timeline editor and edit your video down to the individual frame.

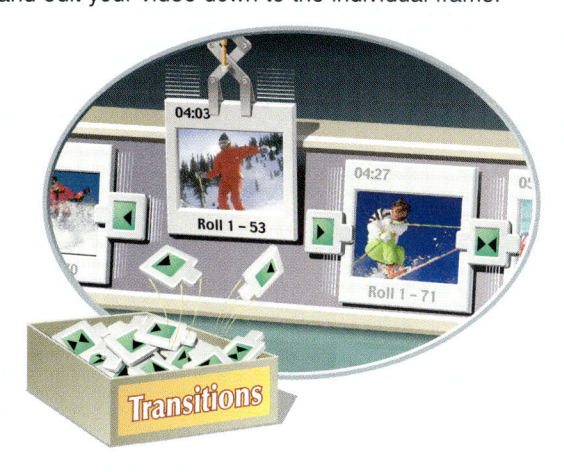

Using Photos in Movies

iMovie gives you complete access to your iPhoto Library so you can mix still sequences into your video. Your still pictures do not have to remain motionless, though. iMovie provides a feature, called the *Ken Burns Effect*, which you can use to pan and zoom over the photos in your movie.

Score Your Movie

iMovie lets you use your iTunes library — including your own GarageBand songs — to score your movie. You can preview songs, search your music collection, and insert a selected song anywhere you like. If your Mac has a microphone, you can even record a voice-over narration.

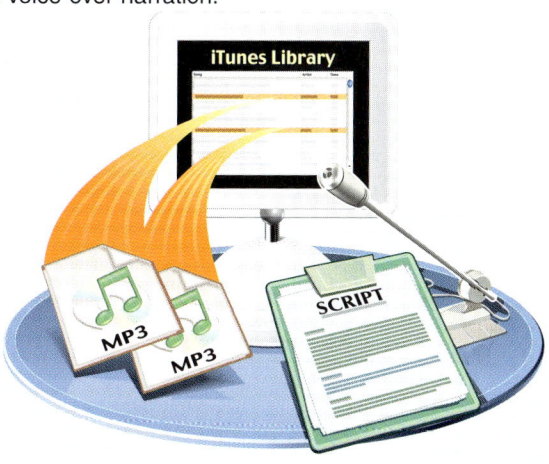

Add Effects

iMovie comes with a large collection of digital video effects that you can apply to your clips. You can supplement these effects with additional video effects available through third-party software companies. You can also add sound effects to your film's soundtrack from the dozens of professionally recorded sound effects that come with iMovie.

11

UNDERSTANDING IDVD

With iDVD you can place your movies and other media on a DVD, complete with high-quality DVD menus that you can play on almost any home DVD player. For more on using iDVD, see Chapters 12 to 14.

Pick a Theme

iDVD comes with an extensive collection of DVD menu themes, suitable for anything from wedding videos to art portfolios. Drop Zone themes let you add your own movies and photos to the menu backgrounds to give your DVD a dynamic, customized design.

Save a Favorite

After you customize one of iDVD's menu themes, you can save it as a favorite design that you can use later in other iDVD projects. iDVD lets you keep your custom themes private or share them with other users on your Mac.

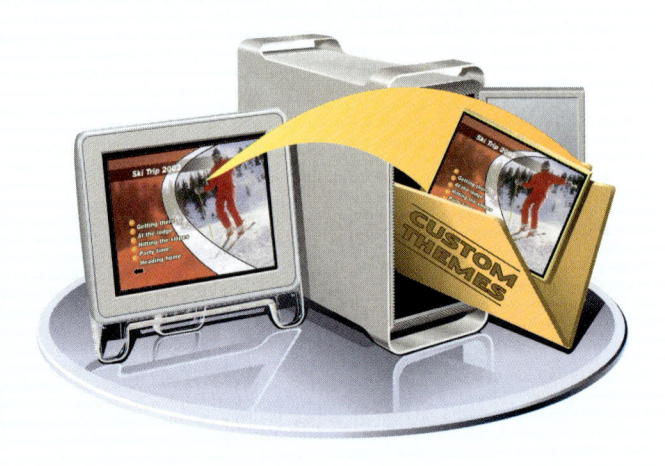

1 Getting Started with iLife

GETTING STARTED WITH ILIFE

Add Movies

iDVD lets you browse all your movie project folders and add your movies to your DVD. If you added chapters to your movie with iMovie, iDVD creates separate scene buttons for each chapter. You can also use your movies as motion backgrounds for your DVD menus.

Create a Slideshow

You can create DVD slideshows from the photos in your iPhoto Library. You can arrange the slides in any order you like and control the slideshow's timing, or set your slideshow up so that you can manually control it with your DVD player's remote control.

Using Songs in Slideshows

You can use songs from your iTunes library, including songs you have composed with GarageBand, as background audio for your DVD menus or your slideshows. When you use a song in a slideshow, you can set the slideshow duration to fit the song's length.

Make a DVD-ROM

You can make a hybrid DVD that plays on both a home DVD player and a computer, and include extra data files and folders that computer users can copy. For example, you can add the original iPhoto pictures that you use in your slideshows or QuickTime versions of the movies you have on your DVD.

13

UNDERSTANDING GARAGEBAND

With GarageBand you do not need to know how to read a note of music to write songs. You can build a song from professionally created samples and add your own additions and changes. GarageBand makes it easy to create custom soundtracks to accompany your iPhoto slideshows and iMovie videos. To learn more about GarageBand see Chapters 15 to 16.

Set Up Tracks

You can create tracks for each instrument or vocal performance you want to include in your song. Tracks can contain performances by software instruments, using GarageBand's built-in synthesizers, or real instruments, using actual recordings to which you can apply filters and effects.

Add Loops

Loops are short pieces of music that are designed to repeat as background accompaniment in songs. GarageBand comes with 1,000 royalty-free loops you can drag, drop, and extend to provide the rhythm and percussion tracks for your own melodies.

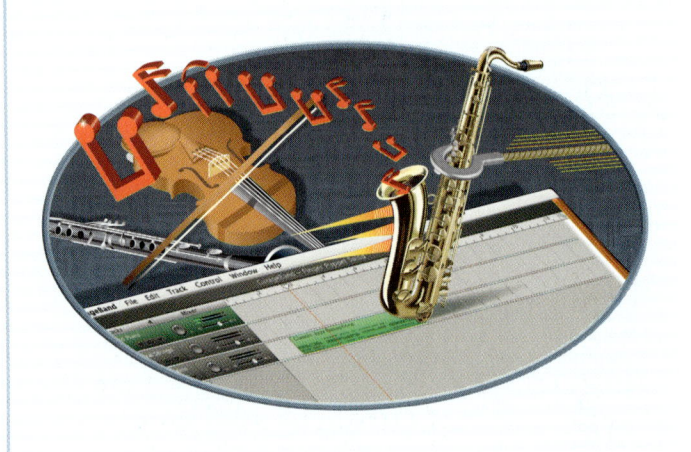

1 Getting Started with iLife

GETTING STARTED WITH ILIFE

Change the Score

Built into GarageBand is an easy-to-use software music editor that lets you fix any bad notes you play on a software instrument. GarageBand's real instrument track editor lets you cut and paste audio recordings as well.

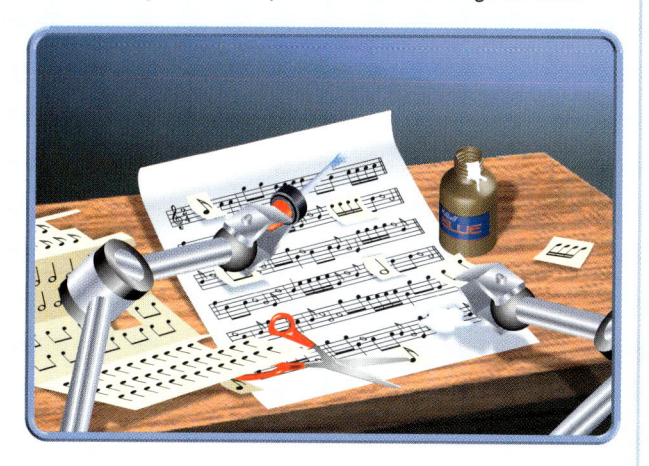

Record a Performance

You can plug any MIDI keyboard into your Mac and record your own performances. If your Mac has an audio input, you can record using microphones and analog instruments like electric guitars.

Mix It Down

You can dynamically control the volume and stereo placement of each of your songs tracks using GarageBand's simple track volume controls to achieve just the right mix of sound.

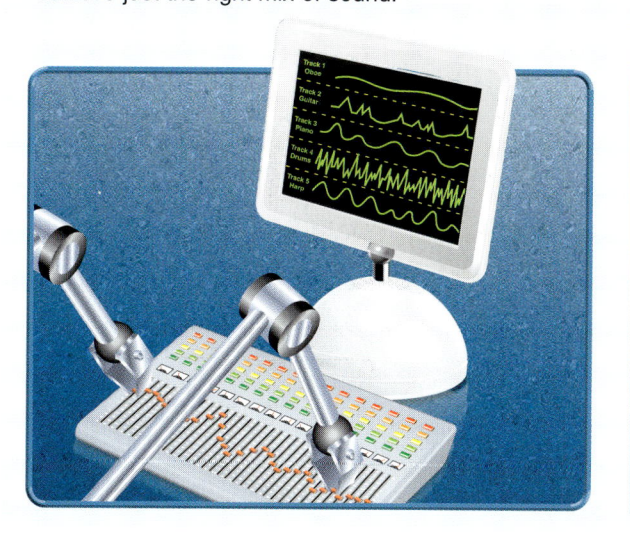

Spread It Around

GarageBand lets you export your songs directly into your iTunes library, where you can burn them to CD or add them to projects you are building in the other iLife programs.

15

EXPLORE THE MACINTOSH DOCK

The Macintosh's Dock, which appears at the bottom of your screen, provides quick access to all of your running and your favorite programs. It comes with icons for some programs already in it, such as the iLife programs.

The Finder

The Finder ( ) is the application that you use to manage the files and folders on your Mac. It is always running. The Finder lets you see the location of your files in windows; it also is the program that displays your Desktop and any icons that are on it. For more on the Finder and the Desktop, see the section "Explore the Finder."

Program Icons

You can open or switch to a program simply by clicking its icon in the Dock. Every running program appears on the Dock with a triangle ( ) beneath its icon. You can click and drag any program icon on your Mac to the Dock to add it, and you can click and drag a program icon off the Dock to remove it.

Contextual Menu

You can `Control`+click, or right-click, the resizing line to display the Dock's contextual menu. You can hide the Dock using this menu to give you more screen room. When you hide the Dock, it temporarily reappears when you move your mouse to the bottom of the screen.

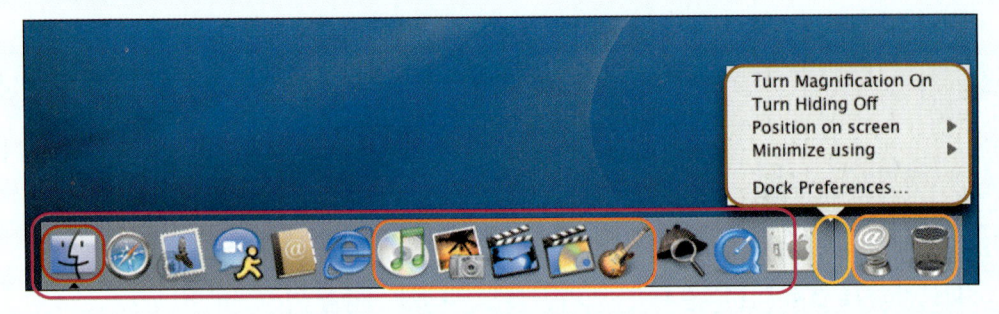

iLife Applications

The five iLife applications are, from left to right, iTunes ( ), iPhoto ( ), iMovie ( ), iDVD ( ), and GarageBand ( ). You simply click the appropriate icon to open the application in which you want to work.

Documents and Trash

Documents, folders, and the Macintosh Trash appear at the right end of the Dock. You click a document or folder to open it. You can click and drag an icon to the Trash from a Finder window or the Desktop to delete it from your Mac. For more on the Finder and the Desktop, see the section "Explore the Finder."

Resizing Line

A thin line appears near the right end of the Dock, separating the application icons from the document, folder, and Trash icons. You click and drag this line up or down to make the Dock bigger or smaller.

START AND QUIT AN ILIFE APPLICATION

1 Getting Started with iLife

GETTING STARTED WITH ILIFE

With your iLife application icons in the Dock, it takes just a single click to start one up.

This task demonstrates how to start and quit the iTunes application, but the steps are the same for the other iLife applications, as well as for nearly all other Macintosh applications. Note that if an application has never been run on the Mac before, it may present a license agreement window and setup window before its main window appears.

START AND QUIT AN ILIFE APPLICATION

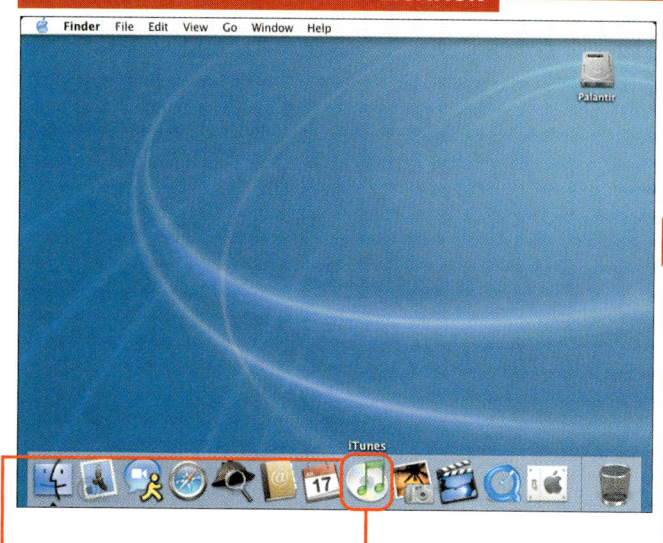

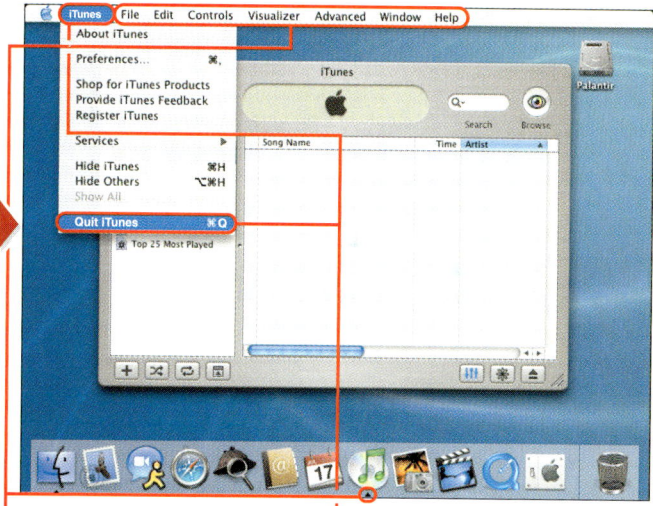

START AN APPLICATION

1 In the Dock, move your mouse to the iLife icon you want to start.

■ The name of the icon appears.

2 Click the icon.

■ The icon bounces as the program begins running.

■ The iLife application window opens.

■ A triangle (▲) appears beneath the application's icon in the Dock.

■ The application's menus appear, and its name appears to the right of the menu.

QUIT AN APPLICATION

1 Click the application's name.

2 Click **Quit**.

■ The application window closes and ▲ disappears from beneath the application's Dock icon.

17

EXPLORE THE FINDER

You can have thousands of files and folders on your Mac. The Macintosh Finder is the program that lets you manage all these files and folders. Finder windows can display your files and folders as icons, as items in a list, or as items arranged in a column view that shows you exactly where they are located on your Mac.

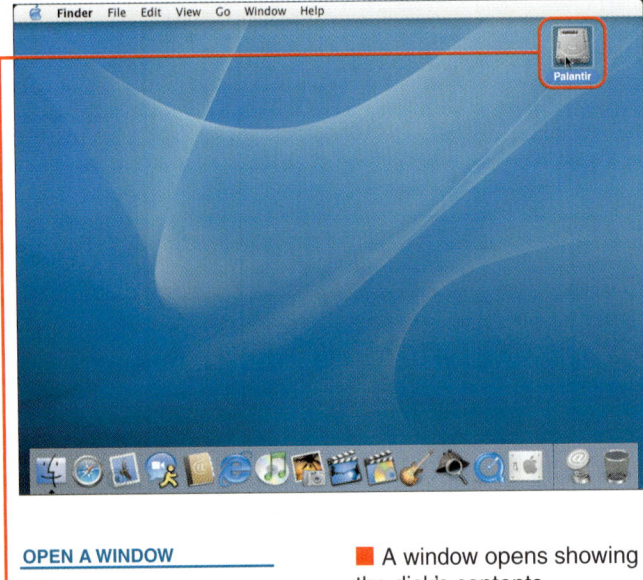

EXPLORE THE FINDER

OPEN A WINDOW

1 Double-click the hard disk icon.

■ A window opens showing the disk's contents.

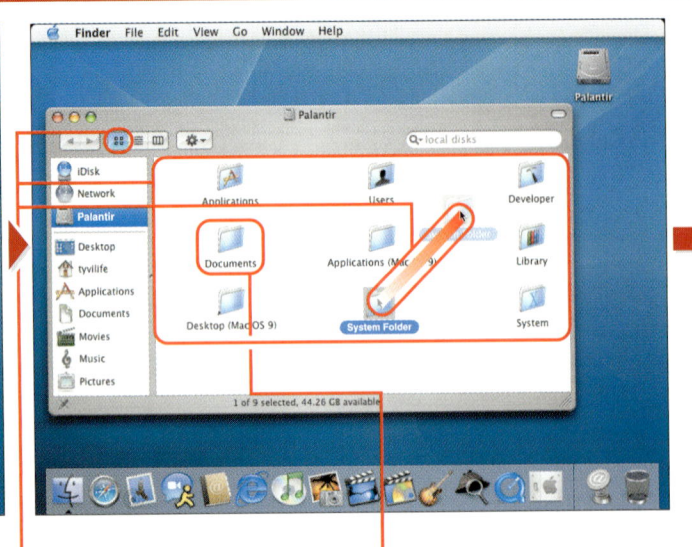

USING THE ICON VIEW

2 Click the Icon portion ( ) of the View button.

■ The window's contents appear as icons ( ).

■ You can click and drag to arrange them.

■ You can double-click to see its contents.

■ You can press ⌘ and double-click to see its contents in a new Finder window.

18

1 Getting Started with iLife

GETTING STARTED WITH ILIFE

What is the Desktop?

The Desktop appears as the image behind all your windows. The Finder lets you click and drag icons from Finder windows to the Desktop so you can quickly get at them. The Desktop view is actually a special view of the Desktop folder inside your Home directory. You can open that folder to see the folders and documents that you have on your Desktop in a standard Finder window.

What is the Home directory?

The Home directory is the folder that contains all your personal files and folders. Each user on a Mac has his or her own Home directory. The Home directory's name is the name you use when you log into your account on the Mac. The Home directory contains, among other things, a Pictures folder for your iPhoto pictures, a Music folder for your iTunes songs, and a Movies folder for your iMovies projects. You can click the Home icon ( ) in any open Finder window, or type Shift + ⌘ + H, to open a Finder window for your Home directory.

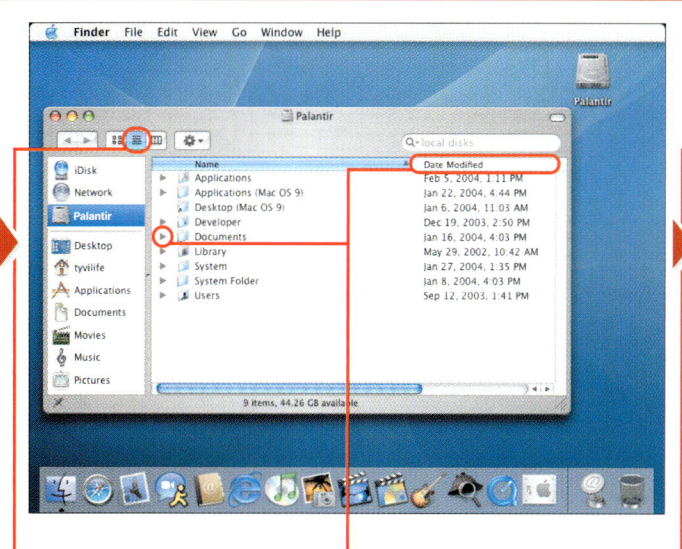

USING THE LIST VIEW

3 Click the List portion ( ) of the View button.

■ The window's contents appear as a list.

■ You can click a column heading to sort the list.

■ You can click the column head again to reverse the sorting order.

■ You can click ▶ to see the folder's contents.

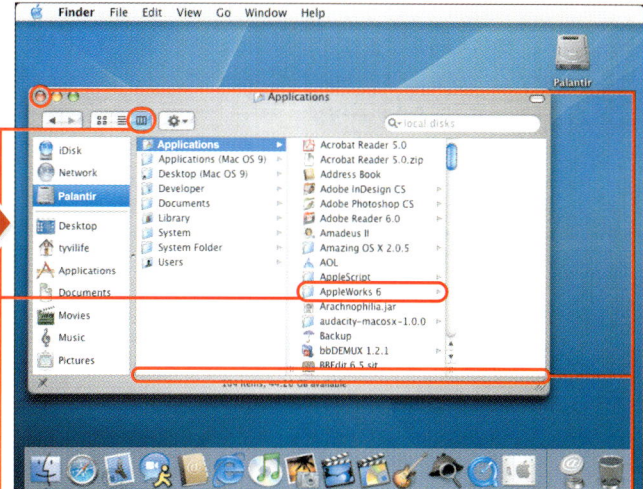

USING THE COLUMN VIEW

4 Click the Column portion ( ) of the View button.

■ The window appears in a column view.

■ You can click 📄 to view the contents in the column to the right.

■ As more columns appear, a scroll bar lets you scroll the view left or right.

5 Click the Close button ( ).

■ The window closes.

19

OPEN AND SAVE FILES

When you use the iLife applications, you will need to open or save files from time to time. The standard Macintosh Open and Save dialogs let you select which files to open, and let you decide where and with what names you save files.

The Open and Save dialogs appear in response to certain menu commands; for example, the Import or Add commands, as well as the Open command, present Open dialogs. The Export and Save commands present Save dialogs. This task uses iTunes to present an example of how these dialogs work.

OPEN AND SAVE FILES

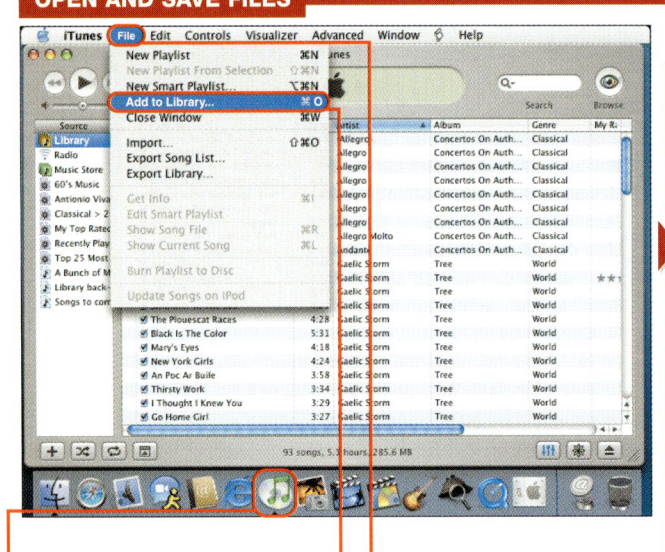

SEE AN OPEN FILE DIALOG

1 Start an iLife application.

Note: See the section "Start and Quit an iLife Application" for more information on how to start an iLife application.

2 Click **File**.

3 Click **Add to Library**.

■ An Open dialog appears.

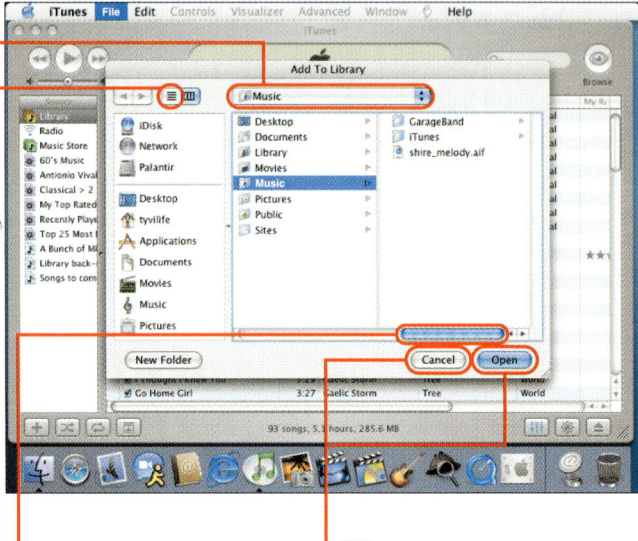

■ You can click and drag the scroll bar to move among columns.

■ You can click here to go quickly to recently used locations.

■ You can click 􀀁 to switch to a list view.

4 Click **Cancel**.

■ The dialog closes.

■ You can click **Open** to open a selected file or folder and close the dialog.

20

1 Getting Started with iLife

GETTING STARTED WITH ILIFE

TEACH YOURSELF

What is a sheet?

A *sheet* is a dialog that slides out from, and is attached to, the title area of another window. Sheets keep the dialogs associated with the windows to which they refer. You often see Save dialogs presented as sheets to let you know which window the Save dialog affects.

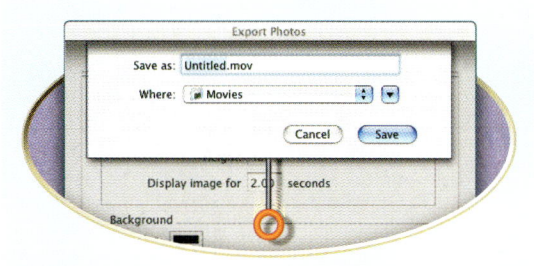

TEACH YOURSELF

What is the sidebar that appears on Finder and File Open and Save dialogs?

The top part of the sidebar contains all the local disks and network locations available to your Mac. The bottom part displays common and favorite locations. Click an icon in the sidebar to display its contents in the window or dialog. You can drag folders to the bottom part of the sidebar in a Finder window to add them to the sidebar; to remove them from the sidebar just drag them off. Consult your Macintosh's Help menu for more information.

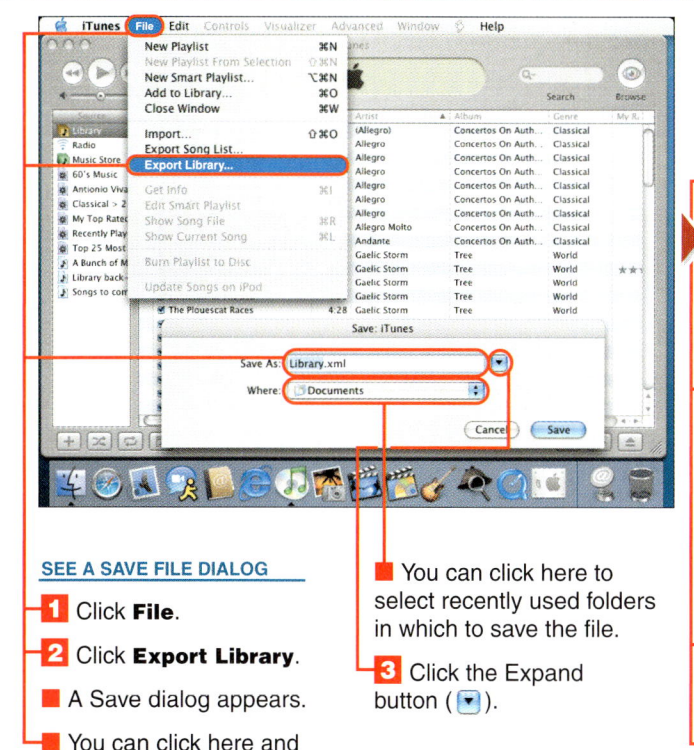

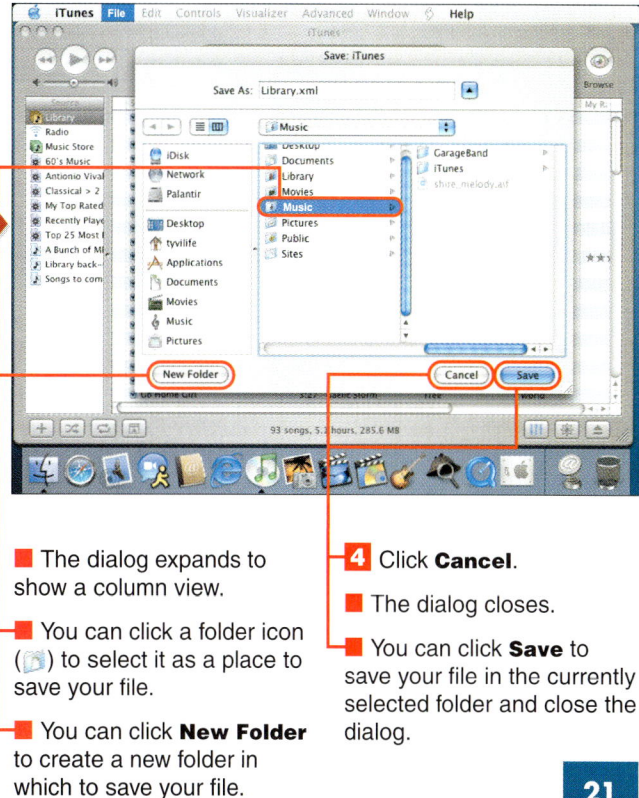

SEE A SAVE FILE DIALOG

1 Click **File**.

2 Click **Export Library**.

■ A Save dialog appears.

■ You can click here and type a filename.

■ You can click here to select recently used folders in which to save the file.

3 Click the Expand button (▼).

■ The dialog expands to show a column view.

■ You can click a folder icon (📁) to select it as a place to save your file.

■ You can click **New Folder** to create a new folder in which to save your file.

4 Click **Cancel**.

■ The dialog closes.

■ You can click **Save** to save your file in the currently selected folder and close the dialog.

21

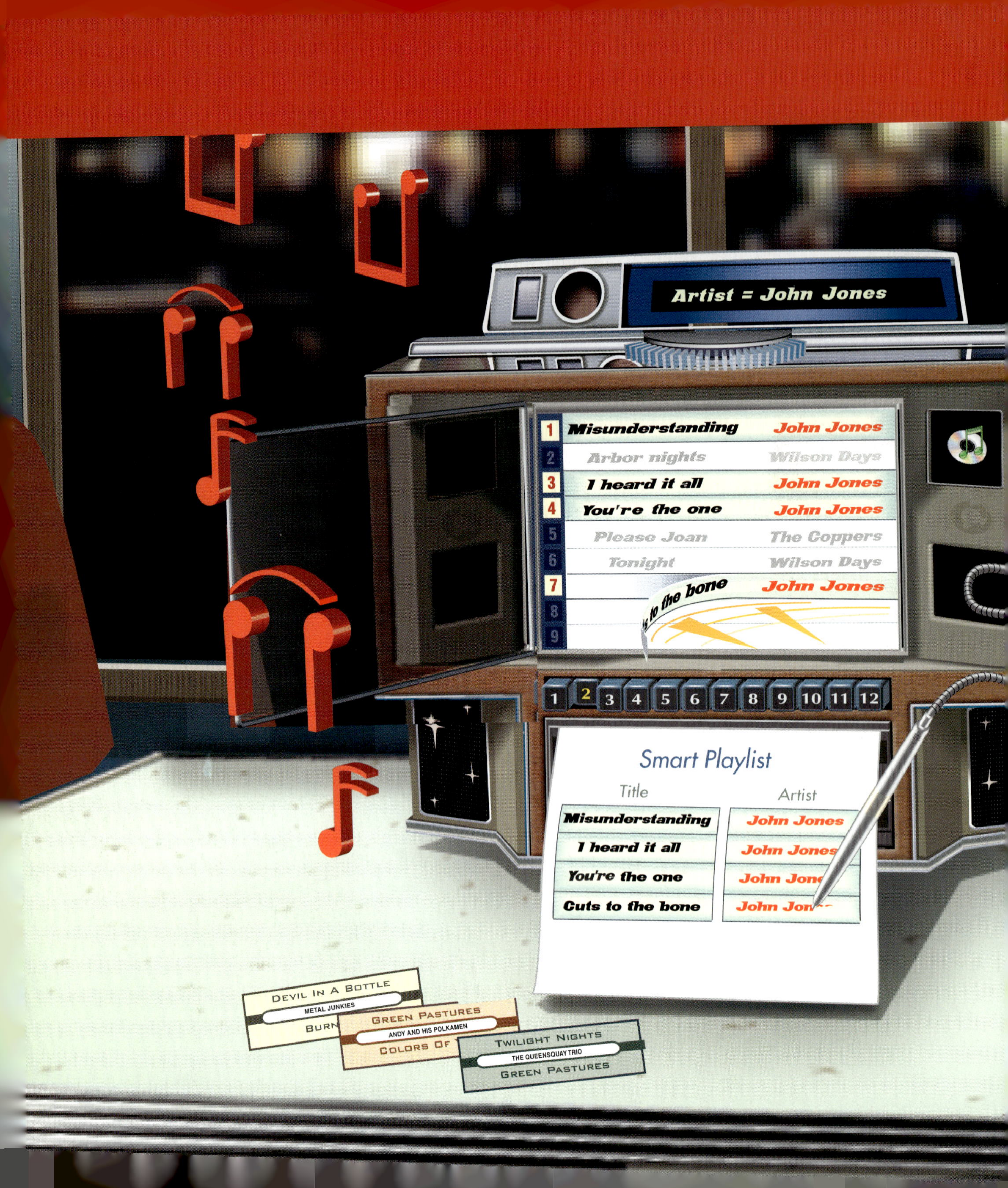

Artist = John Jones
1 Misunderstanding John Jones
2 Arbor nights Wilson Days
3 I heard it all John Jones
4 You're the one John Jones
5 Please Joan The Coppers
6 Tonight Wilson Days
7 John Jones
1 2 3 4 5 6 7 8 9 10 11 12
Smart Playlist
Title
Artist
Misunderstanding
John Jones
I heard it all
John Jones
You're the one
Cuts to the bone
Devil In A Bottle
Metal Junkies
Green Pastures
Andy and His Polkamen
Twilight Nights
The Queensquay Trio
Green Pastures

PART II

Working with iTunes

2 iTunes Basics
Pages 24–45

3 Creating Playlists and Burning Disks with iTunes
Pages 46–57

4 Using the iTunes Music Store
Pages 58–67

5 Using Advanced iTunes Features
Pages 68–87

SET UP ITUNES

You can set iTunes to control how it displays your music collection, how it plays music, how it imports music, and how it burns CDs.

SET UP ITUNES

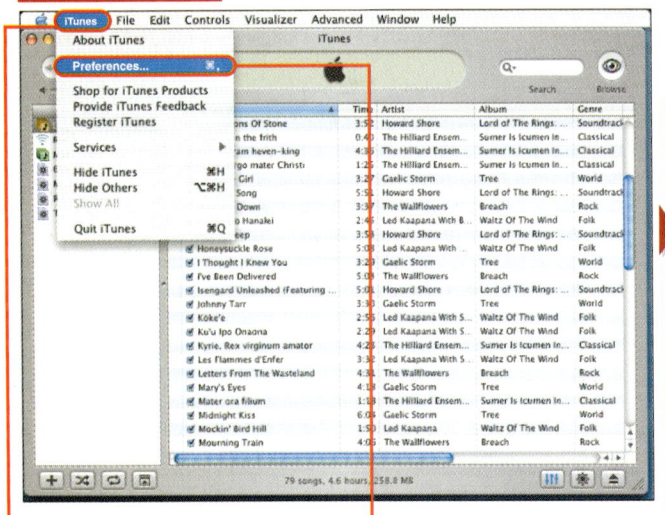

OPEN THE PREFERENCES WINDOW

1 Click **iTunes**.

2 Click **Preferences**.

- iTunes' Preferences window appears.

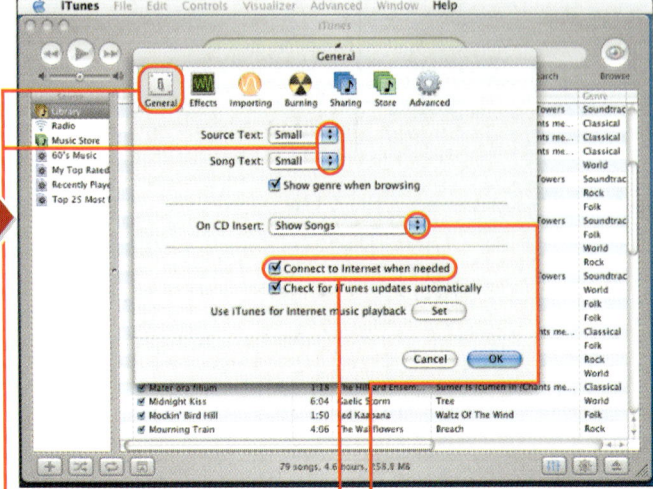

GENERAL PREFERENCES

3 Click the **General** icon.

- The General settings appear in the window.

4 Click here to change the text size for source and song lists that iTunes displays.

5 Click here to select what iTunes does when you insert a CD in your Mac.

6 Click the **Connect to Internet when needed** option to automatically connect to the Internet (☐ changes to ☑).

2 iTunes Basics

WORKING WITH ITUNES

What does the Sound Enhancer do?

Similar to the Surround or 3D setting on some hi-fi systems, the Sound Enhancer makes the music sound a bit "richer" and it amplifies the stereo separation. In rare cases it may cause some slight audio distortion. If so, you can adjust the slider (▢) to a lower setting or disable the **Sound Enhancer** option (☑ changes to ▢).

What does the Sound Check feature really do?

When you add a new song to iTunes, the program examines the sound information that makes up the song and computes how much to adjust the song's playback volume. This ensures that the song plays back at more or less the same level as the other songs stored in the iTunes library.

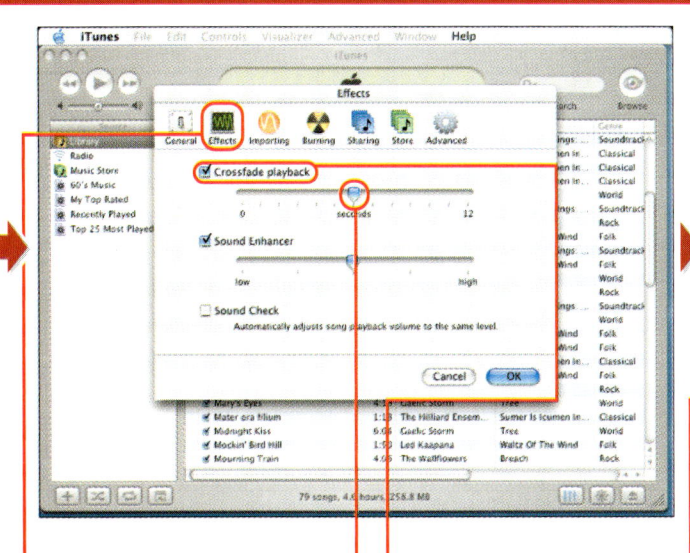

EFFECTS PREFERENCES

7 Click the **Effects** icon.

■ The Effects settings appear in the window.

8 Click the **Crossfade playback** option (▢ changes to ☑) to allow the playback of one song's end to overlap the next song's beginning.

9 Click and drag the slider (▢) to change the crossfade duration.

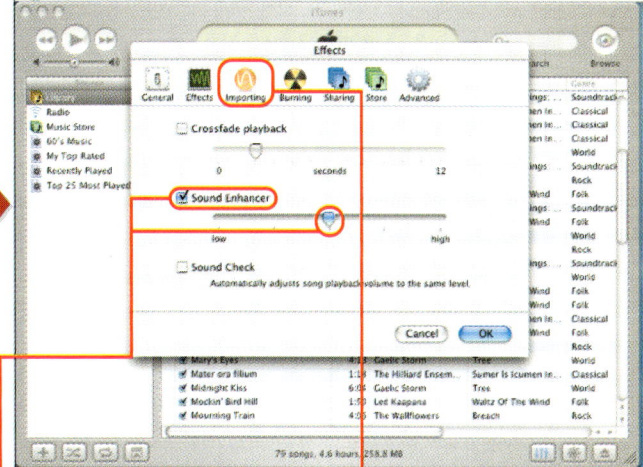

10 Click the **Sound Enhancer** option to activate it.

11 Click and drag ▢ to adjust how strongly the iTunes Sound Enhancer affects the playback.

12 Click the **Importing** icon.

CONTINUED

25

SET UP ITUNES

You can tell iTunes which kinds of discs you want to make and fine-tune how it imports music. You can also specify the information iTunes displays about the songs in your collection.

SET UP ITUNES (CONTINUED)

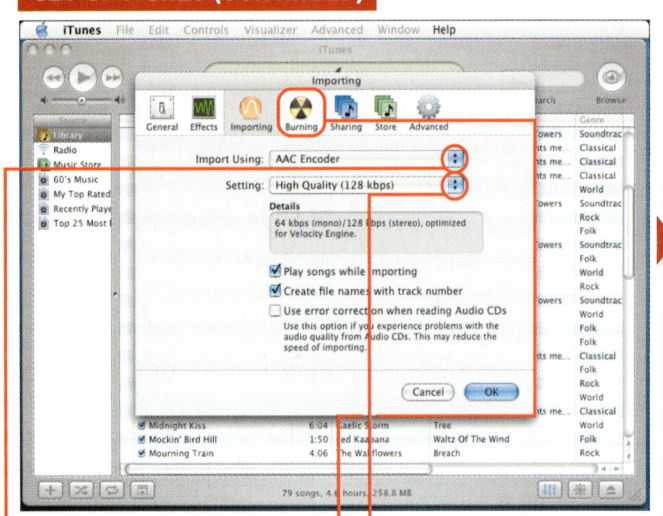

IMPORT PREFERENCES

■ The Importing settings appear.

13 Click here to select an encoder.

14 Click here to select an encoder's settings.

■ Each encoder comes with some preset settings, and you can also customize the settings.

15 Click the **Burning** icon.

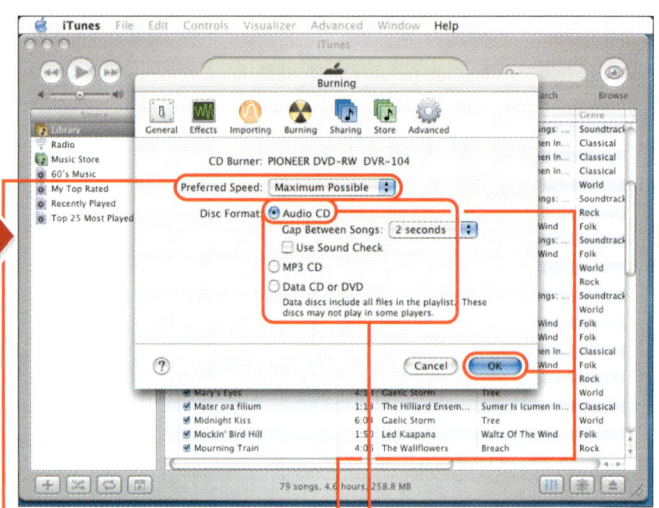

BURNING PREFERENCES

■ The Burning settings appear.

16 Click here to select the speed at which your CD burner will record.

■ You can select a slower speed if your Mac has trouble burning discs.

17 Click a **Disc Format** option (○ changes to ●) to specify the kind of disc you want to make.

■ Selecting the **Audio CD** option lets you specify additional options.

18 Click **OK**.

26

2 iTunes Basics

WORKING WITH ITUNES

TEACH YOURSELF: What do the different encoders do?

They affect how much room the music files take up on your Mac's hard disk, and how good the sound quality is. Both the AAC and MP3 encoders compress the sound, which can reduce the sound's quality; the WAV and AIFF encoders do not compress the sound, but the files they produce take up much more disk space — and do not play on all devices.

TEACH YOURSELF: Why would I want to make a data CD or DVD?

You use data CDs or DVDs to make back-up copies of your music files. This is particularly useful for music that you buy from the iTunes Music Store. You can also use data discs to move your music to another computer. For more on the Music Store, see Chapter 4.

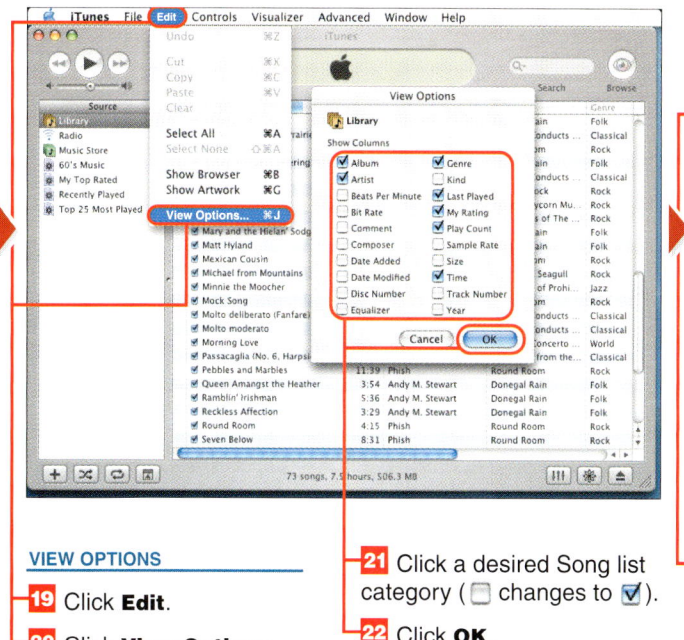

VIEW OPTIONS

19 Click **Edit**.

20 Click **View Options**.

■ The View Options dialog appears.

21 Click a desired Song list category (☐ changes to ✓).

22 Click **OK**.

■ The category you clicked appears in a separate column in the Song list.

■ You can click a column heading to sort the Song list by that category.

■ You can click it again to reverse the sort order.

■ You can click and drag a column's heading to move it left or right.

■ You can click and drag the separator line between column headings to adjust the width of the column to the left of the cursor.

■ Each item in the Source list remembers its view settings.

27

PLAY A CD

iTunes turns your Mac into a very smart audio CD player that can download song title and album information for your CD from the Internet if you have a connection.

Before playing a CD, you may want to set your preferences to show songs when you insert a CD and to connect to the Internet to do so. For more on setting preferences, see the section "Set Up iTunes."

PLAY A CD

■ Insert an audio CD into your Mac.

■ The Accessing CDDB display appears briefly as iTunes retrieves song titles from the Internet.

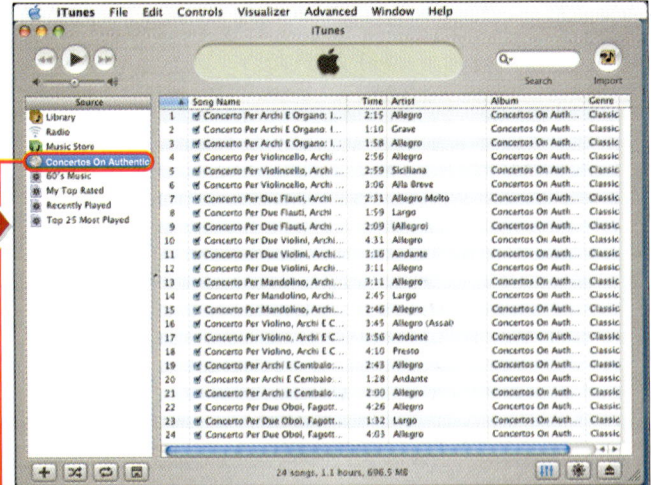

■ The CD's title appears selected in the Source list and its track titles appear in the Song list.

■ If your Mac cannot connect to the Internet or if the CD is not in the database, you see generic track titles.

Note: After iTunes obtains a CD's track list, it remembers it and does not need to access the Internet for that CD again.

28

2 iTunes Basics

WORKING WITH ITUNES

The song names in iTunes' Song list do not match what is printed on my CD liner notes. What can I do?

Page 78 shows how to change information on a song you have imported, but the technique described there also works for the song information on an audio CD.

Can I use the keyboard to control CD playback?

Yes, you can. Click **Controls** to view some of the more common keyboard playback commands. Also, iTunes' **Help** menu has a **Keyboard Shortcuts** entry that shows you even more shortcuts.

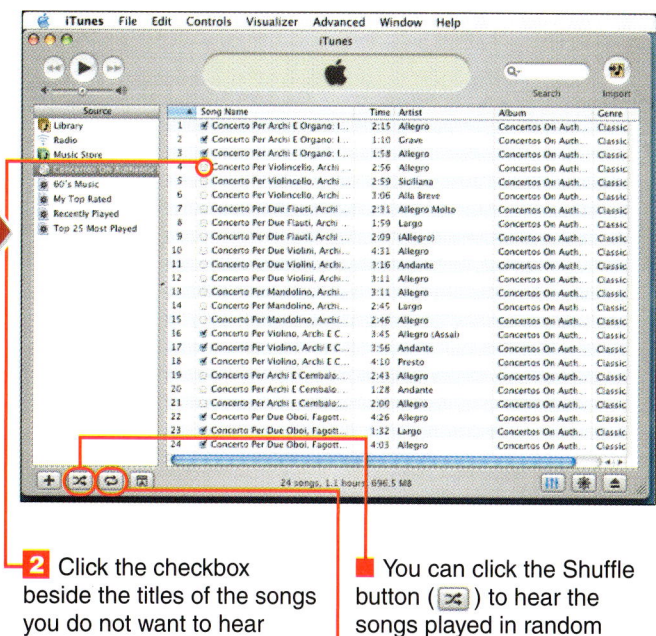

■ **2** Click the checkbox beside the titles of the songs you do not want to hear (☑ changes to ☐).

■ You can click the Shuffle button (⋈) to hear the songs played in random order.

■ You can click the Repeat button (⟲) to have the CD start playing again when it has played all the songs.

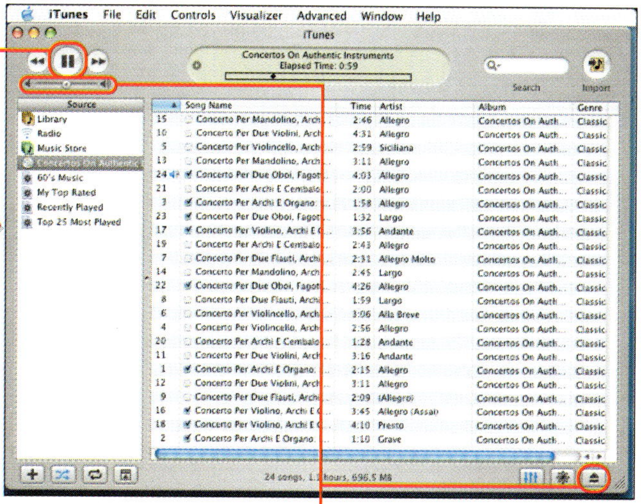

■ **3** Click the Play button (▶ changes to ❚❚).

■ The CD plays.

■ You can click ❚❚ again to pause the playback.

■ You can drag the volume slider (●) to adjust the playback volume.

■ **4** Click the Eject button (⏏) to eject the CD from your Mac when you're done.

29

RIP A MUSIC CD

You can create an extensive library of music on your Mac by importing — also known as *ripping* — CDs with iTunes.

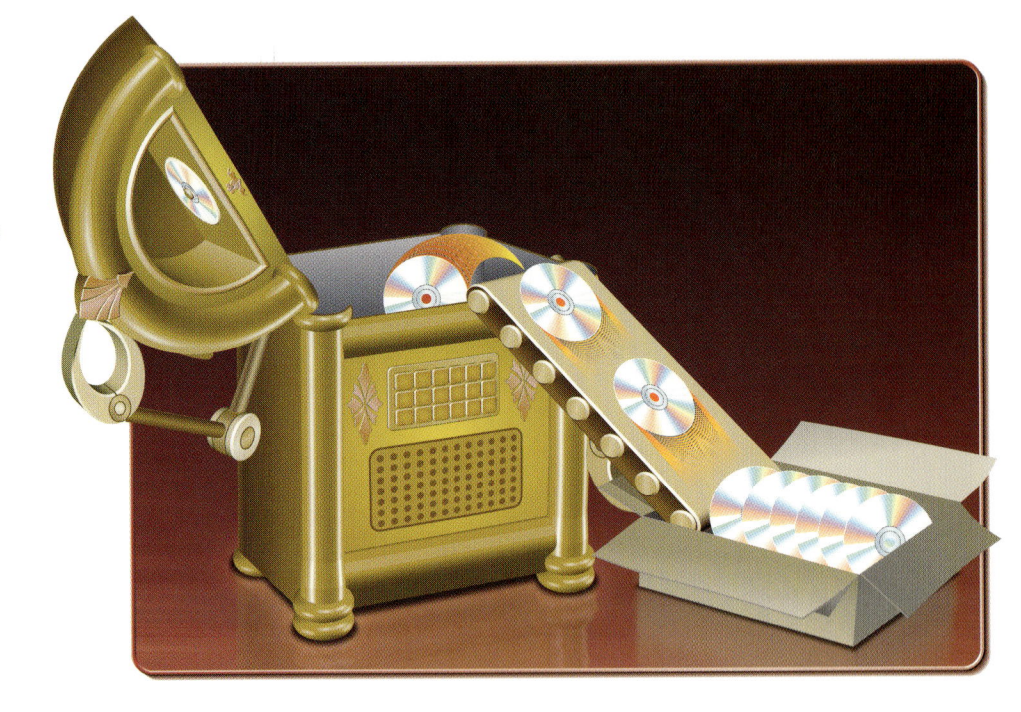

To rip your CDs, you may want to set your preferred import preferences. For more information, see the section "Set Up iTunes."

RIP A MUSIC CD

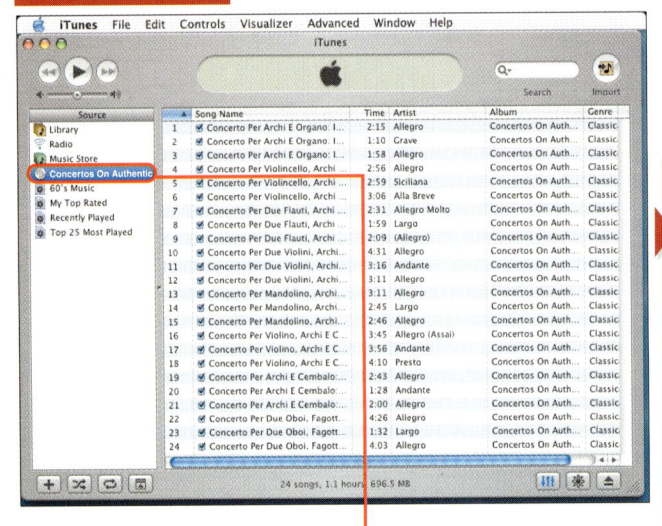

1 Insert an audio CD into your Mac.

■ The CD's title appears in the Source list and its track titles appear in the Song list.

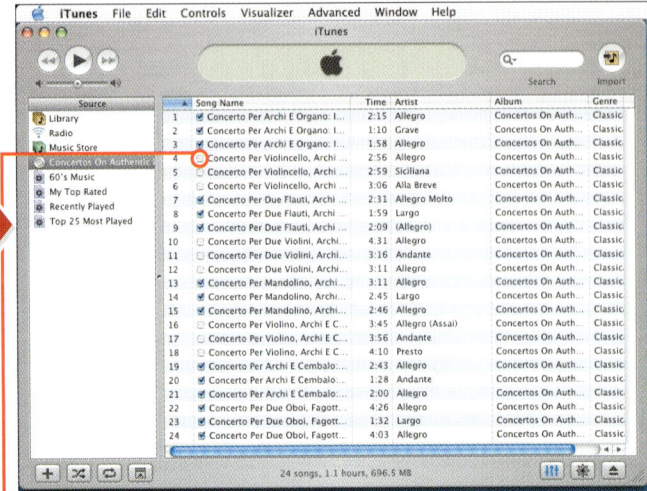

2 Click the checkbox beside those songs that you do not want to import (☑ changes to ☐).

■ You can press and hold down the ⌘ key when you click to uncheck or check all the Song list's checkboxes at once.

30

2 iTunes Basics

WORKING WITH ITUNES

TEACH YOURSELF

How do I play a song after I have imported it?

Find the song in your Library's Song list and simply double-click it. You can also click it once and then press `Return`.

TEACH YOURSELF

Can I import the same song twice, using two different encoders?

Yes. You can change the Import settings in the iTunes Preferences window to the new setting and then import the song again. When you do, iTunes asks you if you want to import the same song again, and whether you want to replace the existing imported song in your library. For more information on setting the iTunes Preferences window, see the section "Set Up iTunes."

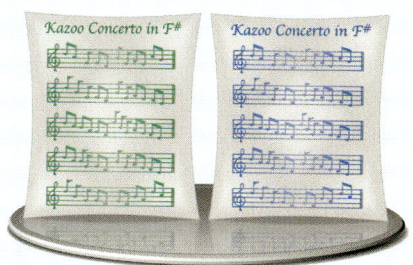

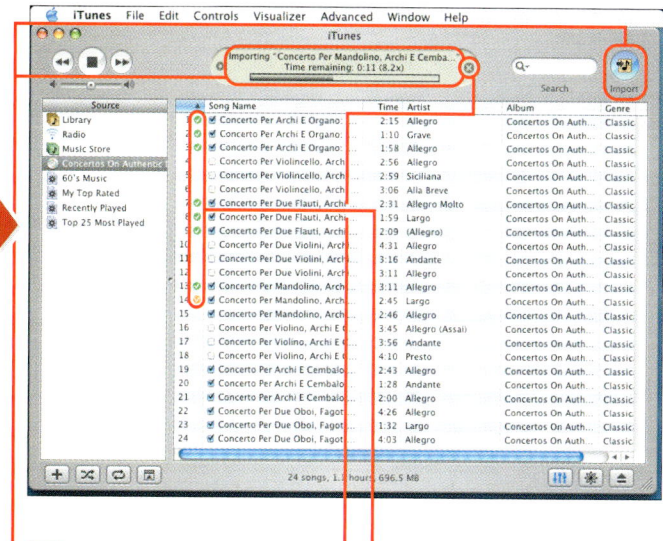

3 Click the **Import** button.

■ iTunes displays the import's progress.

■ When a song completely imports, a green checkmark (✓) appears beside it to let you know it is done.

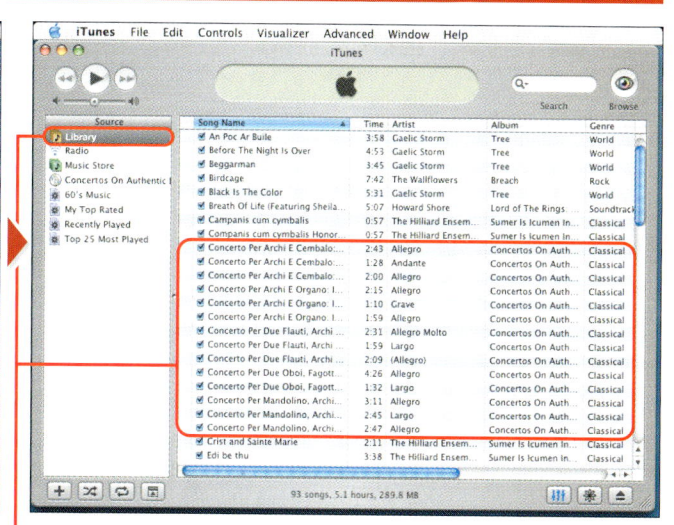

■ You can click the Cancel icon (✕) to stop the import before it finishes.

■ You can click **Library** in the Source list to see the imported songs in your Library.

31

SEARCH THE MUSIC LIBRARY

You can find any song in your iTunes Library with just a few taps on your keyboard even if your music collection contains hundreds or even thousands of songs.

SEARCH THE MUSIC LIBRARY

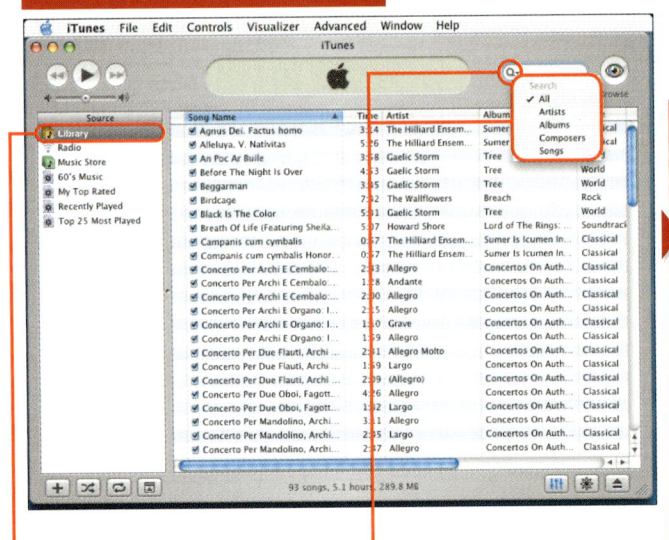

■ **1** Click **Library** in the Source list.

■ You can click the Magnifying Glass (🔍) and click a search category on the menu that appears.

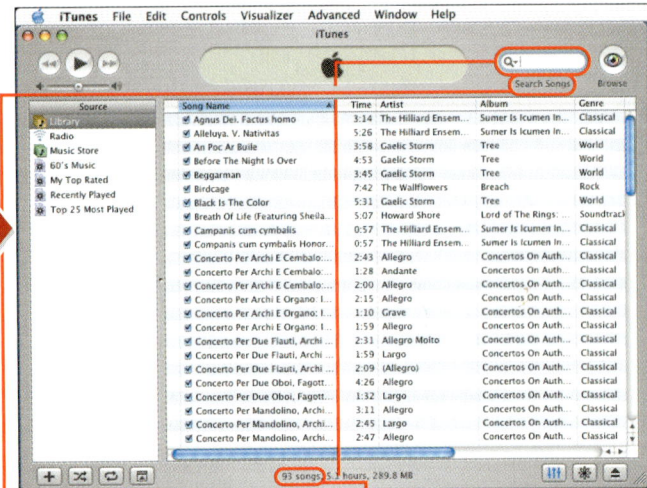

■ The label below the search entry area shows the current search category, or shows Search if you have not selected a category.

■ The number of songs you currently have in the Song list appears here.

■ **2** Click in the search field.

■ **3** Type a single letter.

32

2 iTunes Basics

WORKING WITH ITUNES

How do I search my music library using a search category — such as the genre — that does not exist in the Search field's menu?

Some of the column categories — such as the genre or the date last played — in your Song list do not appear in the Search field's menu. You cannot search using these categories with the Search field, but you can click the column heading in the Song list to sort the list by that category. Then you can easily scroll to the specific item you want.

Can I do "wildcard" searches?

You can type spaces to separate single letters or groups of letters in the search box. This displays song listings that contain only those distinct letters and letter groups. For example, "ga ma" shows both "Wol**ga**ng A**ma**deus Mozart" and "M**a**xwell **Ga**rvey."

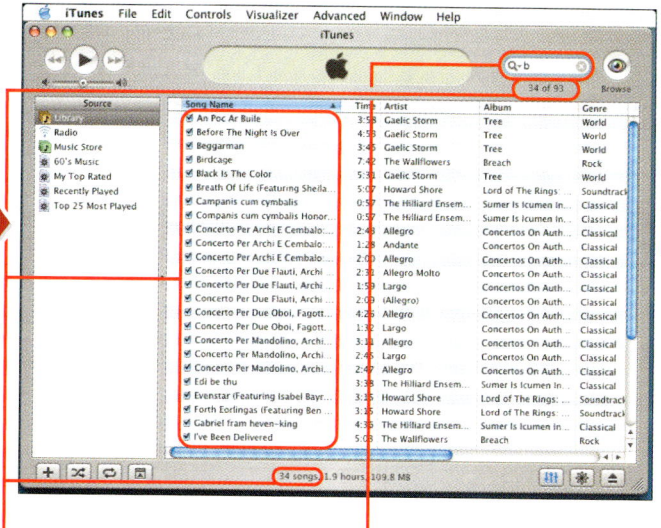

■ Only song listings that contain the letter you typed appear in the list and the number of songs in the list changes.

4 Type a few more letters.

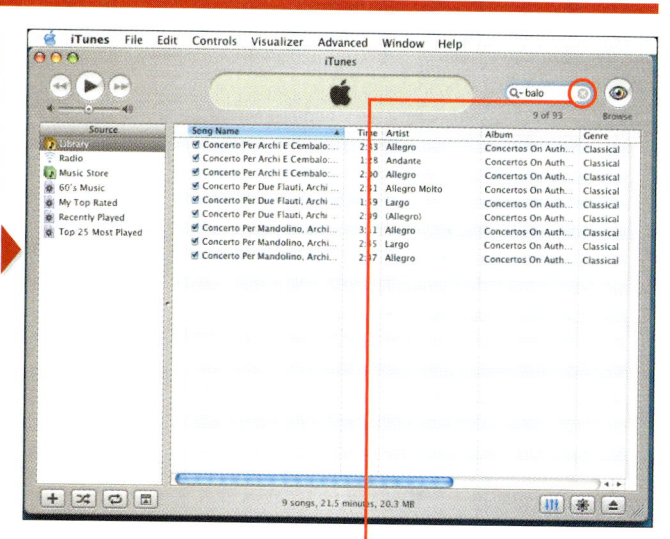

■ The Song list immediately updates.

■ You can click ⊗ to show the entire Song list again.

33

BROWSE THE MUSIC LIBRARY

You can browse through your music collection by genre, artist, and album to view only the songs or albums you want with just a few clicks.

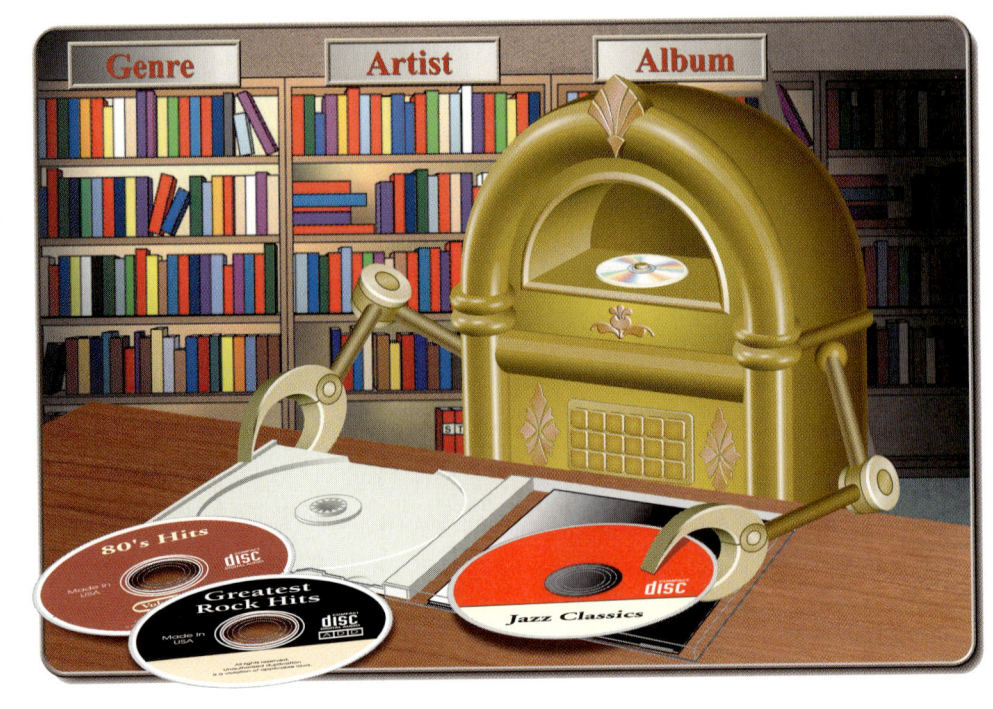

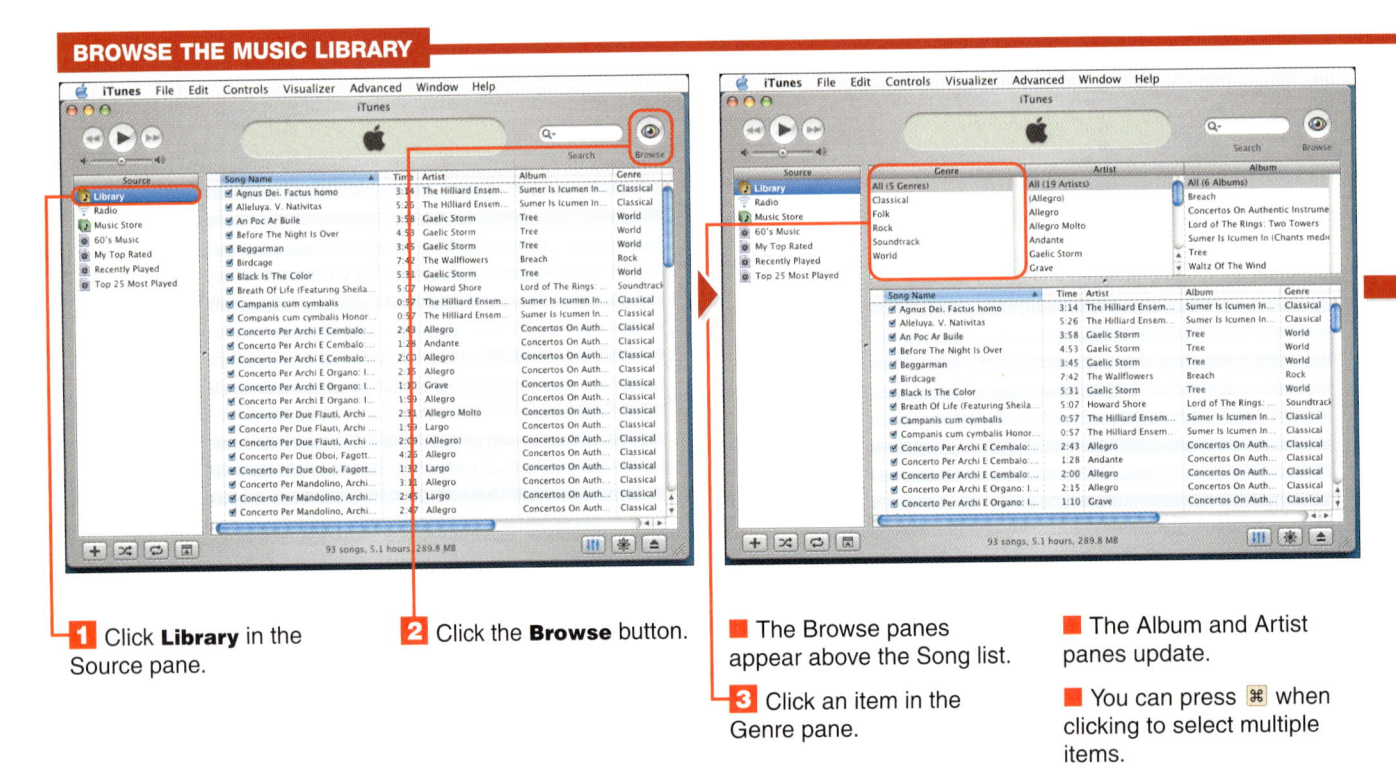

BROWSE THE MUSIC LIBRARY

1 Click **Library** in the Source pane.

2 Click the **Browse** button.

■ The Browse panes appear above the Song list.

3 Click an item in the Genre pane.

■ The Album and Artist panes update.

■ You can press ⌘ when clicking to select multiple items.

2 iTunes Basics

WORKING WITH ITUNES

I do not see a Genre column when I click the Browse icon. Why not?

You can show or hide the Genre Browse pane by setting preferences. For more information, see the section, "Set Up iTunes." To show the Genre Browse pane:

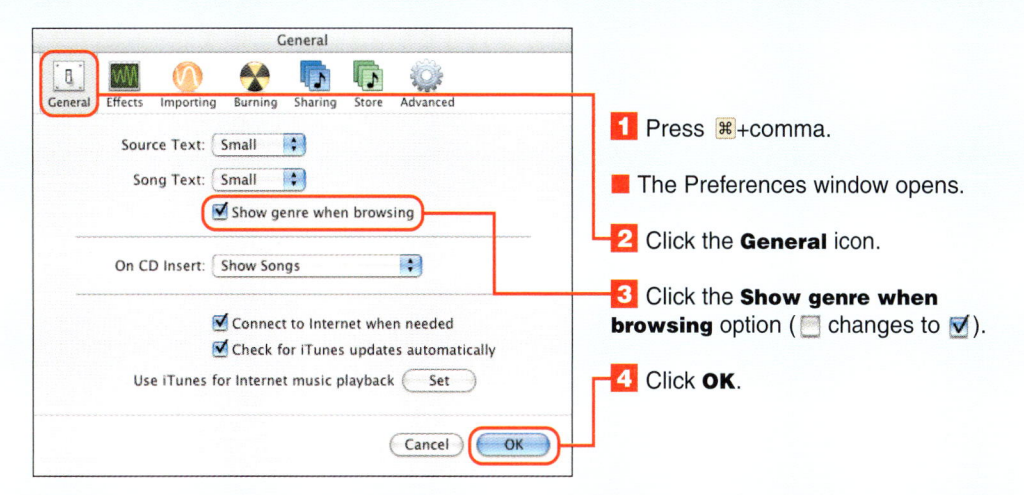

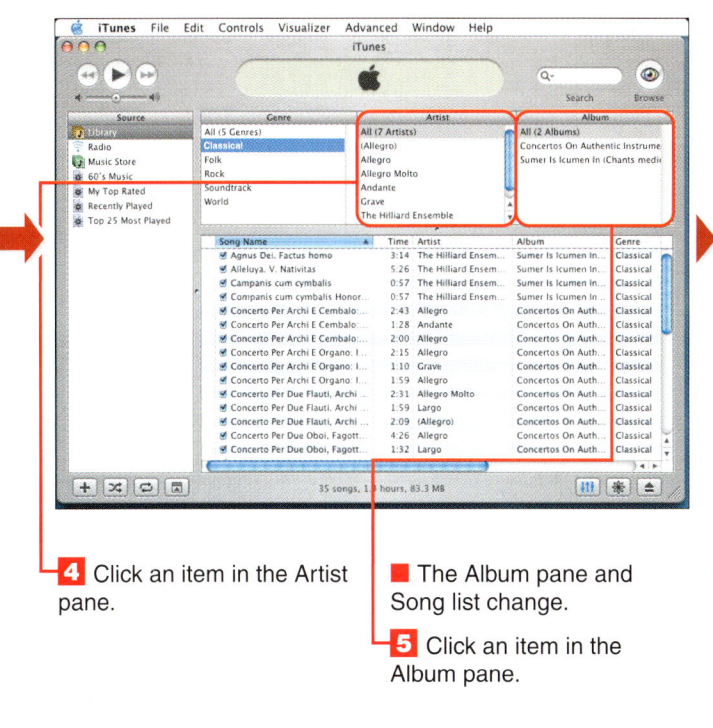

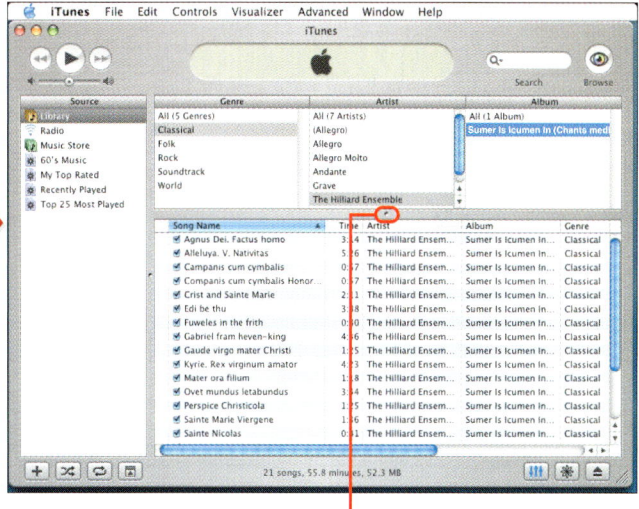

1 Press ⌘+comma.

■ The Preferences window opens.

2 Click the **General** icon.

3 Click the **Show genre when browsing** option (☐ changes to ☑).

4 Click **OK**.

4 Click an item in the Artist pane.

■ The Album pane and Song list change.

5 Click an item in the Album pane.

■ The Song list changes to show only the songs on the selected album.

■ You can click and drag up or down the gray strip that separates the Browse panes from the Song list to change the size of the Browse pane.

35

REMOVE A SONG FROM THE MUSIC LIBRARY

You can remove songs that you no longer wish to hear from your Library and free up some hard disk space.

REMOVE A SONG FROM THE MUSIC LIBRARY

1 Click **Library** in the Source pane.

2 Click a song that you want to remove.

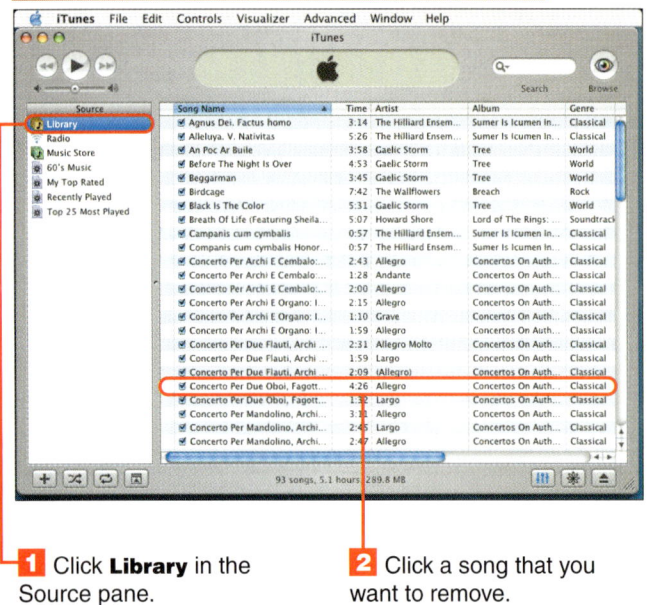

3 Press the Delete key.

■ A dialog appears asking if you want to remove the song from the list.

4 Click **Yes**.

36

2 iTunes Basics

WORKING WITH ITUNES

How can I quickly remove all songs by a particular artist?

Click the **Browse** button. Click the artist's entry in the Artist pane. Press the `Delete` key. You can also delete all the songs on an album or belonging to a specific genre this way.

How can I bypass the dialog that asks me to confirm deletions for just one time only?

Select the song(s) you want to delete. Press ⌘ + `Delete`. This bypasses the dialog that asks you to confirm the deletion. However, iTunes still asks you if you want to move the songs to the Mac's Trash if the songs are in your iTunes Music folder.

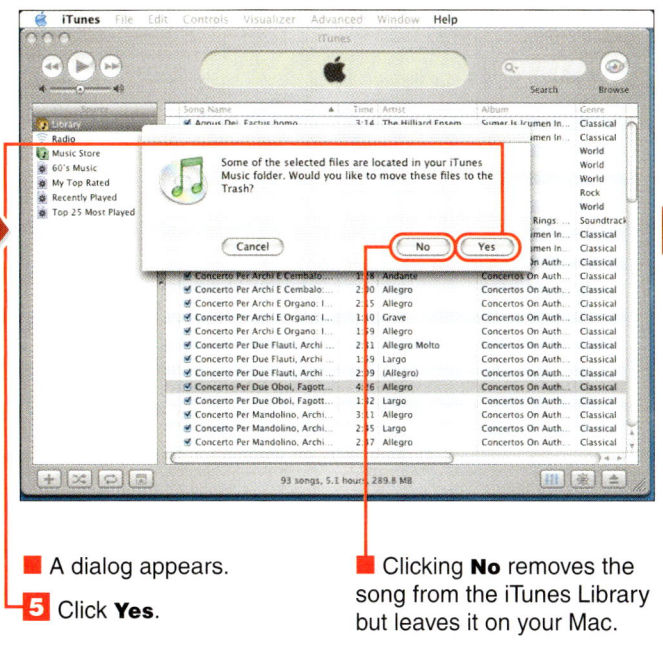

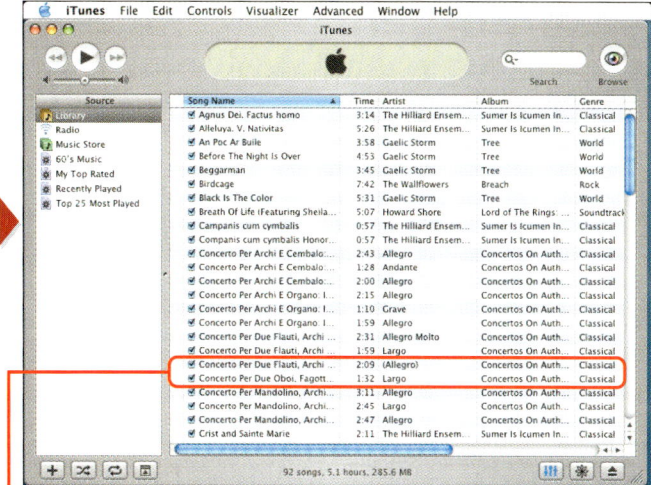

- ■ A dialog appears.
- 5 Click **Yes**.

- ■ Clicking **No** removes the song from the iTunes Library but leaves it on your Mac.

- ■ The song you selected no longer appears in the Song list.

- ■ iTunes removes the song file and moves it to your Trash.

37

RATE A SONG

You can rate the songs in your iTunes music library on a five-star scale so you can quickly find your favorite tunes.

RATE A SONG

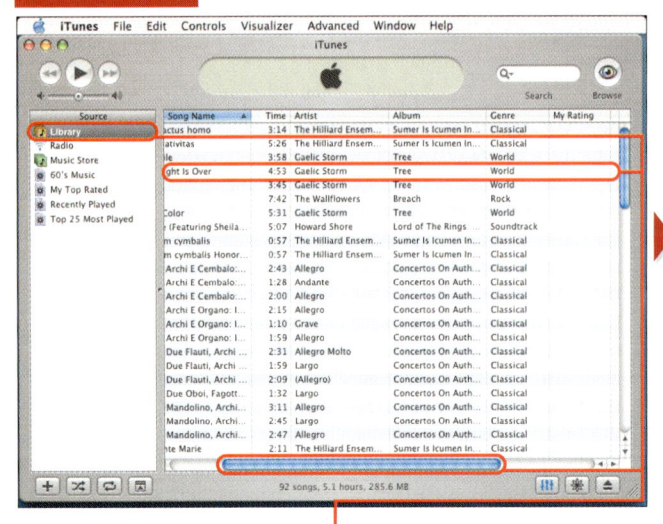

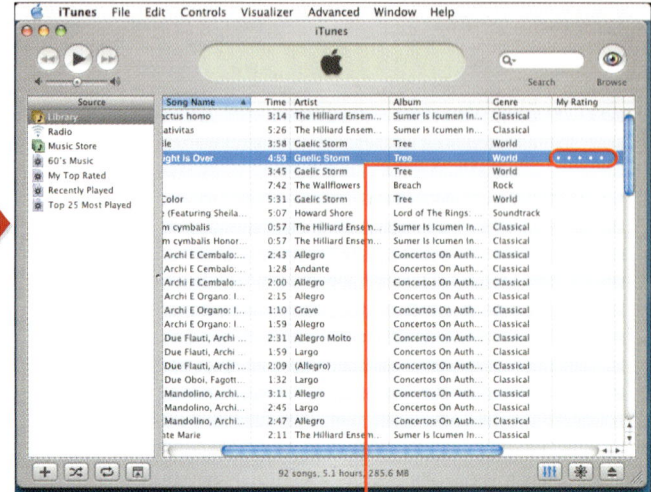

USING THE MOUSE

1 Display the My Rating column in the Song list.

Note: See the section "Set Up iTunes" for how to make this column visible.

2 Click **Library** in the Source list.

■ If necessary, you can scroll the Song list horizontally until the My Rating column appears.

3 Click a song listing.

■ iTunes highlights the song listing and a row of five dots appears in its My Rating column.

4 Click any dot in the My Rating column.

■ Stars replace the dots you click.

2 iTunes Basics
WORKING WITH ITUNES

How do I use my song ratings?

You can sort your Song list by your song ratings so you can quickly find your favorites. Simply click the My Rating column heading to sort the songs by their ratings. You can also make playlists that contain your favorite songs. For more information on making playlists and burning discs in iTunes, see Chapter 3.

How can I set the rating for more than one song at a time?

You can press ⌘ and click on several songs to select all of them. You can press `Control`+click or right-click one of the selected songs to bring up a song menu. Click **My Rating,** and then click a rating. Every selected song gets that rating.

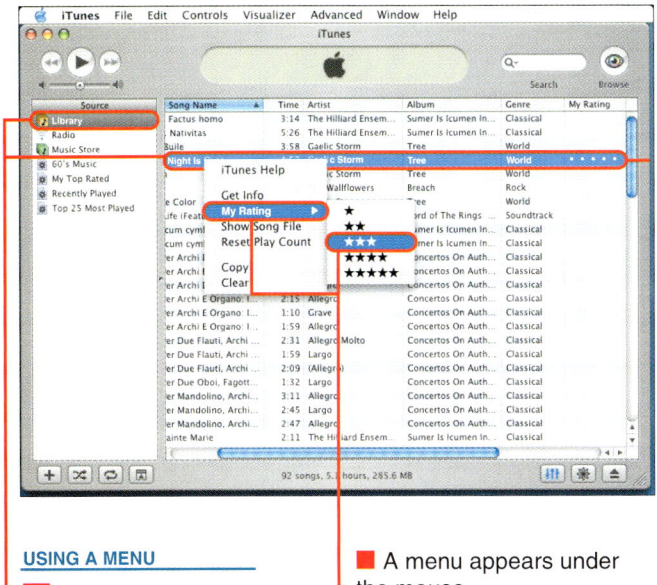

USING A MENU

1 Click **Library** in the Source list.

2 Press `Ctrl`+click or right-click a song.

■ A menu appears under the mouse.

3 Click **My Rating**.

4 Click one of the sub-menu's choices.

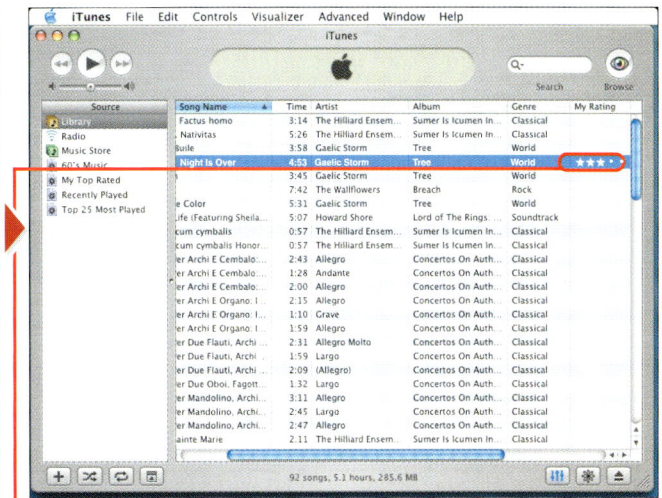

■ Stars appear in the song's My Rating column.

39

PLAY INTERNET RADIO

iTunes can let you hear a number of Internet radio streams selected by Apple, ranging from Pop to Classical to Reggae. For more on playing and adding additional Internet radio streams to your Library, see the section "Add an Internet Radio Station."

To perform the steps in this section, you must have an active Internet connection. To set iTunes to establish an Internet connection when necessary, see the section "Set Up iTunes."

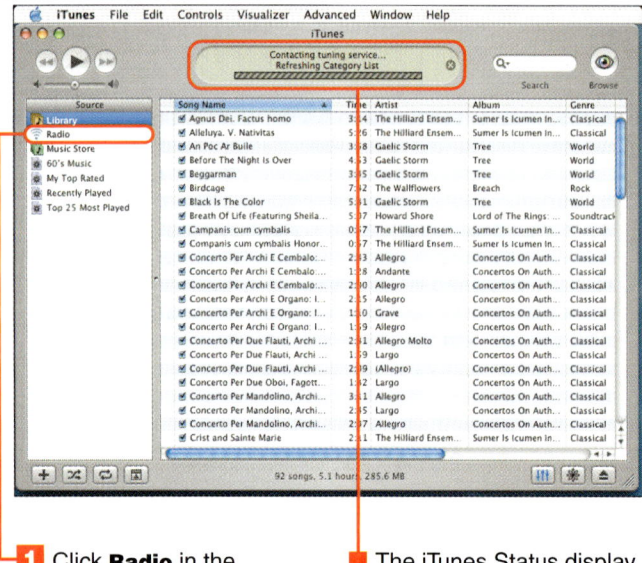

PLAY INTERNET RADIO

1 Click **Radio** in the Source list.

■ The iTunes Status display briefly shows a Contacting tuning service message.

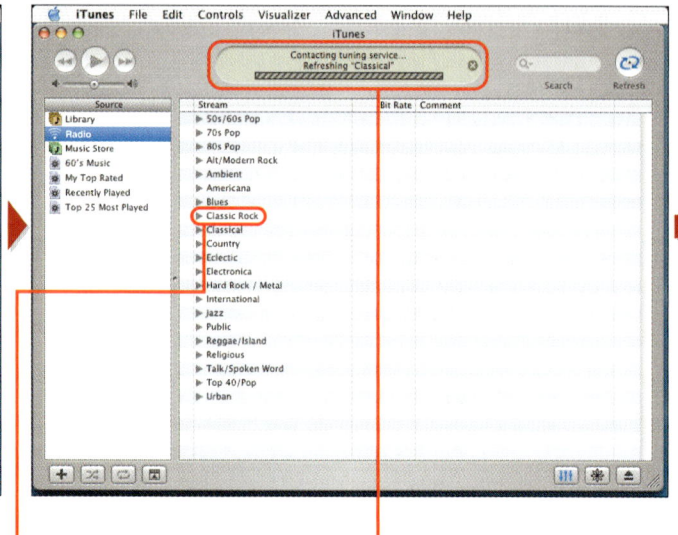

■ iTunes shows you a list of stream categories.

2 Click the ▶ beside a category.

■ The iTunes Status display briefly shows another "Contacting..." message.

40

2 iTunes Basics

WORKING WITH ITUNES

TEACH YOURSELF

Can I listen to Internet radio over a modem connection?

Many of the Internet radio stations offered by iTunes broadcast at modem speeds. If you have a 56K modem connection, look for stations that have a bit rate that is 56 kbps or lower. For slower connections, look for stations that broadcast at 24 kbps or lower.

TEACH YOURSELF

What does it mean when I see a "Rebuffering" message window appear while listening to Internet radio?

To avoid momentary audio drop-outs that transmission errors cause, iTunes stores a few seconds of the music in a buffer as it receives Internet radio information. If iTunes encounters too many gaps, iTunes' buffer empties and the music stops playing while iTunes attempts to refill the buffer.

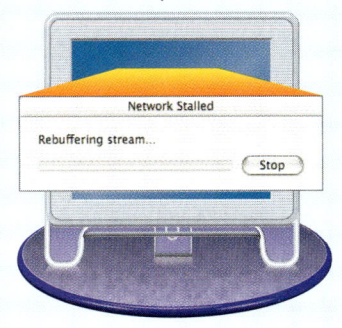

■ The station list for the selected category appears with the number of currently available streams.

3 Click a radio station listing.

4 Press `Return`.

■ The station plays and the iTunes Status display shows the station's information.

Note: Some stations may not play if they have too many listeners connected or are temporarily unavailable for some other reason.

41

ADD AN INTERNET RADIO STATION

You can play Internet radio stations other than the ones that the iTunes' radio list provides and you can add them to your Library. For more about iTunes' radio list, see the section "Play Internet Radio."

To perform the steps in this section, you must have an active Internet connection. To set iTunes to establish an Internet connection when necessary, see the section "Set Up iTunes."

ADD AN INTERNET RADIO STATION

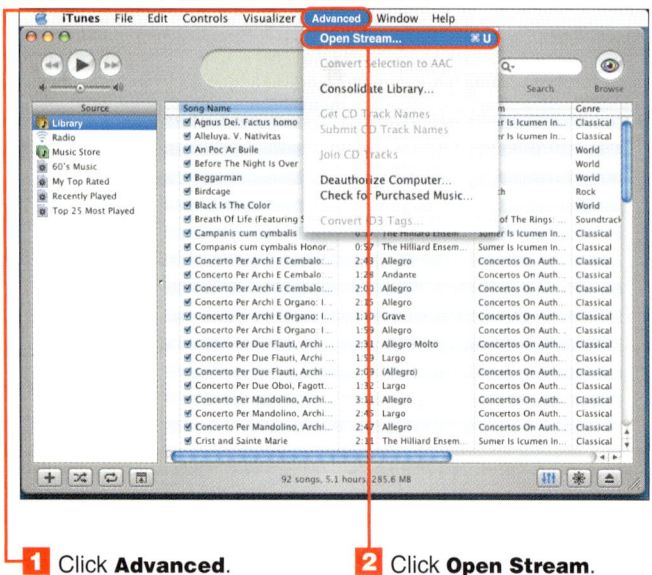

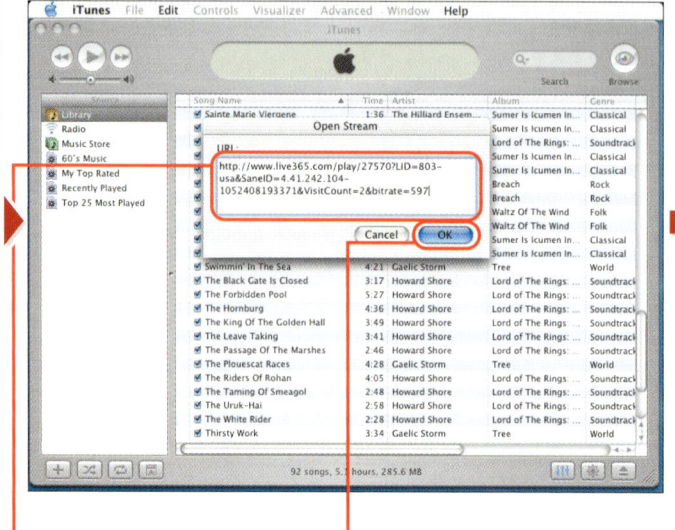

1 Click **Advanced**.

2 Click **Open Stream**.

■ The Open Stream dialog appears.

3 Type or paste the address of an Internet radio station in the URL field.

4 Click **OK**.

Note: Because URLs for Internet are often long and hard to type, you may want to copy and paste them directly from a Web browser or other source.

42

2 iTunes Basics

WORKING WITH ITUNES

How can I find URLs for Internet radio stations?

Open an Internet search engine like Google in your Web browser and search for streaming audio stations. Several sites, such as Live365.com and Shoutcast.com, provide categorized links to many streaming audio stations.

What kind of streams can iTunes play?

iTunes can play MP3 streams. Such streams usually have URLs that end with .pls or .m3u. Some formats, however, require special players and are not compatible with iTunes. Unfortunately, sometimes you can only find out if it is compatible by trial and error.

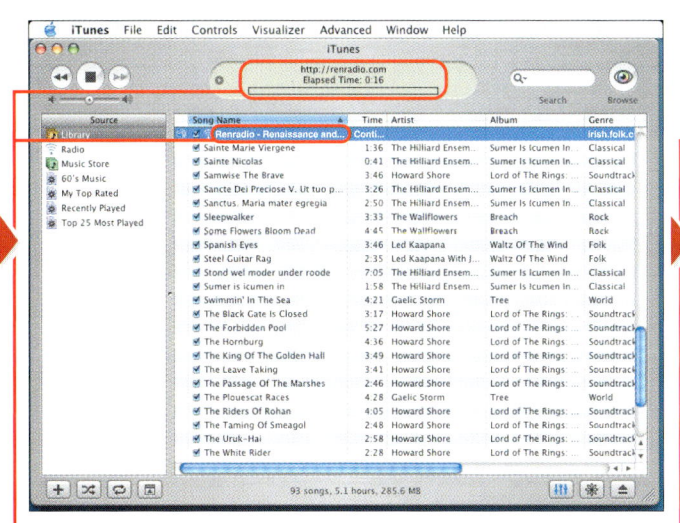

- The radio station appears in the Song list and begins playing.

5 Click the radio station name.

6 Press Enter.

7 Type a suitable name for the station.

8 Press Return.

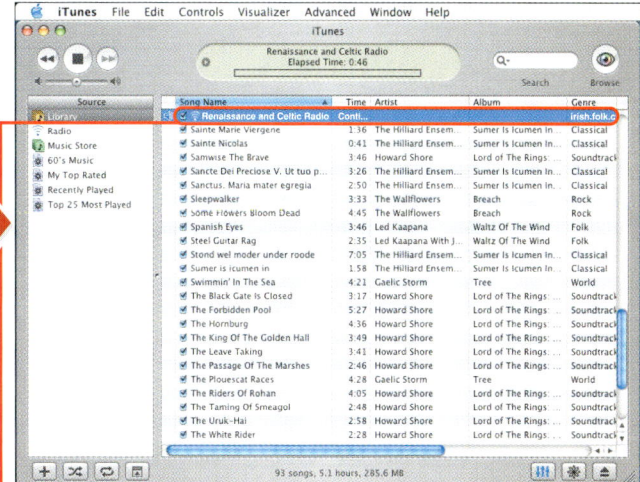

- The radio station is now in your Library with the name that you gave it.

Note: The station may not play if you have an incorrect URL or if the stream format is incompatible with iTunes.

43

SHARE MUSIC OVER A NETWORK

Your friends, family, and co-workers can listen to music from your iTunes Library over a local network. You can have as many as five other iTunes users connected at one time.

Other users see your music using a Shared name, which they see in their iTunes Source list. You may also specify a password, which users must enter to access your shared music.

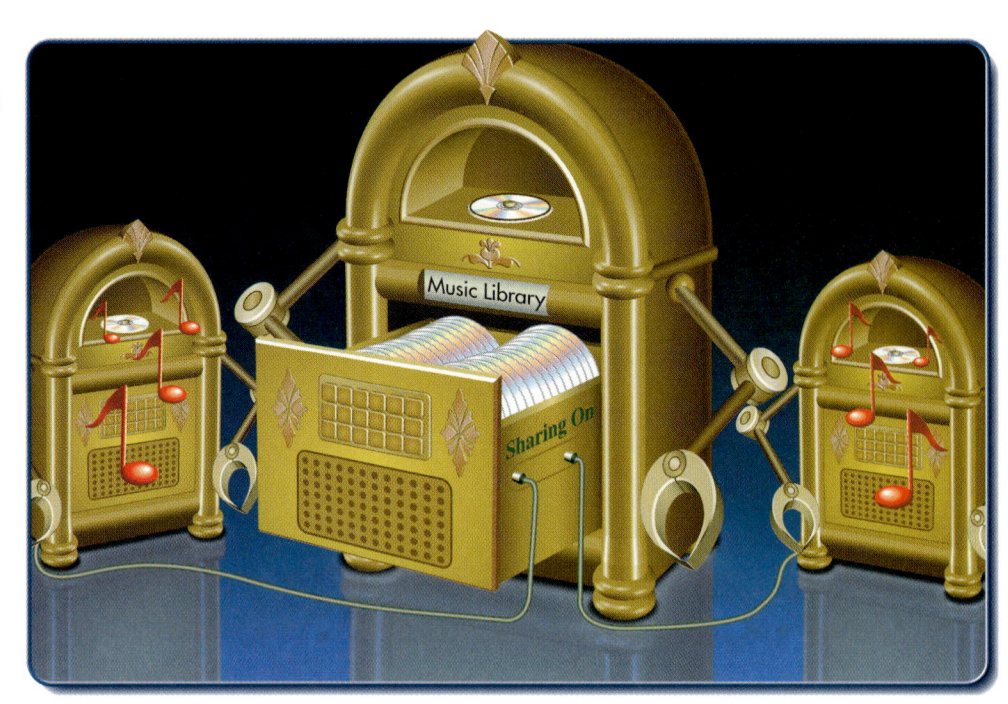

SHARE MUSIC OVER A NETWORK

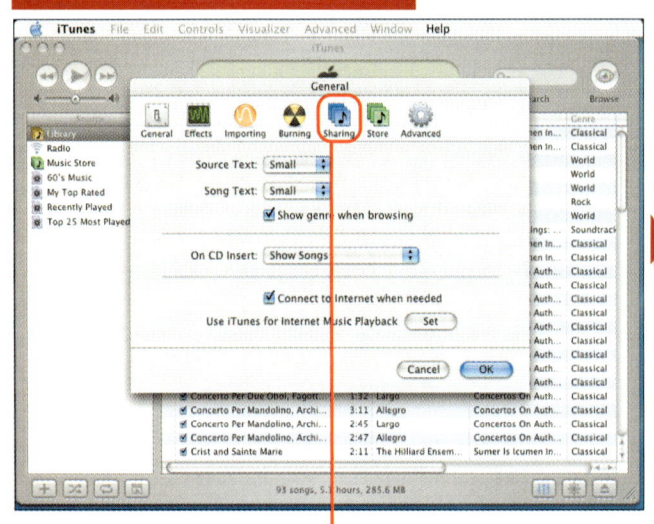

1 Open the iTunes Preferences window.

Note: For more on iTunes Preferences, see the section "Set Up iTunes."

2 Click the **Sharing** icon.

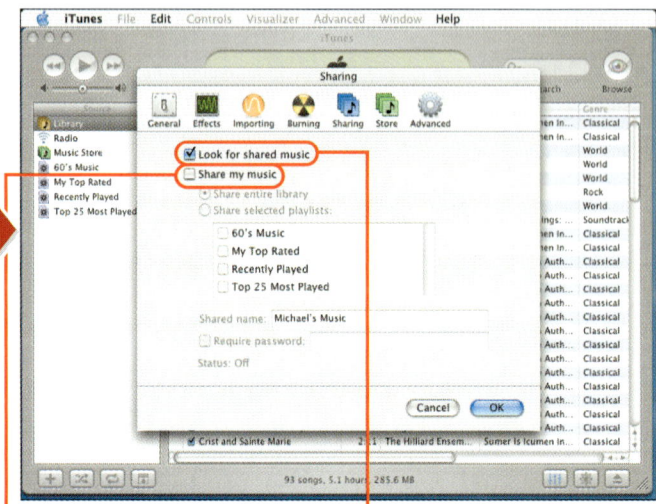

■ The Sharing settings appear.

3 Click the **Share my music** option (☐ changes to ☑).

■ If you do not want to see other iTunes users' music, deselect the **Look for shared music** option (☑ changes to ☐).

44

2 iTunes Basics

WORKING WITH ITUNES

How can I see if someone is listening to my music?

Click the **Sharing** icon in the iTunes Preferences window. The Status area at the bottom of the window shows you how many users are connected to your library. To access the iTunes Preferences window, see the section "Set Up iTunes."

People cannot see some of my music. Why not?

iTunes shares neither QuickTime sound files nor Audible spoken word files you have purchased. It shares music you have purchased from the iTunes Music Store only if you authorize the computers that are connecting to yours. For more on authorizing other computers to play purchased music, see Chapter 4.

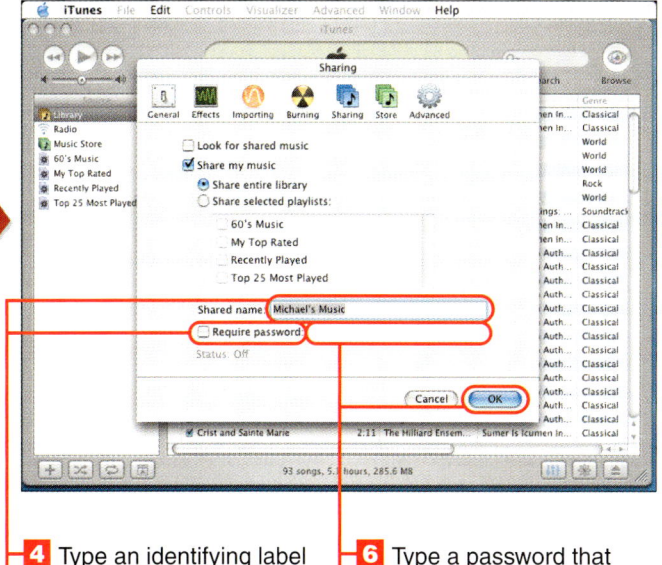

4 Type an identifying label for your shared music.

5 Click the **Require password** option (☐ changes to ☑).

6 Type a password that others must enter to access your music.

Note: For security reasons, do not use your own Mac user password.

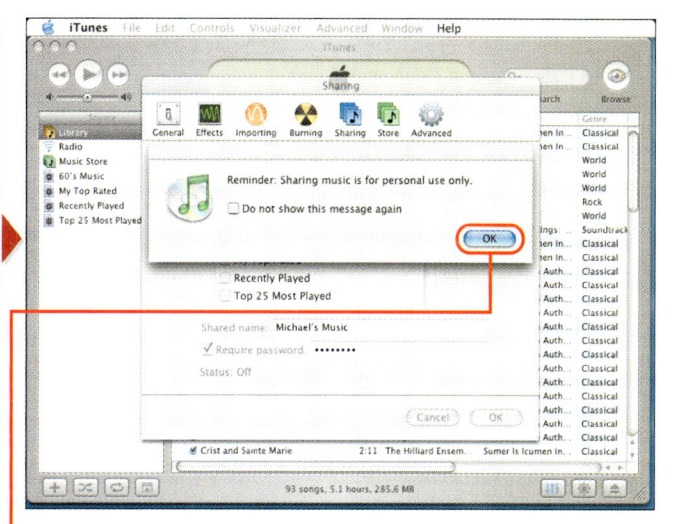

7 Click **OK**.

■ Another dialog window appears.

8 Click **OK**.

■ Both windows close.

■ iTunes now shares your music over your local network.

Note: You can only share your music while you run iTunes.

45

CREATE A PLAYLIST

You can use the songs in your Music Library to create *playlists*, which are individual songs that you group together. For example, you can create a playlist with up-tempo songs for your morning workout, another with soft music for a dinner party, and another with heavy-metal hits to keep your eyes open during an all-night study session.

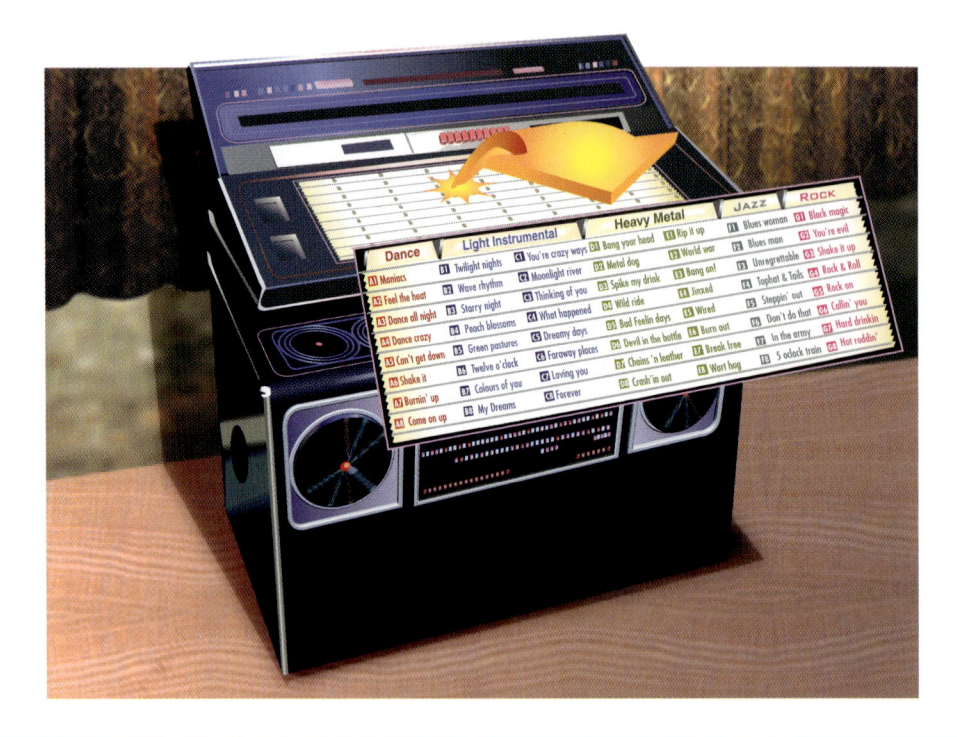

CREATE A PLAYLIST

1 Click **Library**.

2 Click the Create a Playlist button (+).

■ A new playlist appears in the Source list with its name selected for editing.

3 Type a name for the playlist.

4 Press `Return`.

■ The playlist appears in the Source list with its new name.

■ If you have more than one playlist, iTunes moves the renamed playlist to its proper alphabetical position in the Source list.

46

3 Creating Playlists and Burning Disks with iTunes

WORKING WITH ITUNES

What kinds of items can go in a playlist?

Anything that iTunes can play: individual songs you have ripped, songs or audio books that you have purchased from the iTunes Music Store, GarageBand songs you have composed, and even Internet radio stations. For more about ripping a song, see Chapter 2. For more on the iTunes Music Store, see Chapter 4.

Does removing songs from a playlist erase them from my Mac?

No. The items in a playlist simply refer to the actual items in your iTunes Library. Removing the item from a playlist only removes the reference. You can also place references to the same song into several different playlists without taking up any extra disk space on your Mac. To remove an entire playlist, click to select it in the Source list and press `Delete`.

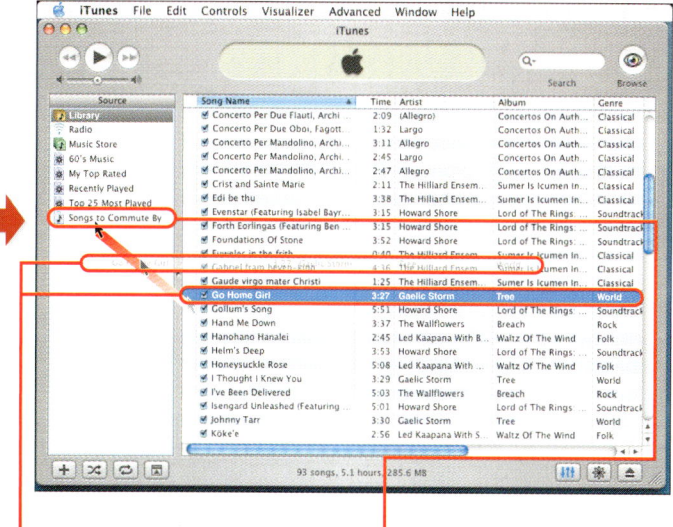

5 Click and drag a song entry in the Song list.

■ A translucent version of the song entry follows the cursor as it moves.

6 Position the cursor over the name of a playlist in the Source list and release the mouse.

■ The playlist name blinks once and the translucent image vanishes from under the cursor.

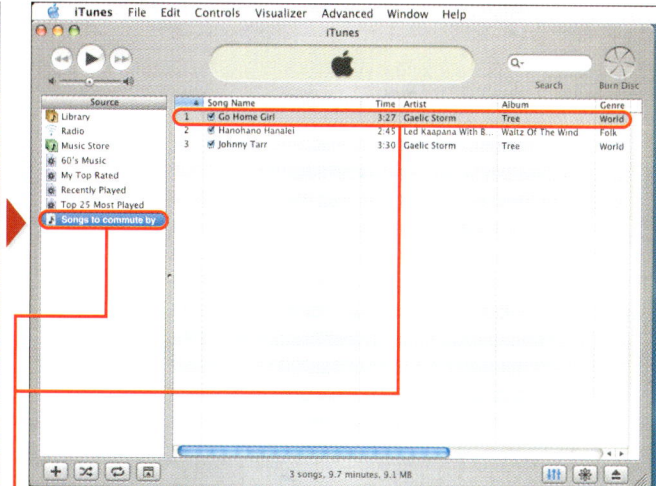

7 Click the playlist.

■ The song you dragged appears in the playlist.

■ You can press `Shift` + click, or ⌘+click, to select several songs and then drag them all at once to a playlist.

47

REARRANGE A PLAYLIST

The songs you place in a playlist normally play in the order in which you added them. But you can change that order any time you like, either by sorting the playlist, shuffling it, or manually dragging the songs into the exact order you want.

REARRANGE A PLAYLIST

ARRANGE BY SORTING

1 Click a playlist in the Source list.

2 Click a column heading in the Song list.

■ iTunes sorts the playlist by that column.

■ You can click the same column heading again to reverse the Song list's sorting order.

■ The songs play in the sorted order.

ARRANGE BY SHUFFLING

1 Click a playlist in the Source list.

2 Click the leftmost column heading in the Song list.

■ The playlist appears in its normal play order.

3 Click the Shuffle button (⤨).

■ The order of the song titles changes randomly.

■ You can click ⤨ again to return to the unshuffled play order.

48

3 Creating Playlists and Burning Disks with iTunes

WORKING WITH ITUNES

How can I sort a playlist and then manually adjust the sorted order?

iTunes has a menu that lets you copy a playlist's sorted or shuffled order so that you can use it as the normal play order.

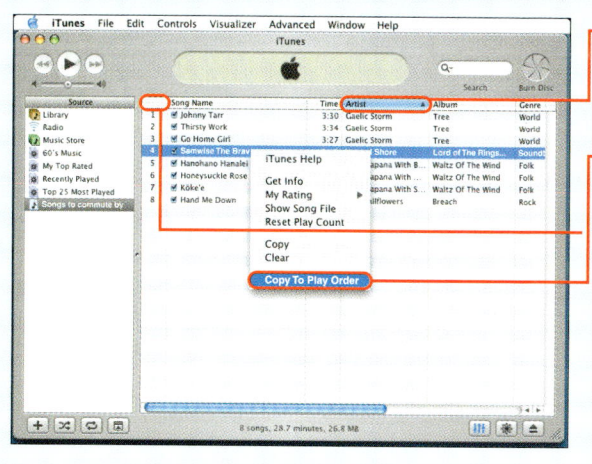

1 Sort the playlist by clicking a column heading.

2 Press `Control` and click one of the songs.

3 In the menu that appears, select **Copy to Play Order**.

4 Click the Song list's leftmost column heading.

■ The play order retains the sorted order you chose.

■ You can now make further play order adjustments by following the steps for manually arranging the playlist.

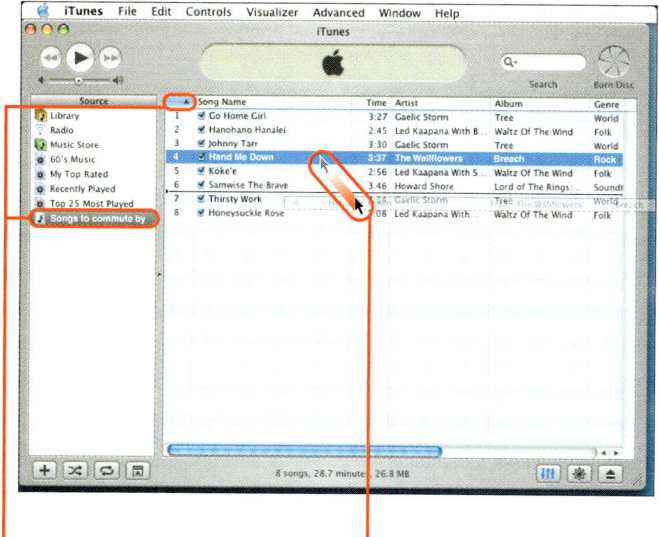

ARRANGE MANUALLY

1 Click the playlist in the Source list.

2 Click the leftmost column heading in the Song list.

3 Click and drag a song in the Song list.

■ A translucent song listing follows the mouse, and a black line appears between the songs in the Song list closest to the cursor.

4 Release the mouse when the black line appears where you want the song to go.

■ The song moves to its new position in the Song list.

49

BURN A STANDARD AUDIO CD

You can burn a playlist to an audio CD with iTunes and play it in any CD player. This allows you to take your music to work, to a party, or on your daily jog.

You need a CD burner attached to your Mac if one is not built in; most commercial CD burners are compatible with iTunes.

Please note that you can only copy copyrighted material for personal, non-commercial use, and that you cannot redistribute this material without permission from the copyright holder.

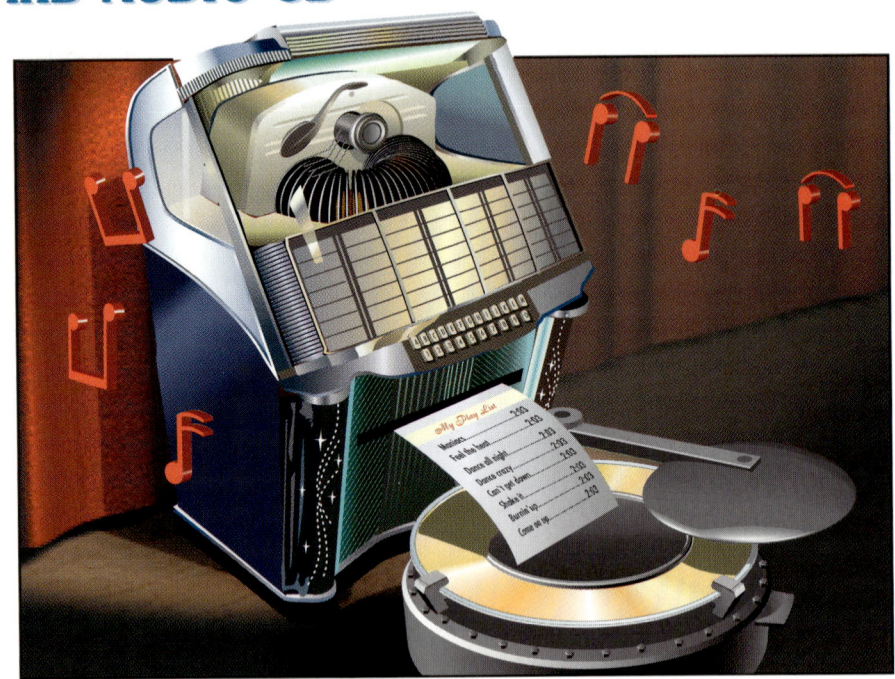

BURN A STANDARD AUDIO CD

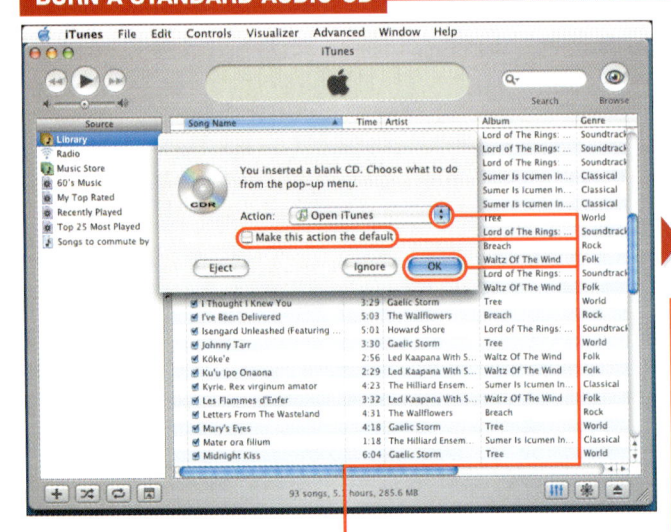

1 Set iTunes' Burning Preferences to burn an audio CD.

Note: For more on setting up Preferences, see Chapter 2.

2 Insert a blank CD-R in your CD burner.

■ A window appears.

3 Click here and select **Open iTunes**.

■ You can click here (☐ changes to ☑) if you always want iTunes to open when you insert a blank CD.

4 Click **OK**.

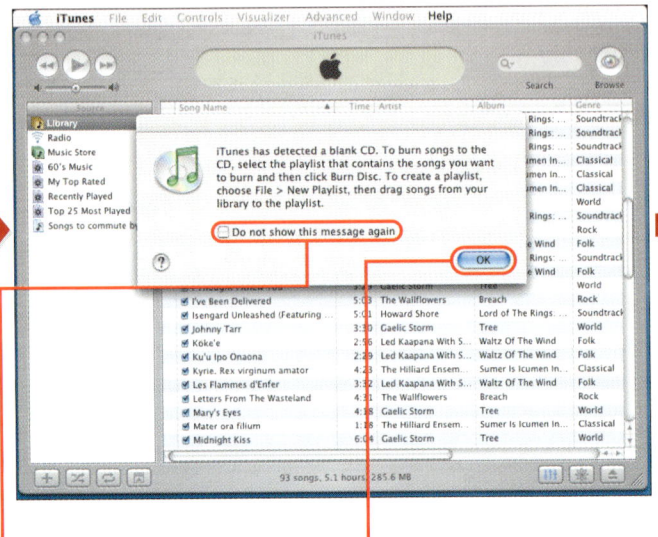

■ Another window appears with some basic instructions for CD burning.

■ You can click the **Do not show this message again** option (☐ changes to ☑) if you do not want to see this instruction message every time you insert a blank CD.

5 Click **OK**.

■ The window closes.

50

3 Creating Playlists and Burning Disks with iTunes

WORKING WITH ITUNES

Can I use an erasable CD-RW to create an audio CD?

iTunes lets you use CD-RWs to make audio CDs, but most consumer CD audio players have trouble reading them. They do play in your Mac, however.

What happens if my playlist is too big to fit on an audio CD?

Standard audio CDs can hold about 74 minutes of sound; 700MB CDs can hold a few minutes more. iTunes warns you if a playlist is too long for the CD and gives you the choice of either just burning enough songs to fit or of making an MP3 CD instead. For more information, see the section "Burn an MP3 CD."

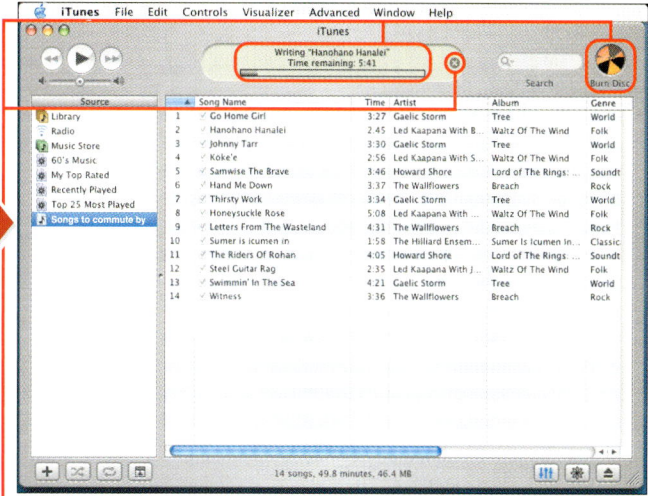

■ **6** Click the playlist in the Source list that you want to burn.

■ **7** Click the **Burn Disc** icon.

■ The Status display prompts you to click Burn Disc.

■ **8** Click the **Burn Disc** icon again.

■ As the Burn Disc icon spins, the Status display shows the burn's progress.

■ You can click the Cancel button (⊗) to cancel the burn.

Note: You cannot reuse a CD-R when you cancel a burn.

■ When the burn finishes, the newly created CD appears selected in the Source list.

51

BURN AN MP3 CD

Some new CD players play both ordinary audio CDs and new MP3-format CDs that hold almost ten times as much music. With iTunes you can burn your own long-playing MP3 CDs for these new CD players.

Because MP3 files are compressed, you can place more songs on an MP3 disc than you can on a standard audio CD.

Please note that you can only copy copyrighted material for personal, non-commercial use, and that you cannot redistribute this material without permission from the copyright holder.

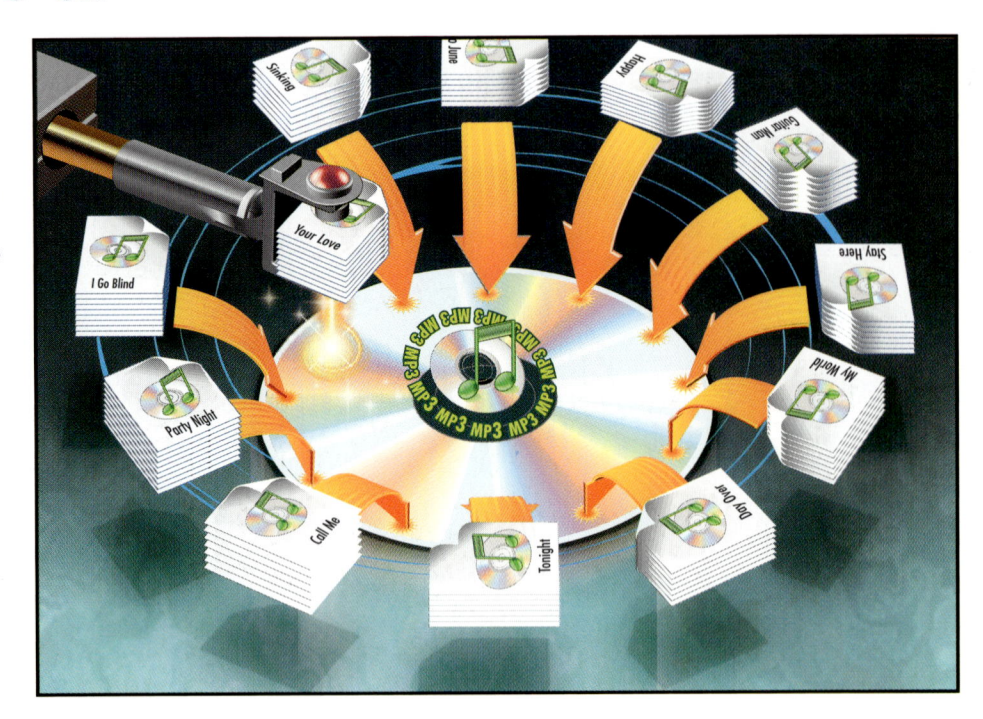

BURN AN MP3 CD

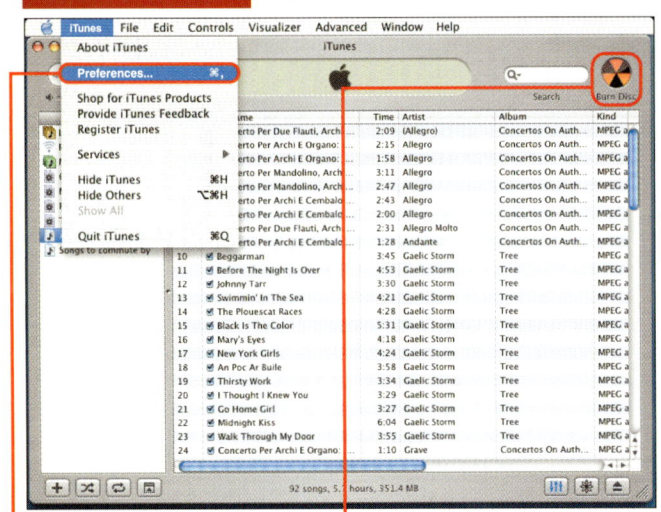

1 Set iTunes' Preferences to burn an MP3 CD.

Note: To set up Preferences, see Chapter 2.

2 Insert a blank recordable CD.

3 Follow steps **3** to **6** in the section "Burn a Standard Audio CD."

4 Click the **Burn Disc** icon.

■ The Status display prompts you to click Burn Disc again.

5 Click the **Burn Disc** icon again.

■ The Burn Disc icon spins, and the Status display shows the burn's progress.

Note: iTunes only copies the songs in your playlist that are compressed in MP3 format to the CD.

■ When the burn finishes, the newly created MP3 CD appears selected in the Source list.

52

BURN AN ARCHIVE CD OR DVD

3 Creating Playlists and Burning Disks with iTunes

WORKING WITH ITUNES

You can back up over 100 songs at a time from your iTunes library to a CD for safekeeping. If your Mac has a DVD burner, you can back up almost 1,000 songs onto a single DVD data disc.

Unlike an MP3 CD, a data CD or DVD can store any of the audio formats that iTunes can play, including purchased music from the iTunes Music Store, Audible book files, and MP4 music. For more on burning MP3 CDs, see the section "Burn an MP3 CD."

Please note that you can only copy copyrighted material for personal, non-commercial use, and that you cannot redistribute this material without permission from the copyright holder.

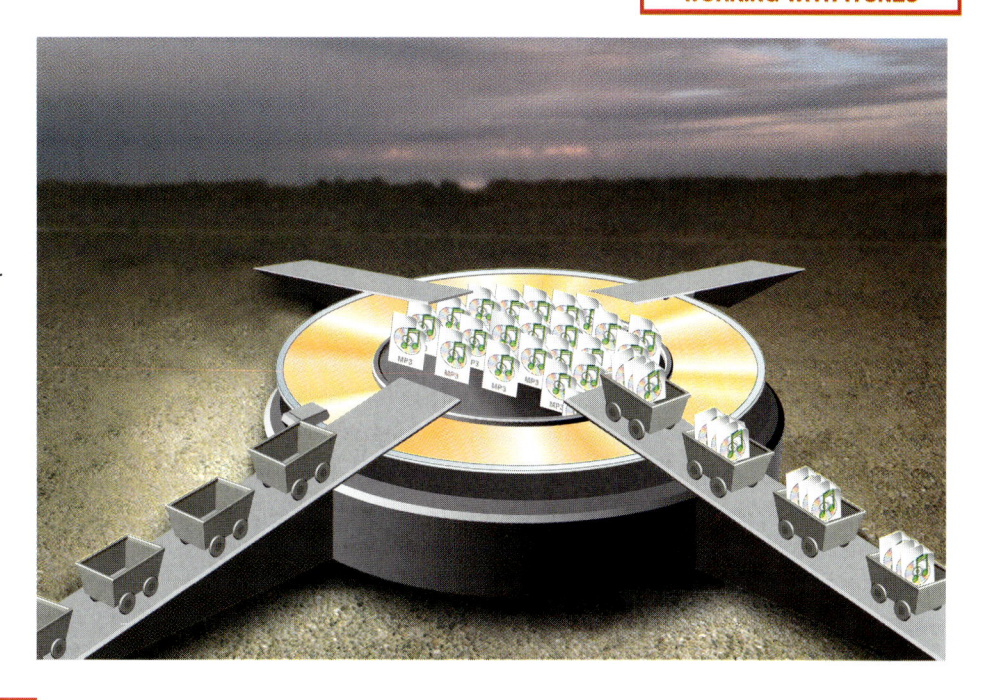

BURN AN ARCHIVE CD OR DVD

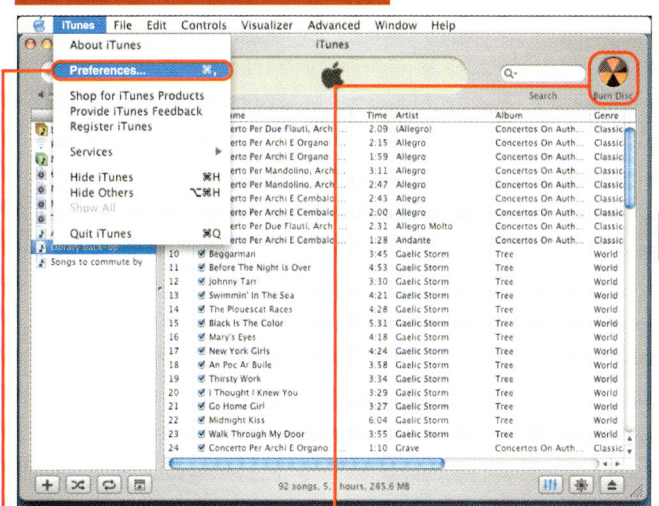

1 Set iTunes' Burning Preferences to burn a data CD or DVD.

Note: See Chapter 2 for more about setting up Preferences.

2 Insert a CD-R or, if your burner supports it, a DVD-R in your disc burner.

3 Follow steps **3** to **6** from the section "Burn a Standard Audio CD."

4 Click the **Burn Disc** icon.

■ The Status display prompts you to click Burn Disc again.

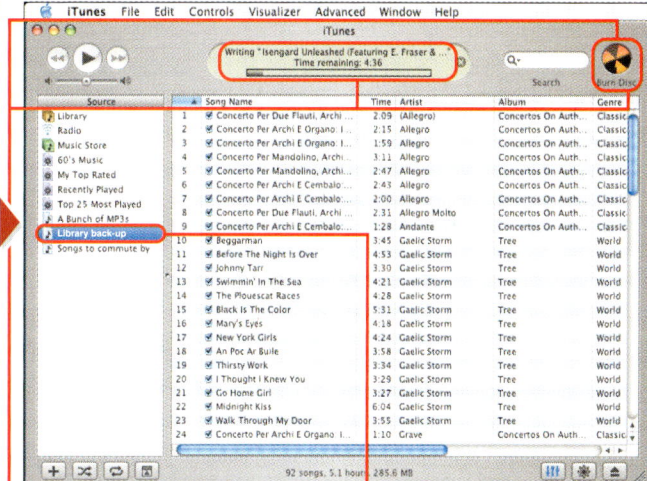

5 Click the **Burn Disc** icon again.

■ The Burn Disc icon spins, and the Status display shows how the burn is progressing.

■ When the burn finishes, the newly created data disc appears selected in the Source list.

53

CREATE A SIMPLE SMART PLAYLIST

You can create Smart Playlists that update themselves when you add songs to or remove songs from your Library. You can create Smart Playlists that contain your current favorite songs, your most recently purchased rap tracks, or a random set of jazz tunes.

The Smart Playlist dialog window provides contextually aware menus and fields that let you specify conditions that a song must meet for it to appear in your Smart Playlist.

CREATE A SIMPLE SMART PLAYLIST

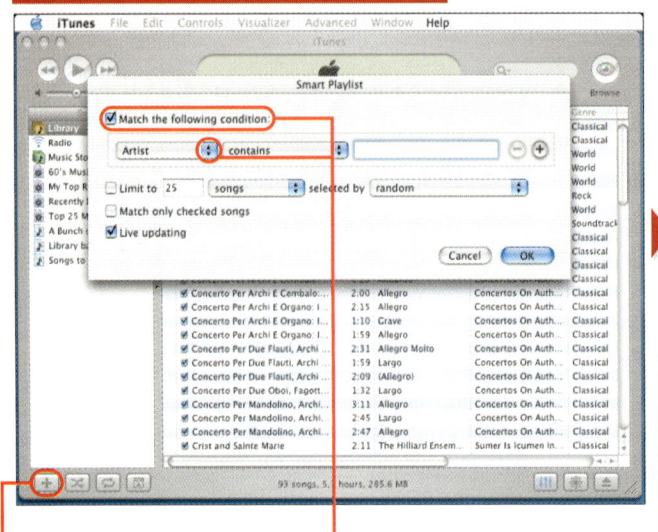

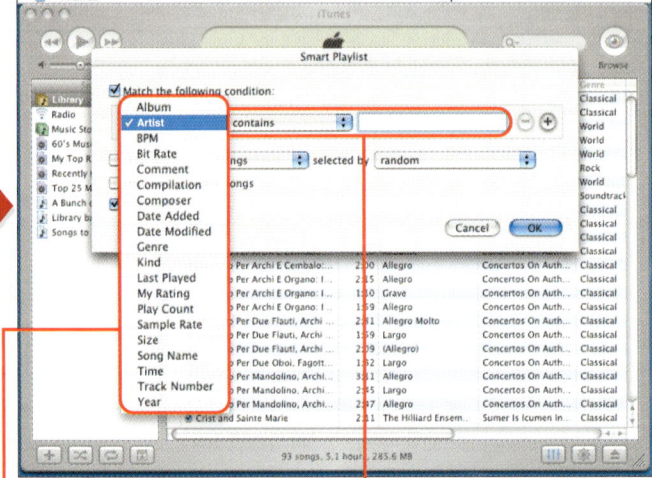

■ **1** Press `option` and then click the Add Playlist button (➕).

■ The Smart Playlist dialog window appears.

■ **2** Click the **Match the following condition** option (☐ changes to ☑).

■ **3** Click the leftmost menu in the Match Conditions panel.

■ **4** Select an item from the menu.

■ The leftmost pop-up menu displays the kind of information you want to match.

■ These items change as necessary to be appropriate for numeric, date, song rating, or textual matches.

54

3 Creating Playlists and Burning Disks with iTunes

WORKING WITH ITUNES

How can I change a Smart Playlist's selection conditions after I have created it?

Click the Smart Playlist's name in the Source list and click **File**, and then **Edit Smart Playlist**. You can also press `Control`, click the Smart Playlist's name, and then select **Edit Smart Playlist** from the menu that appears.

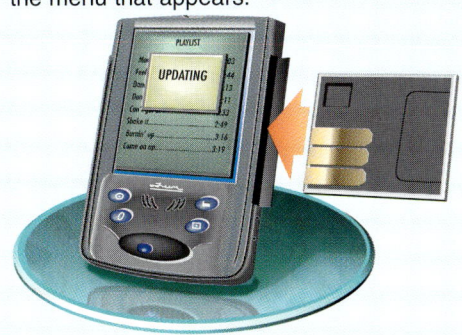

How can I keep iTunes from updating my Smart Playlist when I add songs to my Library?

You may want to keep a Smart Playlist from updating if you plan to use it to make an audio CD but have not yet gotten around to doing so. Make sure that you click the **Live updating** option (☑ changes to ☐) when you create or edit the Smart Playlist. (Note that removing a song from the Library removes it from a Smart Playlist even if you have the Live updating option turned off).

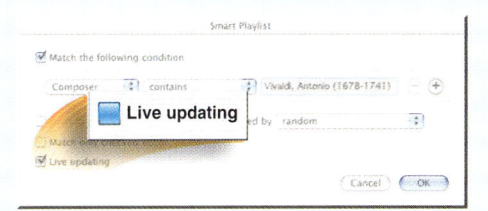

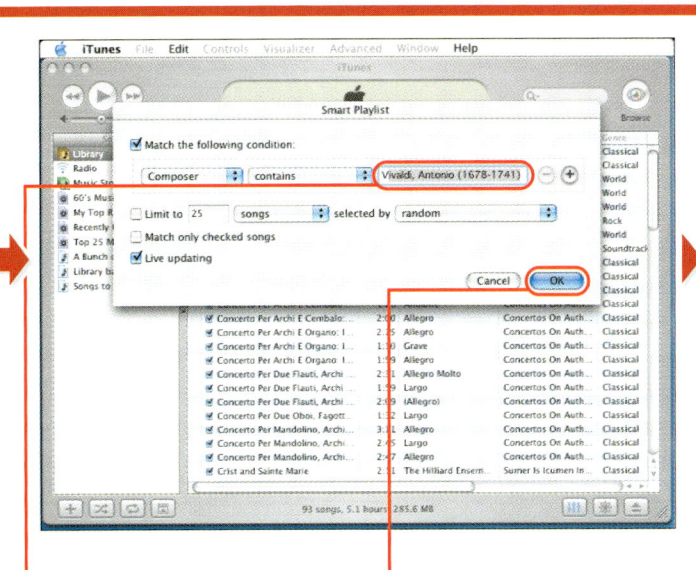

5 Click in the field and type the specific information you want the Smart Playlist's contents to match.

6 Click **OK**.

■ If you are trying to match names or titles, iTunes automatically completes them as you type.

■ The Smart Playlist window closes and the new playlist appears in the Source list with its name selected for editing.

7 Type a name for your playlist.

8 Press `Enter`.

■ Your playlist has the name you typed and is ready for you to play.

55

CREATE AN ADVANCED SMART PLAYLIST

You can add additional conditions to refine how iTunes builds your Smart Playlists. For example, if you want a list of songs that you have played only three times, have two-star ratings or better, *and* last longer than five minutes, iTunes can create one for you.

CREATE AN ADVANCED SMART PLAYLIST

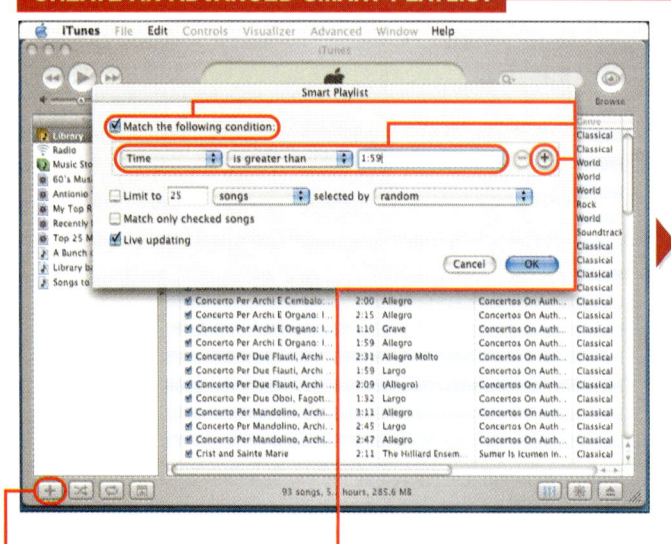

1 Press `option` and then click ➕.

■ The Smart Playlist dialog window appears.

2 Click **Match the following condition** (☐ changes to ☑).

3 Type or select matching conditions in this area.

4 Click the Add Condition (➕) button.

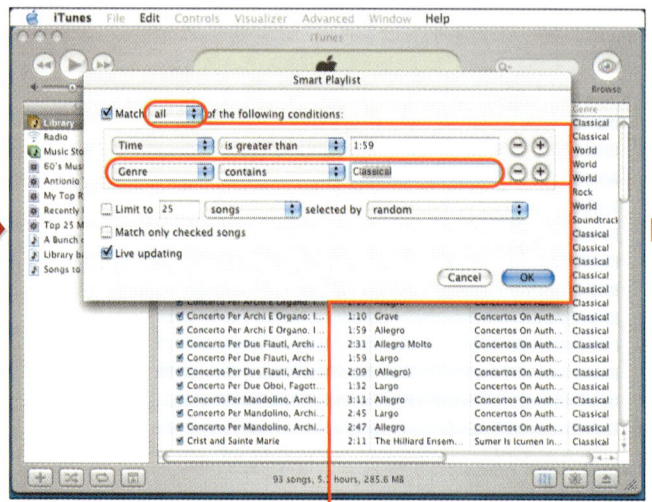

■ The Match Condition panel expands to show another menu and field group.

■ A menu appears in the label beside the Match the following condition checkbox.

5 Click here and select **all** to have songs in the list match all of your conditions, or select **any** to match any of the conditions you specify.

6 Type additional matching conditions using the newly added menu and field group.

56

3 Creating Playlists and Burning Disks with iTunes

WORKING WITH ITUNES

How can I print a list of the songs in a playlist, smart or otherwise?

You can export a Song list to a text file that contains the names of the songs and all their related information, such as date, genre, artist, or time. You can edit, format, and print this list with any word processor. Press `Control` and then click a playlist and select **Export Song List** from the menu that appears. iTunes asks you for a file name and location where you want save the list.

How can I learn more about how to make Smart Playlists?

iTunes comes with several Smart Playlists that you can study and modify, such as '60s Music, My Top Rated, Recently Played, and Top 25 Most Played. Press `Control` and then click any of these Smart Playlists and select **Edit Smart Playlist** from the menu that appears.

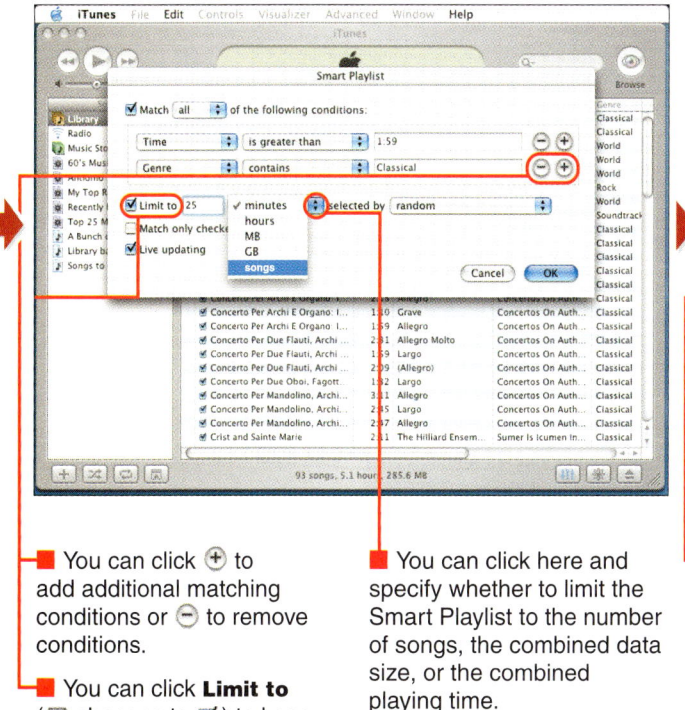

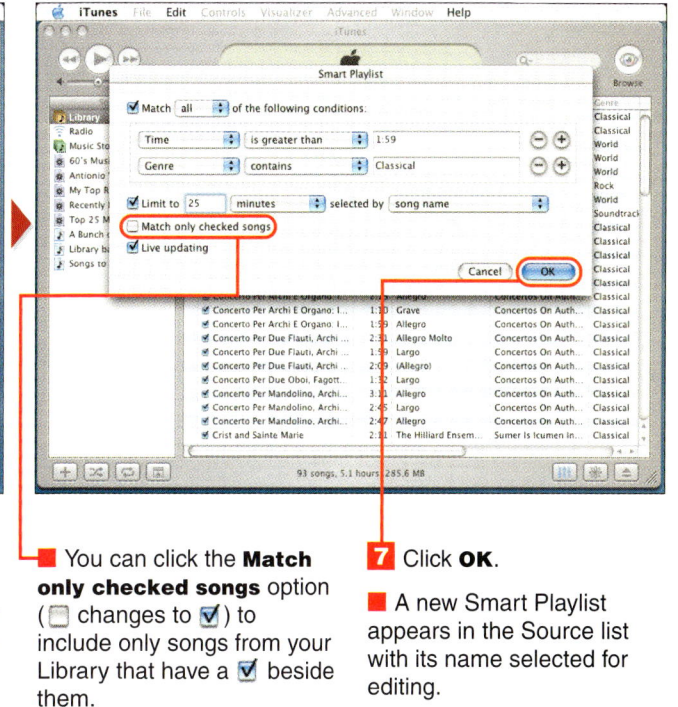

■ You can click ⊕ to add additional matching conditions or ⊖ to remove conditions.

■ You can click **Limit to** (☐ changes to ☑) to keep the playlist below a certain size.

■ You can click here and specify whether to limit the Smart Playlist to the number of songs, the combined data size, or the combined playing time.

■ You can click the **Match only checked songs** option (☐ changes to ☑) to include only songs from your Library that have a ☑ beside them.

7 Click **OK**.

■ A new Smart Playlist appears in the Source list with its name selected for editing.

57

SIGN INTO AND OUT OF THE ITUNES MUSIC STORE

You can sign into the iTunes Music Store whenever you want to buy music online. You should sign out when you are done to keep your account secure.

You use either your Apple ID or your America OnLine screen name to sign in and purchase music, using credit card information that Apple or AOL keeps on file. You can create an Apple ID directly within iTunes or on Apple's Web site at www.apple.com.

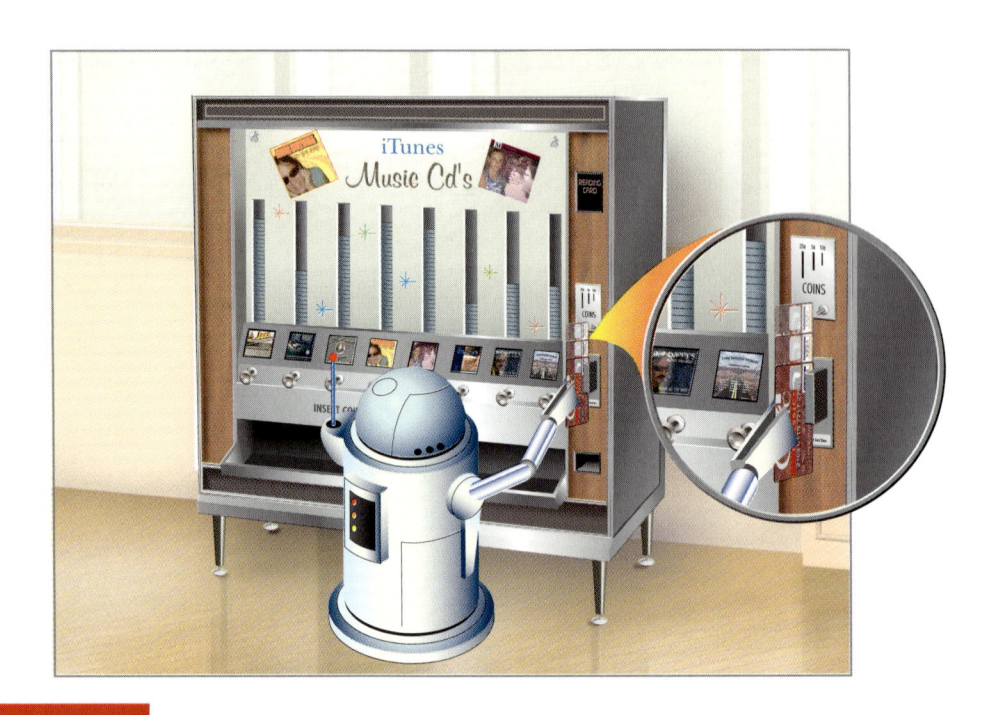

SIGN INTO THE ITUNES MUSIC STORE

1 Click **Music Store** in the Source list.

- The Music Store home page replaces the iTunes Song list.

2 Click **Sign In**.

- A sign-in dialog opens.

3 Type your Apple ID.

- You can click here (○ changes to ●) to use your AOL screen name.
- If you do not have an Apple ID, click **Create New Account** and follow the instructions that appear in the Music Store.

4 Type your Apple ID's or AOL password.

5 Click **Sign In**.

- Your ID appears in the account field.

Note: if you have never used the account with the store, iTunes asks you to supply some information.

58

4 Using the iTunes Music Store

WORKING WITH ITUNES

How can I change my credit card information for my Apple ID?

Follow steps **1** to **3** in this section to sign into your account, but then click **View Account**. When the Music Store displays a form, click **Edit Credit Card** to edit your credit card information.

Can I have more than one Apple Account?

You can have more than one Apple Account if you have more than one e-mail address. Each Apple account ID must be a valid e-mail address. Apple uses the Apple ID address to send you invoices and other information concerning your account.

SIGN OUT OF THE ITUNES MUSIC STORE

■ Click the Account field.

■ A dialog window appears asking for your Apple ID or AOL account password.

■ Click **Sign Out**.

Note: You do not need to type a password to sign out.

■ The Account field says "Sign In" and your Apple ID or AOL account is now signed out.

■ You cannot purchase music from the iTunes Music Store until you sign in again.

Note: If you quit iTunes without signing out, you remain signed in the next time you open iTunes and go to the iTunes Music Store.

59

SEARCH THE ITUNES MUSIC STORE

You can quickly search the thousands of songs in the iTunes Music Store to find albums, artists, composers, and song titles. iTunes' Power Search lets you fine-tune your search.

SEARCH THE ITUNES MUSIC STORE

GENERAL SEARCH

1. Type a word or name in the Search field.

2. Press Enter.

■ The Music Store displays items that match the search term in any of its song name, artist, composer, or album categories.

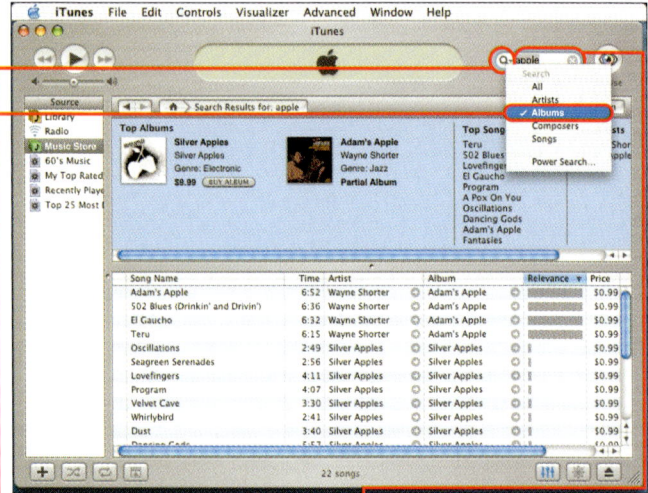

CATEGORY SEARCH

1. Click the Search field's Magnifying Glass (🔍).

■ The search menu appears.

2. Select a search category from the menu.

3. Click in the Search field and type a word or name.

4. Press Enter.

■ The Music Store displays items that match the search term in the selected category.

60

4 Using the iTunes Music Store

WORKING WITH ITUNES

How can I hear a song to see if it is one I want to purchase?

Simply double-click any song in a search result's Song list. The Music Store plays a 30-second sample from the song.

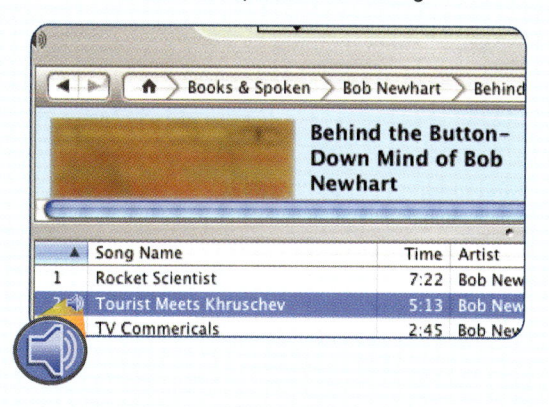

How can I browse the Music Store's inventory?

Click the **Browse** icon (◉) like you would in your own iTunes Library. A three-column browse pane appears that lets you easily examine the Music Store's current inventory. Note that many artists and albums may appear under several different genres.

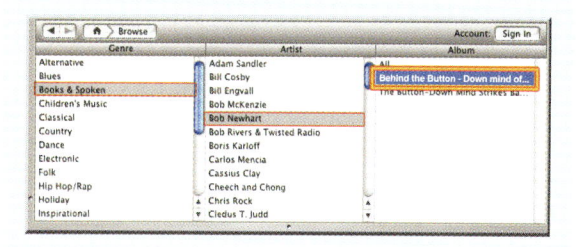

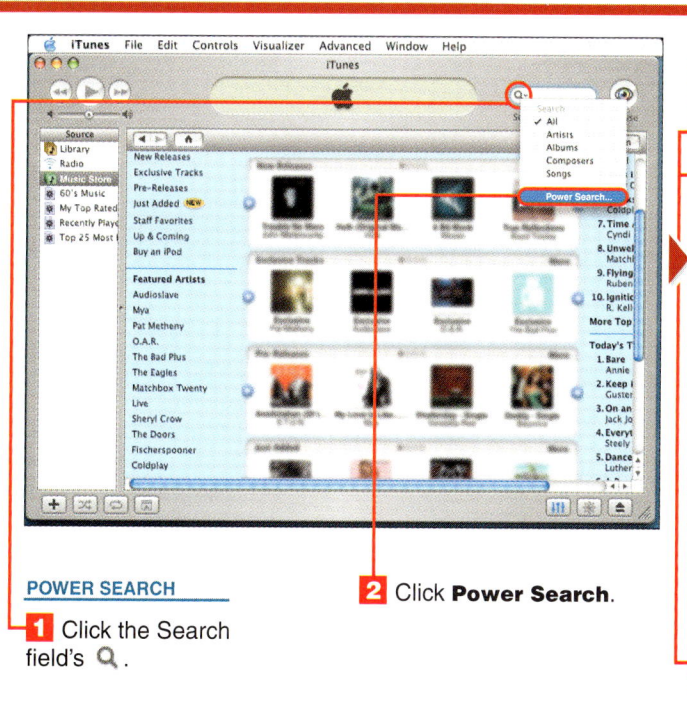

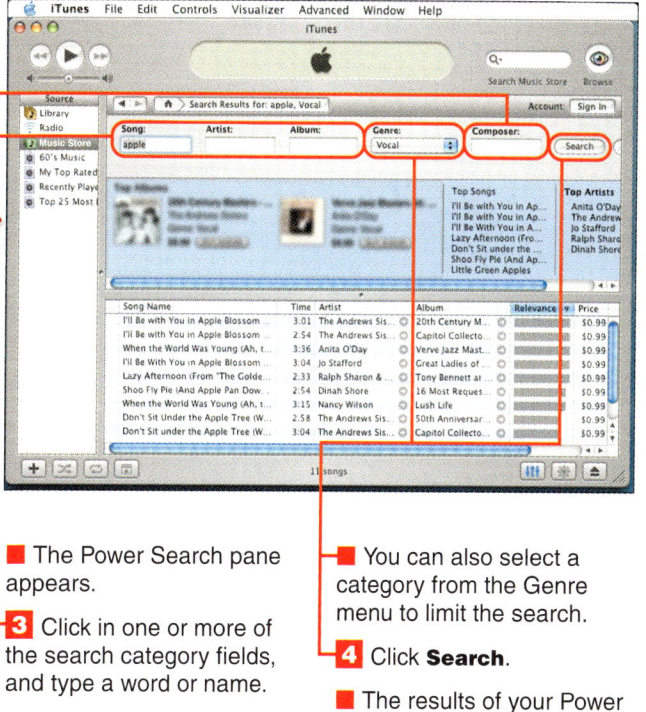

POWER SEARCH

1 Click the Search field's 🔍.

2 Click **Power Search**.

■ The Power Search pane appears.

3 Click in one or more of the search category fields, and type a word or name.

■ You can also select a category from the Genre menu to limit the search.

4 Click **Search**.

■ The results of your Power Search appear.

61

PURCHASE MUSIC WITH 1-CLICK SHOPPING

1-Click shopping lets you buy and immediately download any song or album from the iTunes Music Store that strikes your fancy.

1-Click shopping works best with a high-speed Internet connection; if you have a modem connection, see the section "Purchase Music with the Shopping Cart." Note that to purchase music, you must connect to the Internet and sign in to the Music Store. See the section "Sign Into and Out of the iTunes Music Store" for more on signing into the Music Store.

PURCHASE MUSIC WITH 1-CLICK SHOPPING

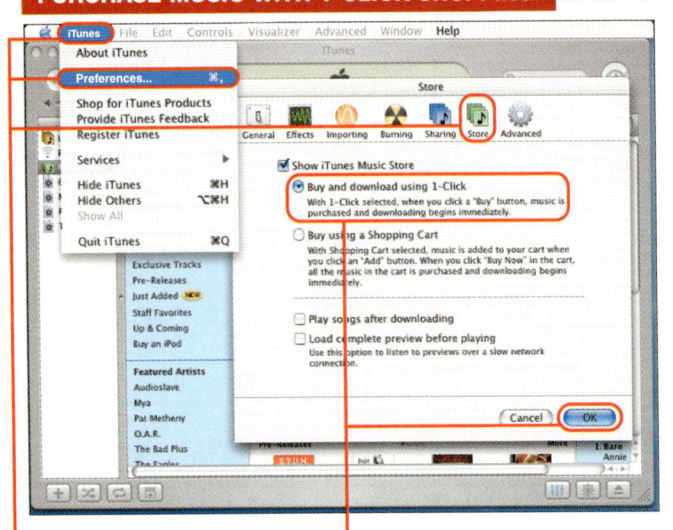

SET UP 1-CLICK SHOPPING

1 Click **iTunes**.

2 Click **Preferences**.

3 In the Preferences window that opens, click the **Store** button.

■ The Store preferences appear.

4 Click the **Buy and download using 1-Click** option (○ changes to ●).

5 Click **OK** to save your preferences.

PURCHASE MUSIC

1 Find a song you want to purchase.

2 Click **BUY SONG**.

Note: For more on finding songs, see the section "Search the iTunes Music Store."

62

4 Using the iTunes Music Store

WORKING WITH ITUNES

What happens if I lose my Internet connection while downloading purchased music?

The Music Store keeps track of the status of music purchases. If a download is interrupted, it usually resumes the next time you open iTunes. If it does not resume, click **Advanced**, and then **Check for Purchased Music**. In the dialog that appears, type your Apple ID or AOL screen name and password and then click **Check**. iTunes shows you the music that you have yet to download.

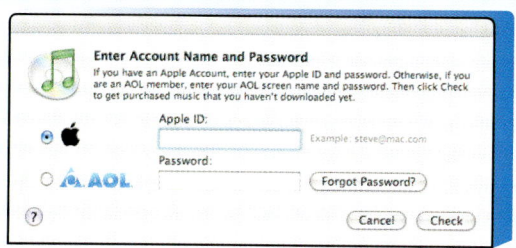

Can I play my purchased music on a Mac other than the one I used to purchase it?

You can authorize up to three Macintoshes at a time to play music purchased with a particular Apple ID. When you add the purchased music to another Mac's Library and try to play it on that Mac, iTunes asks you to authorize the Mac to play it. You must be connected to the Internet at the time you authorize the Mac so that iTunes can update your account information.

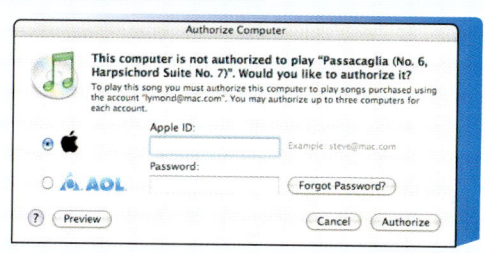

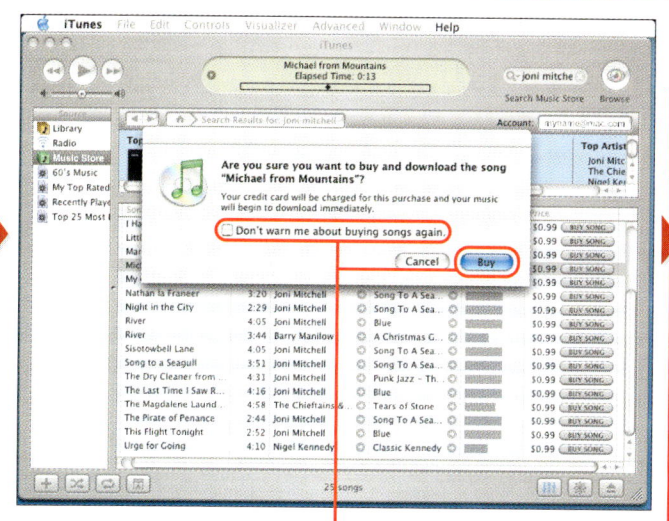

■ A dialog window appears asking you to confirm your purchase decision.

■ You can click the **Don't warn me about buying songs again** option (☐ changes to ☑) if you do not want to see the dialog window each time you buy a song or album.

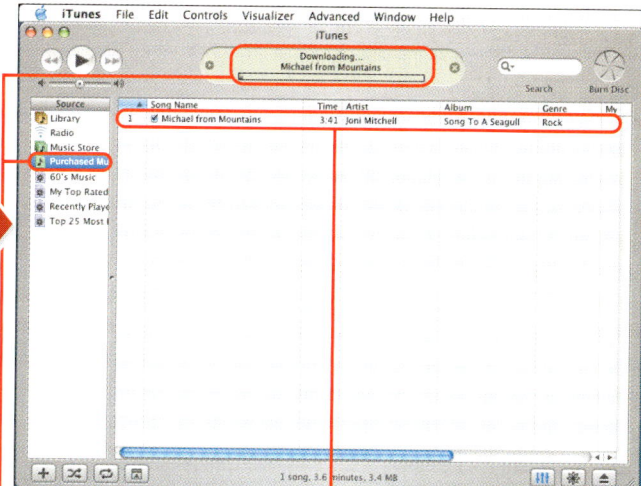

3 Click **Buy**.

■ The Status panel displays the progress of the purchased music's download.

4 Click **Purchased Music** in the Source list.

Note: iTunes creates the Purchased Music playlist the first time you purchase music from the Music Store.

■ The purchased music appears in the Purchased Music playlist.

63

PURCHASE MUSIC WITH THE SHOPPING CART

You use the Music Store's Shopping Cart to collect songs that you are interested in purchasing and then buy them all at once.

You may want to use the Shopping Cart if you have a modem connection to the Internet, because it allows you to finish all of your shopping before you download your purchases, which can take some time over a modem.

You must be connected to the Internet and signed in to the Music Store to purchase music. See the section "Sign Into and Out of the iTunes Music Store" for more information.

PURCHASE MUSIC WITH THE SHOPPING CART

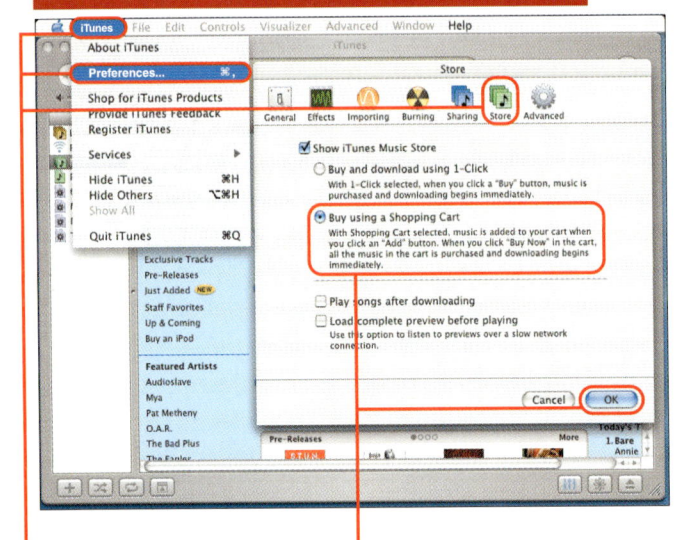

SET UP PREFERENCES

1 Click **iTunes**.

2 Click **Preferences**.

■ The Preferences window opens.

3 Click **Store**.

4 Click the **Buy using a Shopping Cart** option (◯ changes to ⦿).

5 Click **OK**.

■ The Shopping Cart appears in the Source list beneath the Music Store.

PURCHASE MUSIC

1 Find a song you want to purchase.

Note: See the section "Search the iTunes Music Store" for more information.

2 Click **ADD SONG**.

64

4 Using the iTunes Music Store

WORKING WITH ITUNES

TEACH YOURSELF

What happens if I close iTunes when I still have songs in my cart?

The Music Store keeps the songs in your cart and they are available the next time you open iTunes and go to the Music Store. Also, if you open iTunes on a different Mac and sign in with your Apple ID or AOL screen name, the songs appear in the cart on that Mac if you have that Mac set up to use the Shopping Cart.

TEACH YOURSELF

Can I make standard audio CDs with my purchased music?

Yes, but you can only make ten audio CDs from the same playlist if it contains purchased music. To make additional CDs, you must modify the playlist by rearranging the songs, adding songs, or removing songs.

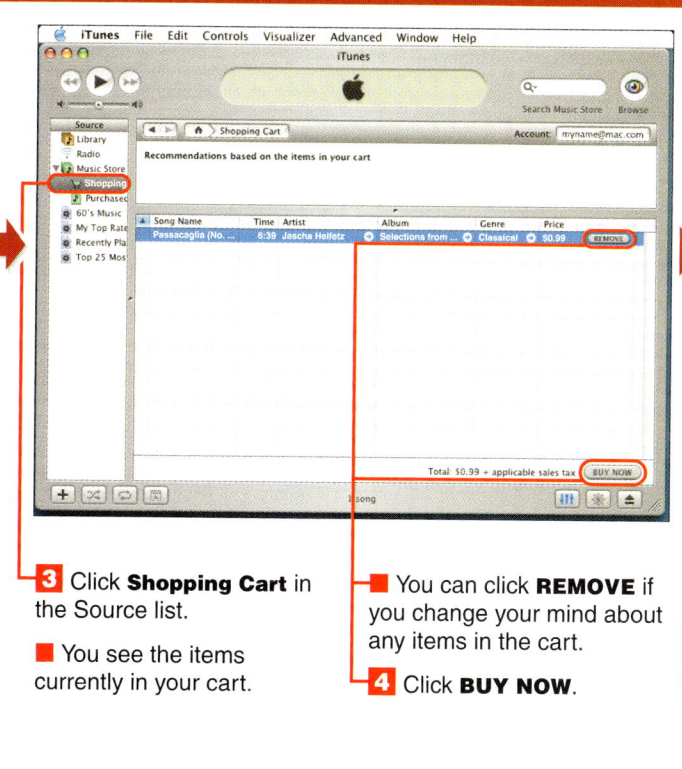

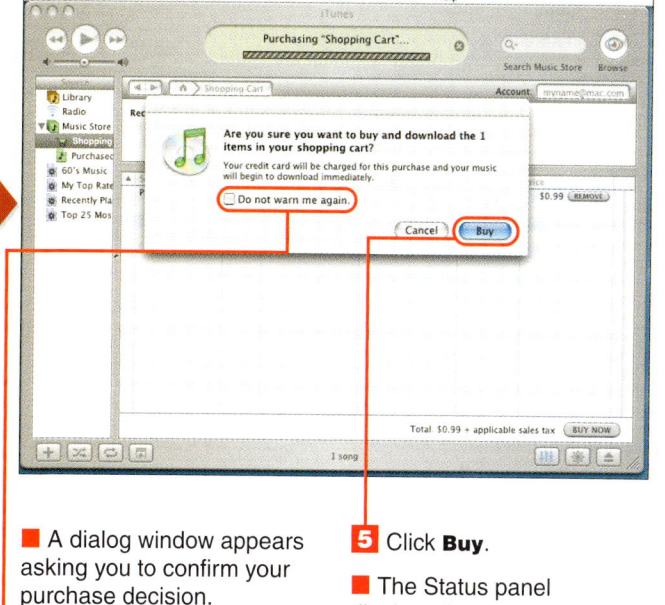

3 Click **Shopping Cart** in the Source list.

■ You see the items currently in your cart.

■ You can click **REMOVE** if you change your mind about any items in the cart.

4 Click **BUY NOW**.

■ A dialog window appears asking you to confirm your purchase decision.

■ You can click the **Do not warn me again** option (☐ changes to ☑) to stop this window from appearing again.

5 Click **Buy**.

■ The Status panel displays the progress of the purchased music's download and the purchased music appears in the Purchased Music playlist.

65

DEAUTHORIZE A COMPUTER TO PLAY PURCHASED MUSIC

Because you can play your purchased music on only three computers at any time, you may find it necessary to remove purchased-music authorization from one computer so you can add it to another; for example, when you purchase a new computer and want to sell or give away your old one.

You need an active Internet connection to deauthorize a computer.

DEAUTHORIZE A COMPUTER TO PLAY PURCHASED MUSIC

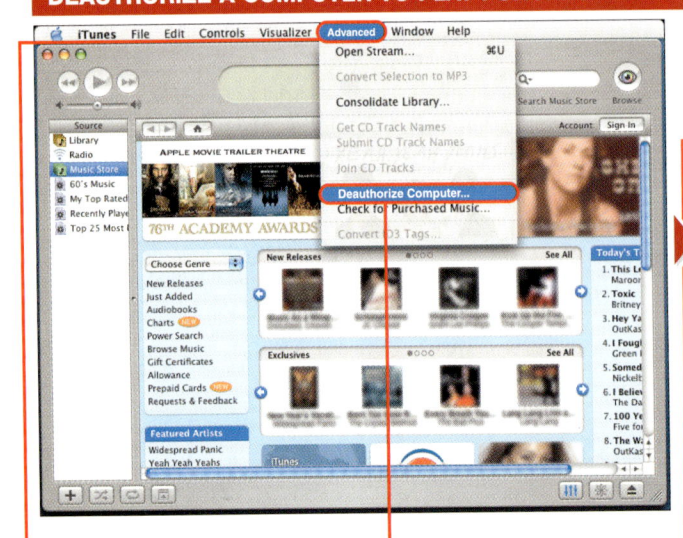

1 Click **Advanced**.

2 Click **Deauthorize Computer**.

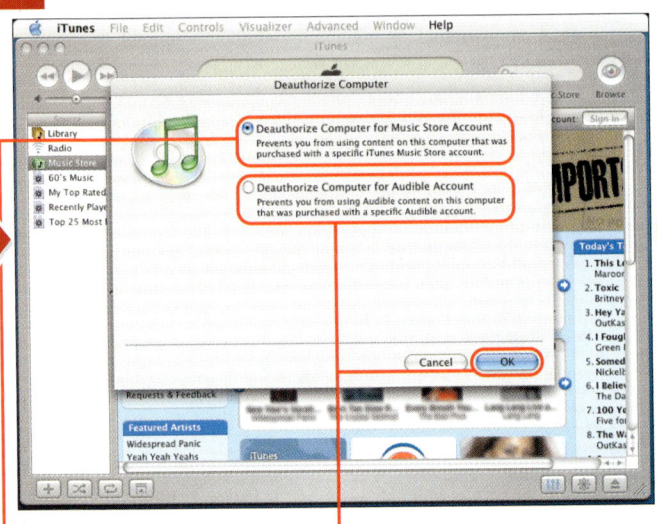

■ A dialog window appears.

3 Click the **Deauthorize Computer for Music Store Account** option (○ changes to ⦿).

■ A similar button lets you deauthorize your computer from an Audible Account, which you need to play audio books purchased from Audible.com.

4 Click **OK**.

4 Using the iTunes Music Store

WORKING WITH ITUNES

My computer was stolen; how can I deauthorize it?

You need to contact Apple's Music Store customer support. There is currently no other way to deauthorize a computer to which you do not have physical access.

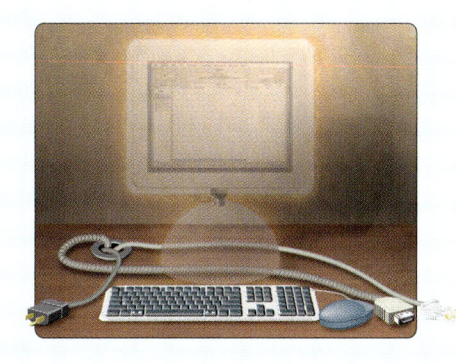

My family members have separate user accounts on my Mac. Can they play my purchased music from their accounts?

Yes. Purchased music authorization applies to the entire computer and not just to an individual user account.

- Another dialog window replaces the first one.
- You can click here to deauthorize an AOL screen name account (○ changes to ●).

5 Type your Apple ID or AOL screen name and password.

6 Click **OK**.

- A message appears informing you that iTunes has deauthorized the computer.

7 Click **OK**.

- You can no longer play music purchased from that account on this Mac.

- If you attempt to do so, iTunes asks you to authorize the computer first.

Note: To authorize a computer, see the section "Purchase Music with 1-Click Shopping."

67

USING THE EQUALIZER

You can use iTunes' Equalizer to adjust the tonal quality of iTunes playback, just like a graphic equalizer on a hi-fi system. You can also assign individual Equalizer settings to any song in your iTunes Library.

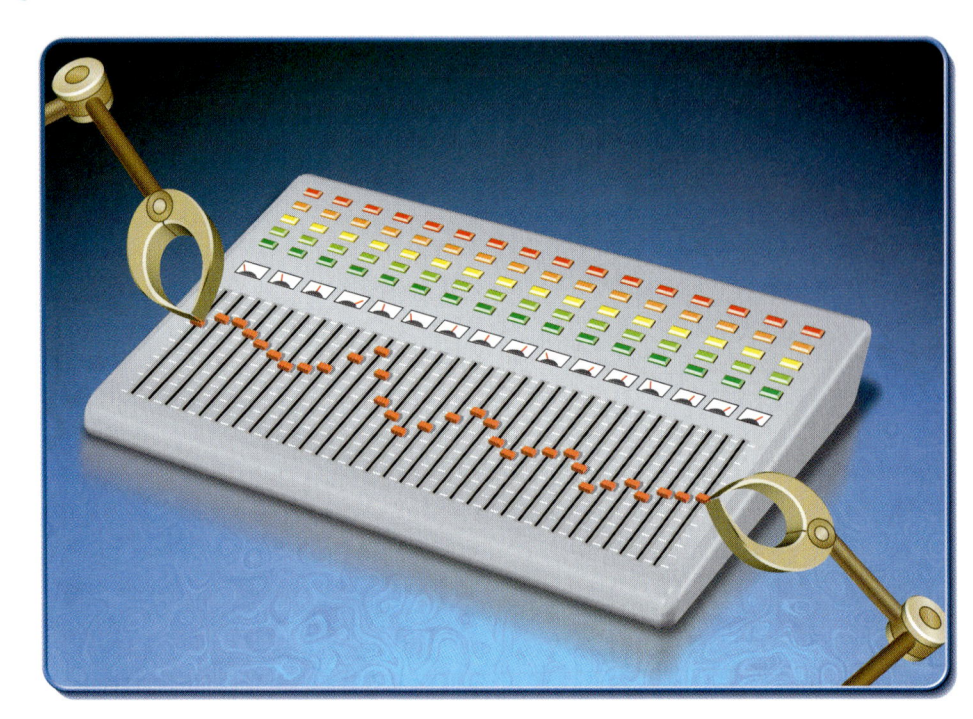

When the Equalizer is on, the Equalizer window's settings apply to songs that have no assigned settings.

USING THE EQUALIZER

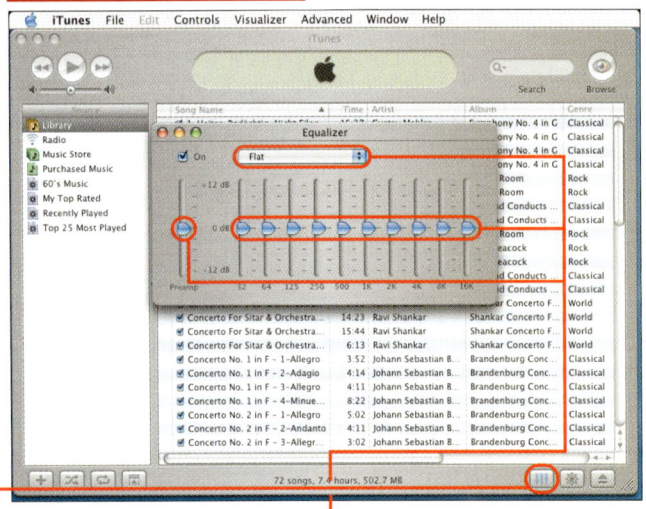

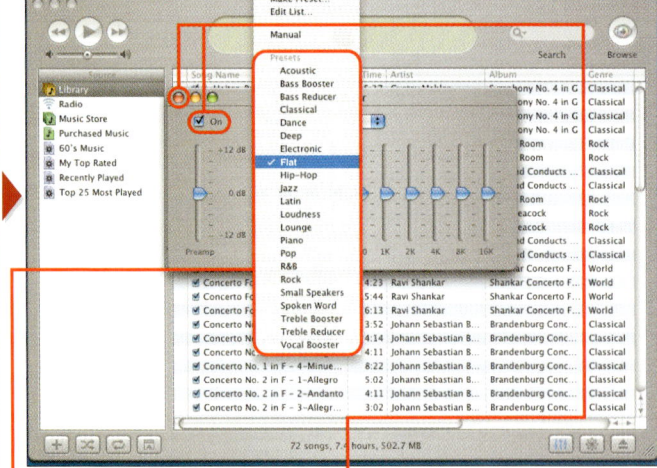

SET THE EQUALIZER

1 Click the Equalizer button (▥).

■ The Equalizer window appears.

■ The Preamp ▶ adjusts overall loudness relative to the iTunes' volume setting.

■ Each ▶ controls the volume of a specific frequency range.

2 Click the Equalizer menu.

3 Select a preset from the menu.

■ When you select a preset, the sliders move to reflect your choice.

■ If you click the **On** option (☐ changes to ☑), the Equalizer remains active even when you close the window.

4 Click ● to close the Equalizer window when you are done.

68

5 Using Advanced iTunes Features

WORKING WITH ITUNES

How can I make my own Equalizer presets?

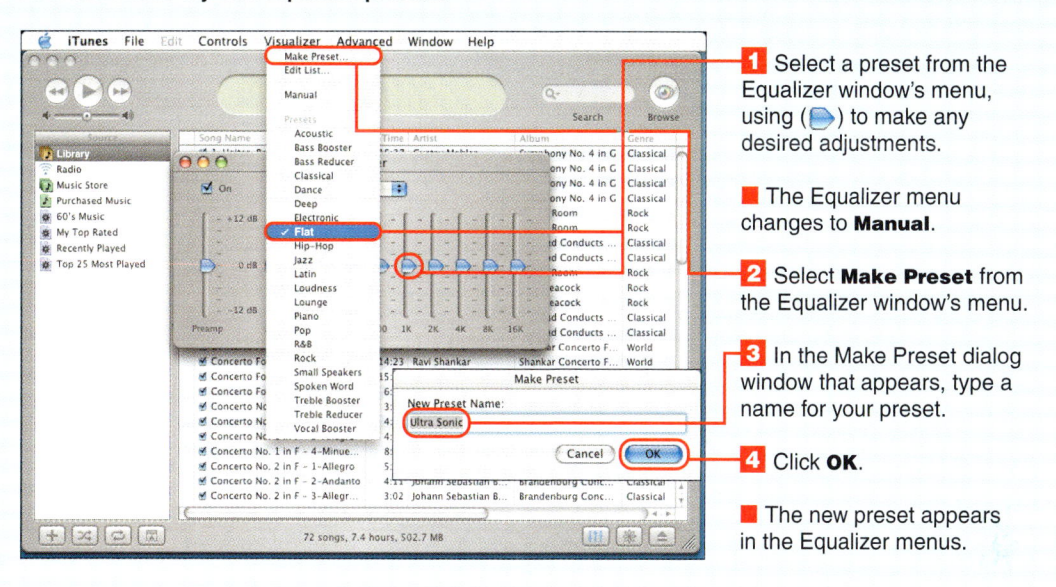

1 Select a preset from the Equalizer window's menu, using ( ) to make any desired adjustments.

■ The Equalizer menu changes to **Manual**.

2 Select **Make Preset** from the Equalizer window's menu.

3 In the Make Preset dialog window that appears, type a name for your preset.

4 Click **OK**.

■ The new preset appears in the Equalizer menus.

ASSIGN AN EQUALIZER SETTING TO A SONG

1 Change the Song list's View settings to show the Equalizer column.

Note: For more on working with the Song list's view settings, see page 27.

2 Click an Equalizer button ( ).

■ A menu of Equalizer presets appears.

3 Select an Equalizer setting from the menu.

■ The song now has an assigned Equalizer setting.

■ You can select **None** to remove the song's assigned Equalizer setting.

69

VIEW AND ADD ALBUM ARTWORK

iTunes can attach pictures, such as album cover art, to any song in your library. You can view these pictures, and you can add pictures to songs you have ripped yourself.

To add a picture of your own, you need to place the picture on your Desktop or in an open Finder window before following the steps in this section. See Chapter 1 for more on working with the Finder.

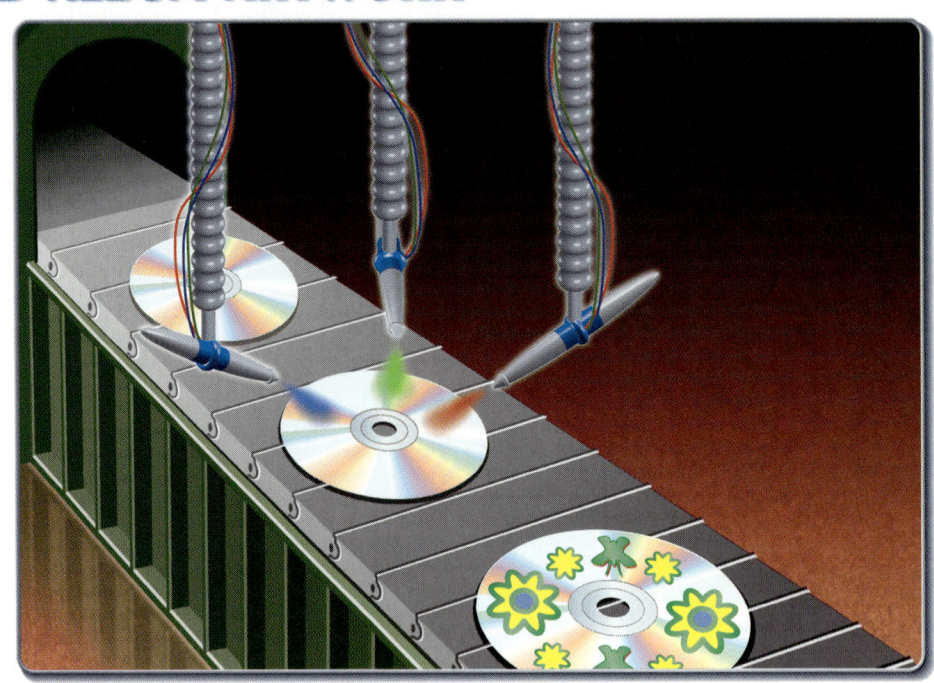

VIEW ALBUM ARTWORK

1 Select a song in the Song list that has a picture associated with it.

Note: Songs purchased from the iTunes Music Store usually have such pictures; songs you obtain elsewhere may have artwork as well.

2 Click the Artwork button ( ).

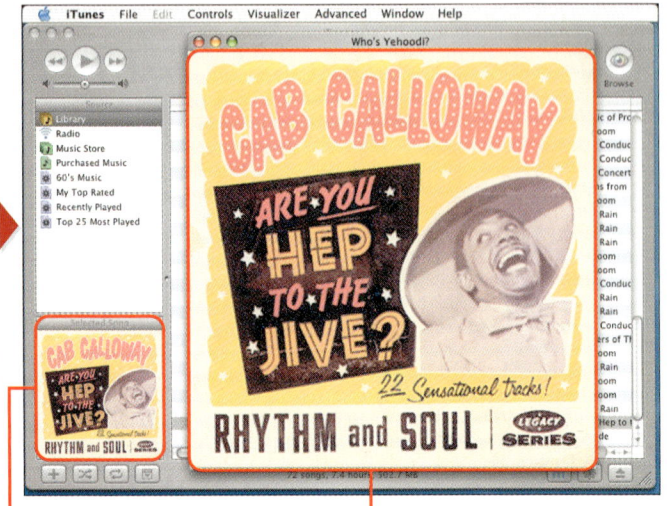

■ A Selected Song panel appears beneath the Source list showing the picture it contains.

■ You can click the picture to see a larger image in a separate window.

70

5 Using Advanced iTunes Features

WORKING WITH ITUNES

Where does iTunes store the song's artwork?

iTunes adds the picture directly to the song file as part of the song's *metadata* — that is, the information about the song itself, such as its title, composer, or date. Because the song file increases in size to accommodate the picture, you may only want to add relatively small image files — approximately 5 to 20K — to your songs to conserve storage space.

Can I only have one picture in a song?

No, you can have several. To add another picture, just drag it to the Selected Song panel. Arrow buttons (◀ ▶) appear at the top of the panel, allowing you to move through the song's pictures.

ADD ALBUM ARTWORK

■ **1** Click a song in the Song list that does not have a picture.

■ The Selected Song panel reads Drag Album Artwork Here.

■ **2** Click and drag a picture from your Desktop or an open Finder window and drop it on the Selected Song panel.

■ You can click and drag here to make the iTunes window smaller in order to see other windows or your Mac Desktop.

■ The picture appears in the Selected Song panel.

71

CHANGE THE IMPORT FORMAT

iTunes 4 usually imports music using the new MPEG-4 AAC format, but you are not limited to that. You can set iTunes to import music using the popular MP3 format, the Windows WAV format, or Macintosh's AIFF.

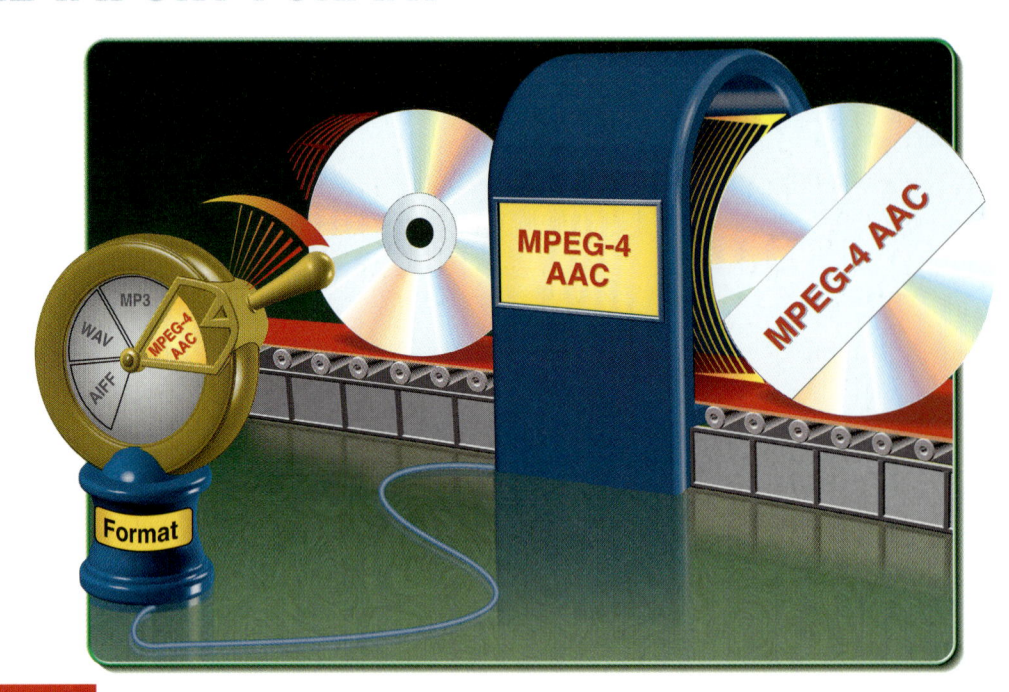

CHANGE THE IMPORT FORMAT

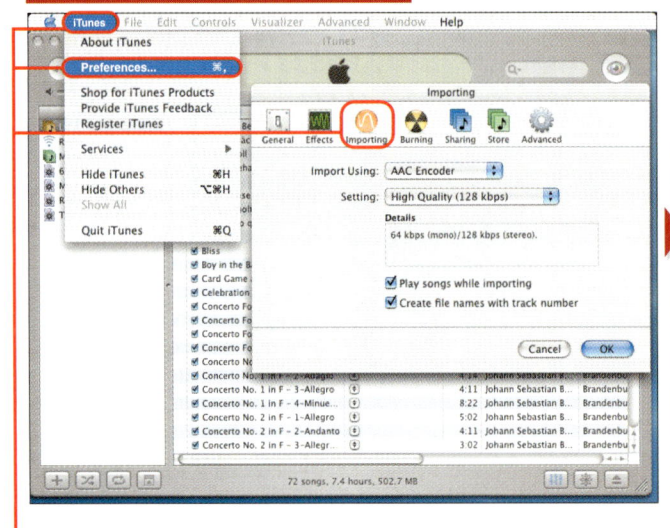

1 Click **iTunes**.

2 Click **Preferences**.

■ The Preferences window appears.

3 Click the **Importing** icon.

■ The Importing pane appears in the Preferences window, with the current import format displayed.

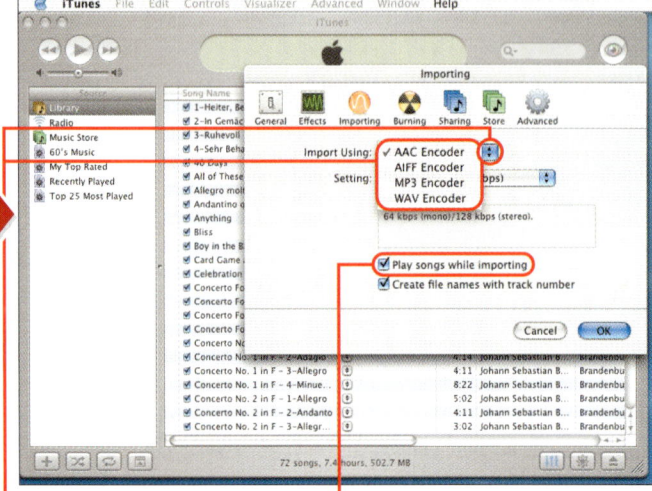

4 Click here and select an encoder.

Note: This example uses the MP3 encoder.

■ The Import Using menu reflects your change, and the Setting menu may also change.

■ You can click the **Play songs while importing** option (☐ changes to ☑) to listen to songs during the import process.

72

5 Using Advanced iTunes Features

WORKING WITH ITUNES

What does changing the Stereo Bit Rate option do?

The Stereo Bit Rate option specifies how many bits of storage each second of stereo music takes up; the larger the number, the bigger the song file size. Higher numbers usually produce better quality sound. For monaural recordings, the bit rate is half of the stereo bit rate.

16 kbps
20 kbps
24 kbps
28 kbps
32 kbps
40 kbps
48 kbps
56 kbps
64 kbps
80 kbps
96 kbps
112 kbps
✓ 128 kbps
160 kbps
192 kbps
224 kbps
256 kbps
320 kbps

What does changing the Sample Rate option do?

A music file comprises many hundreds of thousands of digital measurements — called *samples* — of how loud the music is at any particular moment. The Sample Rate specifies how many times each second the measurement is made (1 kHz is 1,000 samples per second). The more samples per second, the wider the frequency range you can hear; lower sample rates remove higher frequencies, and very low sample rates can produce muffled sound.

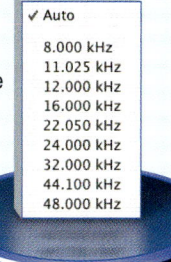

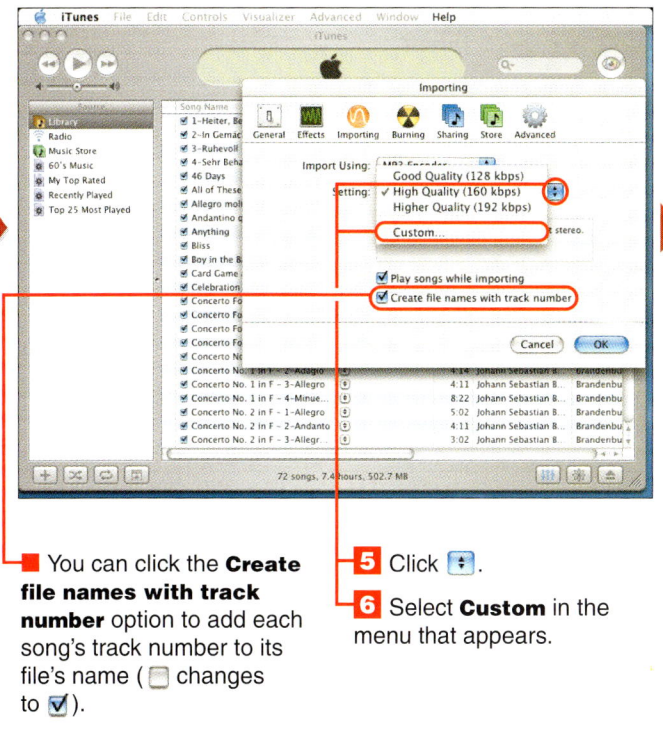

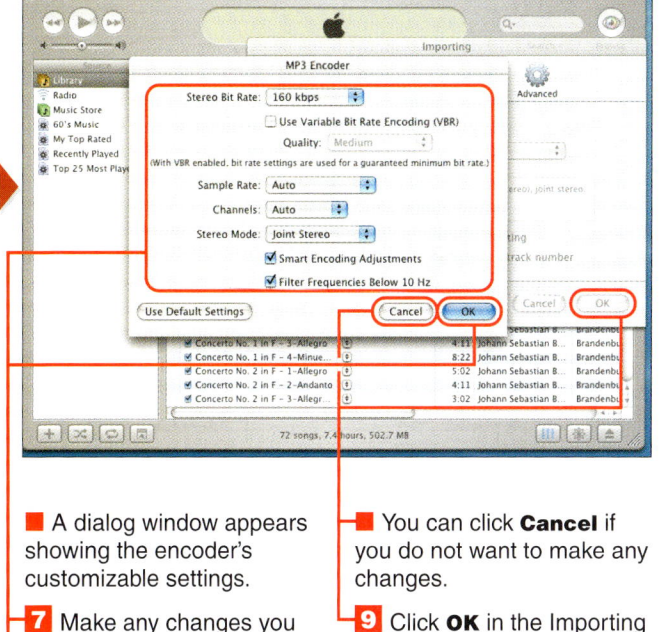

✓ Auto
8.000 kHz
11.025 kHz
12.000 kHz
16.000 kHz
22.050 kHz
24.000 kHz
32.000 kHz
44.100 kHz
48.000 kHz

■ You can click the **Create file names with track number** option to add each song's track number to its file's name (☐ changes to ☑).

5 Click ⇅.

6 Select **Custom** in the menu that appears.

■ A dialog window appears showing the encoder's customizable settings.

7 Make any changes you want to the settings.

8 Click **OK**.

■ You can click **Cancel** if you do not want to make any changes.

9 Click **OK** in the Importing pane.

■ iTunes closes the Preferences window and sets the new import format.

73

CONVERT A SONG'S FORMAT

You can change a song's format even after you import it. You may want to do this to make the song compatible with digital devices that do not play the new AAC format that iTunes uses, or to make MP3 files suitable for burning onto an MP3 CD.

Note: iTunes uses the current import settings when it converts song formats. For more information on how to change these settings, see the section "Change the Import Format."

CONVERT A SONG'S FORMAT

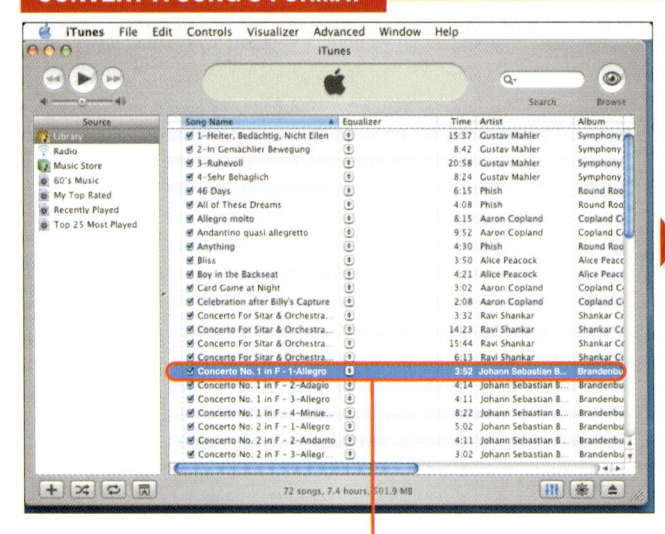

1 Select an import setting for the conversion.

Note: See the section "Change the Import Format" earlier in the chapter for more information.

2 Click the song you want to convert in the Song list.

■ If you want to convert more than one song to the new format, you can **Shift**+click, or ⌘+click, the song list to select several songs at once.

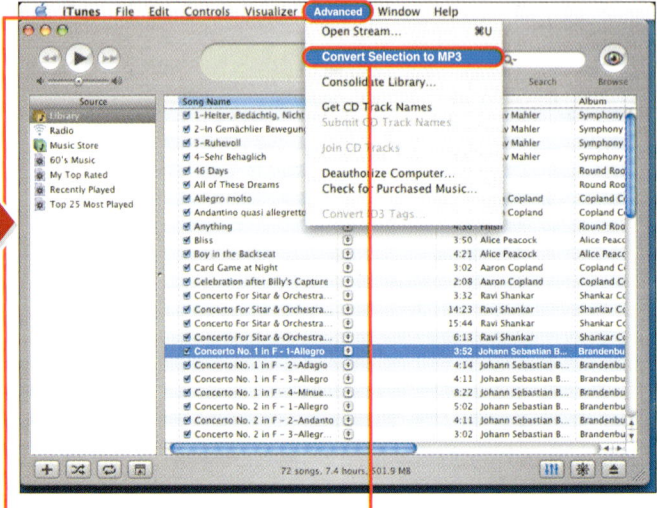

3 Click **Advanced**.

■ The Advanced menu shows a conversion choice that reflects the currently chosen import format, which in this example is MP3.

4 Select **Convert Selection to MP3**.

74

5 Using Advanced iTunes Features

WORKING WITH ITUNES

How seriously does converting a song's format affect the quality of the audio?

That depends on the settings you use for the conversion. Generally, converting between two comparable settings — such as from iTunes' default AAC settings to its default MP3 settings — only slightly degrades the sound quality so that most listeners may not even notice a difference.

I cannot convert the format of songs purchased from the iTunes Music Store. Why not?

The contractual arrangements between Apple and the various music labels that supply songs to the iTunes Music Store require Apple to prevent direct format conversions for purchased music. You may, however, burn the purchased music to an audio CD and then rip the CD in a different format. For more on ripping a CD, see Chapter 2. For more on changing import formats, see the section "Change the Import Format."

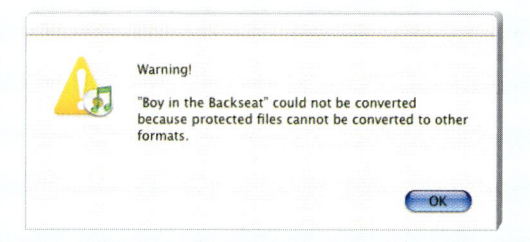

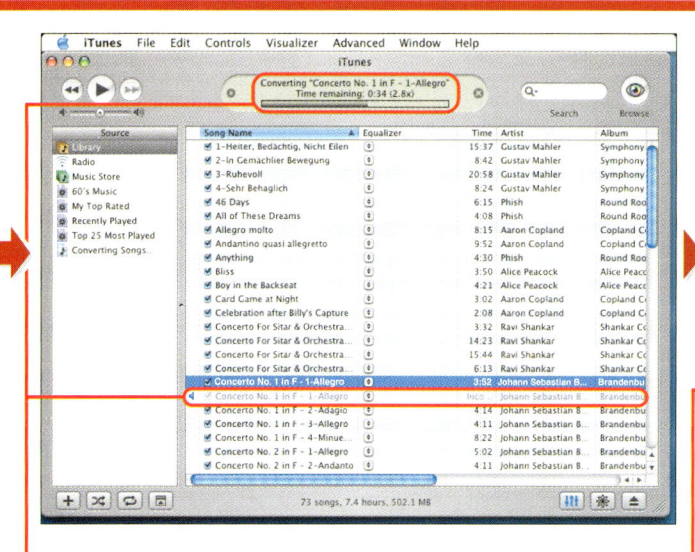

■ iTunes begins converting the song, and the iTunes Status panel shows the conversion's progress.

■ If you select the **Play songs while importing** option in the Importing pane, the song begins playing as iTunes converts it.

Note: For more on the Importing pane options, see the section "Change the Import Format."

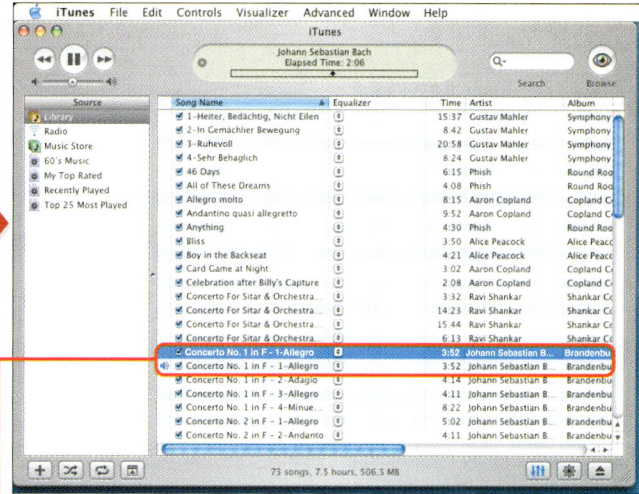

■ The converted song appears in the Song list along with the original song.

75

SET A SONG'S TAG INFORMATION

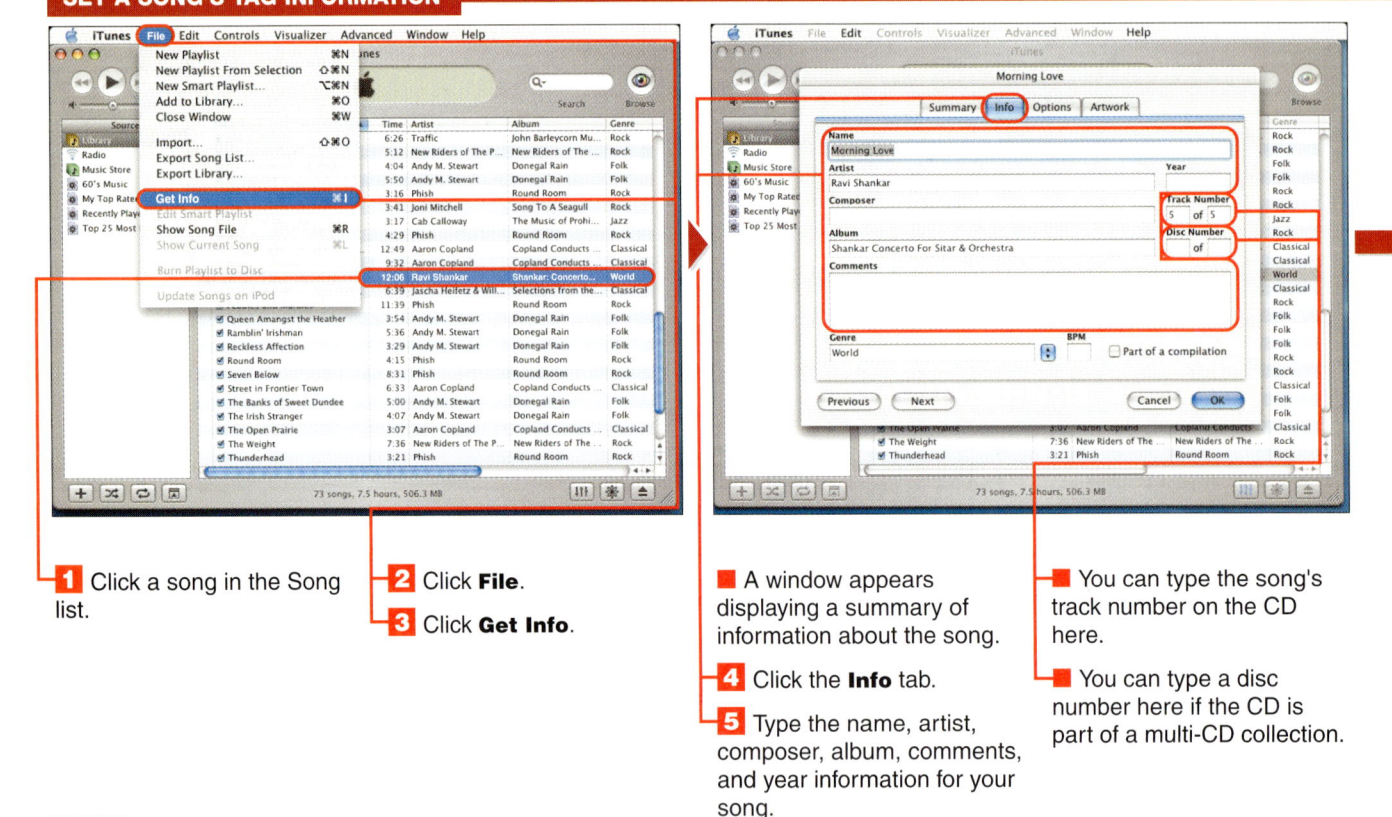

Each song in your iTunes Library has a hidden tag that contains information about that song, such as its title, composer, genre, artwork, equalizer setting, and date of release. iTunes allows you to edit the tag information and to include your own comments in the tag.

To change the information on an entire album, see the section "Change an Album's Tag Information."

SET A SONG'S TAG INFORMATION

1 Click a song in the Song list.

2 Click **File**.

3 Click **Get Info**.

■ A window appears displaying a summary of information about the song.

4 Click the **Info** tab.

5 Type the name, artist, composer, album, comments, and year information for your song.

■ You can type the song's track number on the CD here.

■ You can type a disc number here if the CD is part of a multi-CD collection.

76

5 Using Advanced iTunes Features

WORKING WITH ITUNES

How much information can fit into a song's tag?

iTunes uses the latest standard for MP3 tags — specifically, ID3 version 2.4 — which can store up to 256 megabytes of information. This is enough to hold several books. The AAC files that iTunes can create use a different but similar tag system.

How can I convert my MP3's ID3 tags to the latest version?

The ID3 tag format used in MP3 audio files to store textual information about a song has evolved over the years. Click **Advanced**, and then **Convert ID3 Tags** to display the Convert ID3 Tags window. This window has options that let you convert the tag in an MP3 file to or from any of the previous ID3 versions, and to convert the text in the tag for international use. Older MP3 files may contain earlier forms of the ID3 tag, and some older MP3 players may not be able to interpret the latest ID3 tag version.

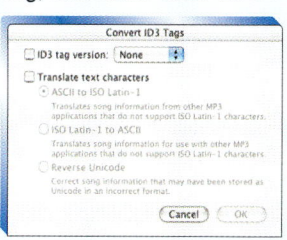

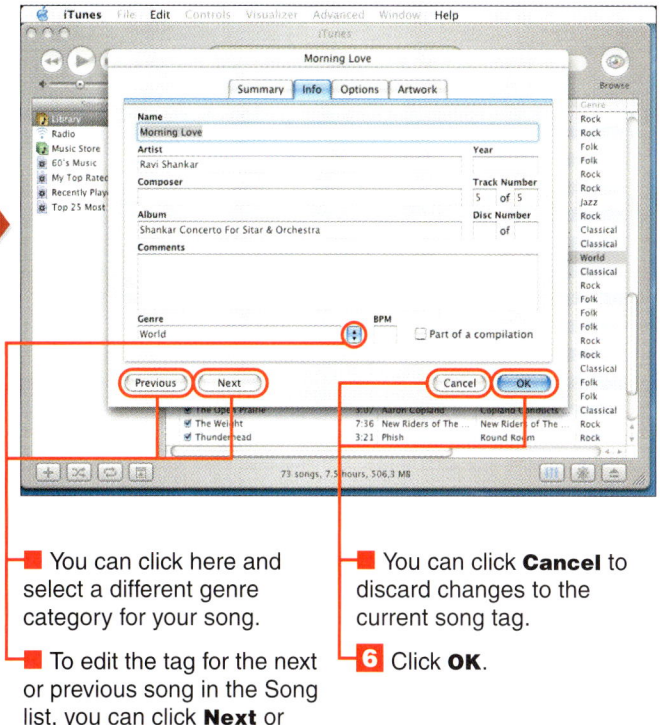

■ You can click here and select a different genre category for your song.

■ To edit the tag for the next or previous song in the Song list, you can click **Next** or **Previous**, and iTunes saves any changes to the current tag before displaying the new one.

■ You can click **Cancel** to discard changes to the current song tag.

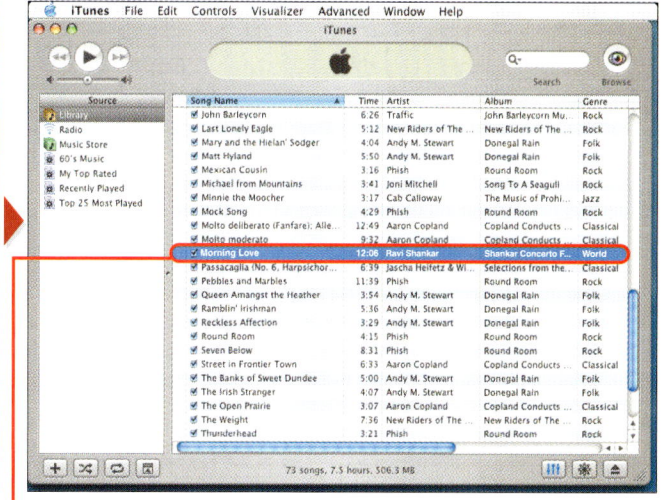

6 Click **OK**.

■ iTunes closes the tag information window and changes the song tag information.

77

CHANGE AN ALBUM'S TAG INFORMATION

When you first play or rip a CD with iTunes, it fetches album and song information from the CDDB (CD database) Internet service. On rare occasions when information is wrong or incomplete, you can easily fix the information.

To change a song's tag information instead of the entire album's, see the section "Change a Song's Tag Information."

CHANGE AN ALBUM'S TAG INFORMATION

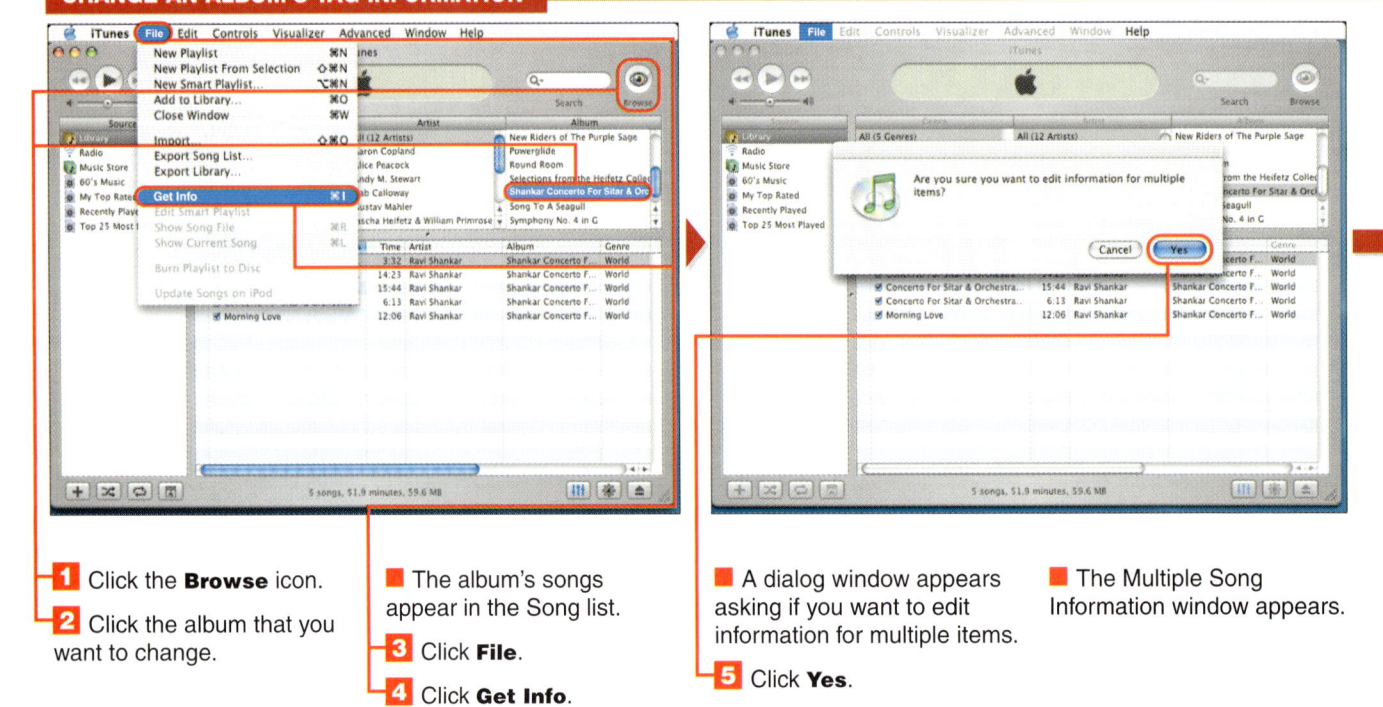

1 Click the **Browse** icon.

2 Click the album that you want to change.

■ The album's songs appear in the Song list.

3 Click **File**.

4 Click **Get Info**.

■ A dialog window appears asking if you want to edit information for multiple items.

5 Click **Yes**.

■ The Multiple Song Information window appears.

78

5 Using Advanced iTunes Features

WORKING WITH ITUNES

How can I make changes to multiple songs that are not part of the same album?

You can press **Shift** and click, or press ⌘ and click multiple songs in the Song list to select them. You can then click **File** and then **Get Info**. When the Multiple Song Information window appears, make your changes as you would with an album. However, be careful, because, as with an album, you cannot undo the changes after you click **OK**.

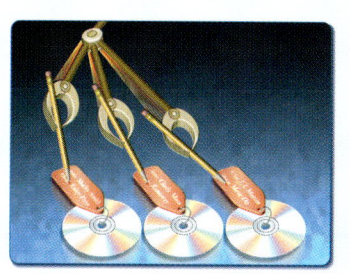

How can I inform the Internet CD database that it has the wrong song information?

Simply make the necessary changes to the CD's album and song information illustrated in this section and the section "Set a Song's Tag Information." Next, click **Advanced**, and then **Submit CD Track Names**. iTunes uses your Internet connection to send the corrected information directly to the CDDB.

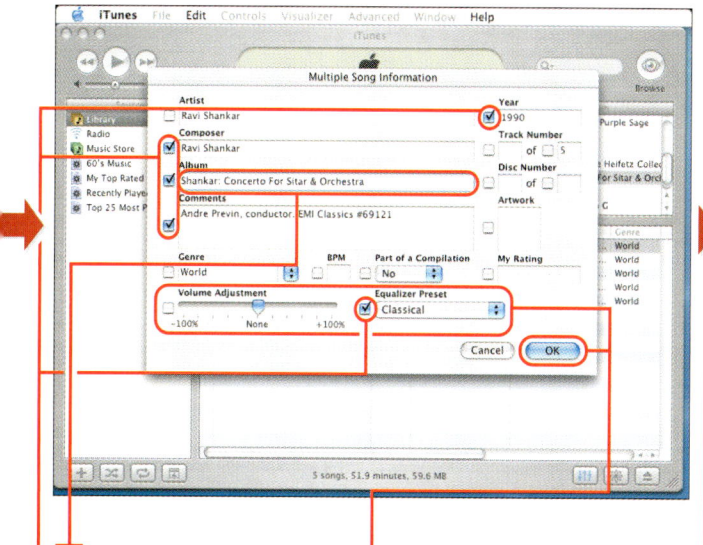

■ **6** Type in any of the fields to make changes to all the album's songs.

Note: See the section "Set a Song's Tag Information" to change these fields for individual songs.

■ ☑ appears beside the modified setting.

■ To discard a change, you can click the checkbox (☑ changes to ☐).

■ You can adjust the volumes of all the album's songs and select an equalizer setting for them.

7 Click **OK**.

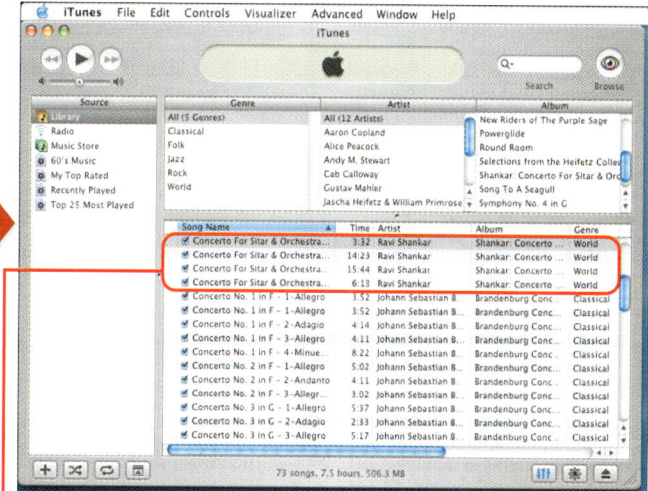

■ The Multiple Song Information window closes and iTunes applies the changes to all the album's songs.

*Note: You cannot click **Edit** and then **Undo** to undo changes to an album's information after you click **OK**.*

79

ADJUST A SONG'S START AND END TIMES

You can set how much of a song's beginning or ending to skip when iTunes plays it. This lets you trim unwanted material like introductions or applause from live recordings to make a better musical listening experience.

ADJUST A SONG'S START AND END TIMES

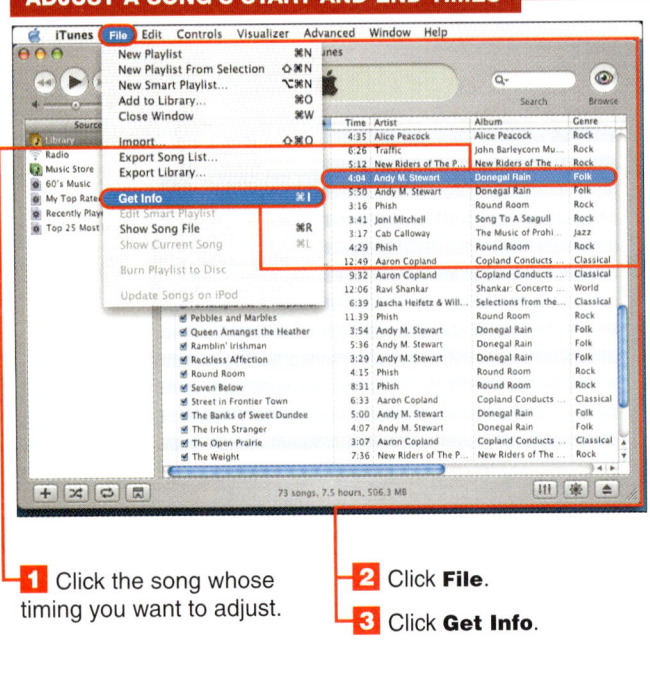

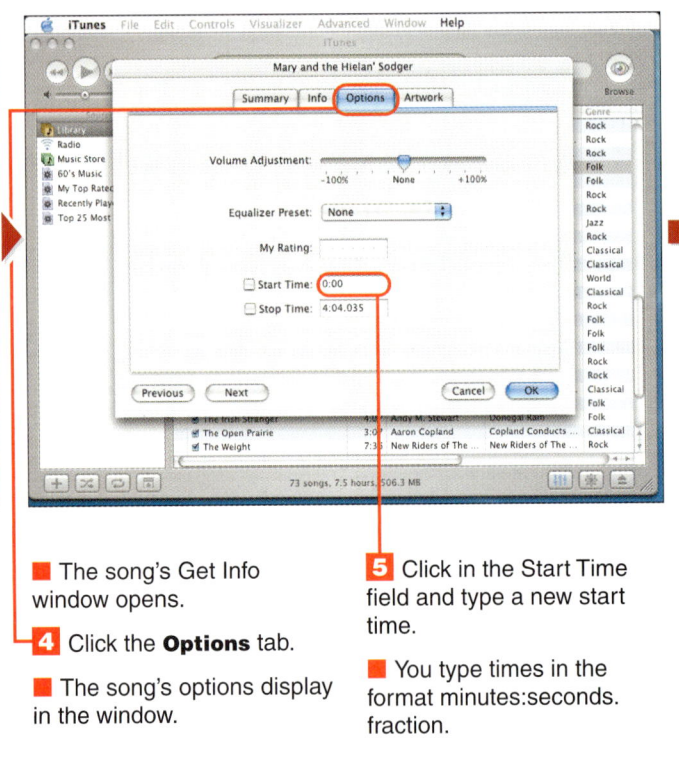

1 Click the song whose timing you want to adjust.

2 Click **File**.

3 Click **Get Info**.

■ The song's Get Info window opens.

4 Click the **Options** tab.

■ The song's options display in the window.

5 Click in the Start Time field and type a new start time.

■ You type times in the format minutes:seconds.fraction.

80

5 Using Advanced iTunes Features

WORKING WITH ITUNES

How do I combine two tracks from the same album on my CD?

You can use the Join CD Tracks command to make iTunes import or play two or more adjacent songs from a CD as a single track. You may want to join tracks on albums that comprise many short tracks or to eliminate the small gaps of silence between tracks.

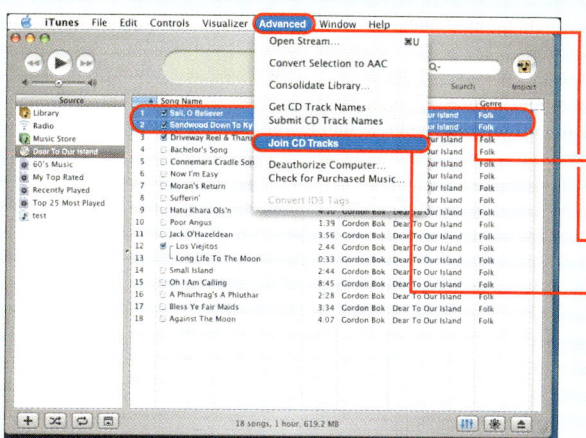

1 Insert a CD.

2 Click the first song you want to join.

3 Press **Shift** and click the last song you want to join.

4 Click **Advanced**.

5 Click **Join CD Tracks**.

■ iTunes marks the tracks as joined in the CD's Song list and remembers this information the next time you insert the CD.

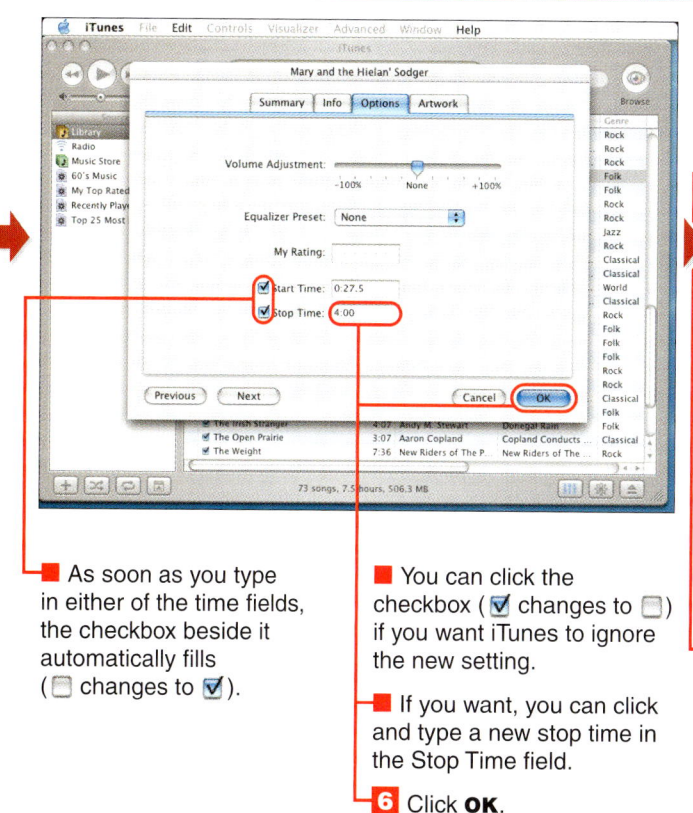

■ As soon as you type in either of the time fields, the checkbox beside it automatically fills (☐ changes to ☑).

■ You can click the checkbox (☑ changes to ☐) if you want iTunes to ignore the new setting.

■ If you want, you can click and type a new stop time in the Stop Time field.

6 Click **OK**.

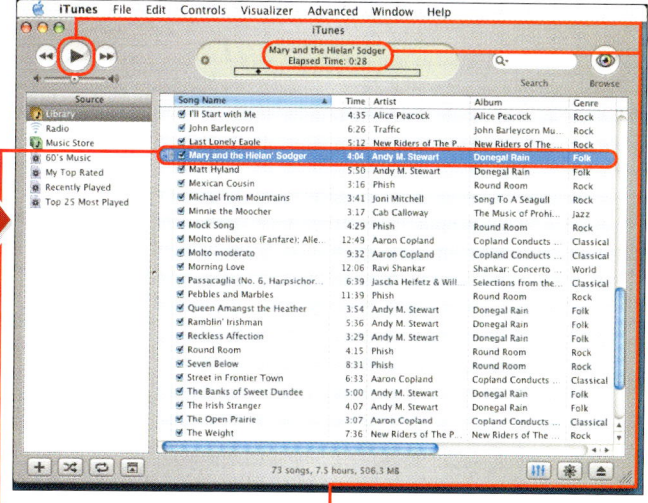

■ The song's Get Info window closes.

■ The song's length appears unaltered in the Song list.

Note: Adjusting a song's start or stop time does not change the song's actual length; it only makes iTunes change where it starts or stops playing the song.

7 Click the Play button (▶).

■ The song begins playing at its new start time.

81

USING THE VISUALIZER

iTunes' Visualizer lets you see your music in bright, swirling colors that seemingly dance to each song's beat and melody. The Visualizer serves no practical purpose — which may be its entire point.

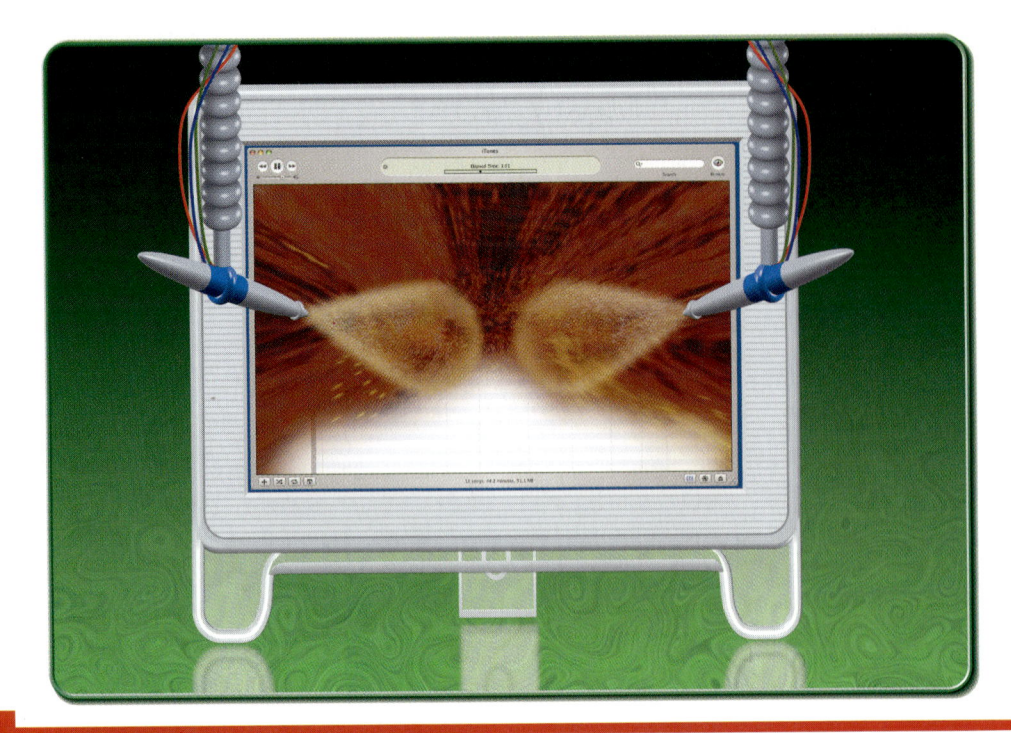

USING THE VISUALIZER

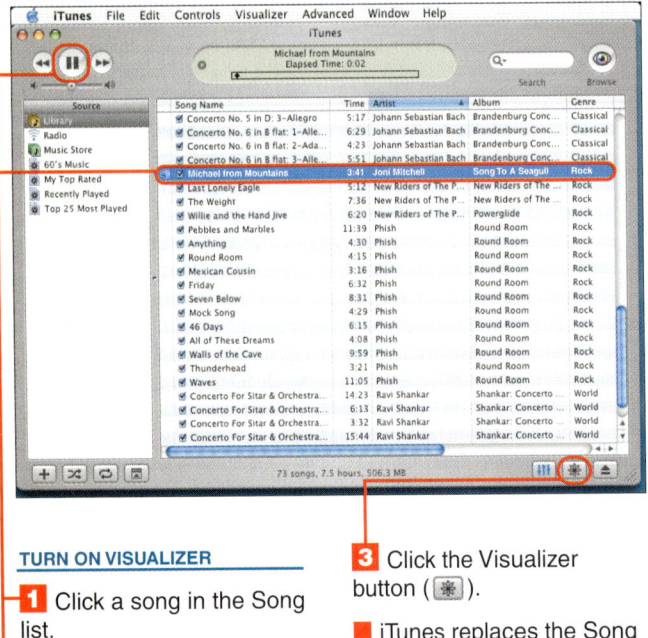

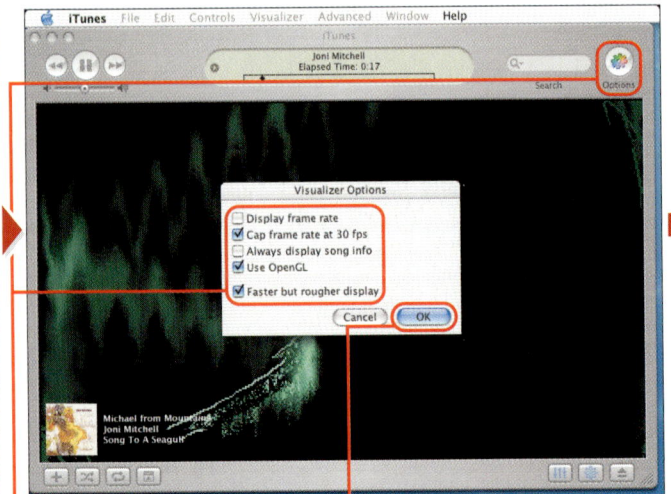

TURN ON VISUALIZER

1 Click a song in the Song list.

2 Click ⏸.

3 Click the Visualizer button (✻).

■ iTunes replaces the Song list and Source list with the Visualizer display.

■ The currently playing song's title briefly appears.

4 Click the **Options** button.

■ The Visualizer Options window appears.

5 Click the options you want (☐ changes to ☑).

■ You can limit the frame rate if the Visualizer is too fast on your Mac.

■ You can choose to keep song titles visible.

■ You can display the Visualizer's frame rate.

6 Click **OK**.

82

5 Using Advanced iTunes Features

WORKING WITH ITUNES

Are other visualizers available for iTunes?

Yes. Apple has released a software development kit that lets programmers build visualizers that plug into iTunes. Among the many available visualizers are ones that display slideshows from folders of pictures, show detailed sound wave information, or fetch and display stock prices from the Internet. To find such third-party visualizers, use an Internet search engine and type **iTunes visual**.

How can I make the Visualizer play more smoothly?

The bigger the display, the more processing the Visualizer uses, and older, slower machines may have difficulty producing a smooth display. Try clicking **Visualizer**, and then selecting a **Medium** or **Small** frame size. Selecting **Faster but rougher display** from the Visualizer Options window can also help.

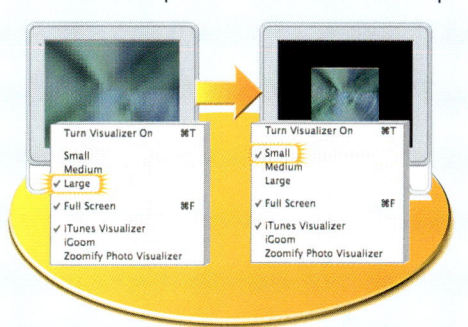

- The Visualizer Options window closes and the settings take effect.

7 Press ?.

- A list of keyboard shortcuts for controlling the Visualizer appears on the display.

8 Press ? again.

- A second list of shortcuts appears.

- You can control many Visualizer settings, and save your favorite settings, with the keyboard.

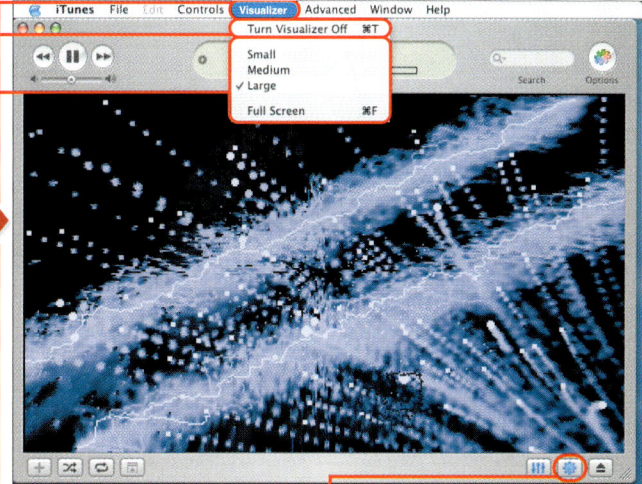

TURN OFF THE VISUALIZER

9 Click **Visualizer**.

- You can click these options to change Visualizer's display size.

10 Click **Turn Visualizer Off**.

- The Visualizer vanishes and the Song list and Source list reappear.

- You can also turn the Visualizer off by clicking when the Visualizer is running.

83

UPDATE SONGS ON AN IPOD

Apple's iPod digital music player and iTunes were literally made for each other. iTunes can exclusively link your iPod to your iTunes Library so that your iPod automatically updates itself with the Library's songs and playlists each time you connect the iPod.

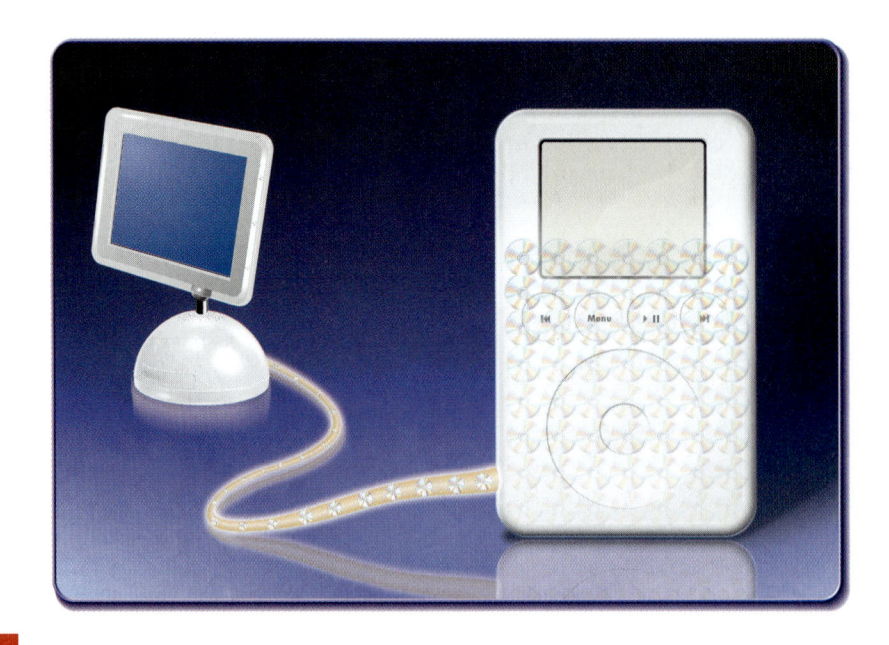

UPDATE SONGS ON AN IPOD

FIRST TIME UPDATE

1 Connect a brand-new iPod to your Mac while iTunes is running.

Note: The iPod's packaging comes with diagrams showing how to connect the iPod to various Mac models.

■ The iTunes Setup Assistant window appears after a few seconds.

2 Click and type a name for the iPod.

3 Click **Done**.

■ iTunes takes a few minutes to copy your entire Library to the iPod.

Note: iTunes does not copy the Library if it is too big to fit on the iPod.

■ The iPod appears in the Source list, where you can view the amount of used space on the iPod.

4 Click the iPod Eject button ( ) to disconnect your iPod.

Note: Do not physically disconnect the iPod until its display indicates that it is safe.

■ The iPod disappears from the Source list.

84

5 Using Advanced iTunes Features

WORKING WITH ITUNES

What happens if I connect my iPod to a different Mac?

iTunes tells you that the iPod is linked to a different iTunes music library and gives you the chance to replace the iPod's contents with the contents of the current iTunes music library.

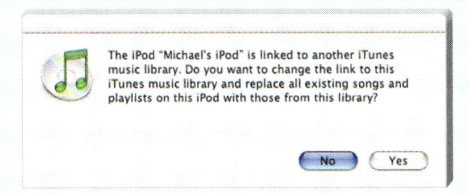

What does the Enable FireWire disk use option do?

Use the **Enable FireWire disk use** option if you want to use your iPod as a portable hard drive as well as a music player. This option makes the iPod appear on your Desktop as a disk drive to and from which you can click and drag files. However, you cannot see your music files because they are protected. Also, each time you connect the iPod, you must use the Finder's Eject command to remove the iPod from your Desktop before you can disconnect it. For more on the Finder, see Chapter 1.

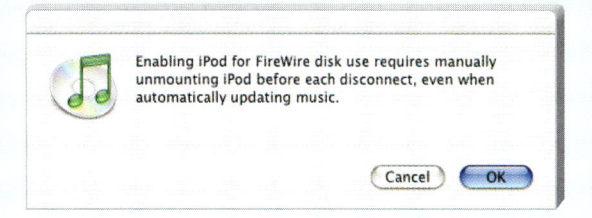

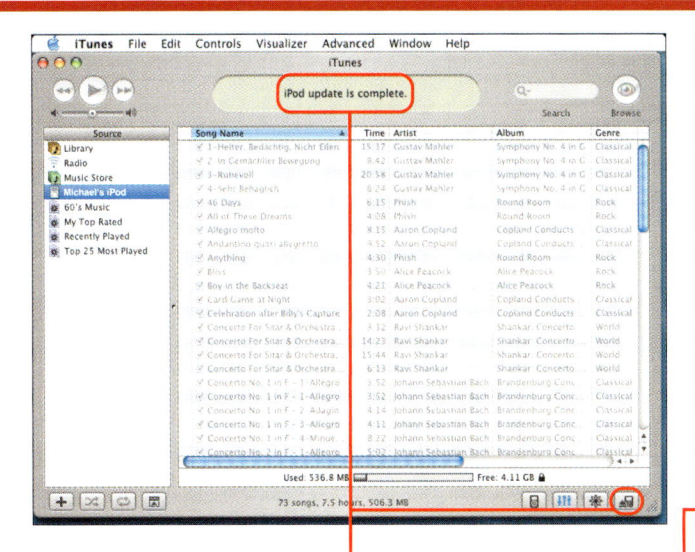

SUBSEQUENT UPDATES

1 Connect your iPod to your Mac.

■ If iTunes is not running, it starts and takes a few seconds to update the iPod.

■ The Status panel tells you when the update finishes.

2 Click 🔲 to disconnect the iPod.

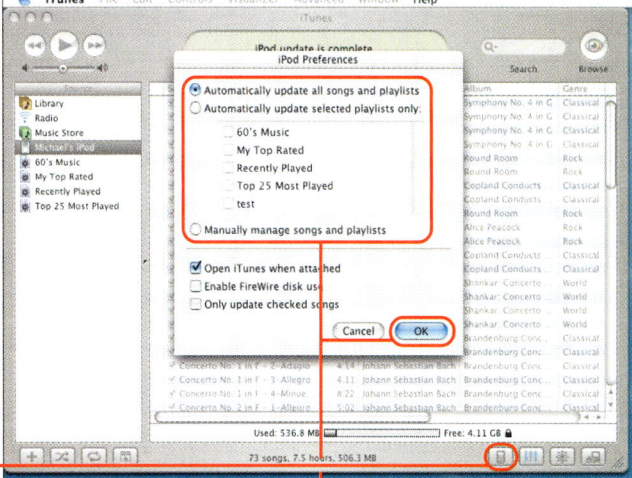

SET IPOD PREFERENCES

1 Connect your iPod.

2 Click the iPod Preferences button (🔲).

■ The iPod Preferences window appears.

3 Select whether you want iTunes to update certain playlists, ignore unchecked songs, or let you manually manage songs and playlists (○ changes to ●).

4 Click **OK**.

■ The iPod remembers your settings.

85

COPY SONGS TO AND DELETE SONGS FROM AN IPOD

When you set your iPod to let you manually manage songs and playlists, you can copy songs to your iPod or delete them when you connect the iPod to any Mac.

Please note that this section assumes you have set your iPod Preferences to manually manage songs and playlists. See the subsection "Set iPod Preferences" in the section "Update Songs on an iPod" for more information.

COPY SONGS TO AN IPOD

1 Connect the iPod.

■ The iPod appears selected in the Source list.

2 Click **Library**.

3 Click and drag a song from the Library's Song list to the iPod and release the mouse.

■ The Status panel states that it is updating the iPod.

■ You can select and drag multiple songs at a time to the iPod.

■ You can also click and drag playlists to the iPod.

■ You can click the **Browse** button to browse your Library and drag genres, artists, or albums to the iPod.

86

5 Using Advanced iTunes Features

WORKING WITH ITUNES

I cannot copy songs from the iPod to my iTunes Library. Why not?

Apple designed the iPod software this way in order to protect iPod users from accidentally infringing copyrights. Copying songs you have purchased and ripped to someone else's iTunes Library can violate copyright law. It does not infringe copyright to copy your own music from your iTunes Library to your iPod.

Do I need to authorize my iPod to play music I have purchased from the iTunes store?

No. The iPod can play any song purchased from the iTunes Music Store. This allows friends and family to share music. It does not, however, encourage copyright infringement, because you cannot copy the music from the iPod to another Mac or play it on another Mac with iTunes — unless you authorize that other Mac.

DELETE SONGS FROM AN IPOD

1 Connect the iPod.

■ The iPod appears selected in the Source list.

2 Click a song in the iPod's Song list.

3 Press `Delete`.

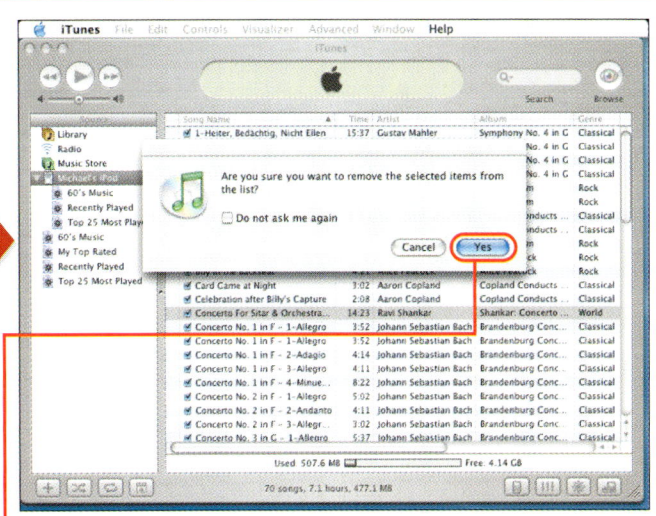

■ A dialog window appears asking if you are sure you want to remove the selected items.

4 Click **Yes**.

■ The window closes.

■ iTunes removes the song from the iPod.

87

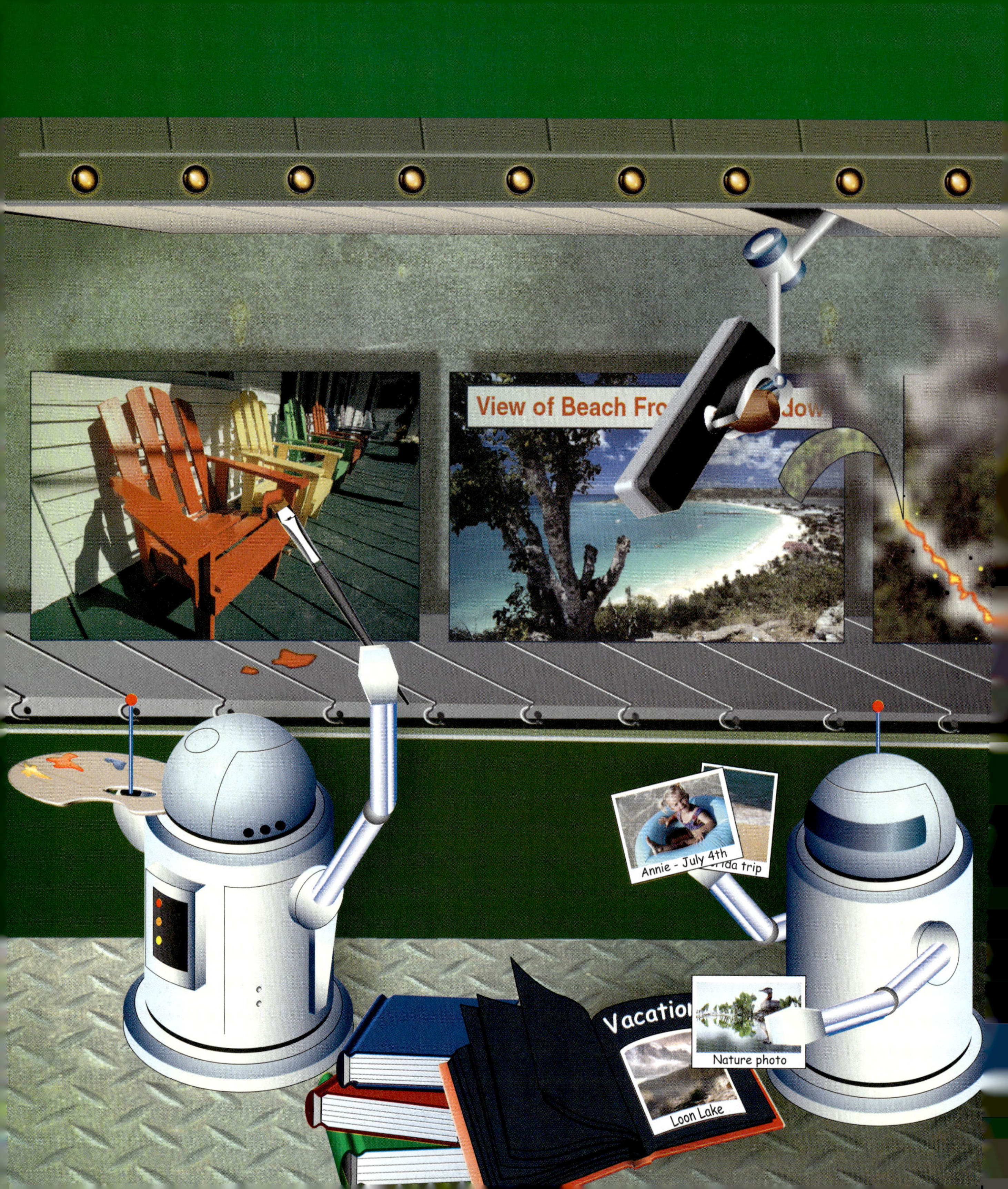
View of Beach
Annie - July 4th
Nature photo
Loon Lake

PART III

Working with iPhoto

You use iPhoto to take control of all your digital photos. You can collect, label, and organize your entire photo collection. You can retouch, crop, and enhance your photos, too. And when you are done, you can use iPhoto to share your photos over the Web, e-mail them to friends and family, and order professional prints and clothbound photo books.

6   iPhoto Basics
Pages 90–119

7   Editing Photos with iPhoto
Pages 120–137

8   Using Photos with iPhoto
Pages 138–173

SET UP IPHOTO

iPhoto requires no special set-up and it is ready to go the first time you use it. However, you can set a few simple preferences to reflect how you want to see and work with your pictures.

This section sets up a new copy of iPhoto; however, you can change iPhoto settings at any time.

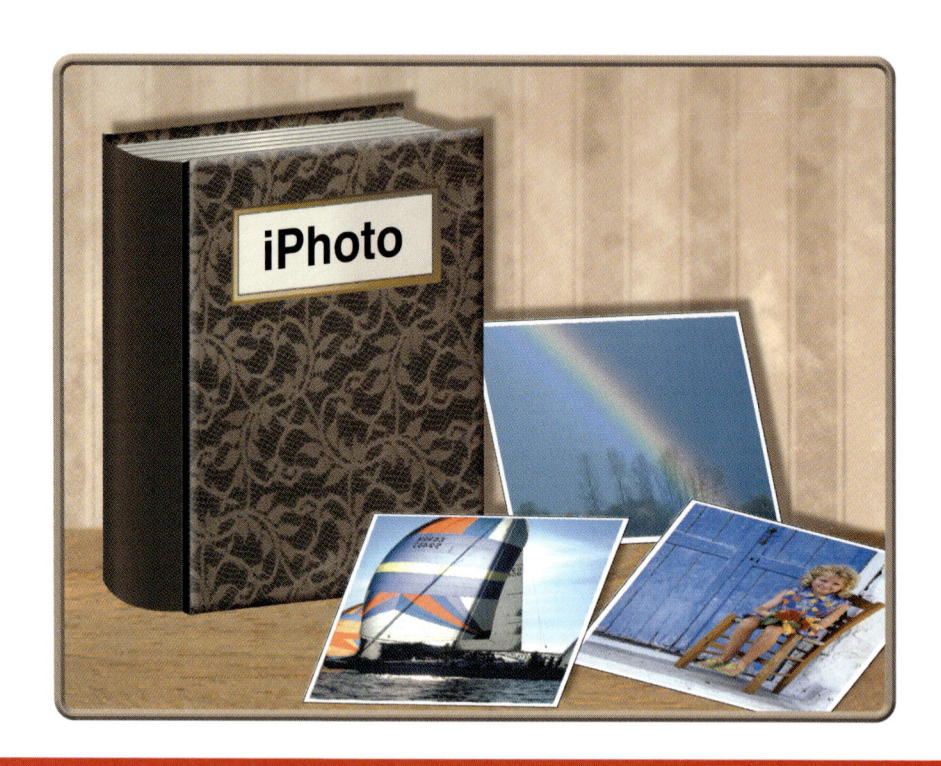

SET UP IPHOTO

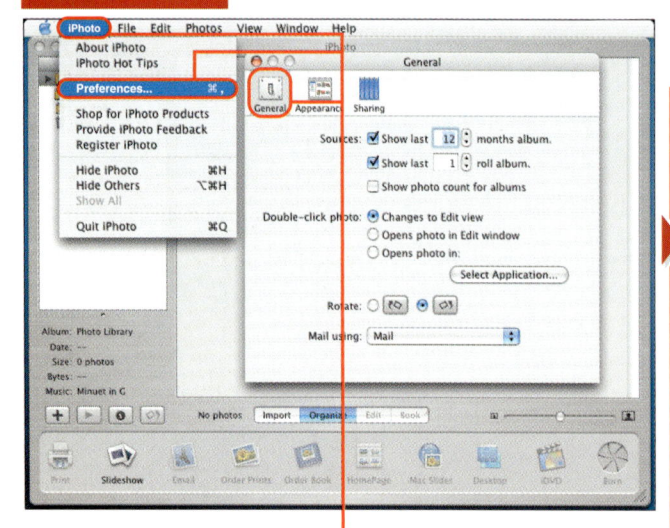

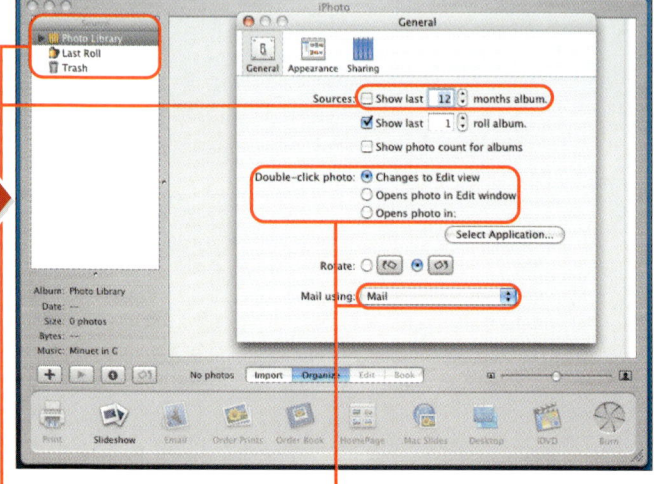

1 Start iPhoto.

Note: See Chapter 1 for more on starting iLife applications.

■ The iPhoto application window appears.

2 Click **iPhoto**.

3 Click **Preferences**.

■ The iPhoto preferences window appears.

4 Click the **General** button.

5 Click **Show last 12 months album** (☑ changes to ☐).

■ The album vanishes from the Source list.

■ Changes to preferences take place immediately.

■ You can click these options (○ changes to ⦿) to specify what happens when you double-click a picture.

6 Click the Mail ⇅.

90

6 iPhoto Basics

WORKING WITH IPHOTO

How many photos can iPhoto hold?

There is no specific limit to the number of photos that iPhoto can manage. If your Mac has enough hard disk space and RAM, iPhoto can handle thousands of pictures at a time.

Do I need an Internet connection to use iPhoto?

You can use iPhoto without an Internet connection to import, edit, organize, or print photos. However, many of iPhoto's features, such as ordering prints or a book, require an Internet connection. A few features, like creating a homepage or a .Mac slideshow, require a .Mac account from Apple.

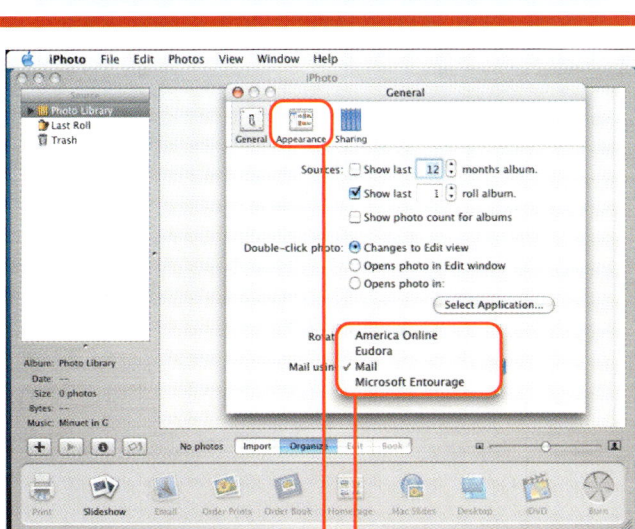

■ The Mail menu displays a choice of mail programs that iPhoto uses when it e-mails photos.

Note: The programs shown on the menu vary depending on the mail programs you have installed on your Mac.

7 Select the e-mail program that you want iPhoto to use.

8 Click the **Appearance** button.

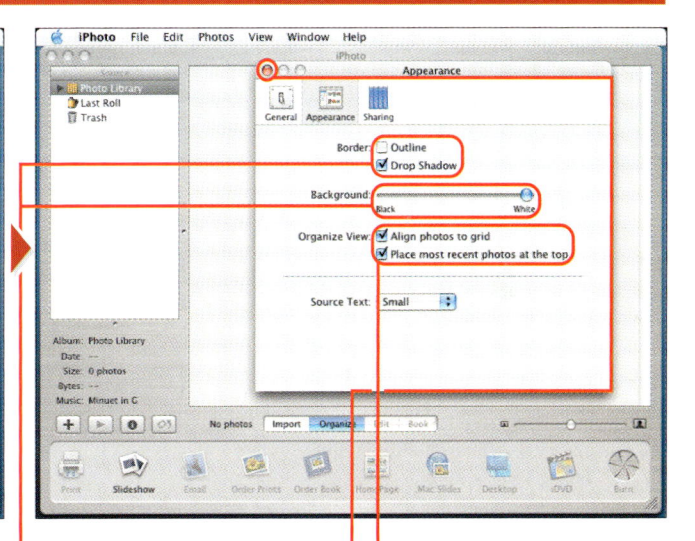

■ You can click these options (☐ changes to ☑) to change how the borders surrounding photos are displayed as you work.

■ You can click and drag the slider ◯ to change the background of the work area.

■ You can click these options to modify how photos are laid out in the Organize view.

9 Click the Close button (◯).

■ The window closes.

91

IMPORT IMAGES FROM A CAMERA

iPhoto can bring photos from your digital camera directly into the iPhoto Library, and erase your camera memory, so that the camera is ready to take more pictures.

Most cameras connect to the Mac using a USB cable, which is usually provided with the camera.

IMPORT IMAGES FROM A CAMERA

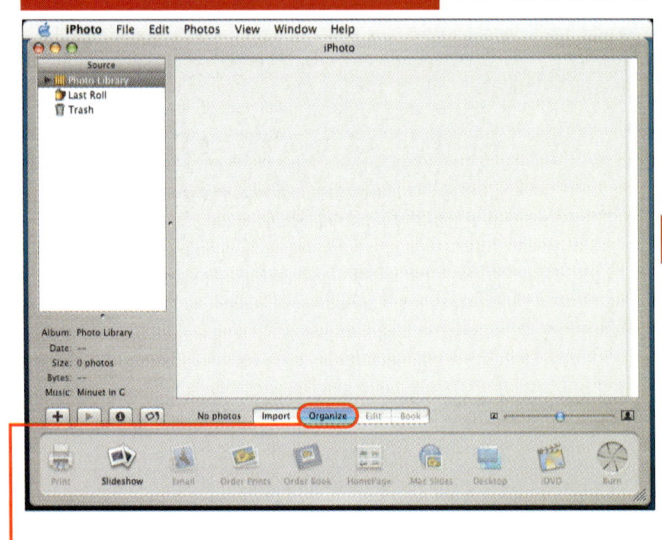

1 Click **Import**.

Note: You may not need to click **Import**; when iPhoto detects a connected camera, iPhoto usually switches automatically to Import view.

■ The Import view appears.

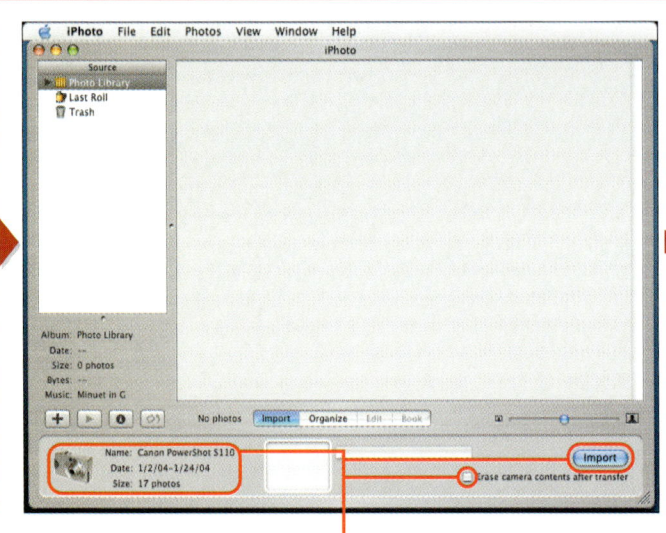

2 Connect your digital camera to your Mac and turn the camera on.

Note: Follow your camera manufacturer's instructions for the precise method of connecting your camera to a computer.

■ The camera's type and the number of photos it contains appear after a few seconds.

■ You can click here (☐ changes to ☑) to erase the camera's contents after importing.

3 Click **Import**.

6 iPhoto Basics

WORKING WITH IPHOTO

Do I need to install drivers or other software to use my camera with iPhoto?

Apple has worked closely with the major digital camera manufacturers to make iPhoto compatible with their cameras. Nearly all digital cameras made in the last two years work with iPhoto without any additional software. See www.apple.com/iphoto/compatibility for a list of compatible cameras.

Does importing photos use up the camera's batteries?

Importing photos uses up some battery power because you have to turn on the camera in order to import photos. If you think your batteries are running low, place fresh batteries in the camera before importing photos to avoid problems. Alternatively, you can use your camera's power adapter, if it has one.

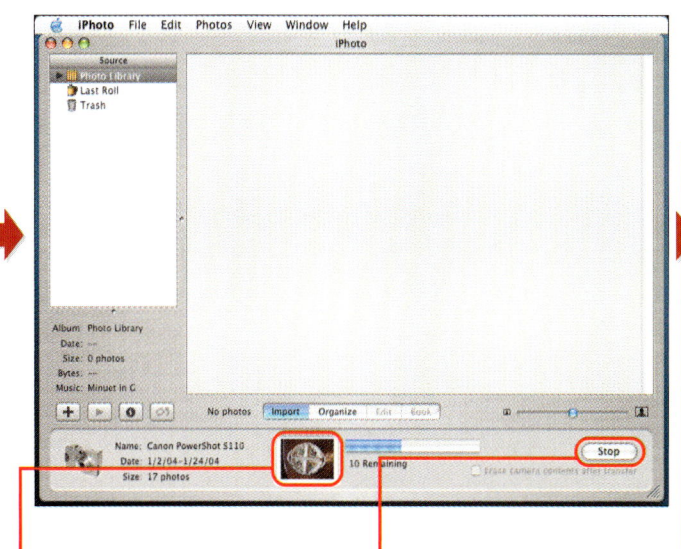

■ The import begins.

■ As iPhoto imports each photo from the camera, a thumbnail of the image appears.

■ You can click **Stop** if you want to end the import process before iPhoto finishes.

*Note: If you selected the **Erase camera contents after transfer** option, stopping the import before it finishes may erase the camera's photos.*

■ When iPhoto finishes importing, iPhoto automatically switches to the Organize view and shows you the photos you have imported.

93

IMPORT IMAGES FROM A CARD READER

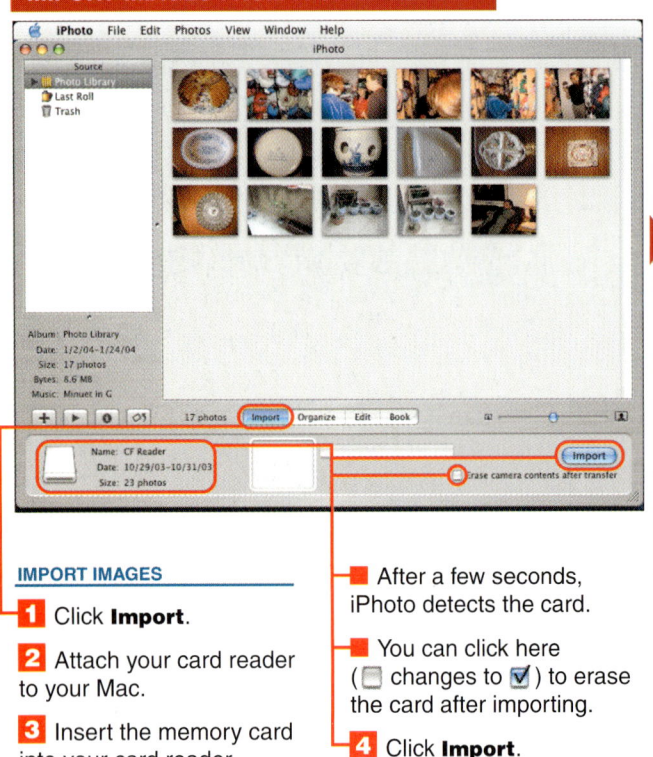

If you want to save your camera's battery power, or if your camera cannot connect to your Mac, you can still import photos from your camera by using a card reader.

Digital cameras usually store their photos on a memory card, which you can remove from the camera and place in a card reader that attaches to your Mac's USB ports. The card appears as a removable disk connected to your Mac. See your card reader's documentation for more on attaching it to your Mac.

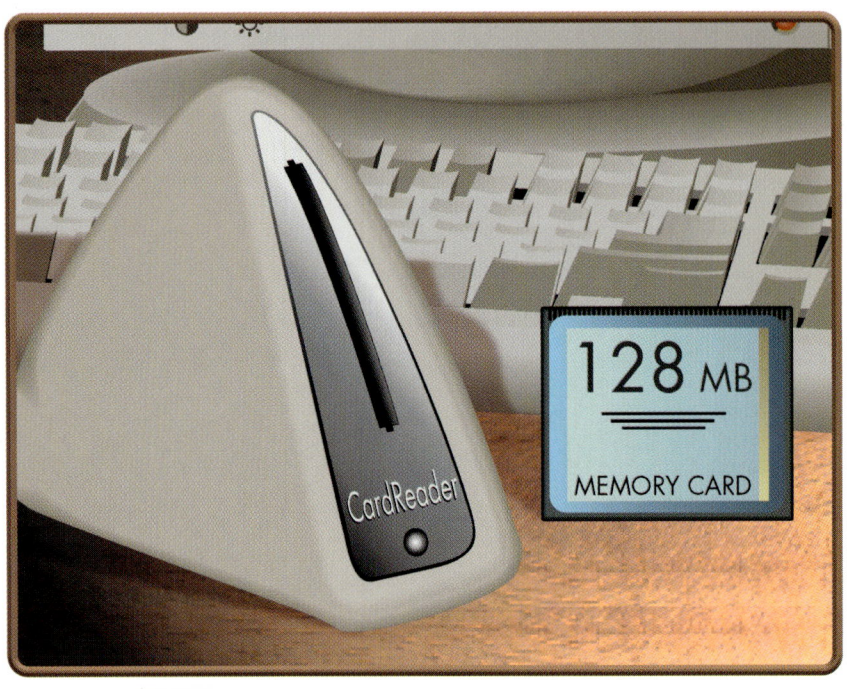

Because your Mac treats the card as a removable disk, you must tell the Mac to eject it before removing the card and disconnecting the reader.

IMPORT IMAGES FROM A CARD READER

IMPORT IMAGES

1 Click **Import**.

2 Attach your card reader to your Mac.

3 Insert the memory card into your card reader.

■ After a few seconds, iPhoto detects the card.

■ You can click here (☐ changes to ☑) to erase the card after importing.

4 Click **Import**.

■ iPhoto imports the photos, displaying thumbnails as it proceeds.

■ You can click **Stop** if you want to end the import process before iPhoto finishes.

94

6 iPhoto Basics

WORKING WITH IPHOTO

Because the Mac treats the memory card as a disk, can I store other files on it?

Yes, but you run a slight risk of making the card unreadable by your camera; consult your camera's manual for details. Also, you cannot use any room taken up by your files for photos.

Does a card reader need batteries?

Nearly all memory card readers get their power directly through the USB connection and do not require another power source.

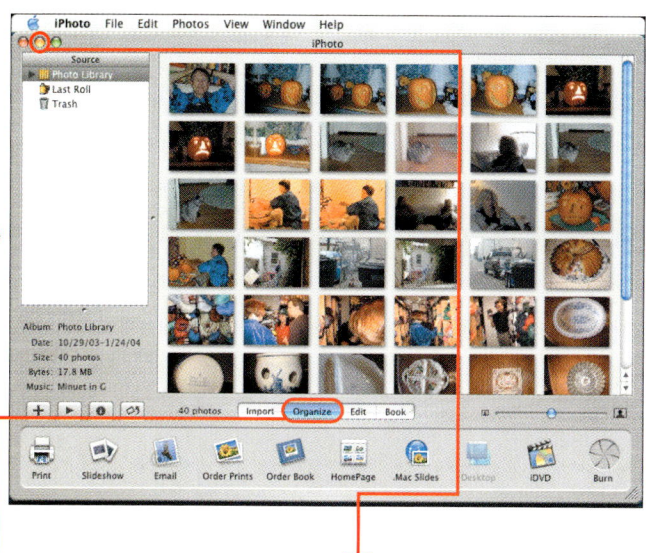

EJECT THE CARD AND DISCONNECT THE READER

■ When the import finishes, iPhoto switches back to the Organize view.

5 Click the iPhoto window's Minimize button ( ).

■ The iPhoto window reduces to an icon in the Dock.

6 Click and drag the card's disk icon to the Dock's Eject icon ( ).

■ The disk icon vanishes from the Desktop.

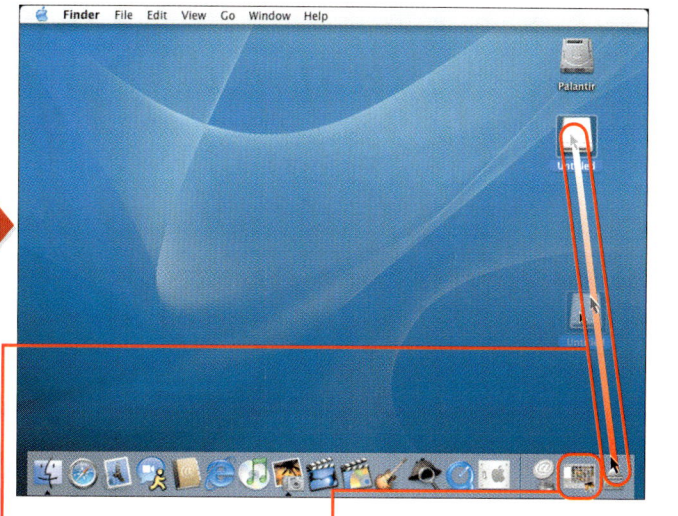

■ You may now remove the card from the reader and disconnect the reader.

7 Click the minimized iPhoto window in the Dock.

■ The iPhoto window expands.

95

IMPORT IMAGES FROM FILES

You can import image files on your Mac into iPhoto, so if someone e-mails photos to you or gives you photos on a disk, you can easily add them to your iPhoto Library.

IMPORT IMAGES FROM FILES

1 Click **File**.

2 Click **Import**.

■ An Import Photos window appears.

3 Navigate to a folder that contains images, and click the folder.

4 Click **Import**.

Note: For more on opening and saving files, see Chapter 1.

6 iPhoto Basics

WORKING WITH IPHOTO

What file formats can iPhoto import?

iPhoto can import any image file format that Apple's QuickTime can read. These formats include JPEG, Windows .BMP, GIF, TIFF, and PNG, among many others. Imported files retain their file types when you copy them into the iPhoto Library.

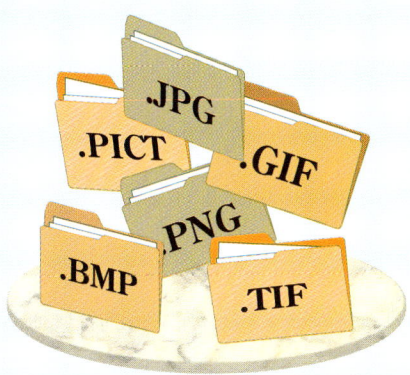

Does iPhoto support drag-and-drop importing?

Yes. You can drag a folder of images, or a folder that contains folders of images, and drop it directly on iPhoto's Photo Library folder. iPhoto imports each folder of images as a separate film roll. For more information, see the next section, "Organize the iPhoto Library by Film Roll."

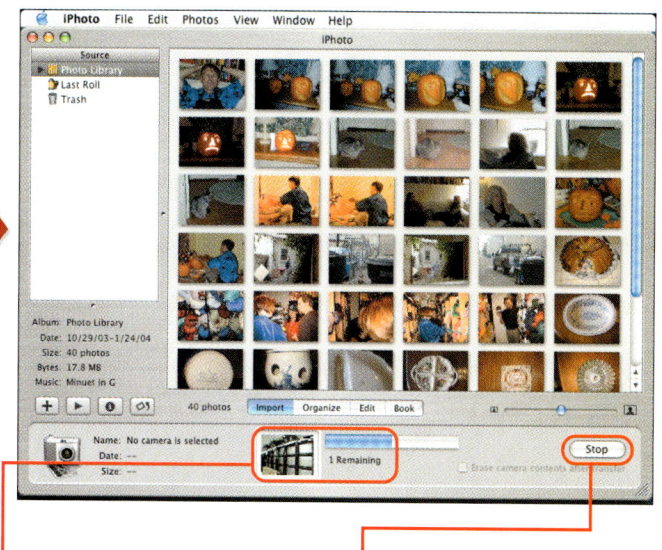

- iPhoto imports the photos from the folder, displaying a thumbnail for each photo.

- You can click **Stop** to end the import process at any time.

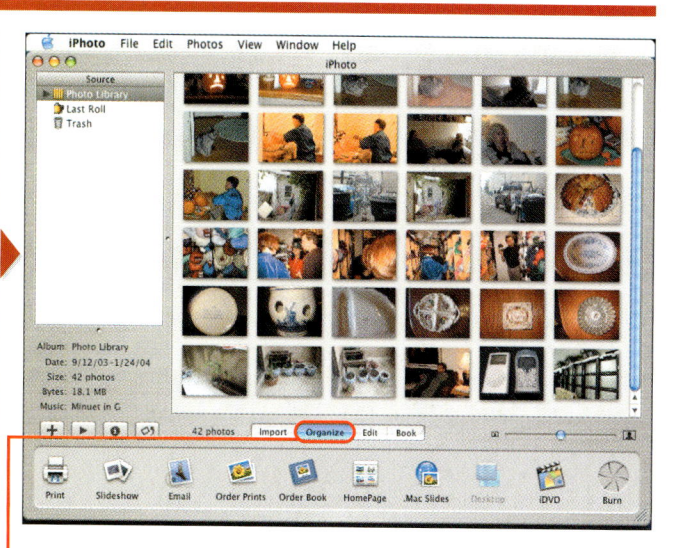

- When the import completes, iPhoto displays the Organize view and adds the imported photos to the iPhoto Library.

97

ORGANIZE THE IPHOTO LIBRARY BY FILM ROLL

Each time you import photos, iPhoto treats them as a roll of film that you have developed. You can see your photos arranged by film roll, and give each roll a name.

ORGANIZE THE IPHOTO LIBRARY BY FILM ROLL

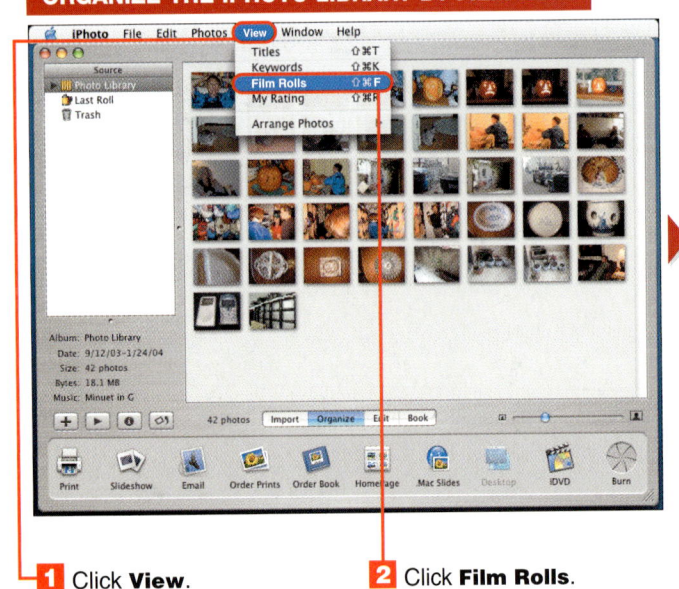

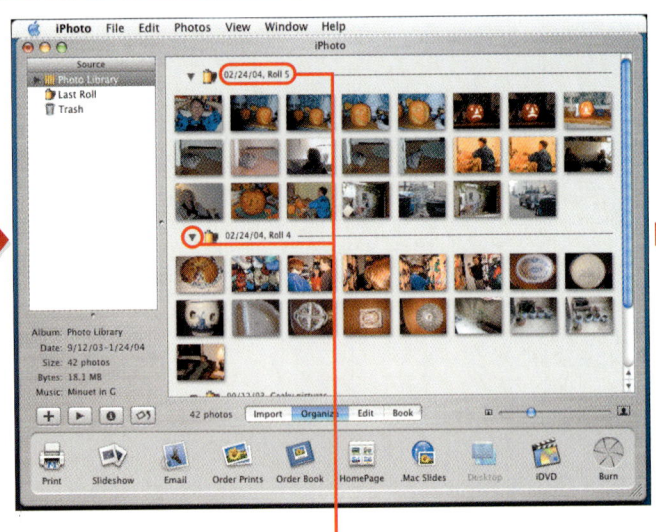

■ **1** Click **View**.

■ **2** Click **Film Rolls**.

■ The Organize view changes to show the film rolls.

■ Each roll displays the date you imported it and the number of photos it contains.

■ **3** Click the Expand button (▼).

6 iPhoto Basics

WORKING WITH IPHOTO

How can I rearrange the order in which iPhoto shows my film rolls?

iPhoto always displays film rolls in the order in which you imported them. You can set iPhoto's Preferences to show the most recent items first or last. For more information, see the section "Set Up iPhoto." You can also change the date and time recorded on the roll to change its place in the list:

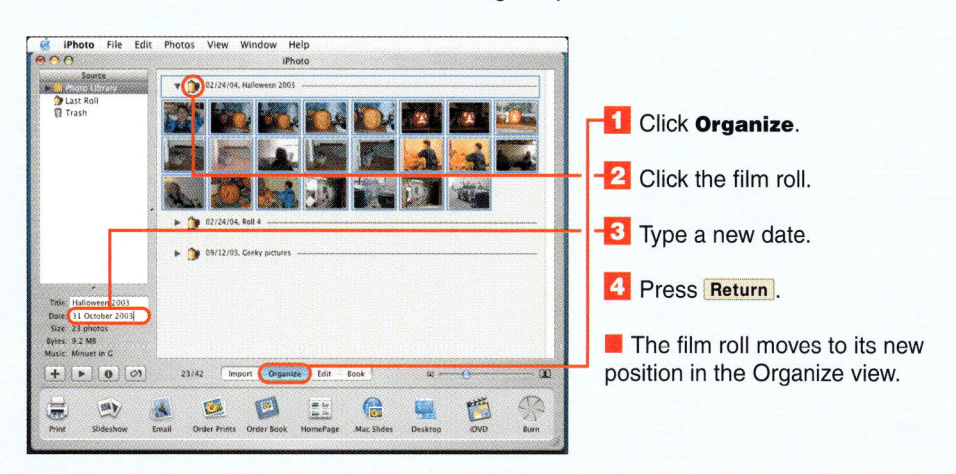

1 Click **Organize**.

2 Click the film roll.

3 Type a new date.

4 Press `Return`.

■ The film roll moves to its new position in the Organize view.

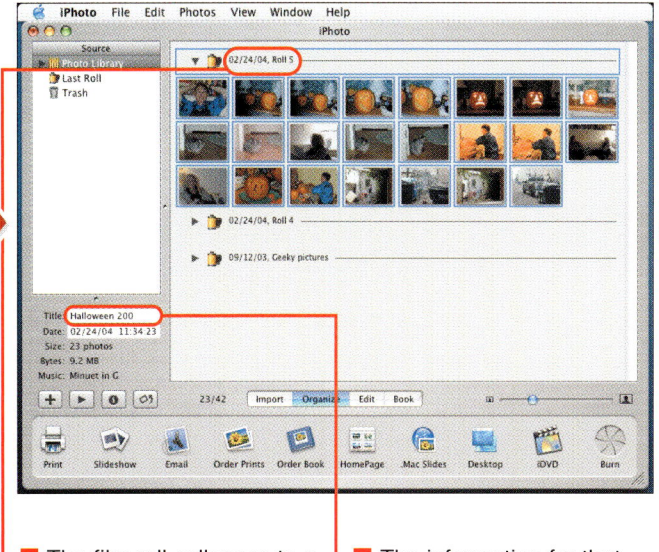

■ The film roll collapses to a single line.

4 Click a film roll's name.

■ The information for that roll appears in the Title and Date fields.

5 Click in the Title field and type a new name for the roll.

6 Press `Enter`.

■ The film roll's new name appears in the Organize view.

99

SET PHOTO TITLES AND DESCRIPTIONS

You can title each of your photos and attach short descriptions to them to help you organize your iPhoto Library.

SET PHOTO TITLES AND DESCRIPTIONS

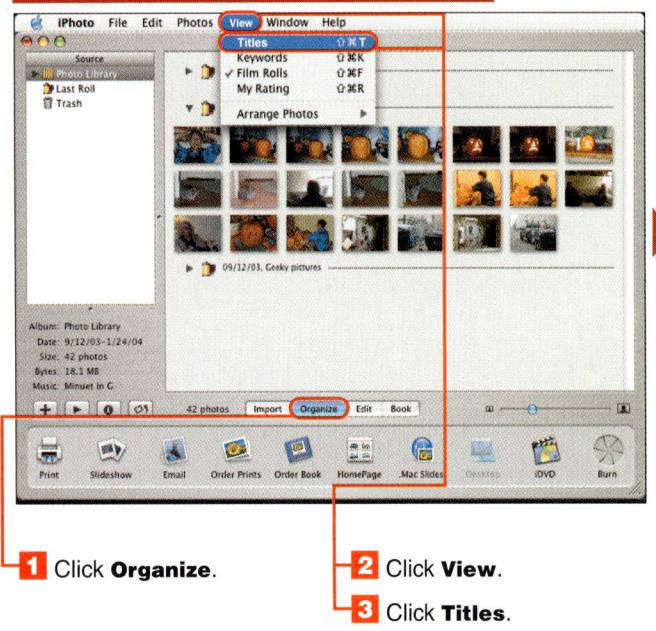

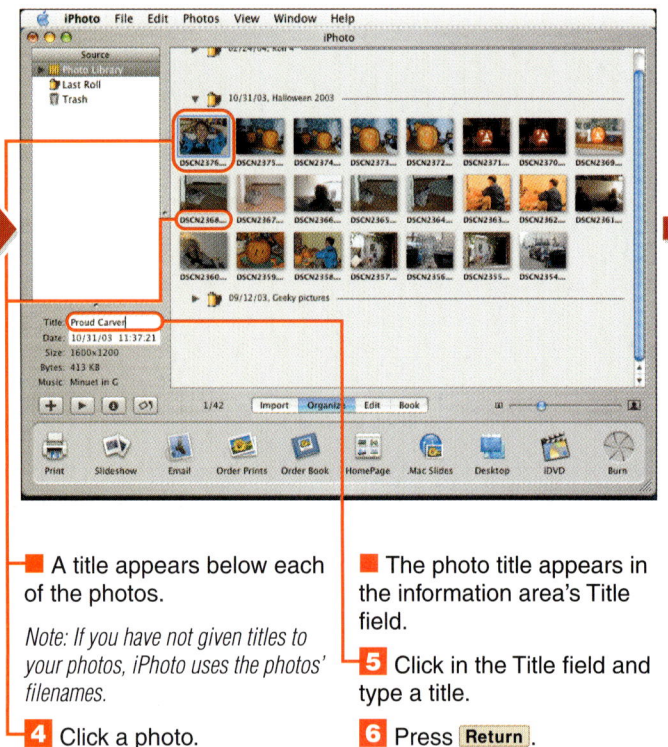

1 Click **Organize**.

2 Click **View**.

3 Click **Titles**.

■ A title appears below each of the photos.

Note: If you have not given titles to your photos, iPhoto uses the photos' filenames.

4 Click a photo.

■ The photo title appears in the information area's Title field.

5 Click in the Title field and type a title.

6 Press Return.

100

6 iPhoto Basics

WORKING WITH IPHOTO

How can I set more than one photo title at a time?

You can give a group of photos standardized titles with the Batch Change command, which you find in the Photos menu. Note that this command also appears in the contextual menu when you `Control`+click, or right-click, a photo.

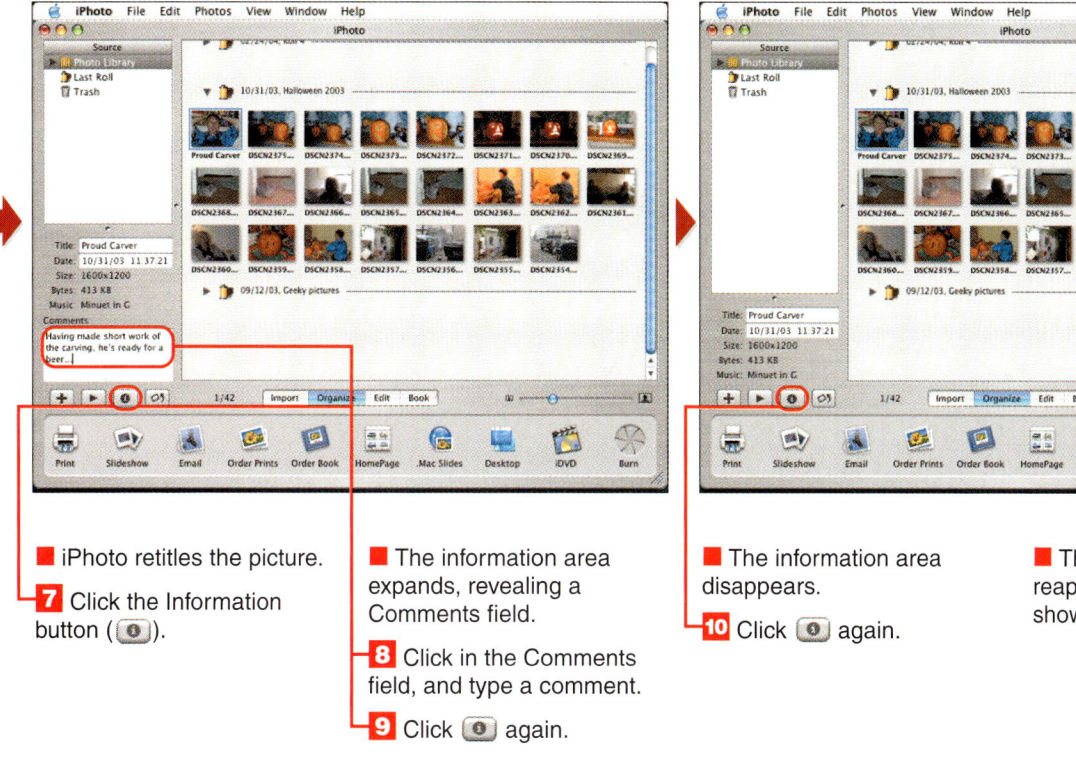

1 `Shift`+click or `⌘`+click multiple pictures.

2 Click **Photos** and select **Batch Change**.

■ The Batch Change sheet appears.

3 Click here and select **Title**.

4 Click here and select **Text**.

5 In the field that appears on the sheet, type a title in the field.

6 Press `Return`.

■ iPhoto retitles the photos you selected.

■ iPhoto retitles the picture.

7 Click the Information button (ⓘ).

■ The information area expands, revealing a Comments field.

8 Click in the Comments field, and type a comment.

9 Click ⓘ again.

■ The information area disappears.

10 Click ⓘ again.

■ The information area reappears, but does not show the Comments field.

101

ASSIGN KEYWORDS TO PHOTOS

You can assign one or more keywords to groups of photos to sort them into categories. For example, you can assign a "Vacation" keyword to all your vacation pictures, or a "Family" keyword to family snapshots to make it easier to find these pictures later.

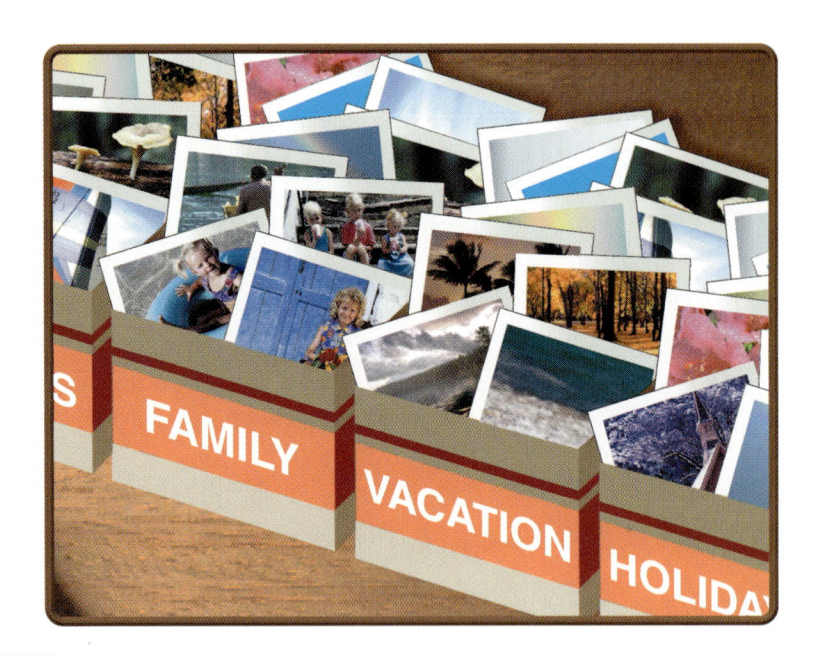

ASSIGN KEYWORDS TO PHOTOS

VIEW KEYWORDS

1. Click **Organize**.
2. Click **View**.
3. Click **Keywords**.

   ■ If any photos have keywords assigned, the keywords appear.

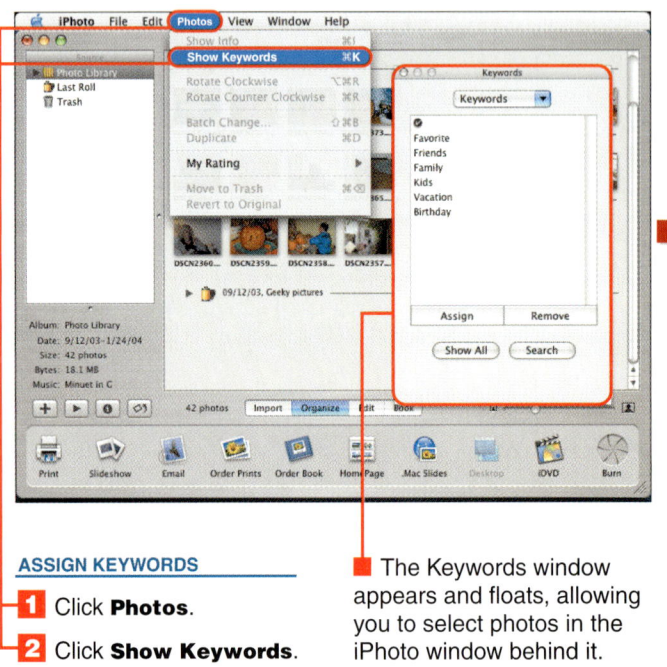

ASSIGN KEYWORDS

1. Click **Photos**.
2. Click **Show Keywords**.

   ■ The Keywords window appears and floats, allowing you to select photos in the iPhoto window behind it.

102

6 iPhoto Basics

WORKING WITH IPHOTO

How can I modify the list of keywords?

The popup menu in the Keywords window allows you to modify iPhoto's list of keywords. You can select **New** from the Keywords menu to add a keyword. You can click a keyword and select **Rename** from the Keywords menu to change a keyword. You can click a keyword and select **Delete** from the Keywords menu to remove a keyword.

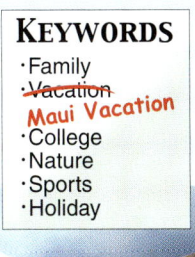

KEYWORDS
- Family
- ~~Vacation~~ Maui Vacation
- College
- Nature
- Sports
- Holiday

How can I rate my photos?

iPhoto allows you to assign star ratings to your photos much in the same way that iTunes lets you rate songs: `Control` +click or right-click on a picture and select a rating from the **My Rating** submenu in the contextual menu that appears.

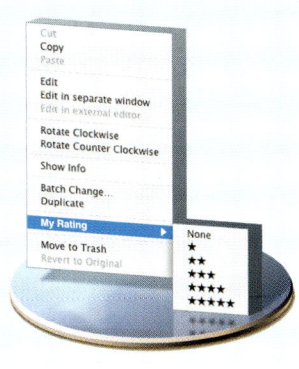

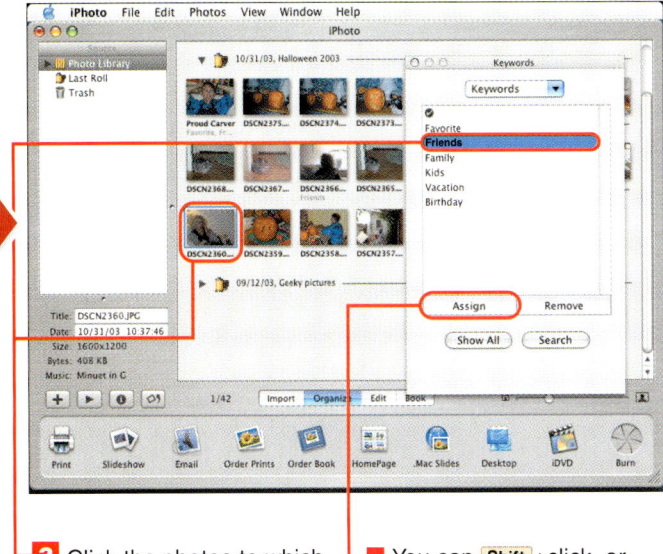

---

3 Click the photos to which you want to assign keywords.

4 Click a keyword in the Keywords window.

■ You can **Shift** +click, or ⌘+click, to select multiple photos or keywords.

5 Click **Assign**.

■ The keyword appears beneath the selected photos.

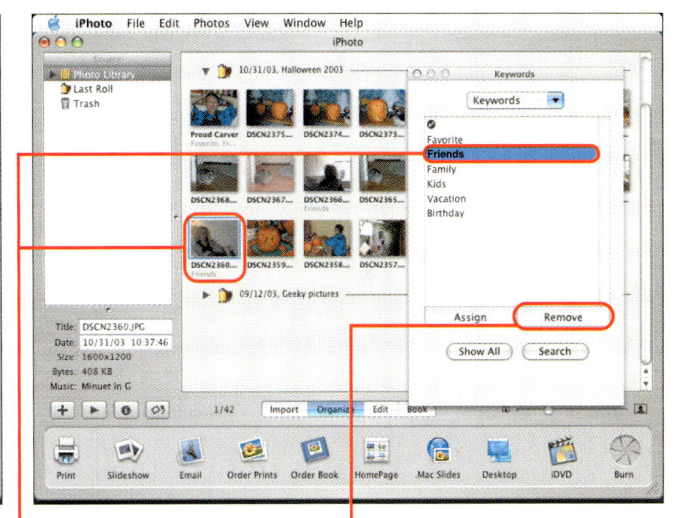

REMOVE KEYWORDS

1 Click the photo from which you want to remove keywords.

■ You can press ⌘+K to open the Keywords window.

2 Click the keyword you want to remove.

■ You can **Shift** +click, or ⌘+click, to select multiple photos or keywords.

3 Click **Remove**.

■ iPhoto removes the keywords from the photos you selected.

103

ORGANIZE THE IPHOTO LIBRARY BY DATE, TITLE, OR RATING

As your photograph collection grows, it may become difficult to find the photos you want. You can arrange your library to sort the photos by date, title, or rating to help you quickly find your photos.

ORGANIZE THE IPHOTO LIBRARY BY DATE, TITLE, OR RATING

ORGANIZE BY DATE

1 Click **Organize**.

2 Click **View**.

3 Click **Arrange Photos**.

4 Click **by Date**.

■ iPhoto arranges the photos by date.

■ The most recent photos appear first if you have selected the **Place recent photos at top** option in the iPhoto preferences' Appearance pane.

Note: See the section "Set Up iPhoto" for more on iPhoto's preferences.

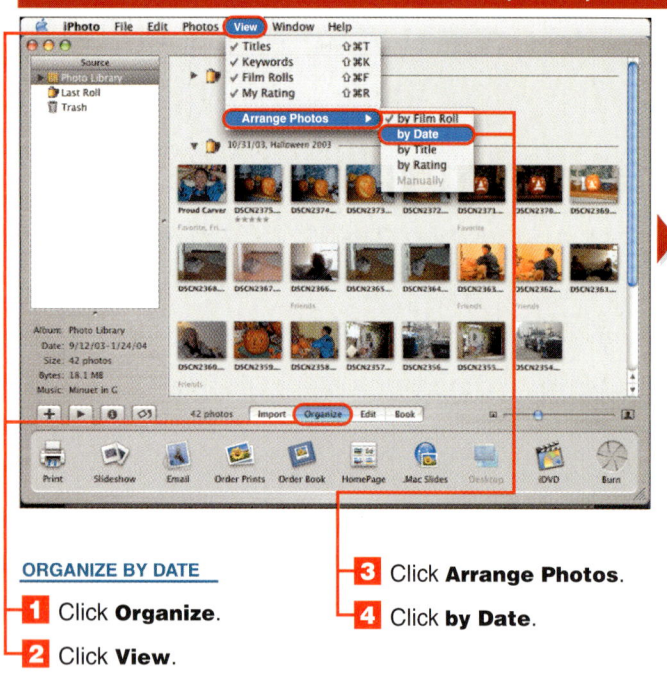

104

6 iPhoto Basics

WORKING WITH IPHOTO

Why is there an option to view photos by date if viewing them by film roll already displays them by date?

When you view photos by date, you no longer see the film-roll dividers. This provides more room to see pictures. Also, when you make an album, you cannot view the album by film roll but you can still arrange the photos by date. For more information, see the section "Create an Album."

I changed the date of a photo by mistake, but I cannot remember its correct date. How can I fix this?

iPhoto always remembers a photo's original date, even if you change it. For more information, see the section "View Photo Information," later in this chapter, to find out how to see the photo's original date, filename, and other information.

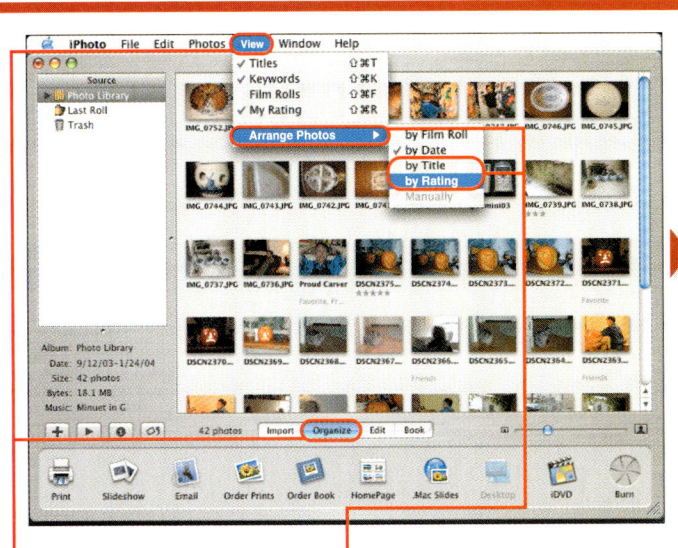

June 19, 2003
(May 22, 2003)

ORGANIZE BY TITLE OR RATING

1 Click **Organize**.

2 Click **View**.

3 Click **Arrange Photos**.

4 Click either **by Title** or **by Rating**.

■ iPhoto arranges the photos alphabetically by title if you selected the **by Title** option, or from most to least stars if you chose **by Rating**.

Note: You do not need to have titles or ratings visible to arrange photos by title or rating.

105

VIEW PHOTO INFORMATION

iPhoto retains and can show you detailed information about your digital photographs. You can use this information to keep track of your photos, and to improve your photographic skills.

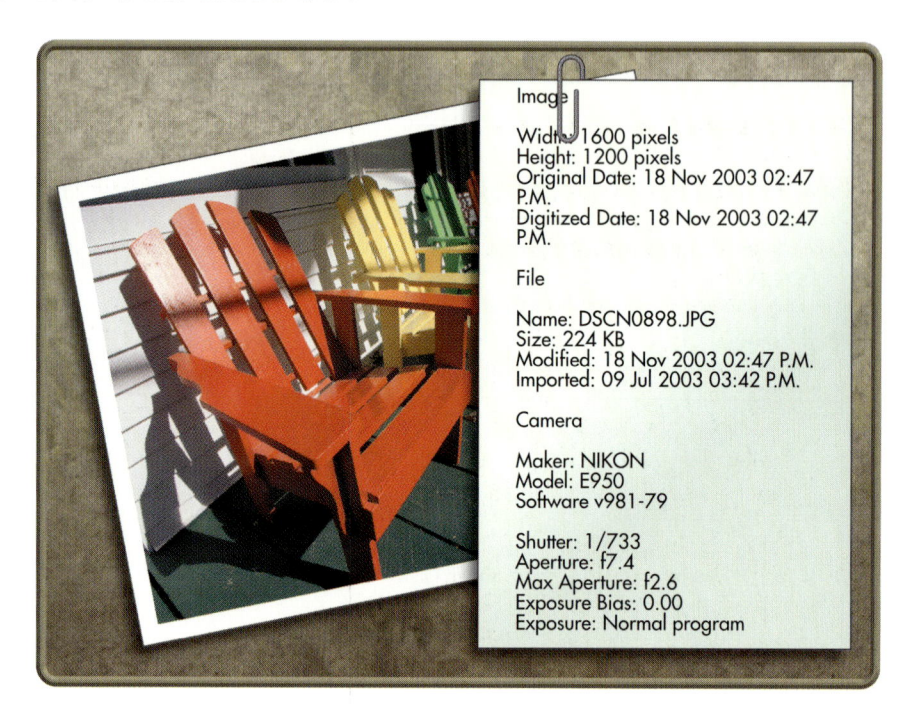

VIEW PHOTO INFORMATION

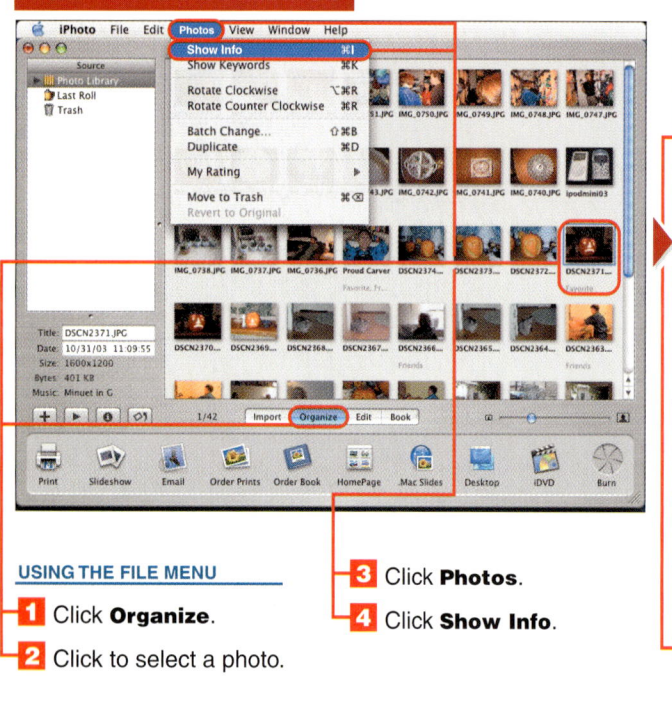

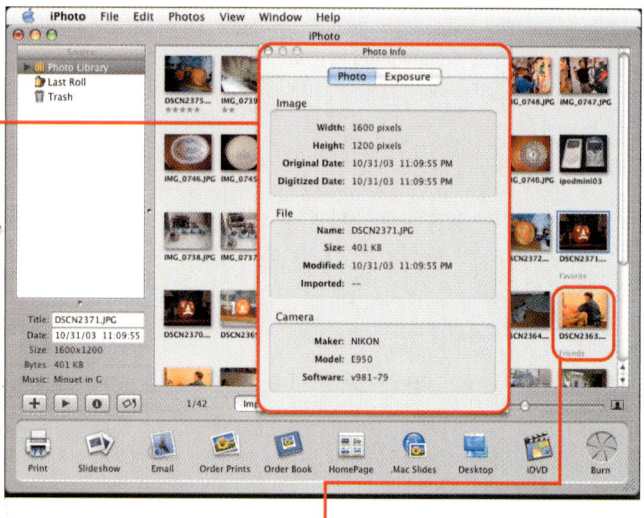

USING THE FILE MENU

1. Click **Organize**.
2. Click to select a photo.
3. Click **Photos**.
4. Click **Show Info**.

■ The Photo Info window appears.

■ The Photo Info window shows detailed information about the selected photo.

Note: The Photo Info window floats, allowing you to click items in the window behind it.

5. Click another photo.

■ The Photo Info window shows that photo's information.

106

6 iPhoto Basics

WORKING WITH IPHOTO

TEACH YOURSELF

Where does the Photo Info window get its information?

Most digital cameras include Exchangeable Image File, or EXIF, information in the photograph files they create. You can find the EXIF standard at www.exif.org/specifications.html.

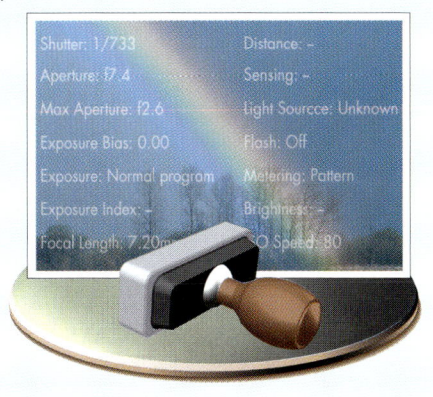

TEACH YOURSELF

Why does the Photo Info window not show the date and title information that I typed into iPhoto's information area?

iPhoto stores the information you type separately from the photo EXIF information. This allows you to always see the original information the camera records, while still letting you change the title and date information in iPhoto to better organize your photographs.

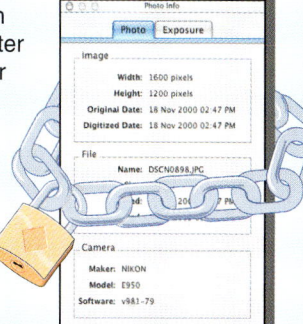

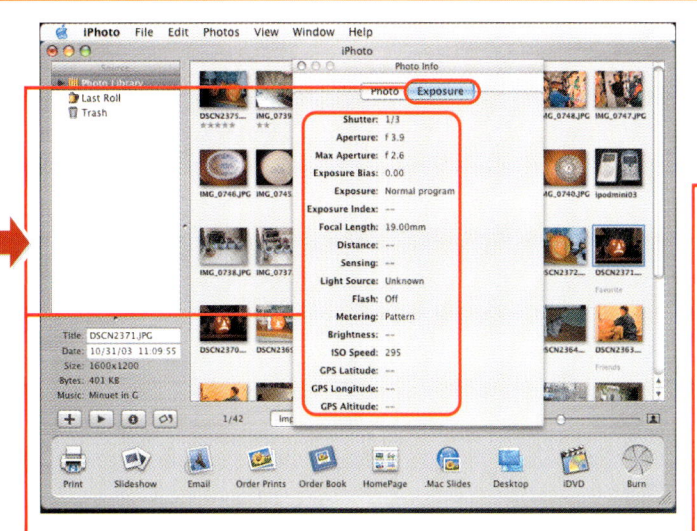

---

6 Click the **Exposure** tab.

■ The Exposure tab displays the camera settings that you used when you took the photo.

■ You can examine the exposure settings to better understand how different camera settings affect your photos.

Note: The recorded photo information may vary from camera to camera, and some of the exposure information fields may be empty.

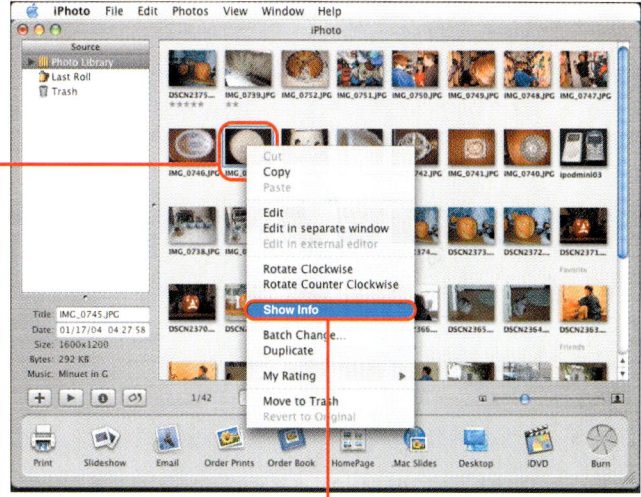

USING A CONTEXTUAL MENU

1 Click **Organize**.

2 `Control` +click a photo.

■ You can also right-click a photo.

■ A contextual menu appears.

3 Click **Show Info**.

■ The Photo Info window appears.

107

ROTATE A PHOTO

When you shoot a photo, you may need to turn the camera 90 degrees for a photo that is taller than it is wide. When iPhoto imports the photo, it appears sideways. You can rotate your photos clockwise or counterclockwise to achieve the orientation you want.

iPhoto lets you set its Rotate button to rotate pictures in the direction you use most often with your camera.

ROTATE A PHOTO

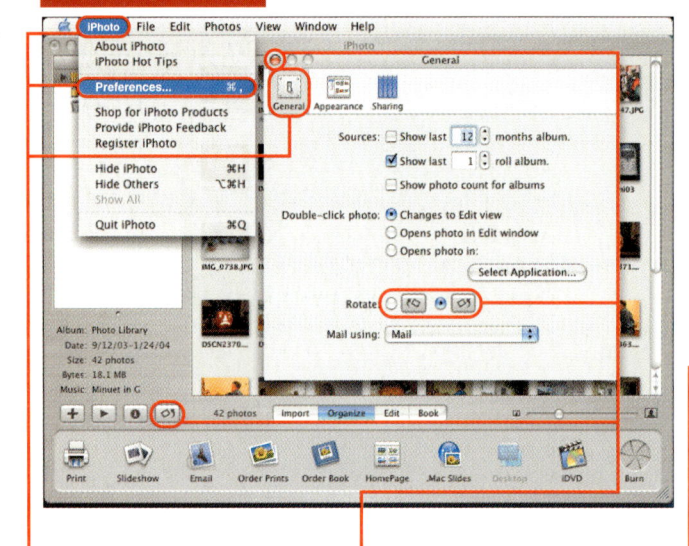

SET PREFERRED ROTATION DIRECTION

1 Click **iPhoto**.

2 Click **Preferences**.

3 In the iPhoto Preferences window, click the **General** button.

4 Click one of the two Rotate buttons, (or), to select the direction you want to rotate your photos.

■ iPhoto's button changes its appearance to indicate your rotation direction choice.

5 Click to close the Preferences window.

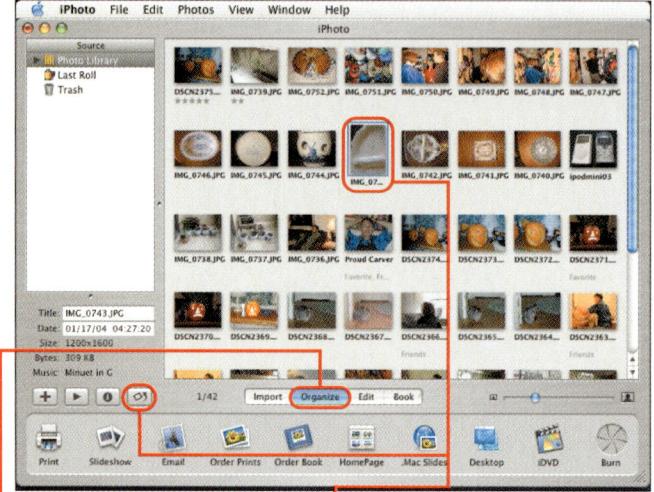

ROTATE A PHOTO IN THE PREFERRED DIRECTION

1 Click **Organize**.

2 Click a photo.

3 Click .

■ iPhoto rotates the photo 90 degrees in the direction indicated by the arrow.

108

6 iPhoto Basics

WORKING WITH IPHOTO

TEACH YOURSELF

When I rotate a photo, its file size changes. How can I prevent that?

You cannot prevent the change in file size, because the act of rotating a photo changes the data in the photo file. However, you can duplicate a photo before you rotate it so you can always have an unmodified copy.

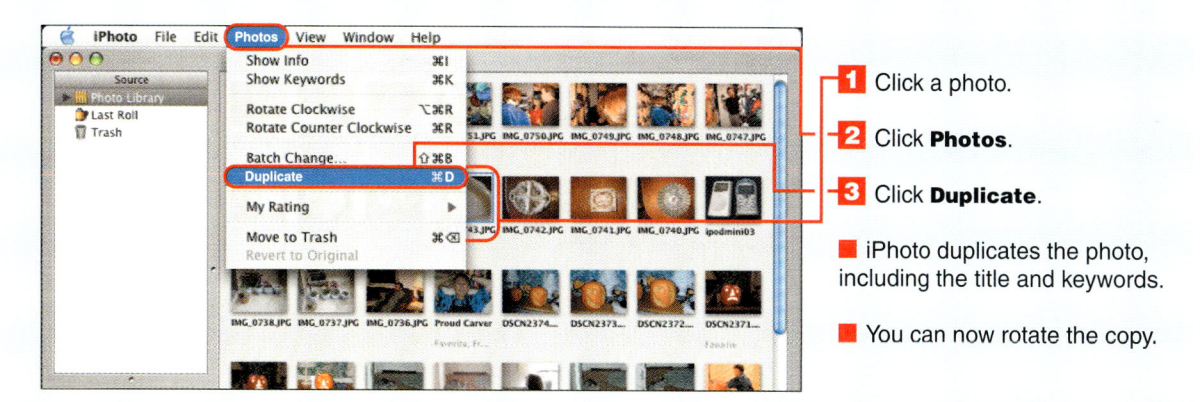

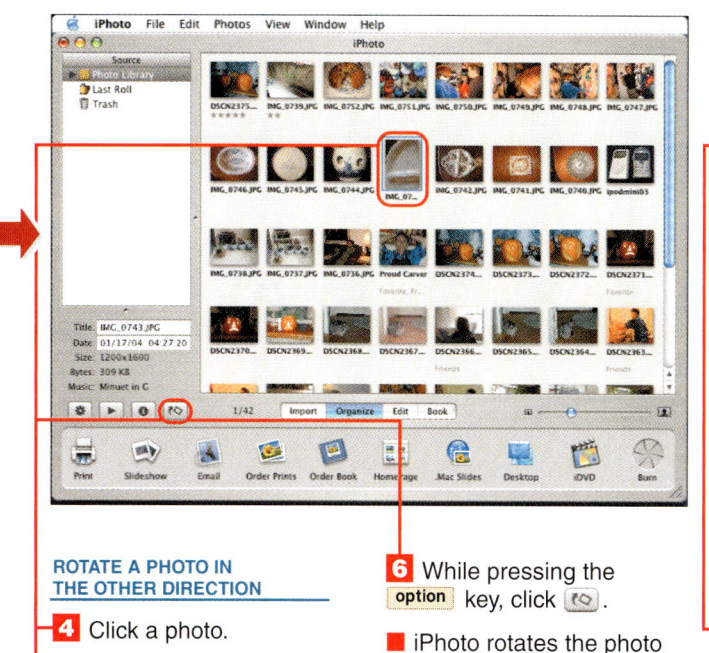

1 Click a photo.

2 Click **Photos**.

3 Click **Duplicate**.

■ iPhoto duplicates the photo, including the title and keywords.

■ You can now rotate the copy.

ROTATE A PHOTO IN THE OTHER DIRECTION

4 Click a photo.

5 Press and hold **option**.

■ The arrow on the Rotate button changes direction.

6 While pressing the **option** key, click.

■ iPhoto rotates the photo 90 degrees in the direction indicated by the arrow.

ROTATE A PHOTO USING A CONTEXTUAL MENU

1 **Control** +click a photo.

■ You can also right-click a photo.

■ A contextual menu appears.

2 Click **Rotate Clockwise** or **Rotate Counter Clockwise**.

■ iPhoto rotates the photo.

109

DELETE PHOTOS FROM THE IPHOTO LIBRARY

Because not every photo is a gem, you may want to get rid of the imperfect shots after you import a set of photos. iPhoto lets you easily delete the photos you do not want to keep, and also gives you a chance to change your mind.

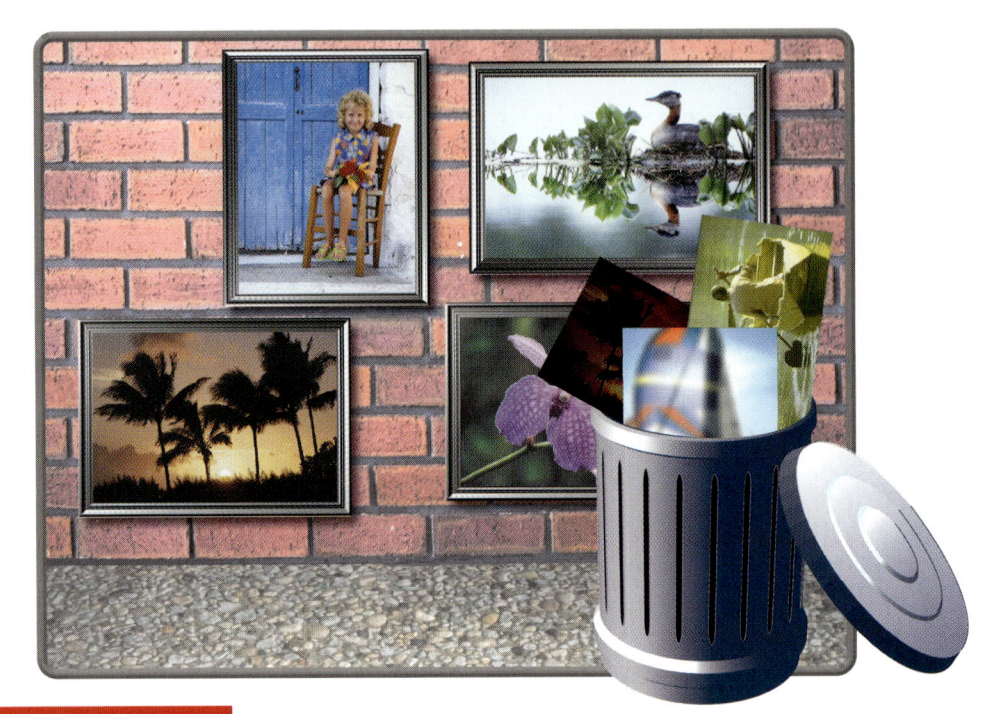

DELETE PHOTOS FROM THE IPHOTO LIBRARY

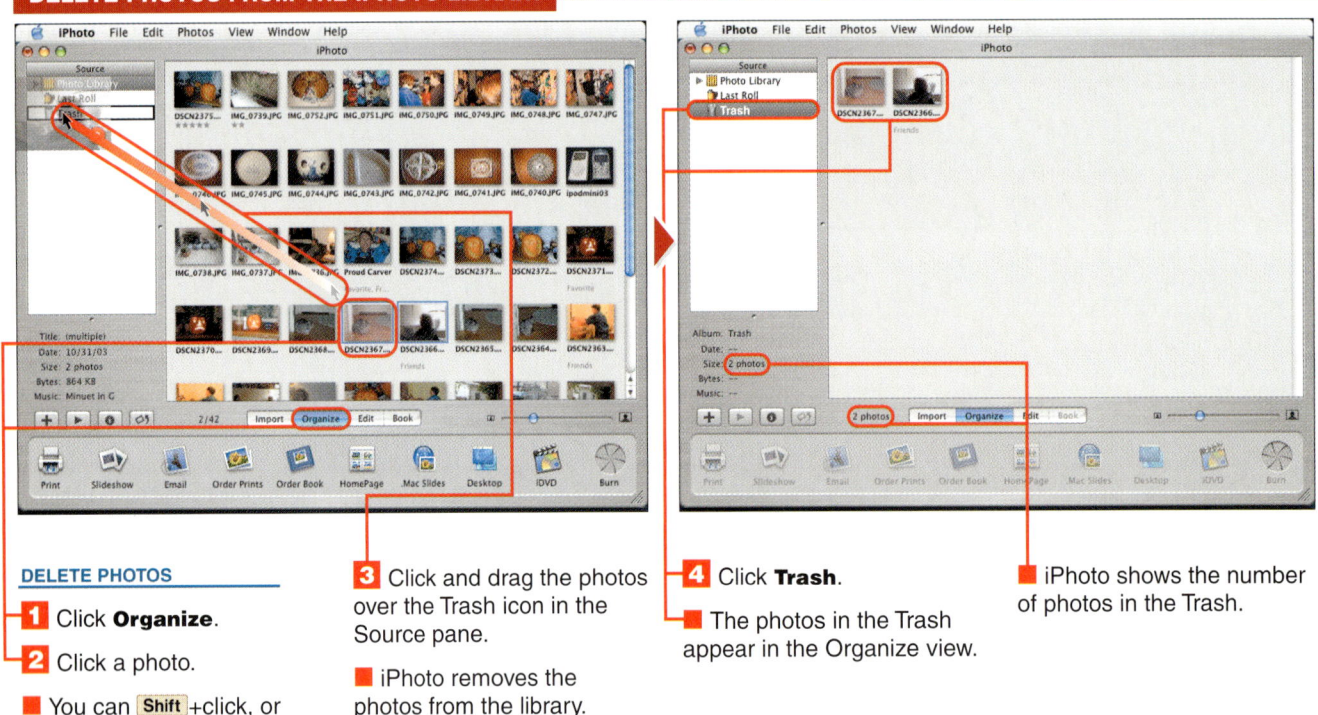

DELETE PHOTOS

1 Click **Organize**.

2 Click a photo.

■ You can Shift+click, or ⌘+click, to select several photos at once.

3 Click and drag the photos over the Trash icon in the Source pane.

■ iPhoto removes the photos from the library.

4 Click **Trash**.

■ The photos in the Trash appear in the Organize view.

■ iPhoto shows the number of photos in the Trash.

110

6 iPhoto Basics

WORKING WITH IPHOTO

I placed some photos in the Trash, but I did not empty it. Later, when I looked in Mac's Trash, they were not there. What happened to the photos?

iPhoto has a separate Trash from your Mac Trash. This arrangement allows you to place your photos in the iPhoto Trash, and place discarded files in the Mac Trash, so that you can empty the Mac Trash without also removing the photos in the iPhoto Trash.

When I click Last Import, I cannot get rid of photos by pressing Delete or by dragging them to the iPhoto Trash. Is there a way around this?

iPhoto's Last Roll collection always contains the last group of photos you have imported. You click the Last Roll icon ( ) to see these photos in the Organize view. You can remove photos simultaneously from this collection and from the iPhoto library and put them into iPhoto's Trash by selecting them and pressing ⌘ + Delete .

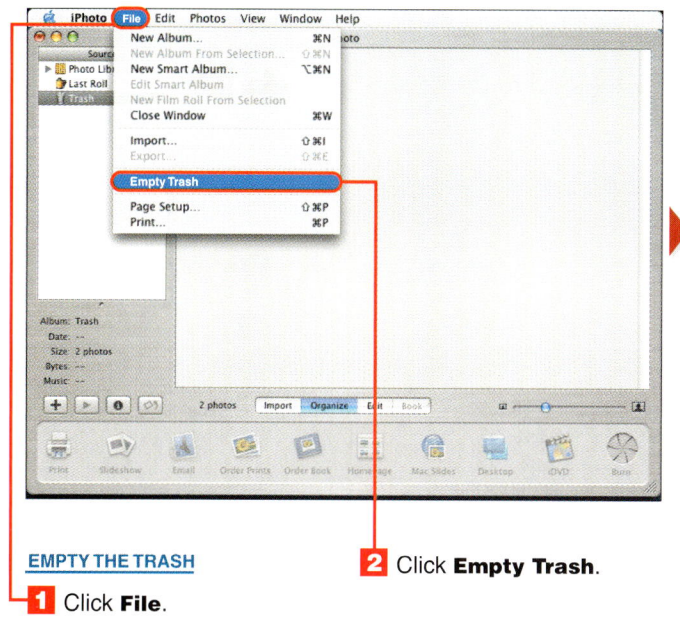

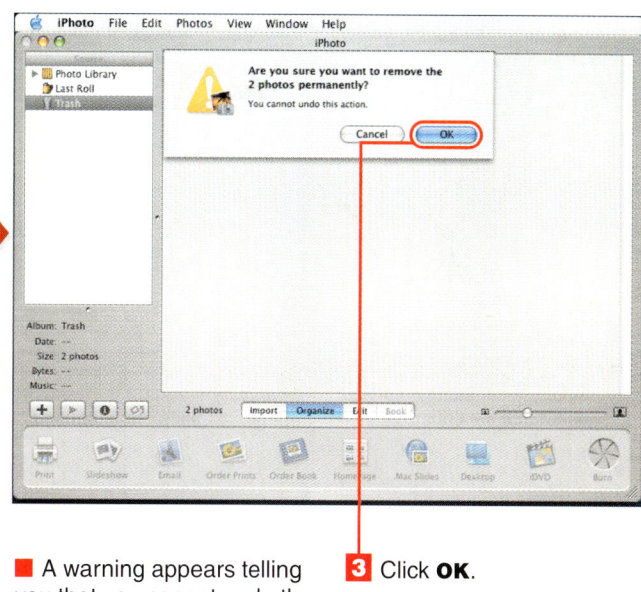

EMPTY THE TRASH

1 Click **File**.

2 Click **Empty Trash**.

■ A warning appears telling you that you cannot undo the action.

3 Click **OK**.

■ iPhoto permanently removes the photos from the library.

111

CREATE AN ALBUM

You can place selected photos into albums, which you can use to create slideshows, photo books, or Web pages.

For more information on creating slideshows, photo books, and Web pages, see Chapter 8.

CREATE AN ALBUM

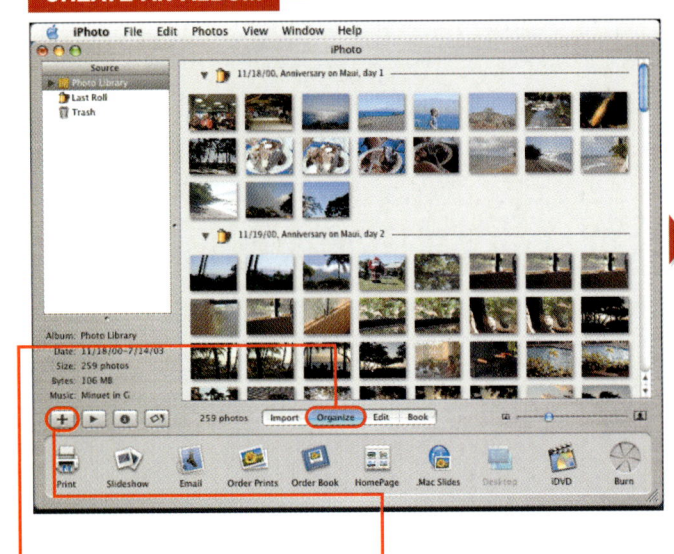

1 Click **Organize**.

2 Click the Add Album button (+).

■ The New Album dialog sheet appears.

3 Type a name for the album.

4 Click **OK**.

112

6 iPhoto Basics

WORKING WITH IPHOTO

How can I quickly create an album?

Select a group of photos in the iPhoto library and simply drag them to the Source pane. You can also select a group of photos and either click **File** and then **New Album from Selection**, or type the keyboard shortcut for that command, Shift + ⌘ + N.

What is the fastest way to import image files to make an album?

Click and drag a folder containing the images from the Finder directly to iPhoto's Source pane. iPhoto imports the photos into the iPhoto Library and simultaneously places them in an album that has the same name as the folder. For more on using the Finder, see Chapter 1.

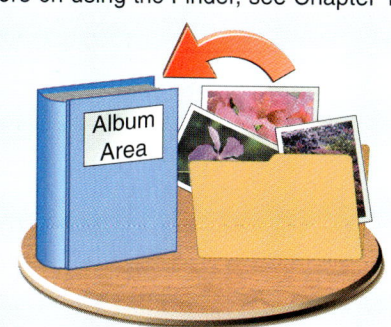

■ An album appears in the Source pane.

5 Select a group of photos from the Organize view.

■ You can Shift+click, or ⌘+click, to select several photos at once.

6 Click and drag the selected photos to the album.

■ As you drag, a transparent image of one of the photos, marked with the number of photos you are dragging, follows the cursor.

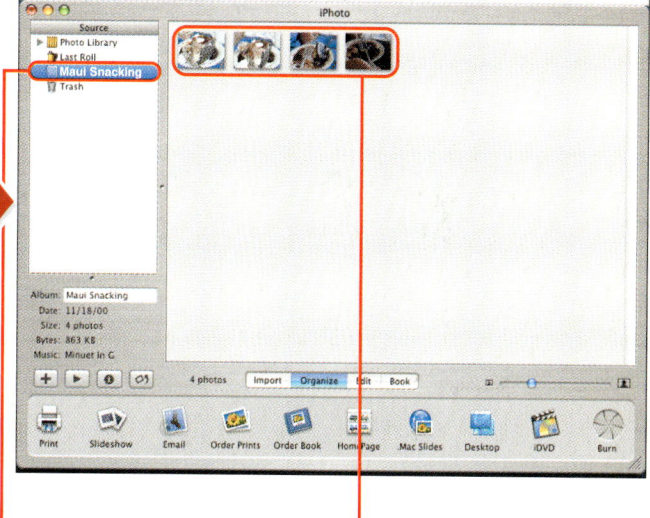

7 Click the album.

■ iPhoto displays the contents of the album.

113

ORGANIZE AN ALBUM

You can organize the photos in your albums by date, title, or rating just like you can in the iPhoto Library. In addition, you can manually arrange the album's photos in any order you like.

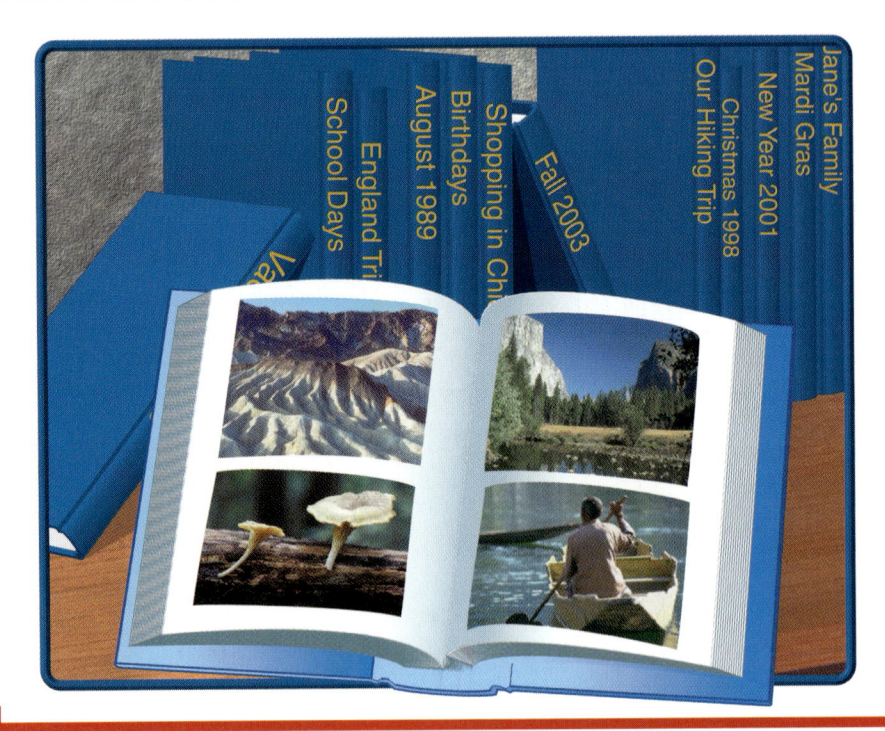

ORGANIZE AN ALBUM

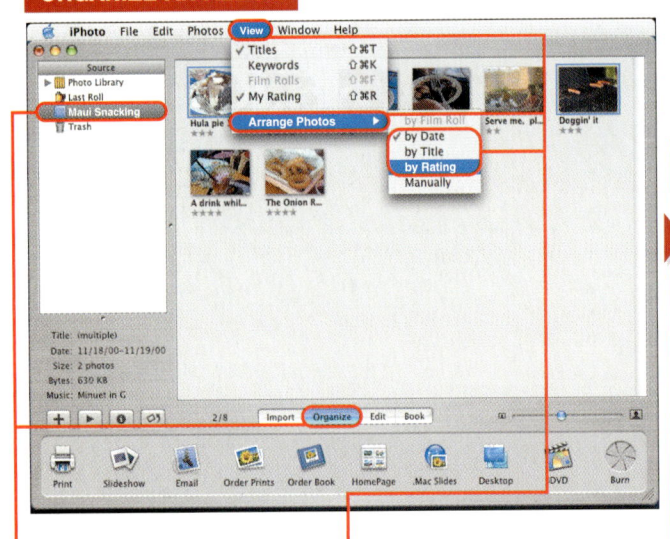

ORGANIZE BY DATE, TITLE, OR RATING

1. Click **Organize**.
2. Click an album.
3. Click **View**.
4. Click **Arrange Photos**.
5. Click either **by Date**, **by Title**, or **by Rating**.

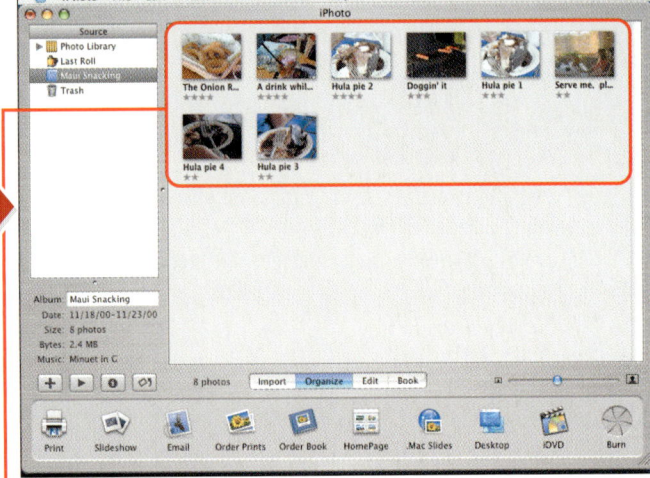

- iPhoto arranges the album by the choice you made.
- By Rating shows photos with ratings from the most to the least stars.
- By Title shows the photos alphabetically.
- By Date shows the photos in date order.

Note: The date order depends on the current preference settings; see the section "Set Up iPhoto" for more on iPhoto's preferences.

114

6 iPhoto Basics

WORKING WITH IPHOTO

What happens if I drag a photo from an album to iPhoto's Trash?

The photo does not appear in the album but it is still in the iPhoto Library. An album only contains references to the photos in your library, not actual images, so the photos do not appear in iPhoto's Trash. If you mistakenly delete a photo from an album, click **Edit**, and then **Undo Remove Photo From Album**.

How can I delete a photo from both an album and the iPhoto Library at the same time?

To remove photos both from an album and from the iPhoto library at the same time, press ⌘ + option + Delete. This keyboard command moves the photos into iPhoto's Trash. For more on deleting photos, see the section "Delete Photos from the iPhoto Library."

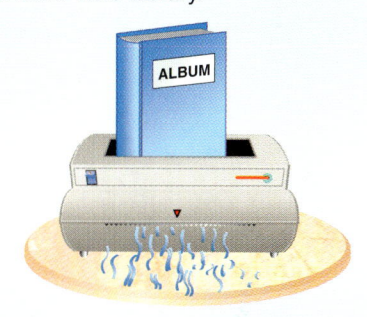

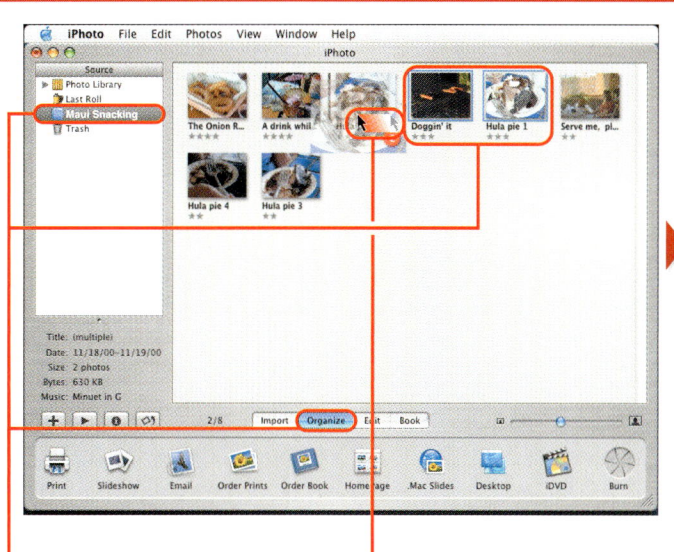

ORGANIZE MANUALLY

1 Click **Organize**.

2 Click an album.

3 Select one or more photos.

■ You can Shift+click, or ⌘+click, to select several photos at once.

4 Click and drag the selected photos to where you want them.

■ As you drag, one of the photos transparent images follows the cursor, and a black line appears.

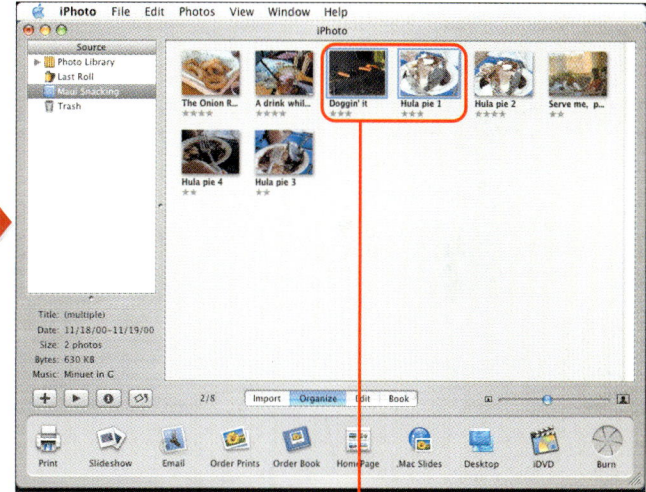

5 Release the mouse where you want the photos to go.

■ iPhoto displays the selected pictures in their new positions.

115

SHARE PHOTOS ON A NETWORK

You can share your photo library or specific albums over a local network with other iPhoto users. For example, students in a computer lab can share photos while working together on a project, or family members can browse each other's vacation photos.

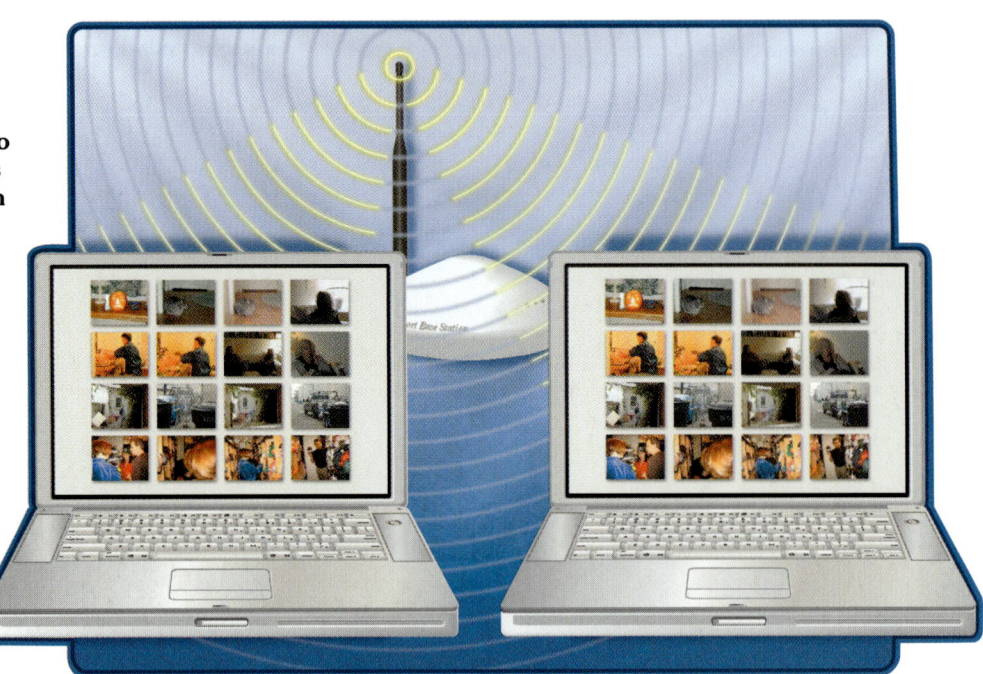

SHARE PHOTOS ON A NETWORK

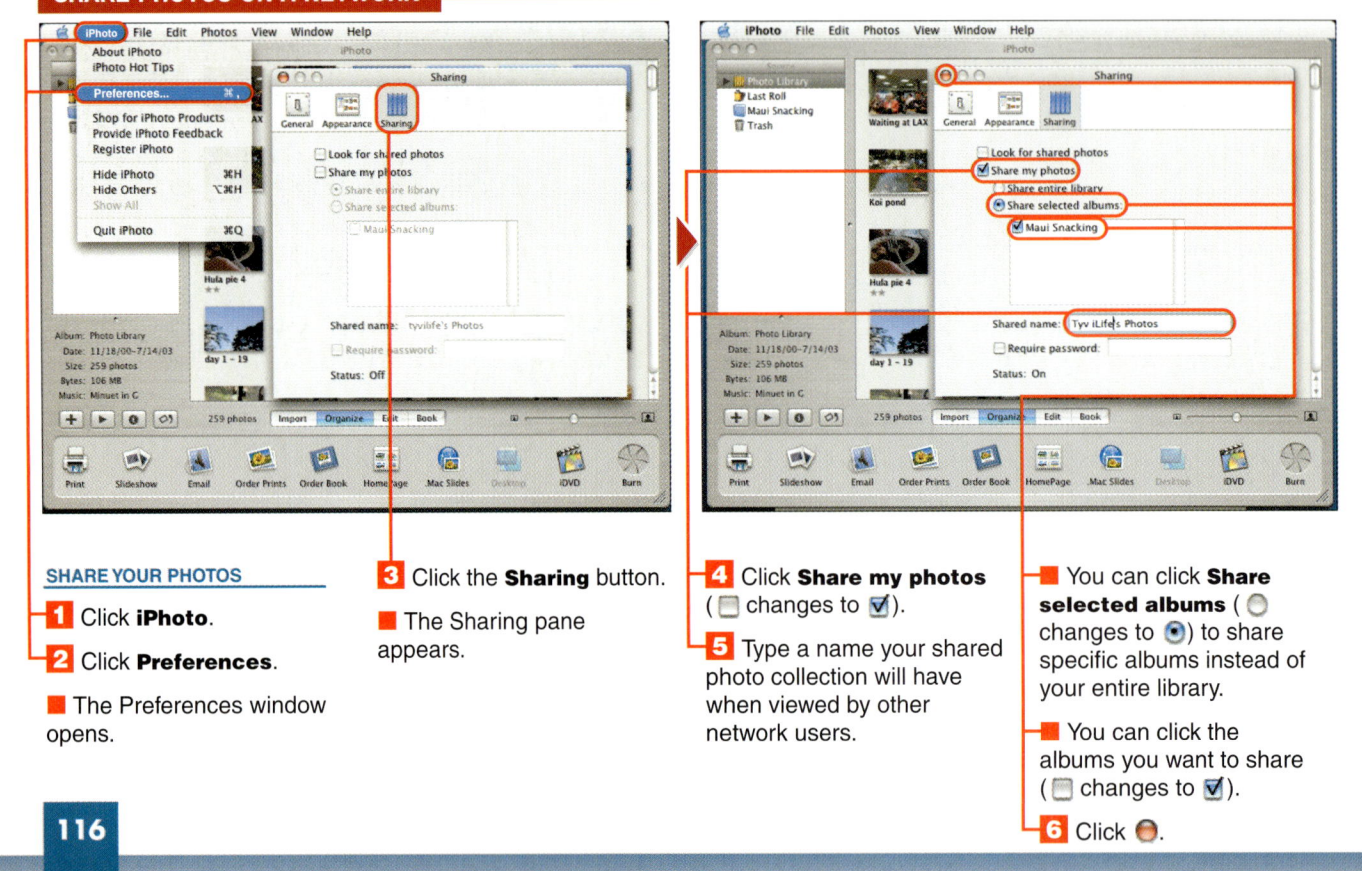

SHARE YOUR PHOTOS

1 Click **iPhoto**.

2 Click **Preferences**.

■ The Preferences window opens.

3 Click the **Sharing** button.

■ The Sharing pane appears.

4 Click **Share my photos** (☐ changes to ☑).

5 Type a name your shared photo collection will have when viewed by other network users.

■ You can click **Share selected albums** (○ changes to ⦿) to share specific albums instead of your entire library.

■ You can click the albums you want to share (☐ changes to ☑).

6 Click ⊙.

116

6 iPhoto Basics

WORKING WITH IPHOTO

I received a Sharing Error message when I tried to share my photos. What happened?

Photo sharing over a network requires that you have certain network *ports* open to receive network communication. The Macintosh firewall software blocks most network ports for security reasons. You can open your System Preferences and turn off the firewall in the Sharing Preferences if that is the problem, or create a firewall setting that opens the port used by iPhoto — port 8770. Consult your Macintosh documentation for more about the firewall and Sharing preferences.

What can I do with a shared photo?

You can view, arrange, and print photos from a shared collection. You can neither copy them to your own library or albums, nor can you burn a disc with them.

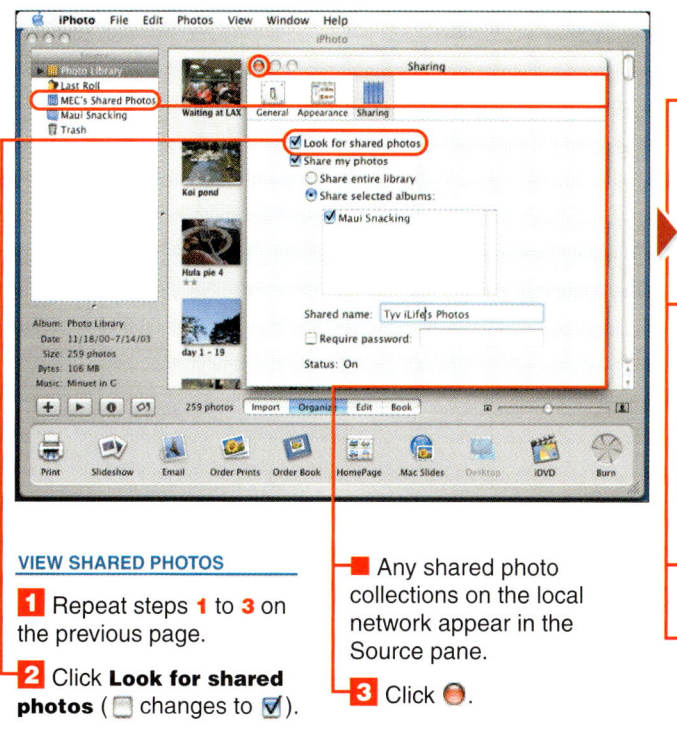

VIEW SHARED PHOTOS

1 Repeat steps **1** to **3** on the previous page.

2 Click **Look for shared photos** (☐ changes to ☑).

■ Any shared photo collections on the local network appear in the Source pane.

3 Click ⏺.

4 Click a shared photo collection.

■ The photos appear in the Organize view.

■ Any shared albums in the collection appear below the collection's name.

117

CREATE A SMART ALBUM

You can create Smart Albums that automatically update their contents based upon conditions you set. You can use Smart Albums to search for and collect pictures by date, title, rating, or a combination of criteria.

CREATE A SMART ALBUM

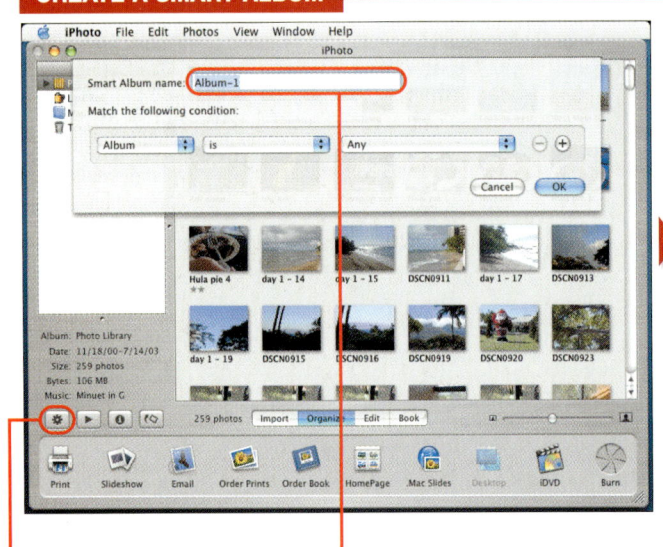

1 Hold down **option** and click the New Smart Album button ( ).

■ The Smart Album sheet appears.

■ You can click **File** and then click **New Smart Album**.

2 Type a name for your Smart Album.

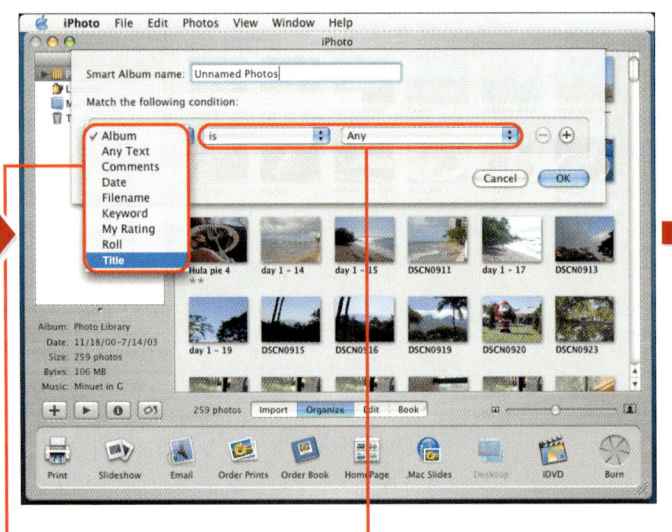

3 Click here and and select the kind of information that your Smart Album's contents should match.

■ The items to the right on the sheet may change based on the choice you make.

Note: Smart Albums are similar to iTunes' Smart Playlists; see Chapter 3 for more about Smart Playlists.

6 iPhoto Basics

WORKING WITH IPHOTO

How can I change the matching conditions that a Smart Album uses?

You can click **File** and then **Edit Smart Album** to see the Smart Album's matching conditions. You can also click **Edit Smart Album** from the contextual menu that appears when you `Control` +click, or right-click, a Smart Album in the Source pane.

How can I arrange photos in a Smart Album?

You can arrange photos in a Smart Album by Date, Title, or Rating. You cannot arrange photos manually nor by film roll in a Smart Album.

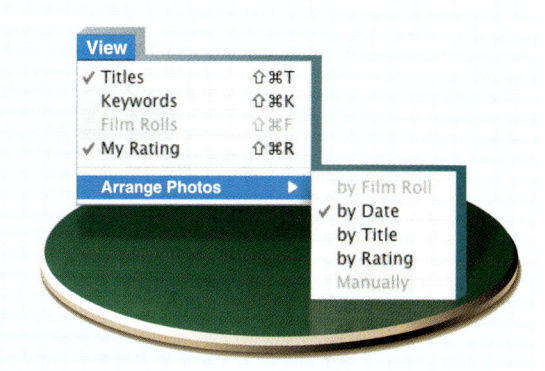

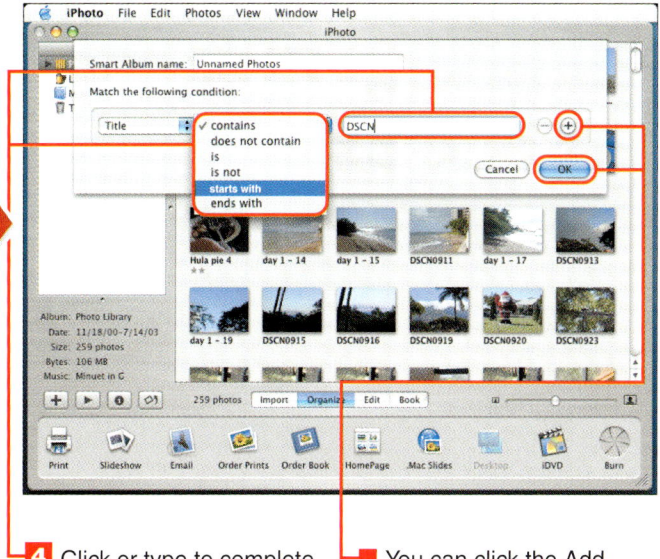

■ **4** Click or type to complete your matching criteria.

■ You can click the Add button (⊕) to add more matching conditions.

■ **5** Click **OK**.

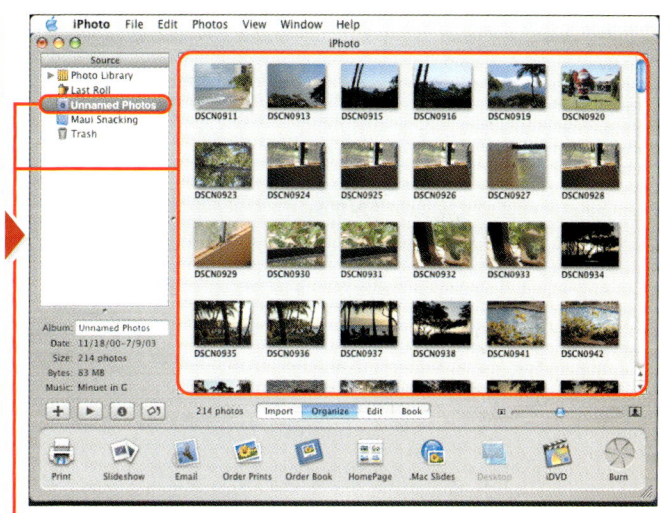

■ The Smart Album appears in the Source pane.

■ The Organize view presents the Smart Album's current contents.

■ Smart Albums automatically update their contents when your iPhoto library changes.

119

ADJUST THE EDIT VIEW

You can zoom into and out of any photo you are editing to give you more control over your work. You can also constrain your editing selections to specific rectangular shapes.

Several of iPhoto's editing tools require that you select part of a photo before you use them. iTool's Constrain menu provides a number of common selection constraints for printing or display use.

ADJUST THE EDIT VIEW

ZOOM THE IMAGE

1 In the Organize view, click a photo.

Note: For more on using the Organize view, see Chapter 6.

2 Click **Edit**.

■ The photo appears in Edit view.

3 Click and drag the size control slider ( ) less than halfway to the right.

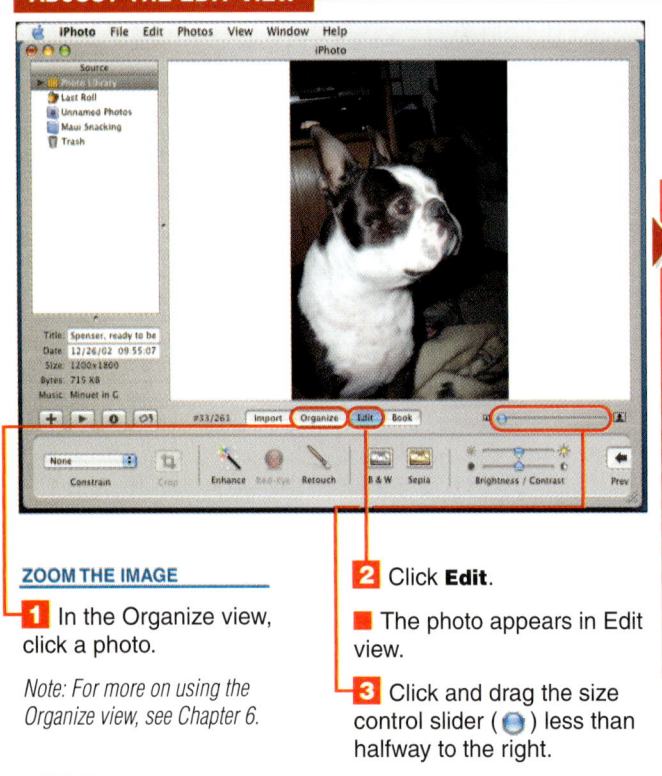

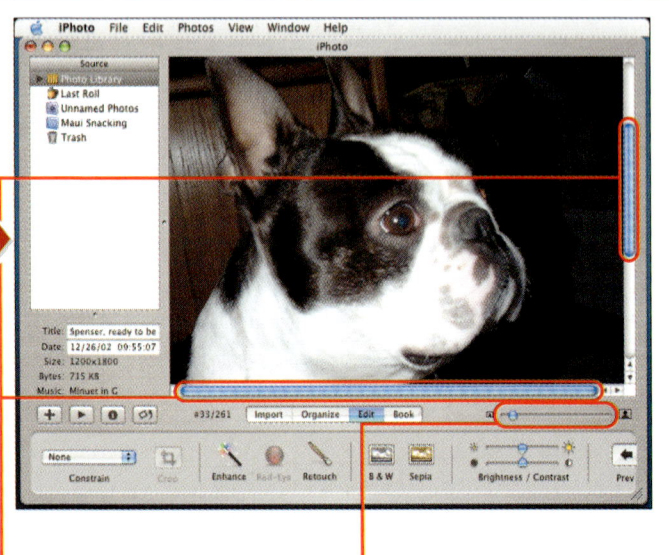

■ The Edit view zooms in and scroll bars appear at the right and bottom.

■ You can click and drag the scroll bars to reposition the visible area of the photo.

■ You can click and drag all the way left to fit the whole photo in the view, or all the way right to zoom to the fullest magnification.

120

7 Editing Photos with iPhoto

WORKING WITH IPHOTO

How can I quickly zoom into the part of the photo on which I want to work?

With no editing tool selected, click and drag over the photo to select the part of it that interests you. Next, click and drag the size control slider ( ) to the right. As you drag, iPhoto attempts to keep the selected part of the picture centered in the Edit view.

I find using the scroll bars to adjust the Edit view awkward. Is there any easier way to move around a magnified photo?

With no editing tool selected, press ⌘ and drag over the photo. The part of the photo on which you click follows the cursor and repositions the visible portion of the photo.

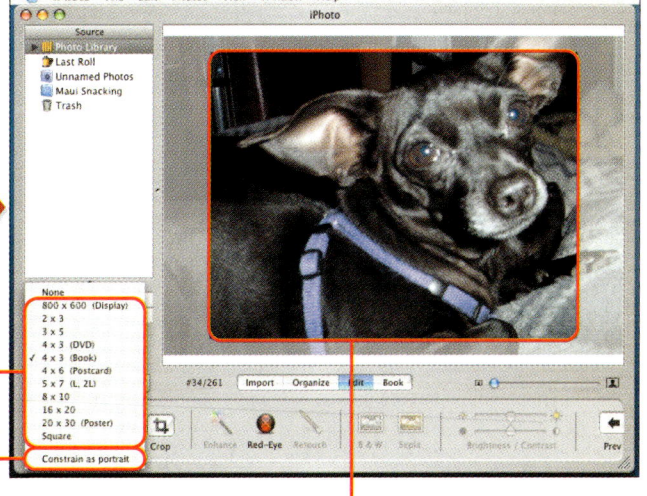

CONSTRAIN THE SELECTION

1 In the Organize view, click a photo.

Note: For more on using the Organize view, see Chapter 6.

2 Click **Edit**.

■ The photo appears in the Edit view.

■ You can click and drag to adjust the photo's magnification.

3 Click the Constrain .

4 Select an item other than None from the menu.

■ You can click **Constrain as portrait** to make a selection taller than it is wide.

■ A selection appears with the width and height ratio you selected.

■ Any selection you make keeps the constraints you selected.

121

SELECT AND CROP A PHOTO

You can crop your photos so they show only the part in which you are interested. Also, by using iPhoto's Constrain menu, you can make sure you crop photos to the right shape for printing or displaying.

Before performing these steps, you may want to enlarge the photo in the Edit view to better see the part of it around which you want to crop. For more on zooming in or out of a photo, see the section "Adjust the Edit View."

SELECT AND CROP A PHOTO

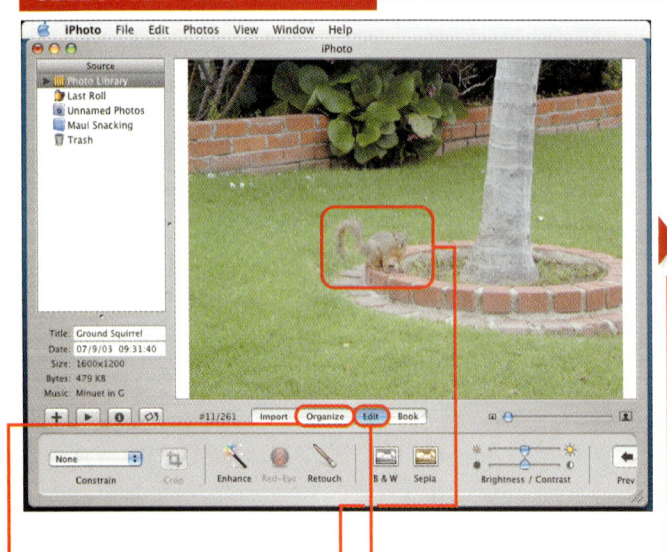

SELECT A PHOTO

1 In the Organize view, click a photo.

Note: For more on using the Organize view, see Chapter 6.

2 Click **Edit**.

3 Click and drag over the part of the photo you want to keep.

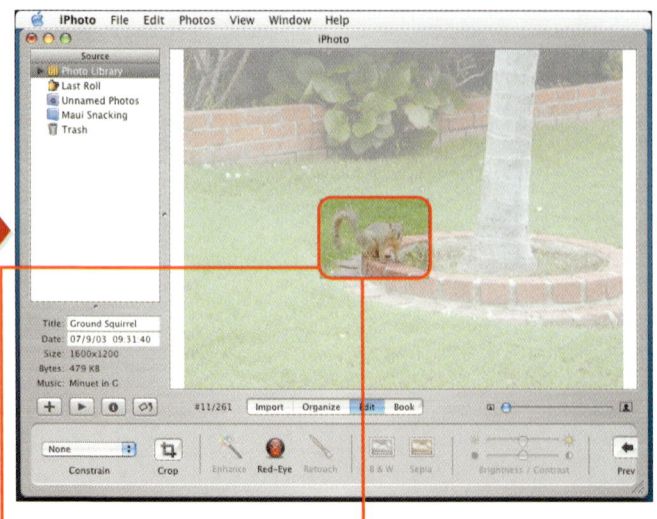

■ The selected area appears bright and clear, while the unselected portion appears muted.

■ You can click and drag the selected area to reposition it.

122

7 Editing Photos with iPhoto

WORKING WITH IPHOTO

What can I do if I accidentally crop too much of the photo?

iPhoto has a powerful Undo capability. Just click **Edit**, and then **Undo Crop Photo** to reverse the effect of your unwanted crop.

I cropped a photo yesterday then did some other work, and today I realize I made a mistake. Is there any way I can start over?

iPhoto keeps a back-up copy of your original photos as they were when you imported them. To start over, click the modified photo, click **Photos**, and then click **Revert to Original**.

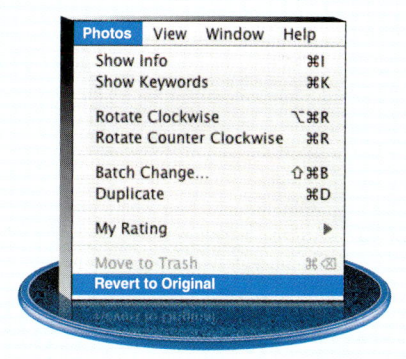

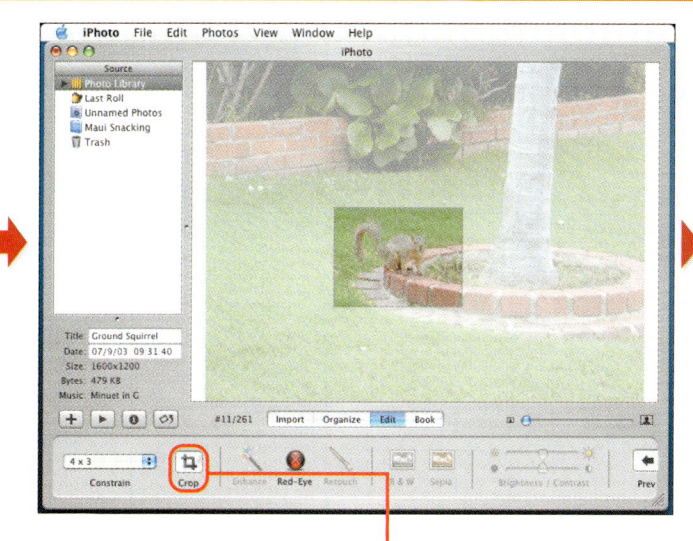

CROP A PHOTO

- The Crop tool becomes enabled when you make a selection.

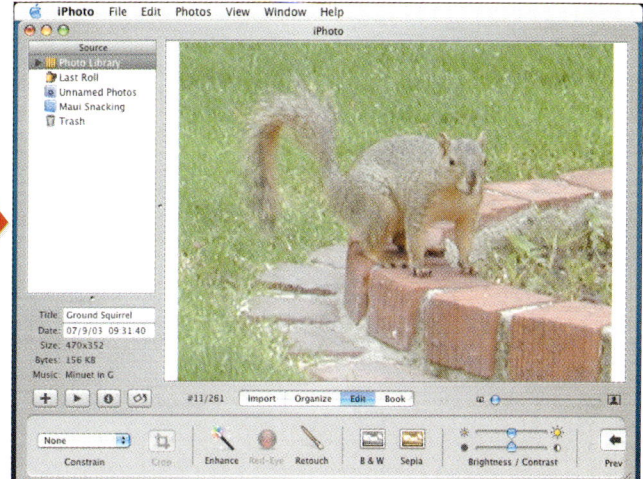

4 Click.

- The unselected portion of the photo vanishes, and the selected area fills the Edit view.

123

ENHANCE A PHOTO'S COLOR

If a photo's lighting makes it look dull or washed out, you can use iPhoto's intelligent Enhance tool to make the photo's colors more vivid.

ENHANCE A PHOTO'S COLOR

1 In the Organize view, click a photo.

Note: For more on using the Organize view, see Chapter 6.

2 Click **Edit**.

3 Click the **Enhance** tool.

■ The Enhance tool darkens for a moment.

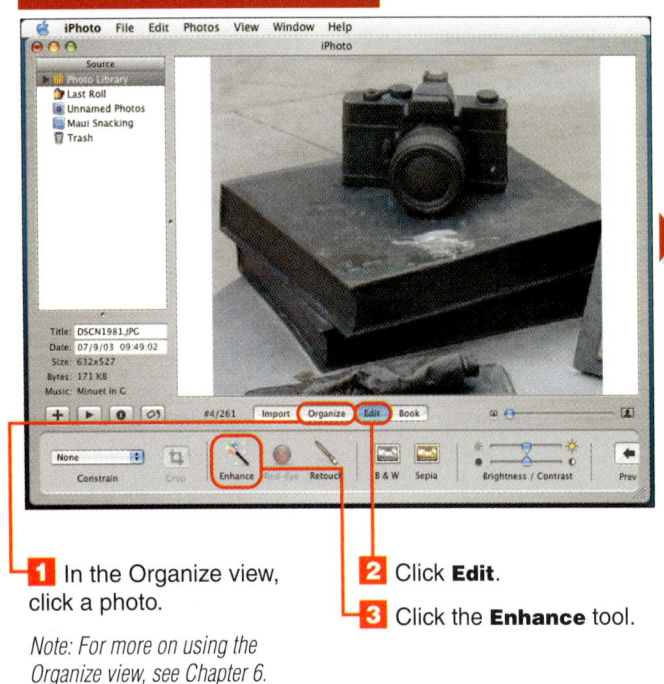

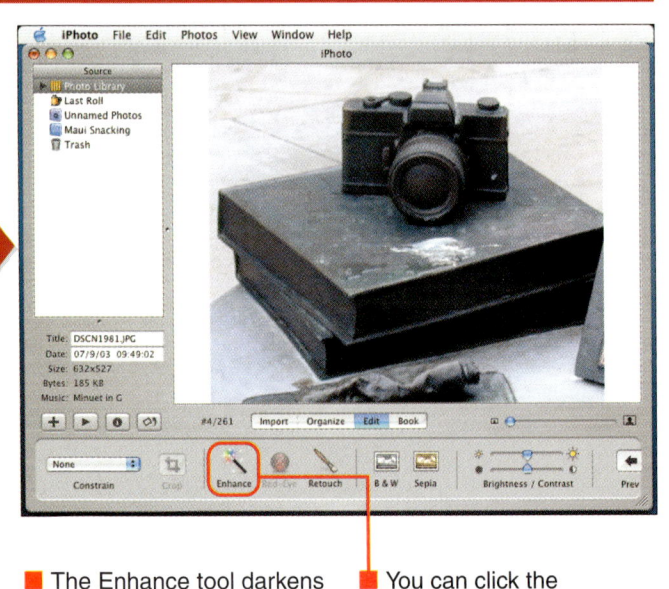

■ The photo's colors appear brighter and more vivid.

■ You can click the **Enhance** tool again to create a more dramatic enhancement, but repeated clicks on the tool eventually cause no further changes.

7 Editing Photos with iPhoto

WORKING WITH IPHOTO

CHANGE A PHOTO TO BLACK AND WHITE, OR SEPIA

You can make a photo look more dramatic or interesting by changing it to black and white, and you can make it look old-fashioned by changing it to sepia tones.

Removing color is particularly useful for digital photos taken in low-light conditions, which can cause color artifacts to appear in the image.

CHANGE A PHOTO TO BLACK AND WHITE, OR SEPIA

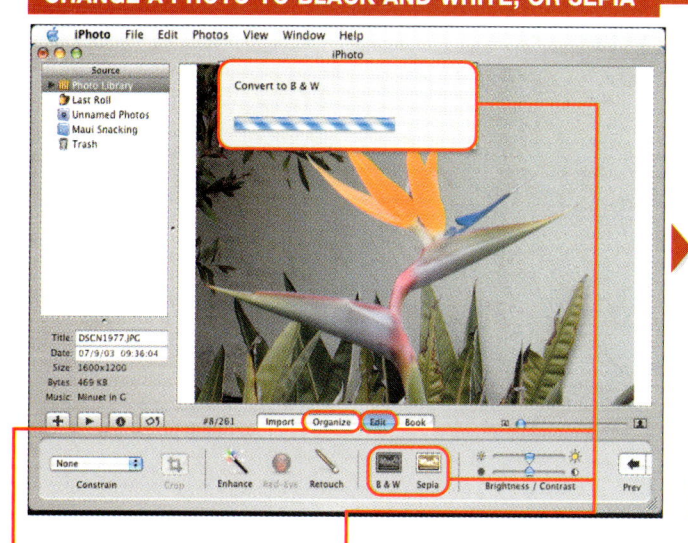

1 In the Organize view, click a photo to convert.

Note: For more on using the Organize view, see Chapter 6.

2 Click **Edit**.

3 Click the **B&W** or the **Sepia** tool.

■ The tool darkens and a Progress sheet appears.

■ The Progress sheet vanishes.

■ The photo appears in black and white if you clicked the B&W tool or in warm sepia tones if you clicked the Sepia tool.

125

ELIMINATE RED EYE

Camera flash units can often make a person being photographed appear to have glowing red eyes. You can use iPhoto's Red-Eye tool to remove this odd effect.

ELIMINATE RED EYE

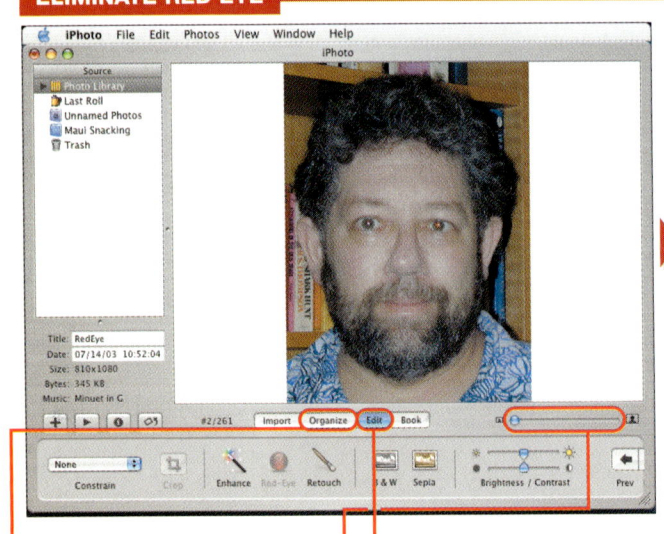

1 In the Organize view, select a photo that suffers from red eye.

Note: For more on using the Organize view, see Chapter 6.

2 Click **Edit**.

3 Magnify the eye area to make the selection easier.

Note: See the section "Adjust the Edit View" to magnify the eye area.

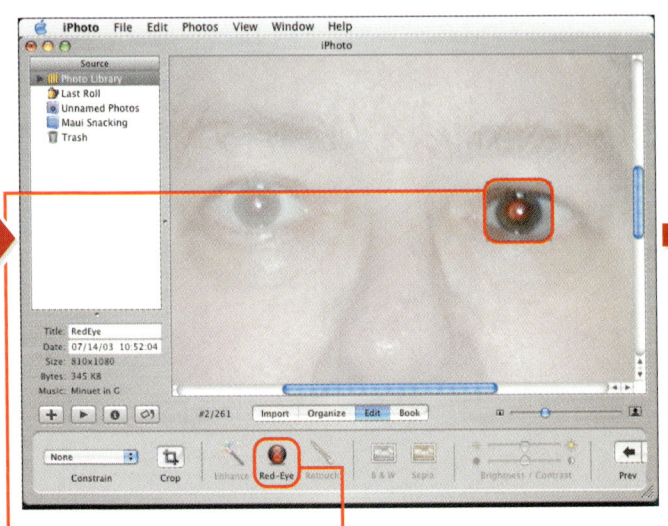

4 Click and drag over the photo to completely select the immediate area around the red eye.

Note: The Red-Eye tool focuses near the center of the selection — if your selection is too tight, the tool may leave some red near the edges.

5 Click the **Red-Eye** tool.

126

7 Editing Photos with iPhoto

WORKING WITH IPHOTO

What causes the Red Eye effect?

The reflection of the camera's flash on the blood vessels in the subject's retina causes the Red Eye effect. The use of telephoto lenses can enhance the effect, and the effect is often more pronounced in photos of people with light-colored eyes.

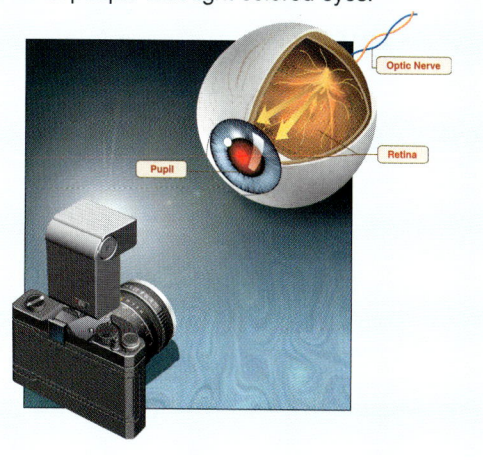

What does the Red-Eye tool actually do?

It removes the red component from the selected area of the photo while leaving other colors untouched. This makes pure red areas look black, while areas that have red mixed with other colors lose their red tint and look darker, leaving the other colors unaffected.

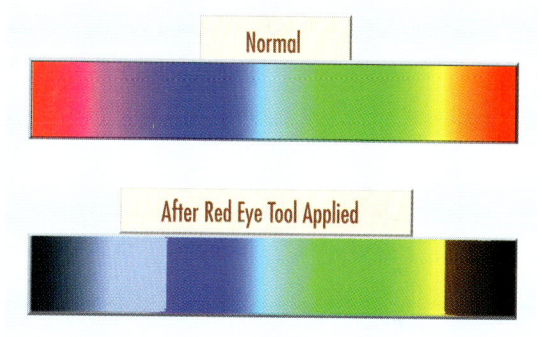

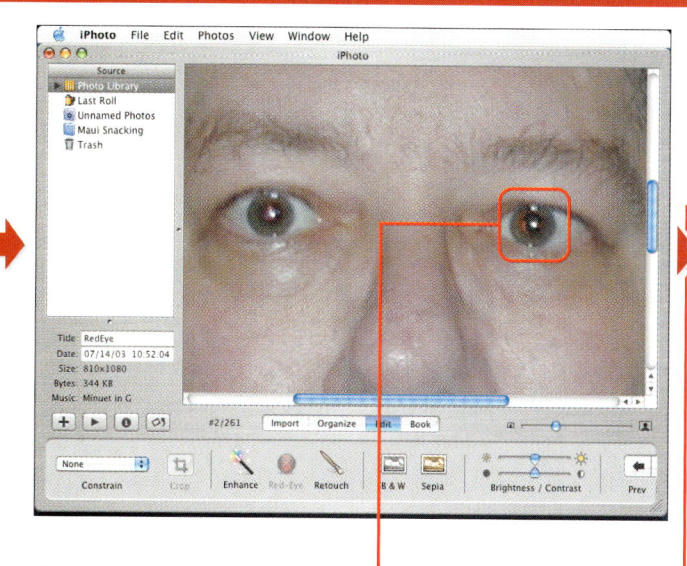

- iPhoto clears the selection.

- The red glow disappears from the eye, leaving the other colors unaltered.

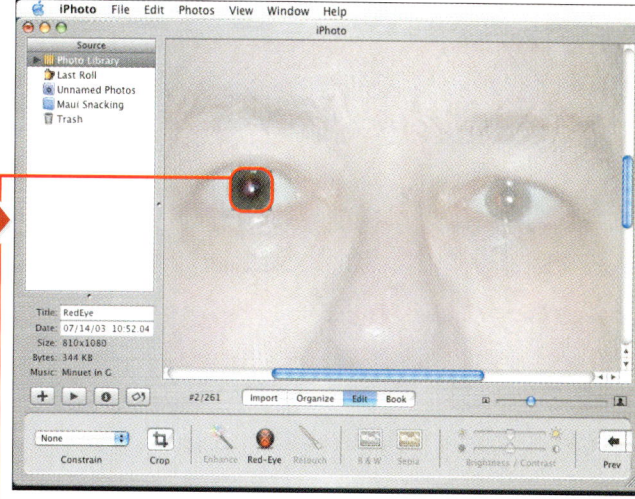

6 Because eyes tend to come in pairs, repeat steps **4** and **5** with the other eye.

- iPhoto clears the selection.

127

RETOUCH A PHOTO

When small flaws, flares, or blemishes mar an otherwise attractive photo, you can use iPhoto's Retouch tool to remove them.

RETOUCH A PHOTO

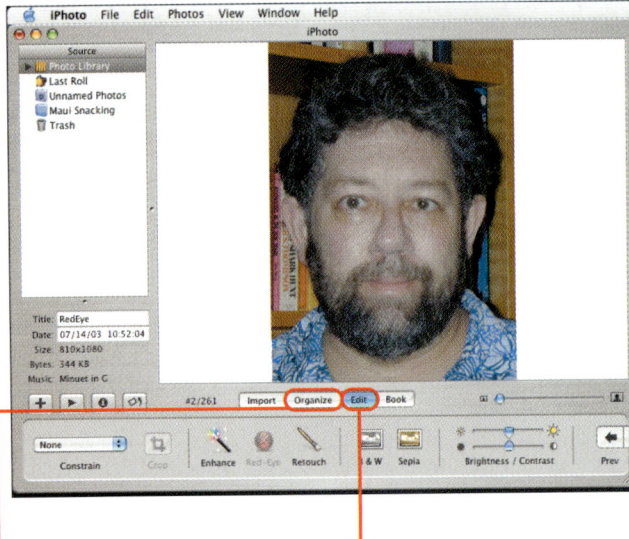

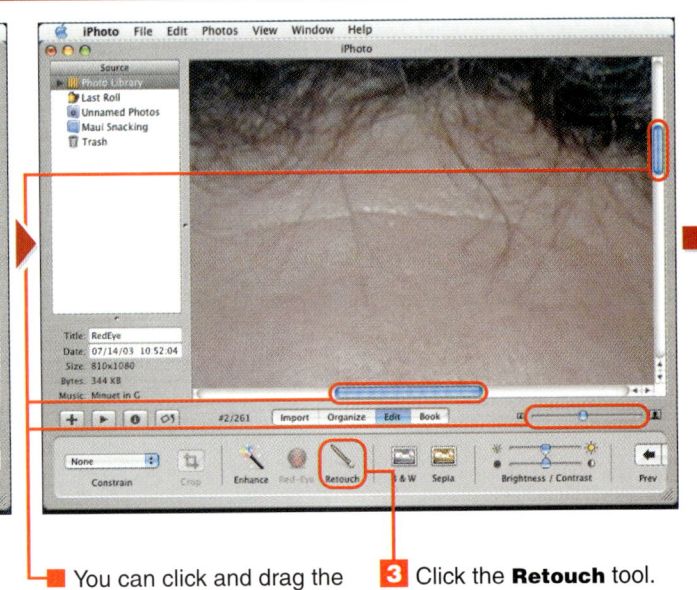

1 In the Organize view, select a photo that exhibits some minor flaws.

Note: For more on using the Organize view, see Chapter 6.

2 Click **Edit**.

■ This example retouches the subject's forehead wrinkle and the shiny areas on the nose and lower lip.

■ You can click and drag the ⊙ and the scroll bars to magnify and center the flaw that needs retouching.

3 Click the **Retouch** tool.

■ The tool displays a white border to indicate it is active.

128

7 Editing Photos with iPhoto

WORKING WITH IPHOTO

How does the Retouch tool work?

As you drag the cursor over a photo, iPhoto attempts to blend the texture of the surrounding area into the area under the cursor. iPhoto also calculates the average of the colors between the area under the cursor and the surrounding area, and changes the colors under the cursor to that average. Because iPhoto applies its changes from moment to moment as you drag, the more you drag back and forth, the smoother and more blended the result becomes.

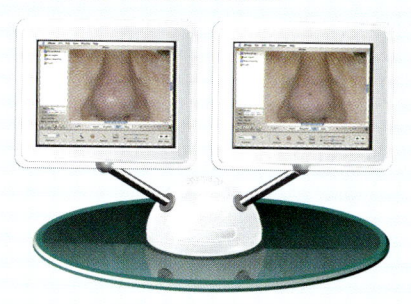

How can I check my retouching work against the original without undoing my work?

Press `Control`. When you do so, iPhoto shows you how the photo looked before your modifications with the current editing tool. Release `Control` to see your changes again. This viewing technique works with all of iPhoto's editing tools.

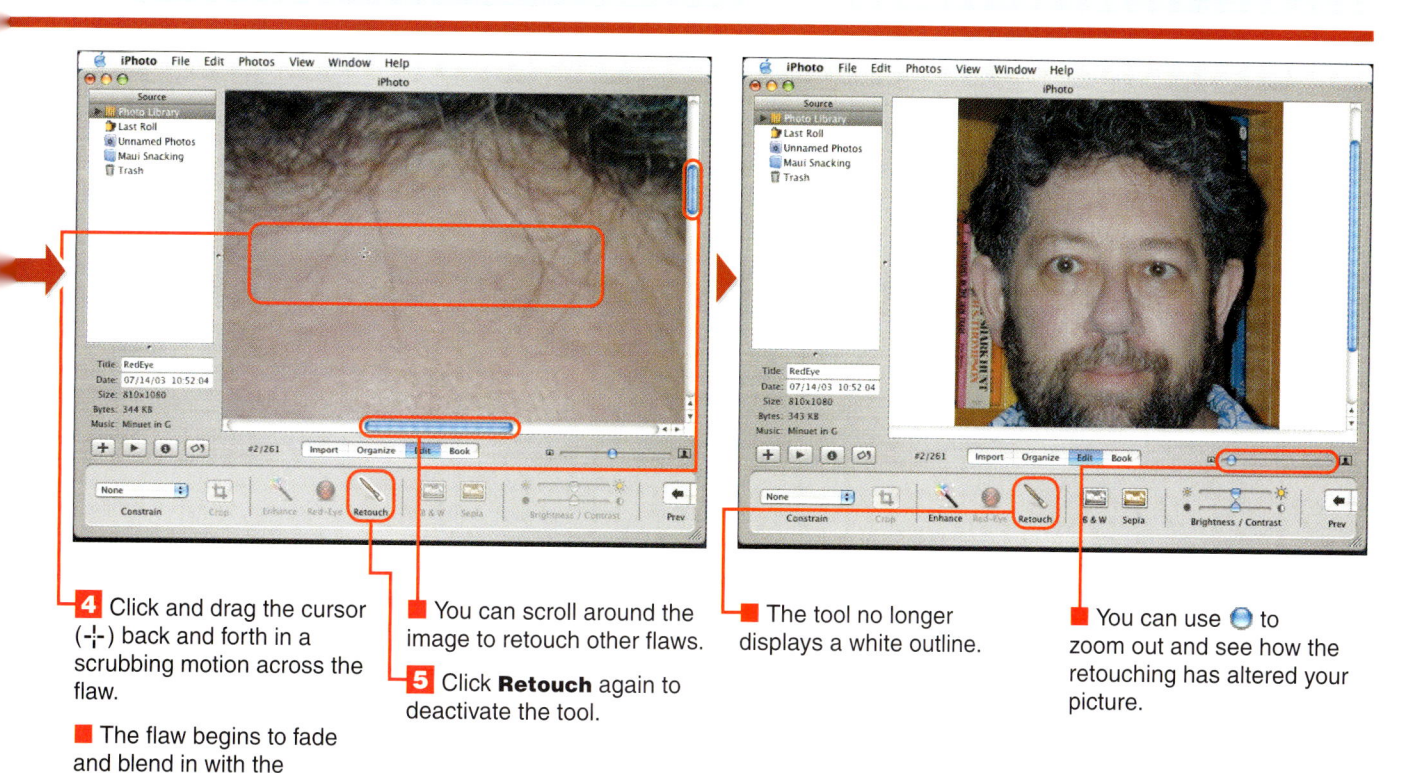

■ **4** Click and drag the cursor (-¦-) back and forth in a scrubbing motion across the flaw.

■ The flaw begins to fade and blend in with the surrounding area.

■ You can scroll around the image to retouch other flaws.

5 Click **Retouch** again to deactivate the tool.

■ The tool no longer displays a white outline.

■ You can use 🔍 to zoom out and see how the retouching has altered your picture.

129

ADJUST BRIGHTNESS AND CONTRAST

You can use iPhoto's Brightness and Contrast controls to help compensate for poor lighting conditions or exposure problems that may afflict your photos.

ADJUST BRIGHTNESS AND CONTRAST

ADJUST BRIGHTNESS

1 In the Organize view, select a photo for which you want to adjust the brightness.

Note: For more on using the Organize view, see Chapter 6.

2 Click **Edit**.

■ In this example, the photo is slightly overexposed and needs to have its brightness setting lowered.

3 Click and drag the Brightness control to the left.

■ The image darkens.

■ In this example, the slightly darker background makes the flowers appear more distinct.

■ You can drag to the right to make the photo lighter.

130

7 Editing Photos with iPhoto

WORKING WITH IPHOTO

What does the Brightness control actually adjust?

The Brightness control proportionally reduces or raises the intensity of each color component of a photo depending on the direction in which you slide it. For many photos, you obtain good results if you adjust the brightness until the very darkest part of the picture looks black.

What does the Contrast control actually do?

The Contrast control regulates the difference between the brightest and darkest parts of a photo. Low contrast makes dark areas less dark and bright areas less bright. High contrast makes dark areas look darker and bright areas look brighter.

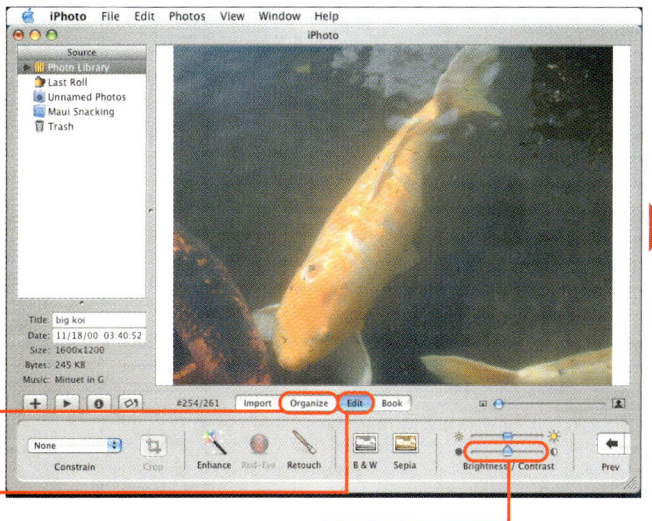

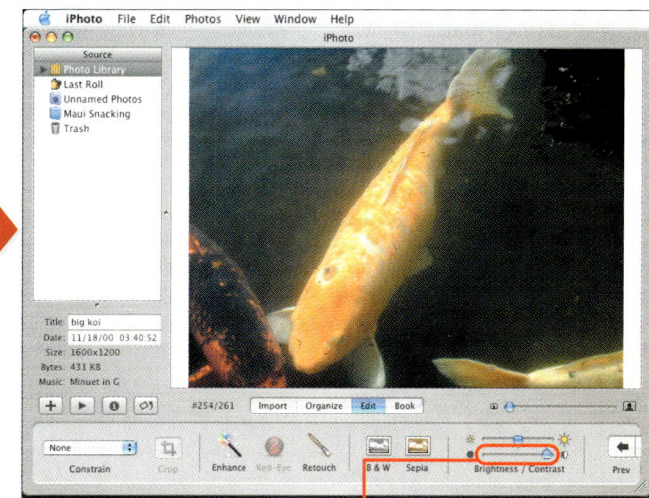

ADJUST CONTRAST

1 In the Organize view, select a photo for which you want to adjust the contrast.

Note: For more on using the Organize view, see Chapter 6.

2 Click **Edit**.

■ This example has a reflection on the water's surface that reduces the contrast between the koi and its surroundings.

3 Click and drag the Contrast control (△) to the right.

■ The contrast increases.

■ In this example, the koi stands out more sharply against its background.

■ You can click and drag △ to the left to reduce the photo's contrast.

131

USING A SEPARATE IPHOTO EDITING WINDOW

In addition to its Edit view, iPhoto lets you edit photos in a separate window. Using a separate editing window, you can still see the contents of your photo library as you edit, and you can edit several photos at a time.

iPhoto's separate editing windows also give you additional editing features, such as the ability to constrain selections to custom aspect ratios.

USING A SEPARATE IPHOTO EDITING WINDOW

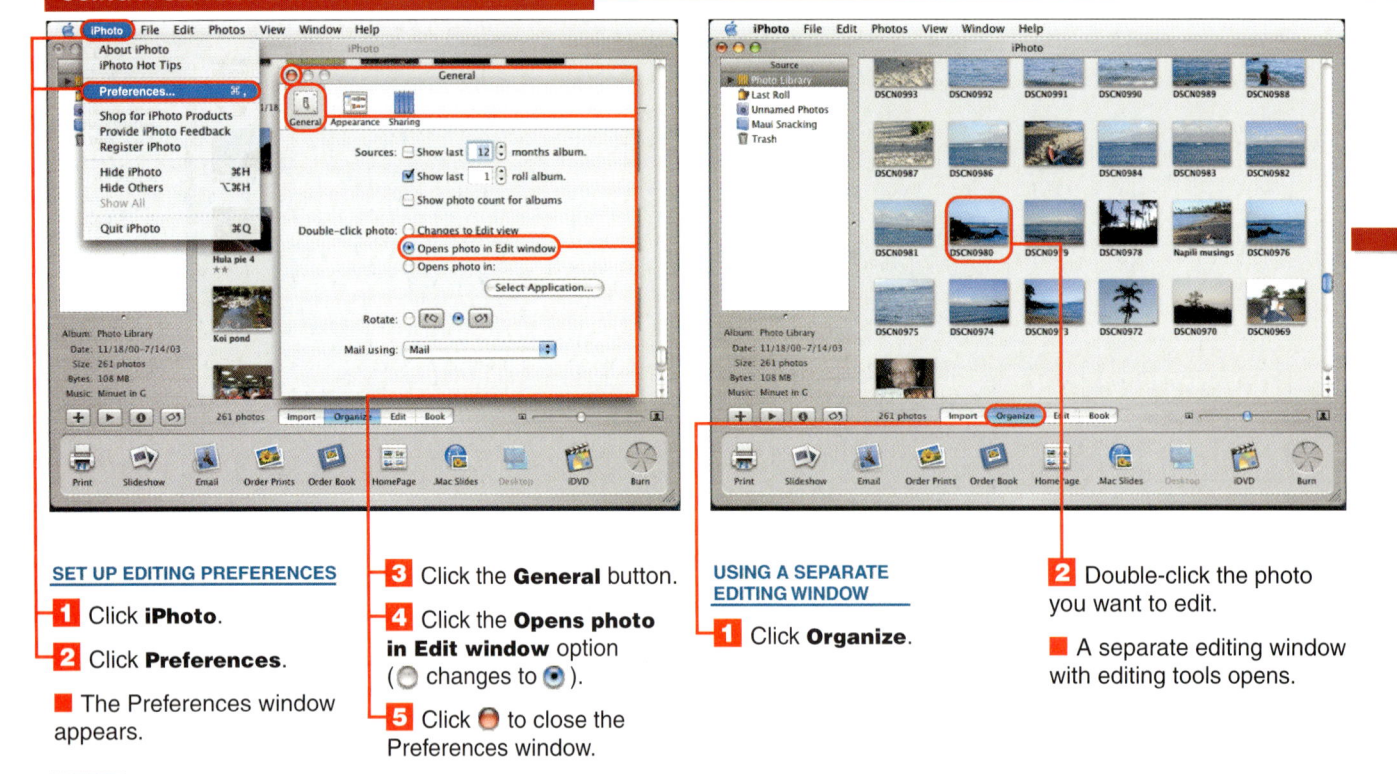

SET UP EDITING PREFERENCES

1. Click **iPhoto**.
2. Click **Preferences**.

■ The Preferences window appears.

3. Click the **General** button.
4. Click the **Opens photo in Edit window** option (○ changes to ●).
5. Click ● to close the Preferences window.

USING A SEPARATE EDITING WINDOW

1. Click **Organize**.
2. Double-click the photo you want to edit.

■ A separate editing window with editing tools opens.

132

7 Editing Photos with iPhoto

WORKING WITH IPHOTO

How can I quickly switch between using a separate editing window and using iPhoto's standard Edit view?

iPhoto has keyboard shortcuts to save you from having to open the Preferences window and changing the setting if, for this one time, you want a separate editing window. If you selected the **Changes to Edit view** option (○ changes to ●) in the Preferences window, pressing `option` while double-clicking a photo opens it in a separate window. Conversely, if you selected the **Opens in Edit window** option, pressing `option` while double-clicking a photo opens it in Edit view.

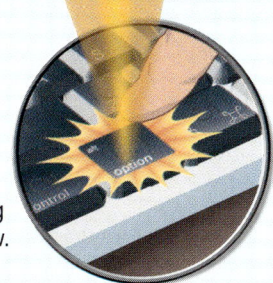

The editing tools in my edit window suddenly vanished! Where did they go?

You may have accidentally clicked the lozenge-shaped button (⬯) in the top-right corner of the editing window. You can click this button to hide the editing tools and click it again to show them.

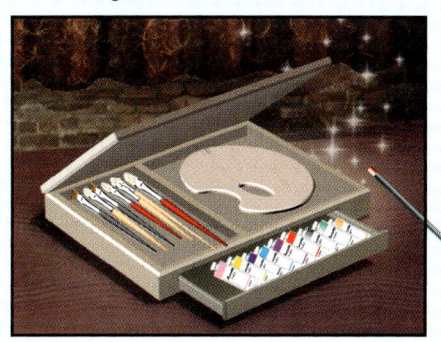

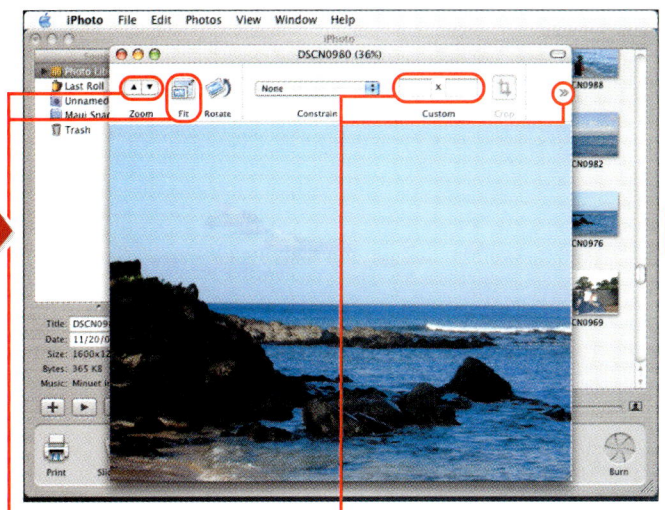

■ **3** Edit your photo.

■ You can click these buttons to zoom in or out.

■ You can click the **Fit** button to zoom the photo to fit in the edit window.

■ You can type values here to specify custom constraint proportions for selections.

■ **4** Click the More Tools button (≫).

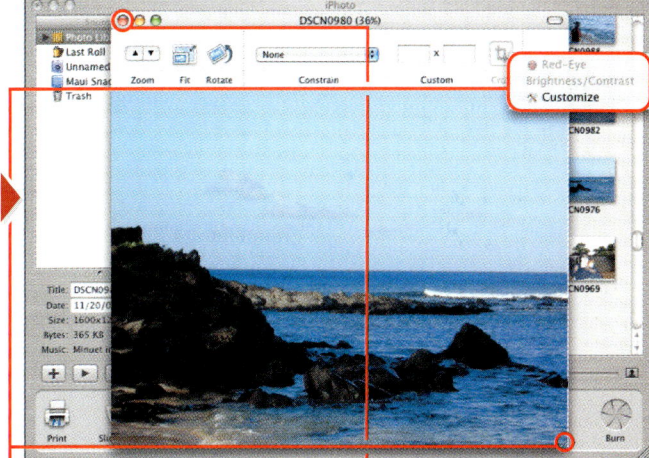

■ A menu containing the tools that cannot fit in the editing window's tool area appears.

■ You can click and drag the lower-right corner of the window to change its size.

■ You can click ⬯ or press ⌘+W to close the window.

133

CUSTOMIZE A SEPARATE IPHOTO EDITING WINDOW

You can add tools to iPhoto's editing windows, and move them around to suit your working style and needs.

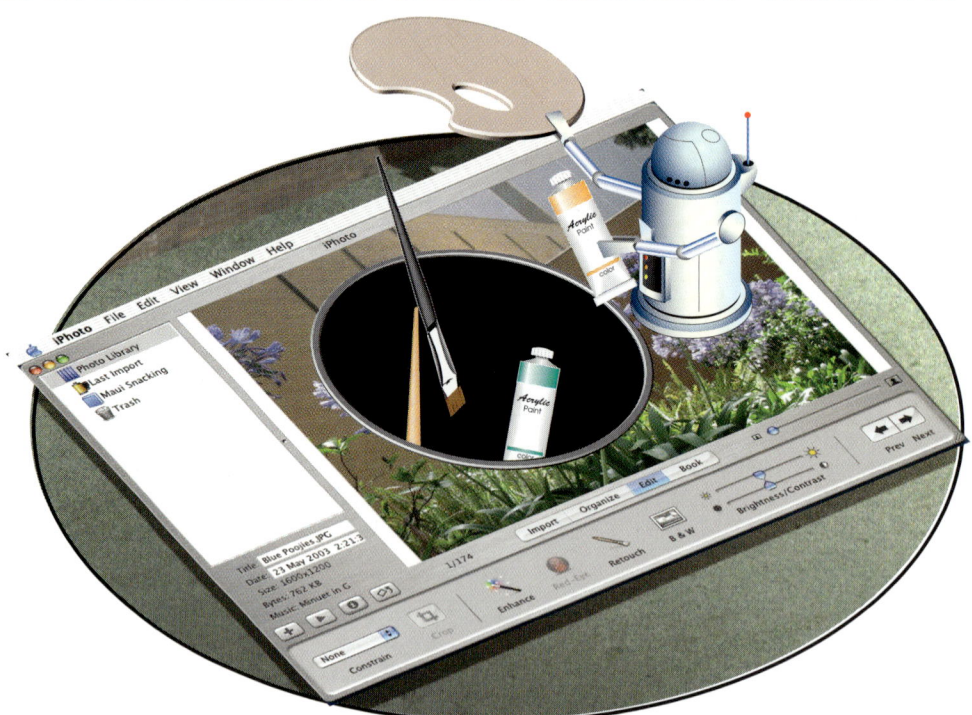

CUSTOMIZE A SEPARATE IPHOTO EDITING WINDOW

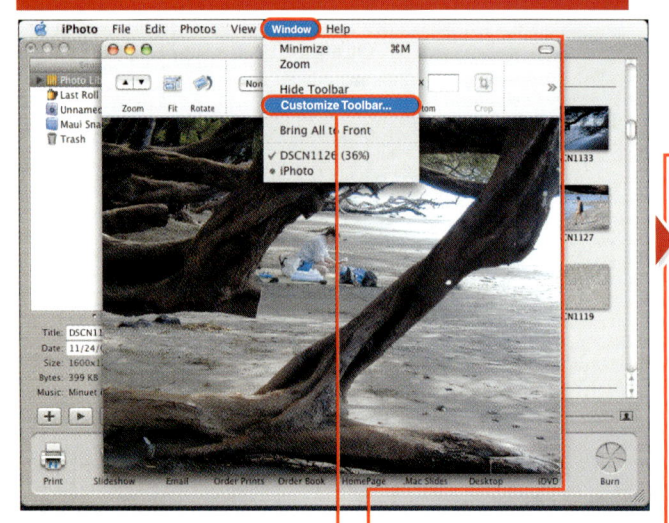

ADDING TOOLS TO THE TOOLBAR

1 Open a photo in a separate editing window.

Note: To open a photo in an editing window, see the section "Using a Separate iPhoto Editing Window."

2 Click **Window**.

3 Click **Customize Toolbar**.

■ A sheet slides out of the window's toolbar.

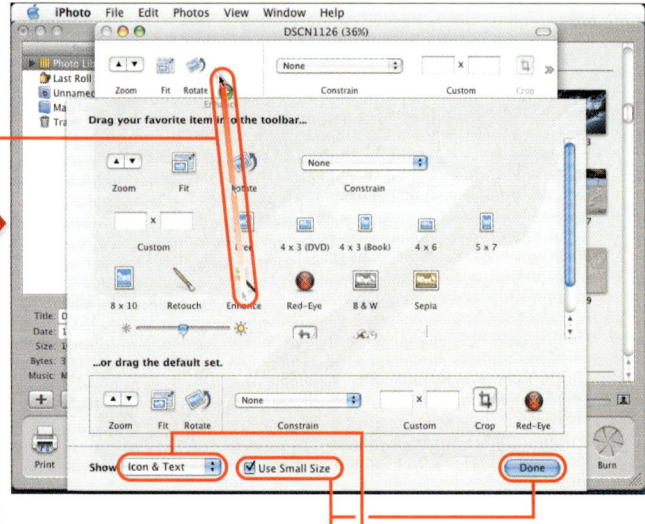

4 Click and drag a tool to the toolbar.

■ As the cursor approaches the toolbar, the other tools move aside to make room.

5 Click here and select whether tools appear as icons, text, or text with icons.

■ You can click here to make the icons smaller (☐ changes to ☑).

6 Click **Done**.

134

7 Editing Photos with iPhoto

WORKING WITH IPHOTO

I have a rather small monitor. How can I make the editing tools in the edit window smaller?

Press ⌘ as you click the lozenge-shaped button (⬭) at the top-right corner of the editing window. Each time you press ⌘ and click ⬭, the tools change appearance. Cycling through the various toolbars displays the following possibilities: Icons with text, Small icons with text, Icons, Small icons, Text, Small text.

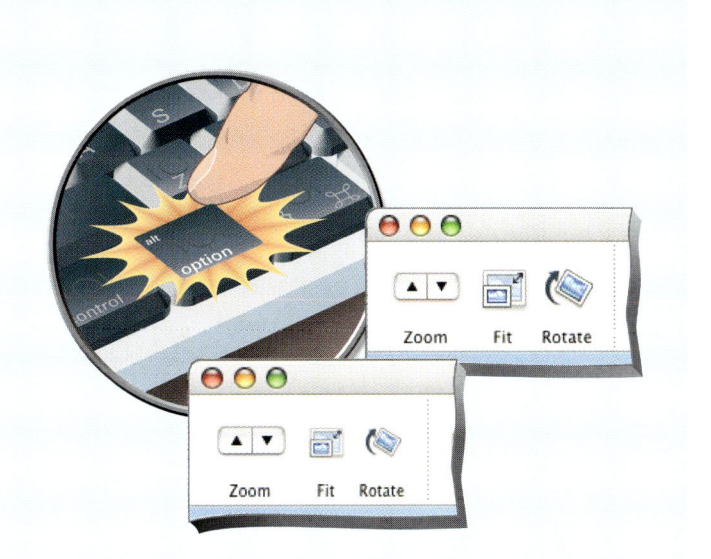

REARRANGE THE TOOLBAR

1 Press ⌘ and drag a tool across the toolbar to where you want it to go.

2 Release the mouse.

■ As you drag the tool, the other tools on the toolbar move aside to make room for it.

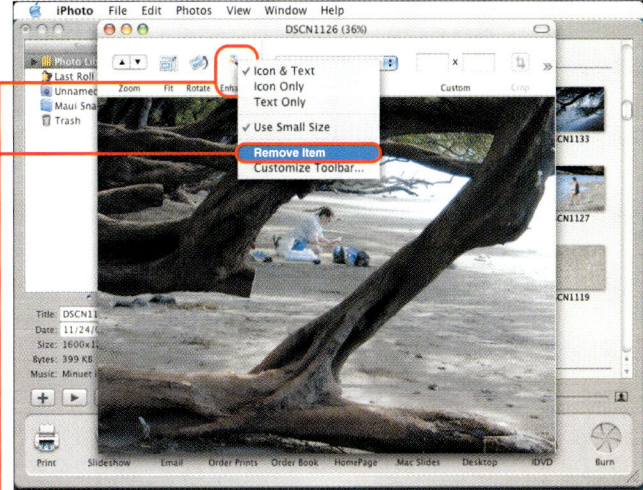

REMOVE A TOOL

1 Press Control and click the tool you want to remove.

2 Click **Remove Item** from the contextual menu that appears.

■ You can also press ⌘ and drag a tool off of the toolbar.

■ The tool disappears.

135

USING A SEPARATE PICTURE EDITING PROGRAM IN IPHOTO

If you need to use more powerful tools to edit your photos, you can set iPhoto to open a photo in another program when you double-click the photo.

A. Photoshop,
1017 Fireworks Way,
Graphic Converter, CA
90403

USING A SEPARATE PICTURE EDITING PROGRAM IN IPHOTO

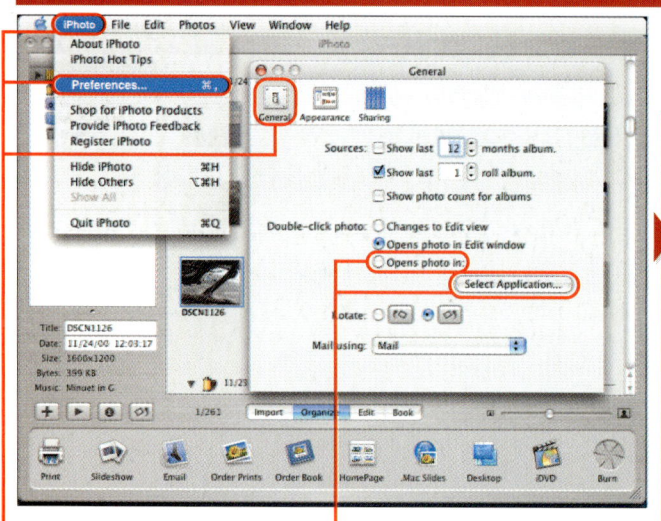

SET A SEPARATE PICTURE EDITOR

1 Click **iPhoto**.

2 Click **Preferences**.

3 In the Preference window, click the **General** button.

4 Click the **Opens photo in:** option (○ changes to ●).

5 Click **Select Application**.

*Note: If you have never clicked the **Opens photo in:** option in iPhoto, iPhoto automatically clicks Select.*

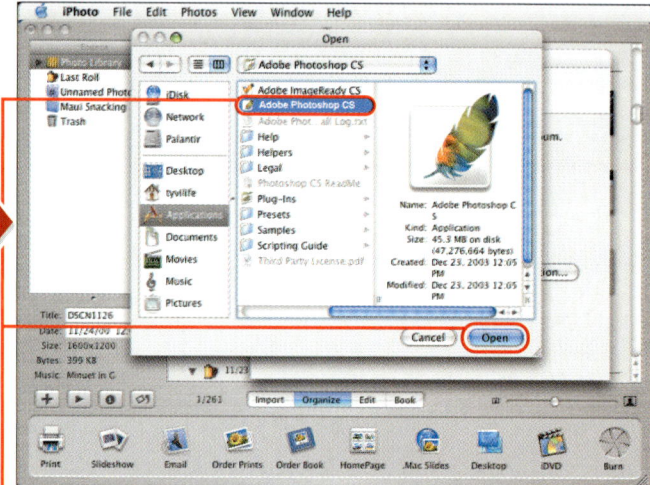

■ An Open dialog window appears.

6 Navigate to the picture editing program you want to use and select it.

7 Click **Open**.

■ The name of the program you select appears in the Preferences window below the Opens photo in: option.

■ The editing program is now set.

8 Close the Preferences window.

136

7 Editing Photos with iPhoto

WORKING WITH IPHOTO

Can I switch between editing in another application or in a separate window without changing my iPhoto preferences?

Yes. Press `Control` and click a photo in the Organize view. You can select either **Edit in separate window** or **Edit in external editor** from the contextual menu that appears. For more on using the Organize view, see Chapter 6.

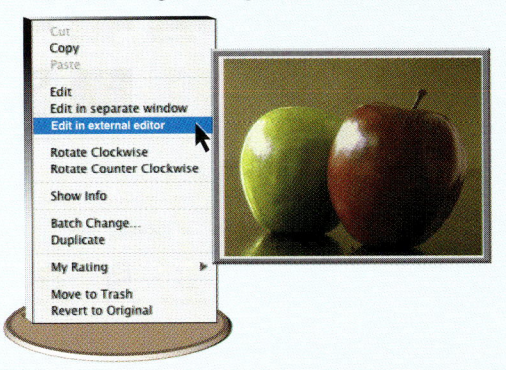

I have a slow computer, and it takes a lot of time to open the separate editing program when I double-click a photo. How can I speed things up?

Start your other editing program before you open iPhoto. When you double-click a photo in iPhoto, the picture quickly appears in a new window in the already running editing program.

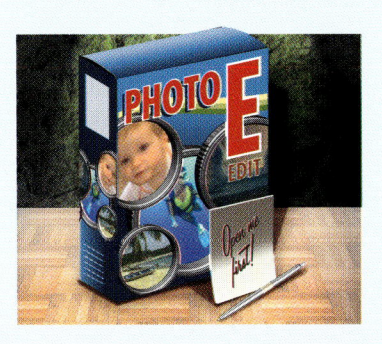

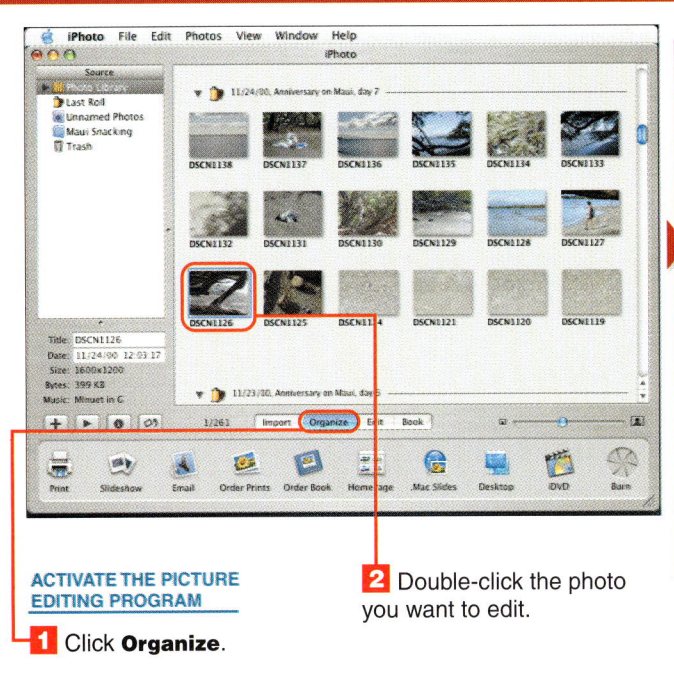

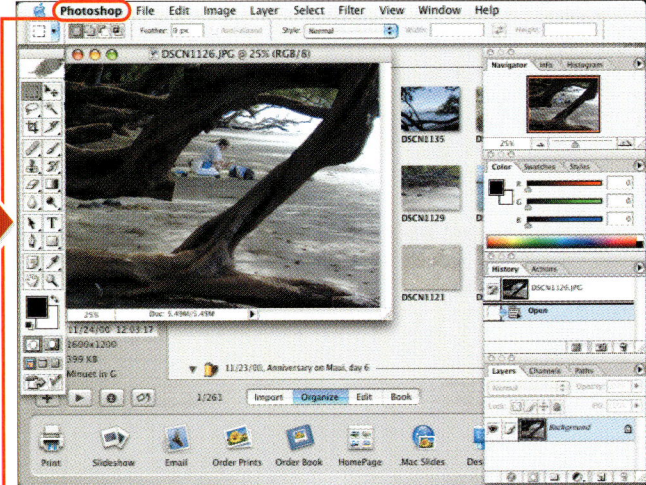

ACTIVATE THE PICTURE EDITING PROGRAM

1 Click **Organize**.

2 Double-click the photo you want to edit.

■ The editing program you set in iPhoto's preferences opens the photo.

■ You can edit the photo and save it in the separate program.

Note: You must use the same name and file type when you save the photo for iPhoto to recognize the changes.

■ When you save, iPhoto changes the photo in the Library and all the albums in which it appears.

137

E-MAIL A PHOTO

iPhoto makes it easy for you to e-mail photos to your family and friends using your favorite e-mail program. You can select the photo sizes and whether to include your iPhoto titles and comments.

This example uses Apple's Mail program. Other mail programs differ in appearance.

E-MAIL A PHOTO

1 Click **Organize**.

2 Click a photo.

■ You can Shift+click, or ⌘+click, to select several photos.

3 Click the **Email** button.

Note: The Email button shows the icon of the e-mail program that iPhoto uses.

■ The Mail Photo dialog window appears.

■ You can click here and select the size of the photos you want to send.

■ You can deselect **Titles** or **Comments** (☑ changes to ☐) if you do not want to include the photo titles or comments in the e-mail message.

■ iPhoto estimates the size of the e-mail message.

4 Click **Compose**.

8 Using Photos with iPhoto

WORKING WITH IPHOTO

How can I use an e-mail program other than Apple's Mail?

You can set the e-mail program you want to use in iPhoto's Preferences window. The Mail menu on the General pane lists the e-mail programs on your Mac that iPhoto recognizes. iPhoto can send photos from most e-mail programs on your Mac. However, the actual e-mail's appearance and capabilities may vary from program to program. For more information on setting up iPhoto's preferences, see Chapter 6.

How many photos can I e-mail at one time?

There is no specific limit to the number of photos you can e-mail. However, most Internet service providers do have limits on how big an e-mail message can be, and it is impolite to send an e-mail message larger than a few hundred kilobytes to people without first asking permission. iPhoto tells you how big the e-mail message is when you send photos.

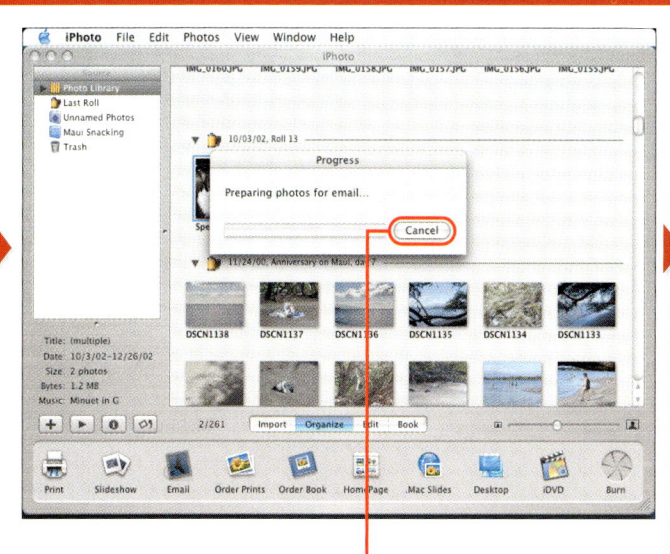

- The Progress window appears.

- You can click **Cancel** if you change your mind.

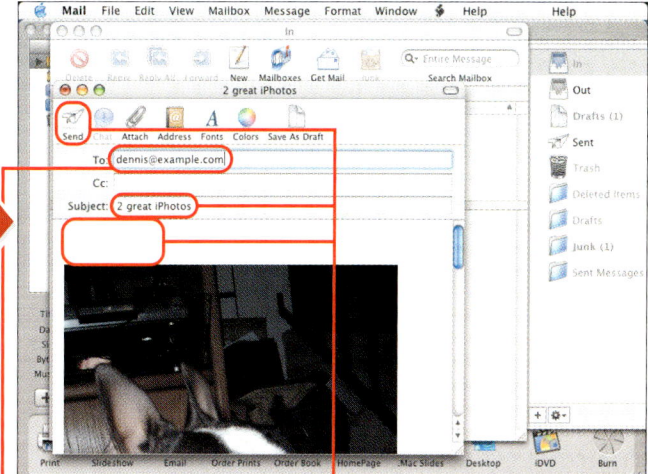

- Your e-mail program opens with a new message containing the photos.

5 Type an address for your message.

- You can change the message's subject, and type additional text in the message.

6 Click the **Send** icon.

- The e-mail program sends your message with the attached photos.

139

PRINT A PHOTO

iPhoto can print your photos in a variety of styles, including contact sheet or greeting card layouts, on any printer attached to your Mac.

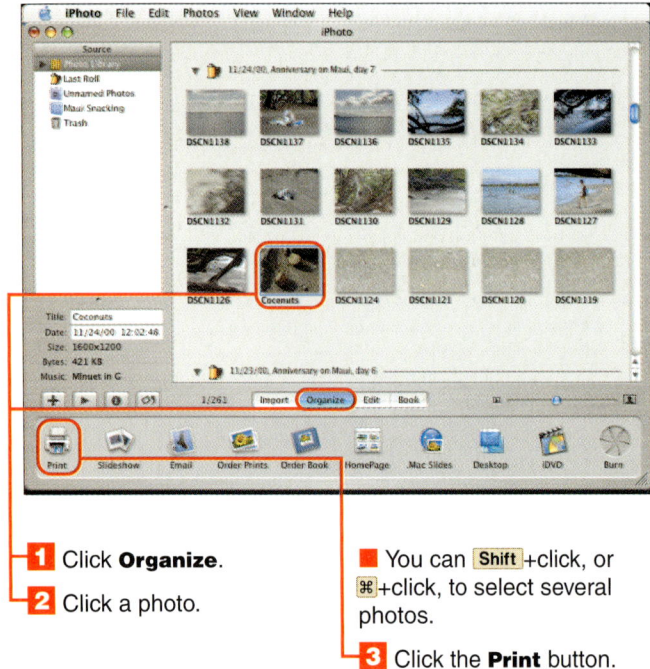

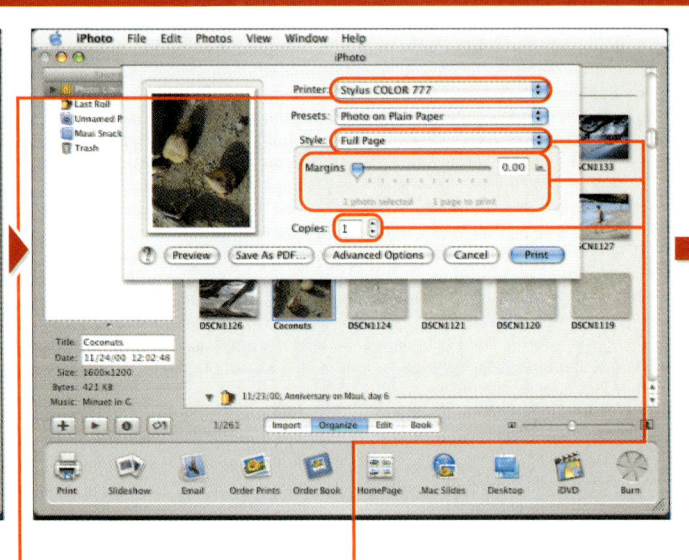

PRINT A PHOTO

1 Click **Organize**.

2 Click a photo.

- You can Shift+click, or ⌘+click, to select several photos.

3 Click the **Print** button.

- The Print dialog sheet appears.

- You can click here to select a different printer if you have more than one printer connected to your Mac.

- You can set or modify printing options for the current printing style here.

- You can click here and select the number of copies you want to print.

4 Click the Style.

140

8 Using Photos with iPhoto

WORKING WITH IPHOTO

How do the Sampler printing templates work?

The Sampler templates, which you select in the Style menu, let you place a number of different-sized photos on a single page. When you select a group of photos and select the **One photo per page** option (☐ changes to ☑), iPhoto prints several photos of different sizes on one page. Clicking the **One photo per page** option provides several samples of a single photo in different sizes on the same page.

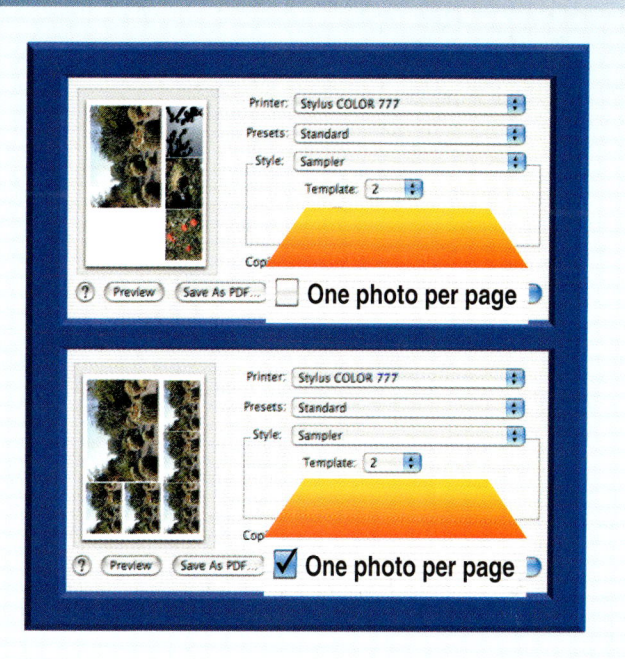

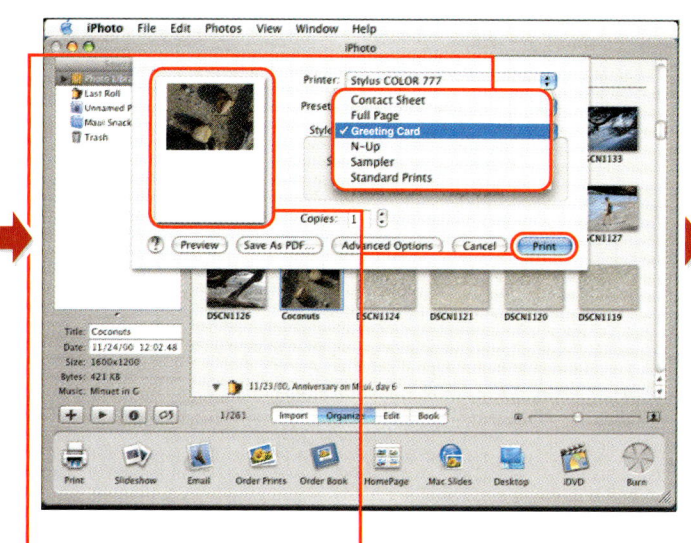

5 Select a printing style.

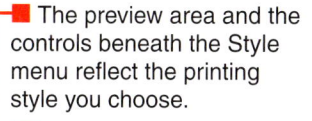

■ The preview area and the controls beneath the Style menu reflect the printing style you choose.

6 Click **Print**.

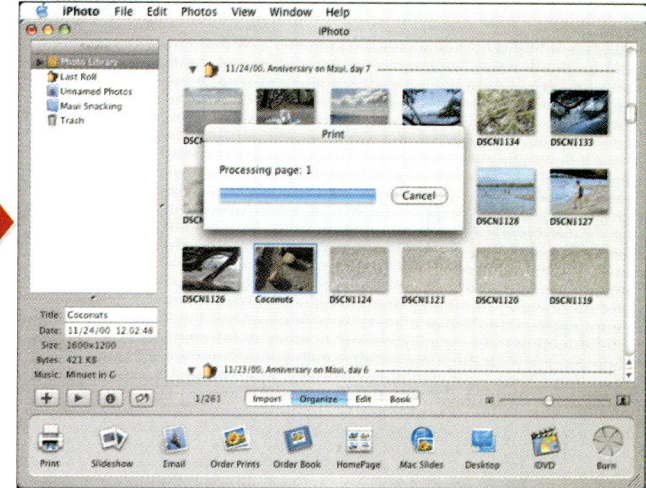

■ A Print dialog window appears, displaying the printing progress.

■ iPhoto prints your photos.

141

CREATE A SLIDESHOW

You can select any group of photos you want and create an on-screen slideshow, complete with accompanying music to show to your family and friends.

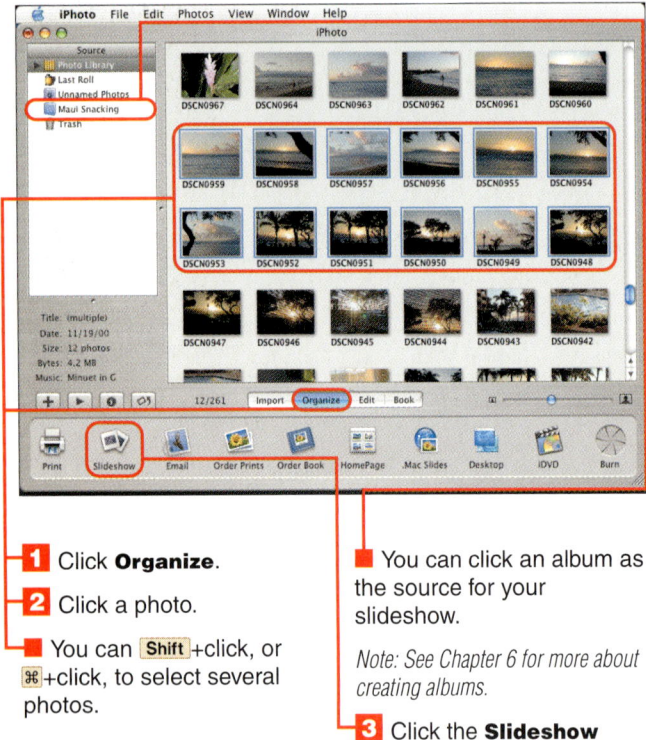

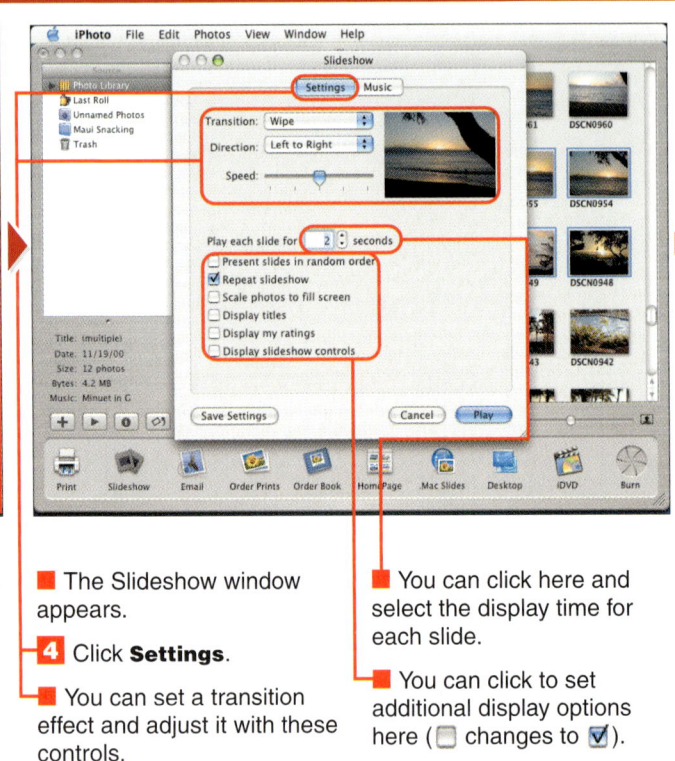

CREATE A SLIDESHOW

■ **1** Click **Organize**.

■ **2** Click a photo.

■ You can Shift +click, or ⌘+click, to select several photos.

■ You can click an album as the source for your slideshow.

Note: See Chapter 6 for more about creating albums.

■ **3** Click the **Slideshow** button.

■ The Slideshow window appears.

■ **4** Click **Settings**.

■ You can set a transition effect and adjust it with these controls.

■ You can click here and select the display time for each slide.

■ You can click to set additional display options here (☐ changes to ☑).

142

8 Using Photos with iPhoto

WORKING WITH IPHOTO

How can I manually move among the slides in my slideshow?

When you pause a slideshow, by pressing `Spacebar`, you can press ◀ and ▶ on the keyboard to move to the previous or next slide.

What do the on screen slideshow controls do?

When you click **Display slideshow controls** in the slideshow settings window, iPhoto gives you a set of controls that let you both navigate and modify slides. In addition to being able to pause, play, and move among slides, you can click controls to rotate photos, assign ratings to them, and remove them from the show.

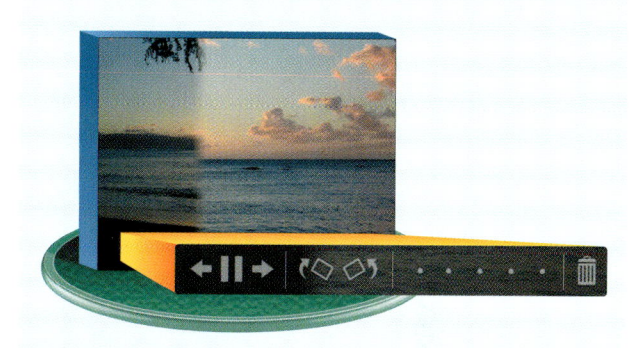

■ **5** Click **Music**.

■ The Music pane appears.

■ You can click to play music during the slideshow (☐ changes to ☑).

■ You can click to select a song from your iTunes library.

■ You can click to select an iTunes playlist.

■ **6** Click **Play**.

■ The slideshow begins.

■ **7** Press `Spacebar`.

■ A pause icon appears briefly, and the slide stops advancing.

■ **8** Press `Spacebar` again.

■ The slideshow resumes.

■ **9** Click the mouse button.

143

SAVE A SLIDESHOW AS A QUICKTIME MOVIE

You can export a set of your photos as a QuickTime movie slideshow, complete with background music. QuickTime movies can play on both Mac and Windows PCs, so you can share your photos with friends who do not have iPhoto or even a Mac.

SAVE A SLIDESHOW AS A QUICKTIME MOVIE

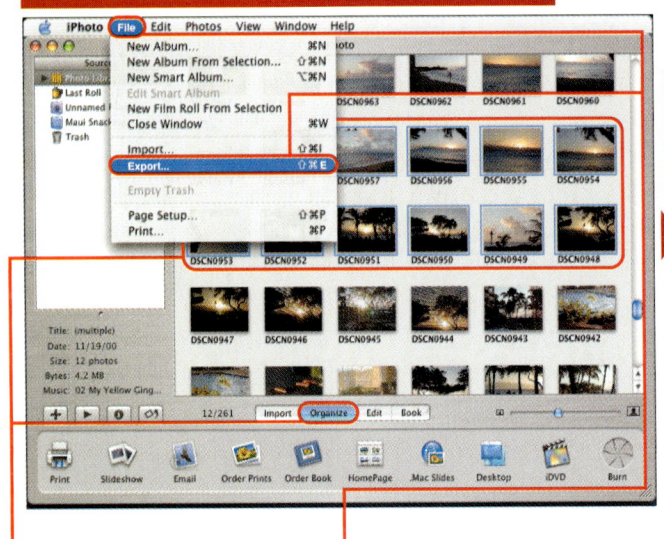

■ 1 Click **Organize**.

■ 2 Click a photo.

■ You can Shift +click, or ⌘+click, to select several photos.

■ 3 Click **File**.

■ 4 Click **Export**.

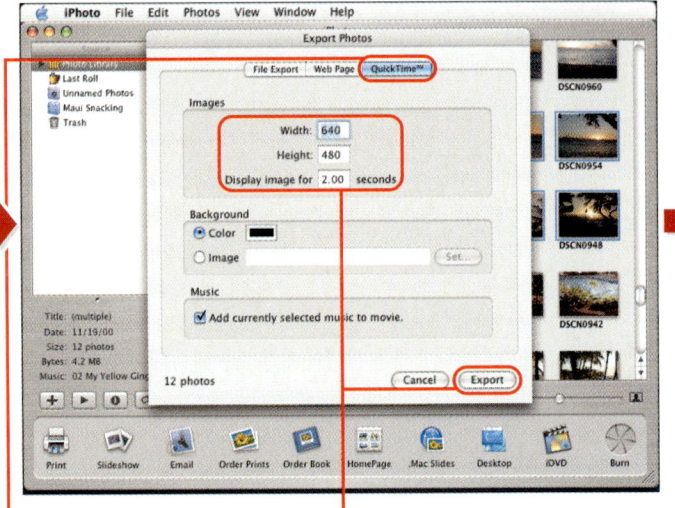

■ The Export Photos dialog window appears.

■ 5 Click the **QuickTime™** tab.

■ The QuickTime Export settings appear.

■ You can type values to specify the size of the images and the display time of each image for the QuickTime movie.

■ 6 Click **Export**.

144

8 Using Photos with iPhoto

WORKING WITH IPHOTO

Why are the images in my QuickTime movie slideshow so much smaller than my iPhoto slideshow?

They do not have to be. You can set the size by typing values in the Width and Height boxes in the iPhoto Export window to make the QuickTime movie image size as large as you want. However, the larger the pictures, the larger the QuickTime movie file you create. iPhoto's default resolution of 640 x 480 is a reasonable compromise that suits most users.

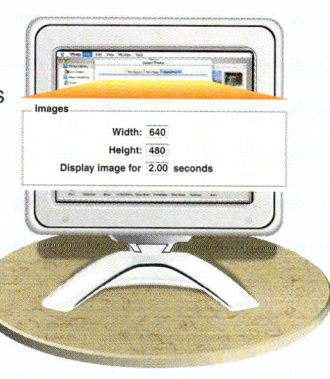

Can I use music purchased from the iTunes Music Store in my QuickTime slideshow?

Yes, but you must authorize your computer to play your purchased music if you want to hear the soundtrack. See Chapter 4 for more information about authorizing your computer to play purchased music.

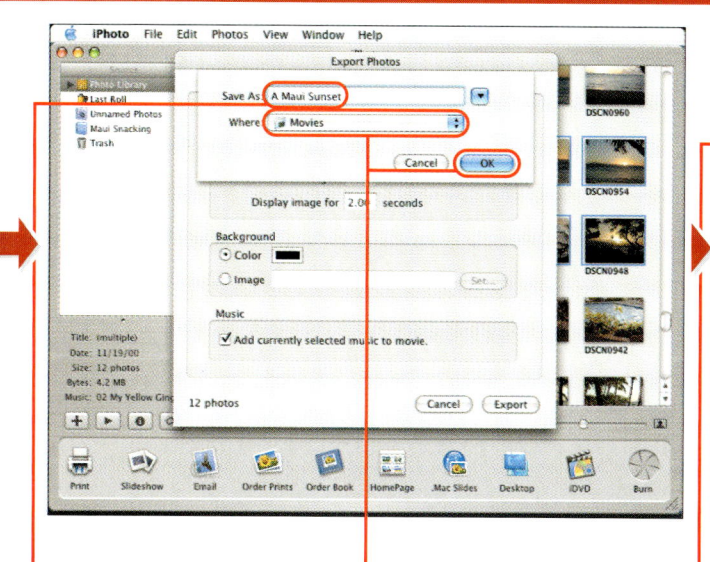

- ■ A sheet slides out from the top of the Export Photos window.

7 Type a name for the QuickTime movie file.

- ■ You can click here and select where to save the QuickTime movie file.

8 Click **OK**.

- ■ An Exporting progress sheet slides out of the top of the Export Photos window, showing you the progress of the export.

- ■ When iPhoto completes the export, the Export Photos window closes.

145

MAKE A SLIDESHOW DVD

The iLife programs work together, so you can create a slideshow with iPhoto and place it on a DVD with iDVD, using music from your iTunes music library. A DVD slideshow lets you share your photos with anyone who has a DVD player.

You can make a slideshow to place on a DVD from any selected group of photos, but it is easiest to use an album as the source for the slideshow.

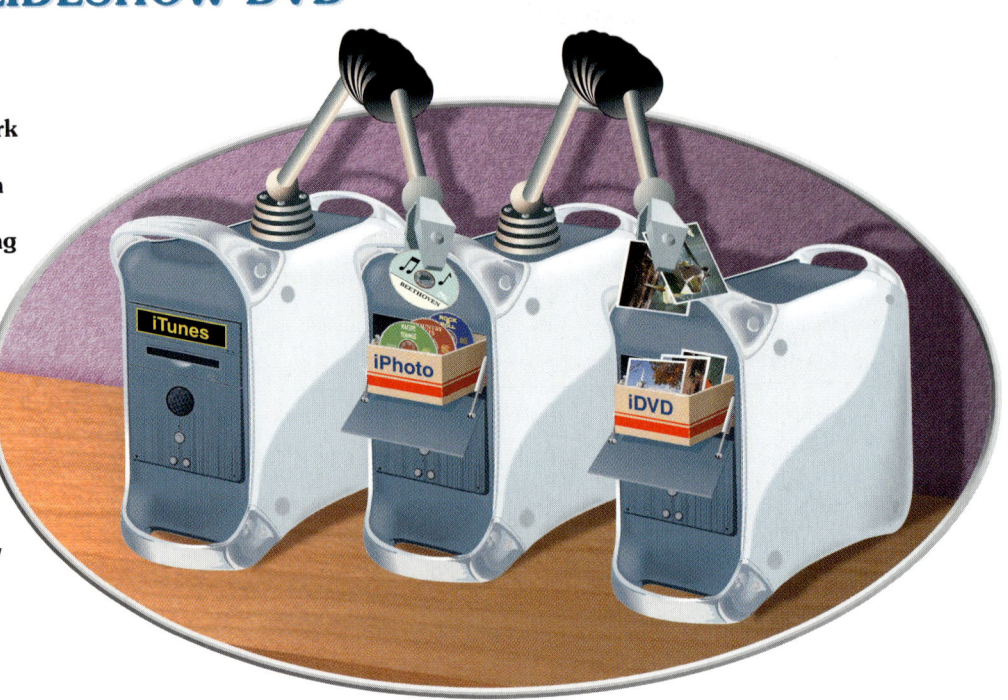

MAKE A SLIDESHOW DVD

1 Click **Organize**.

2 Click an album.

3 Arrange the slides in the order you want to play them.

Note: For more information on organizing an album, see Chapter 6.

4 Click the **Slideshow** button.

■ The Slideshow Settings window appears.

■ You can adjust the display and music settings for the slideshow.

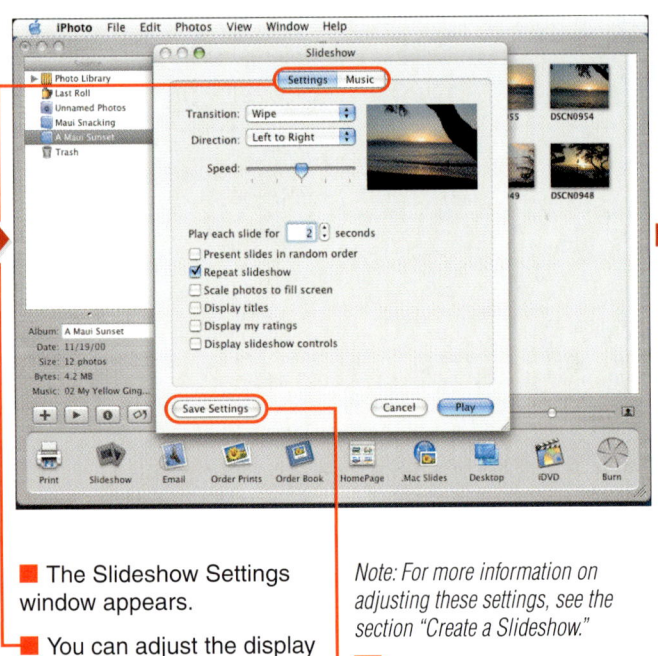

Note: For more information on adjusting these settings, see the section "Create a Slideshow."

5 Click **Save Settings**.

146

8 Using Photos with iPhoto

WORKING WITH IPHOTO

How many slides can I place in a DVD slideshow?

You can have as many as 99 slides in a DVD slideshow. If you need more slides in a single show, you can make a QuickTime movie from a larger slideshow and import the movie into iDVD separately.

I do not see the iDVD button in iPhoto. Why not?

The iDVD button only appears if you have iDVD installed on your Mac. If your Mac cannot run iDVD, the iLife installer does not install it. iDVD requires a G4 Mac or better with a SuperDrive.

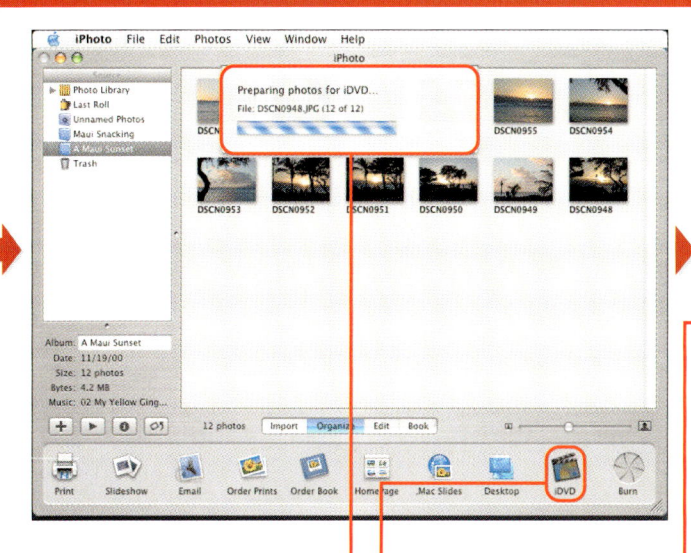

■ The Slideshow Settings window closes.

■ iPhoto saves your changes to the slideshow setting for the album.

6 Click the **iDVD** button.

■ A progress sheet appears.

■ iDVD opens and adds the slideshow to the iDVD project window.

■ iDVD adds the slideshow to the last iDVD project on which you worked.

Note: It may take a number of seconds for iDVD to open. Be patient.

■ You can adjust your slideshow settings using iDVD's slideshow editor.

Note: See Chapters 12 through 14 for more about iDVD.

147

SET UP AN IPHOTO ACCOUNT WITH APPLE

You can set up a secure iPhoto account with Apple to purchase prints and photo books directly through any Mac with an Internet connection.

You must have an active Internet connection and a credit card to complete this task.

SET UP AN IPHOTO ACCOUNT WITH APPLE

1 Click **Organize**.

2 Click the **Order Prints** button.

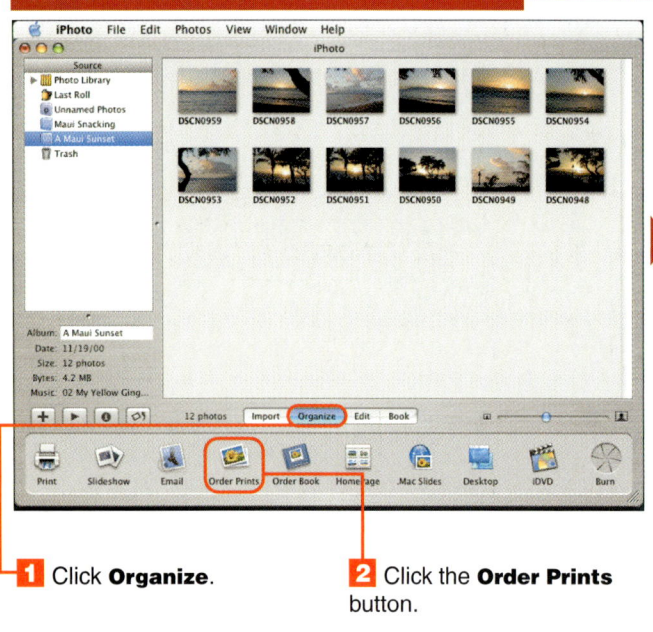

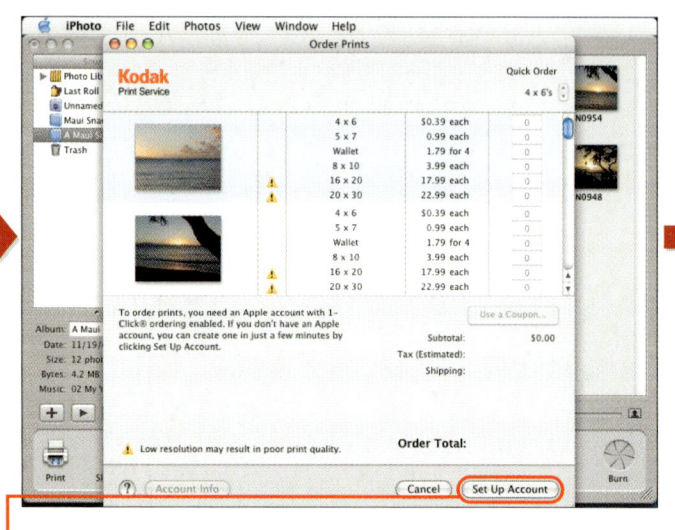

■ The Order Prints window opens.

3 Click **Set Up Account**.

Note: You need to set up your account in iPhoto even if you already have an Apple Account, but you can use the same Apple Account when you do so.

8 Using Photos with iPhoto

WORKING WITH IPHOTO

Do I need to have an iPhoto account to use iPhoto?

No, although you cannot use iPhoto to order books or prints on-line without one.

I live in France. Can I set up an iPhoto account?

iPhoto accounts for ordering books and prints used to be limited to users in the United States and Canada, but Apple has recently made it possible for users in Japan and Europe to order photos as well.

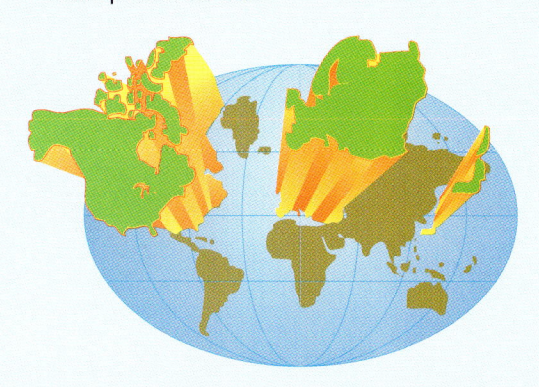

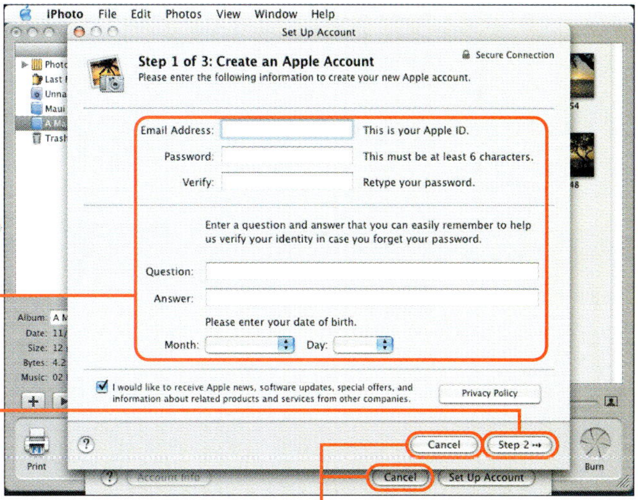

■ The Set Up Account window appears.

4 Click **Create Account**.

■ If you already have an Apple Account, you can type your Apple ID and password and click **Sign In**.

■ The Set Up Account window expands.

■ If you signed in with an existing Apple ID, this screen appears with your account information filled in, however, you still need to complete the set-up process for the account.

5 Type your account information following the on-screen instructions.

■ You can click **Cancel** at any time if you decide not to create an account.

■ When you finish, Apple creates your account and you can click **Cancel** on the Order Prints window if you do not want to order pictures.

149

ORDER PRINTS FROM APPLE

With your Apple Account and an Internet connection, you can order high-quality Kodak prints in a variety of sizes and combinations, from wallet-size to poster-size, and have them mailed to you in a few days.

Please note that this section requires an active Internet connection and an Apple iPhoto Account. For more on setting up an account, see the section "Set Up an iPhoto Account with Apple."

ORDER PRINTS FROM APPLE

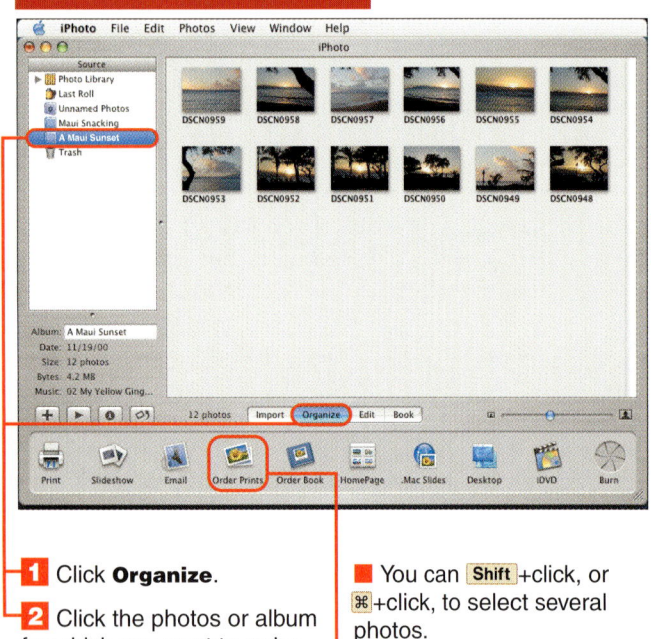

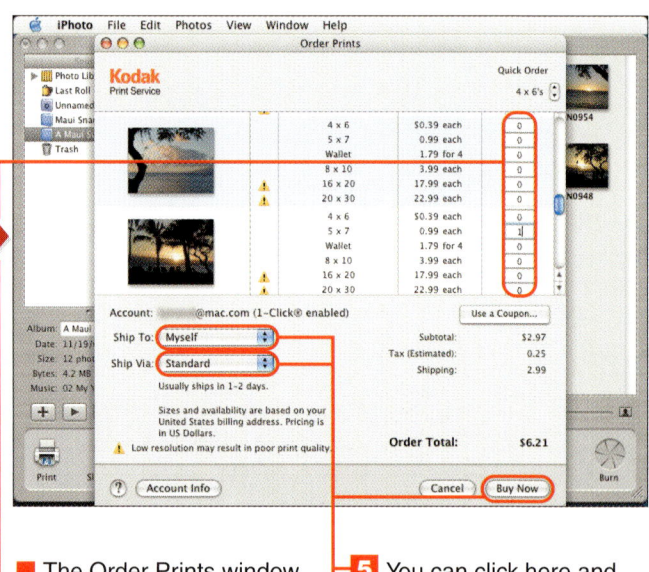

1 Click **Organize**.

2 Click the photos or album for which you want to order prints.

■ You can Shift+click, or ⌘+click, to select several photos.

3 Click the **Order Prints** button.

■ The Order Prints window opens.

4 You can click here and type the number of each size print you want for each photo.

5 You can click here and select a shipping address.

6 You can click here and select a shipping method.

7 Click **Buy Now**.

8 Using Photos with iPhoto

WORKING WITH IPHOTO

I saw a low-resolution warning when I ordered some prints. What does that mean?

When the message, "Low resolution may result in poor print quality," appears on the Order Prints window, it means some of your photos are too small to produce attractive prints. Kodak recommends the following minimum photo sizes for prints. You can see a photo's pixel dimensions in iPhoto's information area below the photo's title and date in the Organize view.

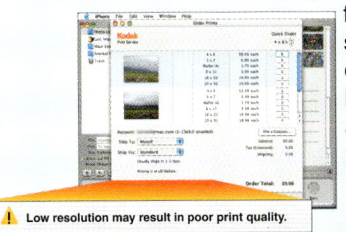

Photo Size	Minimum Pixel Dimensions
Wallet size	640 x 480 pixels
4 x 6 inches	768 x 512 pixels
5 x 7 inches	1152 x 768 pixels
8 x 10 inches	1536 x 1024 pixels

How should I crop photos for ordering prints?

Before ordering prints, crop your photos with the appropriate *aspect ratio* — the relationship between a picture's height and width — for the print size you want. Digital cameras usually produce photos with a 3:4 aspect ratio, while 35mm cameras produce photos with a 4:6 ratio. Therefore, to order a 4 x 6-inch print, crop the picture with a 4:6 aspect ratio. iPhoto's Edit view lets you constrain cropping to various ratios. For more information on selecting and cropping a photo, see Chapter 7.

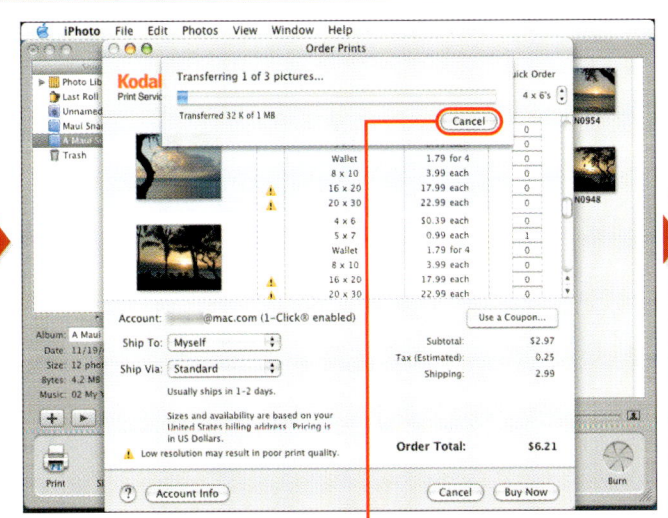

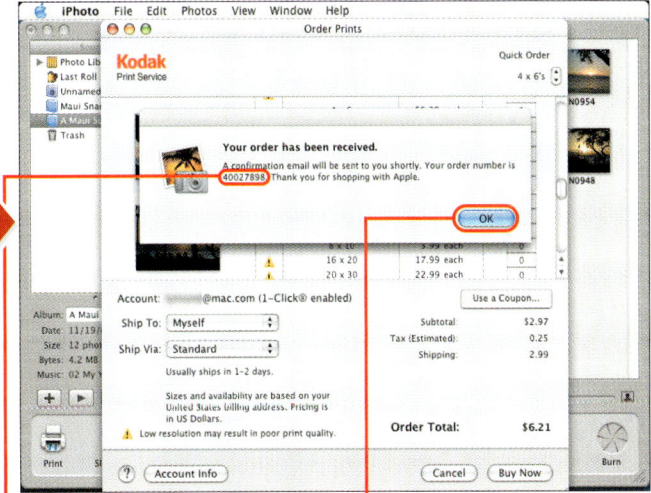

■ iPhoto begins transferring the photos to the printing service.

■ A sheet appears from the top of the Order Prints window and displays the progress of the picture transfer.

■ You can click **Cancel** before the transfer finishes if you change your mind.

Note: The transfer may take several minutes, depending on the number of photos and the speed of your Internet connection.

■ When iPhoto completes the transfer, a confirmation window appears with a confirmation number.

8 Write down your order number for future reference.

9 Click **OK**.

■ The confirmation window and the Order Prints window close.

151

MAKE A PHOTO BOOK

You can produce photo books that present your pictures attractively arranged on each of its pages. You can select a book design from among several available styles. For example, you can present your photos as a portfolio of your photographic work, or as a story, or in the style of a school yearbook.

To arrange pages or change the captions in your photo book, see the sections "Arrange a Photo Book's Pages" and "Add and Change a Photo Book's Captions." To have Apple print your photo book for you, see the section "Preview and Order a Photo Book."

MAKE A PHOTO BOOK

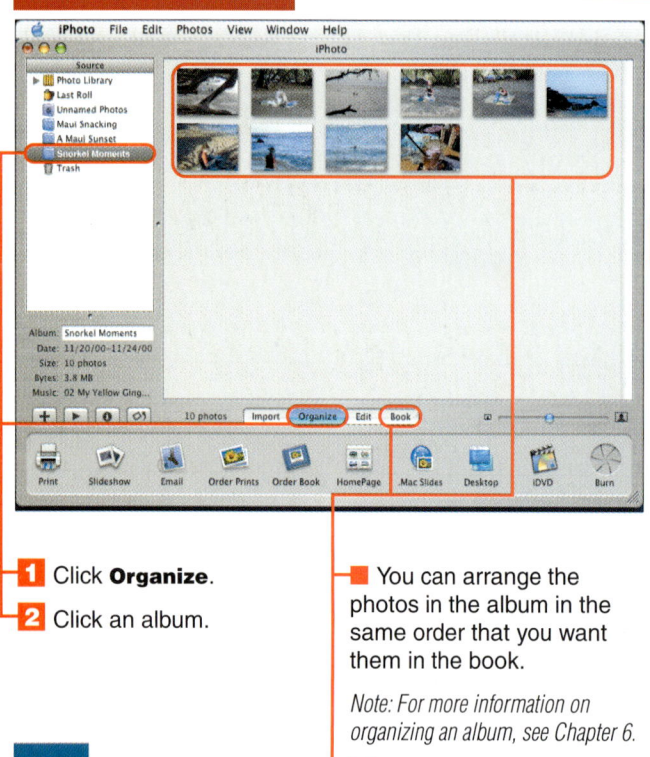

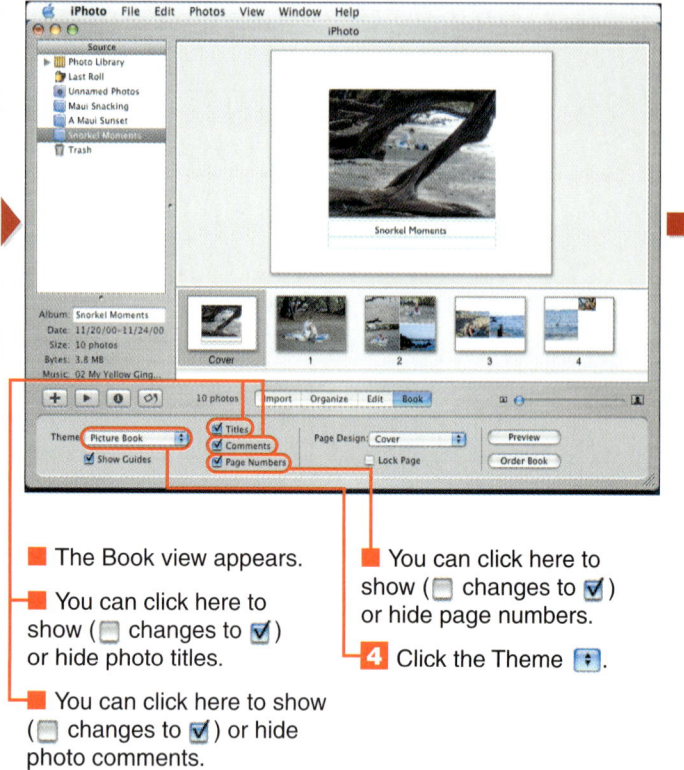

1 Click **Organize**.

2 Click an album.

- You can arrange the photos in the album in the same order that you want them in the book.

Note: For more information on organizing an album, see Chapter 6.

3 Click **Book**.

- The Book view appears.

- You can click here to show (☐ changes to ☑) or hide photo titles.

- You can click here to show (☐ changes to ☑) or hide photo comments.

- You can click here to show (☐ changes to ☑) or hide page numbers.

4 Click the Theme ⬥.

152

8 Using Photos with iPhoto

WORKING WITH IPHOTO

How many pages can I have in a book?

If you print a photo book yourself, you can have as many pages in the photo book as you want. However, if Apple prints the bound photo book, the maximum number of pages is 50. For more on ordering a photo book through Apple, see the section "Preview and Order a Photo Book."

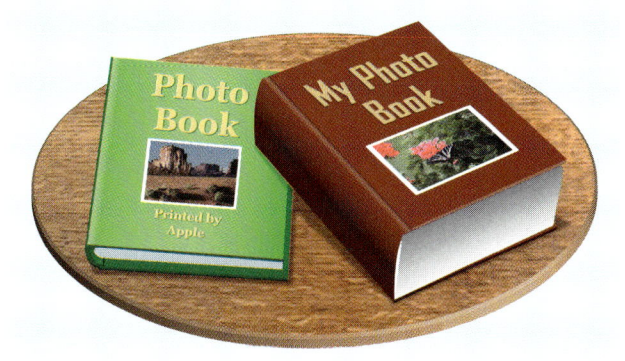

Can I use any picture in my iPhoto Library in a photo book?

Yes, if you print the photo book yourself. When you order a bound book from Apple, you should avoid using black-and-white photos because the printing process that Apple's book service employs does not produce high-quality reproductions of black-and-white photos.

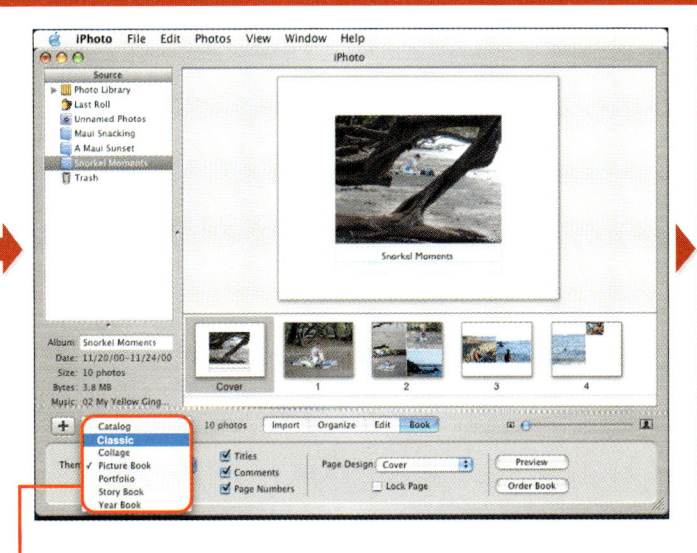

5 Select a theme.

- Each theme has a separate set of page layouts and preferred fonts for titles and comments.
- The page layouts change to match the theme that you select.
- The album retains the book's new theme setting.

153

ARRANGE A PHOTO BOOK'S PAGES

You can change the order of the pages in a book, and you can change the number of pictures that appear on any page. Arranging your pictures in different orders and groups lets you make the perfect photo presentation for your friends, family, or for business.

For more on creating a book, see the previous section "Make a Photo Book." To have Apple publish your photo book, see the section "Preview and Order a Photo Book."

ARRANGE A PHOTO BOOK'S PAGES

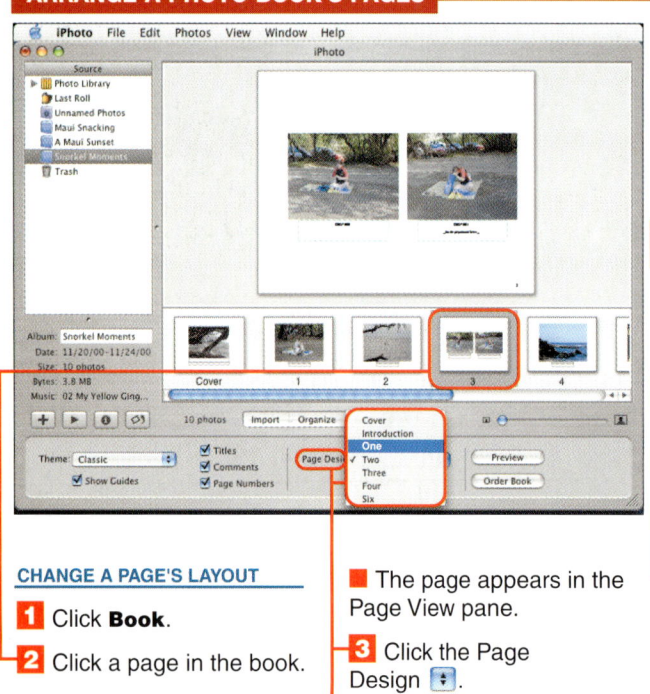

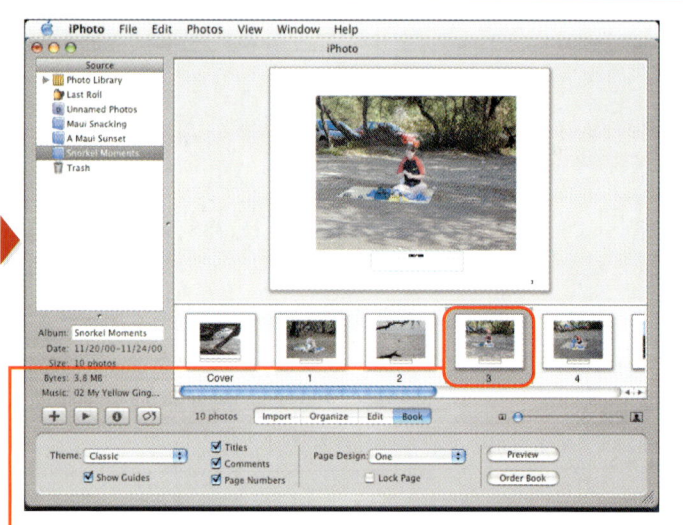

CHANGE A PAGE'S LAYOUT

1. Click **Book**.
2. Click a page in the book.

■ The page appears in the Page View pane.

3. Click the Page Design.
4. Select a page design.

■ The selected page reflects the new page design.

■ The surrounding pages also change to accommodate the new page design.

154

8 Using Photos with iPhoto

WORKING WITH IPHOTO

What does the Lock Page option do?

When you change page layouts in a book, pictures may move from one page to another. You click the **Lock Page** option (☐ changes to ☑) to keep the pictures on a page from moving when you change the layout of another page. A Lock icon (🔒) appears below the page thumbnail beside the page number on locked pages.

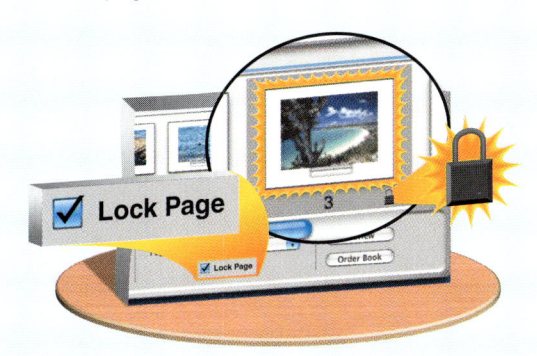

Why does my album's slideshow change when I change the order of the pages in my book?

A book and a slideshow are just different ways to look at the same album. Moving the pages in a book changes the order of the pictures in the album. You need to duplicate the album if you want the pictures in the book to appear in a different order than in the slideshow. To duplicate an album, click it, then click **Photos**, and then click **Duplicate**.

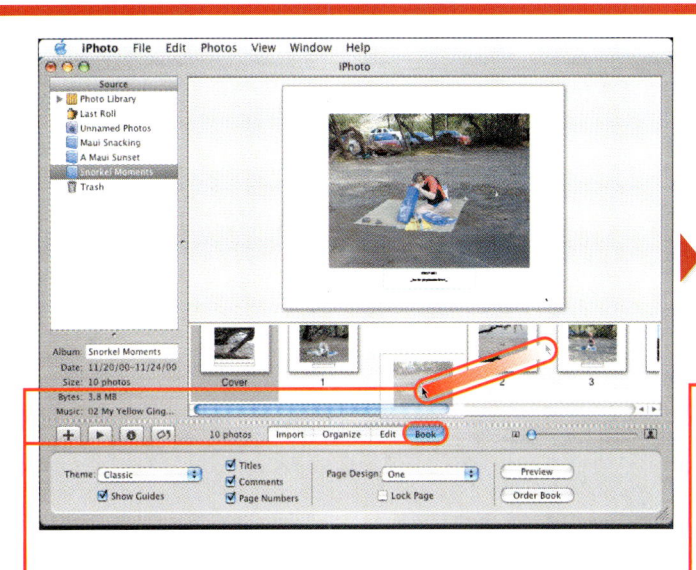

MOVE A PAGE IN A BOOK

1 Click **Book**.

2 Click a page thumbnail and drag it.

■ The thumbnail becomes translucent, and the surrounding thumbnails move out of the way to make space for it as it moves.

3 Release the mouse when the page is where you want it.

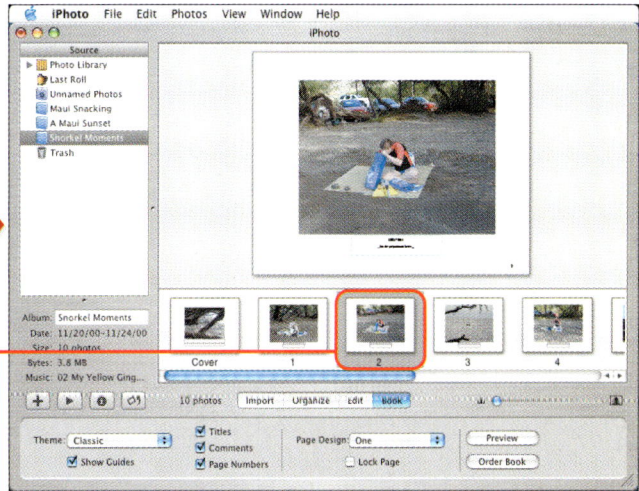

■ The page appears in its new position and the thumbnail becomes opaque.

Note: You cannot move a page to the left of the cover, nor can you move the cover to another position.

155

ADD AND CHANGE A PHOTO BOOK'S CAPTIONS

Pictures in a photo book can use the titles and comments you have given photos as captions. You can edit the captions and change their appearance.

To create a photo book, see the section "Make a Photo Book." To have Apple publish your photo book, see the section "Preview and Order a Photo Book." See Chapter 6 for more about adding titles and comments to photos.

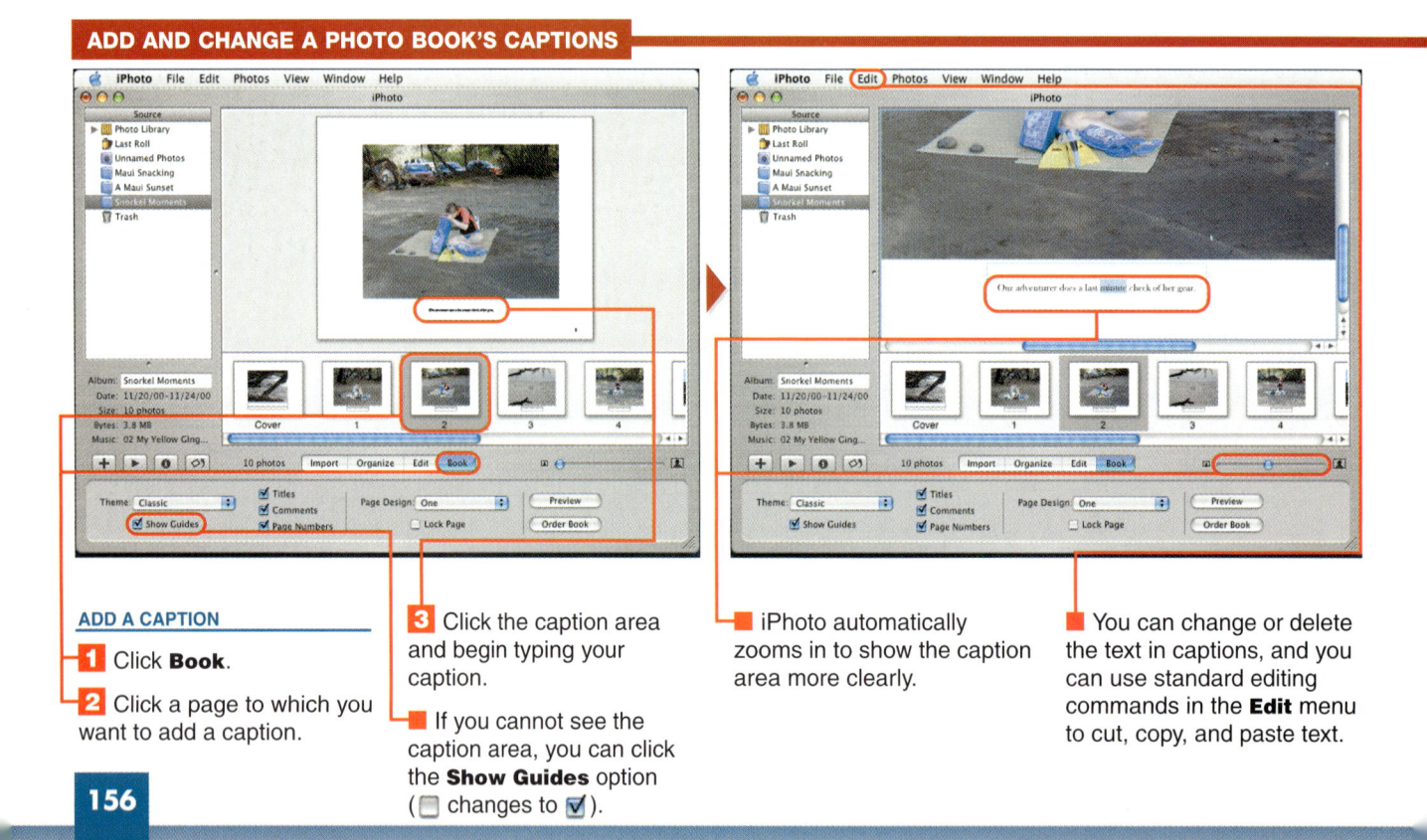

ADD AND CHANGE A PHOTO BOOK'S CAPTIONS

ADD A CAPTION

1 Click **Book**.

2 Click a page to which you want to add a caption.

3 Click the caption area and begin typing your caption.

■ If you cannot see the caption area, you can click the **Show Guides** option (☐ changes to ☑).

■ iPhoto automatically zooms in to show the caption area more clearly.

■ You can change or delete the text in captions, and you can use standard editing commands in the **Edit** menu to cut, copy, and paste text.

156

8 Using Photos with iPhoto

WORKING WITH IPHOTO

The book theme that I am using covers most of my page numbers. Should I hide them?

You should hide them if you plan to use Apple's book service to print a bound book. Apple may cancel Book orders if photos cover more than half the page numbers.

Which fonts can I use in my book's captions?

Although iPhoto lets you use any font installed on your Mac in a photo book, Apple recommends that you only use certain fonts in your books to avoid possible truncated text or a canceled printing order. The recommended fonts are Helvetica, Helvetica Neue, Century Gothic, Papyrus, Gill Sans, Marker Felt, Baskerville, and Brush Script.

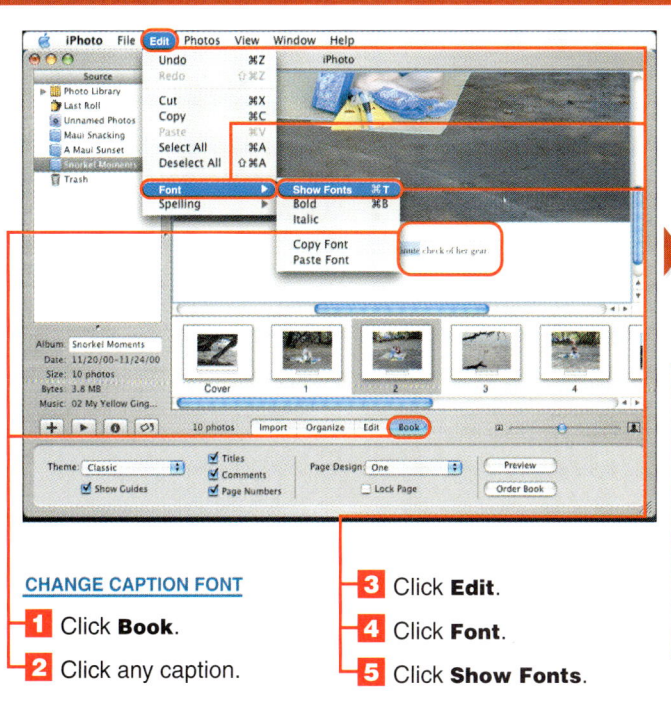

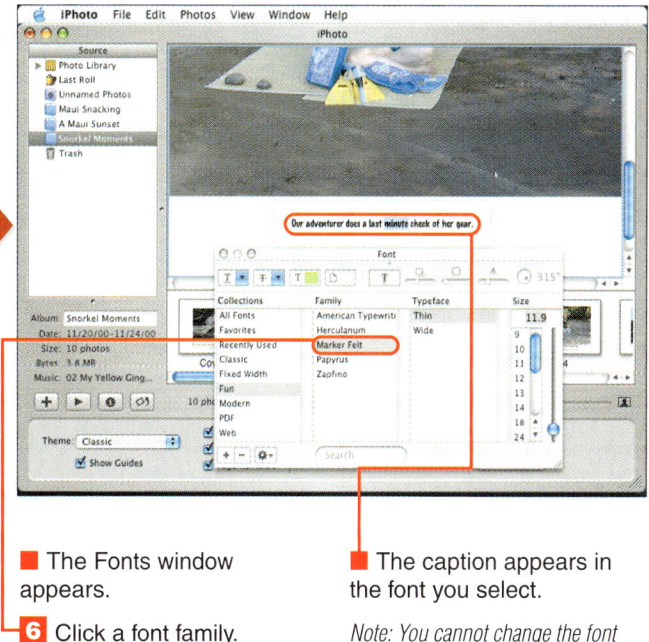

CHANGE CAPTION FONT

1 Click **Book**.

2 Click any caption.

3 Click **Edit**.

4 Click **Font**.

5 Click **Show Fonts**.

■ The Fonts window appears.

6 Click a font family.

■ The caption appears in the font you select.

Note: You cannot change the font size, and you cannot mix fonts in a book's captions.

157

PREVIEW AND ORDER A PHOTO BOOK

You can preview how the pages of your photo book will look when you print them. When you are satisfied, you can order a professionally printed, linen-covered, hardback photo book directly from Apple.

You need an Apple iPhoto Account and an active Internet connection to order a book. See the section, "Set Up an iPhoto Account with Apple" for how to create an iPhoto Account. For more on creating and editing a photo book, see the sections "Make a Photo Book," "Arrange a Photo Book's Pages," and "Add and Change a Photo Book's Captions."

PREVIEW AND ORDER A PHOTO BOOK

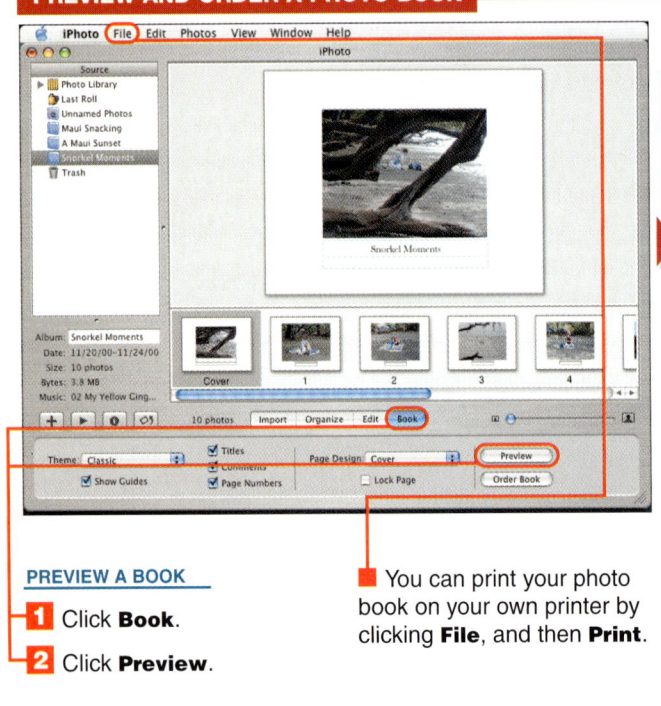

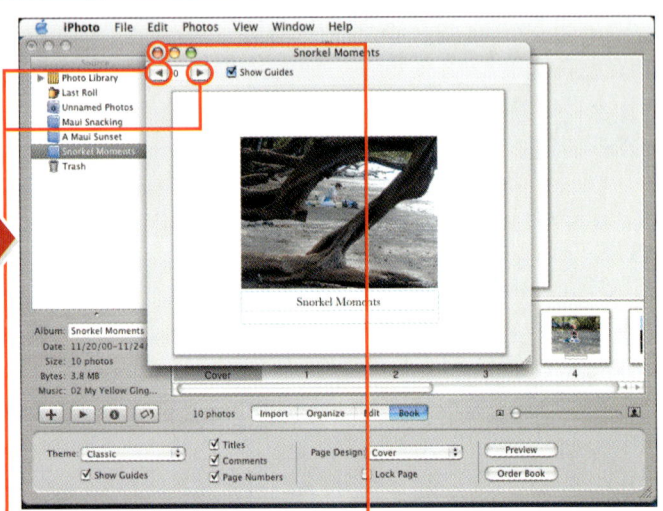

PREVIEW A BOOK

1. Click **Book**.
2. Click **Preview**.

■ You can print your photo book on your own printer by clicking **File**, and then **Print**.

■ A book preview window appears with the title of your book.

■ You can click the Forward (▶) and Back (◀) buttons to move forward or backward through the pages of your book.

■ You can click the Close button (●) when you are done to close the preview window.

158

8 Using Photos with iPhoto

WORKING WITH IPHOTO

When I order a photo book, what does it mean when an exclamation mark appears beside one of my captions?

It means that your caption is too long to fit in the caption area and that some of it will not print. If the bound book that you are ordering contains truncated captions, you receive an additional warning. You may want to delete some text in the caption or change the caption font to one that is more compact. For more information on editing your captions, see the section, "Add and Change a Photo Book's Captions."

How should I crop pictures that I want to use in a book?

iPhoto's book themes are all designed for pictures that have a 4:3 aspect ratio. If you do not crop your pictures to that ratio, Apple may crop or align them incorrectly when it prints the book.

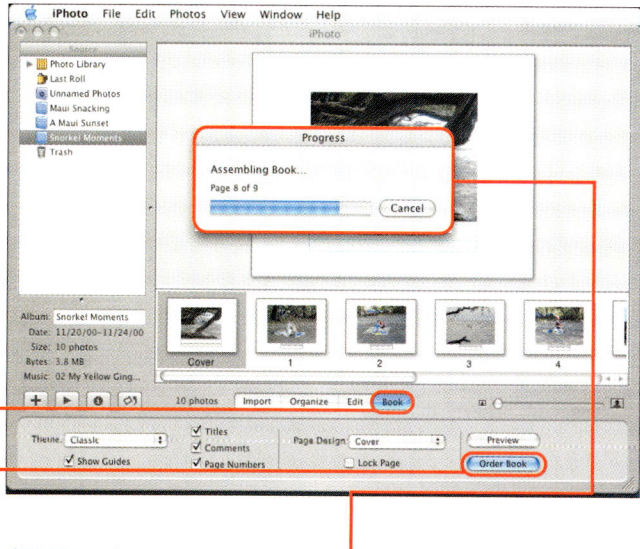

ORDER A BOUND PHOTO BOOK

1 Click **Book**.

2 Click **Order Book**.

■ iPhoto assembles the book.

Note: The minimum number of pages in a bound book is ten; if your book has fewer than ten, you are charged for ten pages.

■ The Order Book window appears.

■ You can click here and select a book cover color.

■ You can type the number of books you want to order here.

3 Click **Buy Now**.

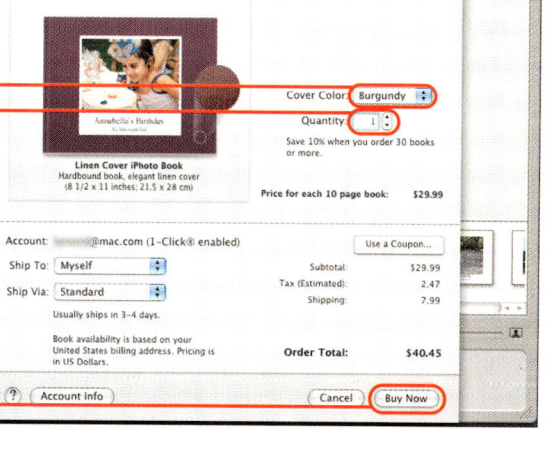

■ iPhoto transfers the book's photos to Apple and presents a confirmation window when the transfer is finished.

Note: It may take several minutes to transfer the photos, depending on their number and the speed of your Internet connection.

159

CREATE A .MAC WEB PAGE

If you have an Apple .Mac subscription, iPhoto can create attractive Web pages containing your photos. You can place your Web pages on your .Mac Web site so you can share them with the world.

Please note that you need an active Internet connection and an Apple .Mac account to complete the steps in this section. You can create a .Mac account from the .Mac preference pane in your Mac's System Preferences.

CREATE A .MAC WEB PAGE

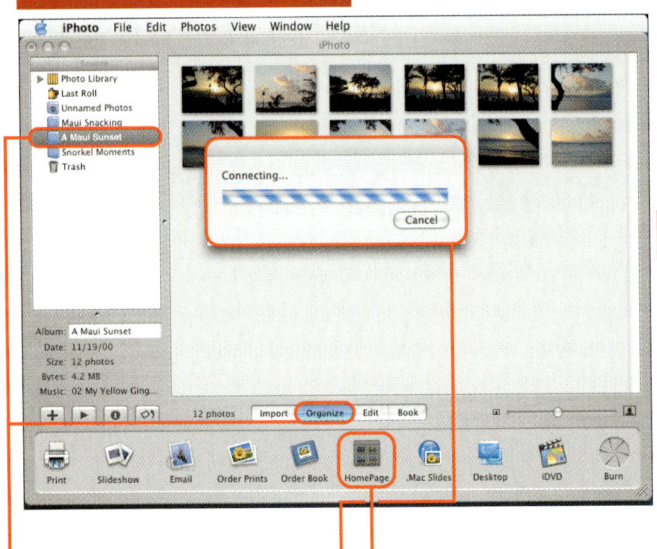

1 Click **Organize**.

2 Click an album that you want to publish.

- You can Shift+click, or ⌘+click, to select individual photos from an album or the iPhoto Library instead.

3 Click the **HomePage** button.

Note: Apple uses the name HomePage for its .Mac Web publishing service.

- A connection dialog briefly appears.

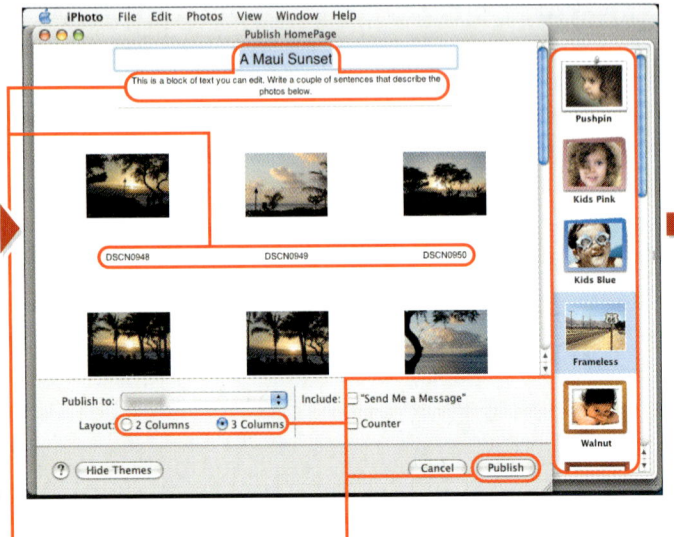

- The Publish HomePage window appears.

- You can click the page and photo captions and type replacement text to edit them.

- You can click a design theme for your Web page.

- You can click here and select a 2-column or 3-column layout (○ changes to ●).

4 Click **Publish**.

160

8 Using Photos with iPhoto

WORKING WITH IPHOTO

What is a .Mac account?

Apple's .Mac is a yearly subscription service that provides on-line storage for files, an e-mail account, its HomePage Web publishing service, and some free software packages. When you first set up your Mac, you are given the opportunity to create a .Mac account. You can also apply for one at any time from the .Mac preference pane in Mac OS X's System Preferences.

How many pictures can I place on my .Mac Web page?

You can have as many as 48 photos on any single .Mac page that you create using iPhoto. However, you can have more than one .Mac photo page on your .Mac Web site.

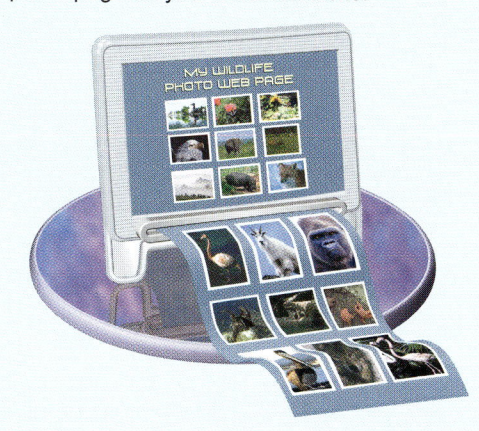

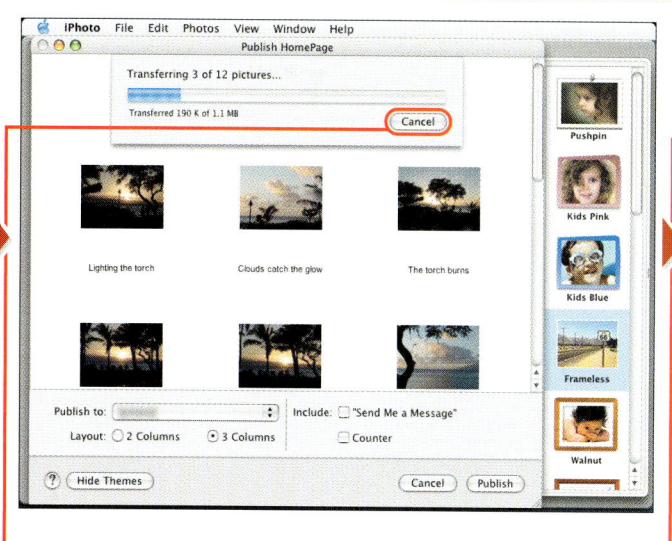

■ A sheet descends from the Publish HomePage window's title informing you of the progress of the photo transfer from your computer to .Mac.

■ You can click **Cancel** if you change your mind.

Note: The photo transfer can take several minutes, depending on the number of photos you are transferring and the speed of your Internet connection.

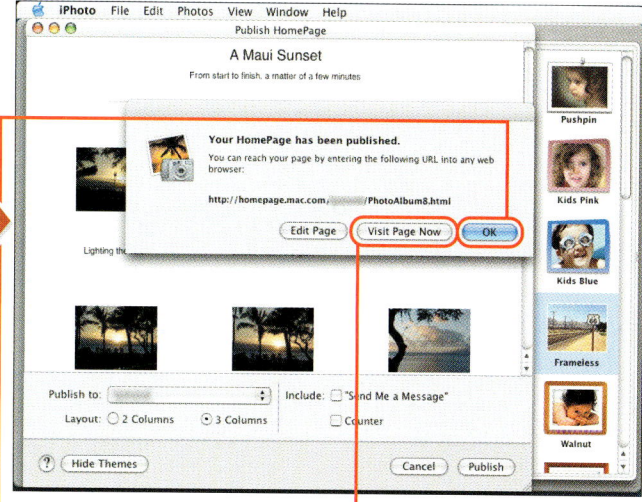

■ A dialog window appears when the transfer completes.

5 Click **OK**.

■ You can click **Visit Page Now** to view the new page in a Web browser.

■ The Publish HomePage window closes.

161

EXPORT WEB PAGES

iPhoto can export Web pages from any album or group of photos. You can use these Web pages on any Web site, regardless of whether you have a .Mac account.

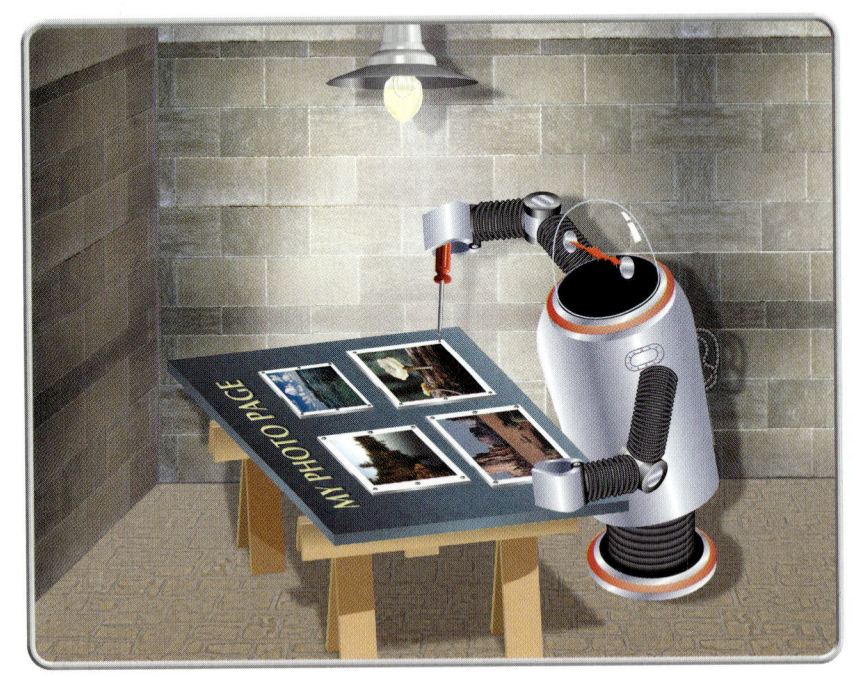

EXPORT WEB PAGES

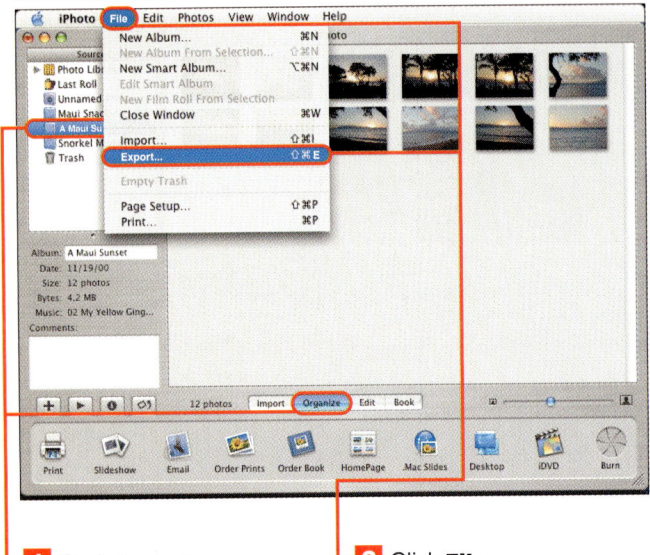

1 Click **Organize**.

2 Select an album that you want to export as Web pages.

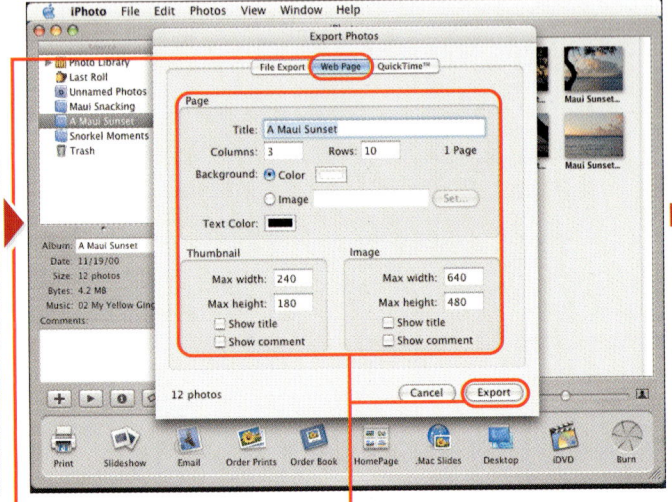

■ You can Shift+click, or ⌘+click, to select individual photos from an album or the iPhoto Library instead.

3 Click **File**.

4 Click **Export**.

■ The Export Photos window appears.

5 Click the **Web Page** tab.

■ The Web Page pane appears in the Export Photos window.

■ You can control the appearance of the exported Web pages by clicking these options or typing values for the various parameters.

6 Click **Export**.

162

8 Using Photos with iPhoto

WORKING WITH IPHOTO

What files and folders does iPhoto create when I export a Web page.

iPhoto creates three folders and one HTML file, and names them after the folder in which you save them. For example, if you export your photos to a folder named Maui Sunset, iPhoto calls the HTML file Maui Sunset.html, the folder containing the photos Maui Sunset-Images, the folder containing the image thumbnails Maui Sunset-Thumbnails, and the folder containing the Web pages for each of the images Maui Sunset-Pages.

What does the Background Image setting do?

You can pick an image that you want to have appear as the background of your Web page. In the Web Page export pane, click **Image** and then click **Set** to select an image from your hard disk to appear as the page's background. If the page is larger than the image you select, the image appears tiled and repeats itself horizontally and vertically as needed. You should select a subtle image for a background so as not to distract your audience from the page's contents.

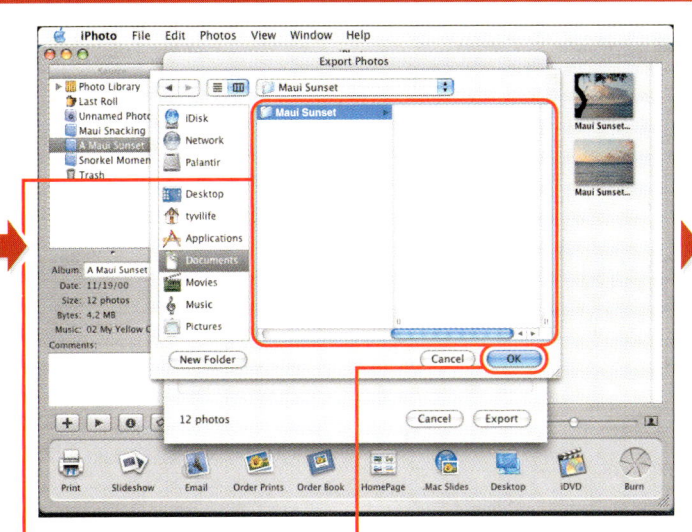

■ A sheet descends from the top of the Export Photos window.

7 Select a destination for the exported Web pages.

Note: See Chapter 1 for more on how to save files on the Macintosh.

8 Click **OK**.

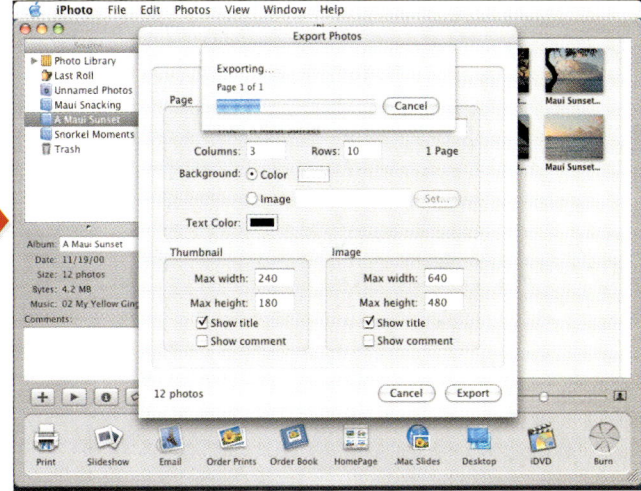

■ A progress sheet descends from the top of the Export Photos window.

■ When the export completes, the Export Photos window closes.

■ iPhoto places your exported Web pages in the folder you selected.

163

PUBLISH A SLIDESHOW ON .MAC

With iPhoto and a .Mac account, you can publish a slideshow of your photos that you can share with your family and friends in the form of a screen saver.

Please note that you need an active Internet connection and an Apple .Mac account to complete the steps in this section and that people viewing the slideshow need Mac OS X 10.2 or higher. See the section "Create a .Mac Web Page" for more on creating a .Mac account.

PUBLISH A SLIDESHOW ON .MAC

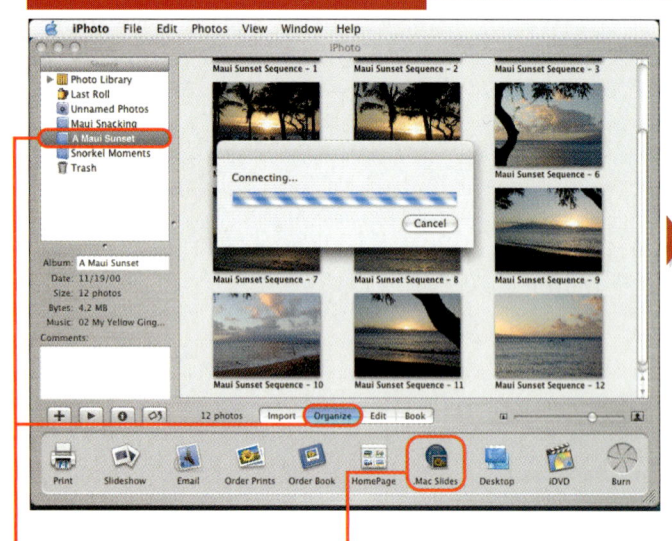

■ **1** Click **Organize**.

■ **2** Select an album that you want to make into a .Mac slideshow.

■ You can Shift+click, or ⌘+click, to select individual photos from an album or the iPhoto Library instead.

■ **3** Click the **.Mac Slides** button.

■ A progress dialog appears as your Mac connects.

■ A dialog window appears, asking you to confirm that you want to publish a slideshow.

Note: If you have previously published a .Mac slideshow, the new one replaces it.

■ You can click **Learn More** to read iPhoto's Help entries regarding .Mac slideshows.

■ **4** Click **Publish**.

8 Using Photos with iPhoto

WORKING WITH IPHOTO

How can other people use my .Mac slideshow?

You and other Mac users can follow these steps to see your .Mac slideshow in Mac OS X 10.3.

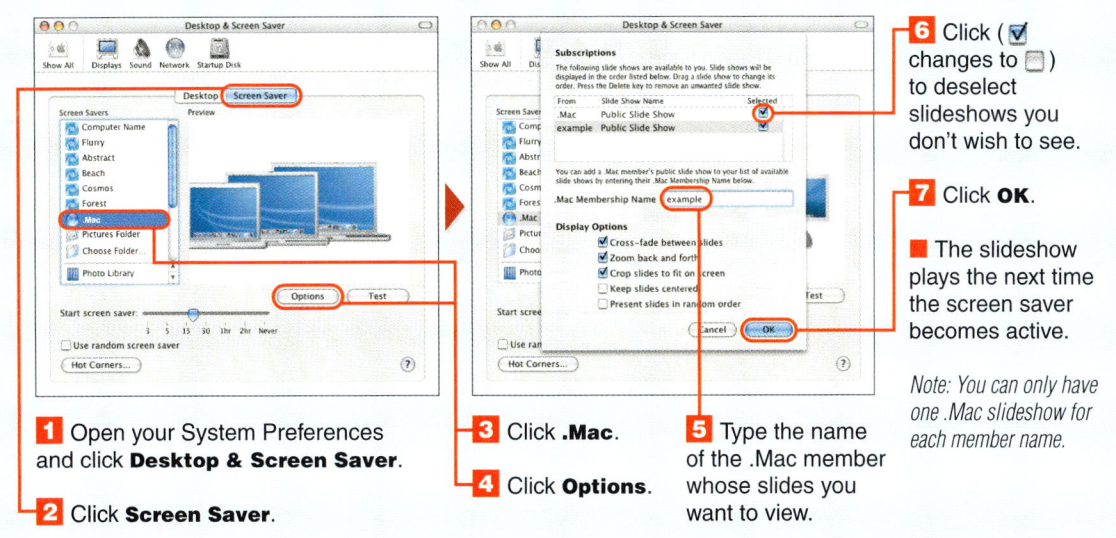

1 Open your System Preferences and click **Desktop & Screen Saver**.

2 Click **Screen Saver**.

3 Click **.Mac**.

4 Click **Options**.

5 Type the name of the .Mac member whose slides you want to view.

6 Click (☑ changes to ☐) to deselect slideshows you don't wish to see.

7 Click **OK**.

■ The slideshow plays the next time the screen saver becomes active.

Note: You can only have one .Mac slideshow for each member name.

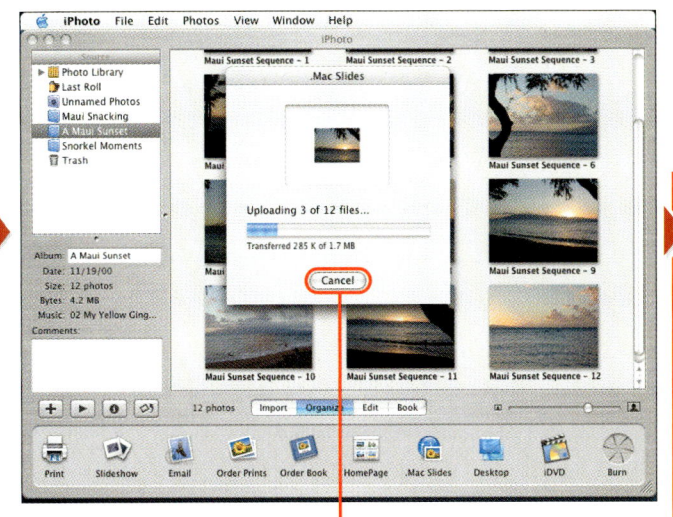

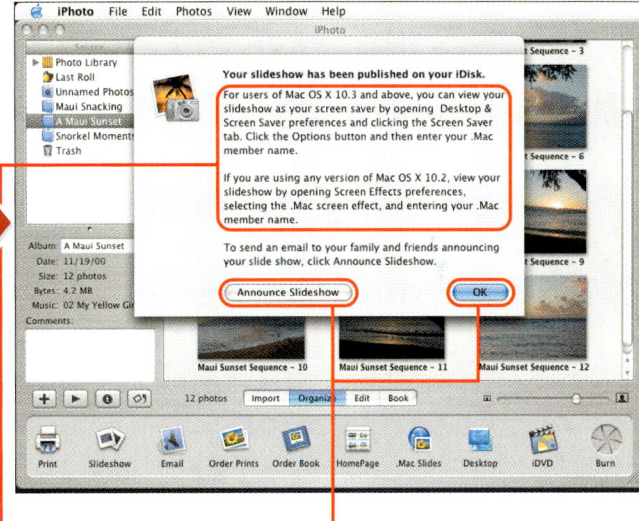

■ The .Mac Slides window appears, showing you the progress of the photo transfer to your .Mac account.

■ You can click **Cancel** if you change your mind about publishing the slideshow.

*Note: Even if you cancel at this point, any previously existing .Mac slideshow is deleted—clicking **Cancel** only cancels the transfer.*

■ A dialog tells you that iPhoto has published the slideshow.

■ The dialog contains instructions for viewing the slideshow.

■ You can click **Announce Slideshow** to open your e-mail program and send e-mail with viewing instructions to your friends.

5 Click **OK**.

■ The dialog window closes.

165

USING A PHOTO AS A DESKTOP PICTURE

You can use any photo in your iPhoto Library as your Mac's Desktop picture. You can even have your Mac's Desktop picture automatically alternate between several photos.

USING A PHOTO AS A DESKTOP PICTURE

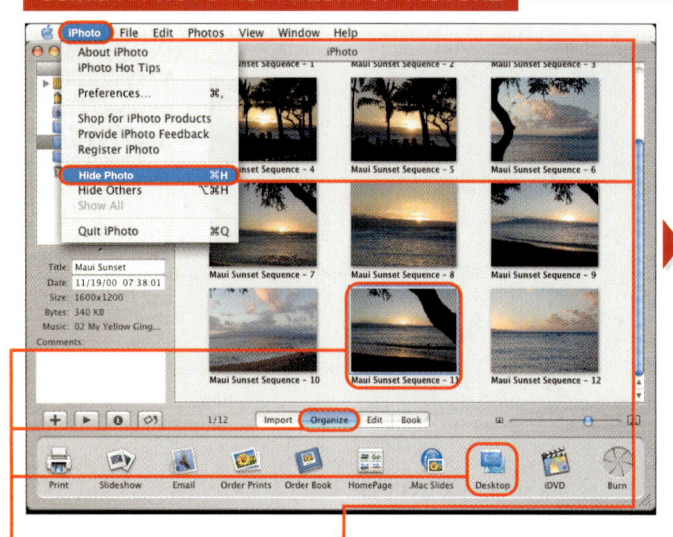

SELECT AND DISPLAY A DESKTOP IMAGE

1. Click **Organize**.
2. Click the image you want to display.
3. Click the **Desktop** icon.

■ The Desktop image changes behind the iPhoto window.

4. Click **iPhoto**.
5. Click **Hide iPhoto**.

■ iPhoto's window disappears, revealing the new Desktop image.

6. Click iPhoto's dock icon to show the iPhoto window.

166

8 Using Photos with iPhoto

WORKING WITH IPHOTO

How can I change back to the standard Desktop picture?

You can change the desktop background back to a standard background by using System Preferences' Desktop & Screen Saver settings. The standard desktop backgrounds are available in the collection called Apple Background Images. You can open System Preferences by clicking the Apple menu ( ) and then selecting **System Preferences**.

How should I crop my photos for use on the desktop?

It depends on the Mac you have and the screen resolution you use. For a 17-inch monitor set to a 1280 x 1024 resolution, you should crop the photo to a 5:4 aspect ratio. For a 17-inch wide-screen iMac set to a 1440 x 900 resolution, the aspect ratio is 8:5. Note that the System Preferences' Desktop preference lets you center, tile, or stretch pictures that do not fit the screen.

SELECT MULTIPLE DESKTOP PICTURES

7 Click **Organize**.

8 Shift +click, or ⌘+click, to select several photos.

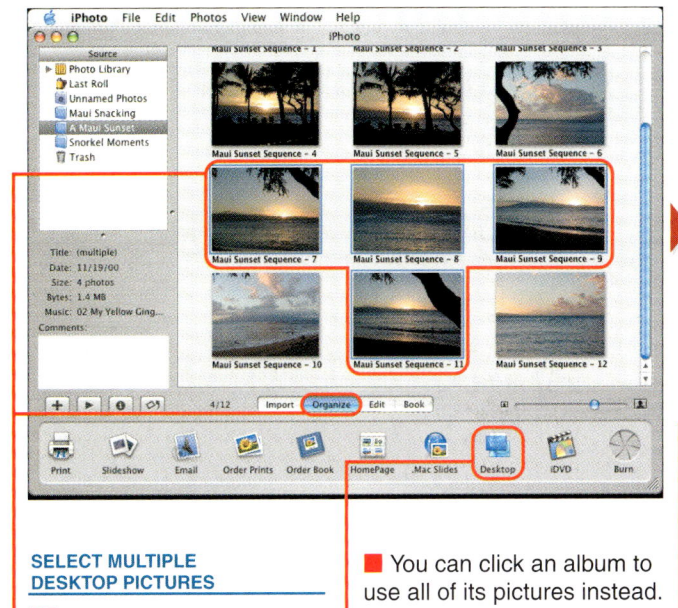

■ You can click an album to use all of its pictures instead.

9 Click the **Desktop** icon.

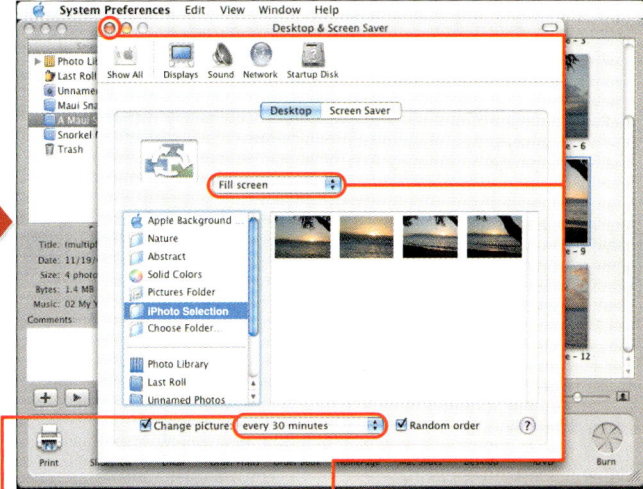

■ System Preferences opens and displays the Desktop pane of the Desktop & Screen Saver preference panel.

■ You can click here and select how often the Desktop picture changes.

■ You can click here and select how the picture appears on the Desktop.

10 Click ● to close System Preferences.

■ The desktop picture periodically rotates among the selected photos.

167

EXPORT PHOTOS TO A HARD DISK

You can export one or more photos to a folder on your hard disk, either in their original sizes and formats, or scaled and converted to a single format. You can then use these pictures in a desktop publishing program or some other application, or give them to someone who does not have iPhoto.

EXPORT PHOTOS TO A HARD DISK

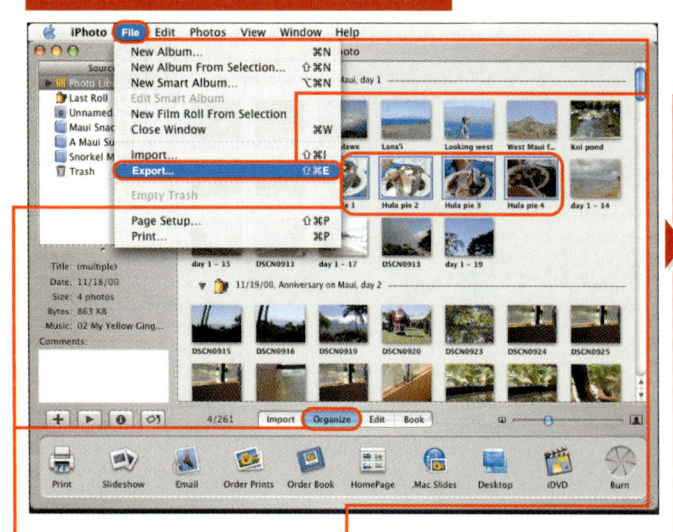

1 Click **Organize**.

2 Click one or more photos.

- You can Shift +click, or ⌘+click, to select several photos.

3 Click **File**.

4 Click **Export**.

- The Export Photos dialog window appears.

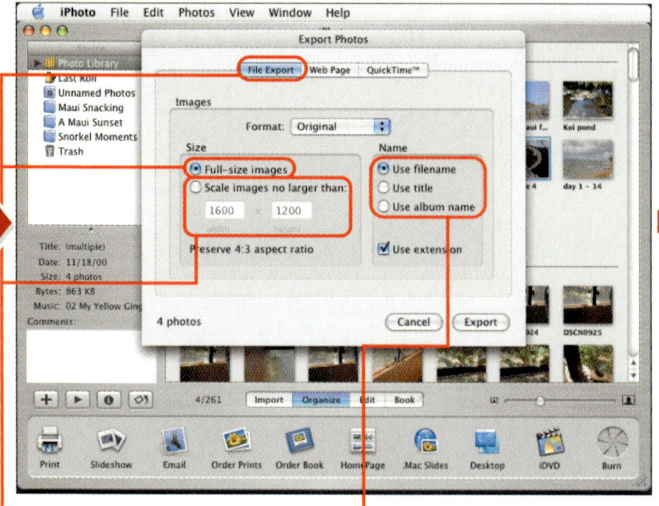

5 Click the **File Export** tab.

- You can click here to export full-sized images (○ changes to ●).

- You can click here (○ changes to ●) and type dimensions to scale your images to a specific size.

- You can click one of these options (○ changes to ●) to specify how iPhoto names exported files.

168

8 Using Photos with iPhoto

WORKING WITH IPHOTO

Why does the height change when I change the width of a photo in the Export Photos window?

iPhoto's export process always keeps the aspect ratios of the photos you export in order to prevent distortion. When you type a width or height, iPhoto calculates the other value to preserve the aspect ratio.

What happens when I type a width or height for a group of photos that have different aspect ratios?

iPhoto still preserves the aspect ratio of each image. The exported photos are never larger than the dimensions you type; for each photo, one of the two dimensions matches one of the dimensions you type, and the other dimension is smaller.

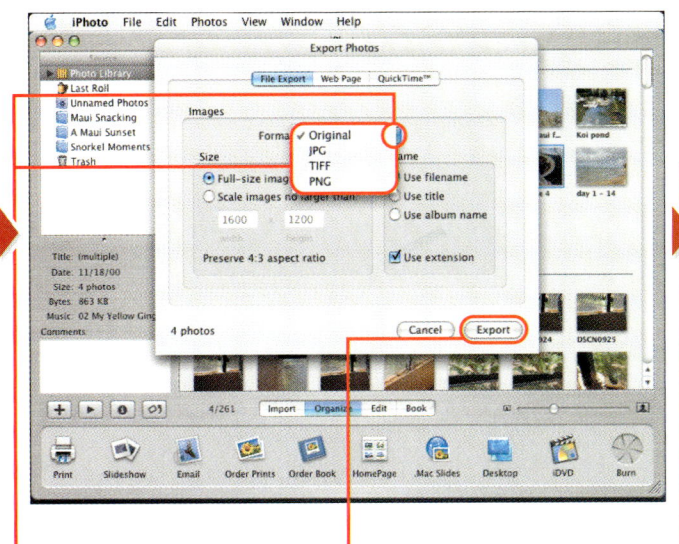

6 Click the Format.

7 Click a single format for all of the exported photos, or select **Original** to let them retain their formats.

Note: iPhoto does not scale TIFF- and PNG-format photos; select JPG if you want to scale the exported photos.

8 Click **Export**.

■ A sheet appears.

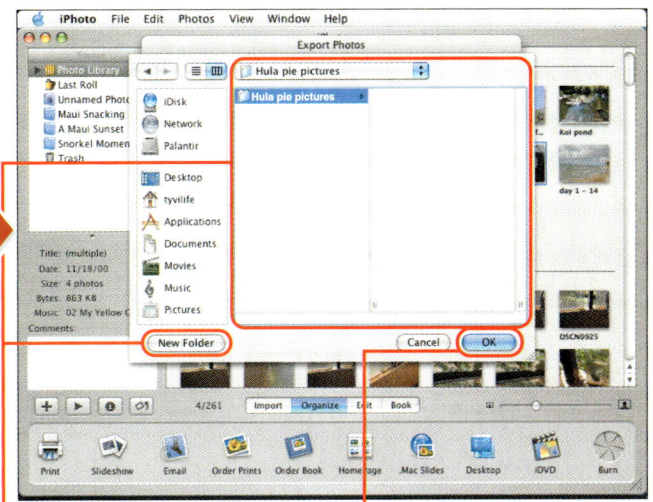

9 Specify where you want to save the exported photos.

Note: See Chapter 1 for more about saving files on the Mac.

■ You can click **New Folder** to create a new folder in which to place the photos.

10 Click **OK**.

■ The Export Photos window closes, and iPhoto saves the exported photos on your hard disk.

169

CREATE A CD OR DVD ARCHIVE

You can safely back up your photos by making an archive of part of or your entire iPhoto Library on CD or DVD. You should perform regular back-ups to protect your photos from hardware failures; the more pictures you take, the more often you should make back-ups.

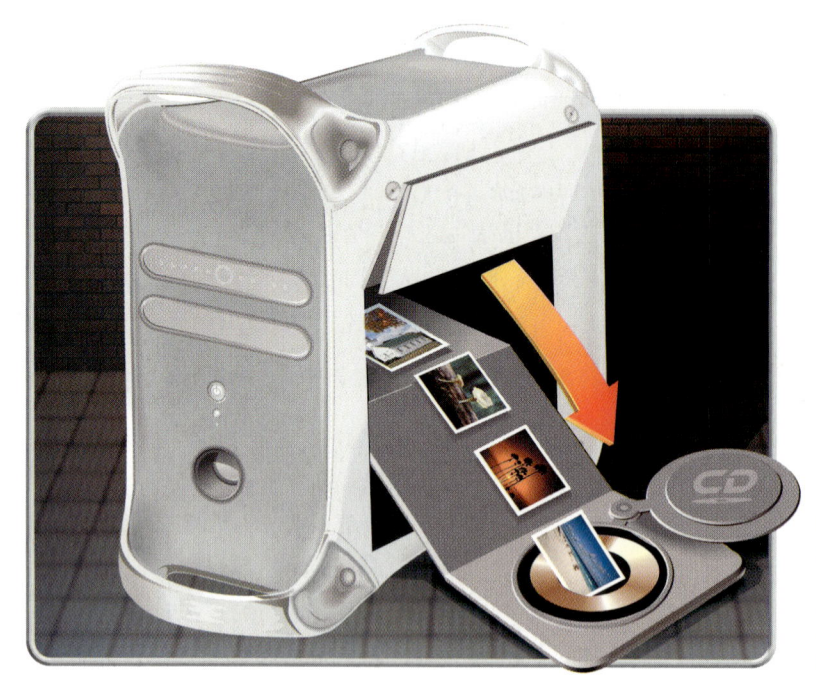

Please note that the steps in this section require a Mac with a CD burner or DVD burner.

CREATE A CD OR DVD ARCHIVE

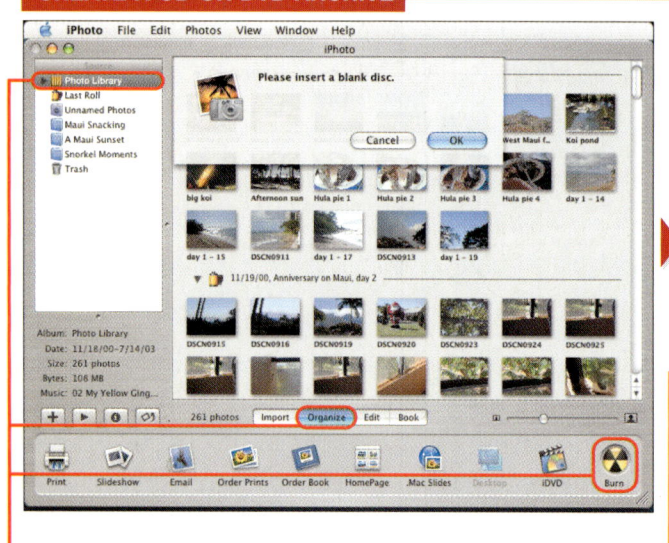

1 Click **Organize**.

2 Select the photos or album that you want to archive.

3 Click the **Burn** button.

■ The Burn icon animates and iPhoto requests that you insert a blank disc.

4 Insert a blank CD-R or DVD-R in your optical disc drive.

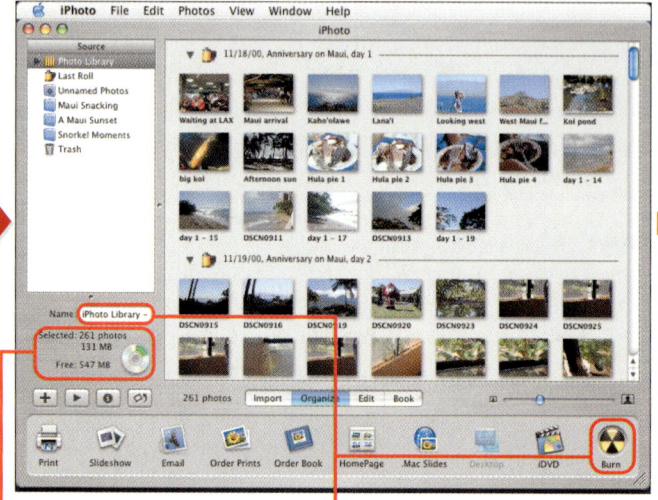

■ The Information area displays how many photos you are burning and how much disc space they require.

5 Click here and type a name for your archive.

6 Click the **Burn** button.

170

8 Using Photos with iPhoto

WORKING WITH IPHOTO

Why am I unable to open my archive CD on a Windows computer?

iPhoto burns Macintosh-formatted archive CDs that the Windows operating system does not recognize. You can make a Windows-compatible CD by first exporting your photos to your hard disk and then burning the CD through the Finder, which produces a Windows-compatible CD. For more information, see the section, "Export Photos to a Hard Disk."

Will CD or DVD archives I made with a previous version of iPhoto work with iPhoto version 4?

Yes, but the reverse is not true: you cannot use a CD or DVD archive made with version 4 of iPhoto with previous versions. You can, however, use the Finder to open the disk and copy the files from it manually into older versions of iPhoto. See Chapter 1 for more about using the Finder.

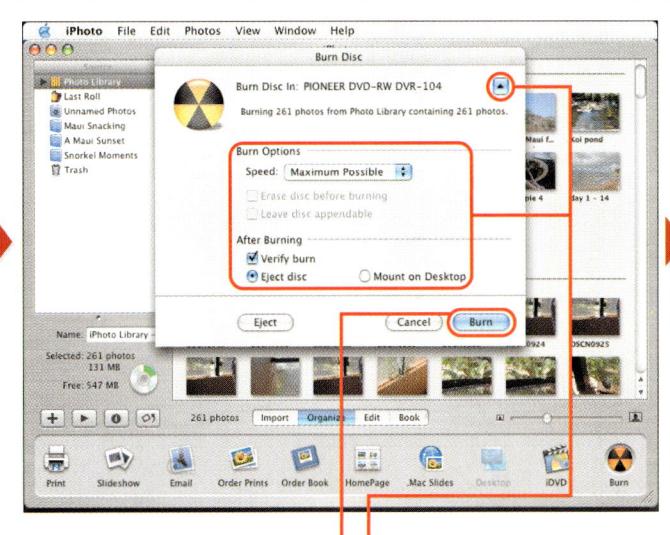

- ■ The Burn Disc dialog window appears, telling you how many photos iPhoto is burning to the disc.

- ■ You can click the button (▲) to expand the window and see additional burning options.

- **7** Click **Burn**.

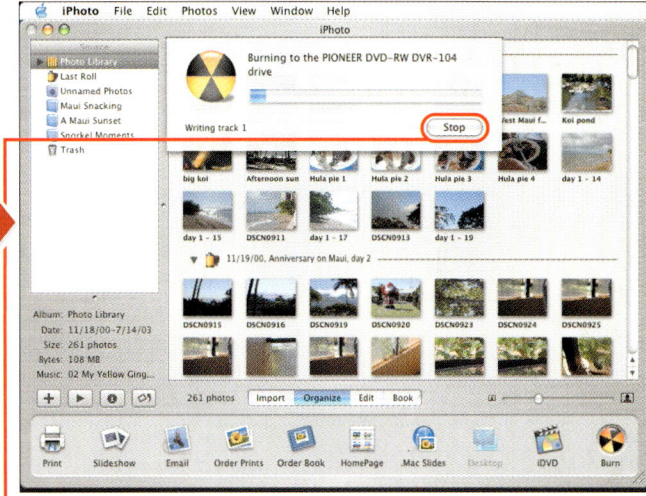

- ■ A Burning dialog window appears, displaying the progress of the disc burning.

- ■ You can click **Stop** to cancel the burning, although this makes the disc unusable.

- ■ When the burning finishes, the Burning dialog window closes, and iPhoto ejects the finished CD.

171

USING AN ARCHIVE CD OR DVD

iPhoto shows you the contents of archive CDs or DVDs that you make, including albums. You can copy photos from the archive to your current iPhoto Library. If you take a lot of pictures, you can keep your iPhoto Library trim and responsive by keeping older pictures in archives, but you can always see them if you need them.

USING AN ARCHIVE CD OR DVD

VIEW AN ARCHIVE DISC

1 Insert an archive CD or DVD into your Mac's optical disc drive.

■ The disc appears in the iPhoto albums list.

■ You can click the Show/Hide arrow to show or hide the albums in the archive.

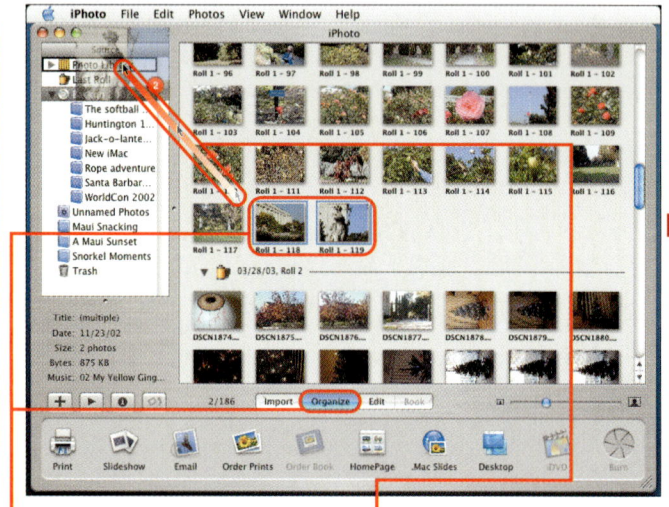

COPY PHOTOS FROM AN ARCHIVE

1 Click **Organize**.

2 Select the photos you want to copy from the archive.

■ You can Shift +click, or ⌘+click, to select several photos.

3 Click and drag any of the selected photos over the iPhoto Library.

■ As you drag, a translucent image of one of the photos follows the mouse; a black frame appears around the Library when the mouse is over it.

172

8 Using Photos with iPhoto

WORKING WITH IPHOTO

How can I restore my iPhoto library from an archive CD or DVD?

iPhoto creates a folder on the archive disc named **iPhoto Library**, which is the same name that iPhoto uses for the iPhoto library it creates in your Pictures folder. If you need to replace the library on your hard disk with your archive, quit iPhoto and use the Finder either to rename the iPhoto Library folder on your hard disk or to move it to another folder. Then copy the iPhoto Library folder from the archive disk to your hard disk. iPhoto uses the library folder you copied the next time you start iPhoto.

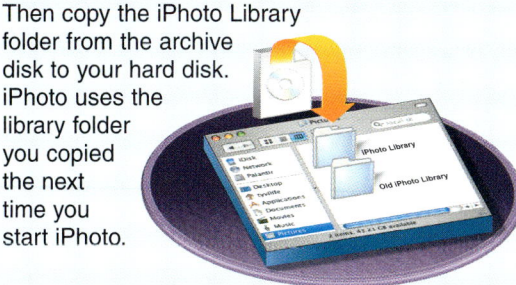

How can I use more than one iPhoto Library?

You can only use one iPhoto Library at a time, but you can have several on your hard disk and switch between them simply by renaming them. Quit iPhoto and use the Finder to rename your iPhoto Library folder, which is usually in your Pictures folder. When you start iPhoto again, it offers to let you find a library or to create a new one.

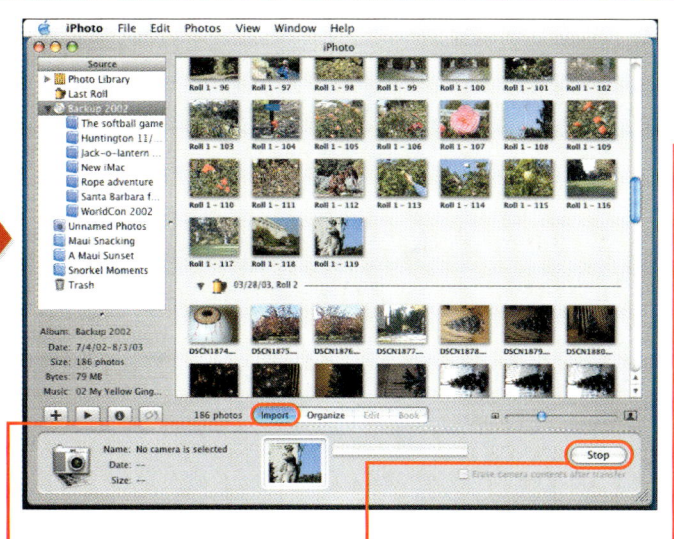

■ **4** Release the mouse button.

■ iPhoto switches to the Import view and displays the progress of the copy.

■ You can click **Stop** to cancel the copy before it is finished.

■ When the copy is complete, iPhoto switches back to the Organize view.

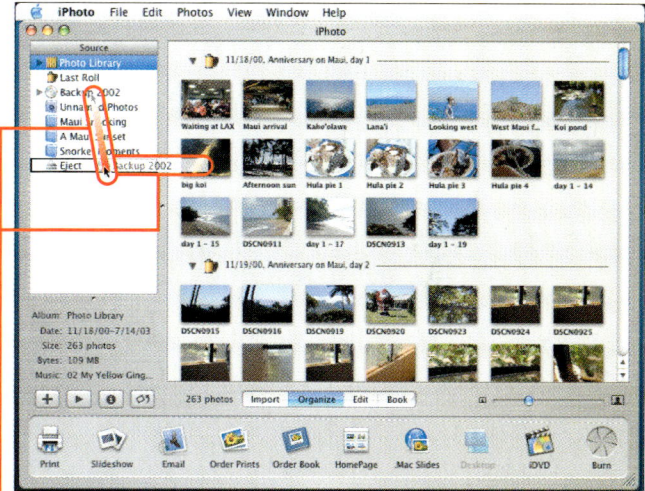

EJECT AN ARCHIVE DISC

1 Click and drag the disc archive toward iPhoto's Trash (🗑).

■ A translucent image of the disc follows the mouse (🗑 changes to ⏏).

■ A black frame appears around the Eject icon when the mouse is over it.

2 Release the mouse button.

■ The Mac ejects the disc.

173

iMovie File Edit View Bookmarks Advanced Window Help
iMovie
Welcome To iMovie
There is no project open. What would you like to do?
Open Existing Project...
Quit
Create Project...
PLAYER
RECORDER

PART IV

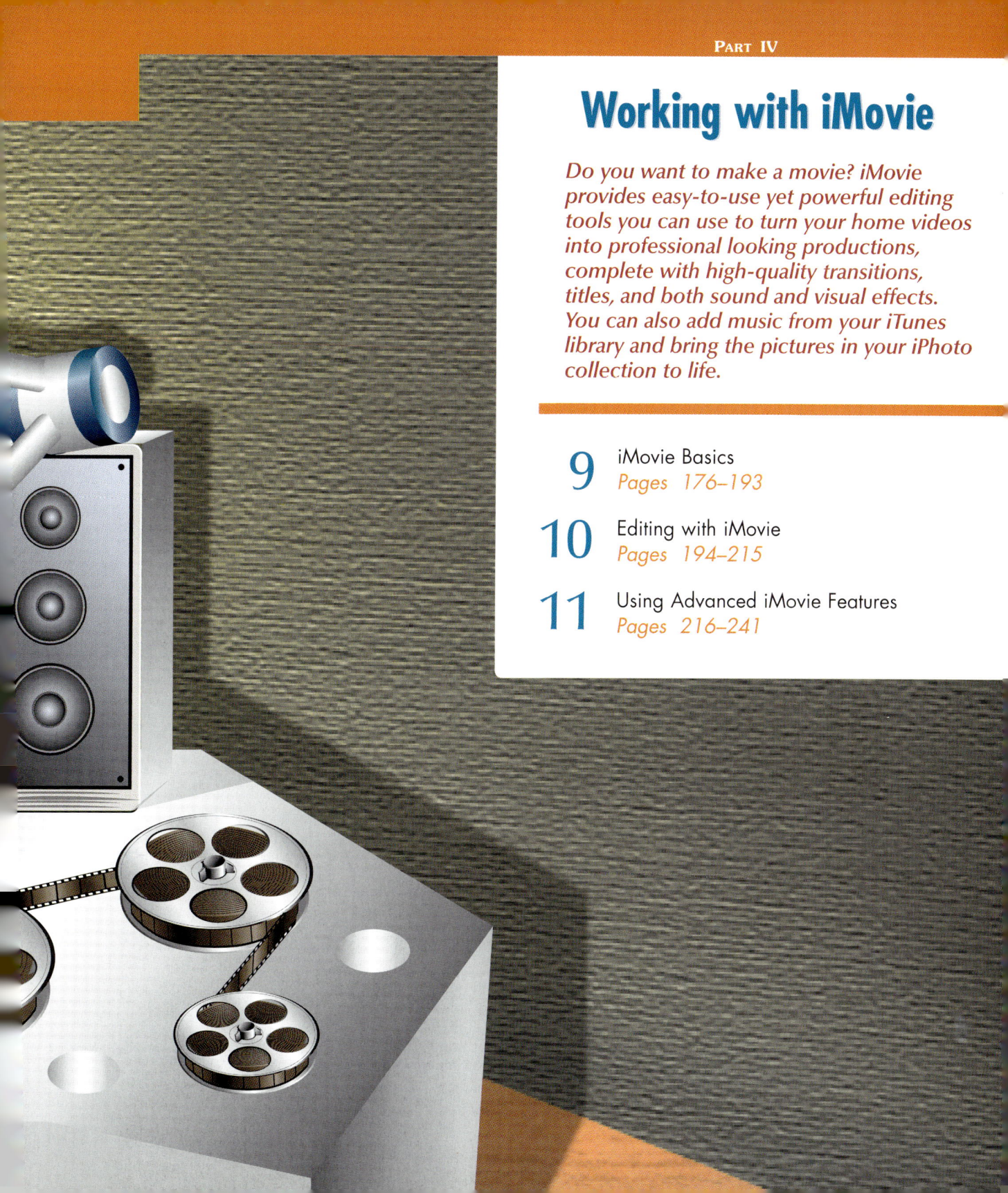

Working with iMovie

Do you want to make a movie? iMovie provides easy-to-use yet powerful editing tools you can use to turn your home videos into professional looking productions, complete with high-quality transitions, titles, and both sound and visual effects. You can also add music from your iTunes library and bring the pictures in your iPhoto collection to life.

9 iMovie Basics
Pages 176–193

10 Editing with iMovie
Pages 194–215

11 Using Advanced iMovie Features
Pages 216–241

SET UP IMOVIE

iMovie comes ready for you to use. Simply create a new project and you can begin assembling your movie.

iMovie comes pre-installed on most Macs and is in the Dock already; if you install iMovie from the iLife installer, the installation process places iMovie in the Dock as well.

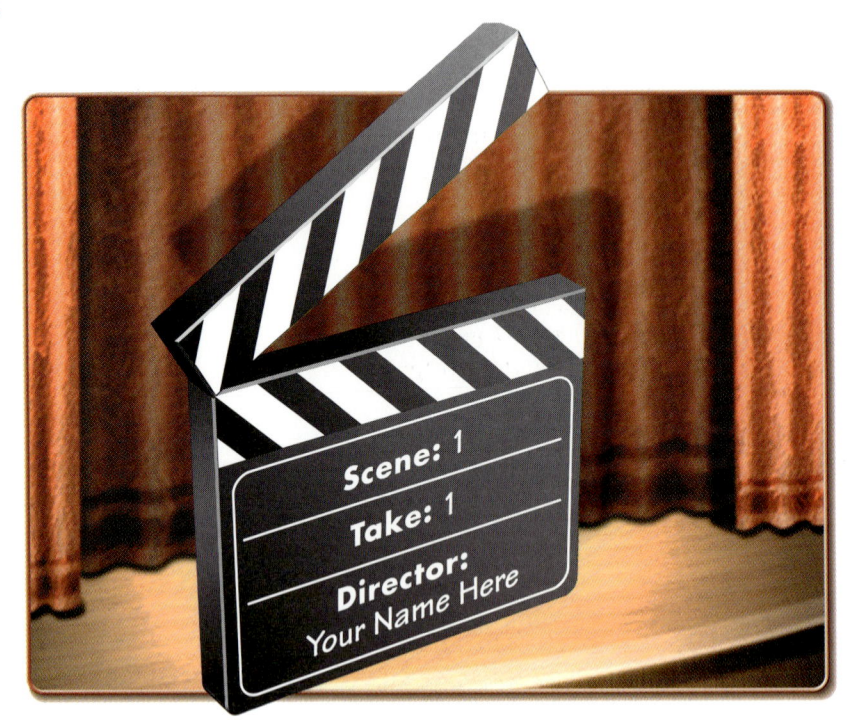

SET UP IMOVIE

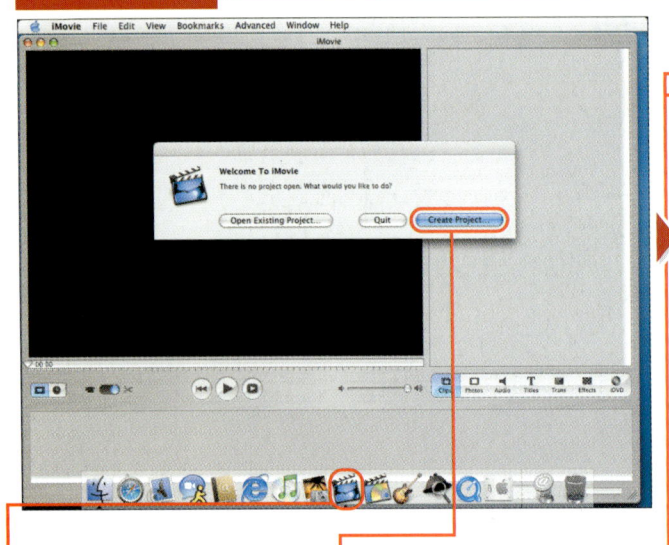

USING THE FIRST TIME

1 Click the iMovie icon ( ) in Dock.

■ The iMovie window appears with a Welcome To iMovie dialog window.

Note: iMovie always attempts to open the last movie project on which you worked. This dialog appears when iMovie cannot find the project, which is the case the first time you use iMovie.

2 Click **Create Project**.

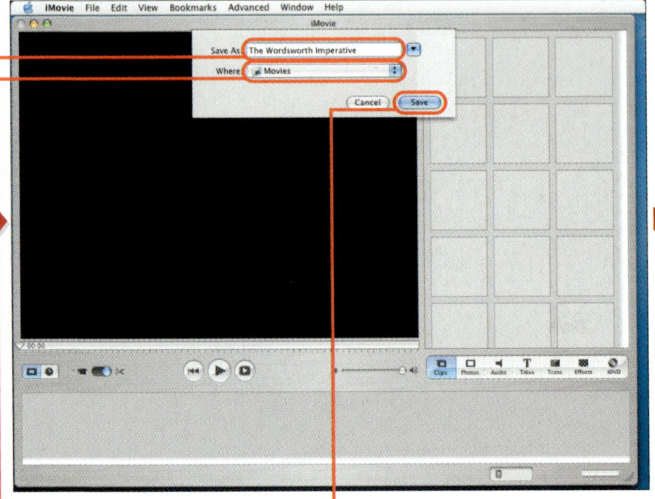

■ A sheet descends from the top of iMovie's window.

3 Click here and type a name for your movie project.

■ By default, iMovie offers to save your movie projects in the Movies folder in your Home directory.

Note: You can, however, save projects elsewhere. See Chapter 1 for more about managing files.

4 Click **Save**.

176

9 iMovie Basics

WORKING WITH IMOVIE

How much disk space does an iMovie project take up?

An iMovie project file itself takes up very little room because it only contains information about how the video clips and other elements of your project are arranged. However, the project's Media folder, which contains the actual video, audio, and other elements in the project, can take up large amounts of storage. For example, a minute of video consumes about 200MB.

Does iMovie work with the new HD (High Definition) video format?

No. iMovie is designed to work with consumer digital camcorders, most of which currently use standard video formats. You can, however, display standard video you create with iMovie on most HD televisions.

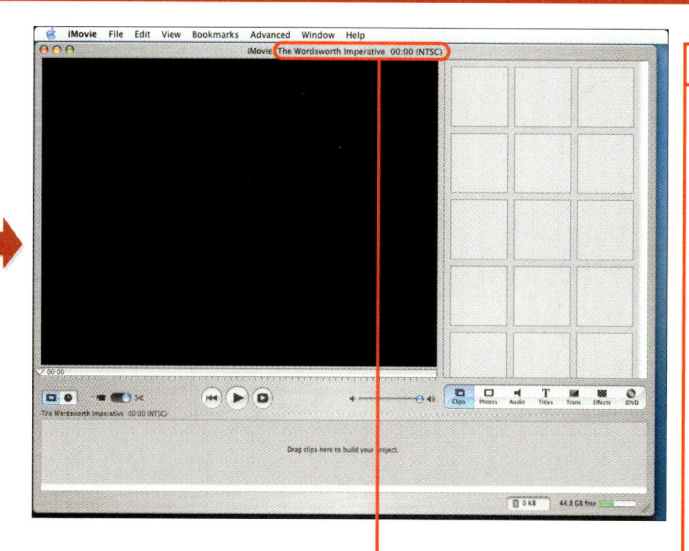

■ iMovie creates a new folder in the location you specified with the name you typed, and saves your iMovie project in it.

■ The name of the project, its current length, and its format appears in the iMovie window.

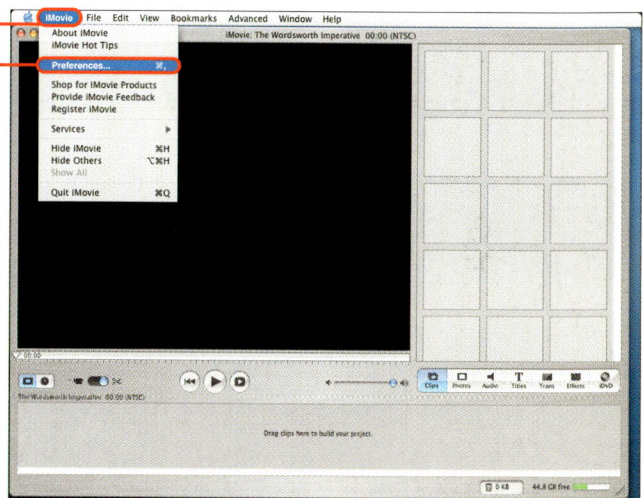

CHANGE IMOVIE PREFERENCES

1 Click **iMovie**.

2 Click **Preferences**.

■ The Preferences window appears.

CONTINUED

177

SET UP IMOVIE

Although iMovie comes with Preference settings that are appropriate for most users, you can change its settings to match your working style or environment.

SET UP IMOVIE (CONTINUED)

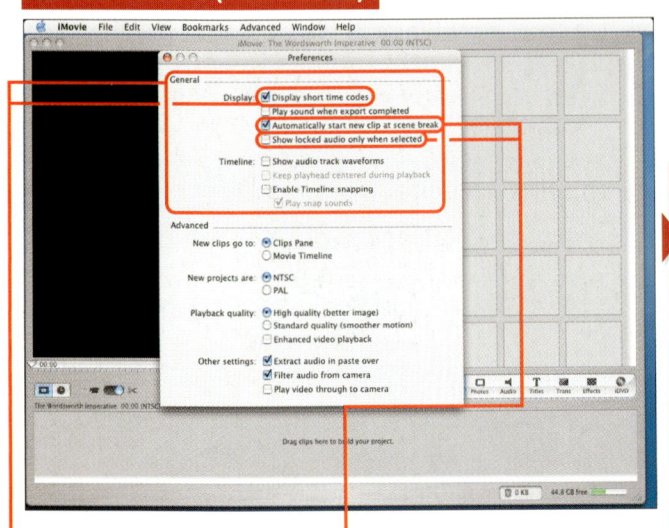

3 Click the General preferences that you want (☐ changes to ☑, or ◯ changes to ⦿).

■ Click here to change how iMovie displays time codes; short time codes can improve performance.

■ Click here to have iMovie create a new clip whenever it detects pauses while importing video.

■ Click here to see locked audio clip marks only when a locked clip is selected in order to reduce visual clutter.

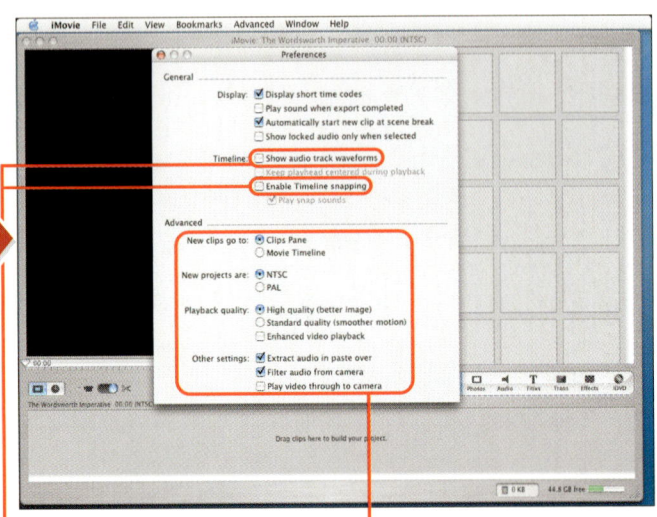

■ Click here to see audio waveforms in the Timeline, which can help you edit audio more precisely.

■ Click here to see indicator snaplines to help you edit more precisely when you drag clips near markers you set or other clip boundaries.

4 Click the Advanced preferences that you want to change.

178

9 iMovie Basics

WORKING WITH IMOVIE

What are NTSC and PAL?

NTSC and PAL are two of the most commonly used television video formats in the world. NTSC, short for National Television System Committee, is the format used for TV in the United States, featuring 29.97 frames of video per second and 525 lines of resolution per frame. PAL, short for Phase Alternating Line, is the format used in much of Europe. PAL uses 25 frames of video per second, and 625 lines of resolution per frame. iMovie can edit video in either format but cannot mix them in a single project.

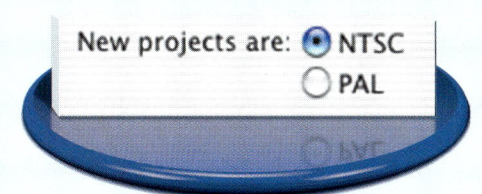

What does the Filter audio from camera setting do?

It sets iMovie to convert the camera's audio signal from the camera's own format to the format that works best with iMovie. In most cases, you should leave this option selected (☐ changes to ☑). If iMovie beeps when you import video, it may be because you did not set this option.

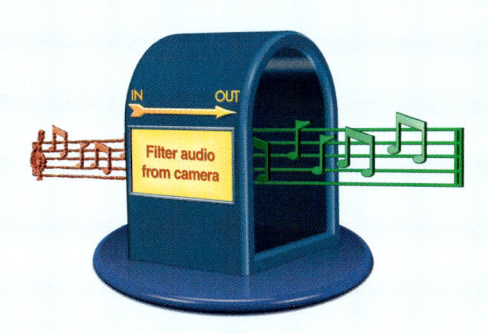

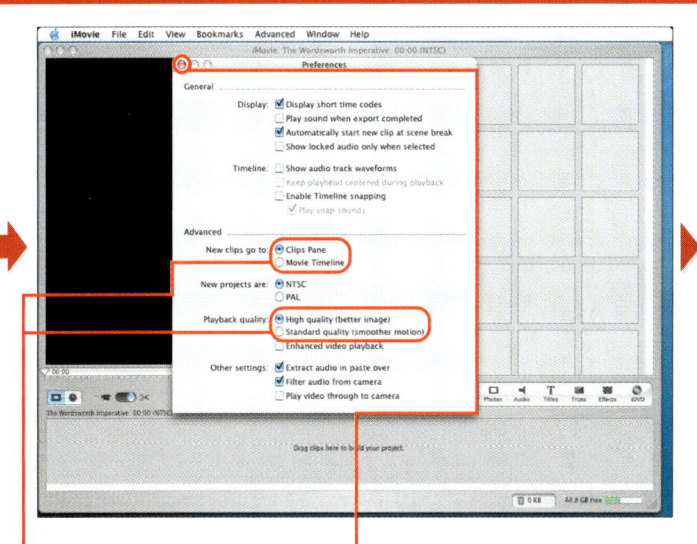

■ Click here to set where iMovie places the clips you import; you can move the clips after you import them.

■ Click here to adjust playback quality while editing; use Standard quality if iMovie skips or stutters.

■ Playback quality settings do not affect the finished movie.

5 Click the Close button (●).

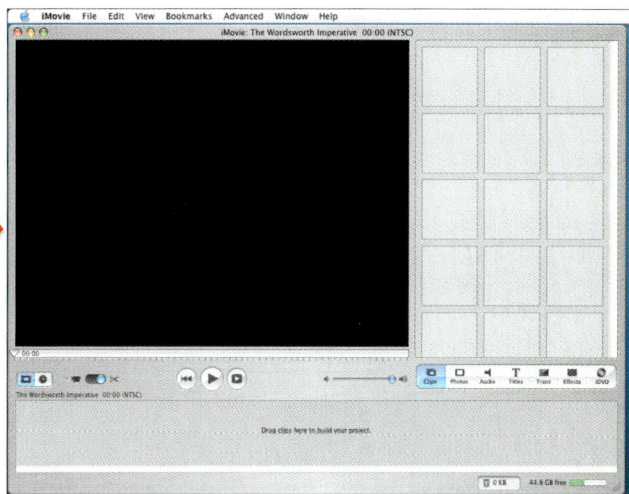

■ The Preferences window closes.

Note: You do not need to close the window to save your preferences; all changes take effect the moment you make them.

179

CONNECT A DIGITAL CAMCORDER

You connect your camcorder to your Mac with a FireWire cable. Doing so allows you to import your movies directly from your camcorder into iMovie. See the next section, "Import Video from a Digital Camcorder," to import your camcorder footage.

FireWire is sometimes called iLink by Sony, and is more formally known as IEEE 1394. Most digital camcorders have FireWire ports.

The steps in this section assume that no camera is attached to the Mac at first.

CONNECT A DIGITAL CAMCORDER

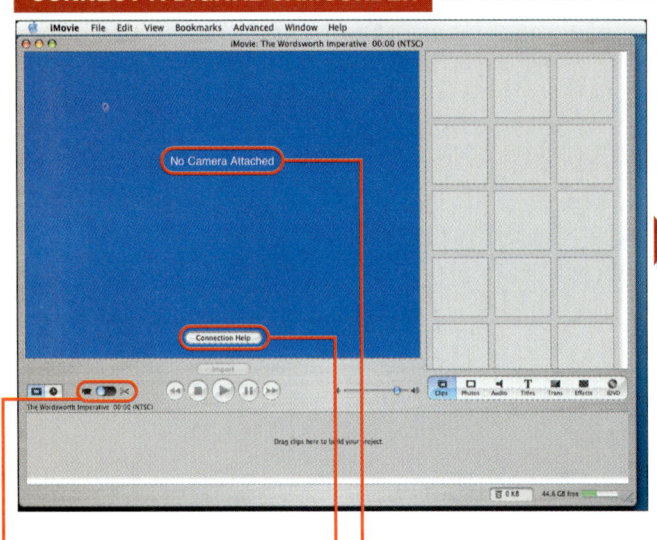

1 Click the mode switch.

■ The switch moves to Camera mode.

■ The Monitor displays a "No Camera Attached" message.

■ You can click here for instructions on connecting a camera.

2 Make sure the camcorder is turned off.

3 Connect the small end of the FireWire cable to the camcorder's FireWire port, making sure that the notch on the cable connector is properly aligned with the port.

4 Connect the large end of the FireWire cable to one of the Mac's FireWire ports, making sure that the narrow end of the cable connector is aligned with the narrow end of the port.

Note: To avoid damaging the ports, do not force the connectors.

9 iMovie Basics

WORKING WITH IMOVIE

Why are the two ends of the camera's FireWire cable different when the two ends of my iPod's FireWire cable are not?

A FireWire cable can have either four or six wires. The six-wire kind can carry power as well as information. You can charge the iPod from your Mac, so it needs a six-wire connector. A digital camcorder uses a separate power cable and does not need power from the FireWire cable, so it only needs a four-wire connector; the four-wire connector also takes up less room on the camera's body.

Do I need to plug the camcorder into an external power source when I use it with iMovie?

You can run your camcorder on battery power when you use it with iMovie, but you should keep an eye on the battery level as you work. It is safer to use a power cable if you plan to work with the camcorder for more than a few minutes.

---

5 Turn the camera's power on and place the camera into VTR mode.

Note: Many cameras combine the power and VTR controls as shown in the example.

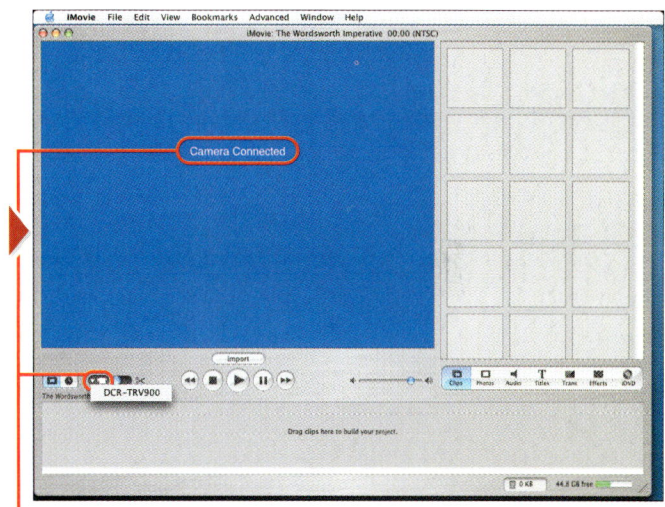

■ iMovie detects the camera and is ready to import video and audio.

6 Click the camera icon (🎥).

■ A menu appears showing the model of camera connected.

■ You can connect several cameras at once and select the one you want to use from this menu.

181

IMPORT VIDEO FROM A DIGITAL CAMCORDER

With just a few clicks, you can watch video from your connected camcorder in iMovie, and then import the video you want to include in your project.

Note that the steps in this section assume that the camcorder contains a tape with recorded video on it.

IMPORT VIDEO FROM A DIGITAL CAMCORDER

PREVIEW VIDEO FROM THE CAMCORDER

1 Connect the camcorder to your Mac.

Note: See the section "Connect a Digital Camcorder" for more information on how to do this.

2 Click the mode switch ( ) if iMovie is not in Camera mode ( ).

3 Click the Play button ( ).

■ The camcorder plays the tape and its contents appear in iMovie's Monitor.

■ You can click ( ) to pause the tape.

■ You can click ( ) to rewind or ( ) to fast forward the tape.

■ You can click ( ) to stop the tape.

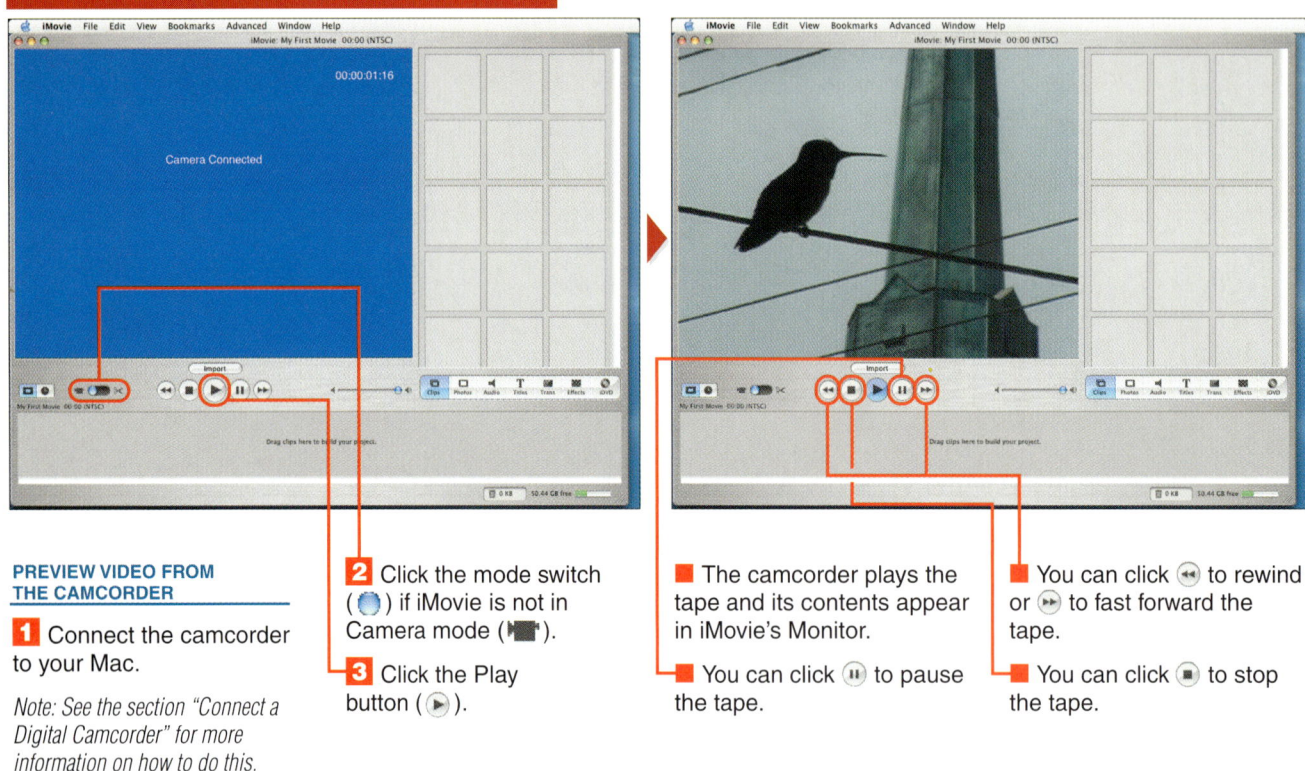

182

9 iMovie Basics

WORKING WITH IMOVIE

Why did iMovie break my 15-minute import into two clips even after I turned off the Automatically start new clip at scene break preference?

Fifteen minutes of digital video takes up about 3GB of storage. Older versions of the Mac operating system, as well as older versions of Windows and many file servers, can only handle files smaller than 2GB. When iMovie imports video, it starts a new clip when the import reaches 2GB in size so that the clips' media files remain compatible with older systems and servers. For more on the preferences available with iMovie, see the section "Set Up iMovie."

How can I rename a video clip?

Click the clip's name and type a new name. You should try to keep the clip's name short so you can read it more easily.

IMPORT VIDEO

1 If iMovie is not already in Camera mode (🎥), click ⬤.

2 Click **Import**.

■ iMovie imports video from the camcorder and places a clip in the Clips Pane.

3 Click ■ to end the import.

■ Each time you click Import, iMovie begins a new clip.

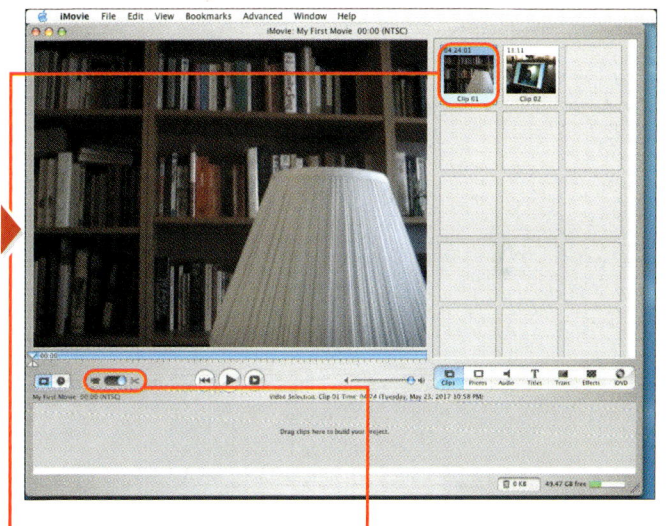

4 Click a clip in the Clips Pane.

■ iMovie switches to Edit mode (✂) and the clip appears in the Monitor.

183

IMPORT VIDEO CLIPS FROM DISK

You can import QuickTime movies and clips from other iMovie projects on your hard disk and add them to your iMovie project.

IMPORT VIDEO CLIPS FROM DISK

1 Click **File**.

2 Click **Import**.

■ A sheet descends from the top of the iMovie window.

3 Navigate to the video you want to import.

4 Click **Open**.

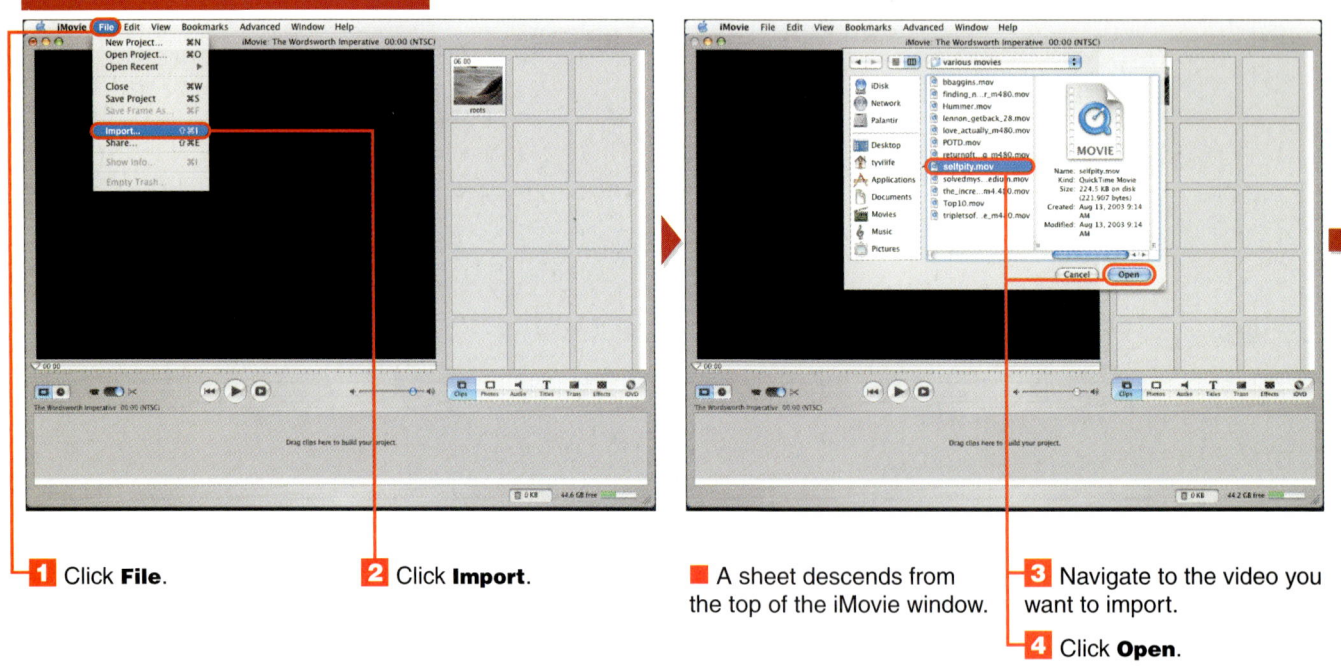

184

9 iMovie Basics

WORKING WITH IMOVIE

Why does my imported QuickTime movie look fuzzy?

iMovie converts imported QuickTime movies into DV clips, which are 720x480 pixels in size. When iMovie scales imported movies to DV format size, it attempts to smooth the image. If the QuickTime movie is much smaller than the DV size, the smoothing can look blurry.

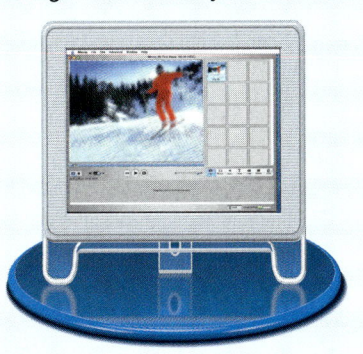

I cannot hear any sound from an imported MPEG-1 movie. Why?

Most MPEG-1 movies do not have a separate sound track; instead the sound is *muxed* — that is, mixed in or multiplexed with the video. iMovie can only extract the video from a muxed MPEG-1 movie.

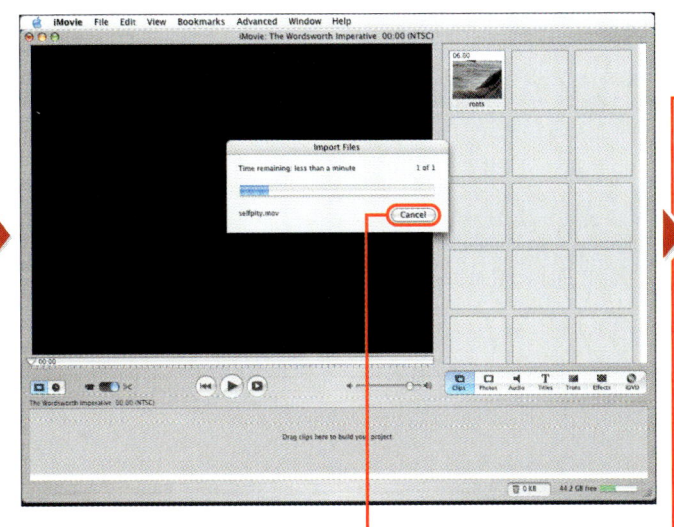

- An Import Files dialog window appears.
- iMovie imports the video, converting it to DV format.

- You can click **Cancel** to halt the import.

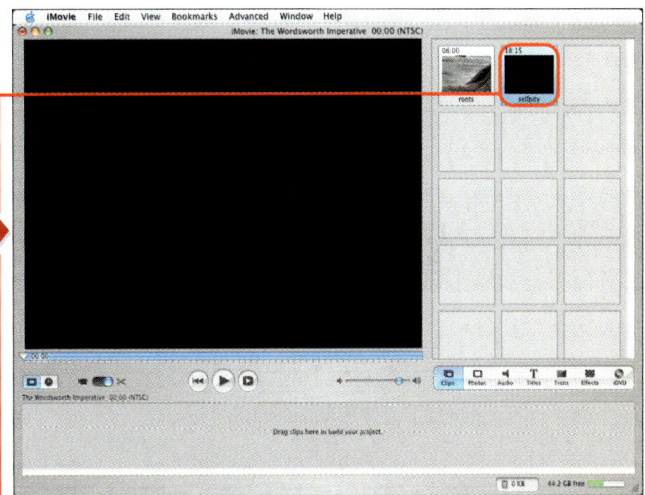

- When the import finishes, the clip appears in the next empty space on the Clips Pane.

185

INSERT AND ARRANGE CLIPS IN A MOVIE

The order of the clips in iMovie's Clips Viewer represents the order in which the clips appear in the movie. You can quickly assemble your movie by dragging clips from iMovie's Clips Pane in any order you like, and you can rearrange the order in which the clips appear just as quickly.

INSERT AND ARRANGE CLIPS IN A MOVIE

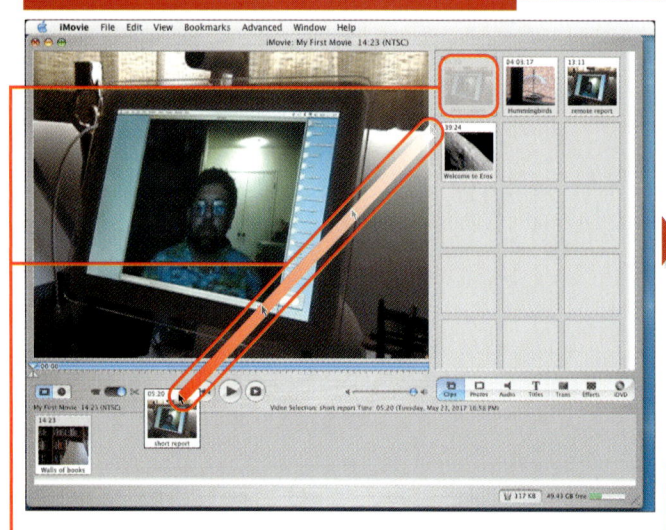

INSERT A CLIP

1. Click a clip on the Clips Pane.

2. Drag the clip towards the bottom of the iMovie window.

■ The clip follows your mouse, leaving a translucent copy on the Clips Pane.

3. When the clip is over the Clips Viewer, release the mouse.

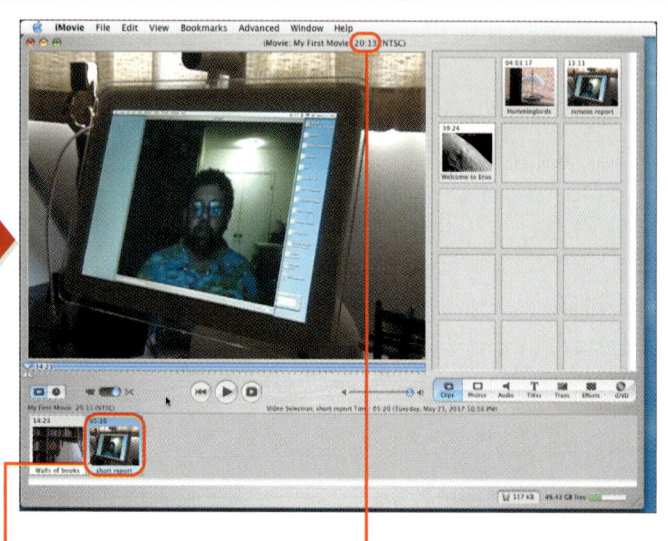

■ The translucent copy of the clip vanishes from the Clips Pane, and the clip is selected in the Clips Viewer.

■ iMovie displays the current length of the movie.

186

9 iMovie Basics

WORKING WITH IMOVIE

How do I play a clip or a movie?

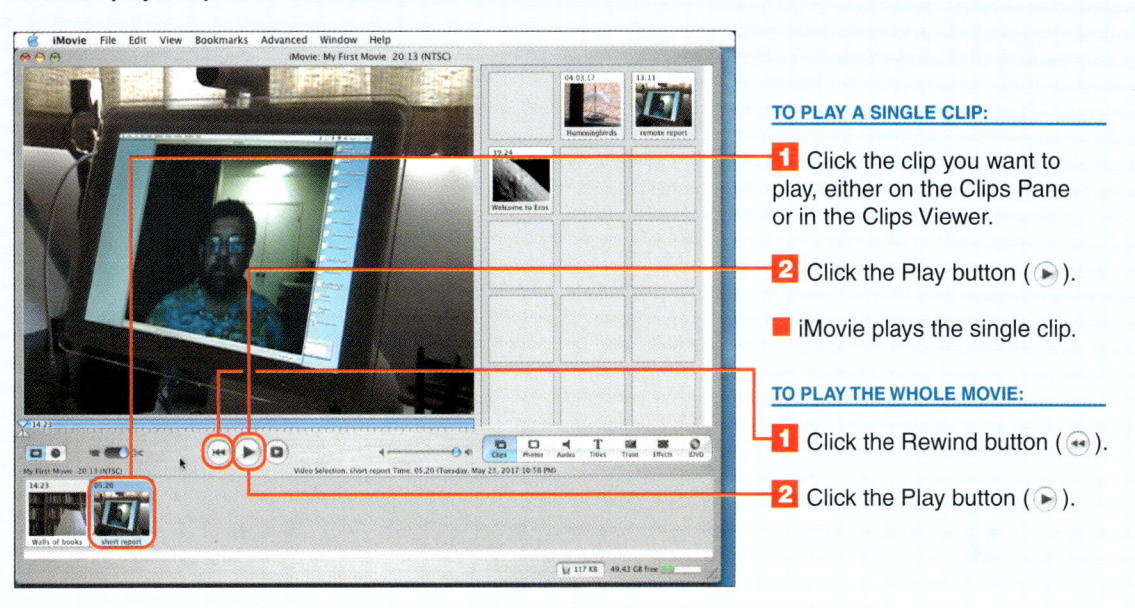

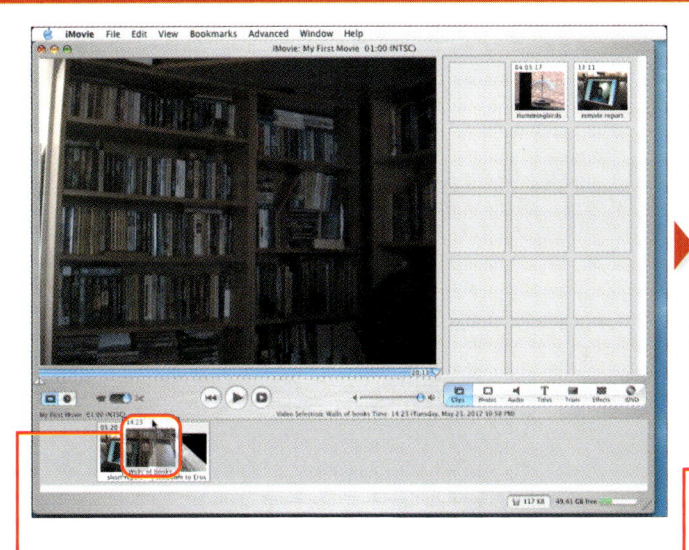

TO PLAY A SINGLE CLIP:

1 Click the clip you want to play, either on the Clips Pane or in the Clips Viewer.

2 Click the Play button (▶).

■ iMovie plays the single clip.

TO PLAY THE WHOLE MOVIE:

1 Click the Rewind button (◀◀).

2 Click the Play button (▶).

ARRANGE CLIPS

1 Click and drag a clip in the Clips Viewer to a new location.

■ The clip follows your mouse.

■ As the clip moves, the other clips move out of the way to make room for it.

2 Release the clip where you want it to appear.

■ The clip appears in its new location in the Clips Viewer.

187

MAKE A CLIP FROM A STILL IMAGE

iMovie can import picture files in any format that QuickTime can understand. This allows you to combine still images and motion video in your movie. QuickTime-compatible file formats include JPEG, TIFF, BMP, and Photoshop, among many others.

When iMovie imports a still image, it uses the photo settings currently in effect in the Photo pane. See the section "Create a Clip from an iPhoto Picture" for more information.

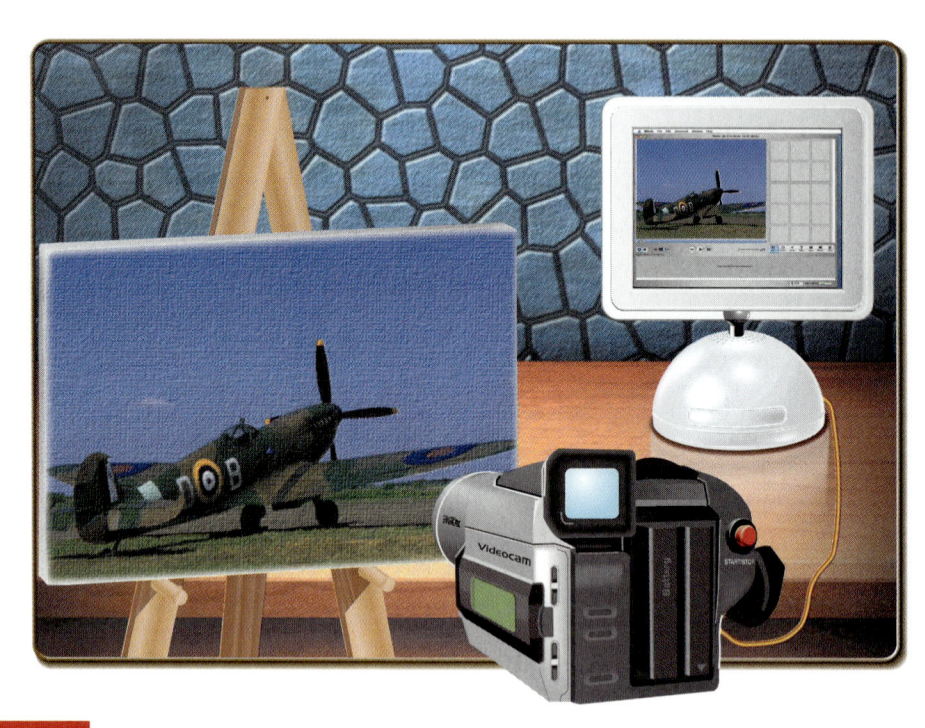

MAKE A CLIP FROM A STILL IMAGE

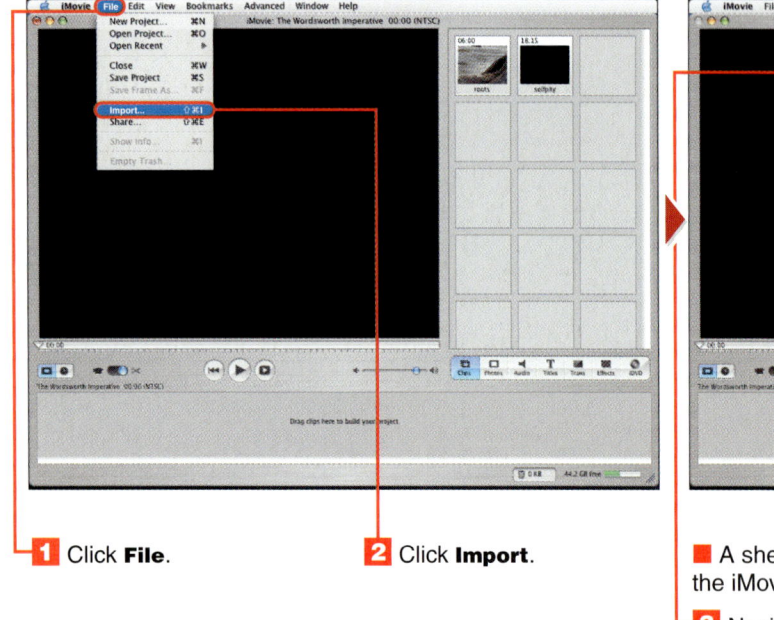

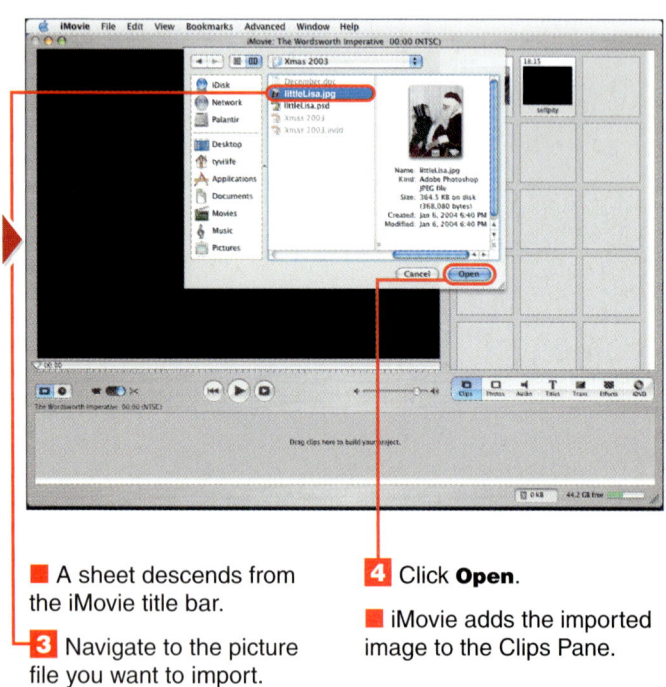

1 Click **File**.

2 Click **Import**.

■ A sheet descends from the iMovie title bar.

3 Navigate to the picture file you want to import.

4 Click **Open**.

■ iMovie adds the imported image to the Clips Pane.

188

CREATE A STILL FRAME FROM A CLIP

9 iMovie Basics
WORKING WITH IMOVIE

You can extract a still frame from any of your clips and use it as a background for titles or to create a freeze-frame effect.

When iMovie creates a still frame clip, it uses the duration currently in effect in the Photo pane. See the section "Create a Clip from an iPhoto Picture" for more information.

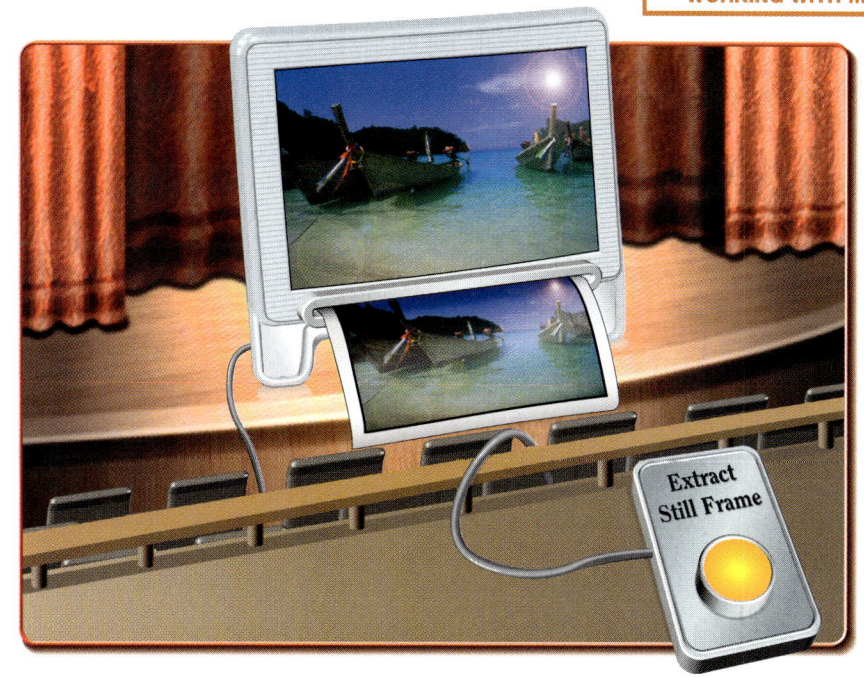

CREATE A STILL FRAME FROM A CLIP

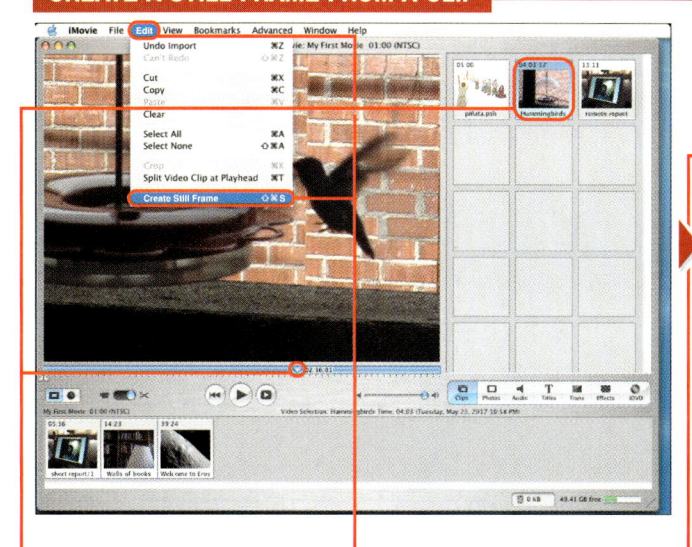

1 Click the clip from which you want to extract a frame.

2 Slide the playhead (▽) to display the frame you want in the Monitor.

■ You can press the ← and → keys to move one frame at a time in either direction.

3 Click **Edit**.

4 Click **Create Still Frame**.

■ The frame appears as a clip on the Clips Pane.

189

CREATE A CLIP FROM AN IPHOTO PICTURE

iMovie gives you complete access to your iPhoto Library and albums. You can create video photo essays or combine your photos with your camcorder footage.

To add motion to your photos, you use an option called the Ken Burns Effect. To learn more about this effect, see the next section, "Adjust the Ken Burns Effect."

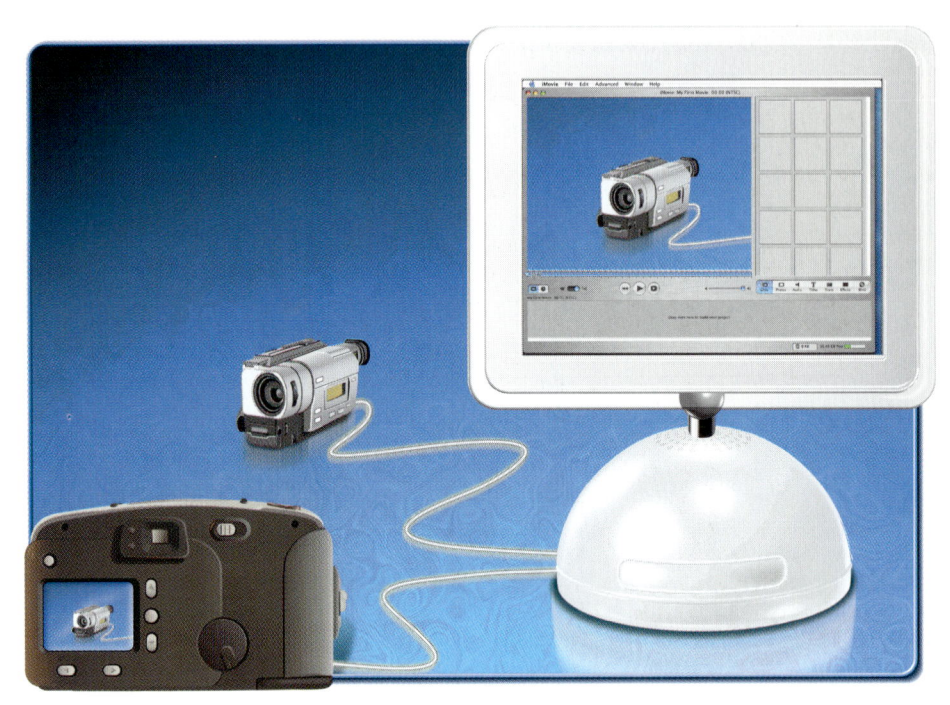

CREATE A CLIP FROM AN IPHOTO PICTURE

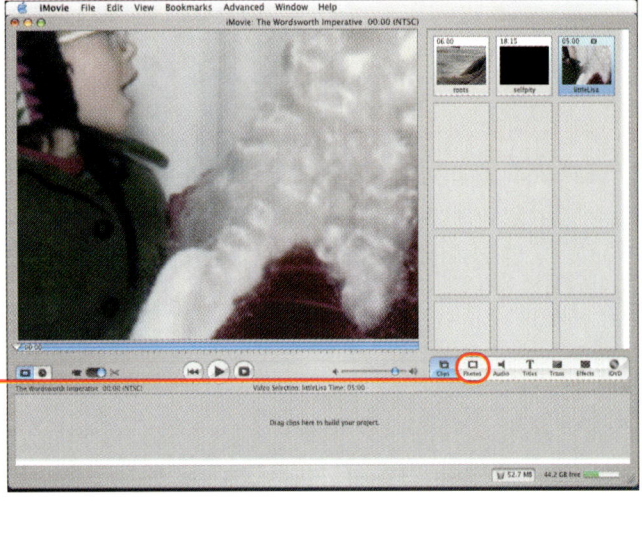

1 Click the **Photos** button.

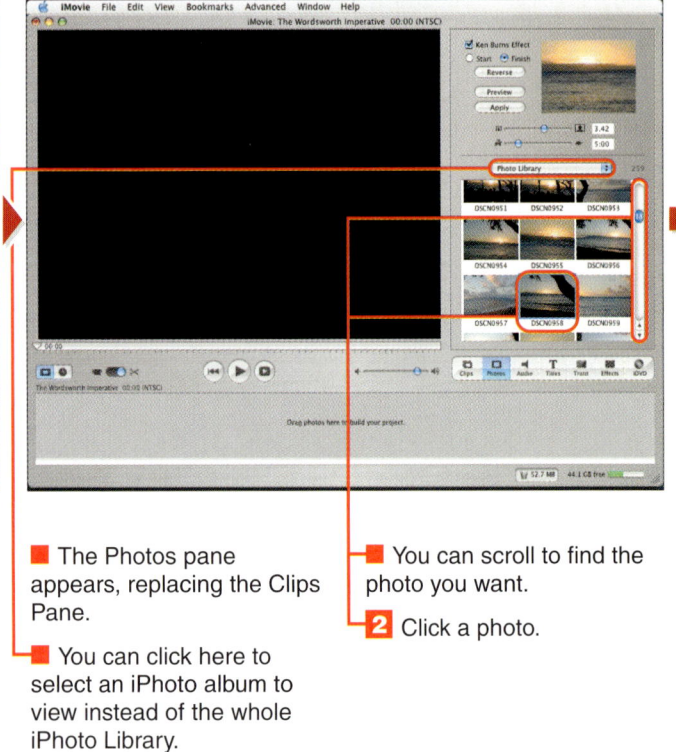

■ The Photos pane appears, replacing the Clips Pane.

■ You can click here to select an iPhoto album to view instead of the whole iPhoto Library.

■ You can scroll to find the photo you want.

2 Click a photo.

9 iMovie Basics

WORKING WITH IMOVIE

Why do I see a black border around some of my photos when I import them into iMovie?

iMovie has to fit still pictures into the standard video frame's 4:3 aspect ratio and it scales photos so that their longest sides fit the frame. A photo that does not have a 4:3 aspect ratio displays black in the empty parts of the frame. To eliminate this effect, crop the photo to a 4:3 aspect ratio, or zoom in on the photo with the Photo pane's zoom slider ( ) until the border disappears.

Why are some of my photos missing in the Photo pane?

The file AlbumData.xml in your iPhoto Library folder in your Pictures folder may be damaged or missing. If the file is not in that folder, open iPhoto and create a new album; this creates a new AlbumData.xml file. If you find the file in the iPhoto Library folder, click and drag the file to the Desktop or the Trash first, and then open iPhoto and create a new album to make a new AlbumData. xml file.

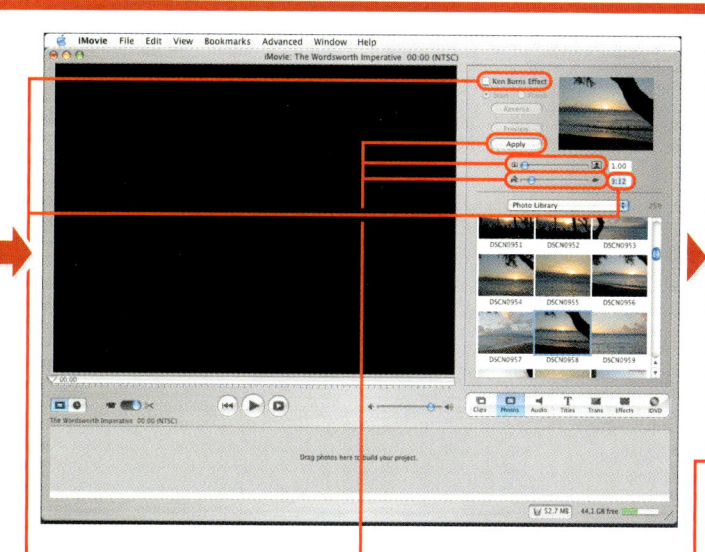

■ **3** Click to deselect the **Ken Burns Effect** option (☑ changes to ☐).

■ Several buttons become disabled in the Photos pane.

■ **4** Click here and type a duration for the clip.

■ You can click and drag the Duration slider ( ) to set a duration.

■ You can zoom in or out by clicking and dragging the Zoom slider ( ).

■ **5** Click **Apply**.

■ The photo appears in the Clips Viewer with the duration you specified.

191

ADJUST THE KEN BURNS EFFECT

You can zoom and pan across imported photos using iMovie's Ken Burns Effect to make your movie more dynamic and visually interesting.

ADJUST THE KEN BURNS EFFECT

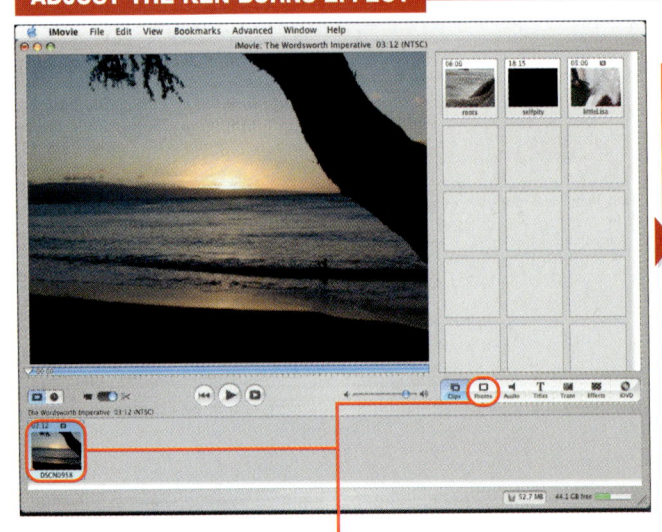

1 Place a still clip in the Clips Viewer.

Note: See the section "Insert and Arrange Clips in a Movie" to add a clip to the Clips Viewer.

2 Click the clip in the Clips Viewer that you want to adjust.

3 Click the **Photos** button.

■ The Photos pane appears with a thumbnail of the selected clip.

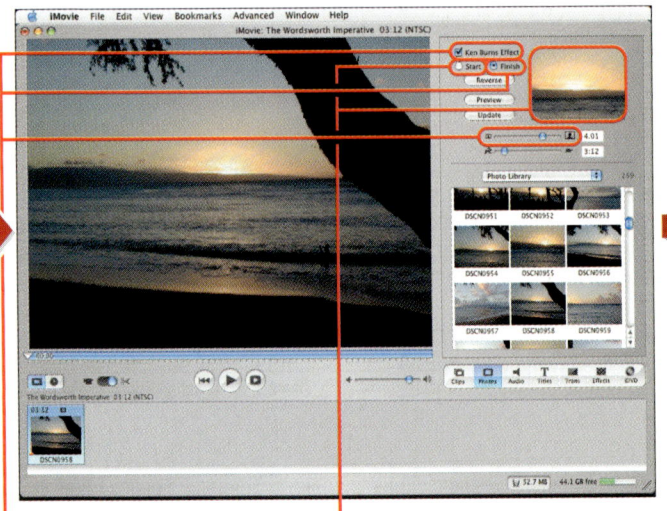

4 Click the **Ken Burns Effect** option (☐ changes to ☑).

5 Click the **Finish** option (○ changes to ◉).

6 Click and drag ⬤ to set how much you want the clip's end to zoom.

7 Hold the mouse down on the thumbnail and drag to show the image you want to see as the clip ends.

8 Click the **Start** option (○ changes to ◉).

192

9 iMovie Basics

WORKING WITH IMOVIE

Why is it called the Ken Burns Effect?

It is named after the American documentary filmmaker Ken Burns, who used the effect extensively in his documentaries about the Civil War, baseball, and jazz, among many others. Mr. Burns has given Apple permission to use his name for the iMovie effect.

How can I start the Ken Burns Effect in the middle of a clip?

Import the clip with the **Ken Burns Effect** option unselected (☑ changes to ☐). Then, split the clip in two and apply the effect to the second half. To learn how to split a clip as well as more on editing with iMovie, see Chapter 10.

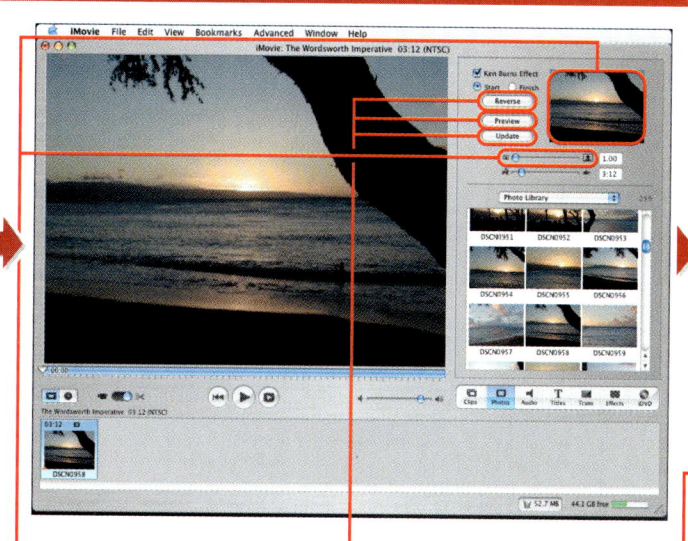

- The thumbnail changes.

9 Click and drag ● to set how much you want the clip's start to zoom.

10 Hold the mouse down on the thumbnail and drag to position the image for the clip's start.

- You can click **Preview** to see the effect.

- You can click **Reverse** to switch the start and finish settings.

11 Click **Update**.

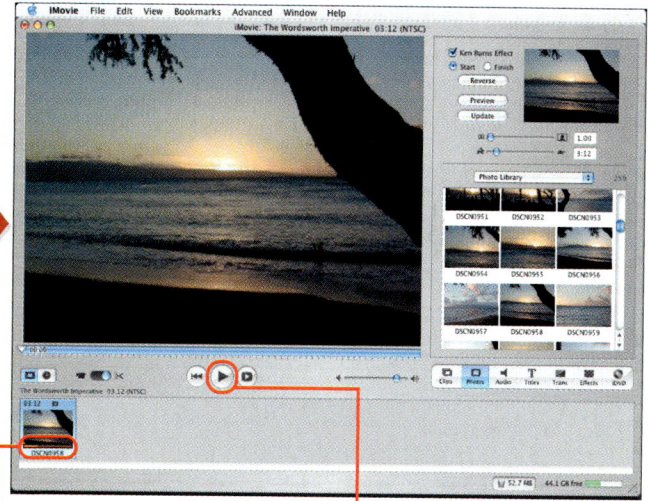

- A red line appears at the bottom of the selected clip in the Clips Viewer and grows brighter from left to right as iMovie renders the effect.

12 Click ▶ to view the completed effect.

193

CROP A CLIP

You can use iMovie's cropping tool to trim the beginnings and ends of your clips so that they contain only the video you need.

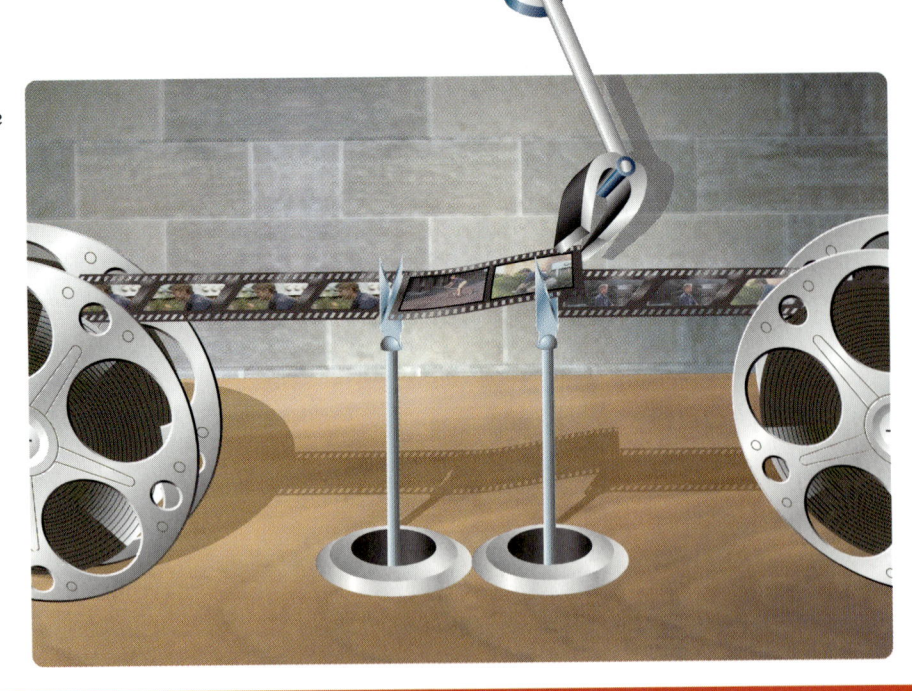

CROP A CLIP

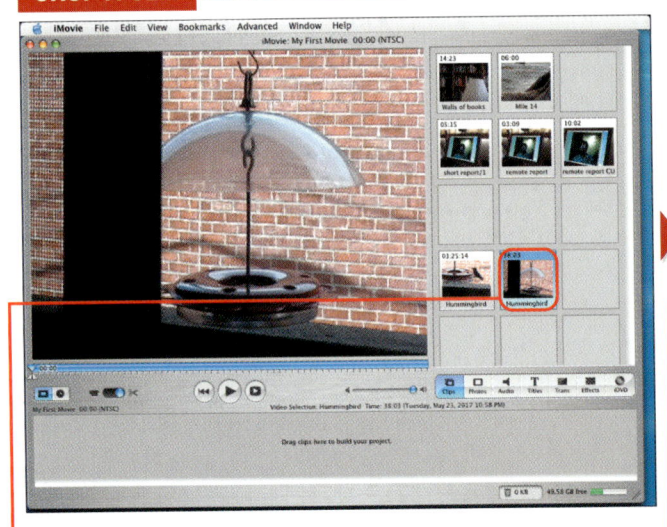

1 Click the clip you want to crop.

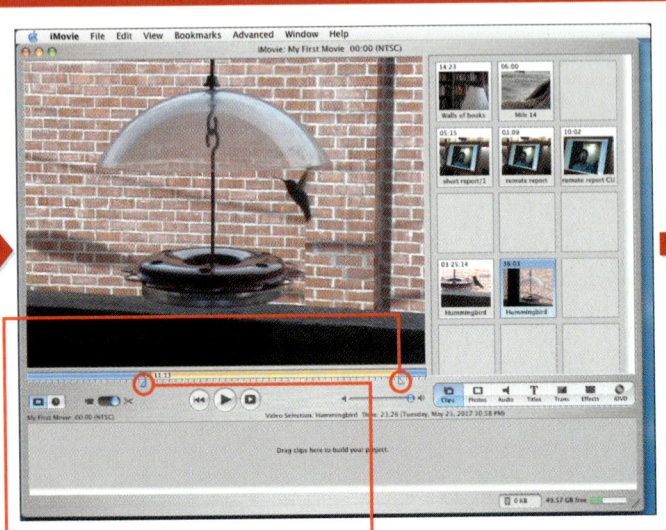

2 Click and drag the right crop marker (◣) to where you want the cropped clip to end.

■ The playhead (▽) follows the crop marker and the monitor displays the video at the playhead's position.

3 Click and drag the left crop marker (◢) to where you want the cropped clip to start.

■ The ▽ follows the crop marker and the monitor displays the video at the playhead's position.

10 Editing with iMovie

WORKING WITH IMOVIE

How can I precisely position the crop marker?

Click and drag either crop marker to a position that is approximately where you want it. Then, press ← to move the marker to the previous frame. Press → to move it to the next frame. You can hold down **Shift** to move the marker ten frames at a time when you press an arrow key. You can *roll* the marker — move it continuously — by holding down an arrow key.

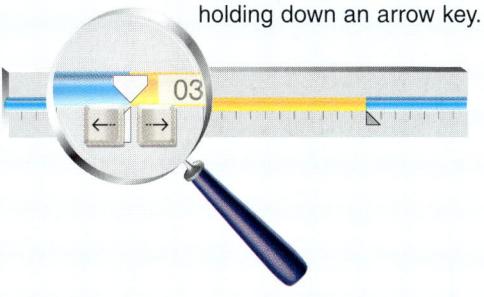

What do the numbers in the time codes mean?

Read from left to right, the time codes display minutes, seconds, and frames. The rightmost number usually ranges from 0 to 29 because NTSC digital video contains 30 frames per second; if you edit PAL video, this number ranges from 0 to 24 to match the PAL frame rate. If you select the **Use short time codes** option (☐ changes to ☑) in iMovie's preferences, iMovie does not show the minutes part of the code for clips or selections that are shorter than a minute. For more on setting up iMovie, including iMovie preferences, see Chapter 9.

Minutes Seconds Frames

03:32:28

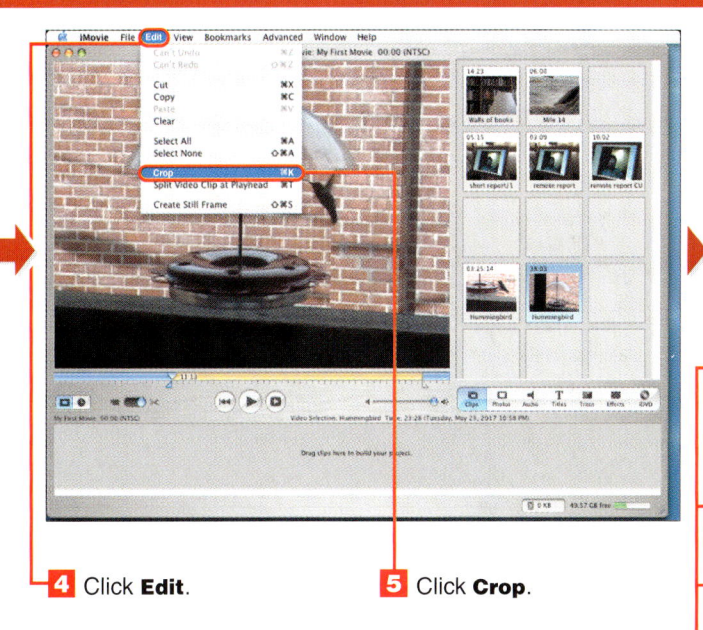

4 Click **Edit**.

5 Click **Crop**.

■ iMovie removes the portions of the clip beyond the crop markers.

■ The size of the iMovie Trash increases.

Note: iMovie keeps the video you removed in its Trash. You can undo the crop until the next time you empty the iMovie Trash. See the section "Using the Trash" for more information.

195

SPLIT A CLIP

iMovie can split a clip in two so you can insert another clip in the middle of a shot or add a transition.

SPLIT A CLIP

1 Click to select a clip.

2 Click and drag ▽ to where you want the clip to be split.

3 Click **Edit**.

4 Click **Split Video Clip at Playhead**.

■ iMovie splits the clip.

■ The new clip has the same name as the one you split, but with a slash (/) and a number added to it.

USING THE TRASH

10 Editing with iMovie

WORKING WITH iMOVIE

iMovie saves video left over from your editing in its Trash so you can undo changes, but you can empty the Trash to reclaim hard disk space.

USING THE TRASH

■ **1** Click the iMovie Trash.

■ You can also click **File**, and then **Empty Trash**.

■ A dialog window appears telling you of the consequences of emptying the Trash.

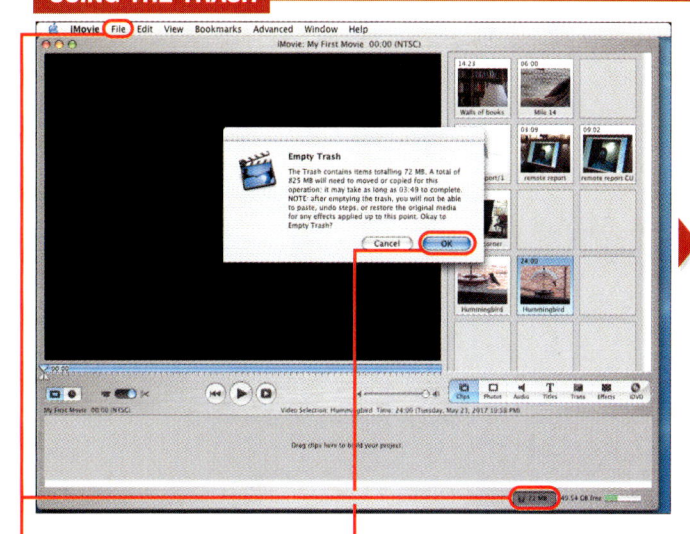

Note: After you empty the Trash, you cannot undo editing actions performed prior to that point.

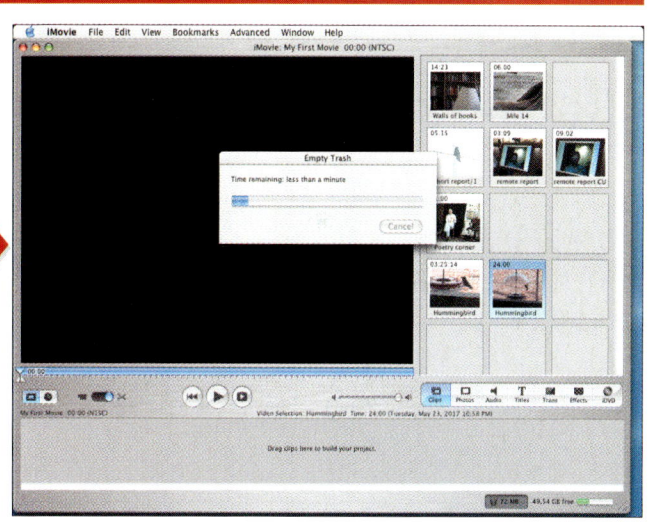

■ **2** Click **OK**.

■ An Empty Trash dialog window appears with a progress bar if the trash takes longer than a few seconds to empty.

Note: After you begin emptying the Trash, you cannot halt the process.

Note: Emptying the Trash can take several minutes if you need to remove large amounts.

■ iMovie empties the Trash.

197

APPLY A TRANSITION TO A SINGLE CLIP

You can drag a transition to the beginning or end of a clip to make the start or end of a clip less abrupt.

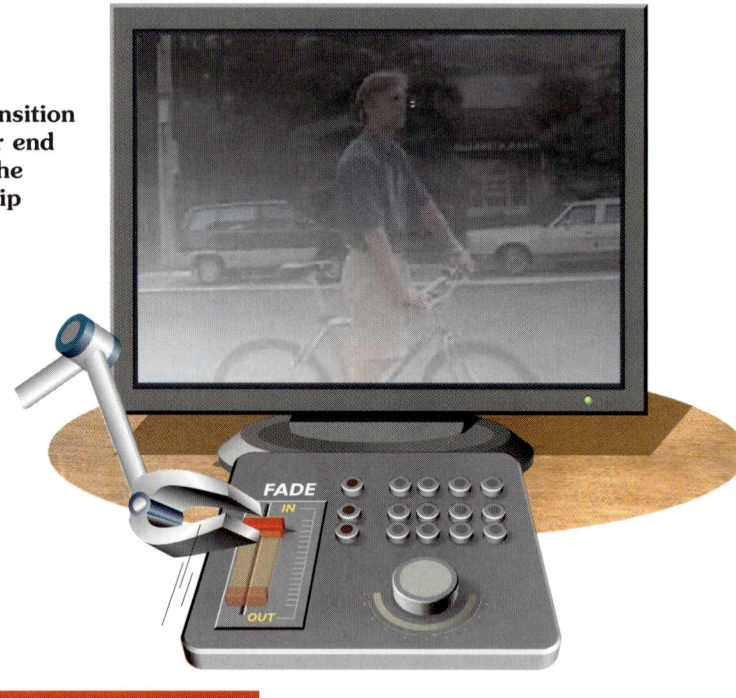

You can only add certain transitions to individual clips. Of these, you can only add some, such as Fade In and Wash In, to the start of a clip, while you can only add others, such as Fade Out and Wash Out, to the clip's end.

You must have a clip in the Clips Viewer to apply a transition to it. See Chapter 9 to learn how to insert and arrange clips in the Clips Viewer.

APPLY A TRANSITION TO A SINGLE CLIP

1 Click and drag ▽ to the place where you want to add the transition.

2 Click the **Trans** button.

■ The Transitions Pane appears.

3 Click a transition that you want to add to a clip.

■ A brief preview of the transition appears in the pane's thumbnail area.

4 Click and drag the Speed slider (●) to adjust the transition's duration.

■ The transition's new duration appears in the thumbnail.

■ You can click **Preview** to see the transition in the monitor.

198

10 Editing with iMovie

WORKING WITH iMOVIE

Why does my clip get shorter when I add a transition in front of it?

The amount of time by which your clip gets shorter is the amount that the transition occupies; the total time taken by the transition together with the clip to which you attach it is the same as the length of the original clip. This means that you cannot add a transition to a clip that is longer than the clip itself.

How can I get rid of a transition?

If you have just added the transition, you can click **Edit**, and then **Undo Add Transition**. Alternatively, you can click the transition itself and press `Delete`.

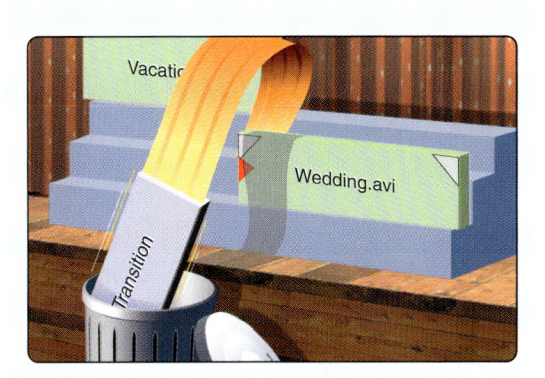

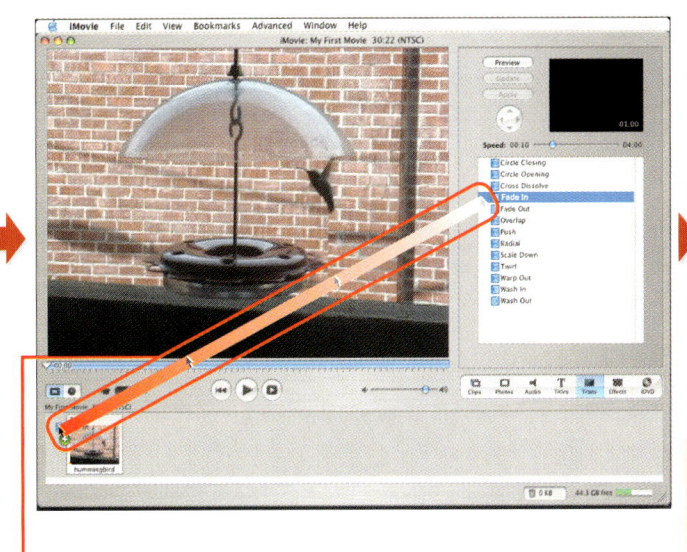

■ **5** Click and drag the transition icon ( ) from the Transitions Pane to the Clips Viewer.

■ As you drag, the clips move aside to make room for the transition.

■ **6** Release the mouse when the transition is where you want it.

■ The transition attaches itself to the clip, and a red line appears indicating that iMovie is rendering the transition.

■ When the red line disappears, you can click the Play button ( ) to view the transition.

199

APPLY A TRANSITION BETWEEN TWO CLIPS

You can drag a transition between two clips to blend them seamlessly.

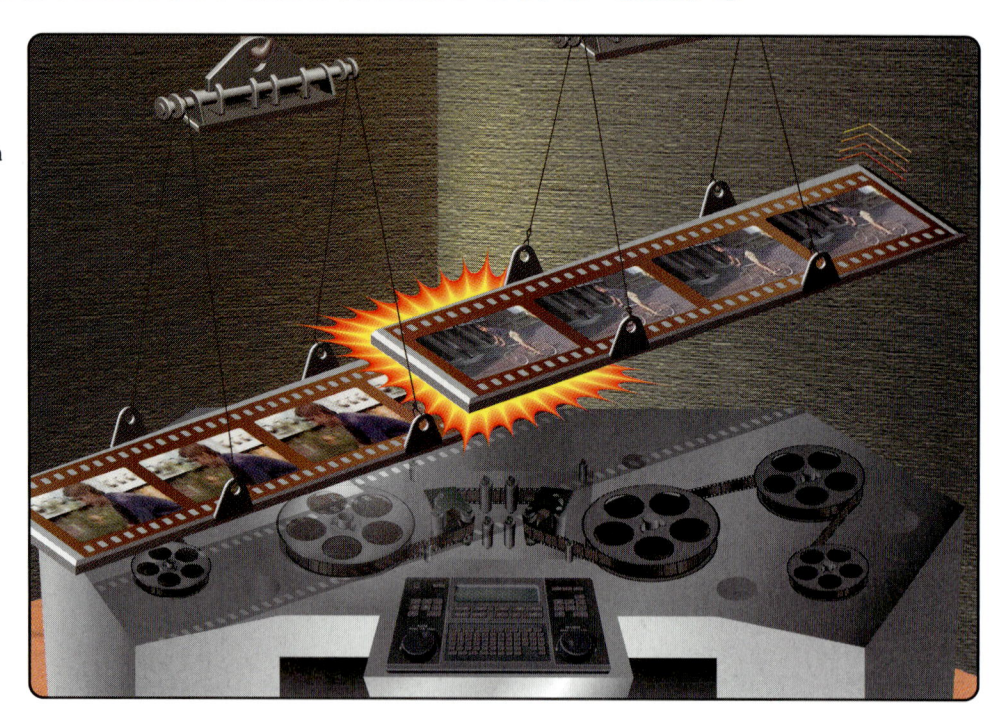

You can only add certain transitions between two clips. Of these transitions, some, such as Cross Dissolve or Push, reduce the length of the movie by combining the parts of the two clips they affect. Others, such as Overlap, copy material from both the clips to keep the length of the movie unchanged.

APPLY A TRANSITION BETWEEN TWO CLIPS

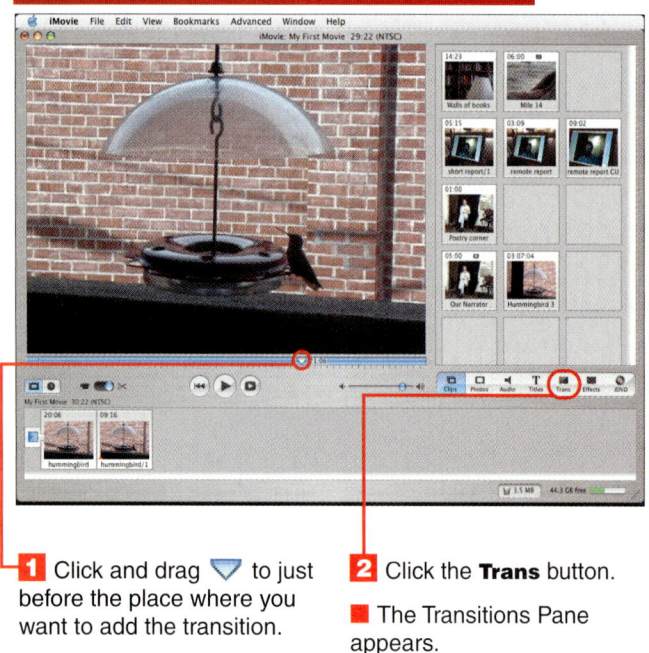

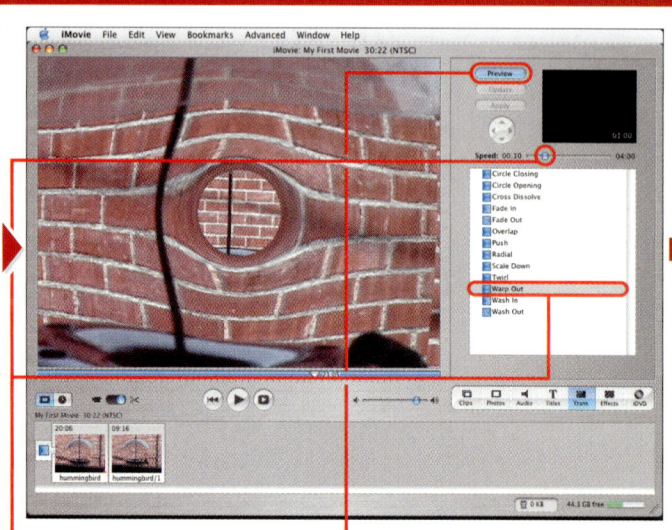

1 Click and drag ▽ to just before the place where you want to add the transition.

2 Click the **Trans** button.

■ The Transitions Pane appears.

3 Click a transition to insert between the two clips.

■ A brief preview of the transition appears in the pane's thumbnail area.

4 Click and drag the ● to adjust the transition's duration.

■ The transition's new duration appears in the thumbnail.

■ You can click **Preview** to see the transition in the monitor.

200

10 Editing with iMovie

WORKING WITH IMOVIE

What is that circular thing near the top of the Transitions Pane?

The circular control ( ) contains four arrow buttons. Some transitions apply motion to the affected clips, and the arrow buttons let you select the direction of the motion. The Push transition is an example: It pushes one scene out of the frame and replaces it with another. The arrow buttons let you determine the direction in which the push occurs.

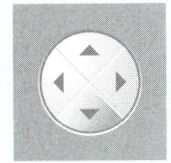

What does the message, "There are not enough video frames around the playhead to preview the title, transition, or effect," mean?

When you click a transition in the transitions pane, iMovie creates a preview of the transition to show in the pane's thumbnail, using the video surrounding the playhead's position to create the preview. iMovie displays the message if it cannot create the preview. You often see the message when you place the playhead over the last clip in the movie, and the transition is the kind that joins two clips. To avoid seeing the message, move the playhead.

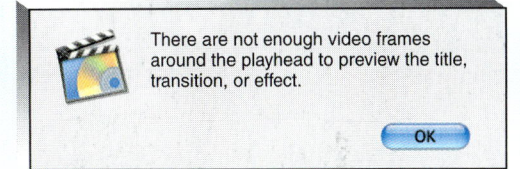

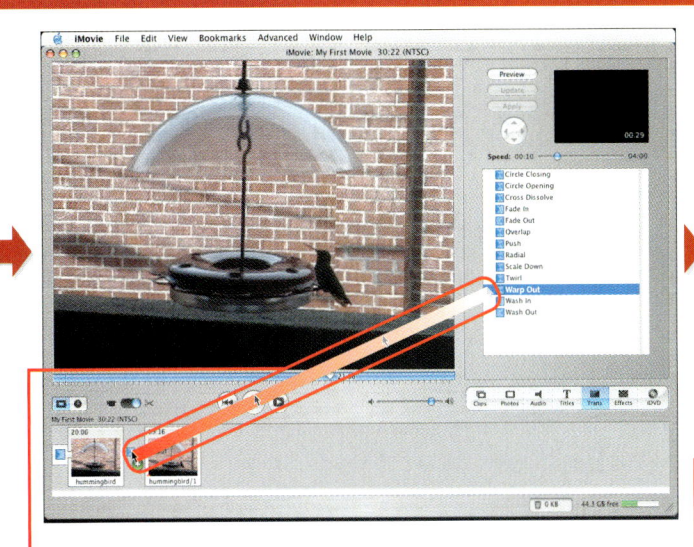

■ **5** Click and drag from the Transitions Pane to the Clips Viewer.

■ As you drag, the clips move around to make room for the transition icon.

6 Release the mouse when the transition is between the two clips.

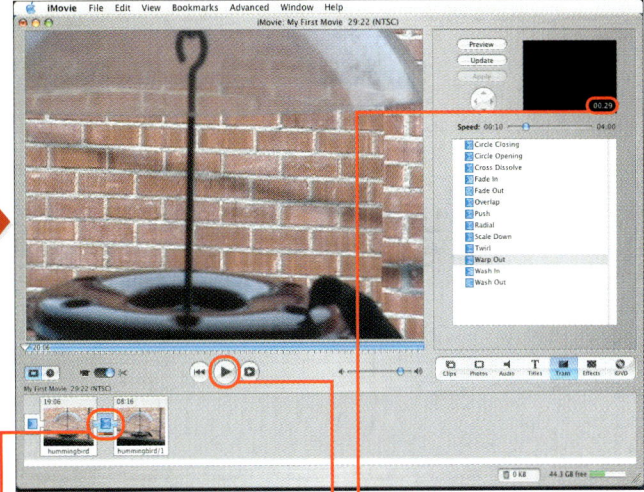

■ The transition attaches itself to both clips, and a red line appears indicating that iMovie is rendering the transition.

■ The duration of the movie is reduced by the duration of the transition.

■ When the red line disappears, you can click ▶ to see the transition.

201

APPLY A VISUAL EFFECT TO A CLIP

You can change the look of a clip, either subtly or dramatically, with a visual effect.

You can use some effects, such as Sharpen, simply to improve a clip's appearance. Other effects, such as Fog or Rain, have uses that are more cinematic or fanciful.

APPLY A VISUAL EFFECT TO A CLIP

1 Click the clip to which you want to apply an effect.

2 Click the **Effects** button.

■ The Effects pane appears.

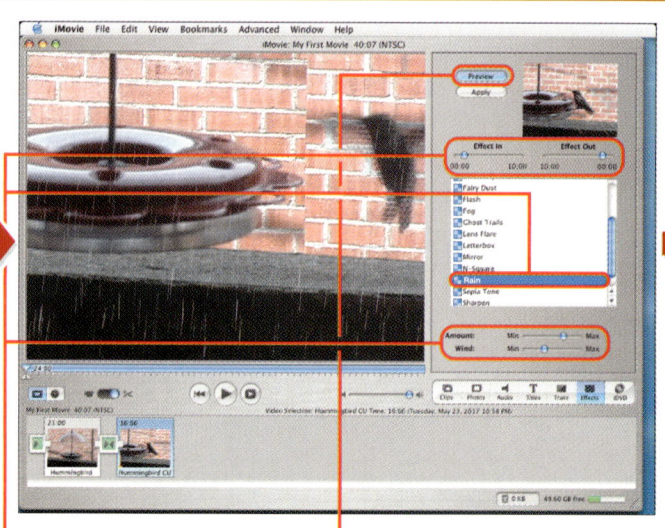

3 Click the effect you want to apply.

4 Click and drag the Effect In and Effect Out to set when the effect appears in the clip.

■ Each effect has additional controls that you can adjust.

■ In this example, the Rain effect has sliders to control the amount of rain and wind it superimposes on a clip.

5 Click **Preview**.

■ The monitor displays the clip with the chosen effect and settings.

202

10 Editing with iMovie

WORKING WITH IMOVIE

Why does an effect seem to begin before the Effect In time, or end after the Effect Out time?

Effects actually apply to an entire clip. An effect fades in until it reaches its full intensity at the Effect In time; similarly, the Effect Out time indicates the moment when the effect starts to diminish.

How can I apply an effect to only part of a clip?

You can select part of a clip by adjusting the crop markers before you apply the effect. See the section "Crop a Clip" for how to manipulate the crop markers. iMovie splits the clip, making the selected portion of the clip — the area between the crop markers — into a new clip, and applies the effect to it.

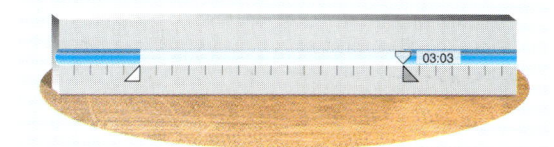

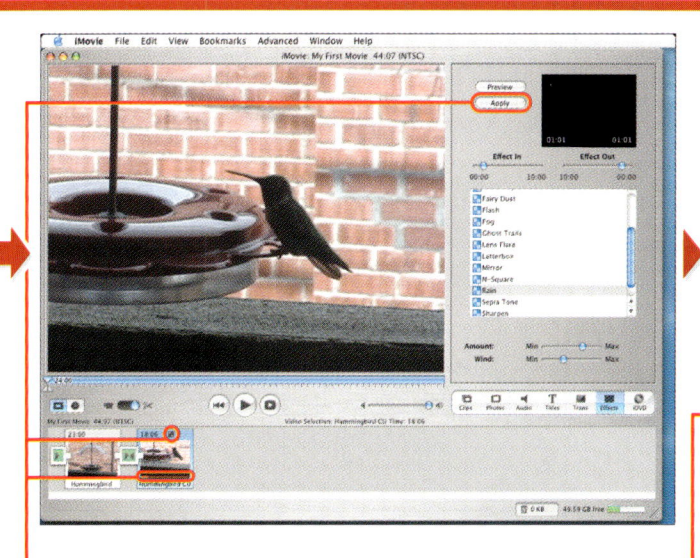

---

6 Click **Apply**.

■ A red line appears below the clip as iMove renders the effect.

■ A small badge (▣) appears on the clip to indicate that it has an effect applied to it.

■ It may take several minutes to render some effects; you can continue working while iMovie renders an effect.

Note: If a clip has a transition applied to it, iMovie warns you that it needs to re-render the transition.

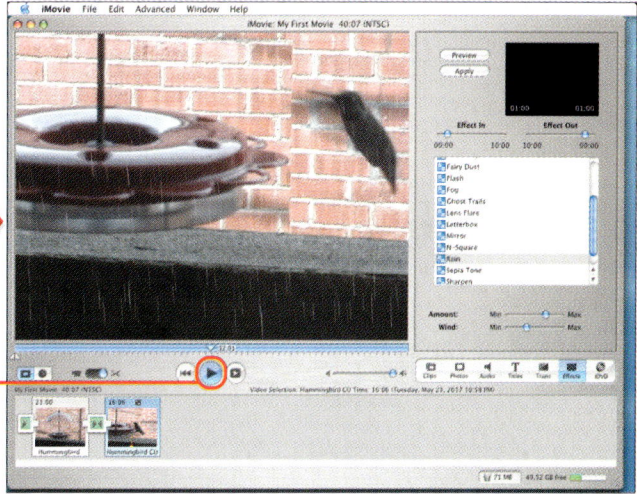

7 Click ▶ when iMovie finishes rendering the effect.

■ The fully rendered version of the effect plays in the monitor.

203

MODIFY A VISUAL EFFECT

If a clip does not look quite as you expected after you apply an effect, you can restore the original clip, change the effect settings, and reapply the effect.

MODIFY A VISUAL EFFECT

1 Click the **Effects** button.

■ The Effects pane appears.

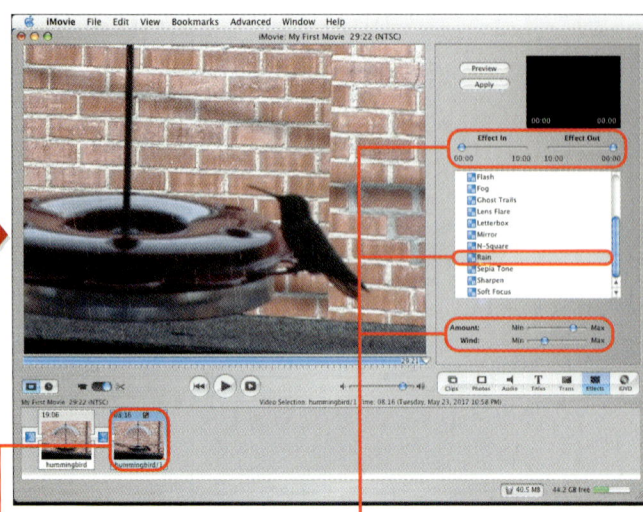

2 Click the clip with the effects you want to modify.

■ iMovie selects the effect in the Effects pane and the effect's controls display the settings the clip uses.

204

10 Editing with iMovie

WORKING WITH iMOVIE

How many steps back can I go with the Edit menu's Undo command?

The Undo command can undo as many as ten major editing actions. Emptying the iMovie Trash, however, resets the Undo command, as does clicking **File**, and then **Save**.

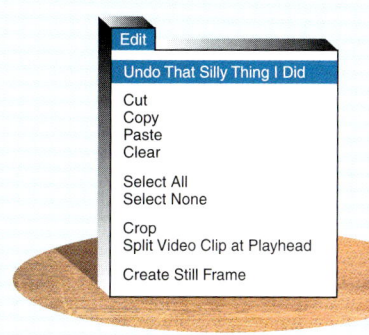

If I have emptied iMovie's Trash, how can I restore a clip to how it looked before I added an effect?

Unfortunately, you cannot restore the clip unless you re-import the video from your camera or hard disk. However, you can duplicate a clip before you apply an effect. To do so, click the clip, click **Edit** and then **Copy**. Next, click **Edit**, and then **Paste**. iMovie duplicates the clip, giving you a back-up copy you can later use if you need it, even if you empty the iMovie Trash.

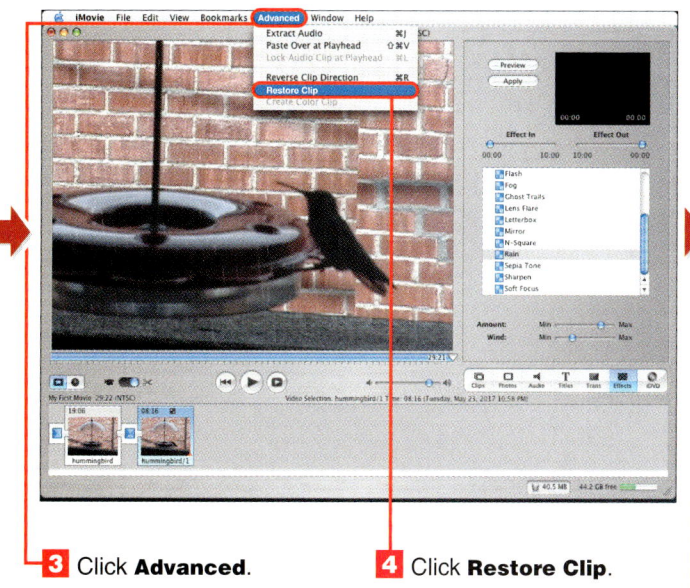

3 Click **Advanced**.

4 Click **Restore Clip**.

■ iMovie removes the effect from the clip (vanishes).

5 Adjust the effect's settings to your liking.

6 Click **Apply**.

■ iMovie applies the new effect settings to the clip and renders it.

205

ADD SINGLE TITLES

You can add animated titles and credits to your movie in a variety of styles.

You should keep your titles short, because a television screen does not have enough resolution to display legible text in a small size, and iMovie shrinks long titles to fit on the screen. A good rule of thumb is to have no more than 35 characters per line.

Note that you can only add titles to clips that are in the Clips Viewer. See page 192 for dragging a clip to the Clips Viewer.

ADD SINGLE TITLES

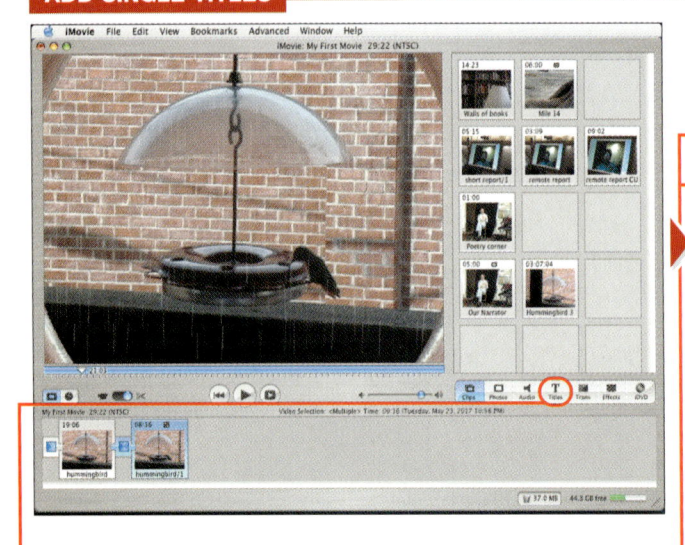

1 Click the **Titles** button.

■ The Titles Pane appears.

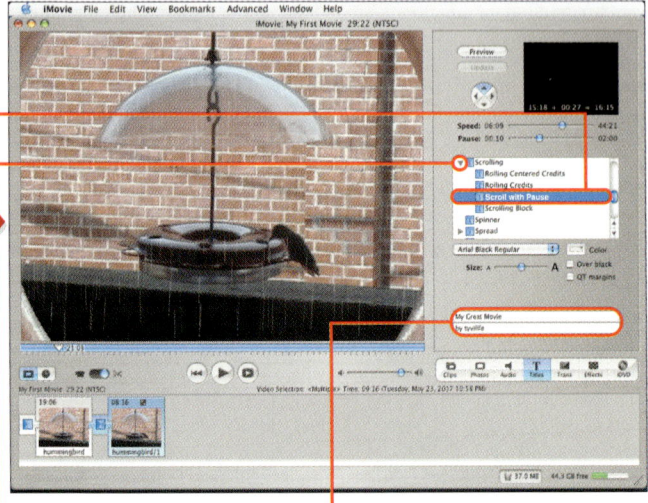

2 Click a title style that you want to use.

■ You can click ▼ to see related versions of some styles.

Note: For this section, avoid styles that have the words "credits" or "multiple" in their names.

■ The pane shows the appropriate controls for the selected style.

3 Click and type the text for the title.

■ Single title styles provide two lines for title text.

206

10 Editing with iMovie

WORKING WITH IMOVIE

How can I place a title in the middle of a clip?

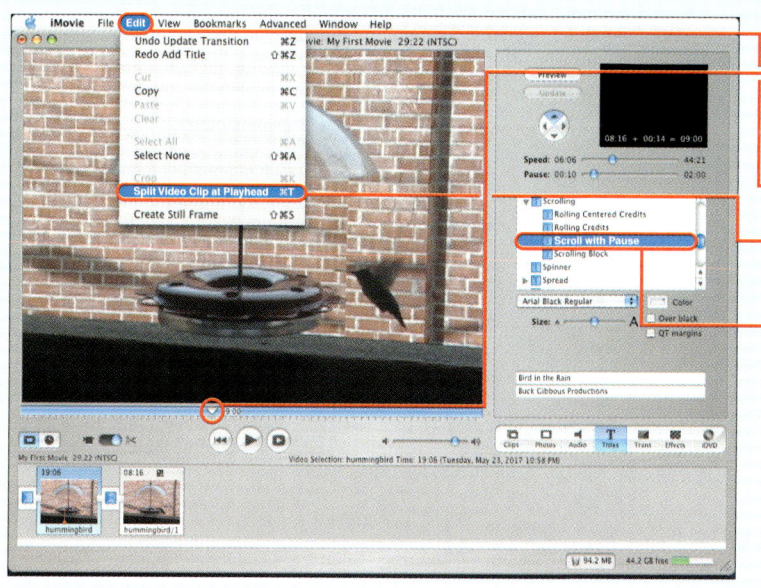

1 Click and drag the playhead (▽) to where you want the title to start.

2 Click **Edit**.

3 Click **Split Video Clip at Playhead**.

4 Click and drag the title between the first and second parts of the clip.

Note: The title should not have a longer duration than the second part of the clip; or iMovie applies the excess to the next clip in the Clips Viewer.

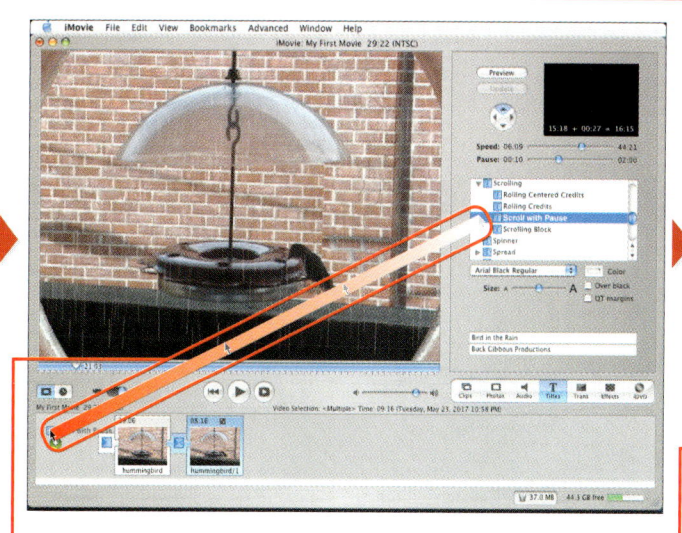

■ **4** Click and drag the title icon (T) to the left of the clip in which you want it to appear.

■ As you drag, the clips move aside to make room for the title.

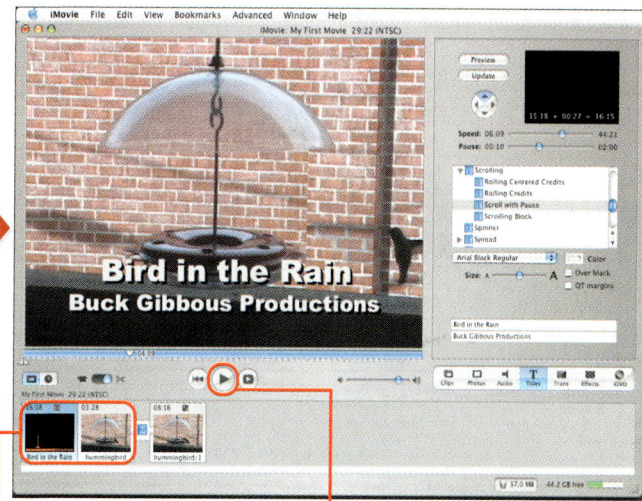

■ iMovie splits the clip to the right of where you dropped the title and renders the title.

■ The clip containing the title displays a title badge (T).

■ You can continue working as iMovie renders.

■ You can click ▶ to see the rendered title.

207

ADD MULTIPLE TITLES

iMovie provides title styles that let you present titles in a sequence, which you can use, for example, to give credit to your cast and crew.

ADD MULTIPLE TITLES

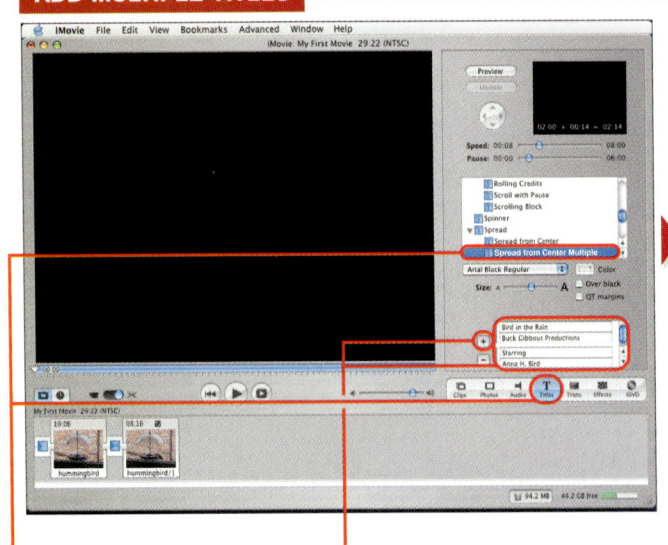

1 Click the **Titles** button.

■ The Titles Pane appears.

2 Click a title style that has the word *multiple* in its name.

■ A multi-line title entry area appears, divided into two-line units with each two-line unit representing one title in the multiple title sequence.

3 Click and type your text in the title entry fields.

4 Click the Add Title button (+).

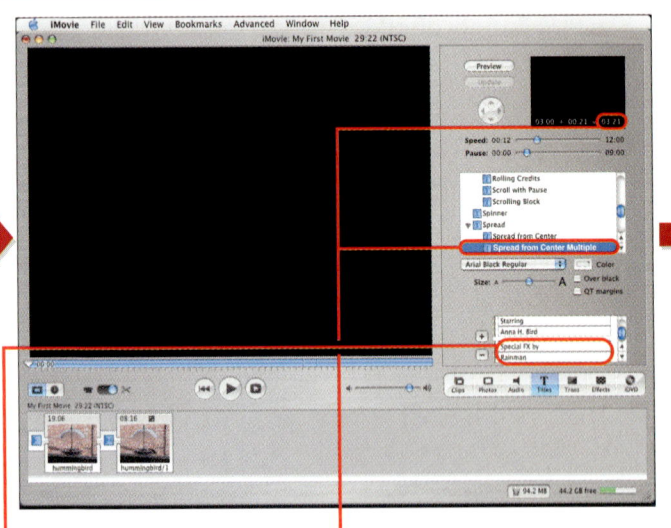

■ A new two-line title appears in the title entry area.

5 Click and type your text in the new title fields.

■ You can press Tab to move between fields.

6 Click the title style again.

■ iMovie calculates the title's new duration and displays it in the title pane's thumbnail.

10 Editing with iMovie

WORKING WITH IMOVIE

How can I rearrange my title sequence?

You can move each two-line title in your title sequence by clicking the gray line to the left of the segment and dragging it up or down in the title entry area; the title entry area scrolls if necessary. Release the mouse when the title is where you want it in the sequence.

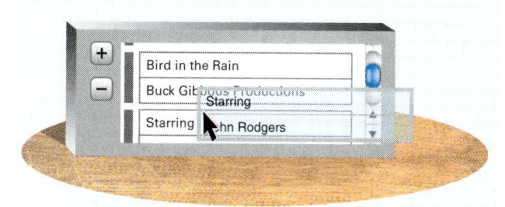

What is the difference between Speed and Pause sliders?

Most title styles both move the titles on the screen and pause them briefly so you can read them. The Speed slider sets how long the animation takes to play, and the Pause slider sets how long the title remains still. The title's duration is the length of the animation plus the length of the pause. iMovie presents the title's total duration in the thumbnail display of the Titles pane as the sum of the durations from the Speed and Pause settings.

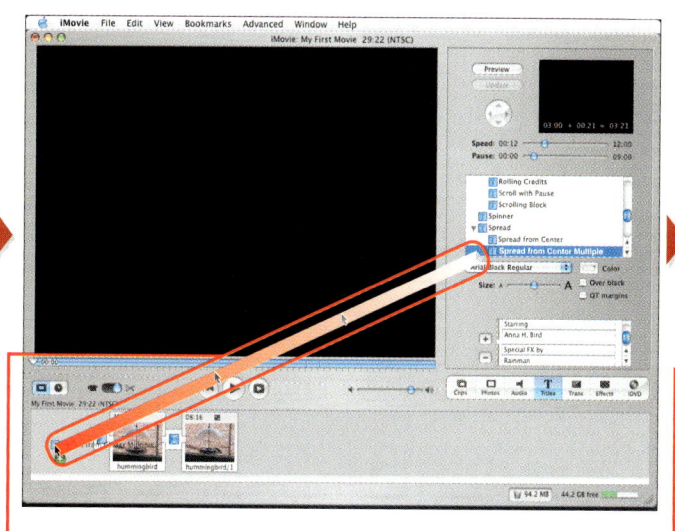

7 Click and drag to the left of the clip in which you want the title sequence to appear.

- As you drag, the clips move aside to make room for the title sequence.

- iMovie splits the clip to the right of where you dropped the sequence and renders the titles.

- You can click and drag ▽ or click ▶ to see the title sequence.

- Each two-line title appears separately when the sequence plays.

209

ADD SUBTITLES

iMovie provides both single and multiple subtitle styles so you can provide a quick translation or give a running text commentary.

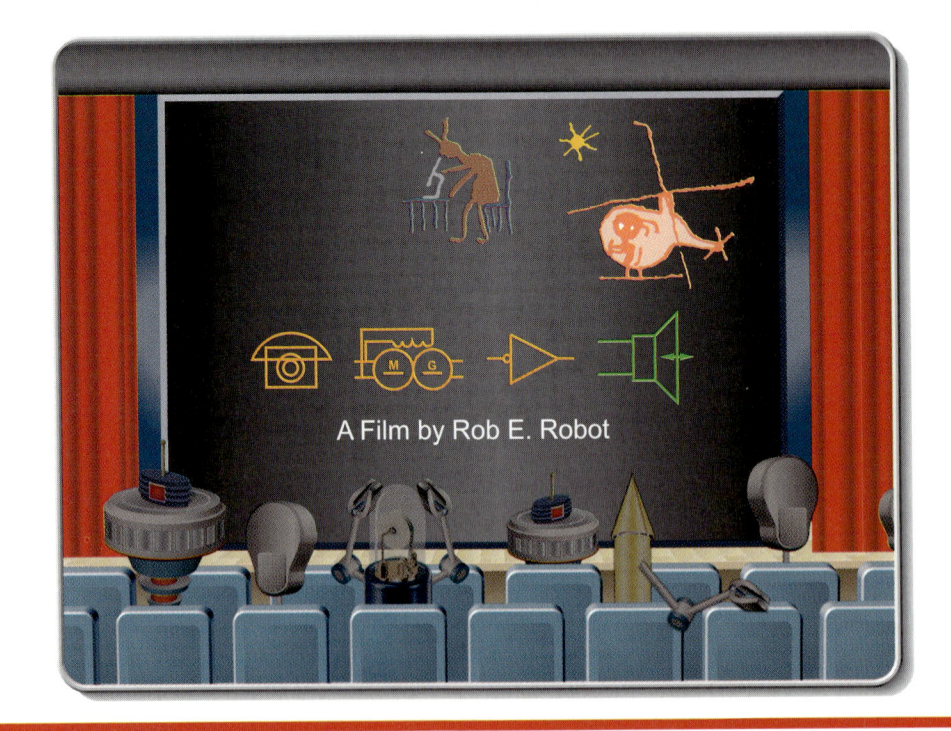

ADD SUBTITLES

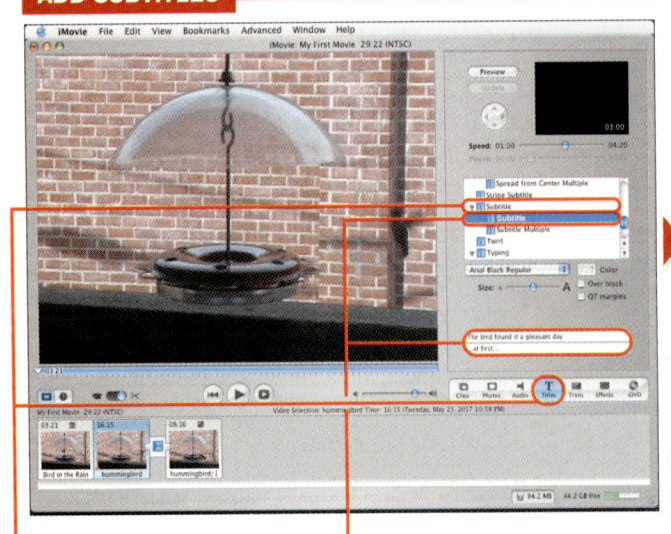

ADD A SINGLE SUBTITLE

1 Click the **Titles** button.

■ The Titles Pane appears.

2 Click **Subtitle**.

■ The subtitle styles appear.

3 Click **Subtitle**.

■ A title entry area appears.

4 Click and type your subtitle text.

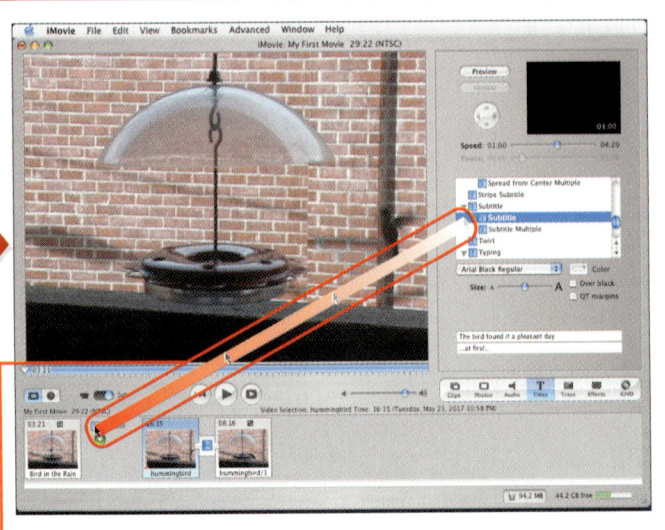

5 Click and drag to the left of the clip in which you want the subtitle to appear and release the mouse.

■ iMovie splits the clip to the right and renders the subtitle clip.

10 Editing with iMovie

WORKING WITH iMOVIE

How can I have long lists of credits like those seen at the end of theatrical films?

Use one of iMovie's Rolling Credits title styles. These styles let you enter text in the same way as iMovie's multiple title styles, but in rolling credits the first line of each two-line title unit appears on-screen in a single line with periods separating the two parts of the title. You can control the speed and direction of the roll with the Titles Pane's speed slider and direction arrow controls, but you cannot pause it.

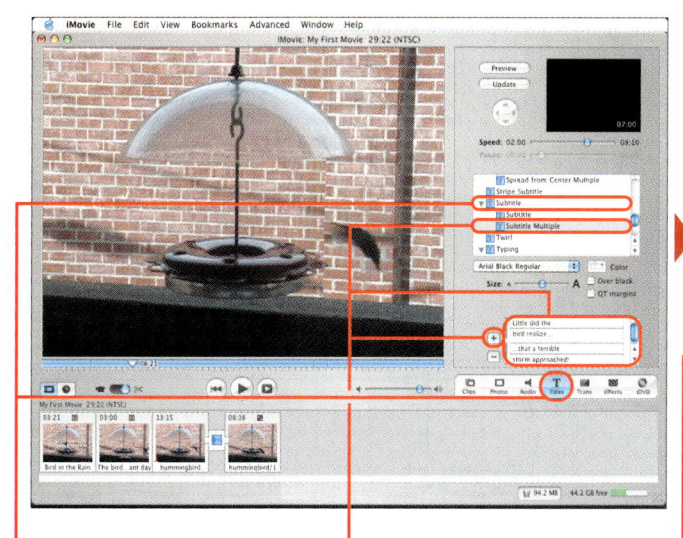

ADD MULTIPLE SUBTITLES

1 Click the **Titles** button.

■ The Titles Pane appears.

2 Click **Subtitles**.

■ The subtitle styles appear.

3 Click **Subtitle Multiple**.

■ A multiple title entry area appears.

4 Click and type your subtitle texts.

■ You can click [+] to add additional subtitles to the sequence.

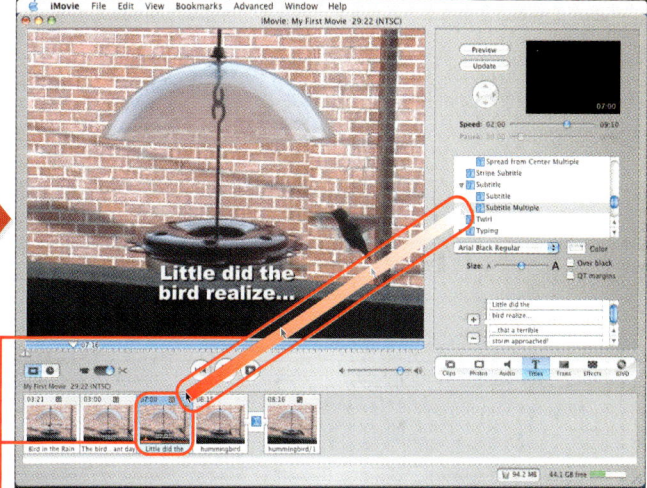

5 Click and drag [T] to the left of the clip where you want the subtitle sequence to start and release the mouse.

■ iMovie splits the clip to the right and renders the subtitle clip.

■ When the movie plays, each subtitle in the sequence appears separately.

211

ADJUST TITLE ANIMATION

You can modify the speed, direction, or style of a title even after iMovie has rendered it.

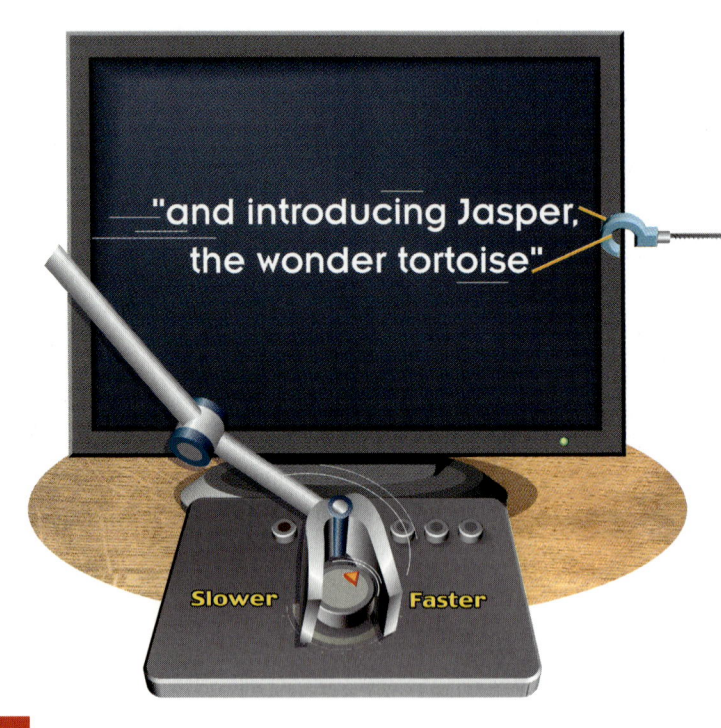

ADJUST TITLE ANIMATION

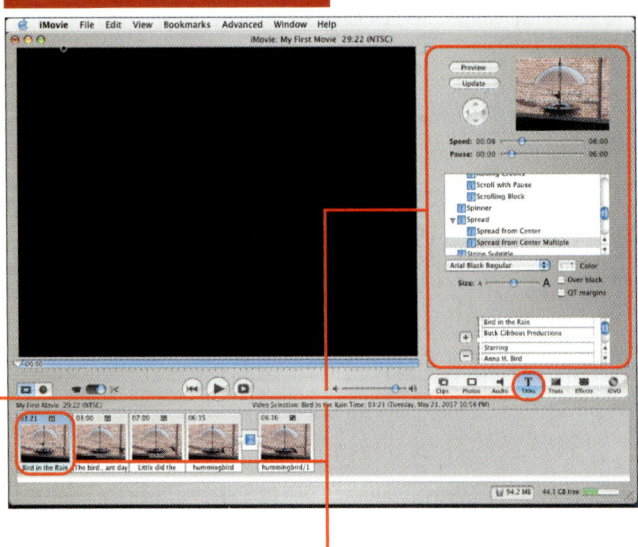

1 Click the **Titles** button.

■ The Titles Pane appears.

2 Click the title clip that you want to adjust.

■ The title clip's settings appear in the Titles Pane.

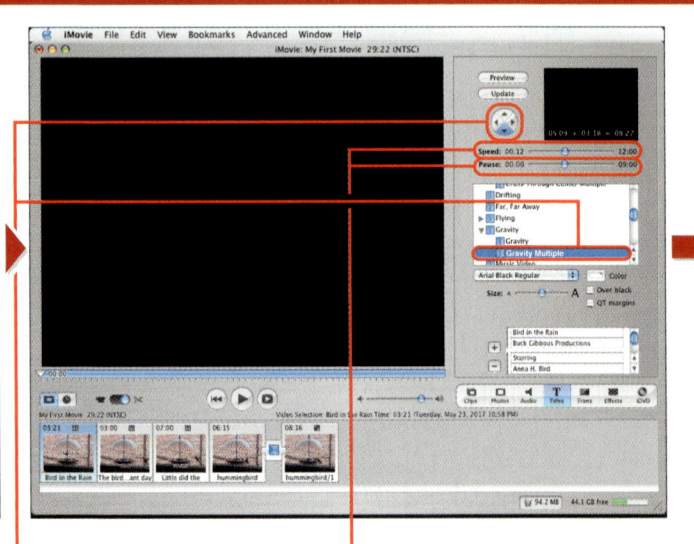

3 Click a different title style.

Note: Different styles have different controls.

■ You can adjust the direction in which the title moves by clicking an arrow button.

■ You can adjust the speed of the title's animation by adjusting the Speed slider ( ).

■ You can adjust how long the title pauses by moving the Pause slider ( ).

212

10 Editing with iMovie

WORKING WITH iMOVIE

Why is some of my text missing in a Scrolling Block title?

You may have placed too much text into it. Apple recommends that Scrolling Block titles not exceed 240 characters in order to avoid truncating the title.

What does the QT Margins checkbox do?

When checked (☐ changes to ☑), the **QT Margins** setting allows iMovie to extend titles to the edge of the frame. You should uncheck this box if you intend to show your movie on a television, as most televisions do not show the complete video frame, and text near the edges of the frame may become lost or distorted.

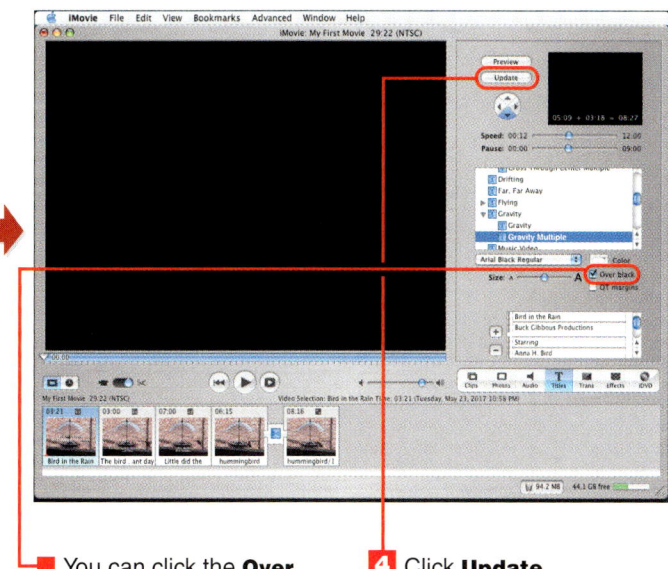

■ You can click the **Over Black** option (☐ changes to ☑) to make the title appear over a black screen rather than over a clip.

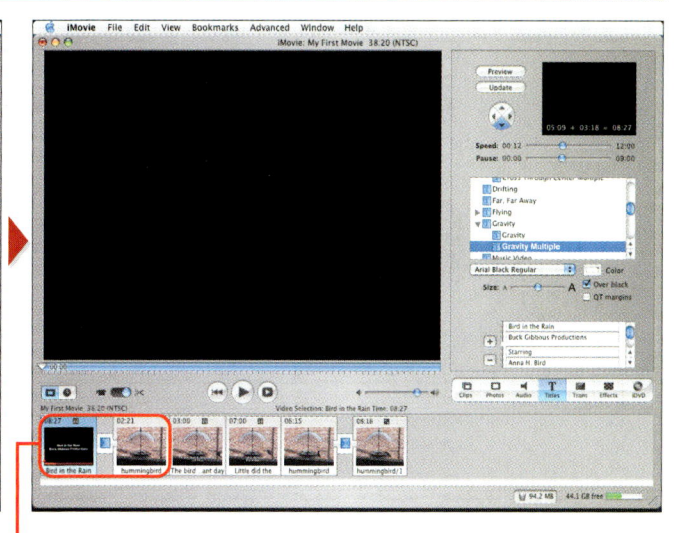

4 Click **Update**.

■ iMovie updates the title, lengthening or shortening the clip to the title's right if necessary.

213

MODIFY TITLE FONT AND COLOR

You can present your titles using any font installed on your Mac, and you can color them in one of over 16 million colors.

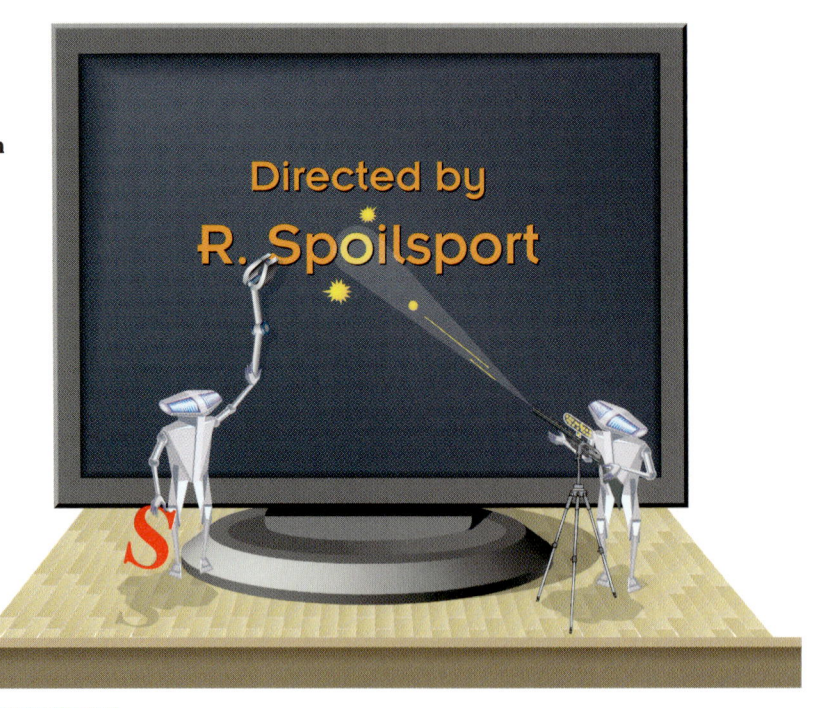

MODIFY TITLE FONT AND COLOR

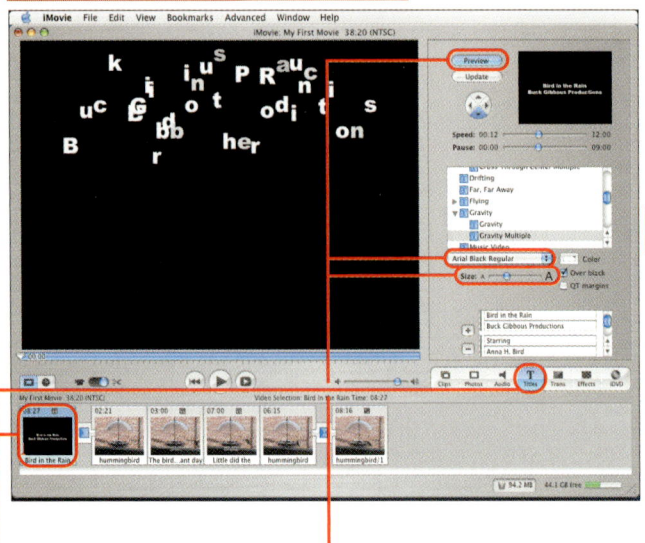

1 Click the **Titles** button.

2 Click the title clip that you want to modify.

3 Click and drag the Font Size slider ( ) to change the title's size.

■ You can click **Preview** to see the effect of the change.

4 Click the Font .

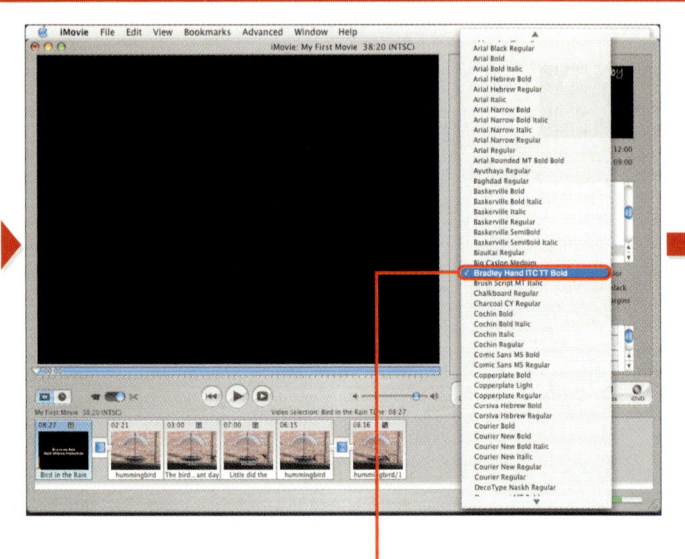

■ A menu appears listing all the available fonts.

5 Select a font.

10 Editing with iMovie

WORKING WITH iMOVIE

Which fonts work the best for titles?

Because televisions have lower resolution than computer screens, text that appears sharp on a computer display may appear less sharp, or even unreadable, on a TV. Large fonts with bold strokes look better on TV than compact fonts with thin lines and serifs.

The centered title style I am using does not actually center the title on the screen. Why not?

iMovie may be having trouble interpreting the font's internal size information correctly. Try using a different font. If that does not work, try placing a few spaces in front of each line of the title to compensate for the problem.

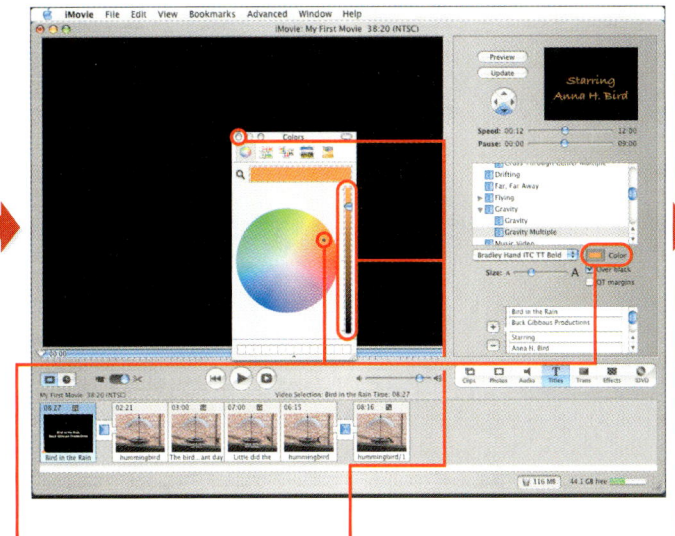

6 Click the Color button ( ).

■ The Colors window appears.

7 Click in the circle to select a new color for the title font.

■ The chosen color appears in the Color button.

8 Click and drag the Colors window's ▣ to change the color's brightness.

9 Click ◯.

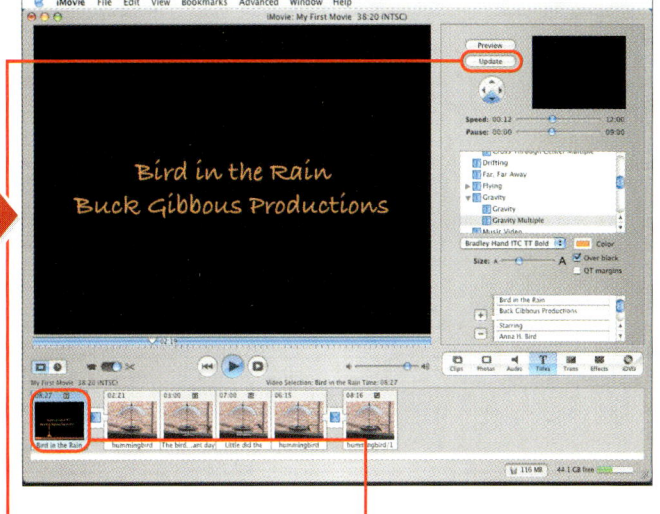

■ iMovie closes the Color window.

10 Click **Update**.

■ iMovie renders the modified title clip.

215

WORK WITH THE TIMELINE

iMovie's Timeline view gives you more control over your movie's timing and allows you to trim clips quickly with the mouse.

iMovie's Clips view lets you arrange the order of the clips in your movie; the Timeline view lets you view and fine-tune the duration of each of the clips in your movie.

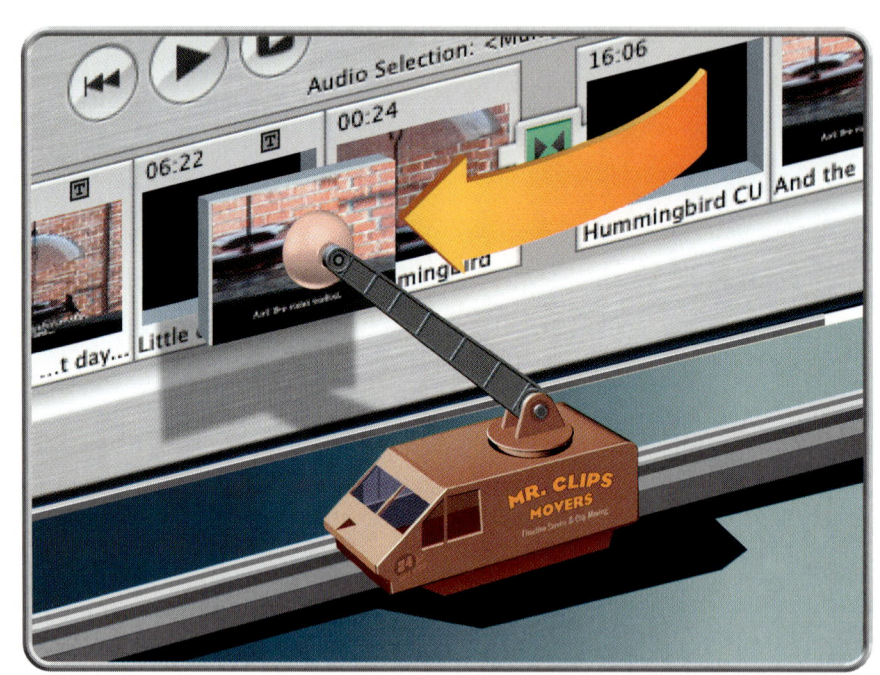

WORK WITH THE TIMELINE

VIEW THE TIMELINE

1 Click the **Clips** button.

2 Click the Timeline View button ( ).

■ The Clips Viewer transforms into the Timeline Viewer.

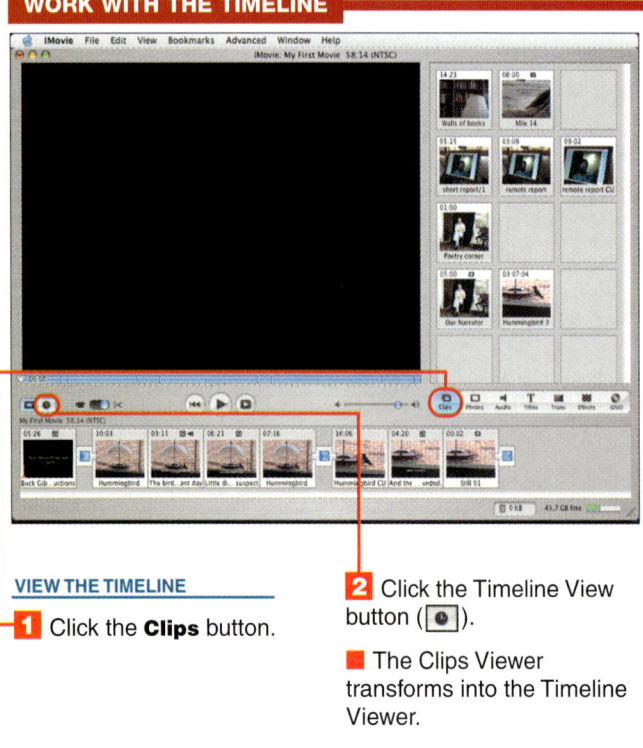

■ The size of a clip in the Timeline is proportional to the clip's duration.

3 Click and drag the Timeline Viewer's playhead ( ).

■ The Monitor's display and change accordingly.

4 Click and drag the Zoom slider ( ) to the right.

■ Zooming the Timeline lets you adjust timings more accurately.

■ The clips in the Timeline widen, and a scroll bar appears beneath the Timeline.

216

11 Using Advanced iMovie Features

WORKING WITH IMOVIE

What are bookmarks and how do I use them?

To quickly move the playhead (▽) to different parts of the movie on which you are working, you can set bookmarks on the Timeline. Bookmarks look like green diamonds (◆) in the Timeline view. Although you cannot see bookmarks in the Clips view, you can still set them and move among them. Follow these steps to set a bookmark:

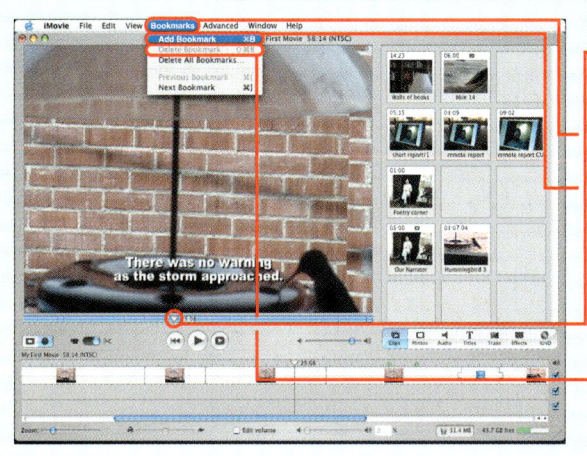

1 Click and drag ▽ to where you want a bookmark.

2 Click **Bookmarks**.

3 Click **Add Bookmark**.

■ iMovie adds the bookmark.

■ You can press ⌘+] or ⌘+[to move to the next or previous bookmark, respectively.

■ You can delete a bookmark by moving to it and then clicking **Delete Bookmark**.

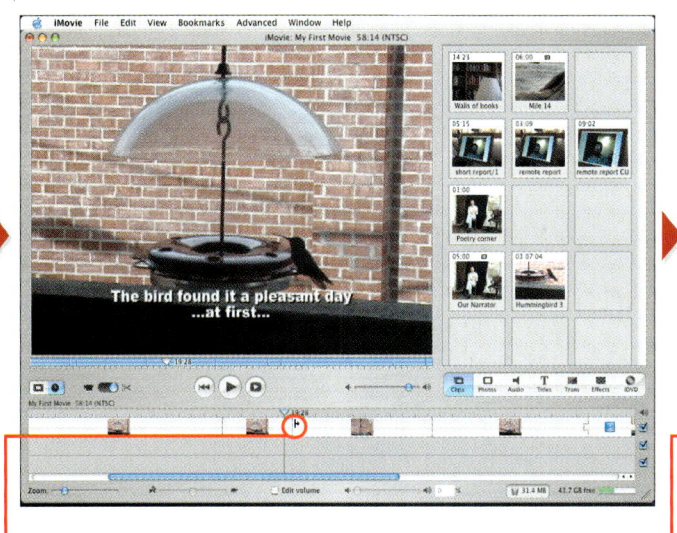

TRIM CLIPS DIRECTLY

5 Place the mouse near the left end of a clip that has rounded corners, which indicates an untrimmed clip.

■ The cursor changes to ╀.

6 Click and drag to the right.

■ The clip becomes smaller and a gap opens to its left.

7 Release the mouse.

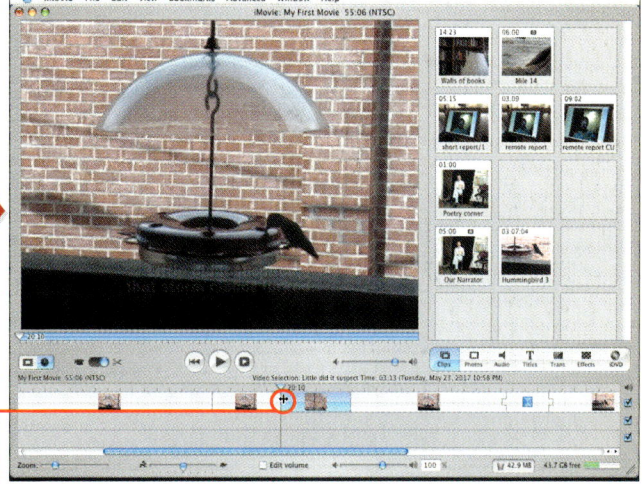

■ The adjacent clips move and the gap disappears.

8 Place the cursor near the left end of the trimmed clip (cursor changes to ↔).

9 Click and drag to the left.

■ The clip grows wider and the clip to the left shrinks as you drag.

10 Release the mouse.

■ The clip remains wider and the clip to the left reverts to its previous size.

CONTINUED

217

WORK WITH THE TIMELINE

You can create black and color clips in the Timeline view to serve as placeholders or as backgrounds for titles, and you can use the audio scrubbing feature to help you match your edits to your movie's soundtrack.

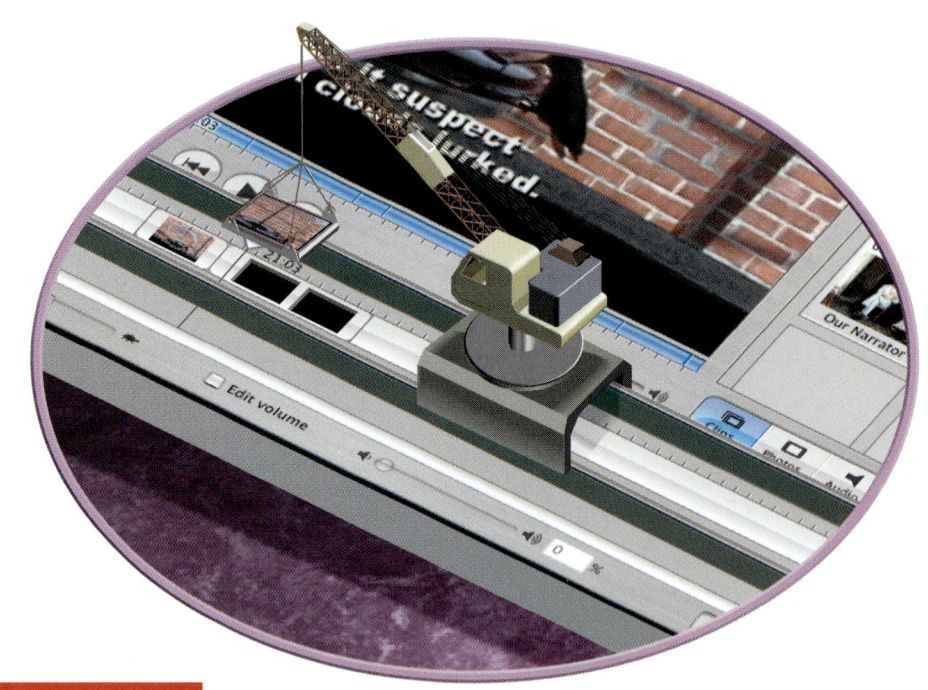

WORK WITH THE TIMELINE (CONTINUED)

CREATE BLACK AND COLOR CLIPS

11 Place the mouse over the center of a clip and click and drag to the right.

■ The clips and all the clips to its right move and a gap opens in the Timeline.

12 Release the mouse.

■ The gap, which remains, is a "black clip" which displays a black screen in the Monitor whenever the ▽ is over it.

13 Press `Ctrl` and click in the gap.

■ A contextual menu appears.

14 Click **Create Color Clip**.

■ A clip appears in the gap.

■ The clip is selected.

218

11 Using Advanced iMovie Features

WORKING WITH IMOVIE

Why are there two playheads?

The Timeline view has a playhead (▽) that you can use in addition to the ▽ beneath iMovie's Monitor. The Monitor's ▽ only controls the currently selected clip, while the Timeline view's ▽ can travel over the entire movie. This can streamline your work when you are making edits back and forth between several clips.

Why does the Timeline ▽ seem to lurch and make a popping noise as I drag it?

You have the **Enable Timeline snapping** and **Play snap sounds** options (☐ changes to ☑) selected in your iMovie preferences. This feature makes the playhead "snap" to the beginning or end of a clip to help you make more precise edits. The snapping noise alerts you when you drag the ▽ over a clip boundary. For more on setting iMovie preferences, see Chapter 9.

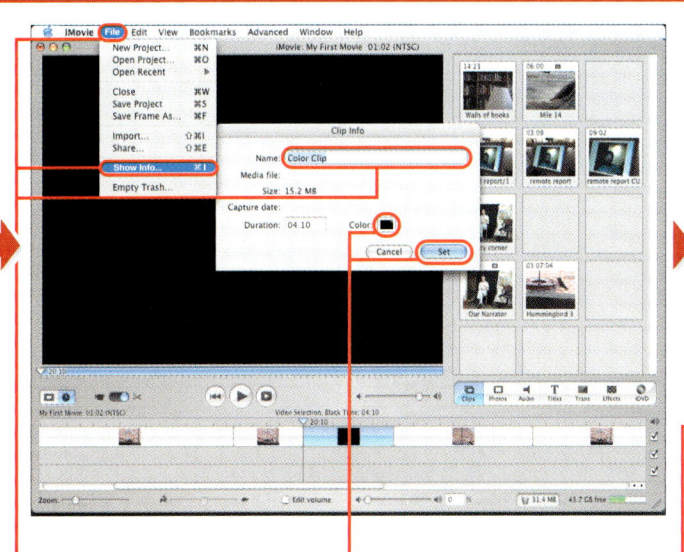

■ **15** Click **File**.

■ **16** Click **Show Info**.

■ A Clip Info window appears.

■ You can click here and type a name for the clip.

■ You can click here to set the color the clip displays.

■ **17** Click **Set**.

■ The clip reflects the changes you made.

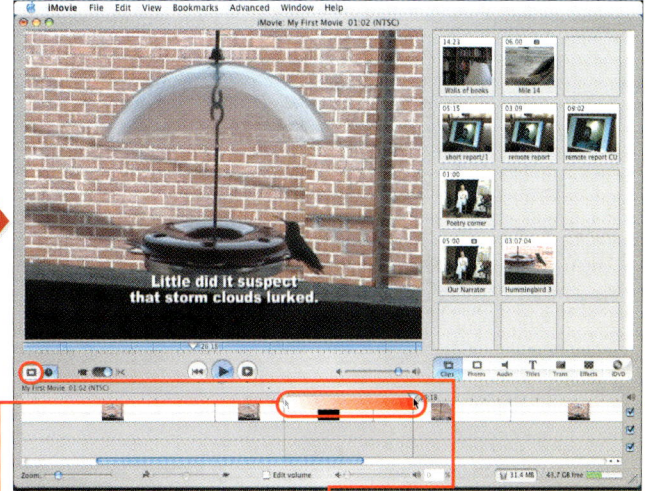

SCRUB AUDIO

■ **18** Press `option` as you drag the Timeline ▽ playhead left and right.

■ As you drag, you can hear the audio from the clip under the playhead.

■ You can use this audio "scrub" feature to help you find where to cut or trim a clip.

■ **19** Click the **Clips** button (▢).

■ The Clips view replaces the Timeline.

219

SEPARATE AUDIO FROM VIDEO

iMovie's Timeline view provides two audio tracks beneath its clips track. You can separate the sound from a clip and place it on one of the audio tracks, and then move the sound elsewhere in your movie, such as beneath a title sequence or a still image.

This section begins with iMovie's Clips view showing. See the section "Work With the Timeline" for how to switch between iMovie's Clips and Timeline views.

SEPARATE AUDIO FROM VIDEO

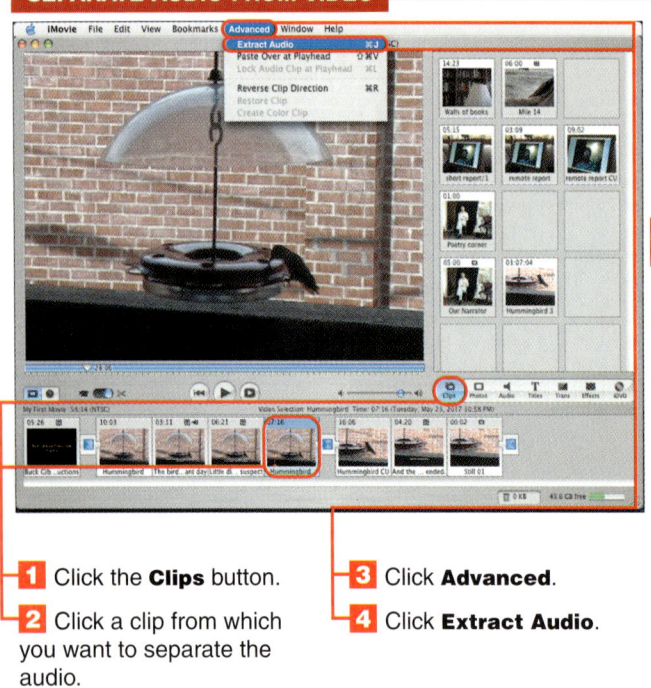

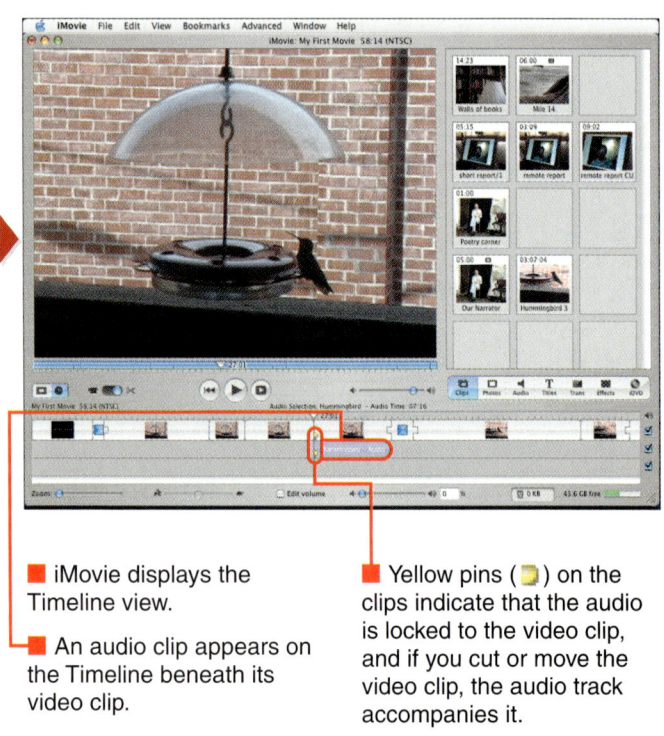

■ 1 Click the **Clips** button.

■ 2 Click a clip from which you want to separate the audio.

■ 3 Click **Advanced**.

■ 4 Click **Extract Audio**.

■ iMovie displays the Timeline view.

■ An audio clip appears on the Timeline beneath its video clip.

■ Yellow pins ( ) on the clips indicate that the audio is locked to the video clip, and if you cut or move the video clip, the audio track accompanies it.

220

11 Using Advanced iMovie Features

WORKING WITH IMOVIE

What do the checkboxes to the right of the Timeline do?

The checkboxes turn the audio on and off for each of the tracks in the Timeline. When you deselect a track's checkbox (☑ changes to ☐), iMovie does not play or export the track's audio.

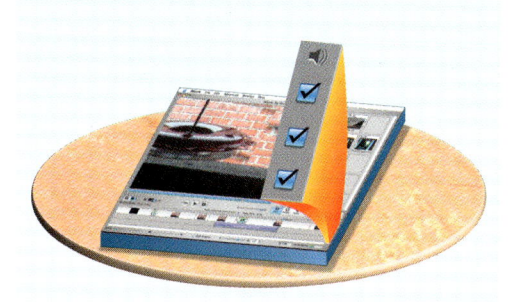

Can I place the sound back in the clip after I separate it?

No, but you do not need to. When you extract a clip's audio, a copy of it remains in the clip with its volume set to 0. You can simply adjust the Timeline Viewer's volume editing controls to make the clip's sound audible again. For more information on how to use these controls, see the section "Adjust Audio Volume."

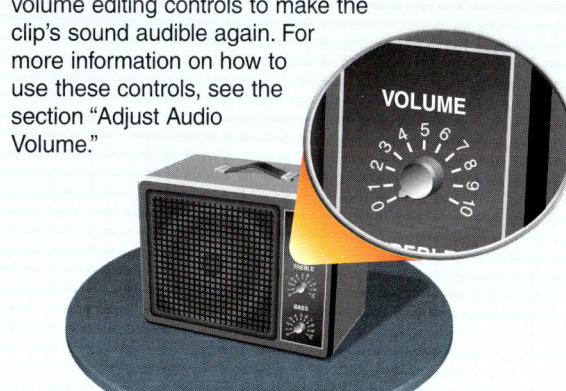

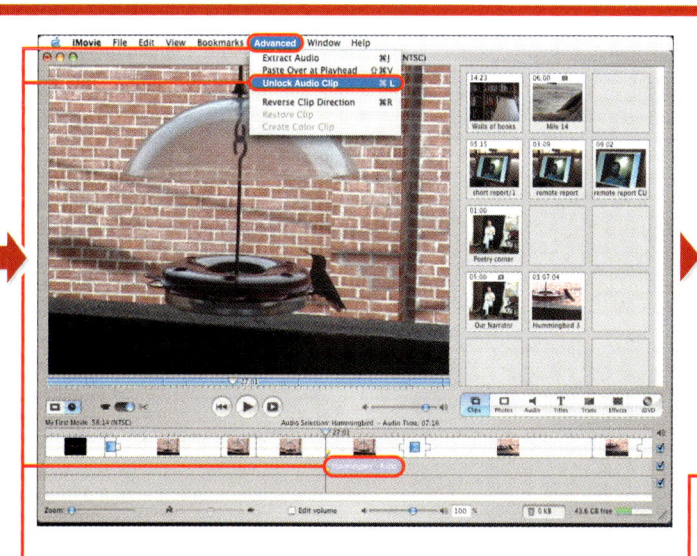

5 Click the audio clip.

6 Click **Advanced**.

7 Click **Unlock Audio Clip**.

■ The audio clip unlocks and the yellow pins vanish.

■ If you later move or cut the video clip, the audio remains in place.

8 Click and drag the audio clip along the Timeline.

■ The audio clip moves to a new position on the Timeline.

■ You can click **Advanced**, and then select **Lock Audio** to lock the audio to the clip it is now under.

221

ADJUST AUDIO VOLUME

You can raise or lower the volume of a movie, a clip, or even part of a clip with iMovie's volume editing controls. You may want to adjust the volume to make the audio in two adjoining clips match, or to compensate for sound that was recorded too low to hear easily.

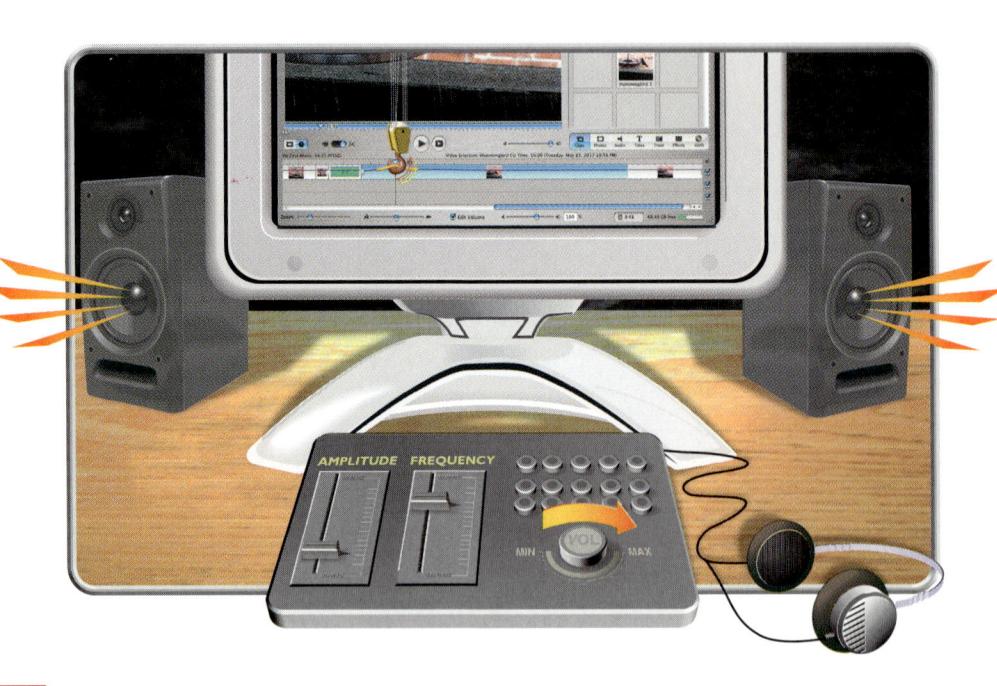

ADJUST AUDIO VOLUME

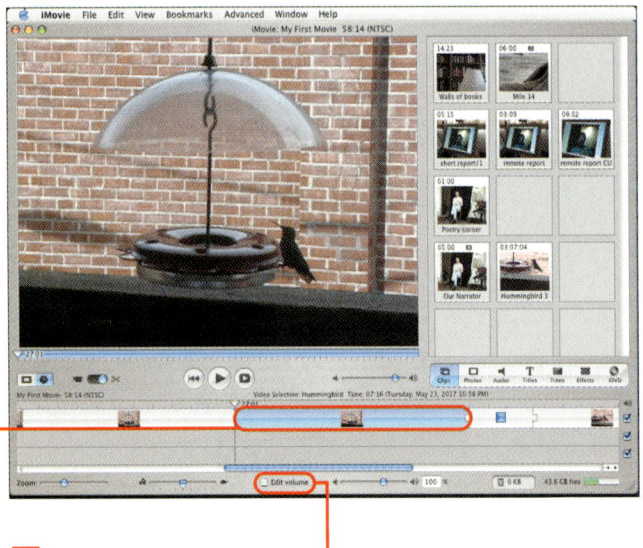

1 In the Timeline view, click a clip for which you want to adjust the volume.

Note: For more on the Timeline view, see the section "Work with the Timeline."

2 Click the **Edit Volume** option (☐ changes to ☑).

■ Colored volume indicator lines representing each clip's volume settings appear on top of the clips.

3 Click and drag the volume slider slightly to the left.

222

11 Using Advanced iMovie Features

WORKING WITH IMOVIE

How can I trim an audio clip?

You can trim an audio clip in the Timeline the same way you trim video clips: position the mouse near the end of the clip (the cursor changes to ├ or ┤), then click and drag to shorten the clip. The trimmed sound remains part of the clip, although it does not play until you empty iMovie's Trash. Note that you cannot trim audio clips if you do not select the **Edit Volume** option (☐ changes to ☑) at the bottom of the screen.

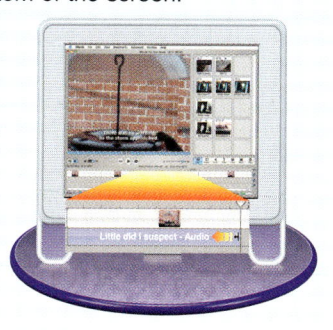

How can I remove a volume change dot that I no longer want?

Click the dot (●) and then press `Delete`. The ● disappears and the clip's volume adjusts itself accordingly.

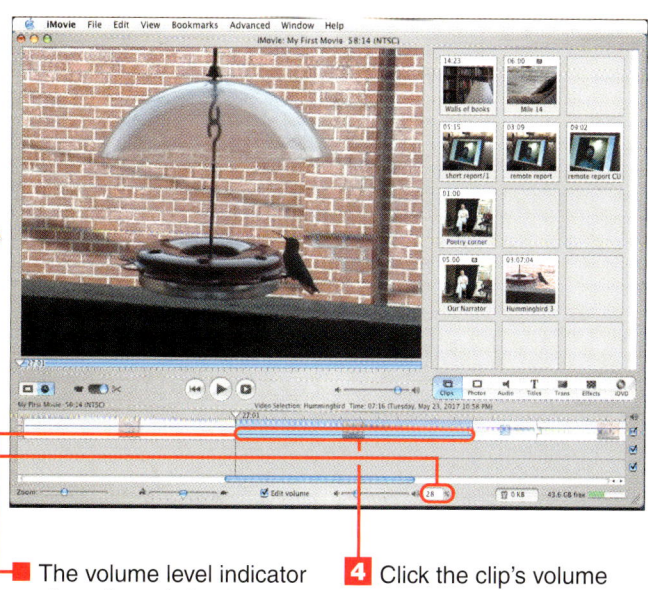

■ The volume level indicator on the selected clip descends to the bottom of the clip and the volume indicator number changes.

4 Click the clip's volume indicator line and drag it slightly upward.

■ A yellow volume control dot (●) and a small anchor dot appear on the volume indicator; a portion of the volume indicator changes color and bends upward following the mouse.

■ You can drag the anchor dot left or right to change the volume indicator's curve, which controls how quickly the volume changes.

223

ADD ITUNES AUDIO TO A MOVIE

iMovie can show you your iTunes music library and playlists, and it lets you add any song from your music collection to one of your movie's audio tracks.

Once you add your iTunes audio, you can adjust the volume of the music. For more information, see the section "Adjust Audio Volume."

ADD ITUNES AUDIO TO A MOVIE

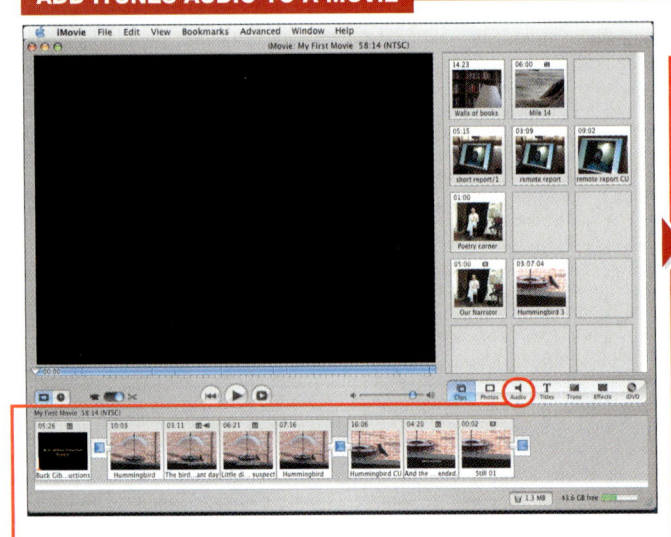

■ 1 Click the **Audio** button.

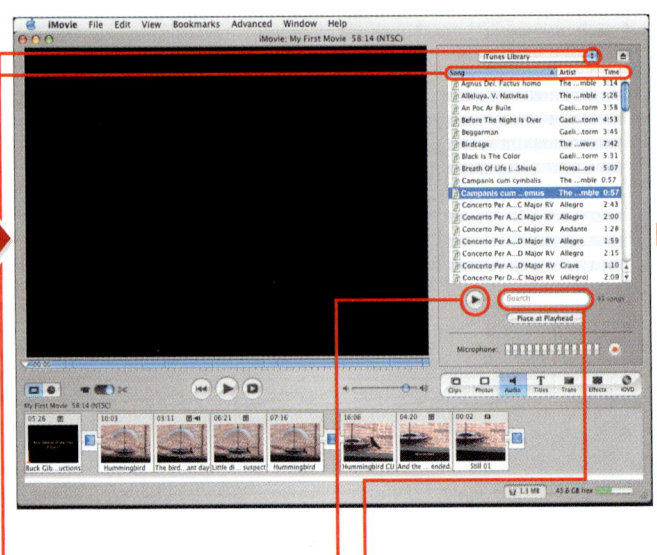

■ iMovie's Audio pane appears, listing the songs in your iTunes Library.

■ You can sort the iTunes song list by clicking the column headings.

■ You can click here and select one of your iTunes playlists from the menu.

■ You can click and type in the Search panel to find a song.

■ You can listen to a selected song by clicking the Play button (▶).

224

11 Using Advanced iMovie Features

WORKING WITH IMOVIE

Can I use songs purchased from the iTunes Music Store in my movies?

Yes, as long as you have authorized your Mac to play them. Note that purchased music is copyrighted, and you may not legally exhibit movies publicly that use copyrighted music without obtaining permission from the music's copyright holder. For more on the Music Store, see Chapter 4.

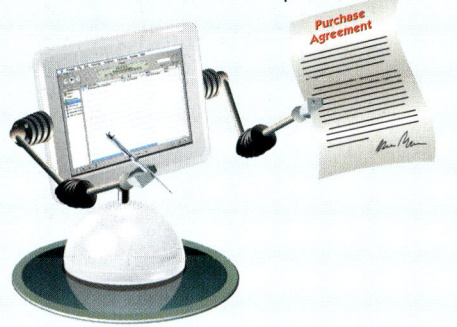

How can I import songs from a CD?

Simply insert an audio CD in your Mac's CD drive. The popup menu in iMovie's Audio pane shows the CD you inserted; you can click your CD and select the track you want in the audio pane just like you can for your iTunes songs. The Audio pane has an eject button that you can click to eject the CD when you are done with it.

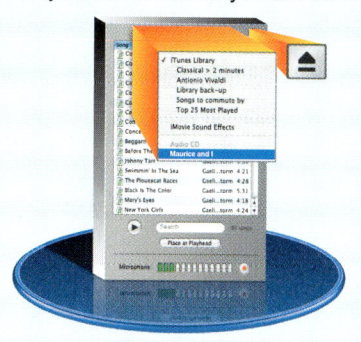

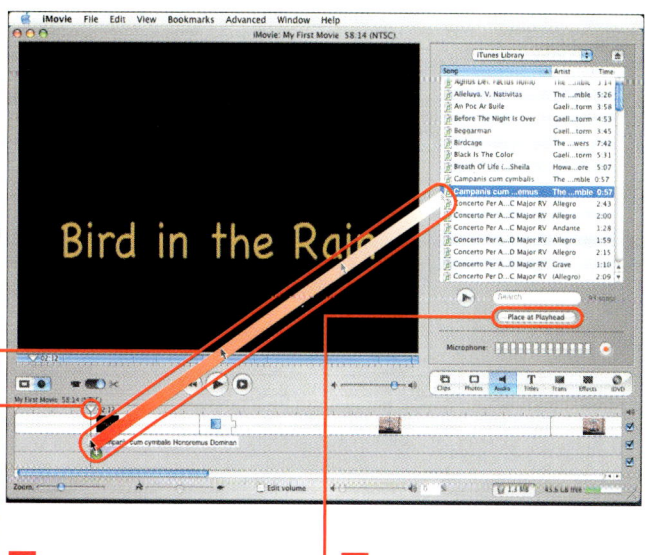

2 Click and drag a song.

■ If the Clips view is visible, the Timeline view appears as you begin to drag the song.

■ The ▽ follows the mouse as you drag over the Timeline.

3 Release the mouse over an audio track where you want the song to start in your movie.

■ You can click **Place at Playhead** to place a song in your movie at the current playhead position.

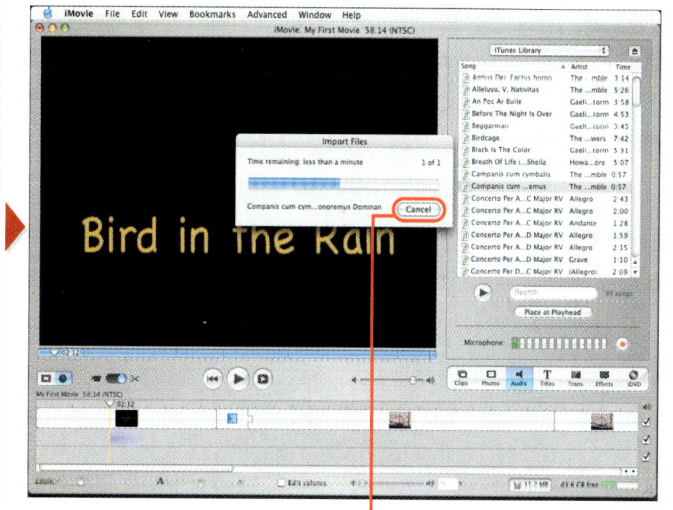

■ iMovie displays an Import Files window showing you the progress of the music import.

■ You can click **Cancel** to stop the import.

■ The song appears in the audio track.

225

ADD IMOVIE SOUND EFFECTS

iMovie comes with collections of sound effects that you can use to add drama, humor, or subtle audio textures to your movies.

ADD IMOVIE SOUND EFFECTS

1 Click the **Audio** button.

■ The Audio pane appears.

2 Click the Audio pane's source.

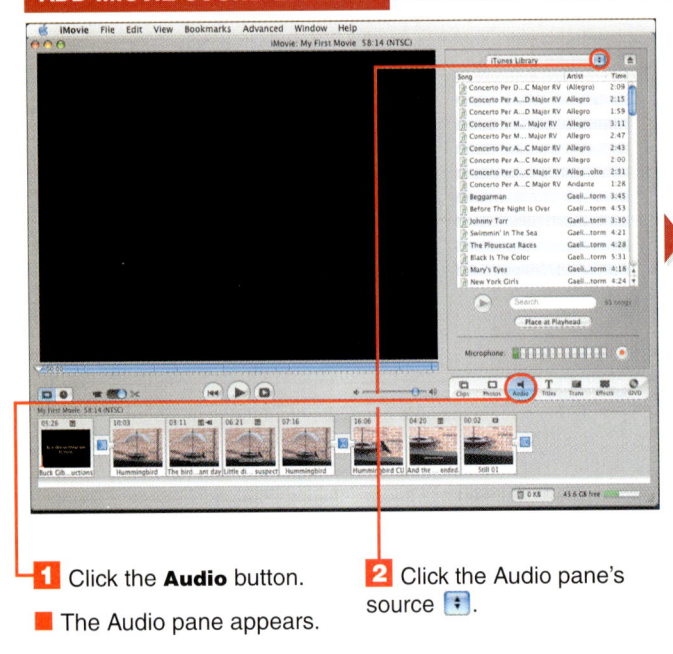

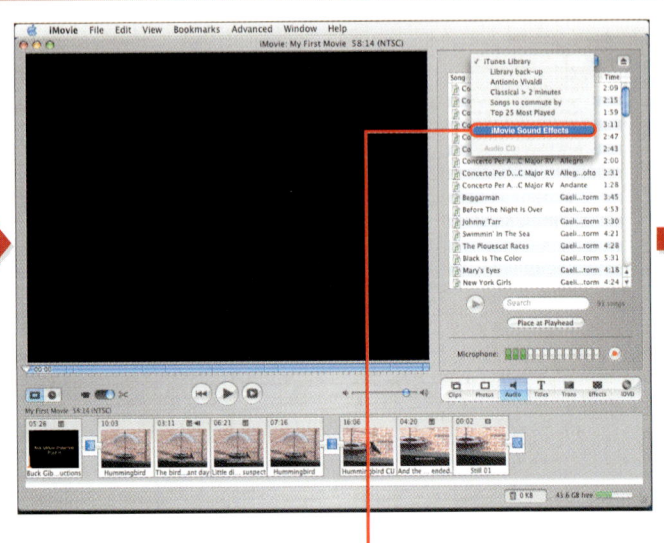

■ A menu appears containing your iTunes playlists and several other items.

3 Select **iMovie Sound Effects**.

11 Using Advanced iMovie Features

WORKING WITH IMOVIE

How can I blend two sounds together?

You can overlap audio clips on either audio track by dragging one clip over the other in the Timeline. Where the clips overlap you hear a mixture of the two sounds.

What does the Show audio track waveforms preference do?

When this preference is selected, iMovie draws a picture of the audio that each audio clip in the Timeline view contains. You can use these pictures to help you find where specific words or sounds occur in the clip. The larger the dark area is at a particular place in the clip, the louder the sound.

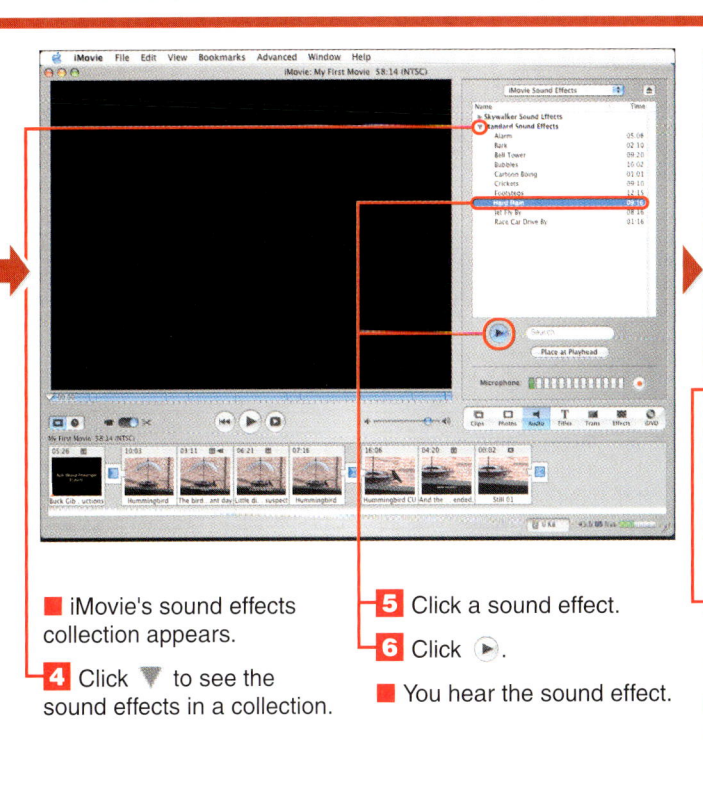

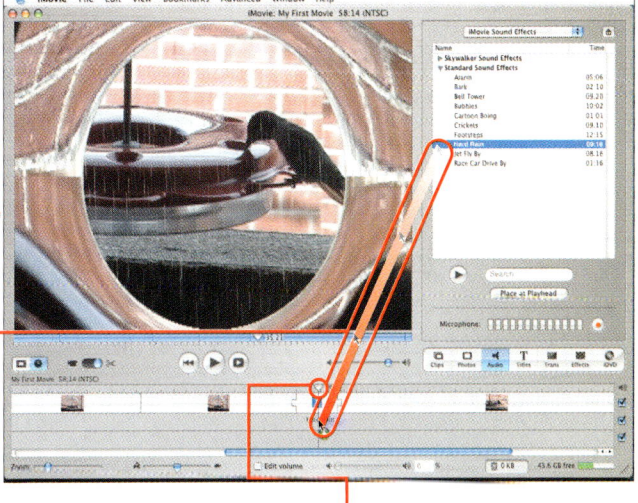

■ iMovie's sound effects collection appears.

4 Click ▼ to see the sound effects in a collection.

5 Click a sound effect.

6 Click ▶.

■ You hear the sound effect.

7 Click and drag a sound effect from the list to your movie.

■ If the Clips view is visible, the Timeline view replaces it.

■ The ▽ moves to follow the mouse.

8 Release the mouse when the sound effect is where you want it.

■ iMovie places the sound in the soundtrack.

227

RECORD NARRATION

If your Mac has a microphone, you can record a voice-over narration directly into your movie.

RECORD NARRATION

1 Click and drag ▽ to where you want the recording to start.

2 Click the **Audio** button.

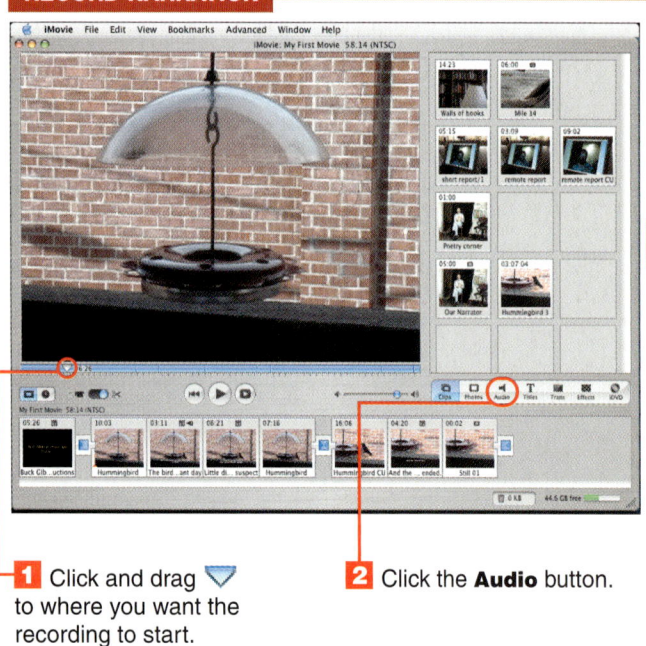

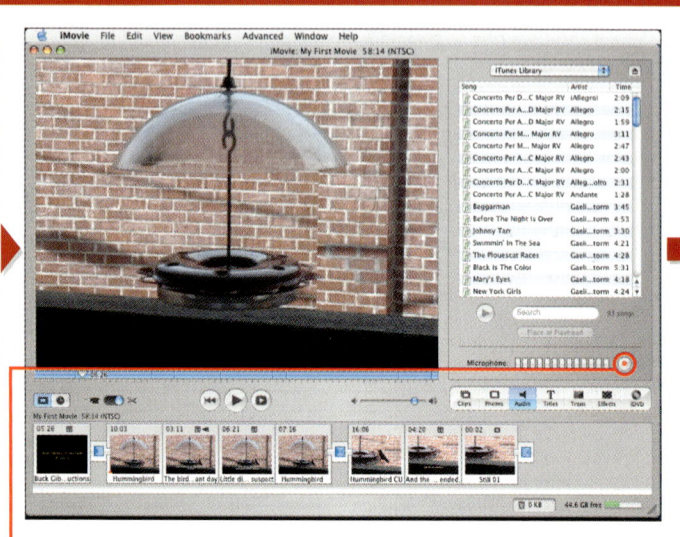

■ The Audio pane appears.

3 Click the Microphone's red button (●).

4 Begin speaking into the microphone.

228

11 Using Advanced iMovie Features

WORKING WITH IMOVIE

What kind of microphone do I need to have in order to record a narration?

In many cases, you already have one built into your Mac, although sometimes it is hard to see. You can tell if you have a microphone by clicking the **Audio** button to open iMovie's Audio pane and then talking. If the microphone indicator in the Audio pane lights up, you have one. Otherwise, you can use almost any inexpensive USB microphone with iMovie. Consult your Mac's documentation for how to add a USB microphone to your Mac.

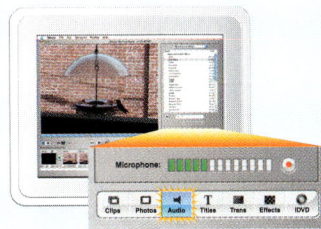

How loudly do I need to speak when I record a narration?

Before you begin recording, open iMovie's Audio pane by clicking the **Audio** button, read your narration, and watch iMovie's microphone meter. If the meter frequently displays yellow and red rectangles toward its right end, you are speaking too loudly; if the meter never displays more than three or four green rectangles, you are not speaking loudly enough.

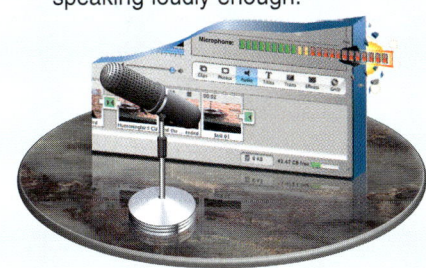

■ If the Clips view is visible, iMovie displays the Timeline in its place.

■ The ▽ moves as iMovie adds the recording to one of the audio tracks.

■ iMovie mutes the other soundtracks as you record.

5 Click ⏺ again.

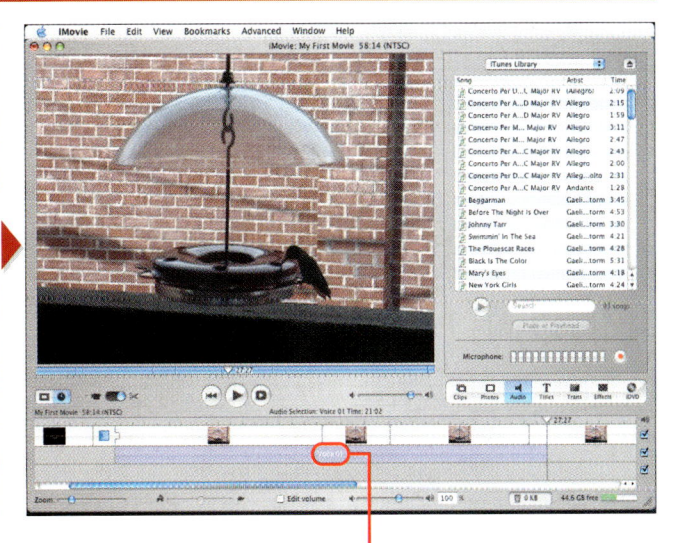

■ iMovie ends the recording and stops the ▽.

■ iMovie labels the audio clip containing the recording Voice followed by a two-digit number.

229

RECORD FROM ISIGHT

You can record from Apple's iSight camera directly into your movie. If you have an iSight and a laptop Mac, you can make videos anywhere without a digital camcorder.

RECORD FROM ISIGHT

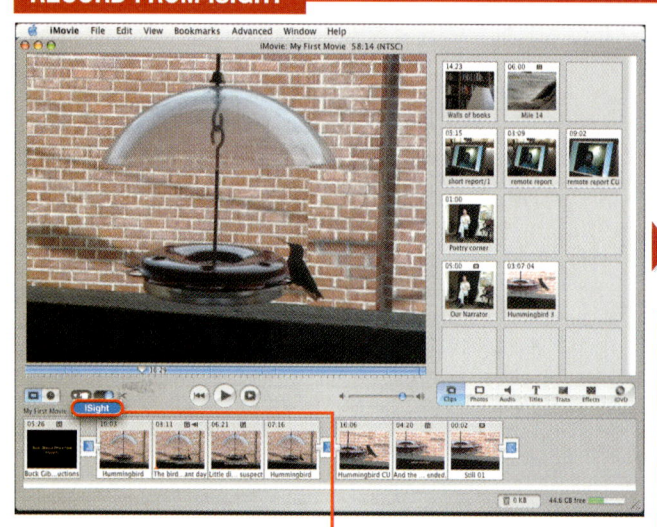

1 Connect your iSight camera to your Mac and make sure your camera's iris is open.

Note: Consult your iSight's documentation to learn more about attaching an iSight to your Mac.

2 Click the camera icon and select **iSight**.

■ iMovie switches to camera mode.

■ The image from the iSight appears in the Monitor display.

3 Click **Record With iSight**.

230

11 Using Advanced iMovie Features

WORKING WITH IMOVIE

How much video can I record at one time with the iSight?

If you have enough disk space on your Mac, you can record about nine and one-half minutes at a time from the iSight. That much video requires between three and four gigabytes of available disk space.

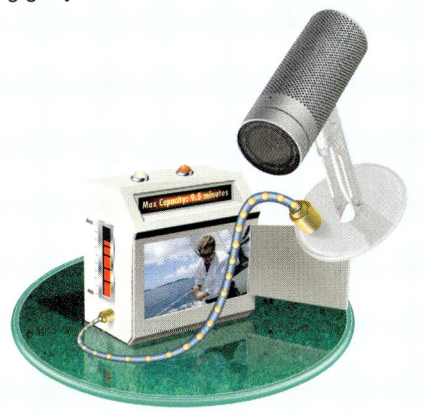

What kind of Mac do I need to use an iSight with iMovie?

The iSight camera requires a Macintosh running at 600MHz or faster with a G3, G4, or G5 PowerPC processor. The camera also requires that the Mac have Mac OS X 10.2.7 or above and a FireWire connector.

- iMovie begins recording.
- A new clip appears in the Clips pane.

4 Click **Record With iSight**.

- The recording ends.
- A dialog appears with a progress bar as iMovie converts the recording to the digital video format it uses.

- You can click **Cancel** to stop the conversion and discard the recording.

231

CHANGE A CLIP'S SPEED

You can slow down a video clip to see the action it contains more clearly, or speed it up for a humorous effect.

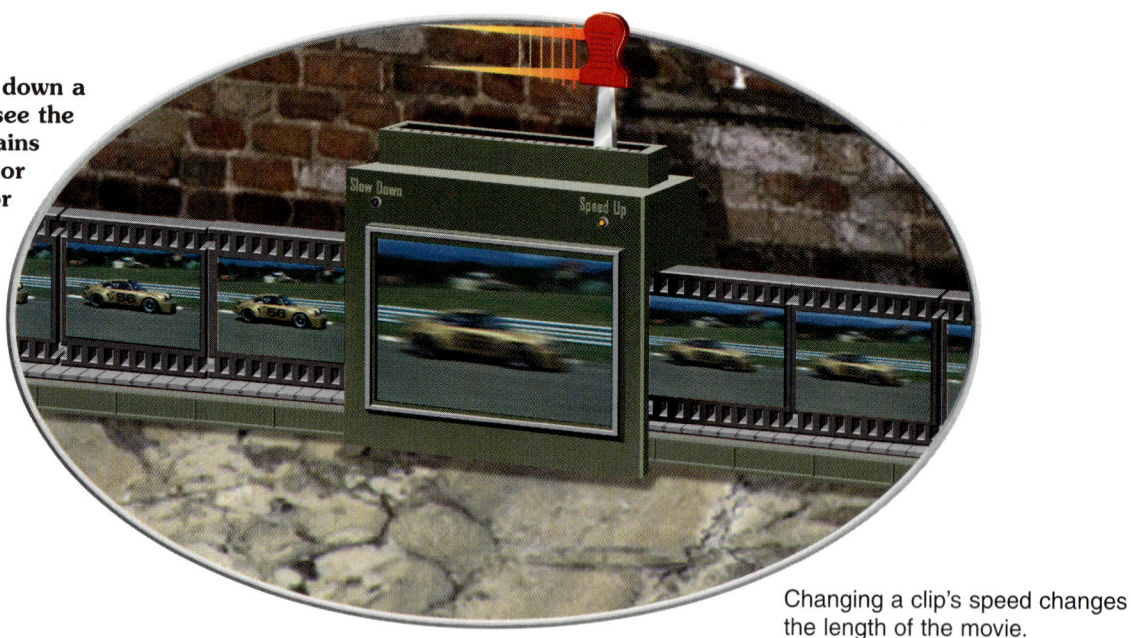

Changing a clip's speed changes the length of the movie.

CHANGE A CLIP'S SPEED

1 Click the **Clips** button.

2 Click [ ] to display the Timeline Viewer.

3 Click the clip for which you want to change the speed.

4 Click and drag the Clip Speed [ ] to the right (toward the [ ]).

■ The clip becomes slower and longer, changing the clip's length.

■ You can slide [ ] to the left (toward the [ ]) to make the clip shorter and faster.

■ Dragging [ ] also changes the clip's audio.

Note: To avoid modifying the clip's audio, you can separate it from the clip first by following the steps in the section "Separate Audio from Video."

232

REVERSE A CLIP'S DIRECTION

11 Using Advanced iMovie Features

WORKING WITH IMOVIE

You can play a clip backward — perhaps to change a camera shot from a zoom-out to a zoom-in or to create an interesting visual effect — with iMovie's Reverse Clip Direction command.

Note that iMovie reverses the clip's audio as well as its video. You can extract the clip's audio track before reversing the clip to avoid this. For more information, see the section "Separate Audio from Video."

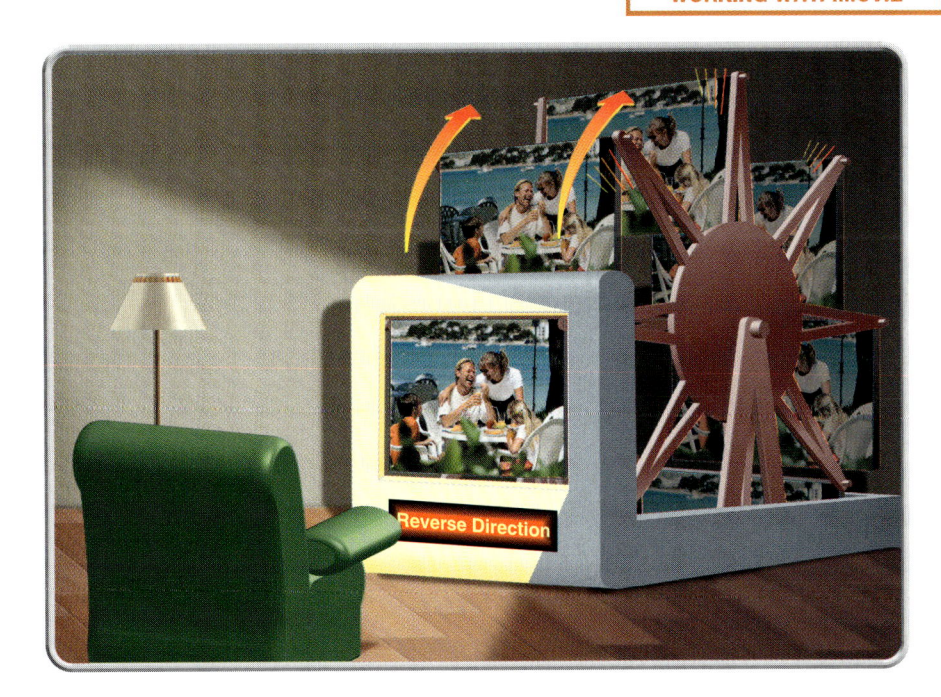

REVERSE A CLIP'S DIRECTION

■ **1** Click the **Clips** button.

■ **2** Click the clip you want to reverse.

■ **3** Click **Advanced**.

■ **4** Click **Reverse Clip Direction**.

■ iMovie reverses the clip.

■ A symbol ( ) appears on the clip in the Clips Viewer.

233

PASTE OVER AT PLAYHEAD

You can paste a clip over a section of your movie, replacing just as much video as is needed to keep the movie's length unchanged. An example of this technique, known as *cross-cutting*, is when you switch between shots of a football quarterback scrambling and his intended pass receiver.

If you set your iMovie preferences to do so, you can also keep the soundtrack of the replaced video to create a *cutaway* edit. For example, you can create a *reaction shot* by pasting over some footage of a person talking with a clip of the person to whom she is speaking.

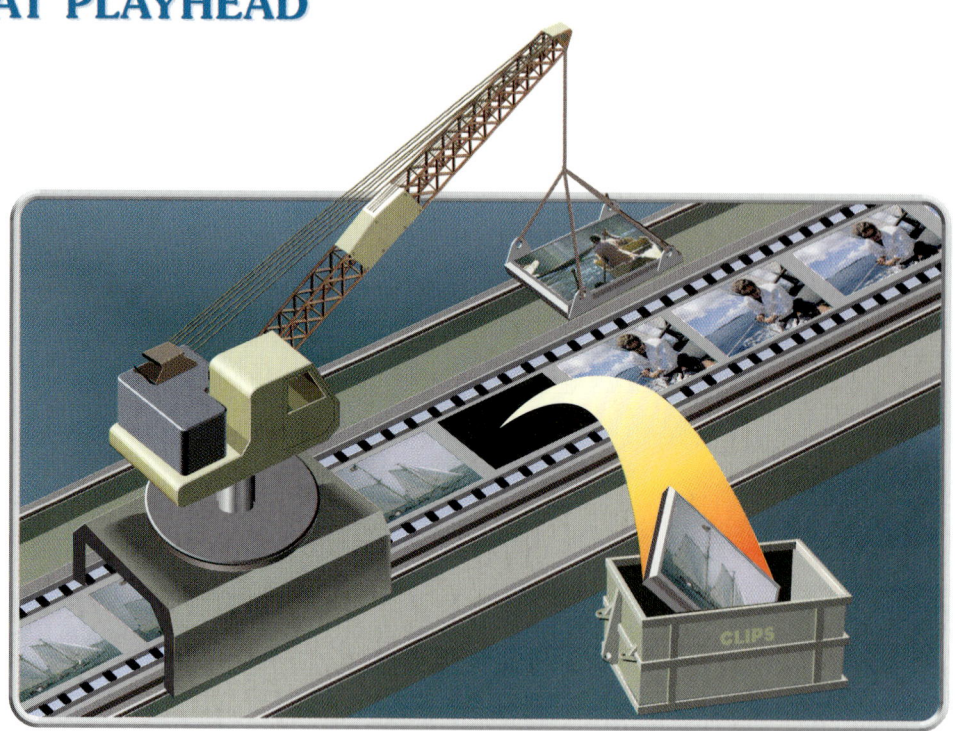

PASTE OVER AT PLAYHEAD

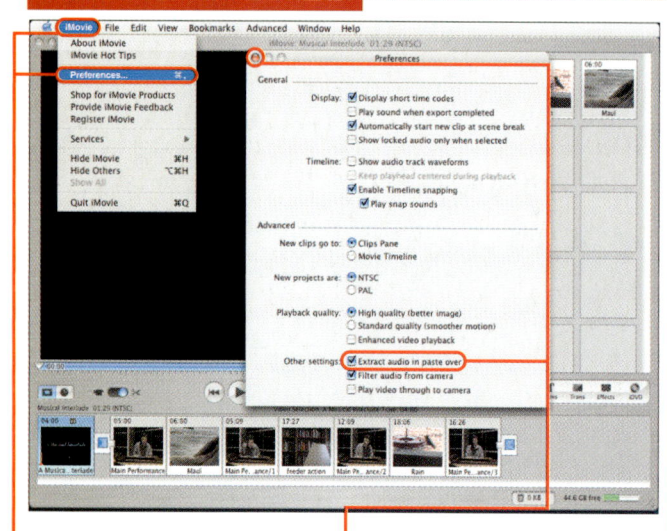

SET AUDIO PREFERENCES

1 Click **iMovie**.

2 Click **Preferences**.

■ The Preferences window appears.

■ You can click the **Extract audio in paste over** option (☐ changes to ☑) if you want to retain the audio track that the new visual material replaces.

3 Click the Close button (●).

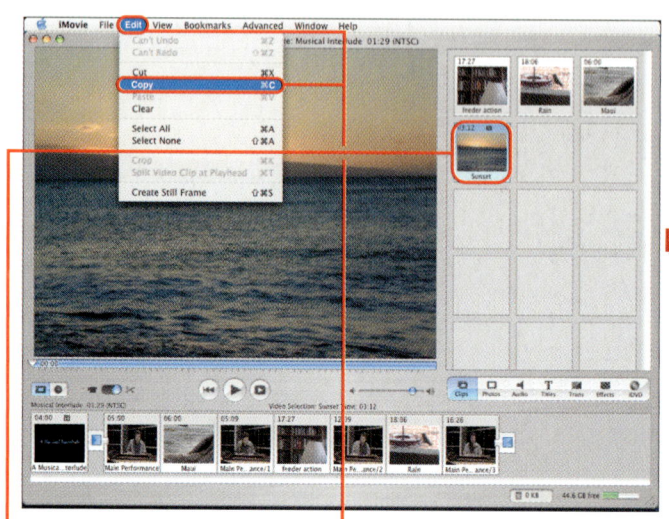

PASTE OVER THE CLIP

1 Click a clip you want to paste over another.

Note: You can use the Monitor's crop markers to select part of the clip; see Chapter 10 for more about using the crop markers.

2 Click **Edit**.

3 Click **Copy**.

234

11 Using Advanced iMovie Features

WORKING WITH IMOVIE

Why do I hear two soundtracks when I paste over a clip?

When you paste over at the playhead and you have set your preferences to extract the original clip's audio, the volume settings of both the extracted audio clip and the pasted clip remain unchanged. You can lower the volume of either clip by clicking the **Edit Volume** option (☐ changes to ☑) and dragging the volume level indicator in iMovie's Timeline Viewer. For more information on lowering the volume, see the section "Adjust Audio Volume."

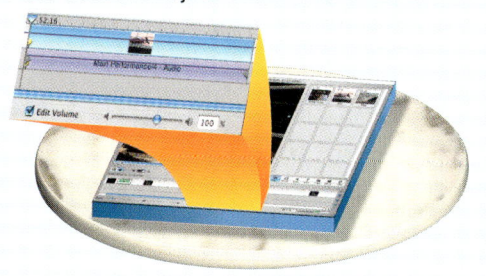

What happens if I simply paste a clip at the playhead instead of pasting over?

iMovie splits the clip at the playhead and inserts the new clip at that point. The movie becomes longer as a result. Note that if your movie contains unlocked audio clips, they retain their positions on the Timeline.

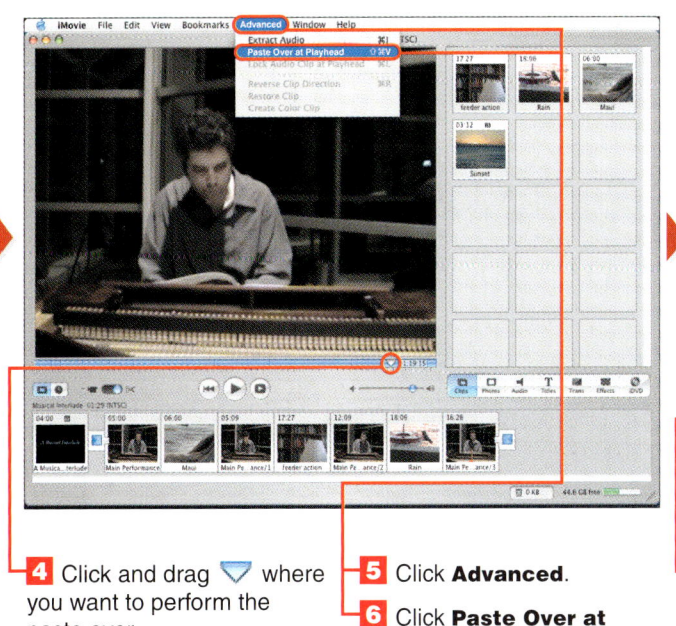

■ **4** Click and drag ▽ where you want to perform the paste over.

■ **5** Click **Advanced**.

■ **6** Click **Paste Over at Playhead**.

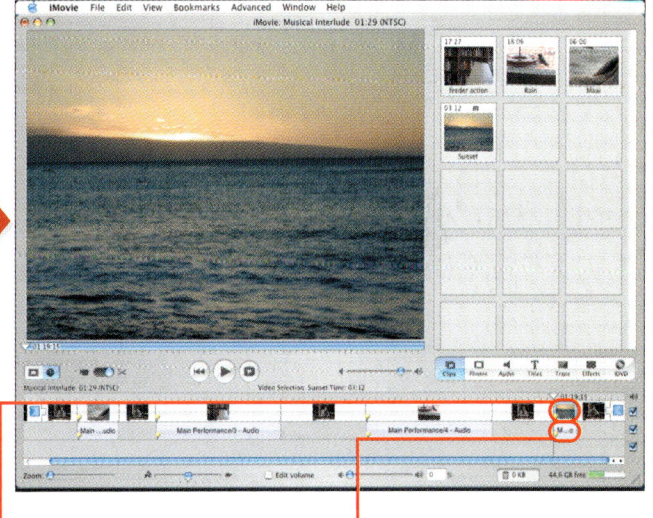

■ iMovie pastes the copied material over the movie starting at the ▽ position.

■ iMovie displays the result of the paste over in the Timeline view if you have selected the **Extract audio in paste over** preference option so that you can see and adjust the retained audio if necessary.

235

ADD CHAPTERS FOR IDVD

You can prepare your movie for iDVD by adding chapter markers to identify important scenes in your movie. iDVD can use your chapter markers to create scene menus automatically on a DVD that you create. Viewers of your DVD can then go immediately to each of the scenes you have marked.

This section assumes you are working in the Clips view; see the section "Work with the Timeline" to learn how to switch between the Timeline and Clips views. See Chapter 13 to learn how to create a DVD scene submenu from a movie created in iMovie that has chapter markers.

ADD CHAPTERS FOR IDVD

1 Click the **iDVD** button.

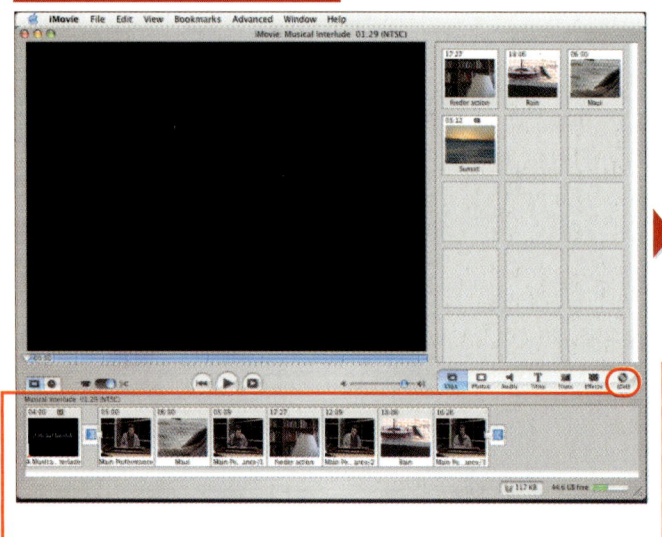

■ The iDVD pane appears.

2 Click and drag ▼ where you want to insert a chapter marker.

3 Click **Add Chapter**.

11 Using Advanced iMovie Features

WORKING WITH IMOVIE

How many chapter markers can I place in a movie?

You can place as many as 99 chapter markers in a movie because that is the maximum number of chapters that iDVD supports. See Chapter 13 for more information about DVD submenus in iDVD.

What is the difference between chapter markers and bookmarks?

iMovie bookmarks let you move quickly to different locations in your movie while you work on a project. They have no names and you cannot export them. Chapter markers have names. You can assign these names, which iDVD retains, when you export your movie to it, for use as movie button names. See Chapter 13 for more information about DVD submenu movie buttons in iDVD.

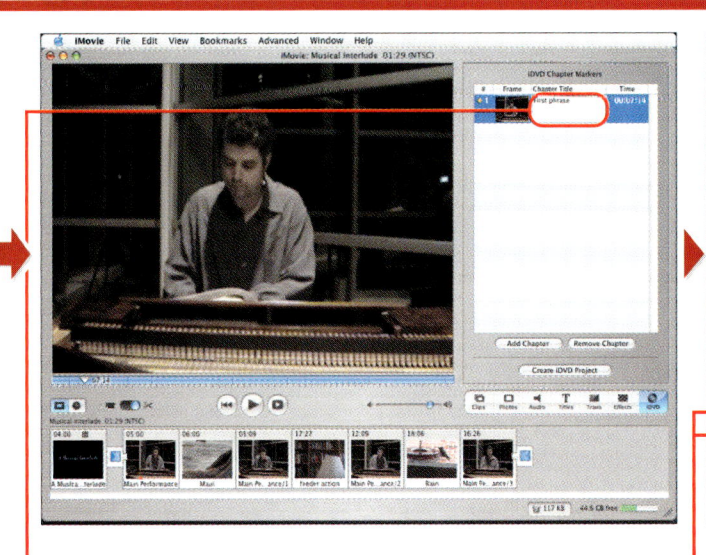

■ A chapter marker entry appears in the iDVD pane with the chapter title's text selected.

4 Click the chapter marker and type a chapter title.

5 Press `Enter`.

■ You can click the chapter title again to select and change it at any time.

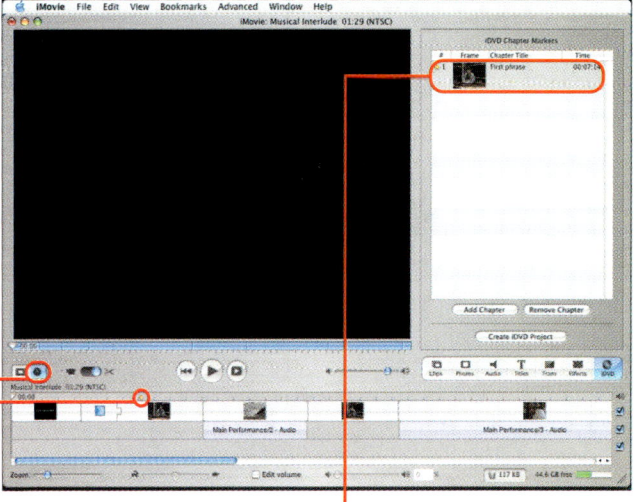

■ If the Clips view is visible, you can click 🔘 to see the Timeline view.

■ The chapter markers appear as yellow diamonds (◆) above the Timeline.

■ You can click a chapter in the iDVD pane to move ▽ to that chapter in your movie; this works in either the Clips view or the Timeline view.

237

EXPORT TO CAMERA

When you finish editing your movie, you can connect your digital camcorder to your Mac and record a perfect copy on tape as a back-up. You can then connect your camcorder to your TV and use your camcorder's VTR function to view your movie or connect the camcorder to a videocassette recorder to record a copy for your family and friends.

Make sure that you have a fresh tape, or one that does not have material on it that you want to keep, to avoid recording over something important.

EXPORT TO CAMERA

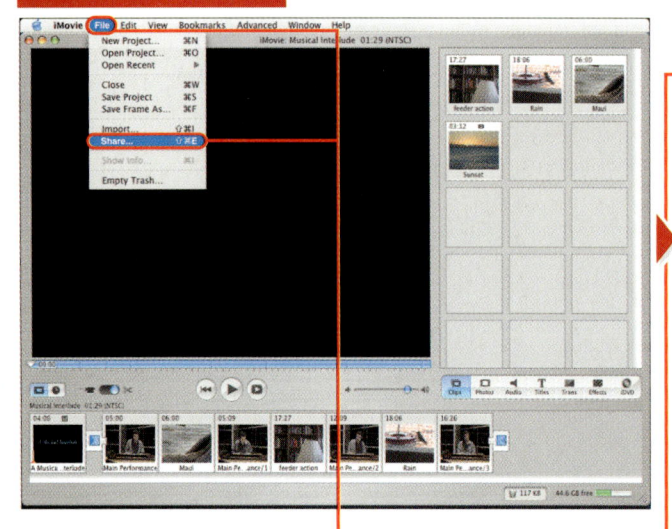

1 Place a writable tape in the camcorder and connect it to your Mac.

Note: For more on connecting a Digital Camcorder, see Chapter 9.

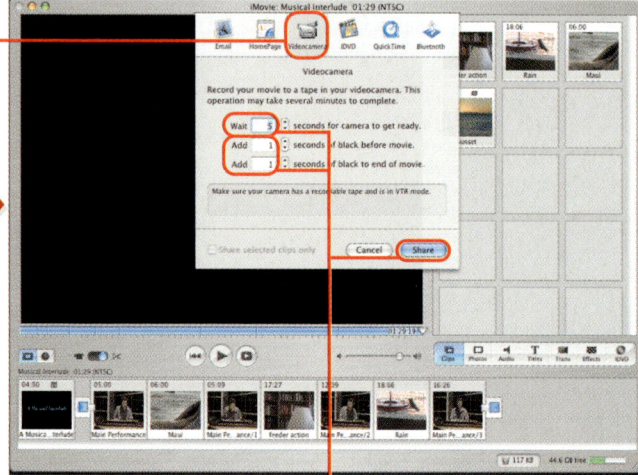

2 Click **File**.

3 Click **Share**.

■ A sheet descends from the top of the window.

4 Click the **Videocamera** button.

■ Videocamera options appear.

■ You can type how long iMovie should wait for the camcorder to get ready.

■ You can type how many seconds of black to add before and after the recording.

5 Click **Share**.

11 Using Advanced iMovie Features

WORKING WITH IMOVIE

How long does it take to export a movie?

It takes just as long to export the movie as it does to play it, plus the time to set up and connect the camera. It is a good idea to open your Mac's System Preferences and set the Energy Saver to prevent your Mac from going to sleep while you are exporting your movie. Consult your Mac's Help menu for more about using System Preferences and the Energy Saver settings.

What can I do if iMovie has trouble controlling my camera?

First, make sure that you have the camera properly connected, set to VTR mode, and that the camera has power or a fully-charged battery. For more on connecting a Digital Camcorder, see Chapter 9. Also, check that the camera has the correct date and time set: if the camera has never had its internal clock set it can confuse iMovie. Consult your camera manual to find out how to reset your camera's date and time.

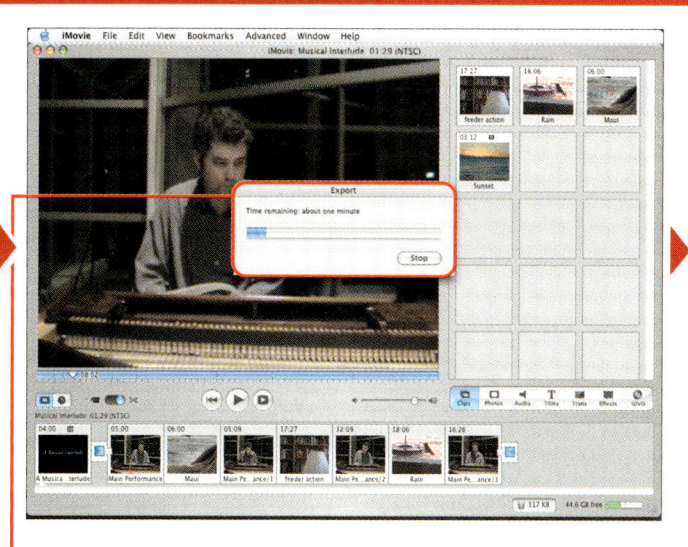

■ The sheet retracts.

■ An Export window appears.

■ iMovie prepares the video for exporting; this usually only takes a few seconds.

■ Your camcorder begins recording.

■ iMovie plays the movie with the sound muted as the camcorder records.

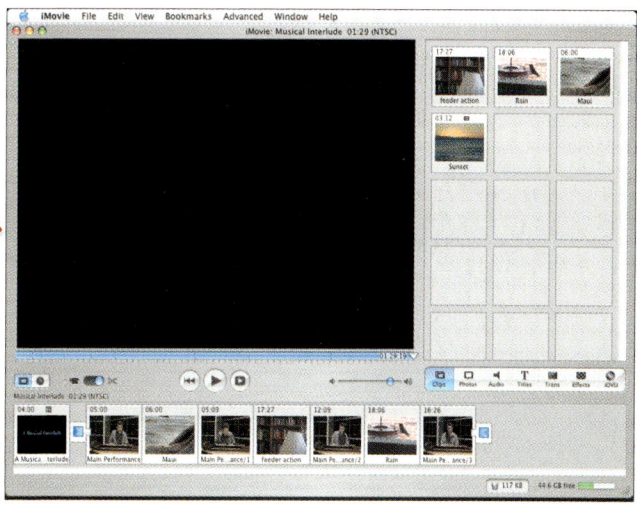

■ The Export window closes when the export completes.

6 Turn off your camcorder and disconnect it from your Mac.

239

SHARE A MOVIE

You can share your finished movie with your family, friends, and colleagues using iMovie's Share feature. You can send your movie as an e-mail attachment, publish it on the Web using your .Mac account, or save it as a file on your hard disk.

When you share your movie, iMovie compresses the movie using Apple's QuickTime in a form appropriate for the way you want to share it. Note that HomePage Web sharing requires a .Mac account.

SHARE A MOVIE

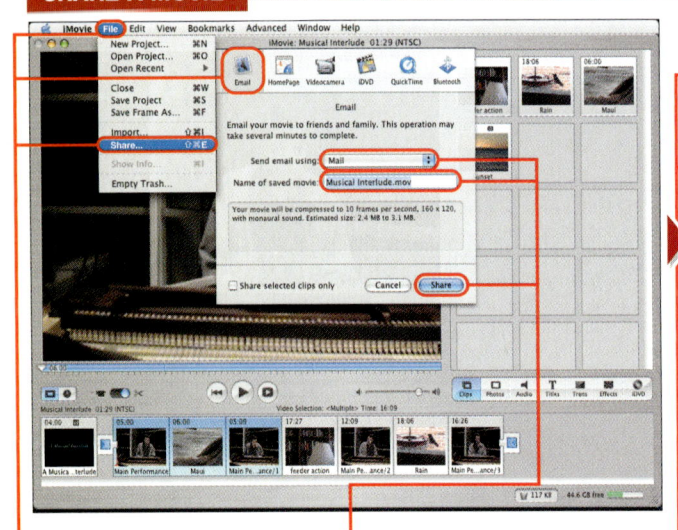

SHARE AS E-MAIL

1. Click **File**.
2. Click **Share**.
3. From the sheet that descends, click the **Email** button.

- You can click here and select an e-mail program.
- You can type the movie's name here.
- You can click **Share** to save the movie and start your e-mail program with the movie attached to a new message.

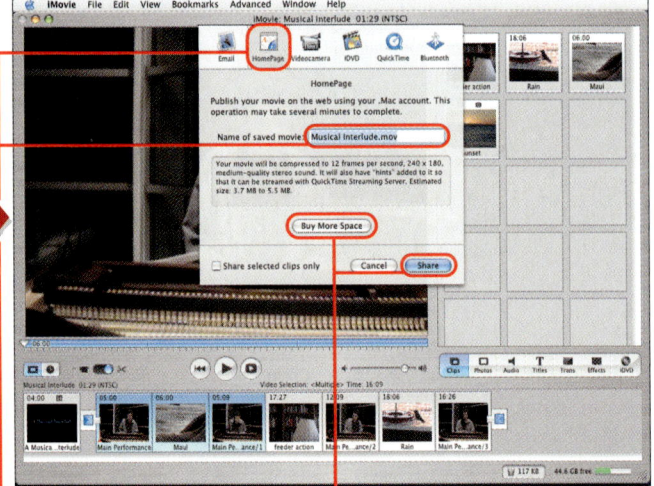

SHARE AS WEB PAGE

4. Click the **HomePage** button.

- Web sharing options appear.
- You can type the shared movie's name here.
- You can click **Buy More Space** to purchase more storage space for your .Mac account.
- You can click **Share** to save the movie as a Web page on your .Mac account's iDisk.

240

11 Using Advanced iMovie Features

WORKING WITH IMOVIE

Where does iMovie store my shared e-mail or Web movies?

iMovie creates a Shared Movies folder inside of your project's folder, and it creates additional folders inside of that to hold the shared movies for each of the different sharing formats you use; for example, the Email folder contains the movies you share as e-mail.

What are the QuickTime sharing options?

iMovie provides five preset QuickTime formats: **Email**, which you can also use for Email sharing, **Web** for use with HomePage sharing, **Web Streaming** for use with Apple's QuickTime Streaming Server software, **CD-ROM**, a larger, high quality format suitable for burning on a CD-ROM, and **Full Quality DV**, a very high quality that takes up about 220MB for each minute of video. You can also select **Expert Settings** to use the full power of Apple's QuickTime software to compress your movie to your own specifications.

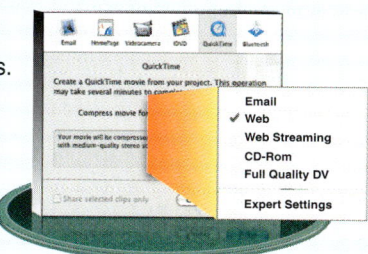

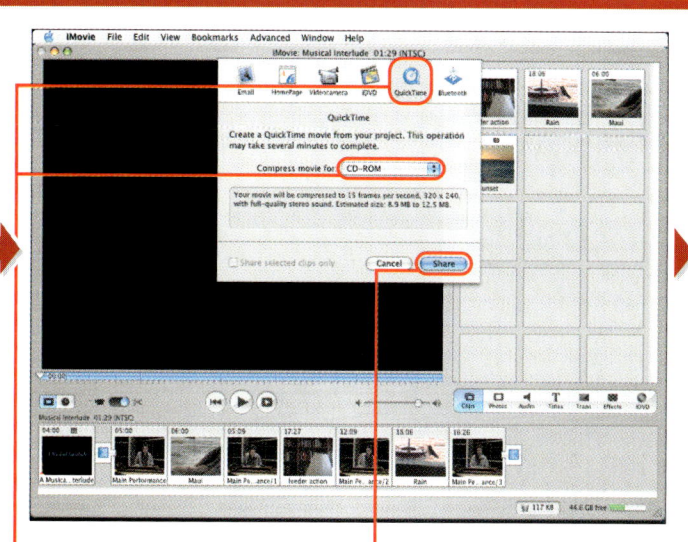

SAVE AS QUICKTIME FILE

■ 5 Click the **QuickTime** button.

■ QuickTime options appear.

■ You can click here and select different QuickTime settings.

■ You can click **Share** to open a file saving sheet, for name and location, to save your movie as a QuickTime file.

Note: See Chapter 1 for more on saving files.

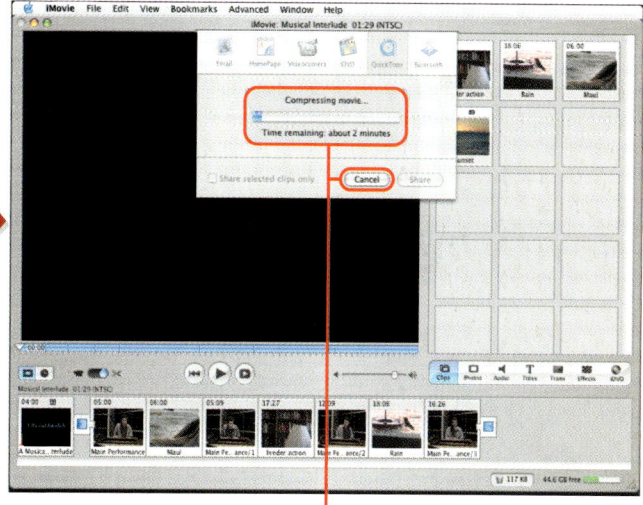

COMPRESS YOUR MOVIE

■ When you click **Share** as Email, HomePage, or QuickTime, iMovie compresses the movie to save disk space.

■ iMovie shows you the progress of the compression and how long it will take.

■ You can click **Cancel** if you change your mind.

241

Put It All Together

Customize Folder Slideshow

PART V

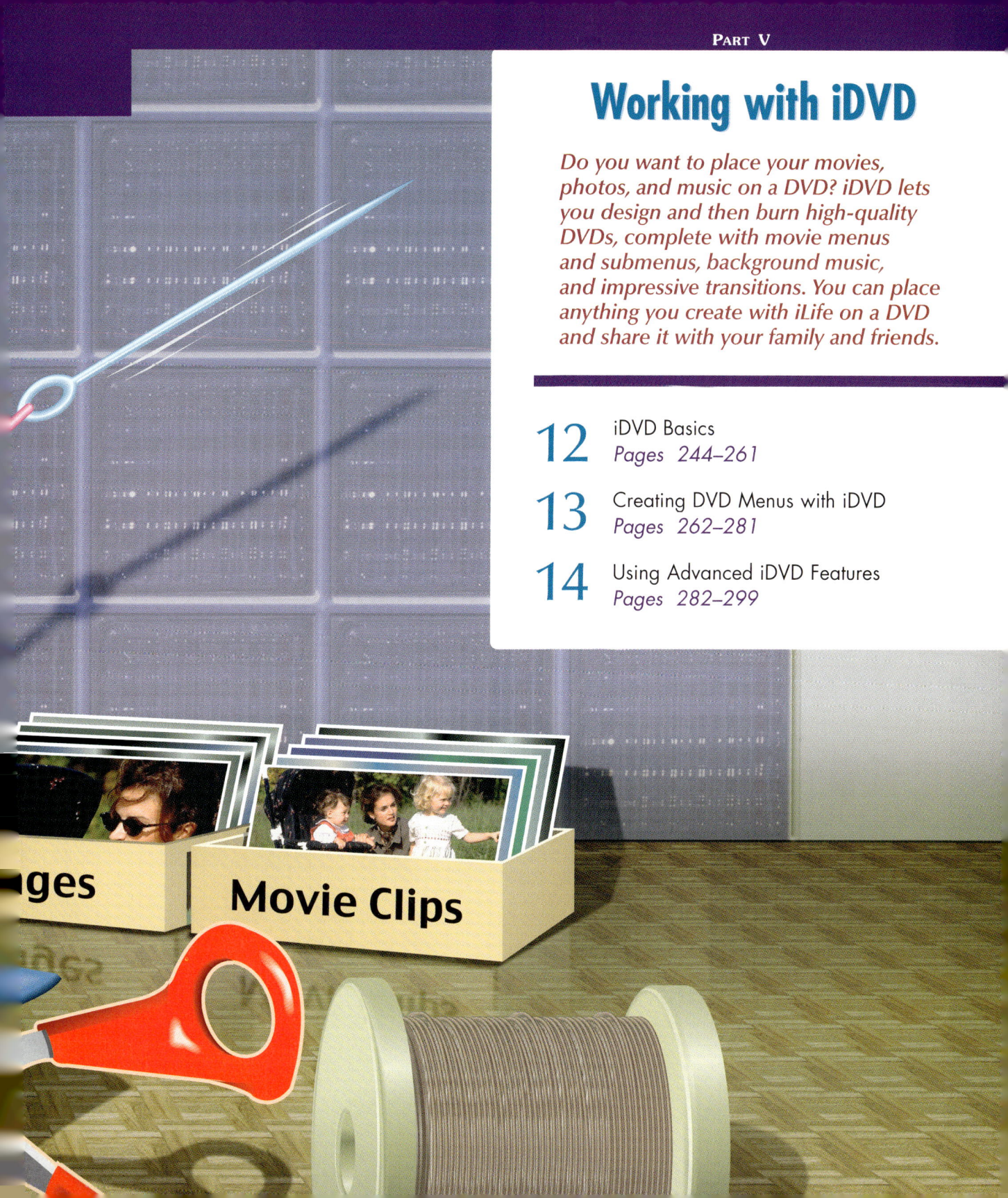

Working with iDVD

Do you want to place your movies, photos, and music on a DVD? iDVD lets you design and then burn high-quality DVDs, complete with movie menus and submenus, background music, and impressive transitions. You can place anything you create with iLife on a DVD and share it with your family and friends.

12 iDVD Basics
        Pages 244–261

13 Creating DVD Menus with iDVD
        Pages 262–281

14 Using Advanced iDVD Features
        Pages 282–299

SET UP iDVD

You can create a DVD project and set its preferences the way you want them. iDVD is pre-installed on most Macs that have SuperDrives and is in the Dock already.

If you install iDVD from the iLife installer, the installation process places iDVD in the Dock as well. You can also find iDVD in your Mac's Applications folder if it is not in your Dock. For more on the Dock, see Chapter 1.

SET UP IDVD

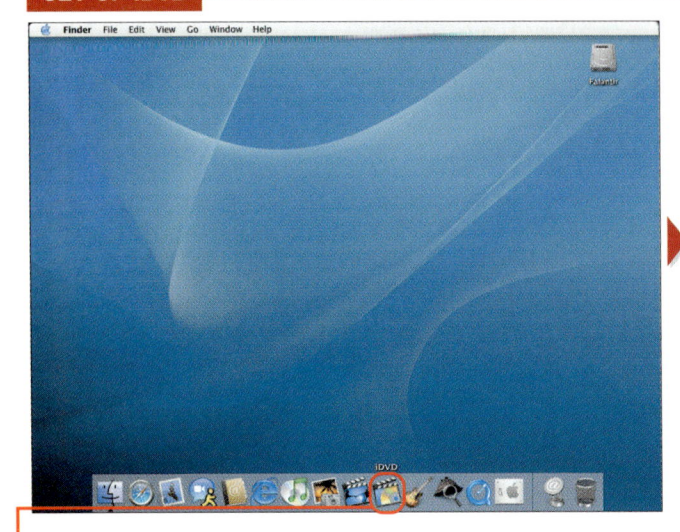

1 Click the iDVD icon ( ) in your Dock.

Note: For more on using the Dock, see Chapter 1.

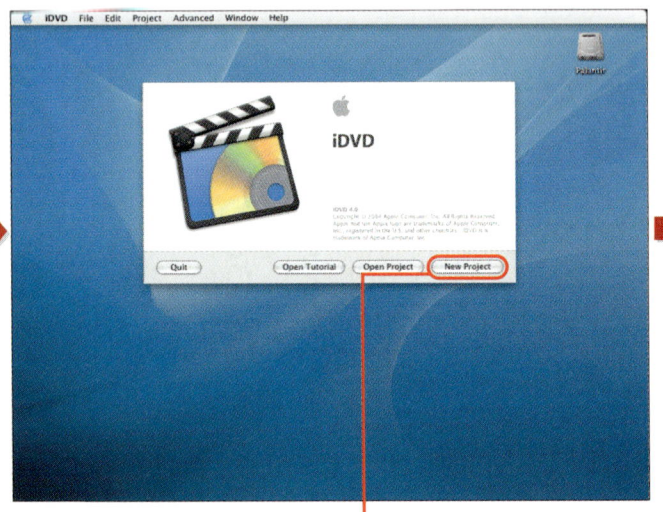

■ An iDVD start-up screen appears.

Note: iDVD always attempts to open the last DVD project upon which you worked. This dialog appears when iDVD cannot find the project, which is the case the first time you use it.

2 Click **New Project**.

244

12 iDVD Basics

WORKING WITH IDVD

How much material can I place on a DVD?

iDVD can store approximately an hour of high-quality video or as much as 2 hours of slightly lower-quality video on a DVD. iDVD reduces the video quality automatically to accommodate longer videos. iDVD also lets you create DVDs that hold data files as well as video, but the more data you have on the DVD, the less video you can store, and vice versa. A DVD-R can hold 4.7GB of data.

What kind of recordable DVDs can I use with iDVD?

The Apple SuperDrive can read and write both DVD-R and DVD-RW, but iDVD can only write to DVD-R. Apple states that the DVD-R format is the most reliable recording format for discs that are intended to play on the widest range of available home DVD players.

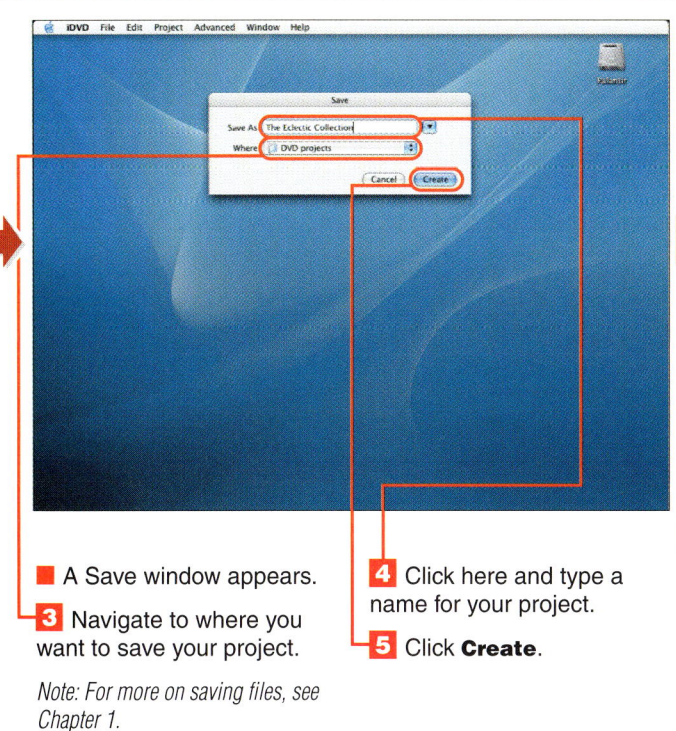

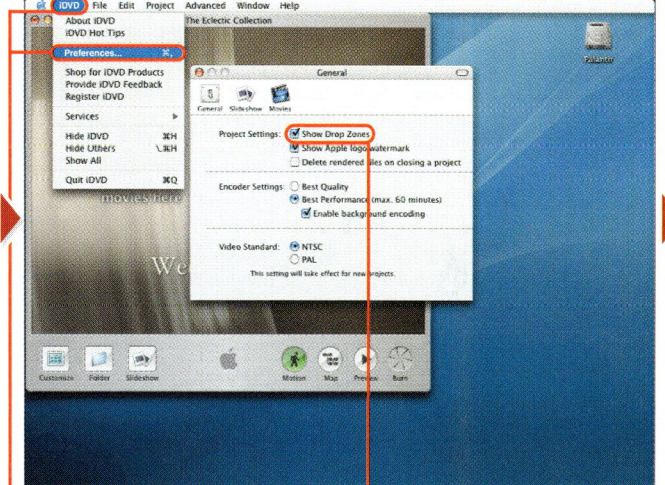

- A Save window appears.
- **3** Navigate to where you want to save your project.

Note: For more on saving files, see Chapter 1.

- **4** Click here and type a name for your project.
- **5** Click **Create**.

- A DVD project window opens and animates.
- **6** Click **iDVD**.
- **7** Click **Preferences**.
- The Preferences window appears, displaying iDVD's General preferences.

- You can click here to hide Drop Zone labels (☑ changes to ☐).
- *Drop Zone* labels show where you can click and drag your own media on a menu.

CONTINUED

245

SET UP iDVD

You can set how iDVD presents its menu themes, and control how it imports photos from iPhoto and movies from iMovie. You can also tell iPhoto where to look for movies on your Mac.

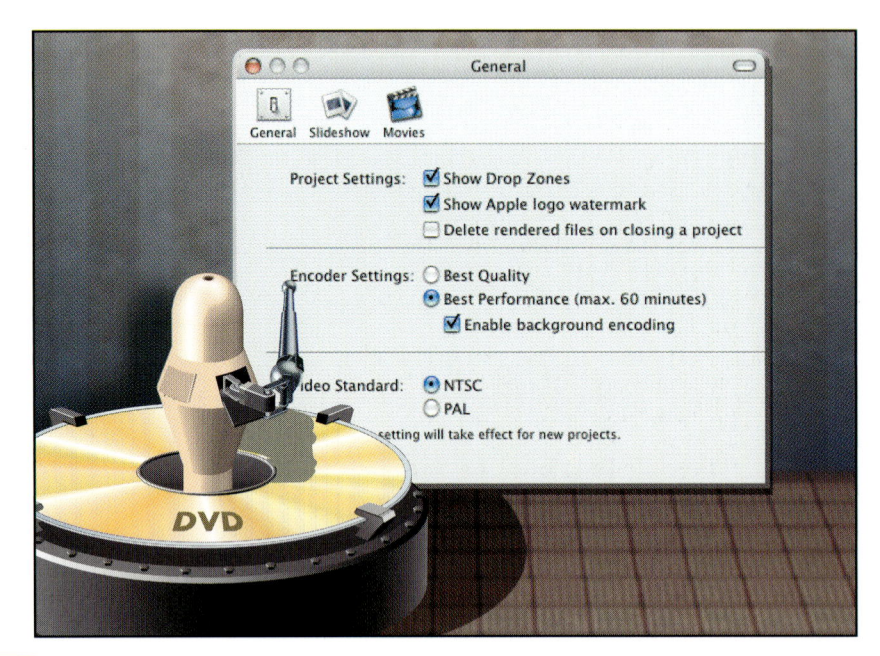

SET UP IDVD (CONTINUED)

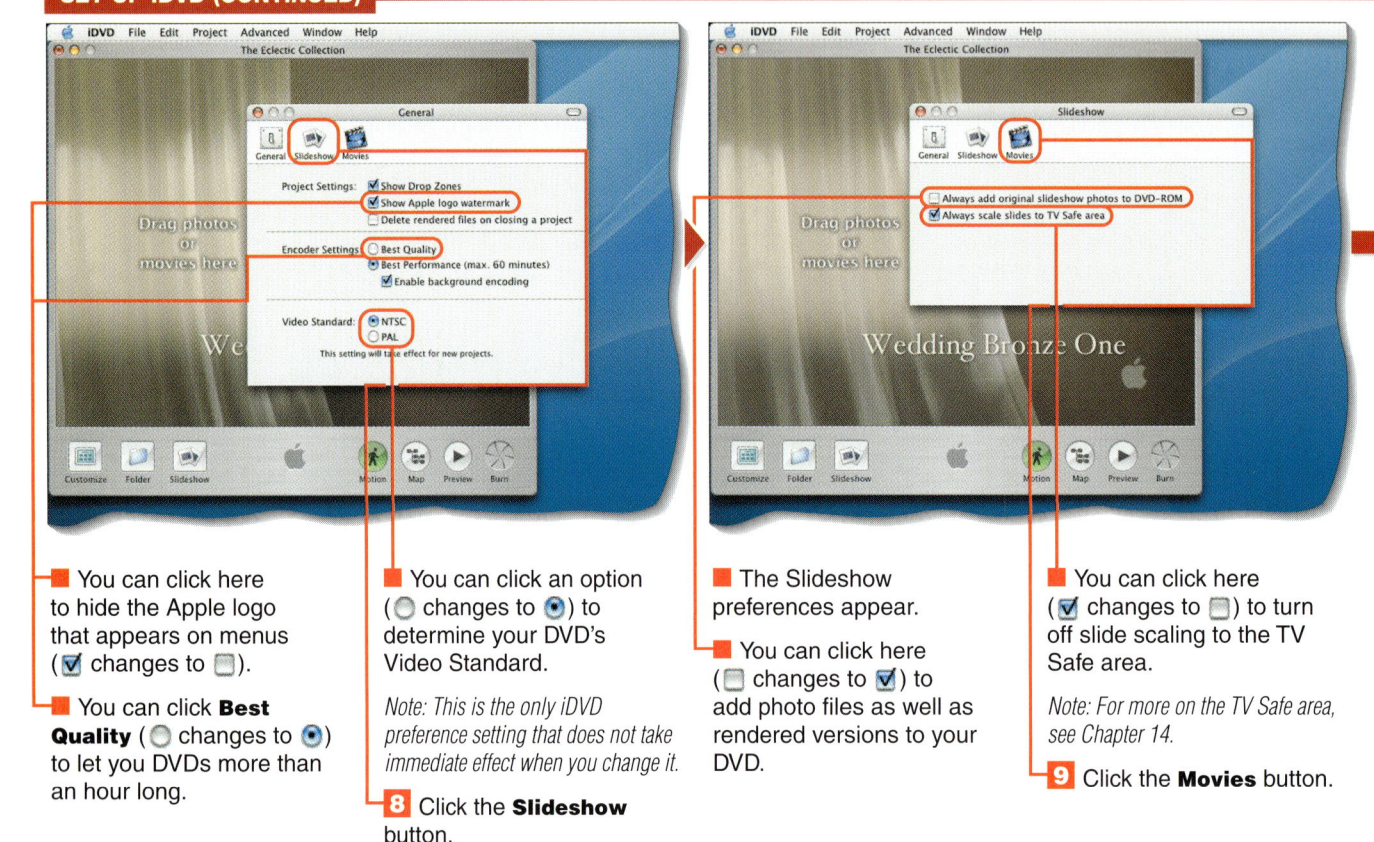

- You can click here to hide the Apple logo that appears on menus (☑ changes to ☐).

- You can click **Best Quality** (○ changes to ●) to let you DVDs more than an hour long.

- You can click an option (○ changes to ●) to determine your DVD's Video Standard.

Note: This is the only iDVD preference setting that does not take immediate effect when you change it.

8 Click the **Slideshow** button.

- The Slideshow preferences appear.

- You can click here (☐ changes to ☑) to add photo files as well as rendered versions to your DVD.

- You can click here (☑ changes to ☐) to turn off slide scaling to the TV Safe area.

Note: For more on the TV Safe area, see Chapter 14.

9 Click the **Movies** button.

246

12 iDVD Basics

WORKING WITH IDVD

What is background encoding?

The movies and photos you add to an iDVD project must be *encoded* — or converted to a DVD-compatible format — which can take some time. When you click the **Enable background encoding** option (☐ changes to ☑) in the General preference window, iDVD immediately begins encoding the items as soon as you add them to your project. This allows you to avoid waiting for iDVD to encode your projects when you are ready to burn your DVD. You can continue working while iDVD encodes your added movies. Note that background encoding is not available for projects that use the **Best Quailty** setting, which allows for longer DVDs.

☑ Enable background encoding

Why should I enable the Delete rendered files after closing a project option?

When you add movies or photos to an iDVD project, iDVD stores a DVD-compatible copy of those items inside of the iDVD project file, which, for a full DVD, can take up almost 5GB. You select the setting, found in the General preference window, to get that space back when you finish burning your DVD and close the project. Note, however, if you later open the project to burn another DVD, iDVD must re-render the video and photos.

☐ Delete rendered files after closing a project

■ You can click these options to determine how iDVD imports movies with chapter markers from iMovie (◯ changes to ◉).

Note: For more on importing movies with chapter markers, see Chapter 13.

■ iDVD can look for movies in folders on your Mac that you add here.

10 Click **Add**.

■ An Open dialog window appears.

11 Navigate to a folder where you want iDVD to look for movies on your Mac.

12 Click **Open**.

■ The Open dialog window closes and iDVD adds the location in the Preferences window.

13 Click ⊖.

■ The Preferences window closes.

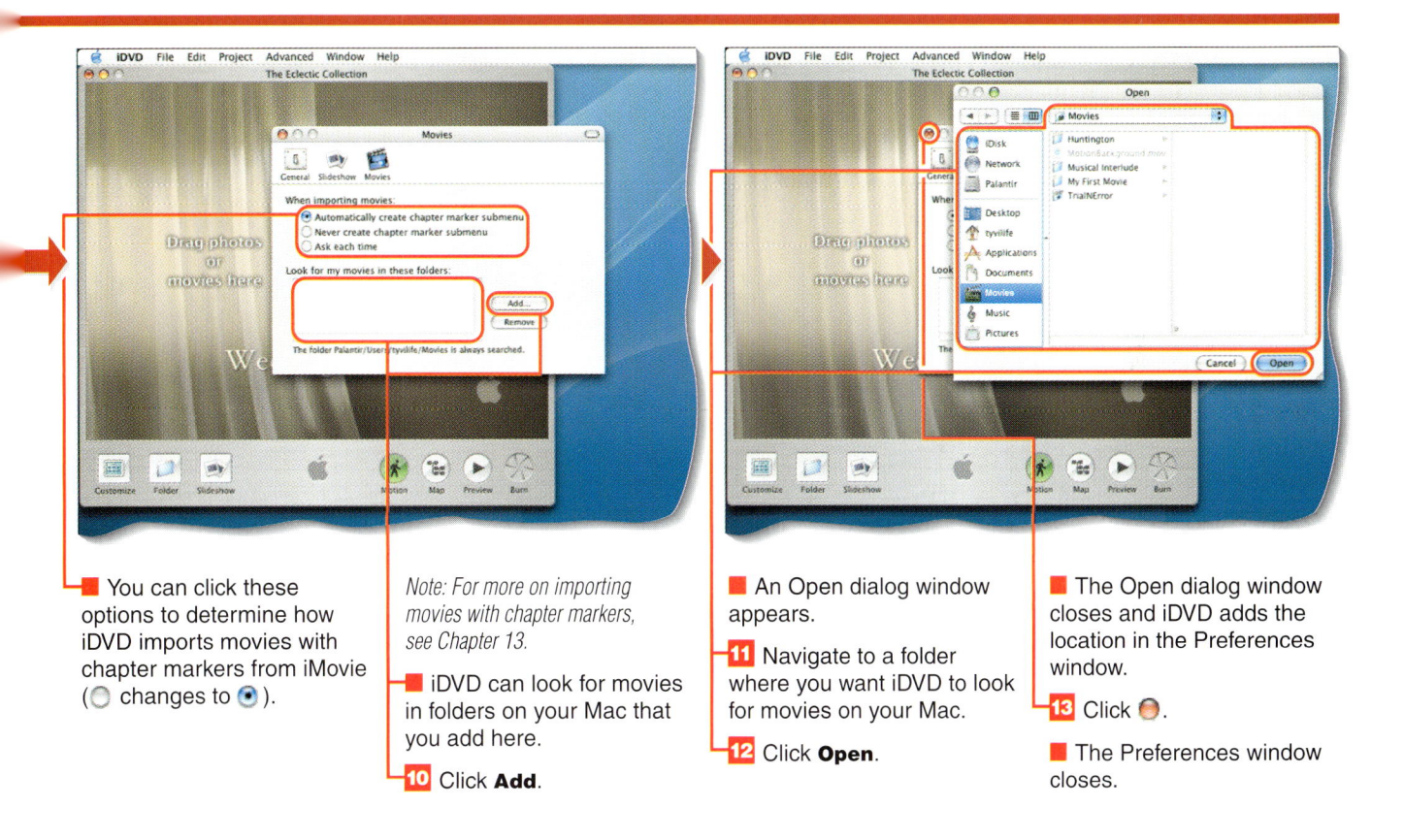

247

SELECT A PICTURE THEME

You can select a simple picture theme for the menus in your DVD project from the themes provided in iDVD's Customize drawer.

A *theme* provides a consistent design for the DVD menus and menu buttons in your iDVD project.

SELECT A PICTURE THEME

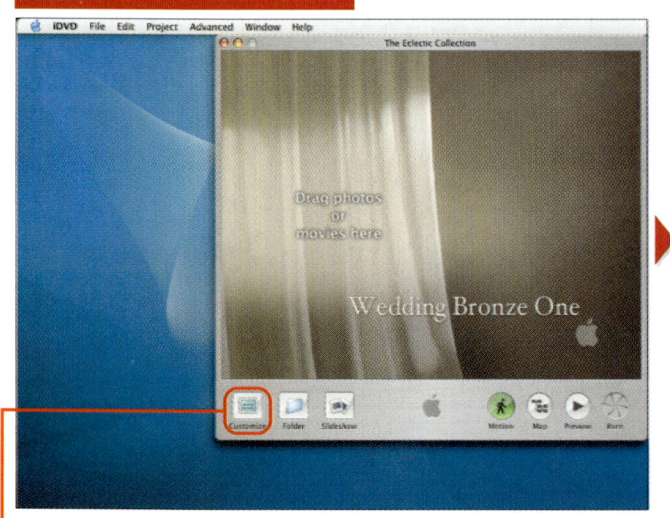

1 Click the **Customize** button.

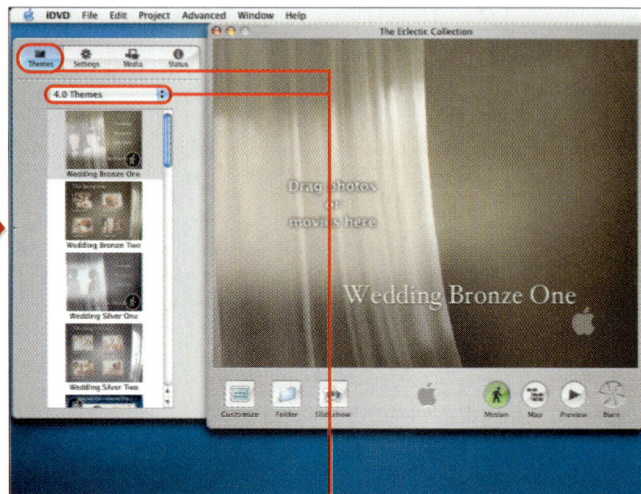

■ The Customize drawer slides out of the left side of the iDVD window.

Note: If your iDVD window is on the left side of your screen, the drawer slides out off-screen where you cannot see it; drag the iDVD window to the right to see the drawer.

2 Click the **Themes** button.

■ The iDVD Themes pane appears.

3 Click the Themes pane's 🔽.

248

12 iDVD Basics

WORKING WITH iDVD

How can I change the background picture in a picture theme?

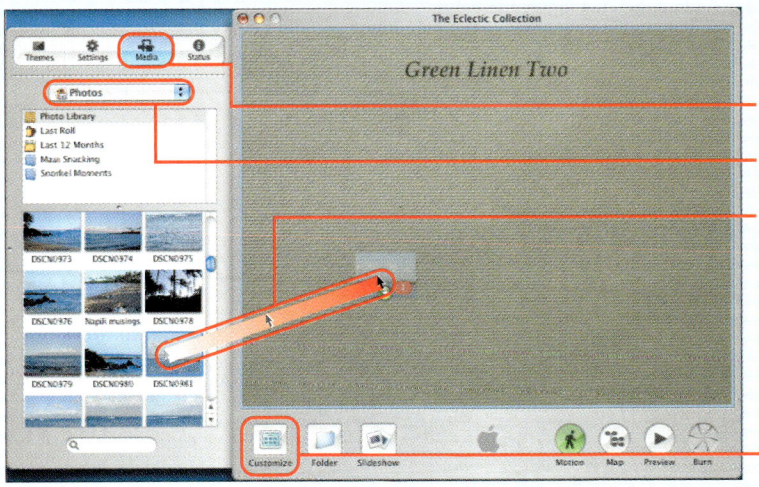

1. Click the **Customize** button to open the Customize drawer.

2. Click the **Media** button.

3. Click here and select **Photos**.

4. Click and drag a picture from your iPhoto library or albums over the menu's background picture and release the mouse.

- iDVD replaces the background picture with the one you dragged.

- You can also drag a picture from any folder on your Mac and drop it on the menu background picture in the iDVD window.

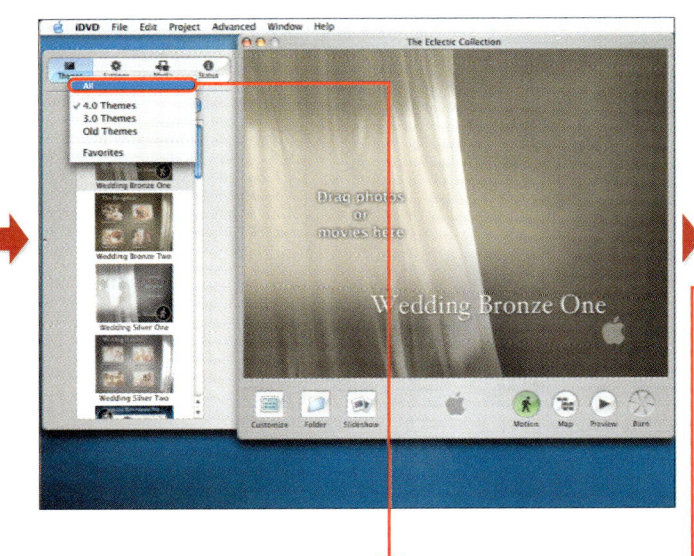

- The Themes menu appears.

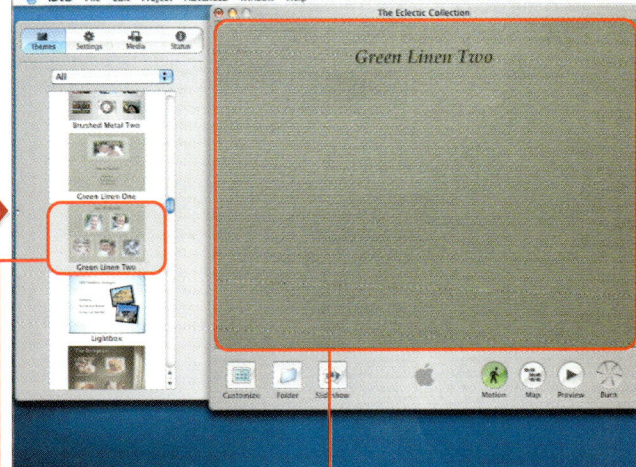

4. Click **All**.

- Additional themes appear in the pane.

5. Click a picture theme.

- This task uses Green Linen Two as an example of a picture theme.

- Other picture themes include Chalkboard, Parchment, Brushed Metal, Brushed Metal Two, Portfolio Color, Portfolio B&W, and Your Photo Here.

- iDVD displays the selected theme.

249

CHANGE A THEME'S AUDIO

Some themes come with audio that plays while you have the DVD's menu on-screen. You can change the theme's audio, or add audio to a silent theme, using the music in your iTunes Library.

CHANGE A THEME'S AUDIO

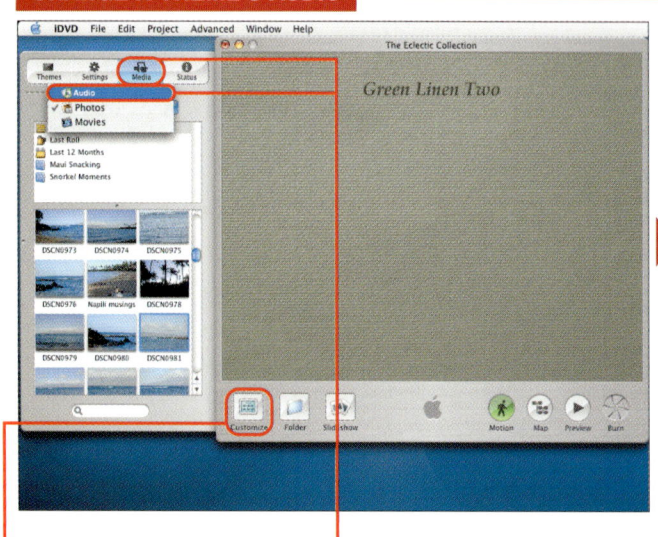

1 Click the **Customize** button.

■ The Customize drawer slides out of the left side of the iDVD window.

2 Click the **Media** button.

3 Click here and select **Audio**.

■ The Audio pane appears and displays the iTunes Library and playlists.

■ You can hear a song by clicking its title and then clicking the Play button (▶).

■ You can click and type here to find a song.

4 Click and drag a song title over the DVD menu and release the mouse.

■ The song starts to play and loops back to the beginning when finished.

5 Click the **Settings** button.

■ The Settings pane appears.

12 iDVD Basics

WORKING WITH IDVD

What do the theme categories in iDVD's theme menu represent?

Each time Apple releases a new version of iDVD, it supplies new themes with new properties. The Old Themes, 3.0 Themes, and 4.0 Themes let longtime iDVD users more easily find the themes with which they are familiar. Note that the Old Themes category is only available when you install iDVD 4 as an upgrade to iDVD 3.

- ✓ All
- 4.0 Themes
- 3.0 Themes
- Old Themes
- Favorites

Is there another way to stop the theme's music from playing while I work?

To just toggle the sound off and on, you can click the speaker icon ( ) in the Setting pane's Audio well. Note that toggling the sound does not affect the finished DVD.

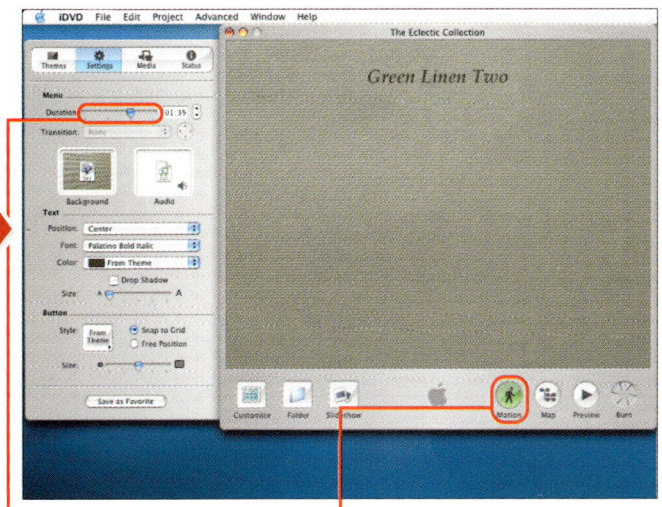

Audio

■ **6** Click and drag the Duration slider ( ) part of the way to the left.

■ The Duration slider controls a theme's audio, as well as any background motion that the theme has.

Note: For more on motion themes, see the section "Select a Motion Theme."

■ The music loops back to the beginning more quickly.

■ **7** Click the **Motion** button.

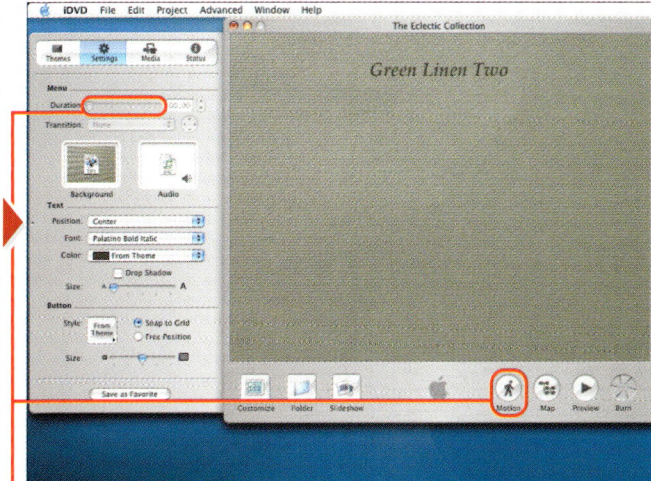

■ The Motion button becomes white and the sound ceases.

■ The Duration slider dims and disables.

■ The Motion button toggles both the theme's audio and video playback.

Note: The Motion button should be on — green — when you preview or burn your DVD.

251

SELECT A MOTION THEME

You can select a DVD menu theme that plays an animated sequence behind the menu's title and buttons to make the menu more visually interesting.

SELECT A MOTION THEME

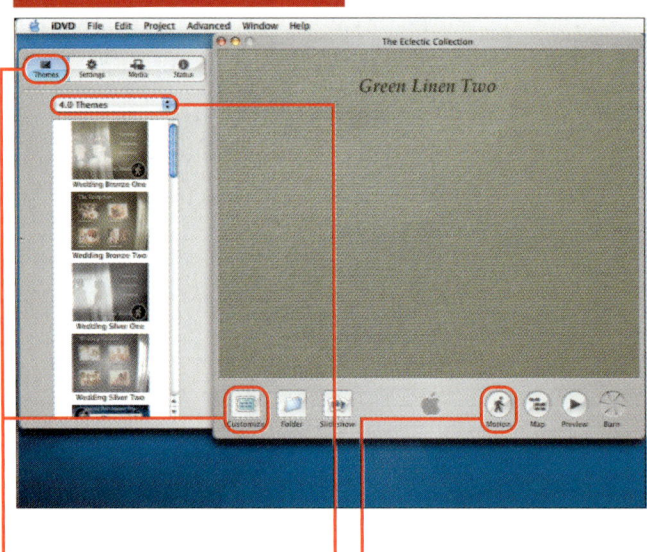

■ **1** Click the **Customize** button.

■ The Customize drawer slides out of the left side of the iDVD window.

■ **2** Click the **Themes** button.

■ If the **Motion** button is white, click it so you can see the motion themes in action.

■ **3** Click and select a theme category.

■ **4** Scroll the Themes pane until you see a theme with a motion badge ( ) on it.

■ **5** Click the motion theme's thumbnail.

■ This task uses the Fish Two theme in the 4.0 Themes collection as an example of a motion theme.

252

12 iDVD Basics

WORKING WITH iDVD

What happens if I click and drag a background picture over a motion background?

The background picture covers the motion background. Any sound associated with the theme, however, keeps playing.

How can I tell which kind of theme is which in the Themes pane?

Unfortunately, Apple has not made it particularly easy to figure out the types of some themes from their thumbnails. Although motion themes have a badge ( ) on them, other types, such as Drop Zone themes or picture themes with audio, are not so clearly marked. In such cases, you must select the theme to see what it does.

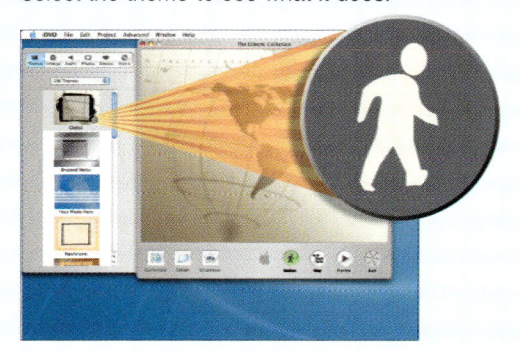

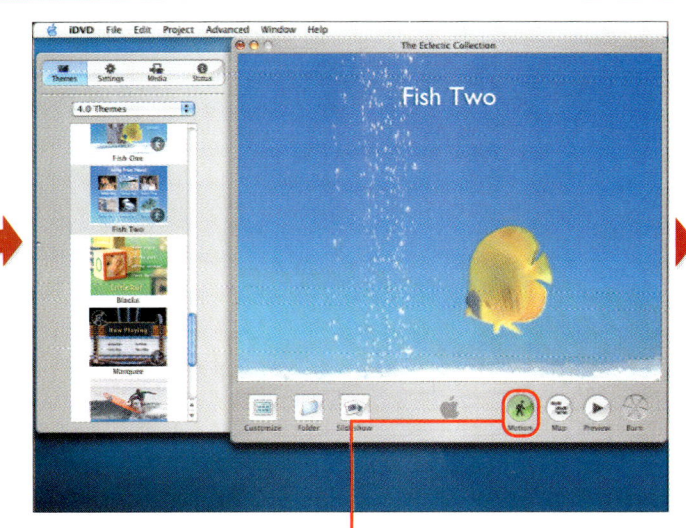

■ The theme appears in iDVD's menu display area.

■ The menu animates.

■ If the theme has sound associated with it, the sound plays.

6 Click the **Motion** button.

■ The theme animation and sound stop, and the menu displays the first frame of its animation.

253

CHANGE A MOTION THEME MOVIE

You can replace the motion background of a menu theme with any movie on your Mac to customize the theme and make it more personal or interesting.

To perform this section, you must have at least one movie in your Movies folder or in another location in which you have set iDVD to look. For more on setting iDVD preferences, see the section "Set Up iDVD."

CHANGE A MOTION THEME MOVIE

1 Click the **Customize** button.

- The Customize drawer slides out of the left side of the iDVD window.

2 Click the **Media** button.

3 Click the Media pop-up menu and select **Movies**.

- The Movies pane appears.

4 Click and drag a movie thumbnail to the Settings button, but do not release the mouse.

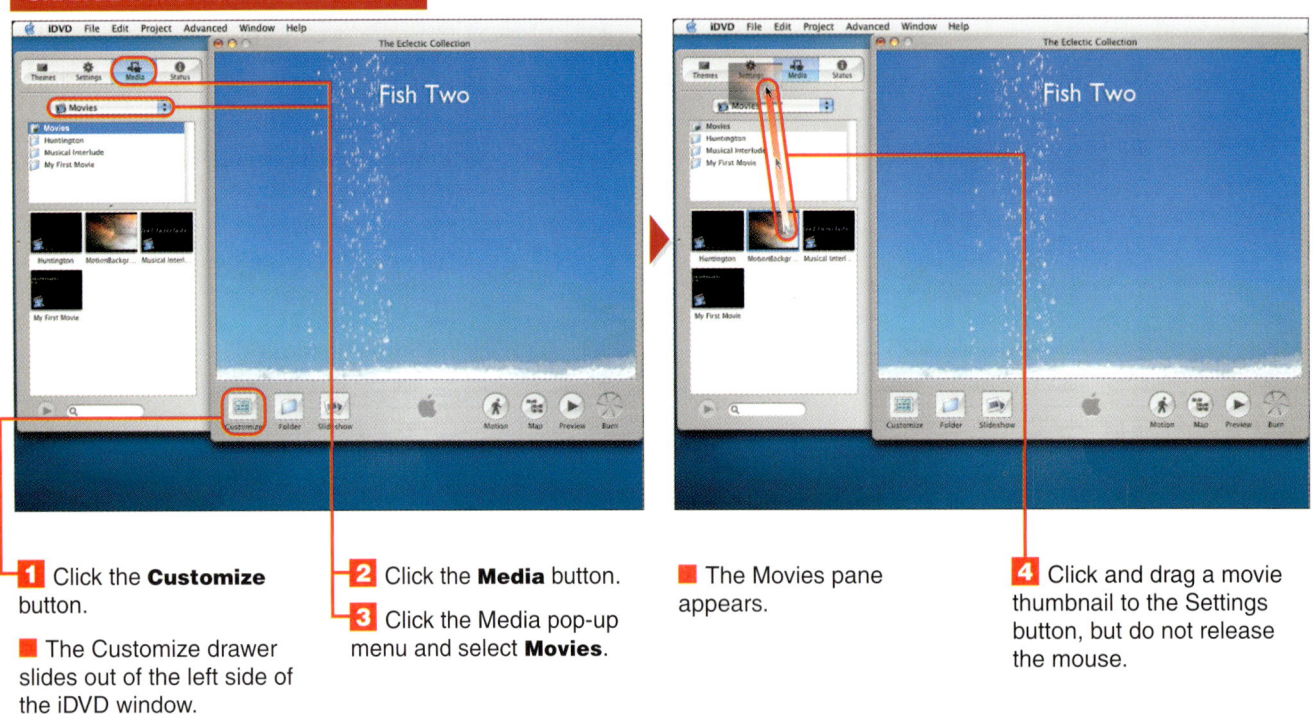

254

12 iDVD Basics

WORKING WITH IDVD

TEACH YOURSELF

How can I remove a previously added background movie or sound from my theme?

In the Settings pane of the Customize drawer, click and drag the movie icon out of the **Background** well — or the sound icon out of the **Audio** well — and release the mouse. The icon vanishes in a puff of smoke.

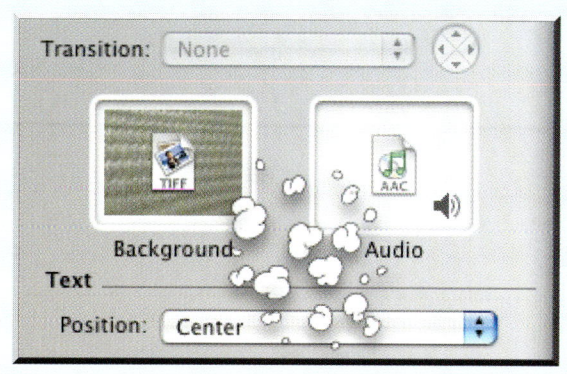

TEACH YOURSELF

How can I add just the sound from one of my own movies to a motion theme?

Click and drag the movie into the Settings pane as shown in this section, but drop the movie icon into the **Audio** well instead of the **Background** well.

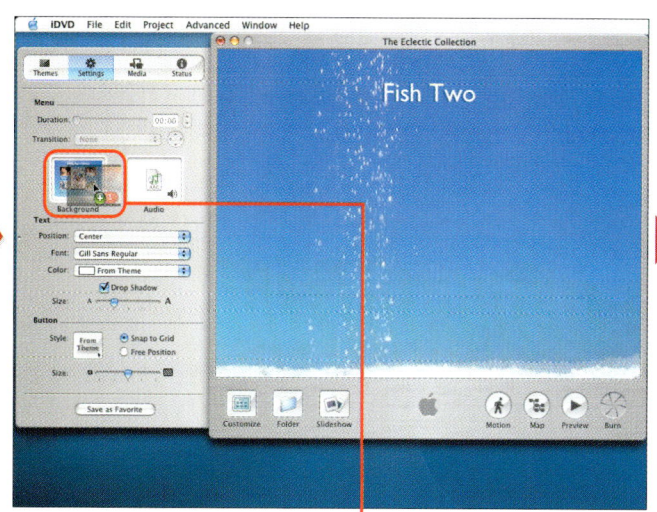

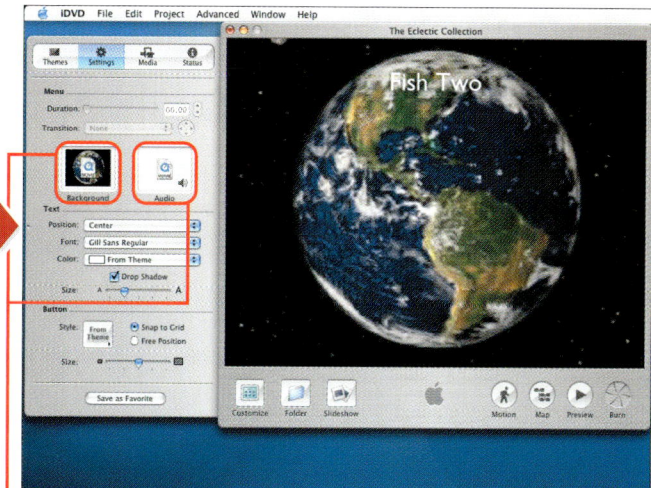

- The Settings pane opens.

5 Continue dragging the movie thumbnail to the **Background** well in the Settings pane.

6 Release the mouse.

- The dragged movie's icon appears in the Background well.

- The dragged movie's soundtrack — if any — appears in the Audio well.

- The dragged movie replaces the background movie in the DVD menu.

255

SELECT A DROP ZONE THEME

iDVD's Drop Zone menu themes let you design DVD menus that display previews or examples of your DVD's contents to inform or intrigue your audience.

SELECT A DROP ZONE THEME

1 Click the **Customize** button.

■ The Customize drawer slides out of the left side of the iDVD window.

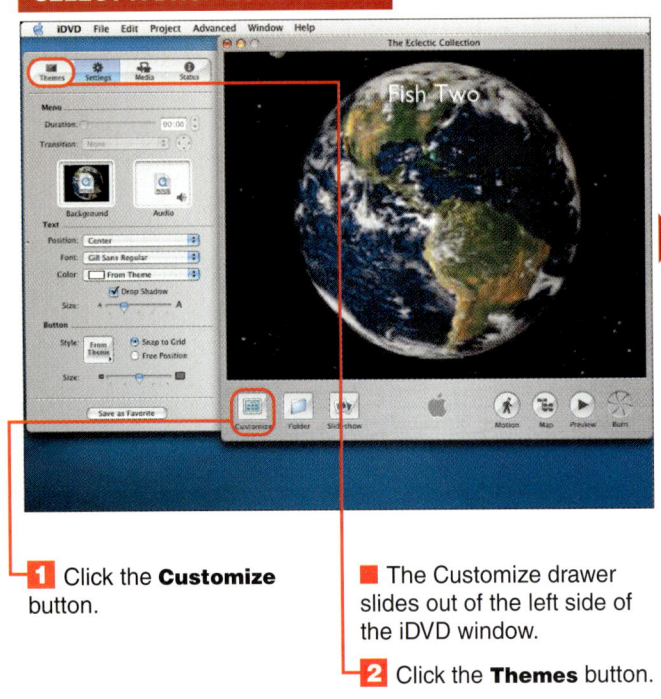

2 Click the **Themes** button.

■ The Themes pane appears.

3 Click and select **All**.

■ Thumbnails for all of the available themes appear in the Themes pane.

256

12 iDVD Basics

WORKING WITH IDVD

What is a *Drop Zone*?

A Drop Zone is an area on a DVD menu's background in which you can display media that you drop on it as part of the menu's design. You can drop items such as your own photos, slideshows, or videos. Drop Zones do not link to any of the DVD's content.

How large a picture can I add to a Drop Zone?

Because the DVD menu itself is only 640 x 480 pixels, any picture you add to a Drop Zone does not need to be larger than that, although it can be. iDVD scales pictures to fit within Drop Zones while maintaining their aspect ratios.

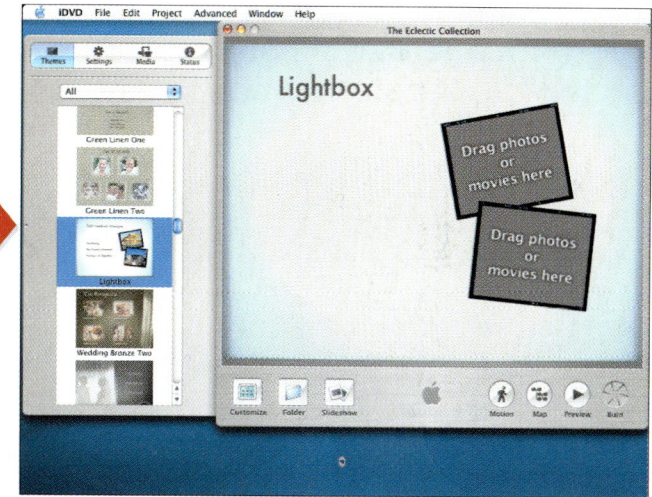

■ **4** Click a Drop Zone theme.

■ Drop Zone themes have areas marked "Drag photos or movies here" when you display them in iDVD's menu display.

Note: The Drop Zone theme does not display this text if you have disabled that preference; see the section "Set Up iDVD" for more information.

■ This examples uses Lightbox as a Drop Zone theme.

■ The Drop Zone theme appears in iDVD's menu display area.

257

ADD MEDIA TO A DROP ZONE THEME

To give your DVD a personalized flare, you can drag and drop photographs and videos into your DVD menu's Drop Zones directly from your movie folders and iPhoto Library.

ADD MEDIA TO A DROP ZONE THEME

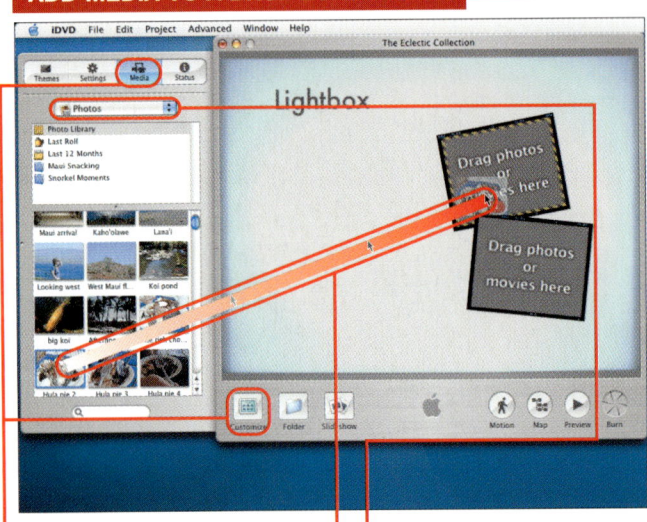

1 Click the **Customize** button.

■ The Customize drawer slides out of the left side of the iDVD window.

2 Click the **Media** button.

3 Click here and select **Photos**.

4 Click and drag a picture from your iPhoto Library over a Drop Zone.

■ The Drop Zone highlights when the mouse is over it.

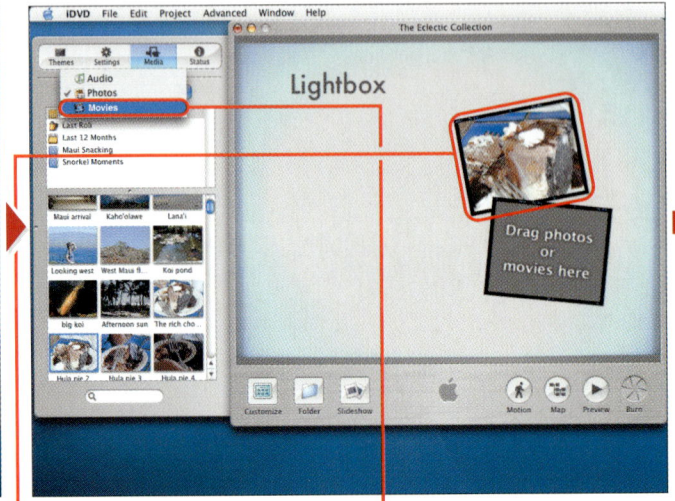

5 Release the mouse.

■ The picture appears in the Drop Zone.

■ You can click and drag the picture to adjust its position in the Drop Zone.

6 Click here and select **Movies**.

■ The Movies pane appears.

258

12 iDVD Basics

WORKING WITH IDVD

How can I place a slideshow in a Drop Zone?

To make a Drop Zone slideshow, drag several photos or an album onto the Drop Zone. A Drop Zone slideshow can display as many as 30 pictures. The Duration slider in the Settings pane controls the speed of the slideshow as well as the durations of the theme's other media. For more on how to adjust the Duration slider, see the section "Change a Theme's Audio."

How can I remove something that I dropped into a Drop Zone?

You can `Control`+click, or right-click the Drop Zone and select **Clear** from the contextual menu. Alternatively, you can simply click and drag the media out of the zone and release the mouse; the material vanishes in an animated puff of smoke.

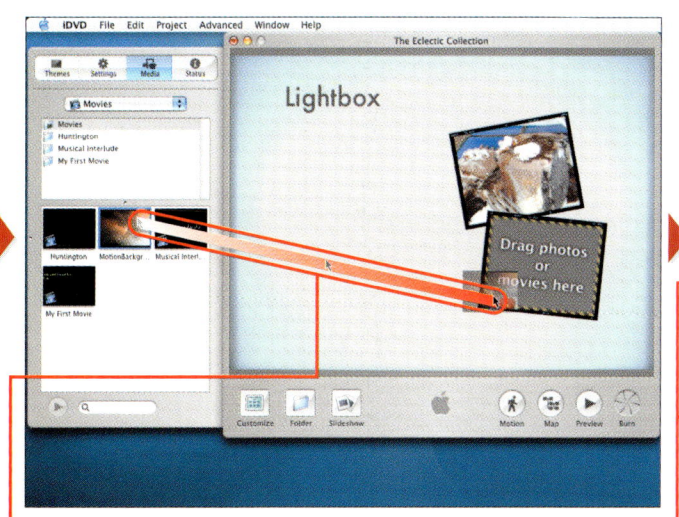

7 Click and drag a movie from the Movies pane over a Drop Zone.

■ A translucent thumbnail of the movie follows the mouse, and the Drop Zone highlights when you place the mouse over it.

8 Release the mouse.

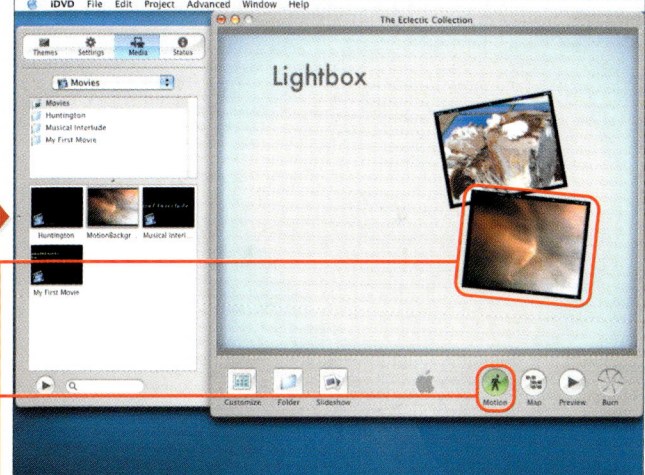

■ The movie appears in the Drop Zone.

■ You can click and drag the movie to adjust its position in the Drop Zone.

■ If the Motion button is green, the movie plays in a loop.

■ You can control the amount the movie plays with the Duration slider ( ) in the Settings pane.

Note: For more on how to adjust the Duration slider, see the section "Change a Theme's Audio."

259

SAVE A MODIFIED THEME AS A FAVORITE

After you customize a menu theme, you can save it as a favorite to use with other projects.

SAVE A MODIFIED THEME AS A FAVORITE

1 Click the **Customize** button.

■ The Customize drawer slides out of the left side of the iDVD window.

2 Click the **Settings** button.

■ The Settings pane appears.

3 Click **Save as Favorite**.

■ A sheet slides down from the top of the iDVD window.

260

12 iDVD Basics

WORKING WITH IDVD

How can I remove a favorite?

iDVD 4 has no built-in ability to remove favorites. Instead, you must quit iDVD and move the favorite file into the Mac's Trash. You can find the favorites you create for yourself in the iDVD folder inside your home directory's Library folder. The iDVD folder contains a Favorites folder that holds your favorites. Favorites you create to share with others are in the iDVD folder inside the Mac's main Library folder.

How do I reset a theme that I have modified?

Open the Themes pane, click another theme, and then click the first one again. iDVD restores the theme's original background and font settings. However, iDVD retains any changes to the title text, Drop Zone media, and menu buttons.

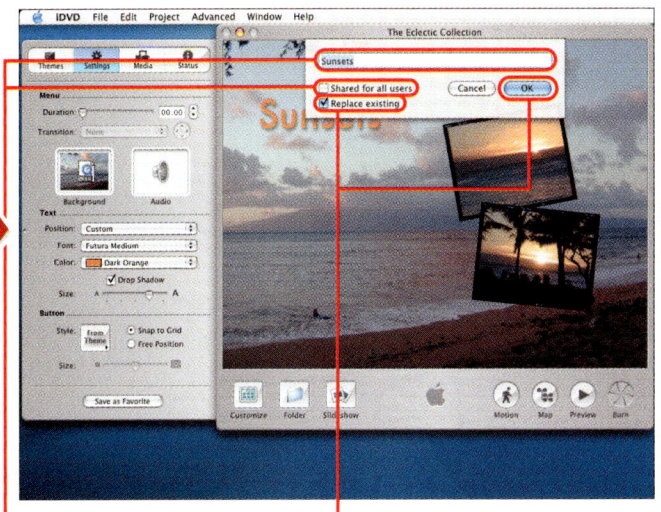

■ **4** Click here and type to give your favorite a name.

■ You can click here if you want other users of your Mac to use the favorite (☐ changes to ☑).

Note: You must have Administrator privileges to save a shared favorite.

■ You can click here if you want to replace any existing favorite with the same name (☐ changes to ☑).

■ **5** Click **OK**.

■ iDVD saves the favorite.

■ **6** Click the **Themes** button.

■ **7** Click the Themes pane's ⇅ and select **Favorites**.

■ Your favorite appears in the pane.

■ Favorite theme thumbnails display a badge (🏃) in their lower-left corners.

261

CHANGE A MENU TITLE'S FORMAT

You can change the font, color, and placement of a DVD menu's title to suit your taste or design requirements.

CHANGE A MENU TITLE'S FORMAT

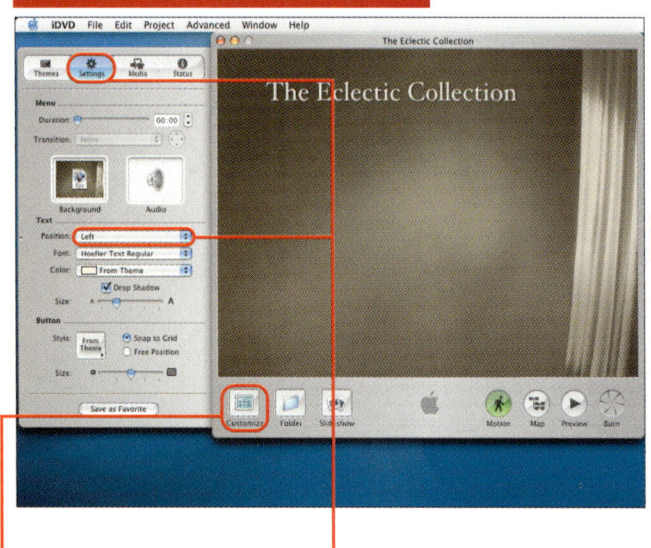

1 Click the **Customize** button.

■ The Customize drawer opens.

2 Click the **Settings** button.

■ The Settings pane appears.

3 Click the Position ⬢.

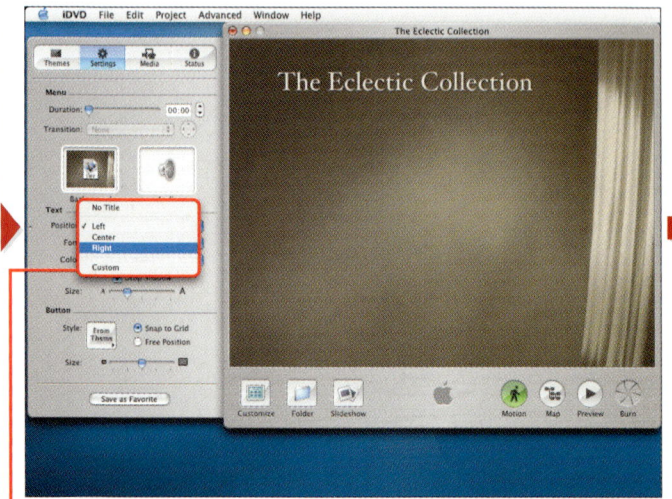

4 Select a Position option or click outside the menu to close it.

■ You can select **Custom**, which allows you to drag the title anywhere on the DVD menu.

■ You can select **No Title** to hide the title.

■ The position choices vary depending on the menu's theme.

262

13 Creating DVD Menus with iDVD

WORKING WITH IDVD

How do you change a DVD menu title's text?

Simply click on it and type. You can also use the standard editing commands in the **Edit** menu to cut, copy, paste, and clear text in the title. You can insert a line break in the title by pressing `Return` or `Enter`.

How much text can I place in a menu title?

You can make titles as long as you like, though you should try to keep them to a few words: the longer the text, the less room you have for other menu buttons. Remember, too, that you are meant to see a DVD menu on a TV screen, which cannot display text as clearly as your Mac's screen. If you use a small, dense font for your title, more words fit on the screen, but you may not find the text very legible when you see it on a TV.

- You can click here and select a title font from any of the fonts installed on your Mac.

- You can click and drag the Size slider ( ) to make the title text bigger or smaller.

- You can click this option (☑ changes to ☐) to turn off the drop shadow cast by the text.

- **5** Click the Color .

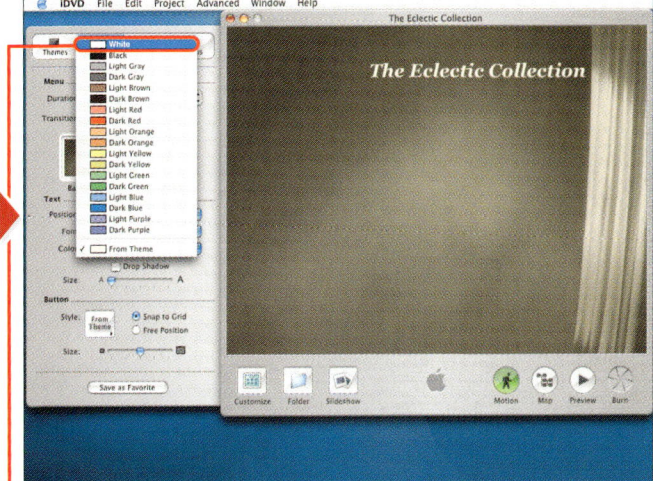

- A Color menu appears.

- **6** Click a color for the title text.

- The title changes color.

263

CREATE A MOVIE MENU BUTTON

You can create a menu button that you can select with your DVD player's remote control to play a movie.

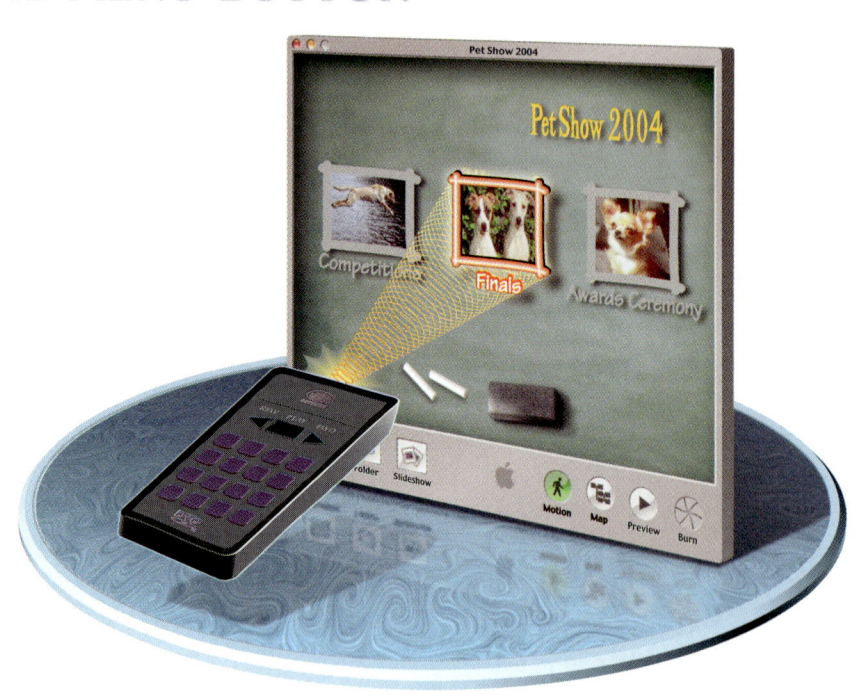

The menu button's appearance depends on the DVD menu's theme. Drop Zone themes create text-only movie buttons, but most other themes create motion menu buttons, which play a small section of its movie in a loop. For more on Drop Zones, see Chapter 12.

This section assumes that your movie does not contain chapter markers. See the section "Create a Scene Submenu from iMovie" for using movies with chapter markers.

CREATE A MOVIE MENU BUTTON

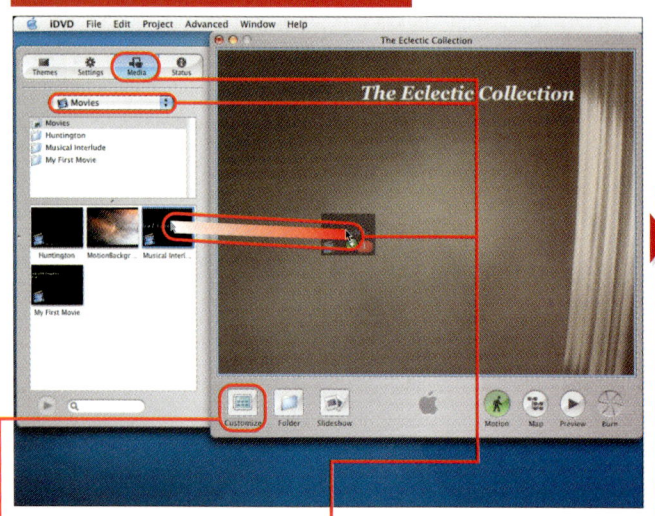

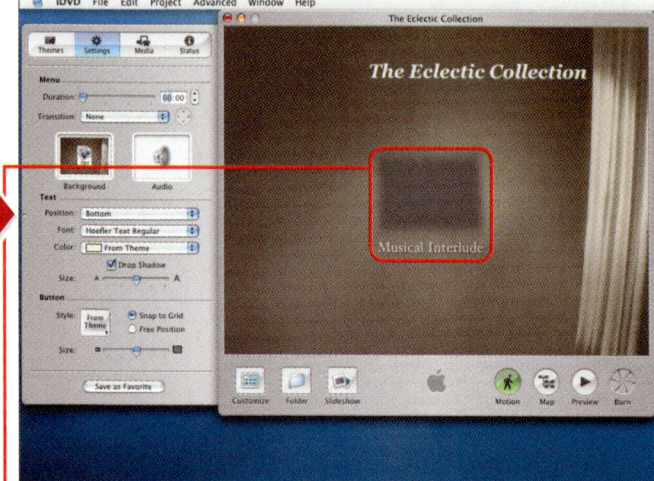

1 Click the **Customize** button.

■ The Customize drawer opens.

2 Click the **Media** button.

3 Click here and select **Movies**.

4 Click and drag a movie from the pane to the DVD menu.

5 Release the mouse.

■ A menu button appears.

■ This task uses the Wedding Bronze Two theme, which creates motion menu buttons.

264

CHANGE A MENU BUTTON'S SHAPE

13 Creating DVD Menus with iDVD

WORKING WITH iDVD

To suit your taste or your project's design needs, you can change a DVD menu button's shape from the one used by menu's theme to one of iDVD's other button shapes.

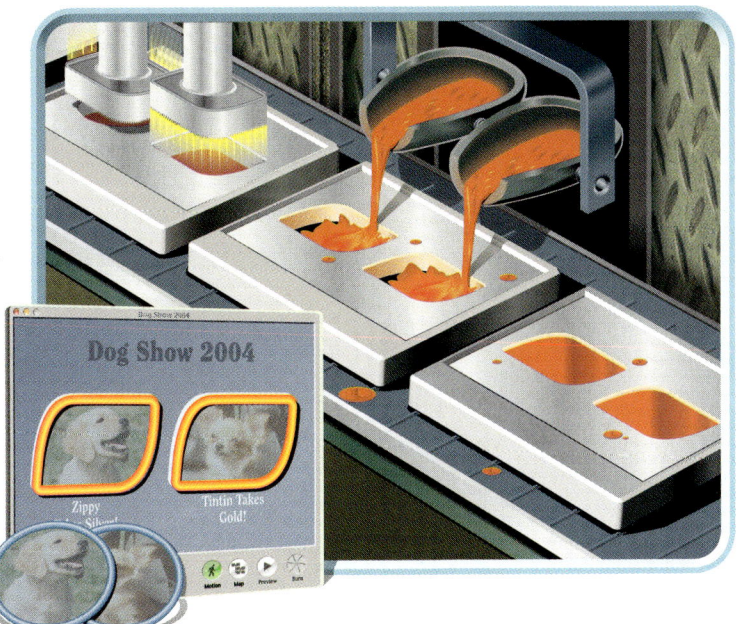

This section requires that the DVD menu have at least one menu button on it. You can change the text-only buttons in Drop Zone themes and other themes to motion menu buttons by giving them a shape as shown in this section.

CHANGE A MENU BUTTON'S SHAPE

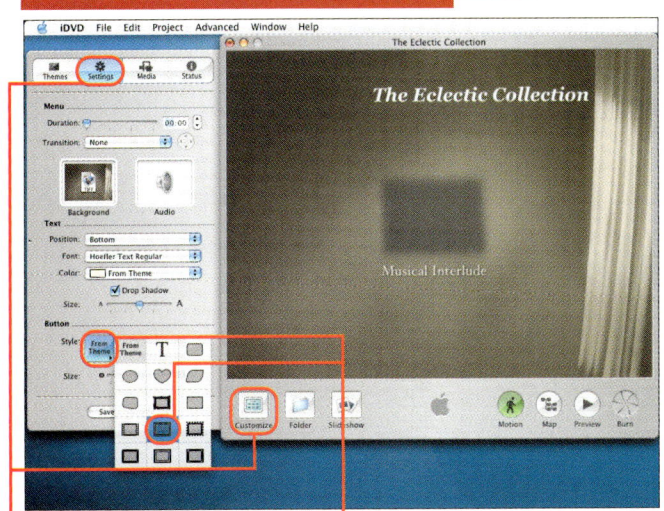

1 Click the **Customize** button.

■ The Customize drawer opens.

2 Click the **Settings** button.

3 Click the button shape menu.

■ A palette menu appears with a selection of button shapes.

4 Select a shape.

■ The Text item (T) creates a text-only button.

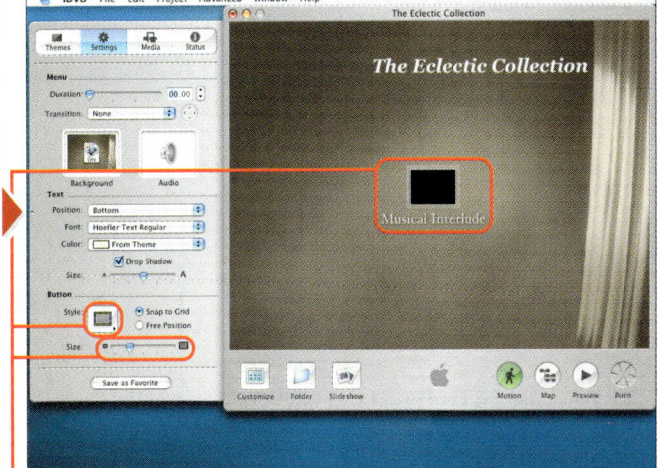

■ The button changes shape.

■ The button shape menu displays the current button shape.

5 Click and drag the Size slider ( ).

■ The button increases or decreases in size.

■ The button shape menu and Size slider affect all the buttons on a DVD menu.

265

CHANGE A MENU BUTTON'S TEXT FORMAT

You can change the size, font, position, and color of menu buttons' text labels to suit your taste or your project's design requirements.

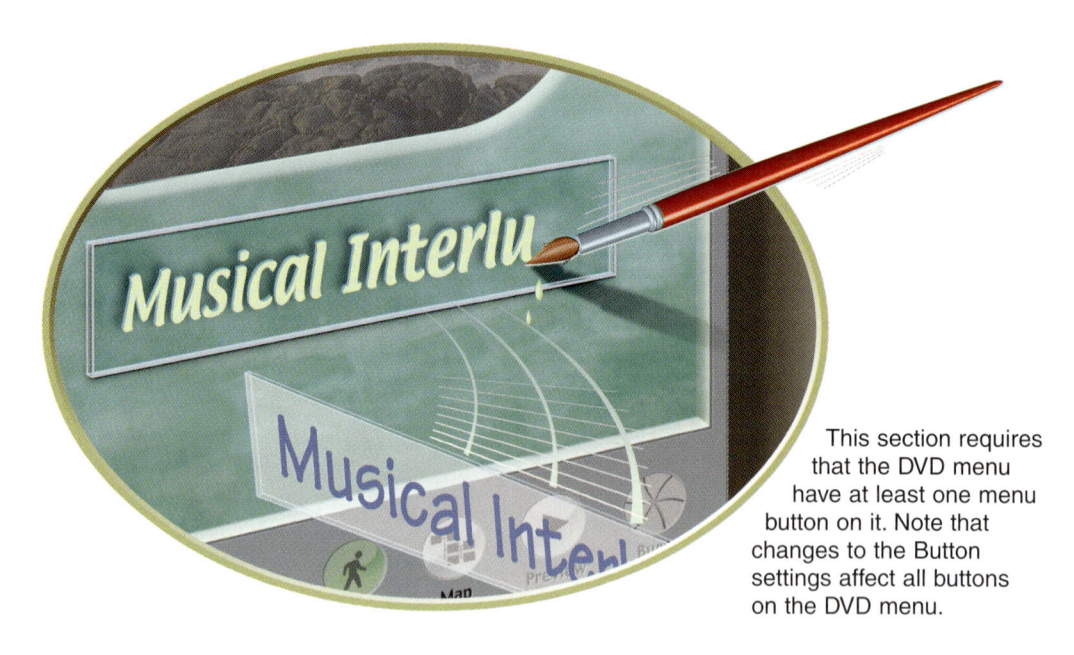

This section requires that the DVD menu have at least one menu button on it. Note that changes to the Button settings affect all buttons on the DVD menu.

CHANGE A MENU BUTTON'S TEXT FORMAT

CHANGE TEXT SIZE

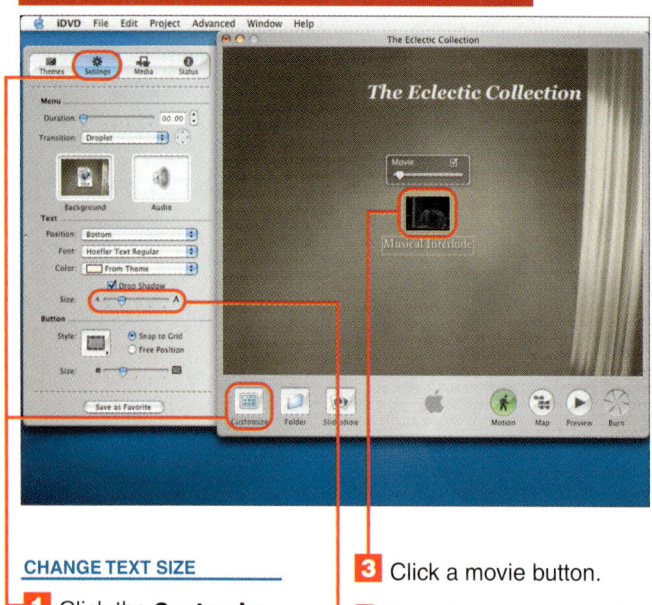

1. Click the **Customize** button.

■ The Customize drawer opens.

2. Click the **Settings** button.

3. Click a movie button.

■ Controls appear around the button.

4. Click and drag the Text slider.

■ The button labels change size.

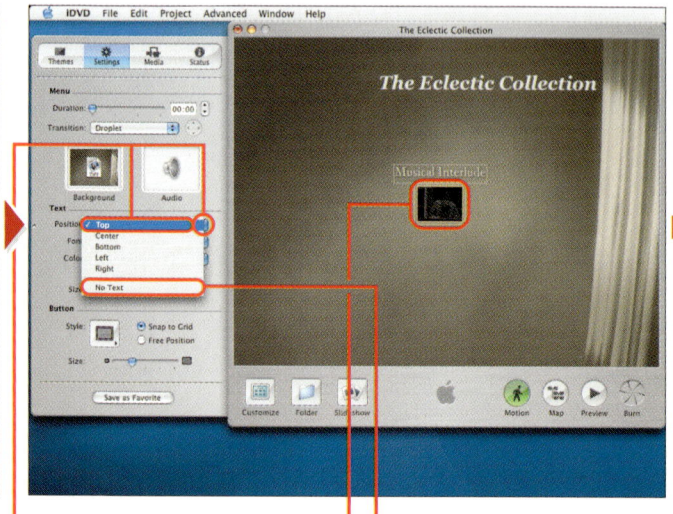

CHANGE TEXT POSITION

5. Click the Position menu.

6. Select an item from the menu.

■ To change the text format on a menu button, do not select **No Text** because it hides menu button labels.

■ The button labels move to the new position.

266

13 Creating DVD Menus with iDVD

WORKING WITH IDVD

How can I add free-floating text to a menu?

You can add text blocks to a DVD menu in order to provide credits or additional information about the DVD. Follow these steps:

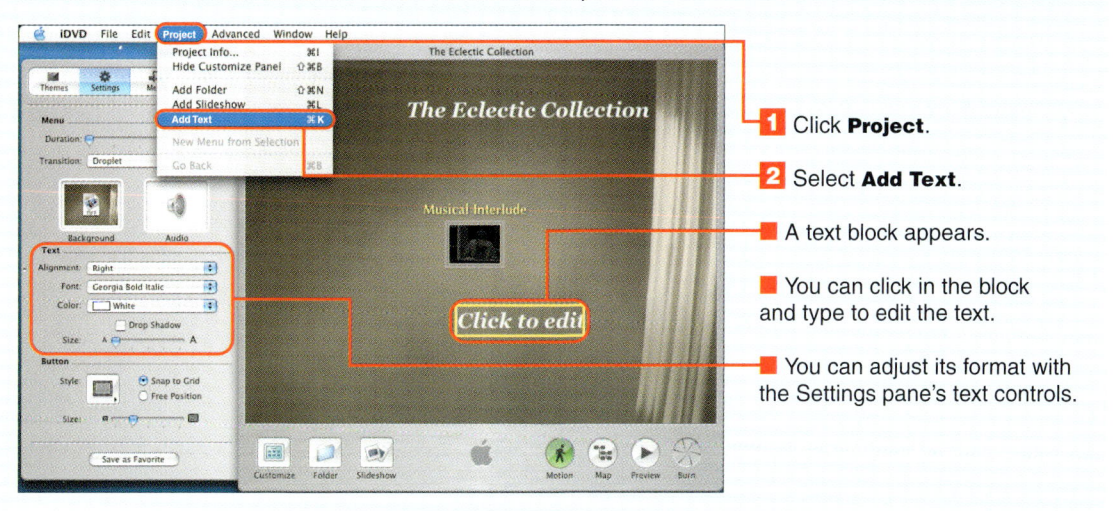

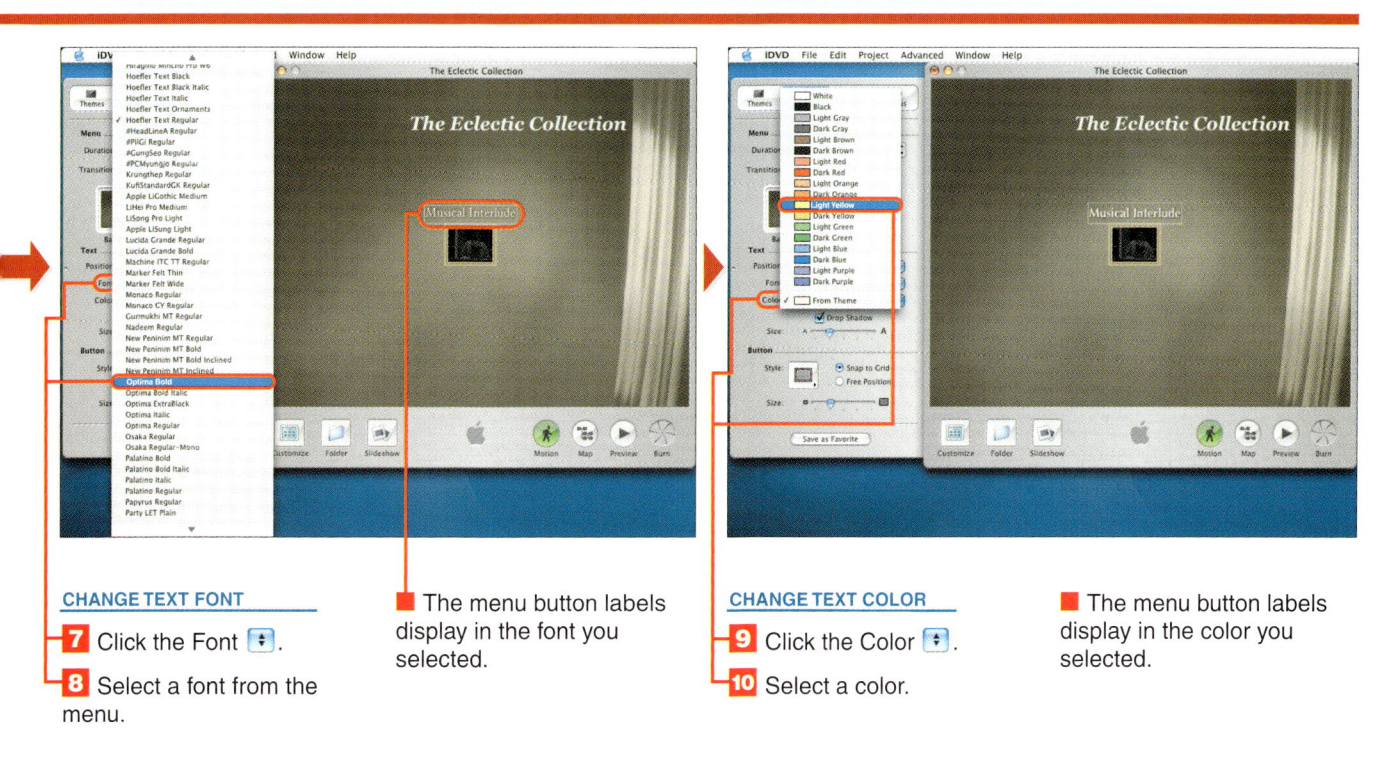

1 Click **Project**.

2 Select **Add Text**.

■ A text block appears.

■ You can click in the block and type to edit the text.

■ You can adjust its format with the Settings pane's text controls.

CHANGE TEXT FONT

7 Click the Font.

8 Select a font from the menu.

■ The menu button labels display in the font you selected.

CHANGE TEXT COLOR

9 Click the Color.

10 Select a color.

■ The menu button labels display in the color you selected.

267

ADD A CUSTOM BUTTON IMAGE OR MOVIE

You can add an image or a different movie to a menu button instead of the one that iDVD normally displays. For example, you may want to use family portraits for the buttons in a DVD containing videos of a family reunion.

This section requires that the DVD menu have at least one menu button on it.

ADD A CUSTOM BUTTON IMAGE OR MOVIE

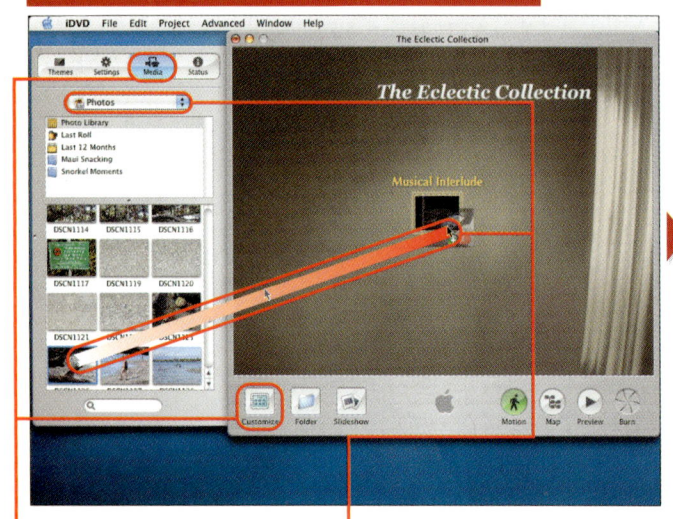

ADD AN IMAGE

1 Click the **Customize** button.

■ The Customize drawer opens.

2 Click the **Media** button.

3 Click here and select **Photos**.

4 Click and drag a photo from the pane over a movie menu button.

■ The button highlights when the mouse is over it.

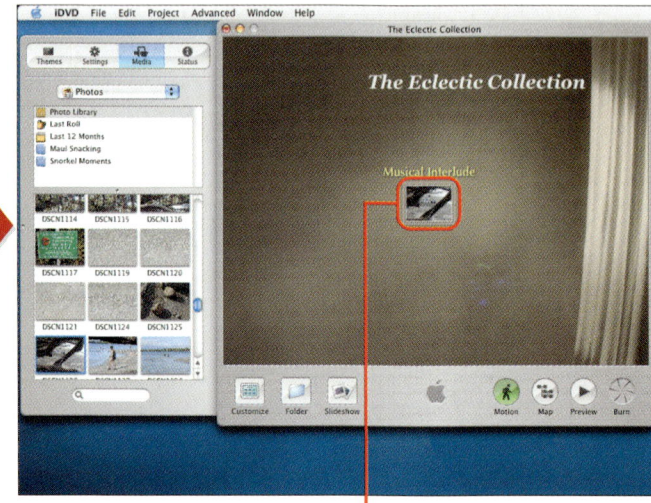

5 Release the mouse.

■ The picture appears on the movie menu button.

268

13 Creating DVD Menus with iDVD

WORKING WITH iDVD

How long can the movies on menu buttons be?

The movies that iDVD displays on motion menu buttons can run as long as 15 minutes before they loop back to the beginning. Note that the Duration slider in iDVD's Settings pane sets the duration for the longest item in the menu, whether it be a background movie, a sound, or the movies displayed in menu buttons.

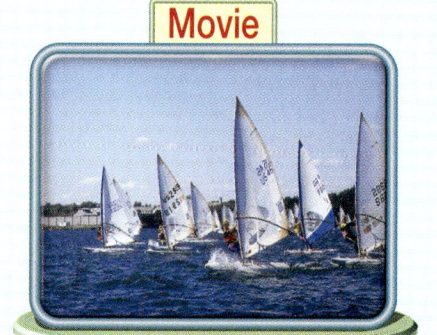

Can I drag several photos or an album onto a movie menu button to create a slideshow preview?

No. A movie menu button can display a movie or a single image like a Drop Zone, but unlike a Drop Zone it cannot display a slideshow; if you drag several pictures at once to a movie menu button, iDVD presents a warning.

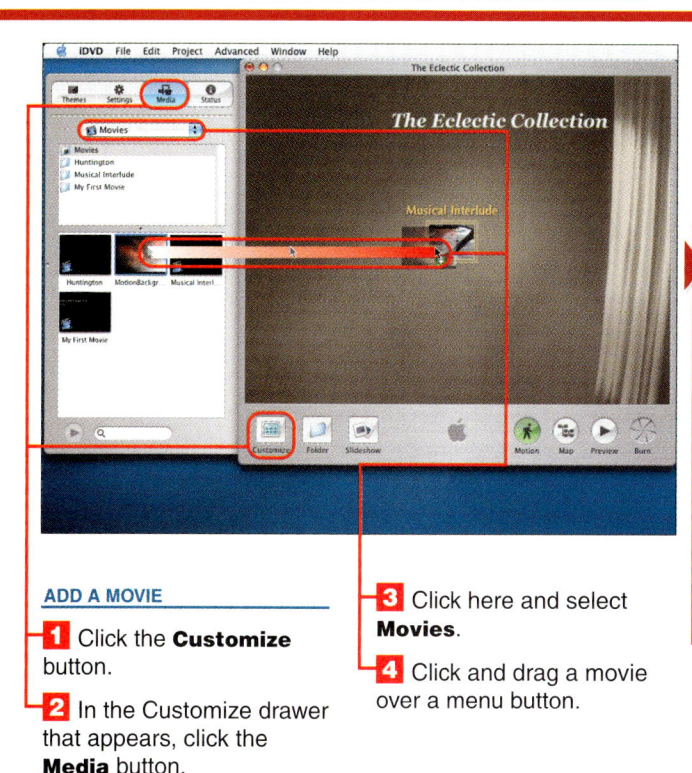

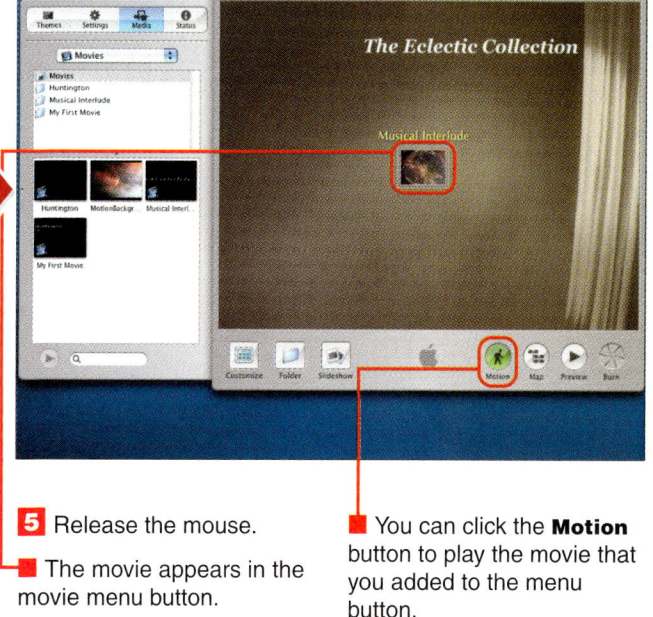

ADD A MOVIE

■1 Click the **Customize** button.

■2 In the Customize drawer that appears, click the **Media** button.

■3 Click here and select **Movies**.

■4 Click and drag a movie over a menu button.

■5 Release the mouse.

■ The movie appears in the movie menu button.

■ You can click the **Motion** button to play the movie that you added to the menu button.

269

ARRANGE MENU BUTTONS

iDVD displays menu buttons in the order that you add them to the DVD menu, but you can arrange the buttons in a different order or place them where you like.

This section requires that the DVD menu have at least two menu buttons on it.

ARRANGE MENU BUTTONS

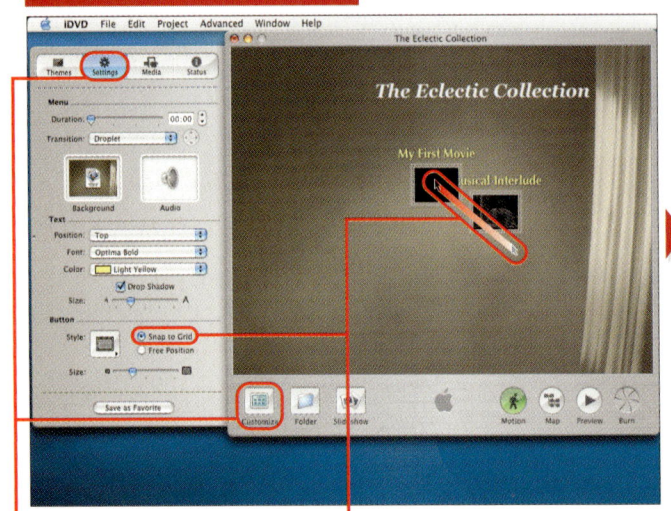

ARRANGE BUTTONS ON A GRID

1 Click the **Customize** button.

■ The Customize drawer opens.

2 Click the **Settings** button.

3 Click the **Snap to Grid** option (○ changes to ●).

4 Click and drag a menu button.

■ The other buttons move out of the way as you drag the button.

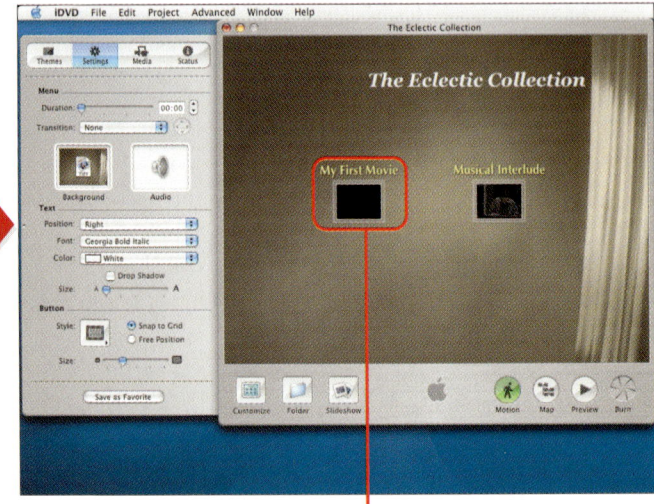

5 Release the mouse.

■ The button snaps to its new position and highlights.

270

13 Creating DVD Menus with iDVD

WORKING WITH IDVD

? The menu buttons do not adjust their positions when I change their label positions. Why not?

Each menu theme that uses motion menu buttons has a layout grid that leaves room for the menu labels on only one of the button's sides. If you change the labels' positions, they may appear on top of other buttons or go off-screen. To fix this, you can either hide the labels, set the labels back to their default position for the theme, or click the **Free Position** option (◯ changes to ⦿) to turn the grid off and then manually arrange the buttons. Note that Drop Zone themes create text-only menu buttons. You must click the **Free Position** option (◯ changes to ⦿) to turn the grid off in Drop Zone themes if you want to change the text buttons to motion menu buttons in Drop Zone frames, or else the buttons will overlap.

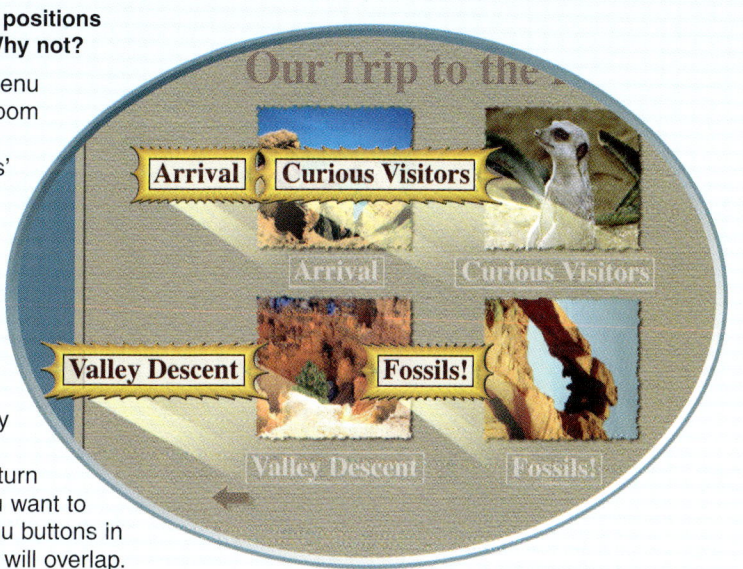

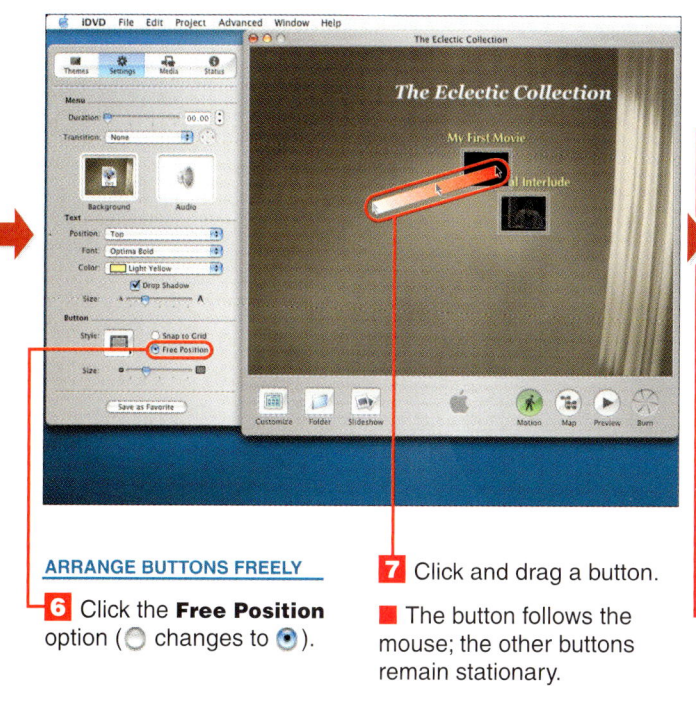

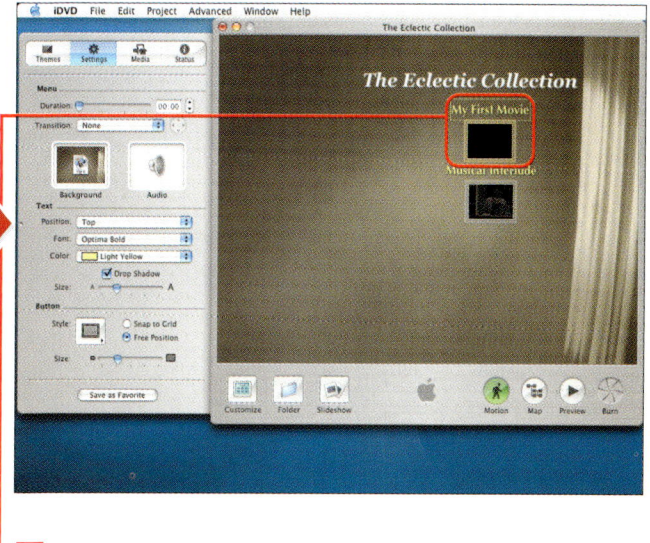

ARRANGE BUTTONS FREELY

6 Click the **Free Position** option (◯ changes to ⦿).

7 Click and drag a button.

■ The button follows the mouse; the other buttons remain stationary.

8 Release the mouse.

■ The button stays where you place it.

■ The button is highlighted.

271

CHANGE A MOTION MENU BUTTON'S START FRAME

When you make a motion menu button, it normally plays from the movie's first frame, but you can change the frame on which it starts so you can display a more visually interesting or informative sample of the movie.

CHANGE A MOTION MENU BUTTON'S START FRAME

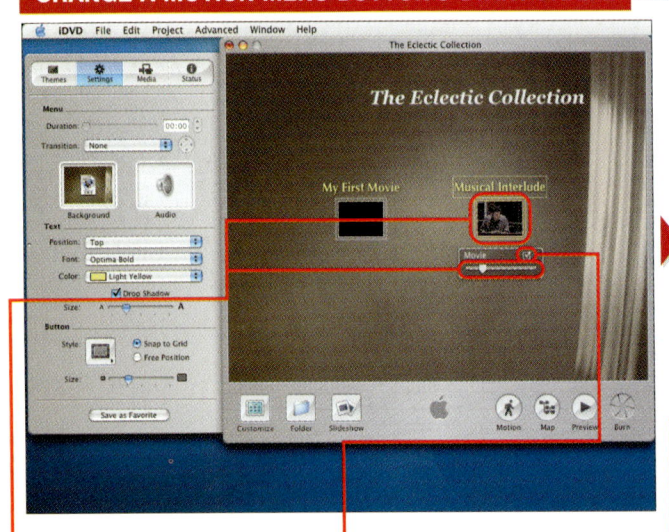

■ **1** Click a motion menu button.

■ The button highlights and a slider appears above it.

■ **2** Click and drag the Movie slider (●).

■ Different frames appear on the button as you drag.

■ **3** Release the mouse when you see the frame you want.

■ If you want the button to display only that frame, you can click the **Movie** option (☑ changes to ☐).

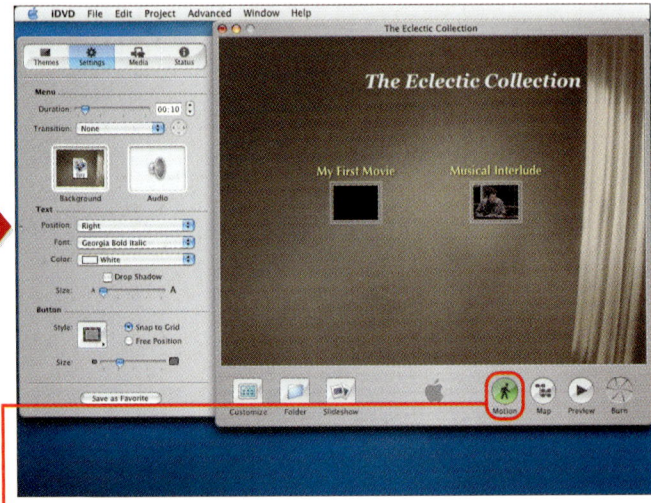

■ **4** Click the **Motion** button.

■ The motion menu button plays starting from the frame you selected.

CHANGE THE MOTION MENU BUTTONS' DURATION

13 Creating DVD Menus with iDVD

WORKING WITH IDVD

The movie displayed on a motion menu button plays in a loop, but you can reduce the loop's duration to suit your taste or the project's design requirements.

CHANGE THE MOTION MENU BUTTONS' DURATION

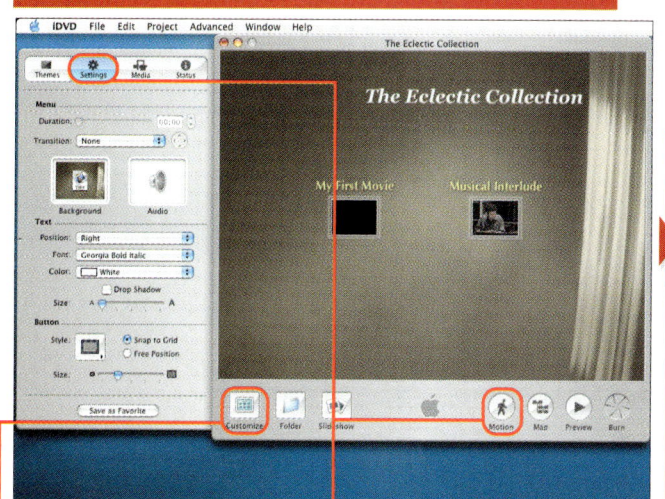

1 Click the **Customize** button.

■ The Customize drawer opens.

2 Click the **Settings** button.

3 If the **Motion** button is white, click it.

Note: You cannot adjust button durations when the Motion feature is turned off.

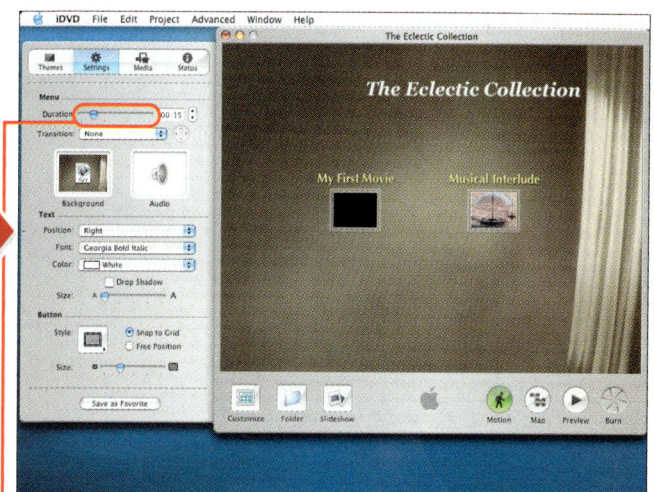

4 Click and drag the Duration slider (●) left or right.

■ The motion menu buttons play their movies, looping after the number of seconds set on the Duration slider.

Note: The Duration slider controls not only the duration all of the DVD menu's motion menu buttons, but also the duration of the background motion and background audio on the DVD menu. See Chapter 12 for more about the Duration slider.

273

CREATE A SUBMENU

You can create submenus in your DVD project that can contain additional menu buttons and that can display different themes. This allows you to organize your DVD's contents more effectively.

CREATE A SUBMENU

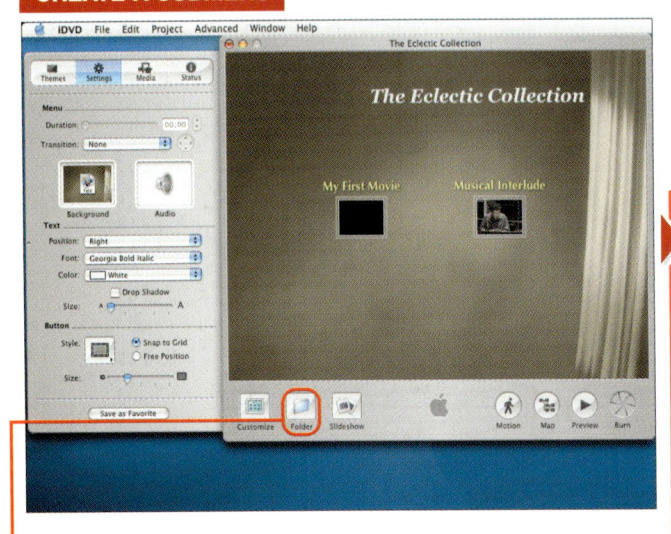

1 Click the **Folder** button.

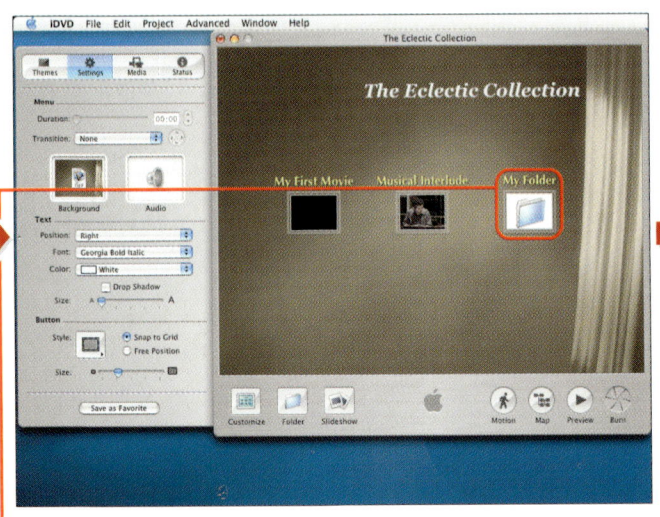

■ A My Folder button appears on the menu.

2 Double-click **My Folder**.

■ A new menu appears with the same theme as the previous menu.

13 Creating DVD Menus with iDVD

WORKING WITH IDVD

How many menu buttons can fit on a DVD menu?

You can have as many as 12, not counting the Back (←) or Next (→) buttons that can appear on submenus. However, most themes are designed to accommodate about six buttons comfortably.

How can I move a movie button to a submenu?

You can use keyboard editing commands to cut a movie button from one menu and paste it on another. To move a movie button, click the button and press ⌘+X . Next, open the submenu and press ⌘+V . The button appears on the submenu.

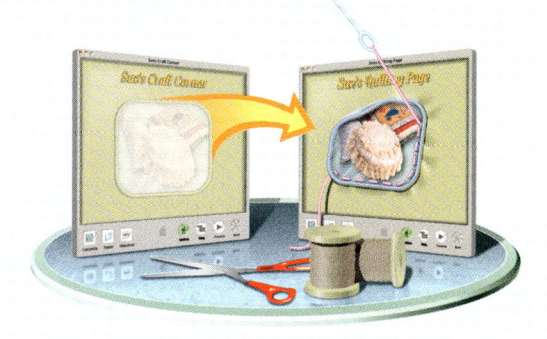

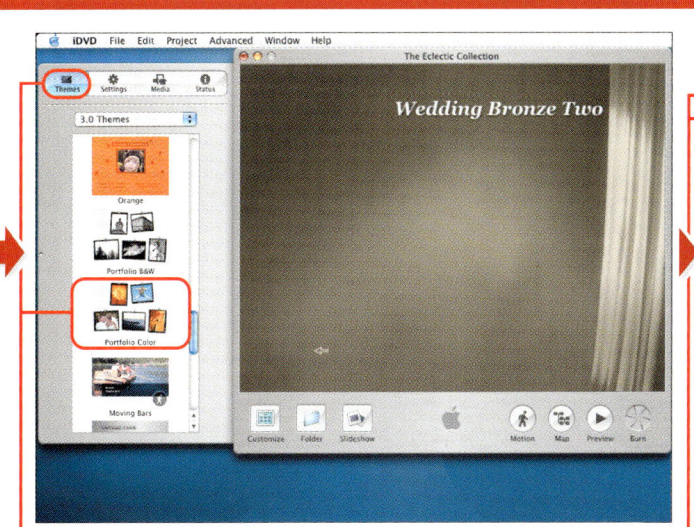

■ The menu has a Back button (←) on it.

3 Click the **Themes** button.

4 Click a theme.

Note: This example uses Portfolio Color, a theme with motion menu buttons. You should skip steps 9 to 14 if you select a theme that uses text buttons.

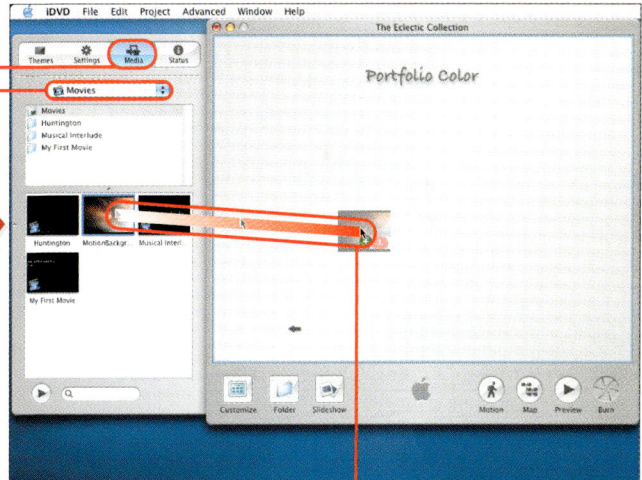

■ The menu changes to reflect the theme you selected.

5 Click the **Media** button.

6 Click here and select **Movies**.

7 Click and drag a movie from the Movies pane to the menu.

8 Release the mouse.

CONTINUED

275

CREATE A SUBMENU

You can customize a menu button that links to a submenu so that it shows a frame from one of the submenu's buttons. This can provide a helpful visual reminder for your DVD's viewers.

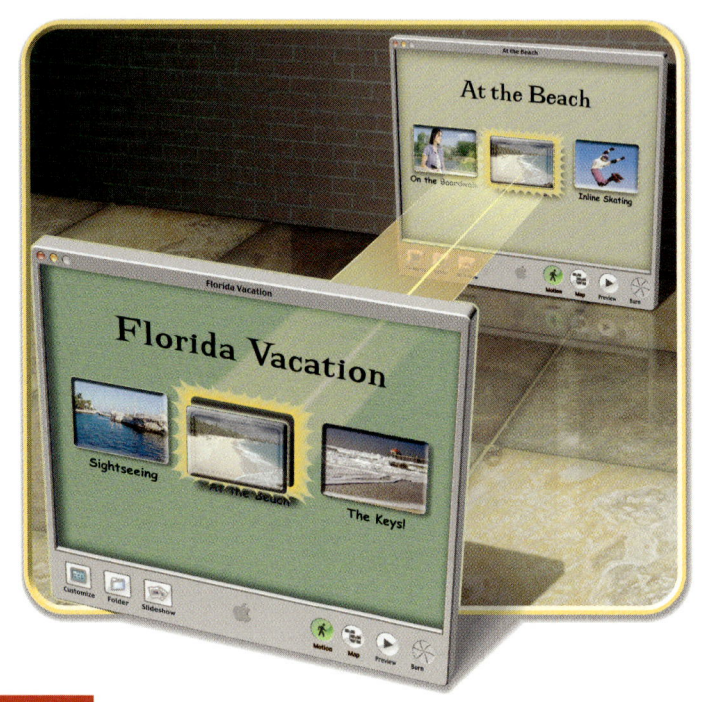

CREATE A SUBMENU (CONTINUED)

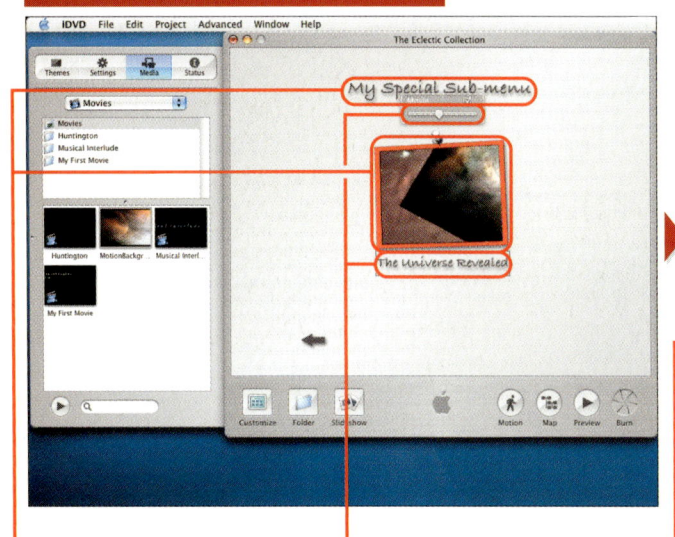

- A movie button appears on the menu.

- You can click here and type a menu's title.

9 Click the menu button.

- A Movie control appears.

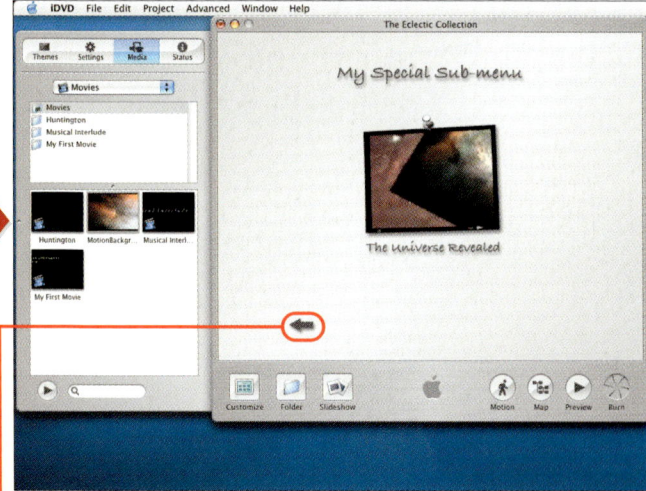

10 Click and drag the Movie slider ( ).

- The movie button displays a new first frame.

- You can click here and type the button's label.

11 Click the menu's ⬅.

276

13 Creating DVD Menus with iDVD

WORKING WITH IDVD

How do I quickly apply the current menu theme to my submenus?

You can click **Advanced**, and then click **Apply Theme to Project** to copy the theme on the currently visible DVD menu to all the menus in your project. To restrict the theme to just the submenus attached to the current menu, click **Advanced**, and then click **Apply Theme to Folders**.

How many submenus can I create?

An iDVD project can contain as many as 99 menus. Most projects, of course, should not require that many menus.

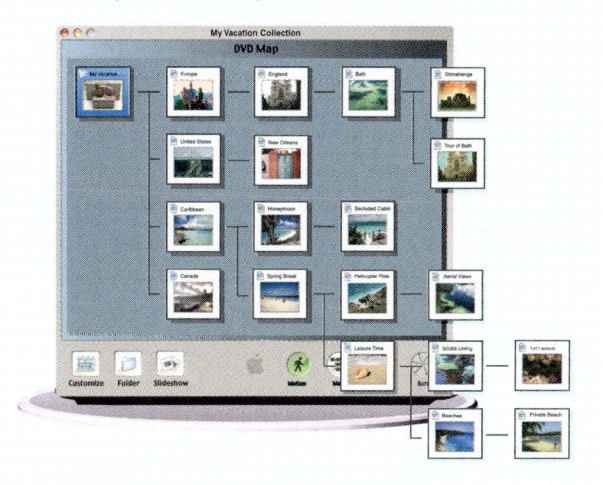

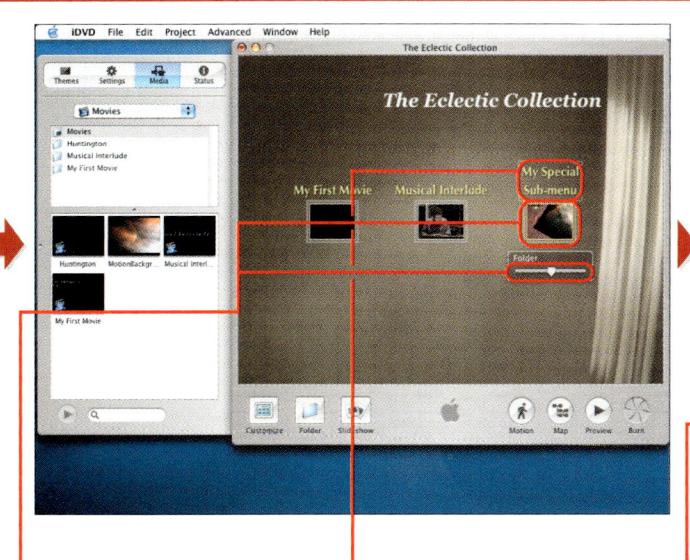

- The main menu appears.
- **12** Click the folder button.
- A Folder control appears.
- **13** Click and drag the Folder slider ( ) to the middle.

- The menu button displays the image from the submenu's movie button.
- The rightmost slider position displays the submenu itself in the button.
- You can click here and type the button's label.

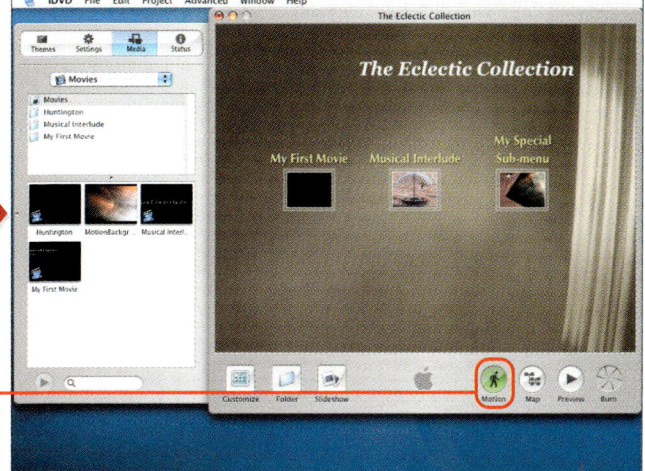

- **14** If the **Motion** button is white, click it.
- Any motion menu buttons begin playing.

- The folder button does not play.

277

CREATE A SCENE SUBMENU FROM IMOVIE

When you import a movie that has chapters, iDVD can create movie buttons and submenus that let viewers go to each chapter with their DVD remote controls.

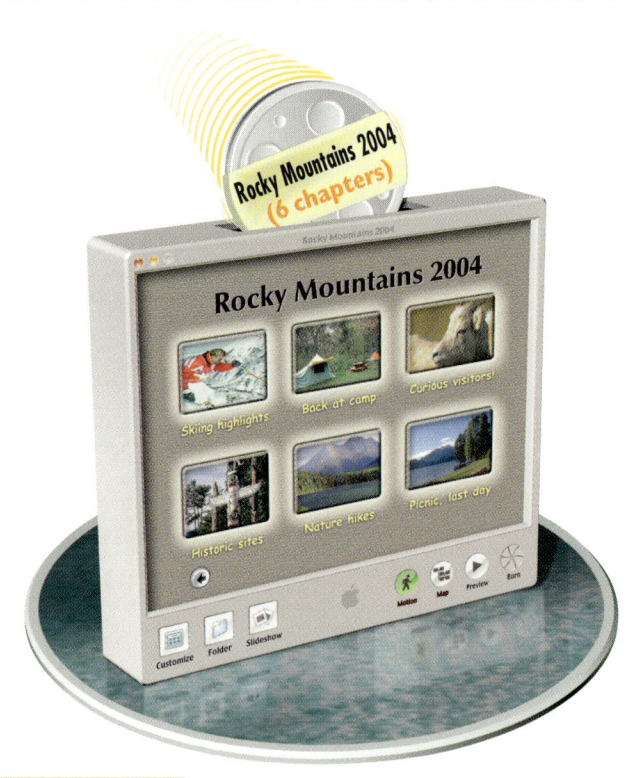

CREATE A SCENE SUBMENU FROM IMOVIE

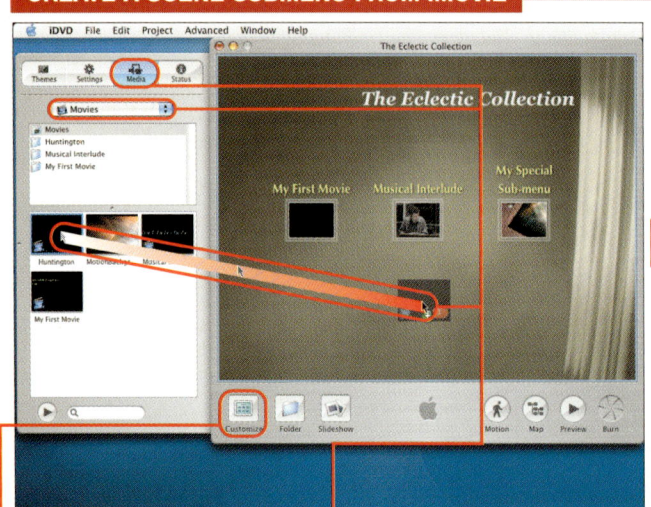

1 Click the **Customize** button.

■ The Customize drawer opens.

2 Click the **Media** button.

3 Click here and select **Movies**.

4 Click and drag a movie with chapters to the DVD menu.

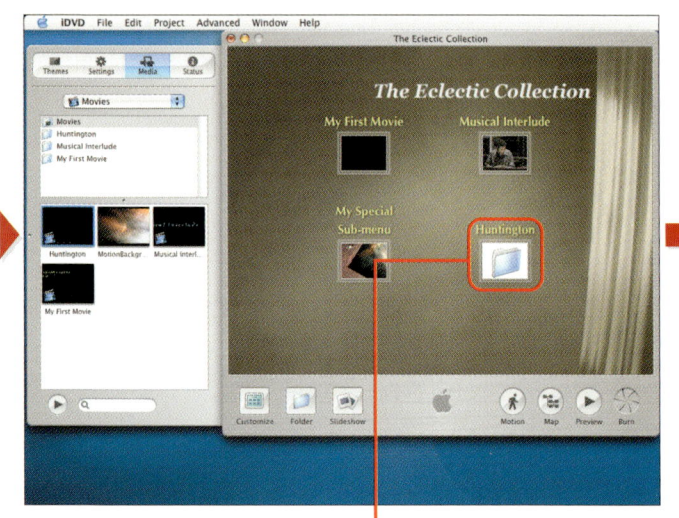

5 Release the mouse.

■ A folder button appears labeled with the movie's name.

6 Double-click the folder button.

278

13 Creating DVD Menus with iDVD

WORKING WITH iDVD

How can I keep iDVD from making submenus when I import a movie with chapters?

Open iDVD's preferences by pressing ⌘+,. Next, click the **Movies** button (📇). You can then click the appropriate option to have iDVD ask you to create submenus or to have iDVD never create submenus from movies with chapters. If you select for the former option, whenever you import a movie with chapters, iDVD displays a dialog window, from which you can select whether or not to create submenus.

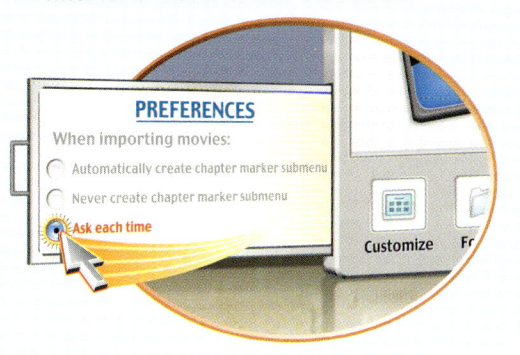

What happens if I drag a movie with many chapters to a DVD menu?

When you drag a movie with many chapters to an empty menu, iDVD creates multiple linked Scene Selection submenus. On the first Scene Selection submenu it creates, iDVD places as many movie buttons as the menu theme is designed to display, along with a Next button (→). This → links to the movie's next Scene Selection submenu, and so on.

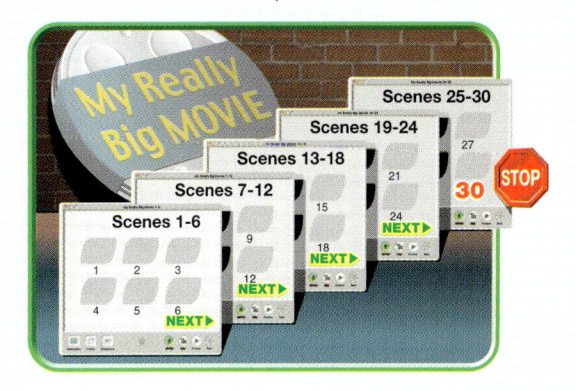

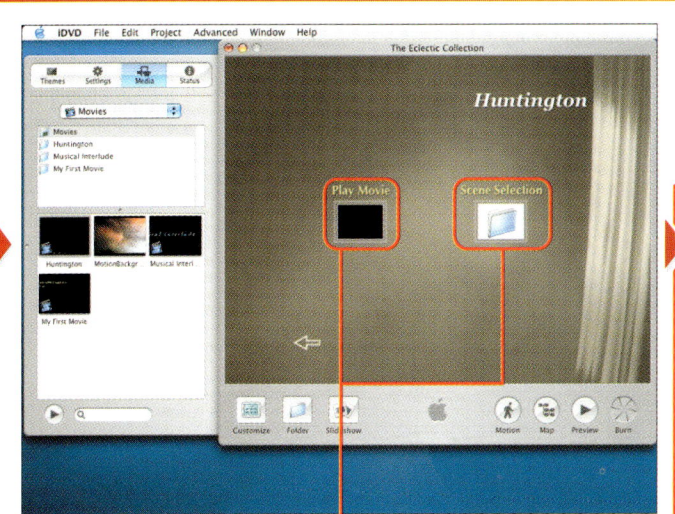

■ A DVD menu appears, titled with the movie's name.

■ The menu has a Play Movie button that viewers can select with their DVD controls to view the entire movie.

7 Double-click the **Scene Selection** folder button.

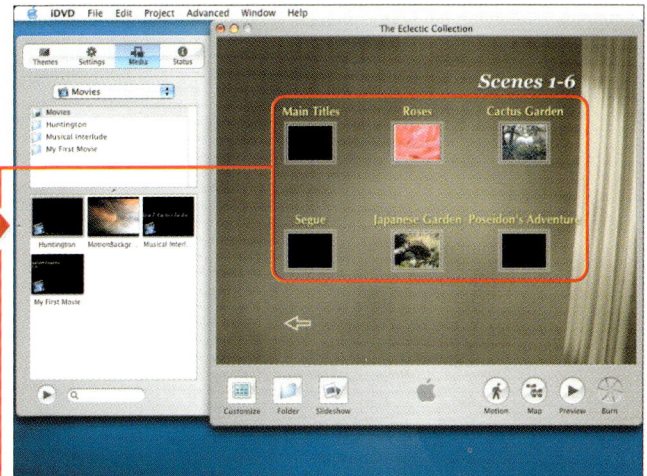

■ A DVD menu appears, labeled with the scenes it contains.

■ The menu contains movie buttons for the movie's first chapters.

■ Viewers can select a scene selection movie button with their DVD controls to view the movie starting at that scene.

279

USING THE MAP

As a DVD project becomes more complex, it can become more difficult to remember which menus contain what. The iDVD Map lets you see the arrangement of your DVD's menus and move among them.

USING THE MAP

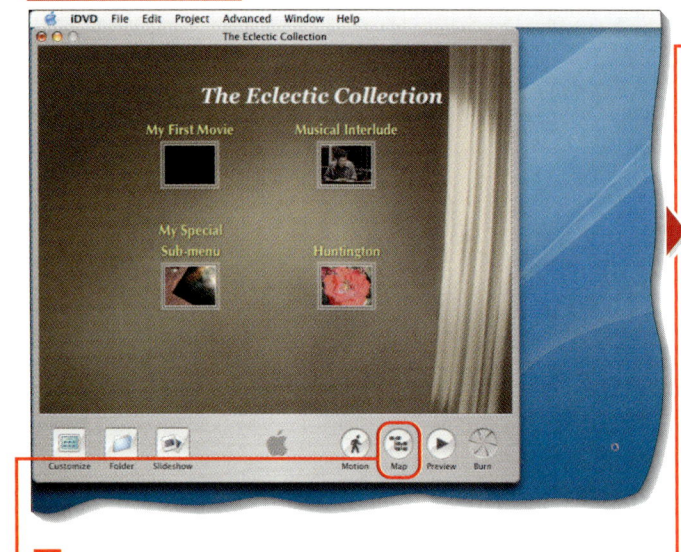

1 Click the **Map** button.

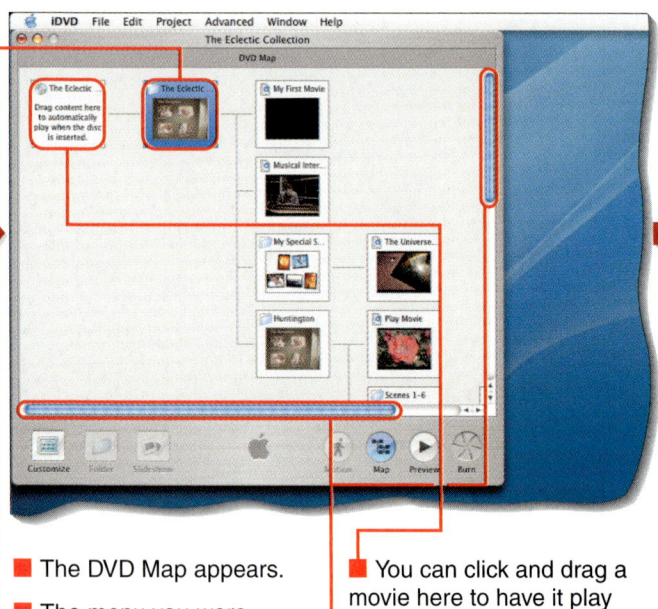

- The DVD Map appears.
- The menu you were viewing when you clicked **Map** is highlighted.

- You can click and drag a movie here to have it play when you insert a disc in a DVD player.

2 Drag the scroll bars to see more of the Map.

13 Creating DVD Menus with iDVD

WORKING WITH iDVD

What else can I do with the Map?

You can set individual movies to loop when played, which is useful for DVDs designed to play unattended in kiosks, for example. To set a movie to loop, perform the following steps:

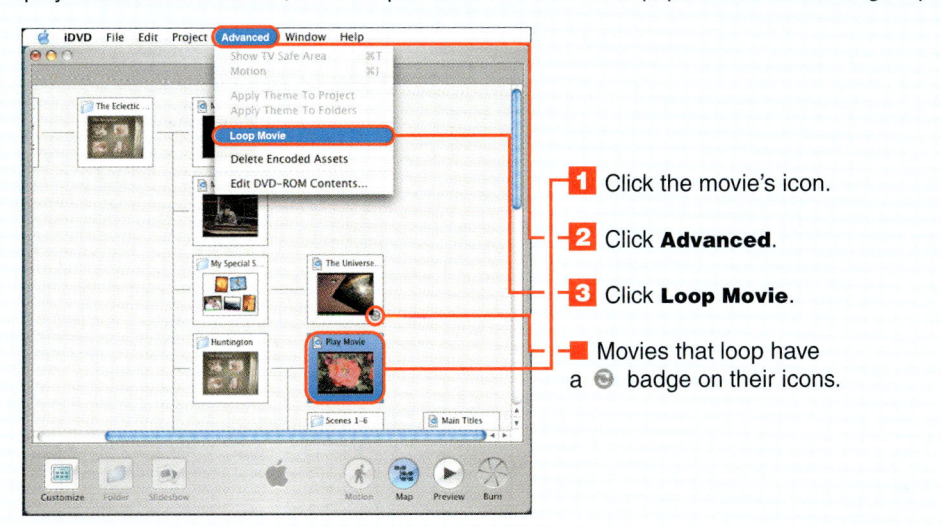

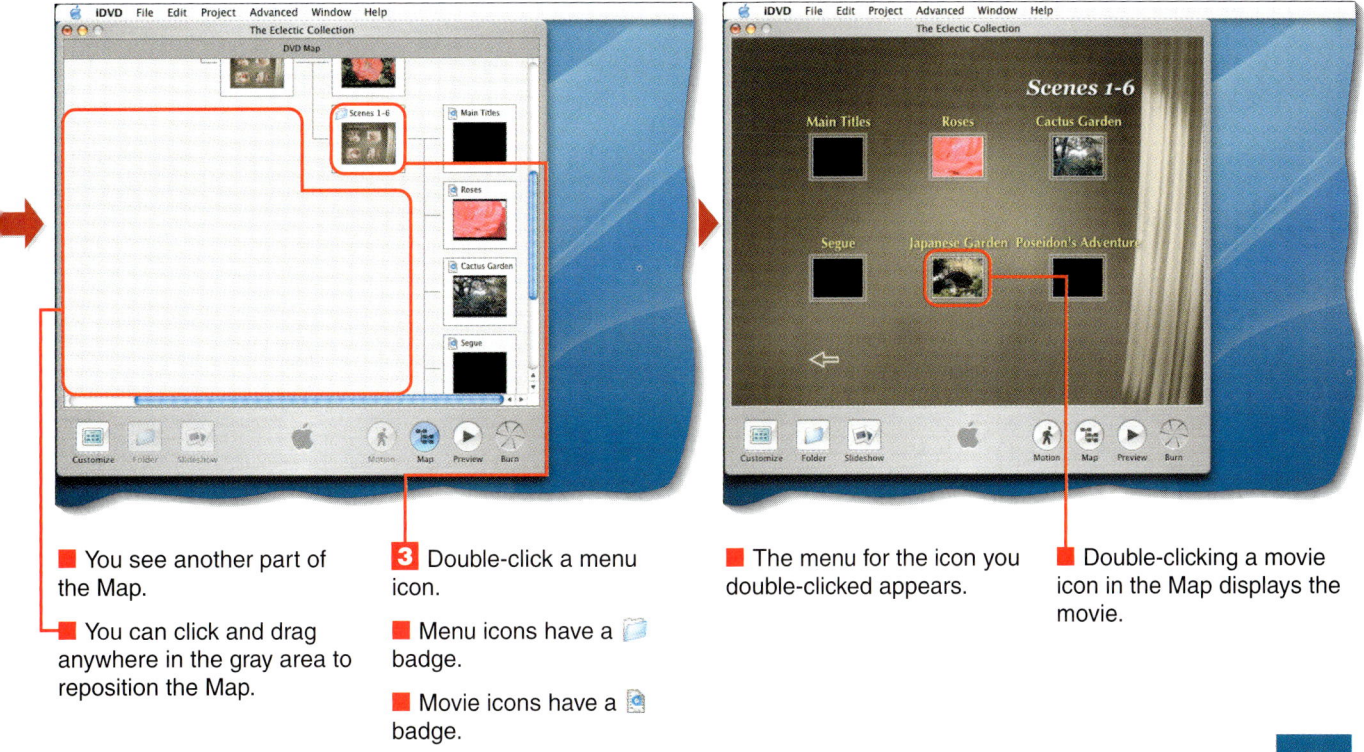

1 Click the movie's icon.

2 Click **Advanced**.

3 Click **Loop Movie**.

■ Movies that loop have a ⟲ badge on their icons.

■ You see another part of the Map.

■ You can click and drag anywhere in the gray area to reposition the Map.

3 Double-click a menu icon.

■ Menu icons have a 📁 badge.

■ Movie icons have a 🎬 badge.

■ The menu for the icon you double-clicked appears.

■ Double-clicking a movie icon in the Map displays the movie.

281

CREATE AND ADD PHOTOS TO A SLIDESHOW

You can create photo slideshows to place on your DVD using the pictures and albums from your iPhoto Library so you can share your photos with anyone who has a TV and a DVD player.

CREATE AND ADD PHOTOS TO A SLIDESHOW

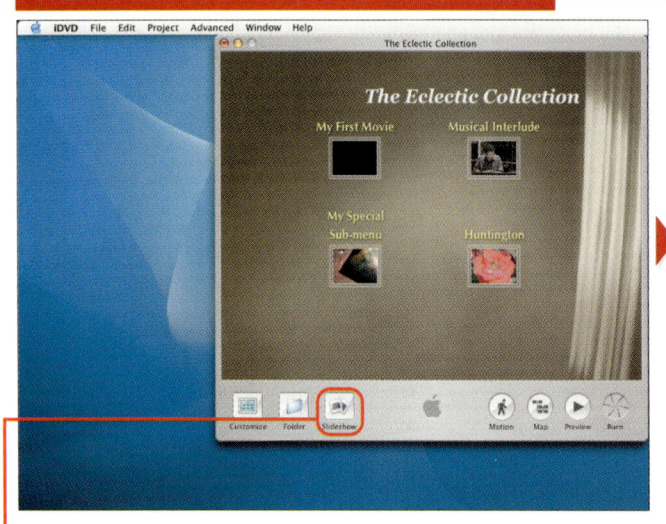

CREATE A NEW SLIDESHOW

1 Click the **Slideshow** button.

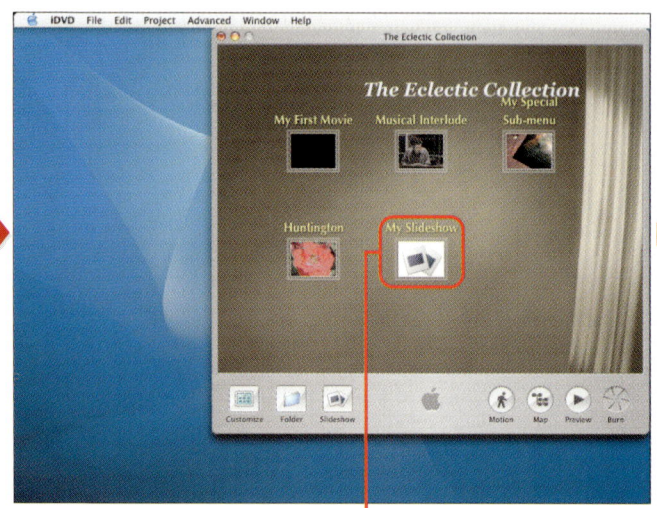

■ A slideshow menu button appears on the DVD menu.

2 Double-click the slideshow menu button.

14 Using Advanced iDVD Features

WORKING WITH iDVD

How many slides can I have in an iDVD slideshow?

Each slideshow can have as many as 99 slides in it. Because an iDVD project can have as many as 99 slideshows, you can place a grand total of 9,801 slides on a DVD using iDVD.

Can I use photos and pictures that are not in my iPhoto Library in an iDVD slideshow?

Yes, you can use any type of picture that QuickTime can open. Click and drag the picture files you want to include in your slideshow from a Finder window or from your Desktop to iDVD's Slideshow Editor to have iDVD add them to your slideshow. For more on the Finder, see Chapter 1.

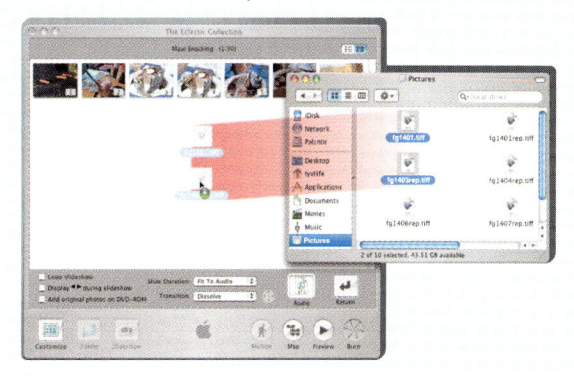

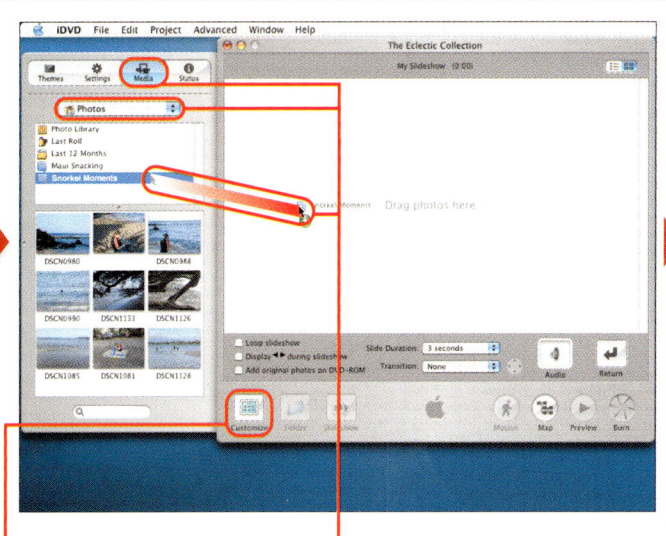

ADD AN ALBUM TO A SLIDESHOW

■ The Slideshow editor appears in the DVD display area.

3 Click the **Customize** button.

4 Click the **Media** button.

5 Click here and select **Photos**.

6 Click and drag a photo album over the Slideshow Editor.

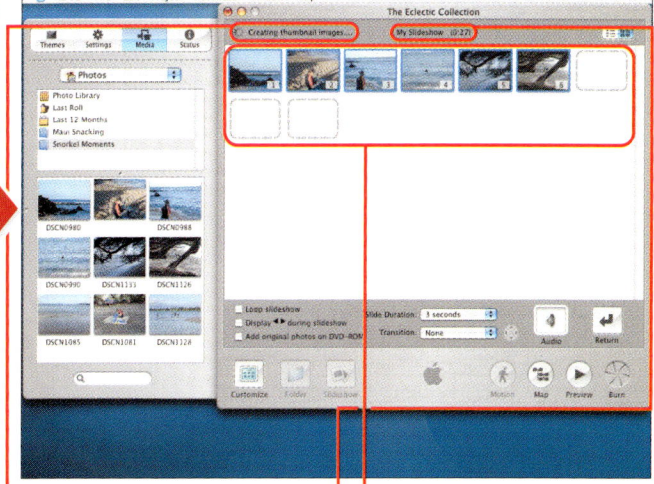

7 Release the mouse.

■ iDVD displays a progress indicator as the pictures import.

■ The album's pictures appear in the Slideshow Editor as thumbnails.

■ iDVD displays the current duration of the slideshow.

CONTINUED

283

CREATE AND ADD PHOTOS TO A SLIDESHOW

You can add pictures to a slideshow, or instantly make a new slideshow from an iPhoto album.

CREATE AND ADD PHOTOS TO A SLIDESHOW (CONTINUED)

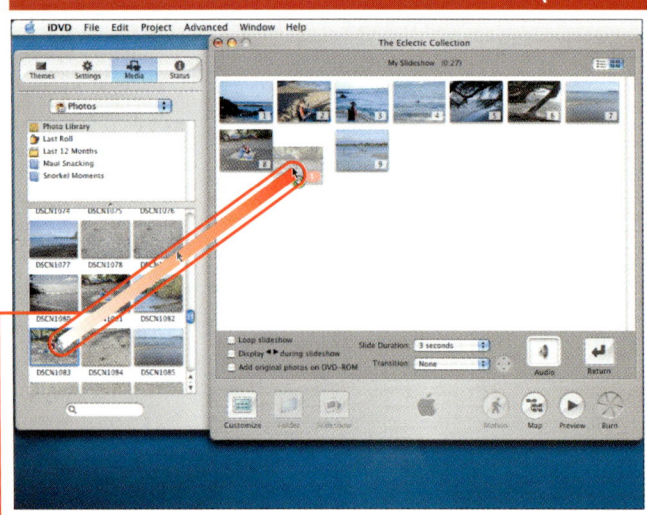

ADD INDIVIDUAL PHOTOS TO A SLIDESHOW

8 Click and drag a photo over the Slideshow Editor.

■ You can Shift+click or ⌘+click to select multiple photos.

■ As the mouse moves over the thumbnails, the thumbnails move aside to make room for the picture.

9 Release the mouse.

■ The picture thumbnail appears where you released the mouse.

10 Click the **Return** button.

■ The DVD's menu replaces the Slideshow Editor.

284

14 Using Advanced iDVD Features

WORKING WITH iDVD

How do I remove a picture from a slideshow?

Select one or more pictures that you want to remove, and then press Delete. Alternatively, you can click **Edit**, and then **Delete**.

On iDVD's Slideshow Editor, what does the Add original photos on DVD-ROM option do?

When you select the **Add original photos on DVD-ROM** option (☐ changes to ☑), iDVD creates a folder on the DVD you burn that contains the photos in the slideshow, so that people viewing the DVD on a computer can copy them. By default, iDVD selects this option automatically if you select the iDVD Slideshow Preference option, **Always add original slideshow photos to DVD-ROM** (☐ changes to ☑). For more on copying files to a DVD, see the section "Add Data Files to a DVD." For more information on setting iDVD Preferences, see Chapter 12.

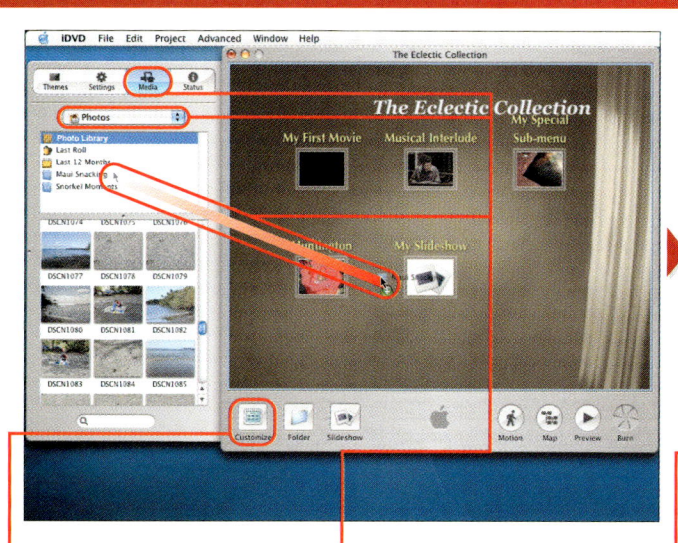

CREATE A SLIDESHOW FROM AN IPHOTO ALBUM

1 Click the **Customize** button.

■ The Customize drawer opens.

2 Click **Media**.

3 Click here and select **Photos**.

4 Click and drag a photo album over the DVD menu.

5 Release the mouse.

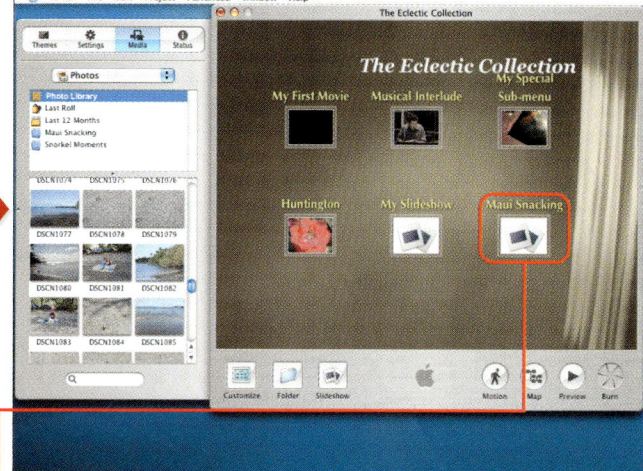

■ A slideshow menu button appears on the menu with the name of the album you dragged.

■ You can double-click the slideshow menu button to see the Slideshow Editor and to modify the slideshow's contents.

285

ARRANGE PICTURES IN A SLIDESHOW

You can quickly and easily rearrange the order in which the slides in your slideshow appear so that your slideshow can tell a story or make a point.

ARRANGE PICTURES IN A SLIDESHOW

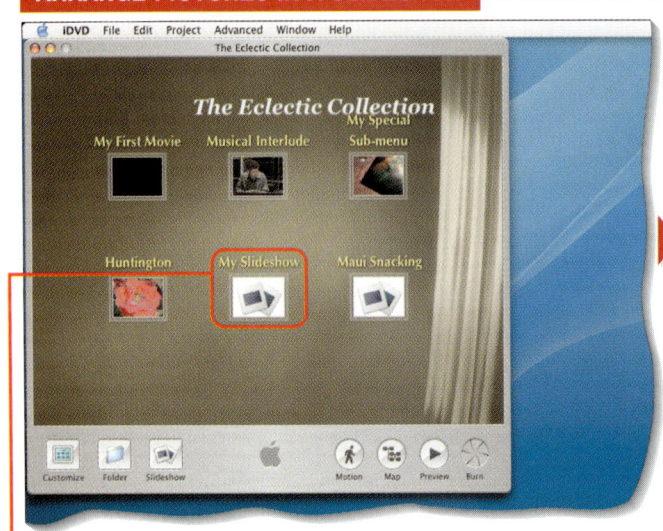

ARRANGE IN THUMBNAIL VIEW

1 Double-click the slideshow menu button for the slideshow you want to rearrange.

■ The slide editor replaces the DVD menu.

2 Click and drag a slide to where you want it.

■ The other slides move to make room.

3 Release the mouse.

■ The slide appears where you released the mouse.

286

14 Using Advanced iDVD Features

WORKING WITH IDVD

What kinds of transitions can I place between slides?

iDVD 4 provides six transitions that can appear between slides: Cube, Dissolve, Droplet, Mosaic, Page Flip, and Wipe. You can control the direction of the Cube, Mosaic, Page Flip, and Wipe transitions. Transitions play when you move from one slide to the next, but not when you go to a previous slide. Note that adding transitions takes up some space on the DVD and requires extra encoding time when you burn the disc. For more on burning a DVD, see the section "Burn a DVD."

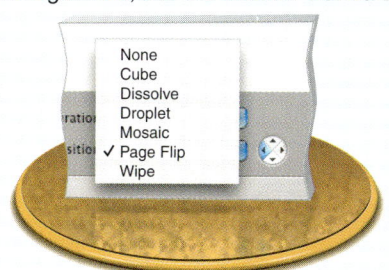

If I delete a slide from a slideshow when the Add original photos on DVD-ROM option is checked in the Slideshow Editor, does iDVD remove the slide file from the DVD-ROM?

No. However, you can update the files that you store on the DVD-ROM portion of the disc by clicking the **Add original photos on DVD-ROM** option (☑ changes to ☐) and then clicking it again (☐ changes to ☑). iDVD rebuilds the list of included photo files to match the modified slideshow. See the section "Add Data Files to a DVD" for more about adding files to a DVD-ROM.

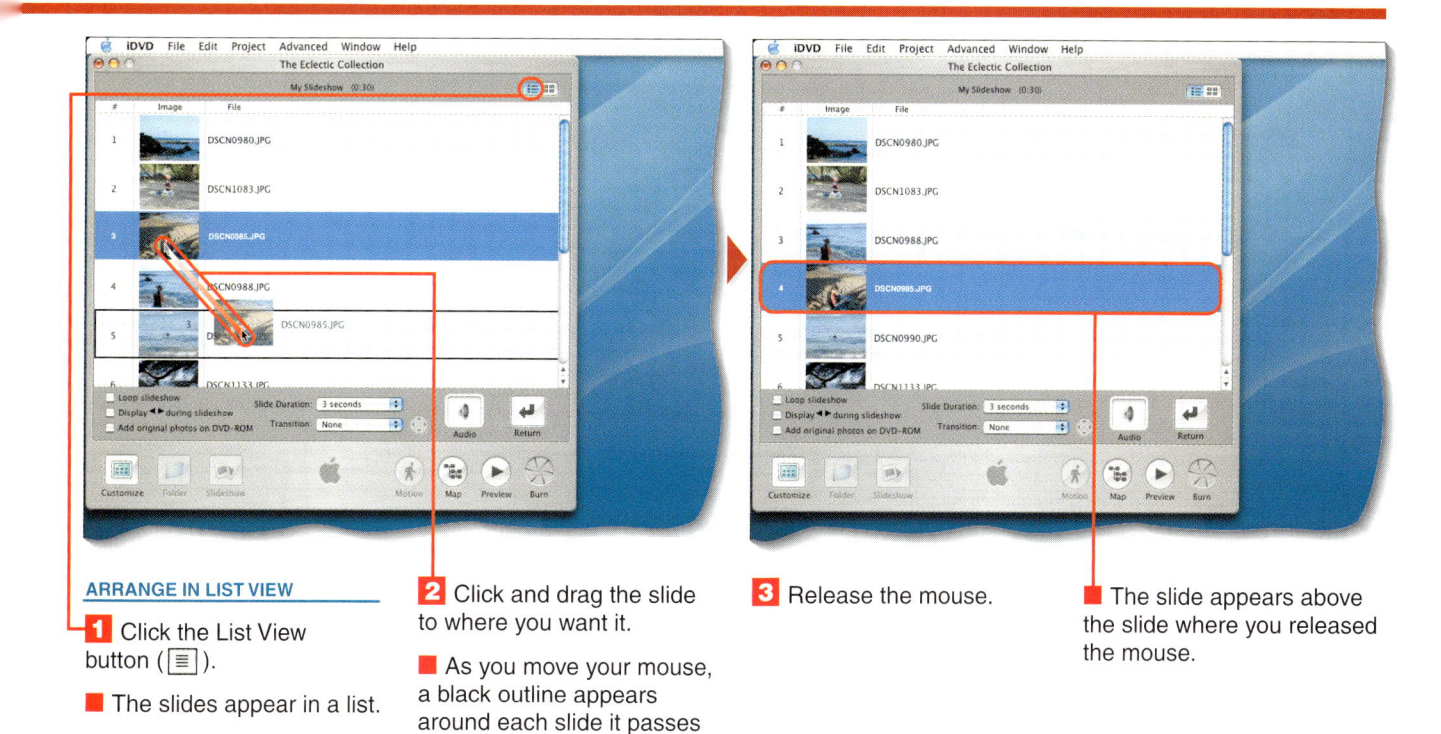

ARRANGE IN LIST VIEW

1 Click the List View button (☰).

■ The slides appear in a list.

2 Click and drag the slide to where you want it.

■ As you move your mouse, a black outline appears around each slide it passes over.

3 Release the mouse.

■ The slide appears above the slide where you released the mouse.

287

CHANGE A SLIDESHOW'S DURATION

You can set your slideshow to advance automatically at several different speeds, or advance slides manually.

CHANGE A SLIDESHOW'S DURATION

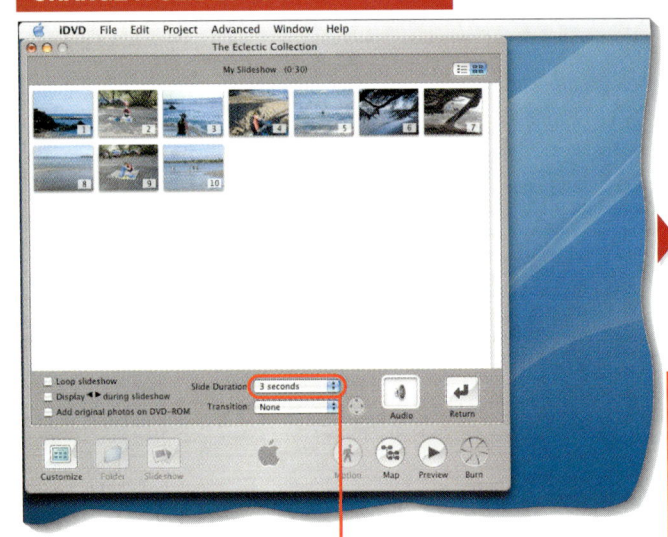

1 Open the Slideshow Editor for the slideshow you want to modify.

Note: See the section "Create and Add Photos to a Slideshow" for how to open the Slideshow Editor.

2 Click the Slide Duration.

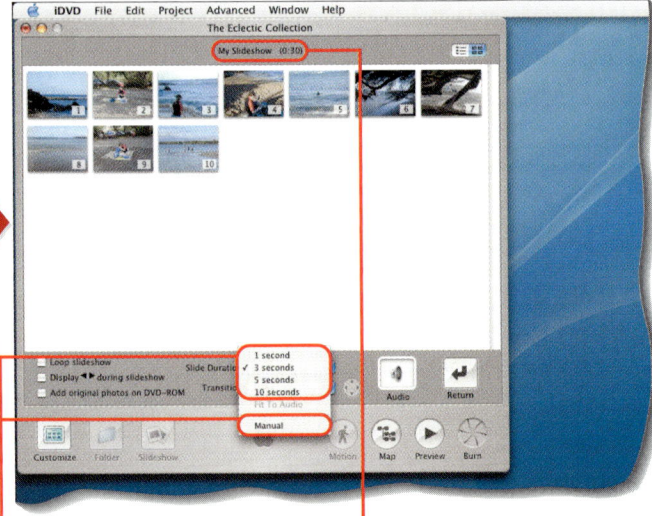

3 Select how long to display each slide on the screen before the DVD advances to the next screen.

■ The **Manual** option leaves each slide on-screen until you advance to the next with the DVD control.

■ The Slideshow Editor displays the slideshow's new duration.

288

14 Using Advanced iDVD Features

WORKING WITH iDVD

CHANGE A SLIDESHOW BUTTON'S IMAGE

You can select a slide from the slideshow to appear on the slideshow's menu button. You can also place a different photo or movie on a slideshow button to make it more attractive or informative.

CHANGE A SLIDESHOW BUTTON'S IMAGE

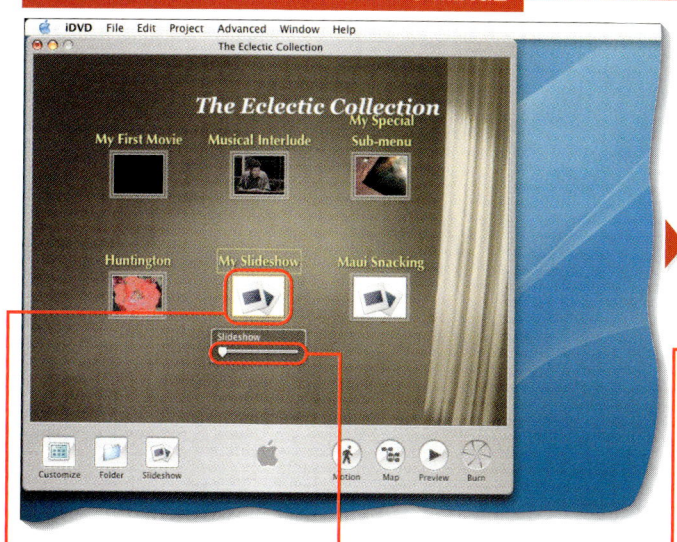

1 Click a slideshow menu button.

■ The menu button highlights and a Slideshow slider (🔹) appears below it.

Note: In some themes, 🔹 may appear above the menu button.

2 Click and drag 🔹 to the right.

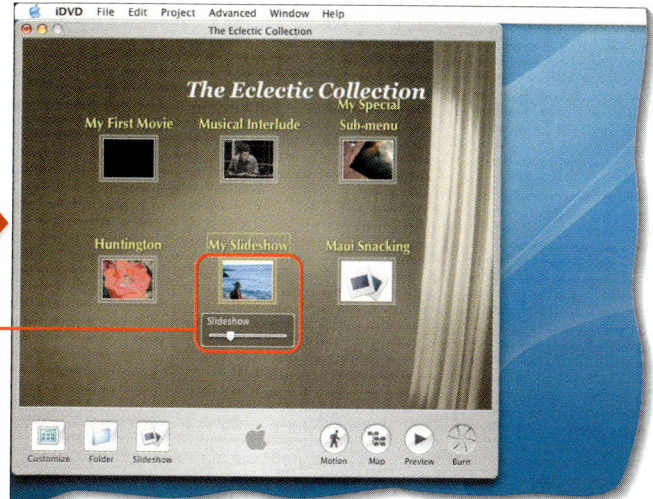

■ As you drag the slider, different pictures from the slideshow appear on the menu button.

■ You can drag a single photo from the Media pane to the slideshow menu button to give it a custom image.

■ If you drag multiple photos to the slideshow menu button, iDVD adds those photos to the slideshow.

■ You can drag a movie from the Media pane to the slideshow menu button to make the button into a motion menu button.

289

ADD AUDIO TO A SLIDESHOW

You can accompany your slideshow with music from your iTunes Library to make the slideshow more entertaining.

ADD AUDIO TO A SLIDESHOW

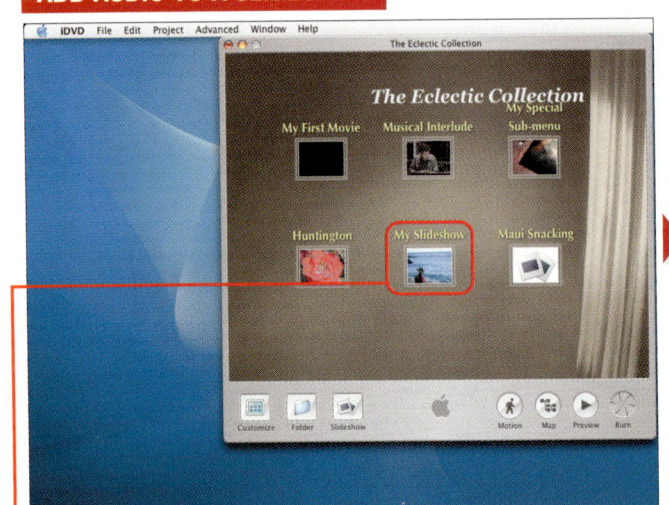

1 Double-click the menu button of the slideshow to which you want to add audio.

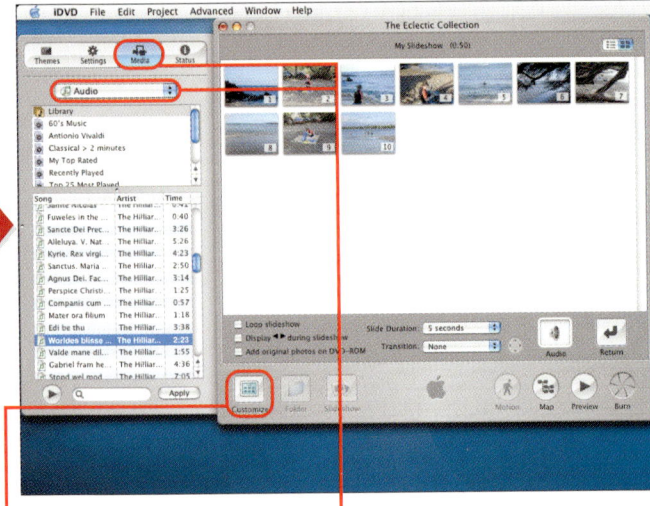

■ The Slideshow Editor replaces the DVD menu.

2 Click the **Customize** button.

■ The Customize drawer opens.

3 Click the **Media** button.

4 Click here and select **Audio**.

■ The Audio pane appears.

290

14 Using Advanced iDVD Features

WORKING WITH IDVD

Can I select a different slide duration setting for a slideshow that has attached audio?

iDVD does not let you select a manual duration for slideshows with attached audio, but you may select any of the other duration choices from the Slide Duration menu. If the audio is longer than the combined durations of all the slides, the slideshow ends after the last slide; if the audio is shorter than the combined slide durations, the sound loops until the last slide appears.

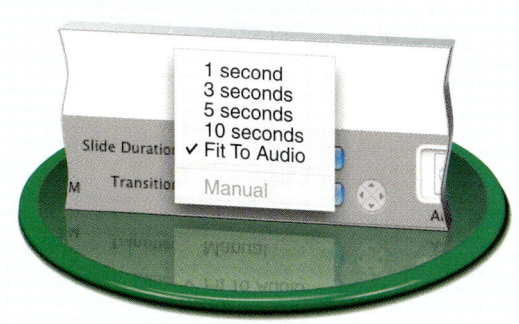

How do I remove a slideshow's audio?

In the Slideshow Editor, click and drag the audio icon out of the Audio well. The icon vanishes in a puff of animated smoke. You can also drag a different song into the Audio well from the Audio pane to replace the slideshow's attached audio.

■ **5** Click and drag a song from the Audio pane to the Audio well in the Slideshow Editor.

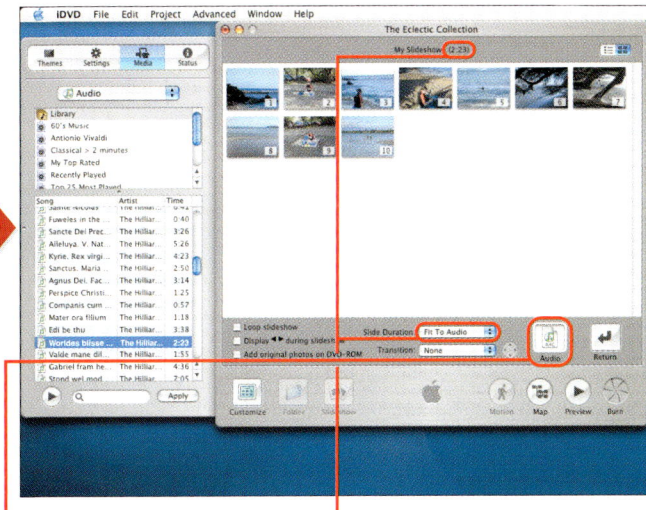

■ An audio icon appears in the Slideshow Editor's Audio well.

■ The Slide Duration menu changes to Fit to Audio.

■ The slideshow's duration changes.

291

CHECK AN IDVD PROJECT'S STATUS

Before you burn your DVD you can check its playing time, the amount of data the DVD will contain, and whether iDVD has encoded all the movie files for playback in the MPEG-2 format to make sure that your project is ready to burn.

iDVD can encode movies into the MPEG-2 format while you work; see Chapter 12 for more information about background encoding, and see the section "Burn a DVD" to learn how to burn a DVD.

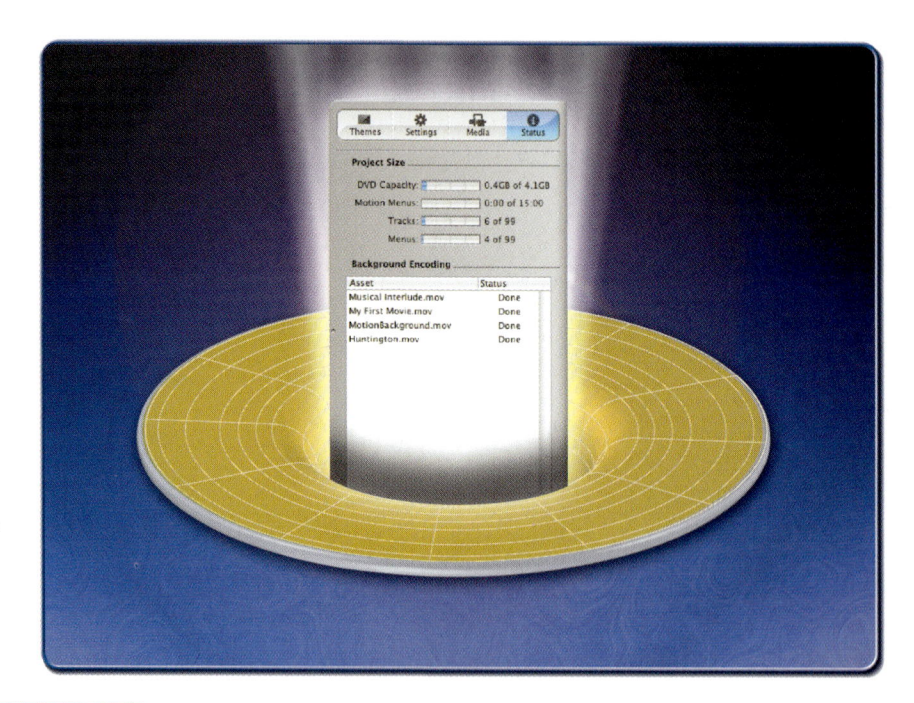

CHECK AN IDVD PROJECT'S STATUS

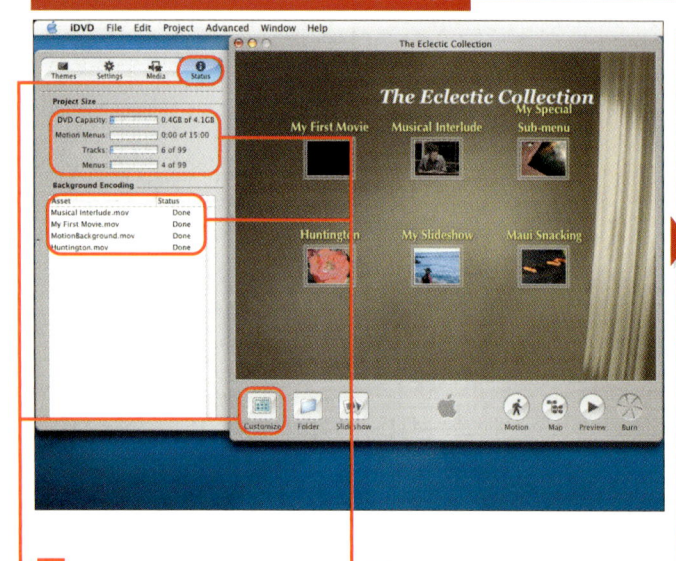

1 Click the **Customize** button.

2 In the Customize drawer, click the **Status** button.

■ You see a list of the movie files that iDVD will include on the DVD and whether iDVD has encoded the movies.

■ You can see how much of the DVD your various media are using.

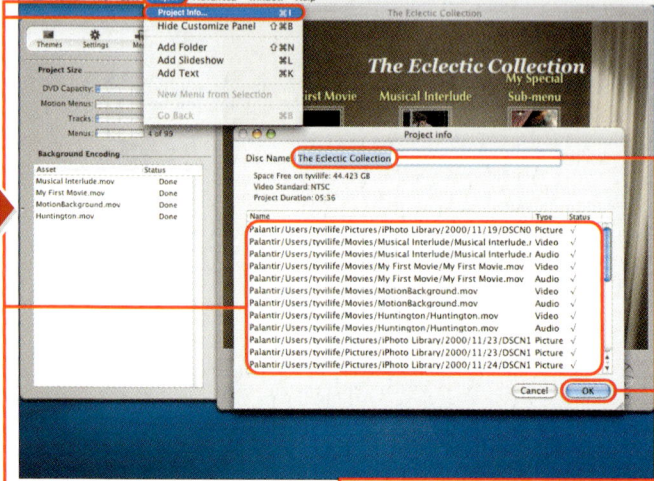

3 Click **Project**.

4 Click **Project Info**.

■ The Project Info window appears.

■ The window lists all the files that the DVD will contain, along with their types and their status.

■ You can click here and type a name for the disc.

5 Click **OK**.

■ The Project Info window closes.

CHECK THE TV SAFE AREA

14 Using Advanced iDVD Features

WORKING WITH IDVD

Often, television sets crop the edges of the images they display. iDVD can show you the TV Safe Area. Knowing where this area is allows you to place your DVD menu buttons so they are visible when your DVD plays on a TV.

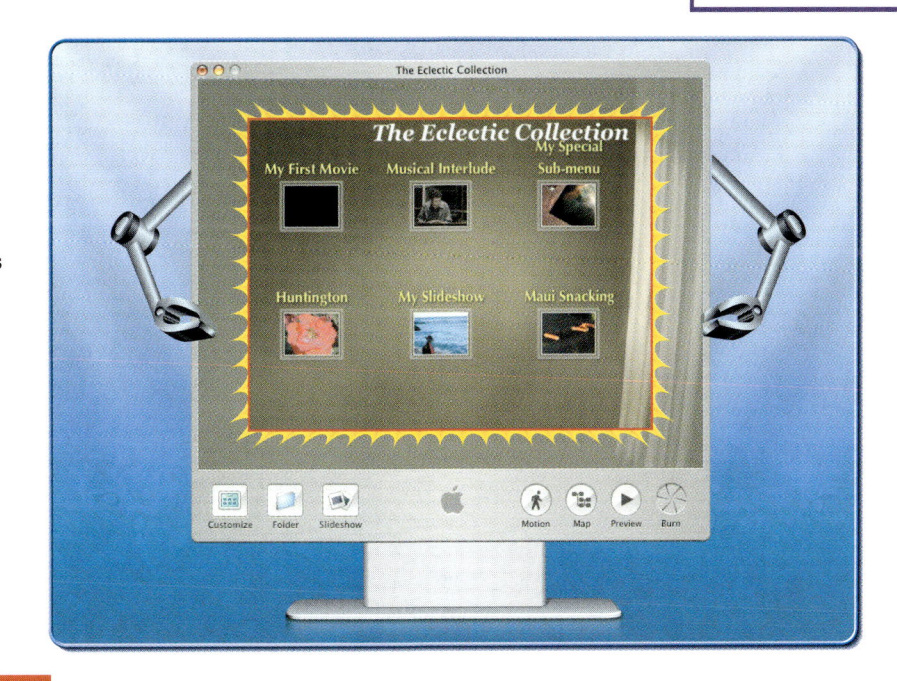

CHECK THE TV SAFE AREA

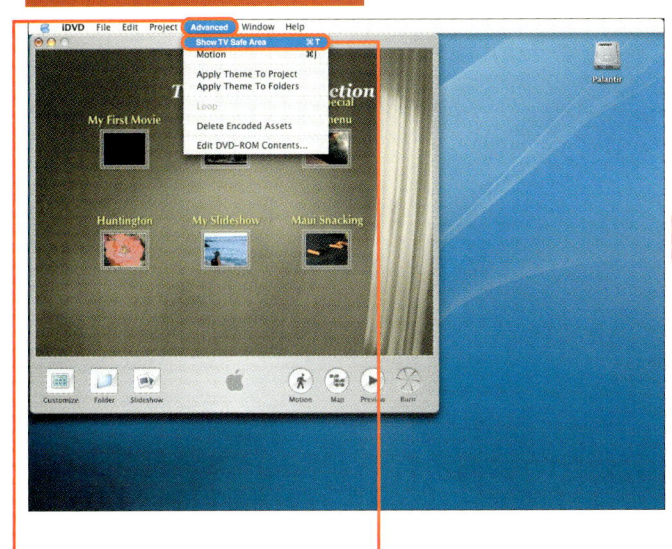

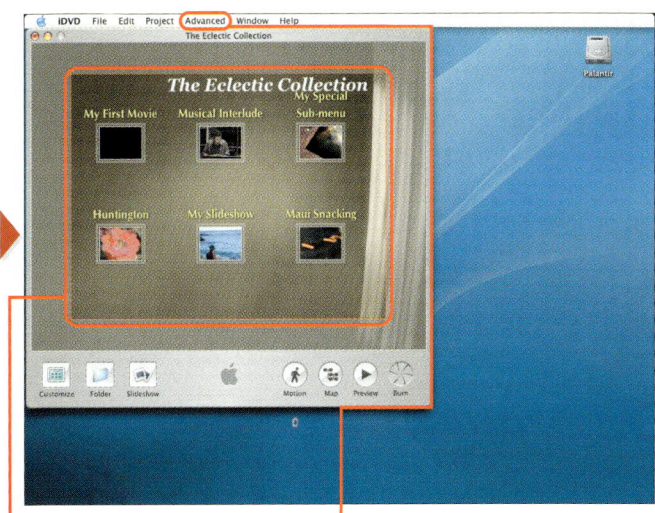

1 Click **Advanced**.

2 Click **Show TV Safe Area**.

■ A box outlines the TV Safe Area.

Note: Each iDVD theme automatically positions menu buttons inside the safe area unless you select ***Free Position*** *in the button settings. See Chapter 13 for more on arranging menu buttons.*

Note: See Chapter 12 for more on setting iDVD's Slideshow preferences to scale slides to fit the TV Safe Area.

■ You can click **Advanced** and select **Hide TV Safe Area** to stop seeing the TV Safe Area.

293

PREVIEW A DVD

You can preview your DVD using an on-screen DVD control to check how the finished DVD will play.

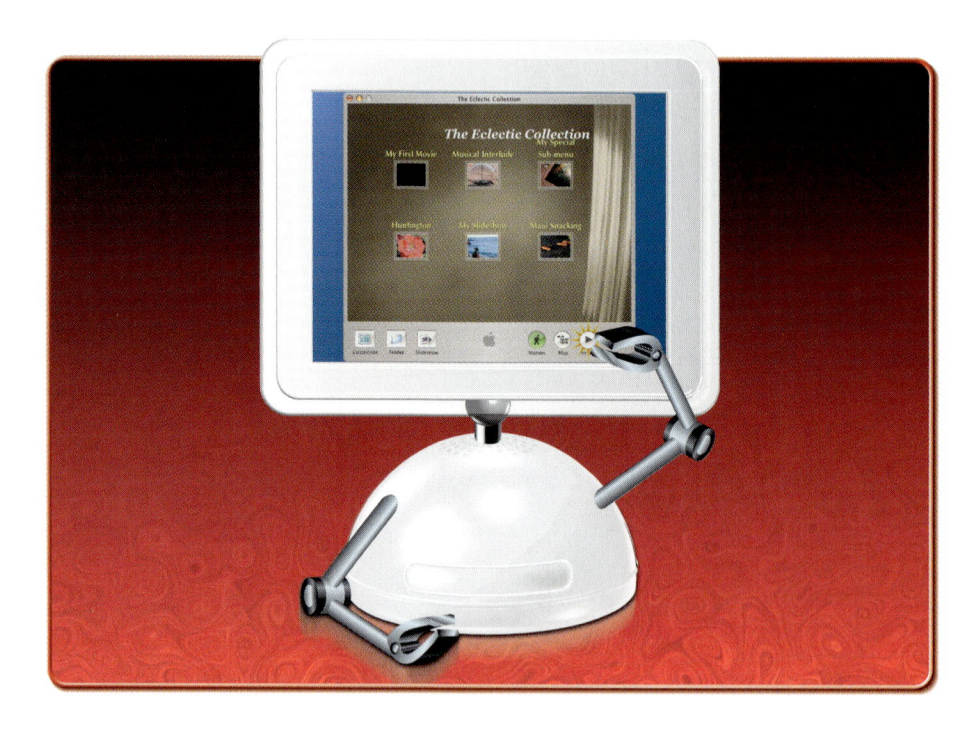

PREVIEW A DVD

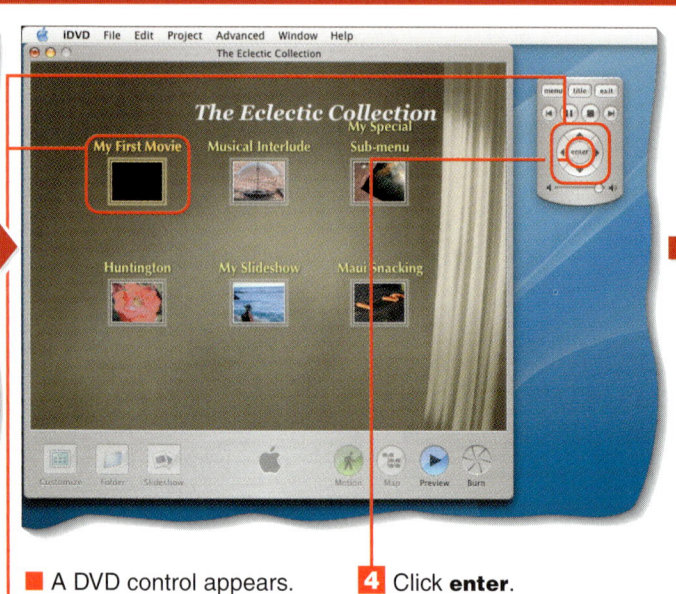

1 Click the **Motion** button.

*Note: iDVD does not preview motion menu buttons unless you enable the **Motion** button.*

2 Click the **Preview** button.

- A DVD control appears.
- iDVD highlights the first menu button.

3 Click the control's arrow buttons to select the menu button for the movie you want to play.

4 Click **enter**.

- The movie begins to play.

294

14 Using Advanced iDVD Features

WORKING WITH IDVD

How can I add transitions between menus?

The Transition popup menu in the Settings pane lets you assign a transition that plays when you click any of the menu buttons on a DVD menu. iDVD 4 provides six transitions: Cube, Dissolve, Droplet, Mosaic, Page Flip, and Wipe. You can control the direction of the Cube, Mosaic, Page Flip, and Wipe transitions. Note that some transitions may appear uneven when you preview a DVD project, but they will appear properly on the finished DVD. Note also that adding transitions takes up some space on the DVD and requires extra encoding time when you burn the disc.

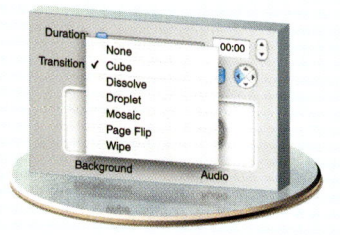

While previewing a movie, I accidentally pressed the control's menu button. How can I pick up where I left off in the movie?

When you click **menu** or **title** on the Preview mode's DVD control, you can get back to the same place in the movie or slideshow you were viewing by clicking **menu** again.

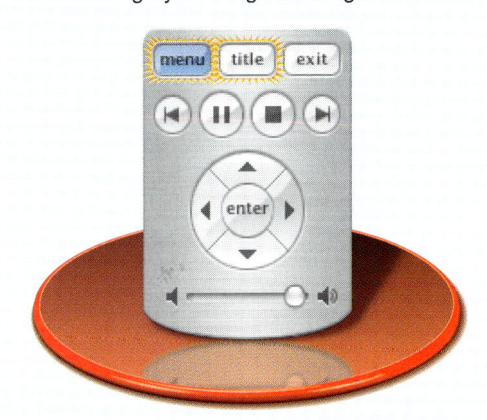

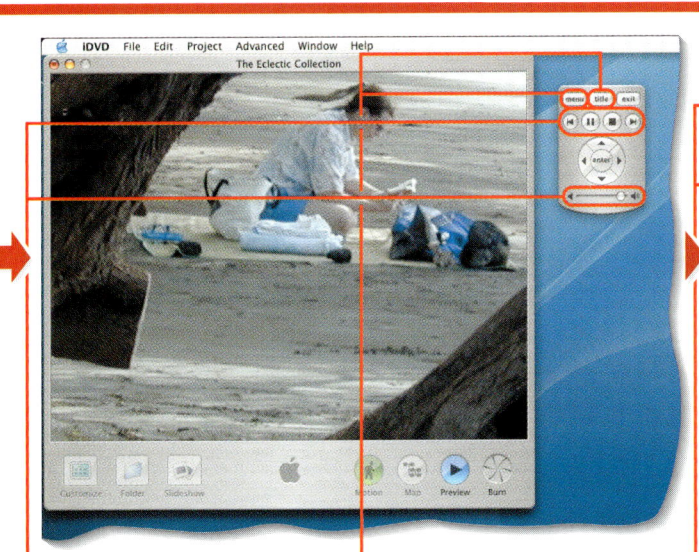

- You can click the pause (▮▮), rewind (◀◀), and fast forward (▶▶) controls to navigate through the movie.

- You can control the movie's volume by clicking the dragging the slider (○).

- You can click **menu** to return to the DVD menu that contains the button for this movie.

- You can click **title** to return to the DVD's top menu.

- When previewing slideshows, you can click the left and right arrow buttons to move between slides.

5 Click **exit**.

- The on-screen DVD control disappears.

- Preview mode ends.

295

ADD DATA FILES TO A DVD

In addition to movies and slideshows, you can include data files on your DVD that others can copy to their computers.

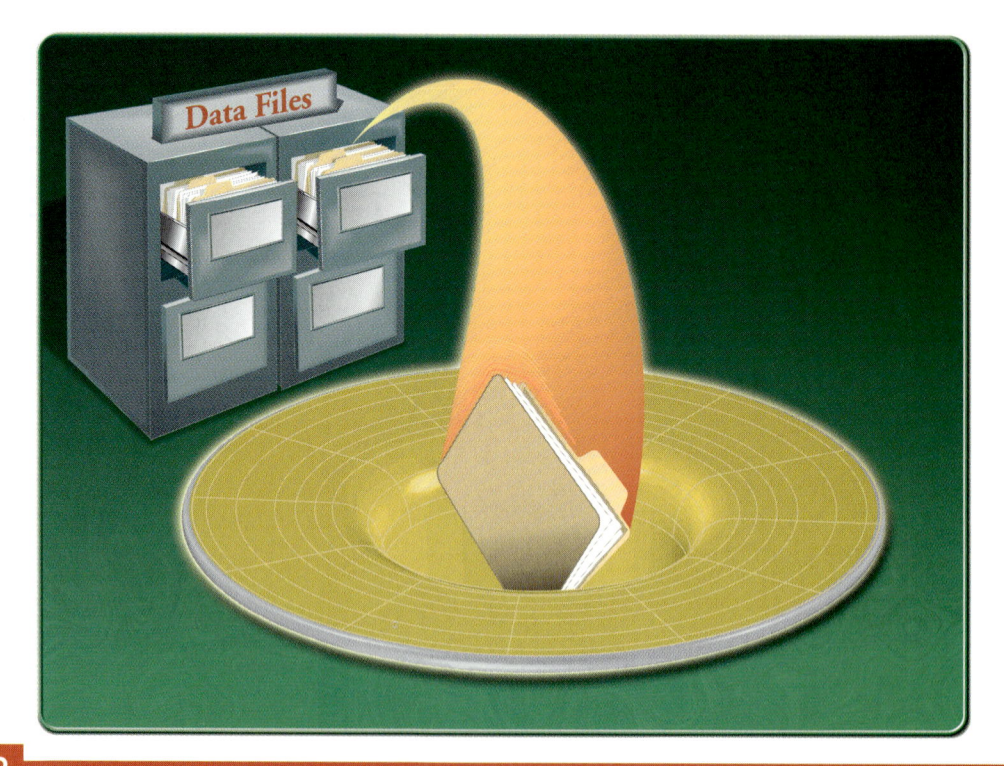

ADD DATA FILES TO A DVD

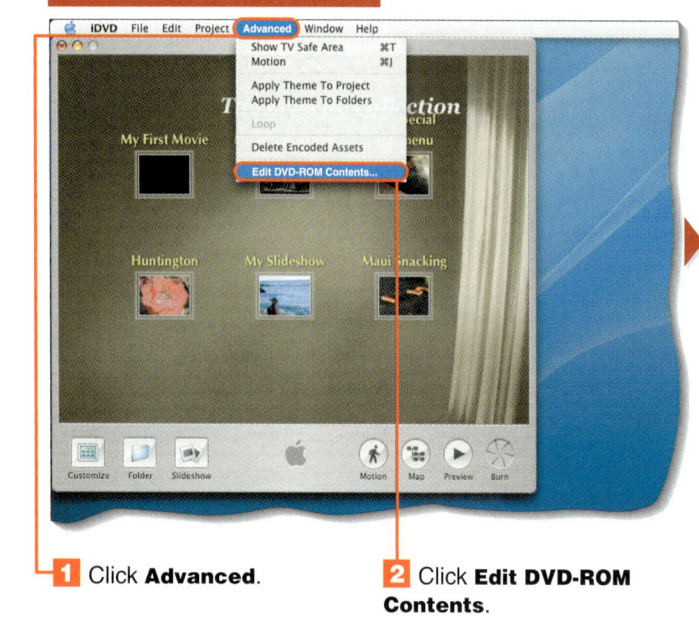

1 Click **Advanced**.

2 Click **Edit DVD-ROM Contents**.

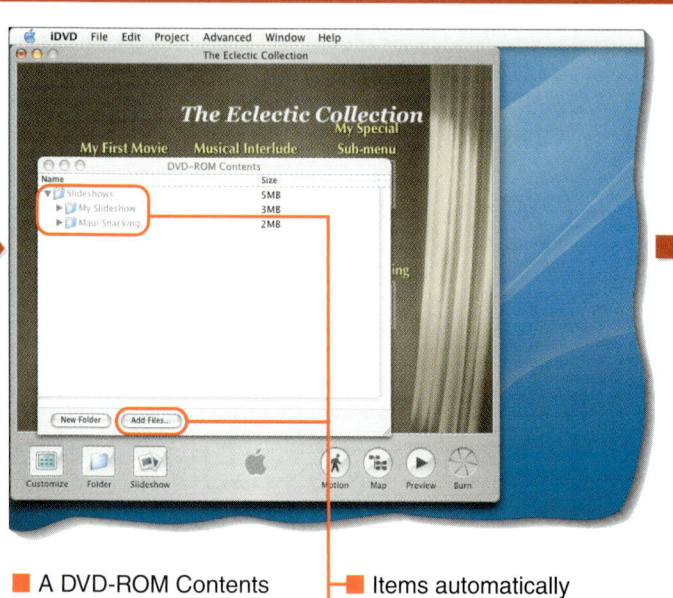

■ A DVD-ROM Contents window appears.

■ Items automatically included by iDVD, such as the original pictures that make up a slideshow, appear in gray.

3 Click **Add Files**.

296

14 Using Advanced iDVD Features

WORKING WITH IDVD

What does the New Folder button on the DVD-ROM Contents window do?

You click **New Folder** to place a new, empty folder on the DVD-ROM. To rename the folder, you can click the folder name and type a new name. You can add files and folders from your hard disk to this new folder, or drag other files and folders already on the DVD-ROM into it. Note that if you have iDVD automatically include the photos in your DVD's slideshows, iDVD does not let you drag the slideshow folders or their contents into a DVD-ROM folder that you create. See Chapter 12 to learn how to set iDVD's preferences to include slideshow photos on your DVD.

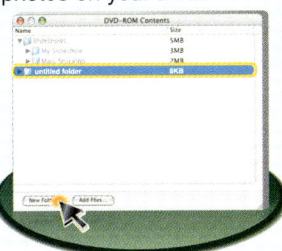

Why do some of the file names in my DVD-ROM contents list appear red?

If you include a file from your hard disk on the DVD-ROM contents list, and then move the file, rename it, or delete it from your hard disk, iDVD displays the file's name in red to indicate that it can no longer find the file.

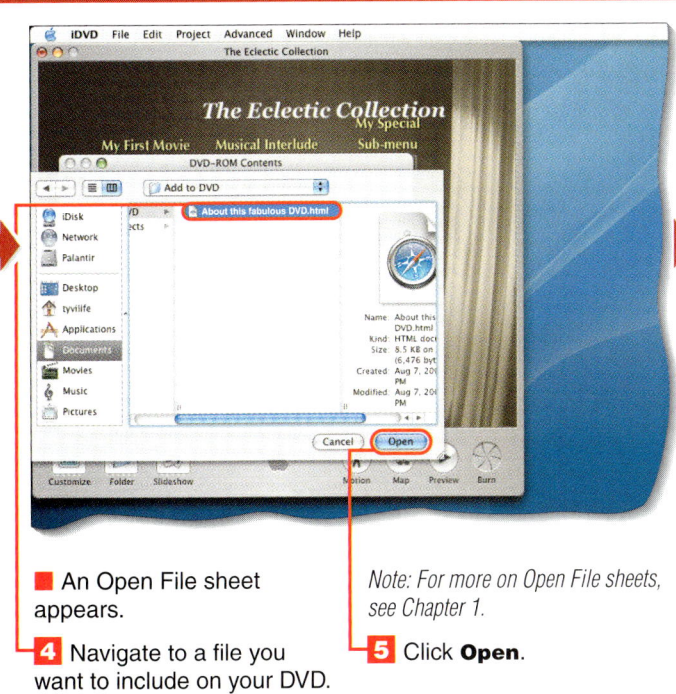

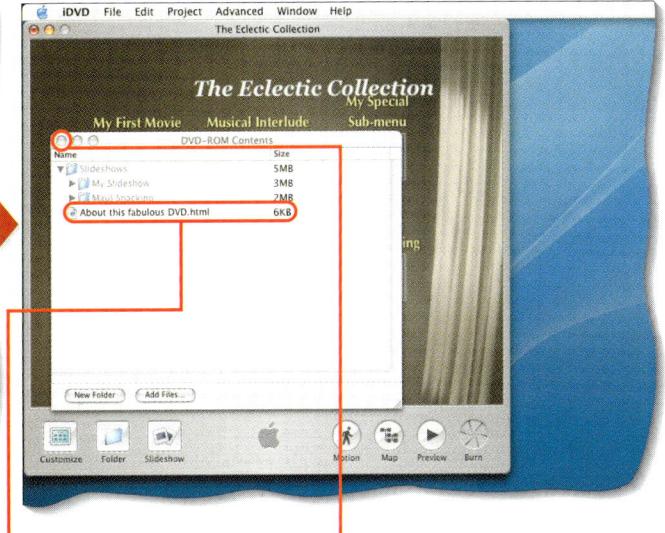

■ An Open File sheet appears.

■ Navigate to a file you want to include on your DVD.

Note: For more on Open File sheets, see Chapter 1.

5 Click **Open**.

■ The file appears in the DVD-ROM Contents window.

■ You can drag files and folders into this window from a Finder window.

Note: See Chapter 1 for more about Finder windows.

■ You can remove a file by clicking it and pressing `Delete`.

6 Click the close button (○) to close the DVD-ROM Contents window.

297

BURN A DVD

When your DVD project is ready, you can burn a DVD that you can then play on a home DVD player or any computer with a DVD drive.

Before you burn your DVD, you should check its status and preview it to make sure it is ready for burning; see the sections "Check an iDVD Project's Status" and "Preview a DVD".

BURN A DVD

1 Click the **Motion** button.

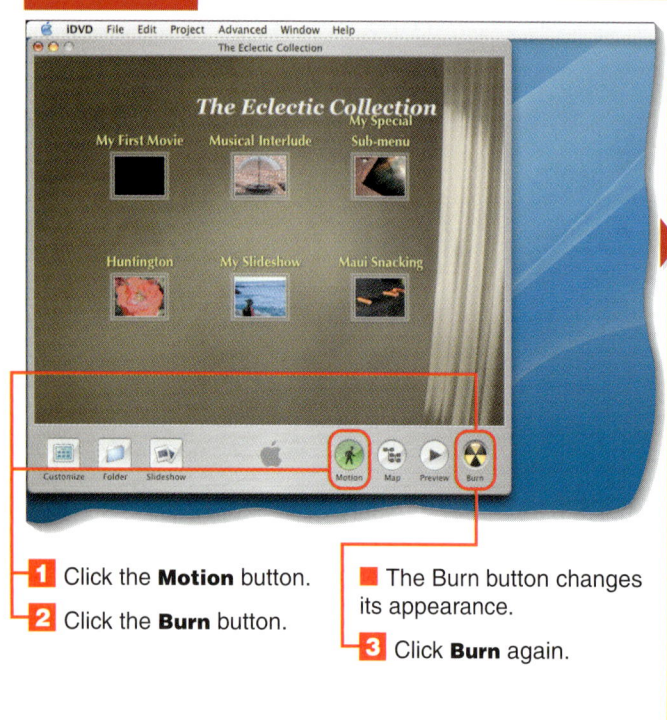

2 Click the **Burn** button.

■ The Burn button changes its appearance.

3 Click **Burn** again.

■ The DVD menu area becomes black and the iDVD icon appears on it.

■ A sheet descends asking you to insert a blank DVD-R.

■ You can click **Cancel** to stop the DVD burn process.

■ If you have a tray-loading SuperDrive, the tray comes out.

4 Place a blank DVD-R in the SuperDrive; close the drive if necessary.

298

14 Using Advanced iDVD Features

WORKING WITH IDVD

Can I burn a disc with the Motion button turned off?

Yes. If you do so, iDVD warns you, but lets you proceed if you want. If you decide to go ahead, motion menus, background video and audio, transitions, and Drop Zone video do not play on the finished disc.

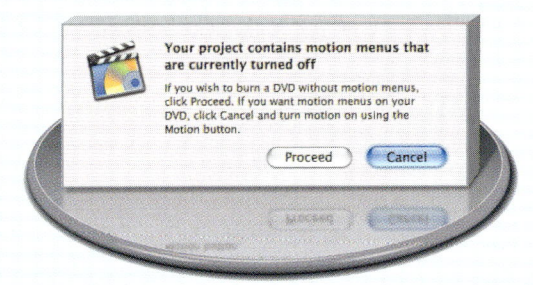

What are the four stages of DVD burning?

When iDVD burns a DVD, it performs four separate but related processes. First, it prepares the disc to receive the information, which takes less than a minute. Second, it renders and encodes motion menus and Drop Zone videos, slideshows, and transitions; this process can take a number of minutes. Third, it encodes the movies and slideshows; if you have background encoding enabled, this process may go quickly, but it can take as much as twice the time it takes to play the movies being encoded. Finally, iDVD burns the DVD, which can take up to an hour, depending on the amount of material you want to place on the DVD.

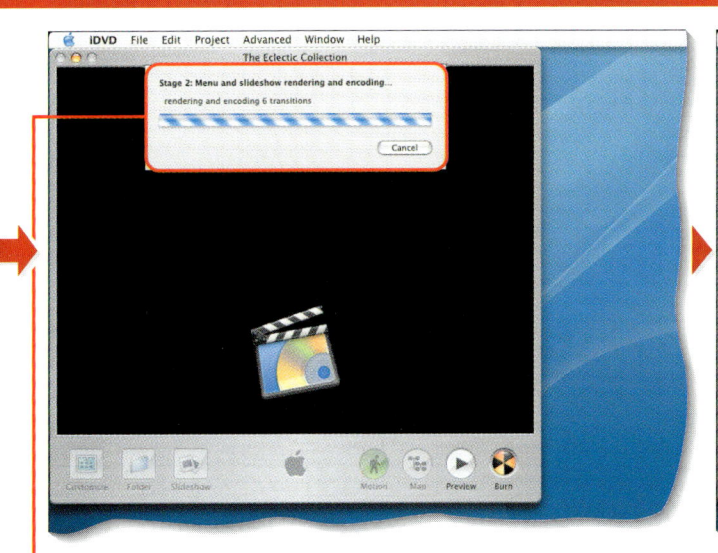

- A progress sheet appears.

- As iDVD proceeds, the sheet displays the stage of the burning process.

Note: Burning a DVD can take several hours, and requires a good deal of computer processing power; Apple recommends you refrain from using other applications that may place heavy demands upon your computer while iDVD burns a disc.

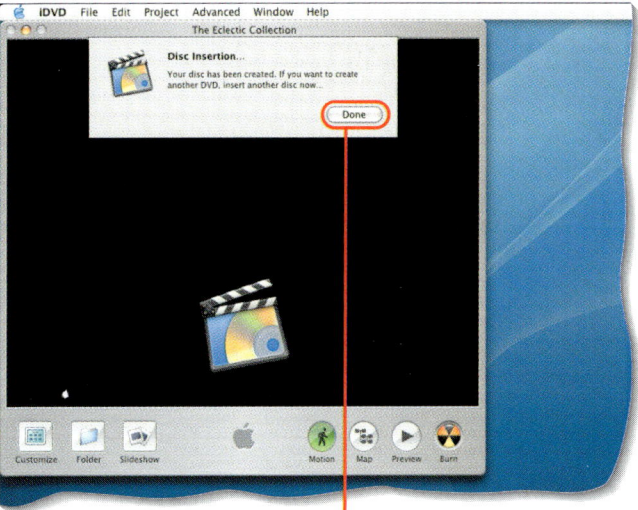

- iDVD ejects the disc when it finishes and tells you to insert another disc if you want to burn another one.

5 Click **Done**.

- The DVD menu appears and the burn button closes.

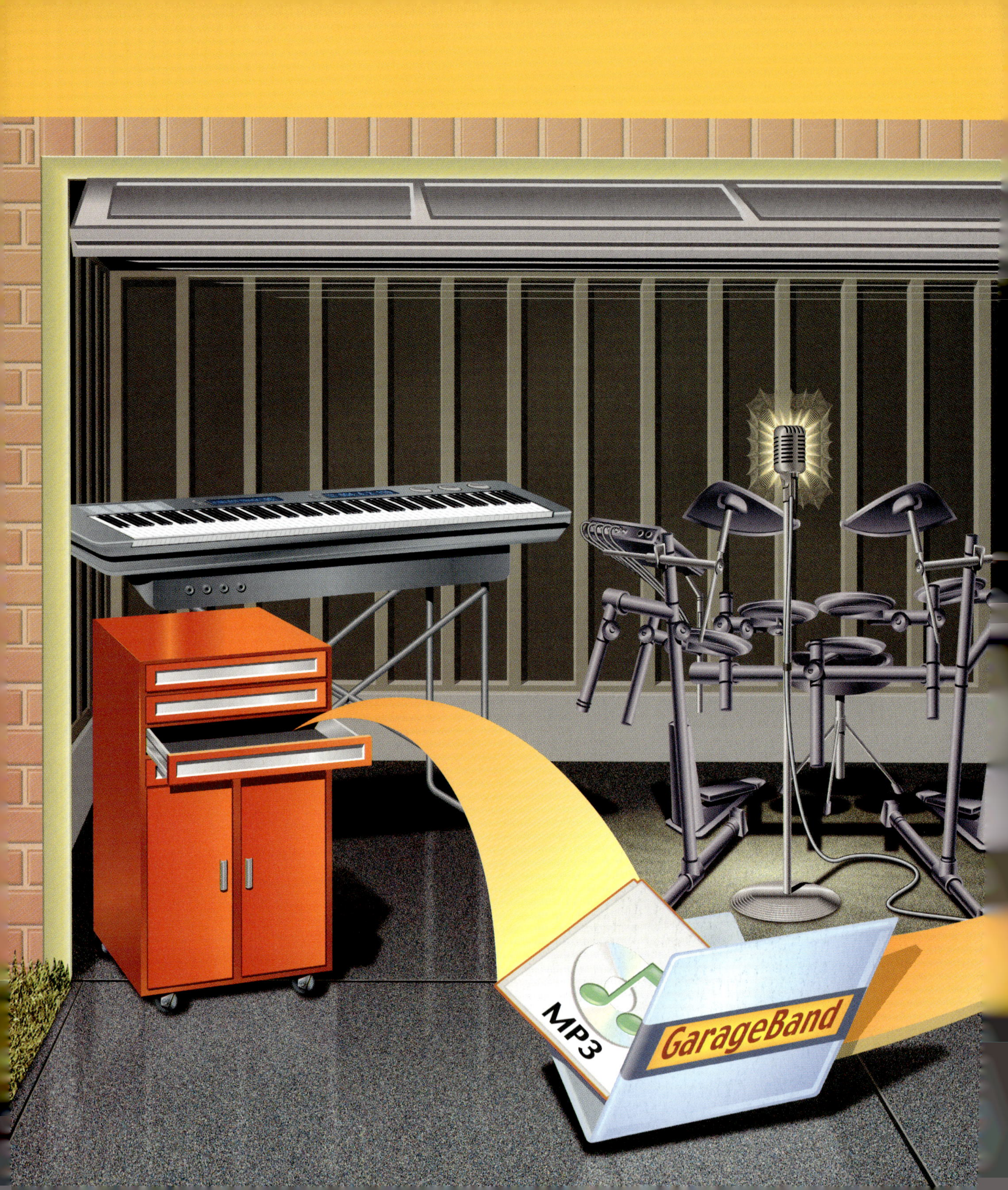
MP3
GarageBand

PART VI

Working with GarageBand

With GarageBand, you do not have to be a musician or even be able to read music to unleash your inner Mozart or McCartney. You can turn your Mac into a powerful and easy-to-use home recording studio, where you can produce and polish your own songs. When you are finished laying down your latest hit, GarageBand lets you add it to your iTunes library so you can use it with all other iLife programs.

15 GarageBand Basics
Pages 302–313

16 Make Music with GarageBand
Pages 314–331

SET UP GARAGEBAND

When you open GarageBand the first time, it is ready for you to create a new song and start making music, but you can adjust some simple settings to tune its performance and behavior to your Mac.

The first time you use GarageBand it creates a GarageBand folder in your Home directory's Music folder.

SET UP GARAGEBAND

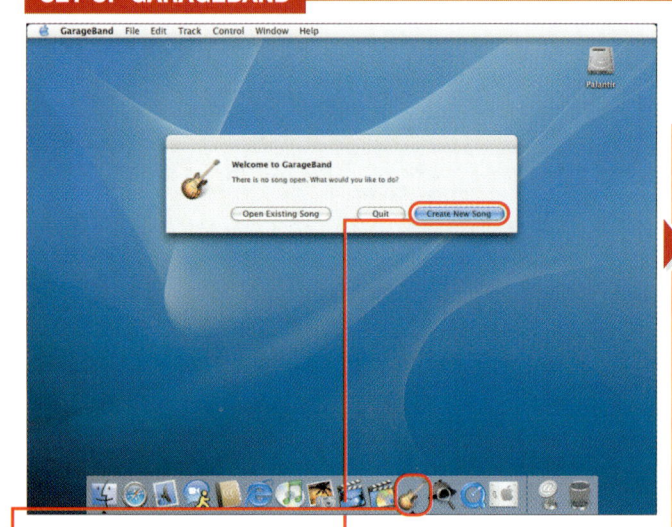

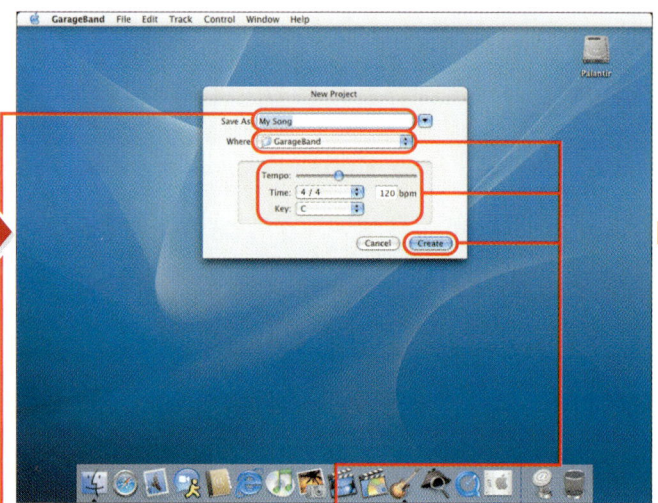

START GARAGEBAND

1 Click the GarageBand icon ( ) in the Dock.

Note: For more on the Dock, see Chapter 1.

- The icon bounces and GarageBand starts up.
- The Welcome to GarageBand dialog appears.

2 Click **Create New Song**.

CREATE A NEW SONG

- The New Project window appears.

3 Type a name for your song.

- You can click here to select a folder in which to save your song.
- You can click and drag or type to modify your song's tempo, time signature, and key.

4 Click **Create**.

15 GarageBand Basics

WORKING WITH GARAGEBAND

What is a time signature?

A song's time signature indicates how many beats of music occur in each *measure* or *bar* of music, and what portion of a whole note each beat represents. For example, 4/4 time, GarageBand's default, has four beats per measure with each beat being a quarter note. You can see the measure and beat markings on GarageBand's beat ruler.

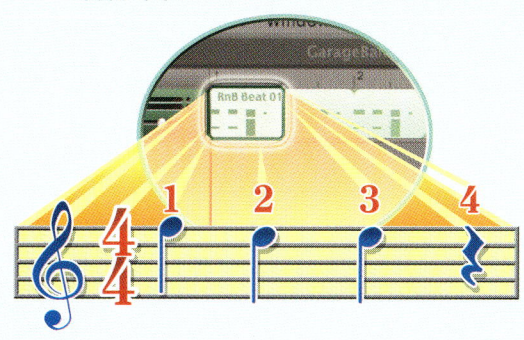

What is a tempo?

A song's tempo indicates how many beats there are per minute (*bpm*). GarageBand's default is 120 bpm, or two beats per second.

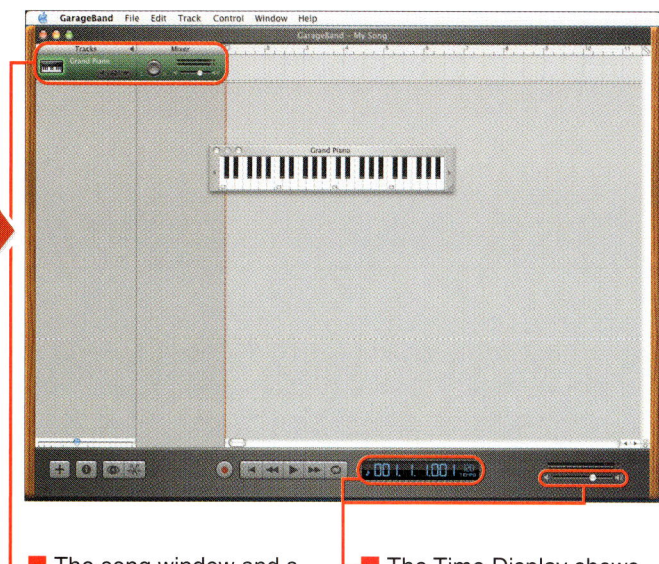

- The song window and a floating music keyboard window open.

- GarageBand automatically adds an instrument track to the song's timeline.

- The Time Display shows the song's tempo and the current playhead position in measures, beats, and ticks.

- You can drag the Master Volume control ( ) to adjust the song's overall volume.

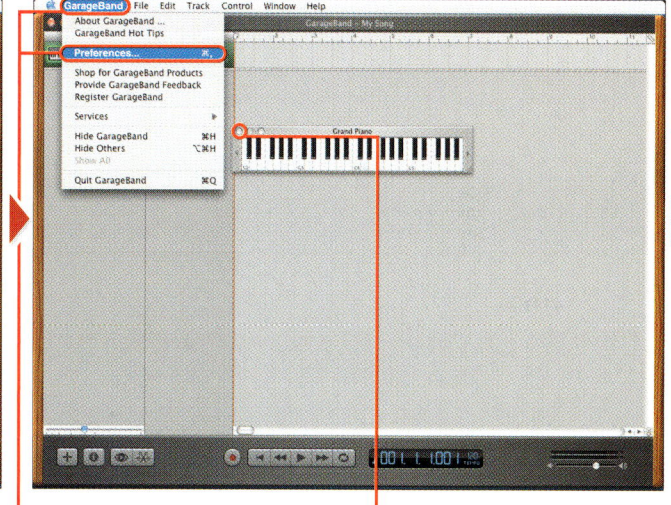

SET PREFERENCES

5 Click **GarageBand**.

6 Click **Preferences**.

- You can click the floating keyboard's close button ( ) to hide it.

CONTINUED

303

SET UP GARAGEBAND

You can set the number of instruments and tracks a song can have to suit your Mac's capabilities. You can also determine how GarageBand labels your songs when you export them to iTunes.

GarageBand's preferences take effect the moment you make any changes.

Testing...1, 2, 3...Testing

SET UP GARAGEBAND (CONTINUED)

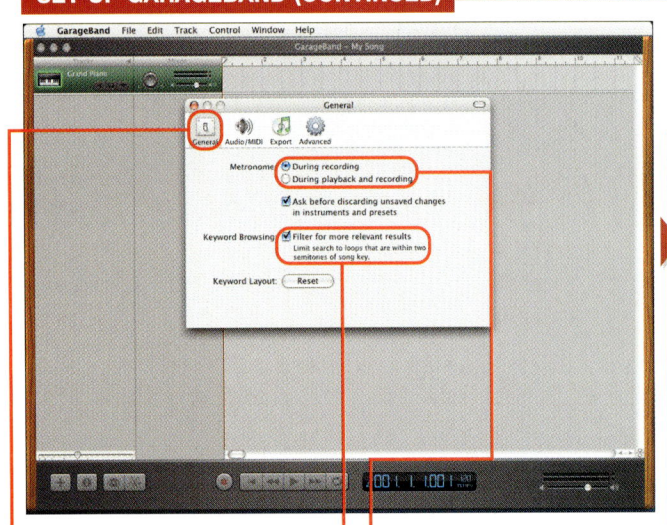

GENERAL PREFERENCES

- The GarageBand Preferences window appears.

7 Click the **General** icon.

- The General preferences appear.

- You can click here to select metronome settings.

- You can click this option (☐ changes to ☑) to browse for appropriate musical samples for your song.

AUDIO/MIDI PREFERENCES

8 Click the **Audio/MIDI** icon to view more preferences.

- You can click here and select which connected audio devices to use to record and play back sound.

- You can click this option (◯ changes to ◉) to improve GarageBand's performance on slower Macs.

- GarageBand displays any detected MIDI instruments here.

304

15 GarageBand Basics

WORKING WITH GARAGEBAND

What is MIDI?

MIDI stands for *Musical Instrument Digital Interface,* and it is the standard way that electronic musical instruments exchange information. MIDI instruments generate note, volume, and other information in a simple numeric form that a musical synthesizer, like your Mac running GarageBand, can use to create sounds.

How can I save a song

Click **File**, and then **Save**. GarageBand normally saves songs in the GarageBand folder in your Home directory's Music folder. You should save your song periodically as you work to avoid losing changes if something goes wrong.

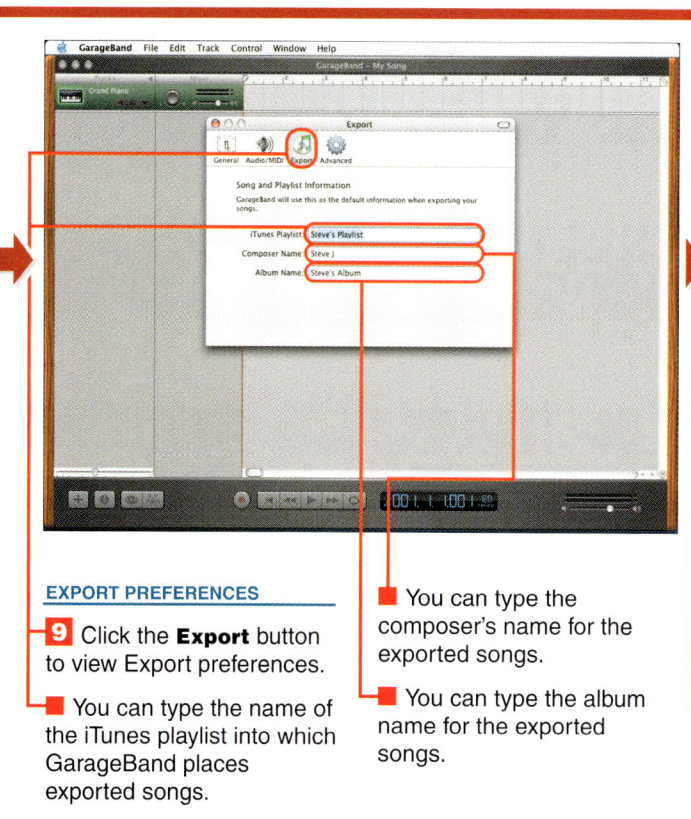

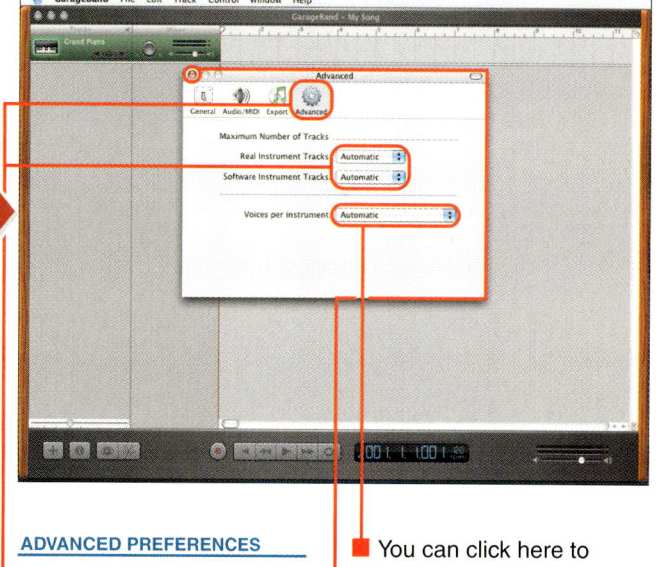

EXPORT PREFERENCES

■ 9 Click the **Export** button to view Export preferences.

■ You can type the name of the iTunes playlist into which GarageBand places exported songs.

■ You can type the composer's name for the exported songs.

■ You can type the album name for the exported songs.

ADVANCED PREFERENCES

■ 10 Click **Advanced** to view Advanced preferences.

■ You can click here to select how many instrument tracks songs can contain.

■ You can click here to select how many notes each instrument can play at once.

Note: To improve performance on slower Macs, select fewer instruments and voices.

■ 11 Click ⊙.

305

CREATE A SOFTWARE INSTRUMENT TRACK

You can create a software instrument track to contain music that comes with GarageBand or that you play yourself on a MIDI instrument connected to your Mac.

Each software instrument track plays the notes you place into it. Using GarageBand's music synthesizers, you can make your music sound as though any one of dozens of available musical instruments is playing it. Most songs you create will contain several tracks.

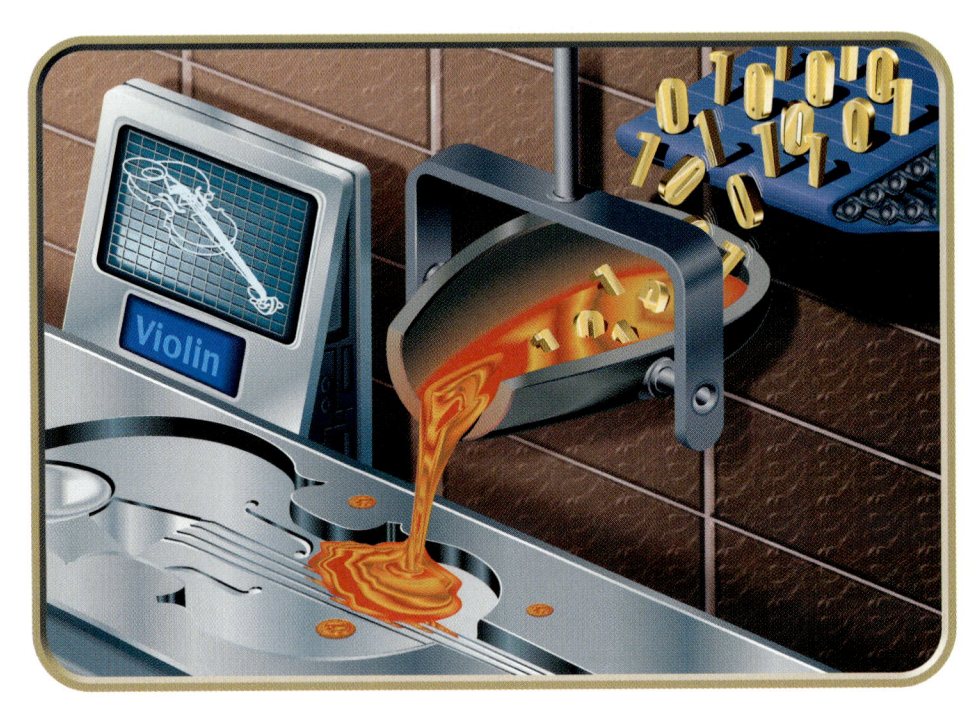

CREATE A SOFTWARE INSTRUMENT TRACK

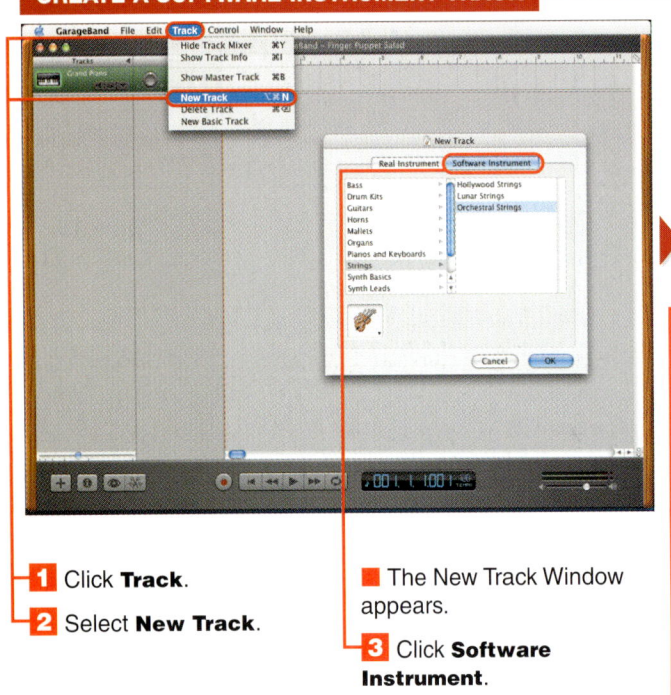

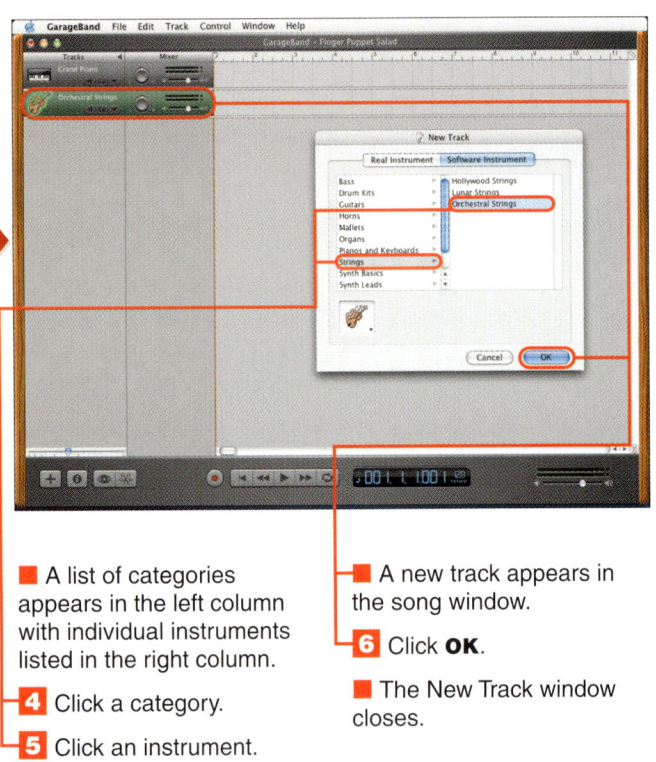

1 Click **Track**.

2 Select **New Track**.

■ The New Track Window appears.

3 Click **Software Instrument**.

■ A list of categories appears in the left column with individual instruments listed in the right column.

4 Click a category.

5 Click an instrument.

■ A new track appears in the song window.

6 Click **OK**.

■ The New Track window closes.

CREATE A REAL INSTRUMENT TRACK

15 GarageBand Basics

WORKING WITH GARAGEBAND

You can create a real instrument track to contain both music that comes with GarageBand or music that you record yourself, such as the notes you play on a flute into a microphone that you have attached to your Mac, or as notes you play on an electric guitar that is directly connected to your Mac.

Each real instrument has its own preset music filters that alter the recording to make it sound like various instruments.

CREATE A REAL INSTRUMENT TRACK

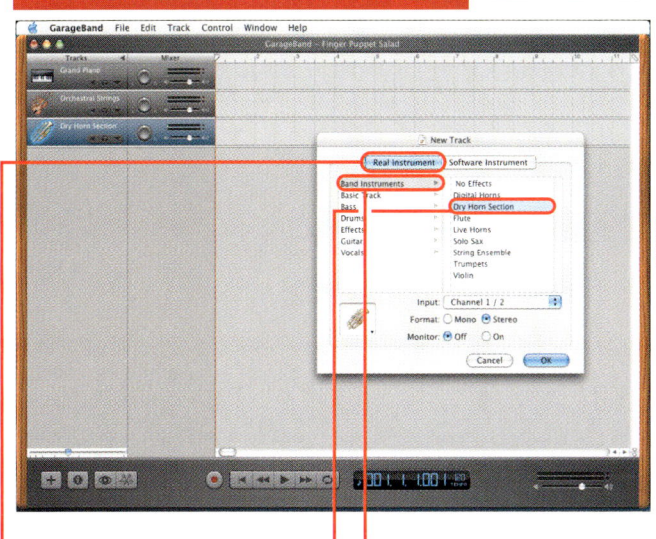

1 Open the New Track Window.

Note: For more information, see the section "Create a Software Instrument Track."

2 Click **Real Instrument**.

3 Click an instrument category in the left column.

4 Click an individual instrument in the right column.

■ A real instrument track appears.

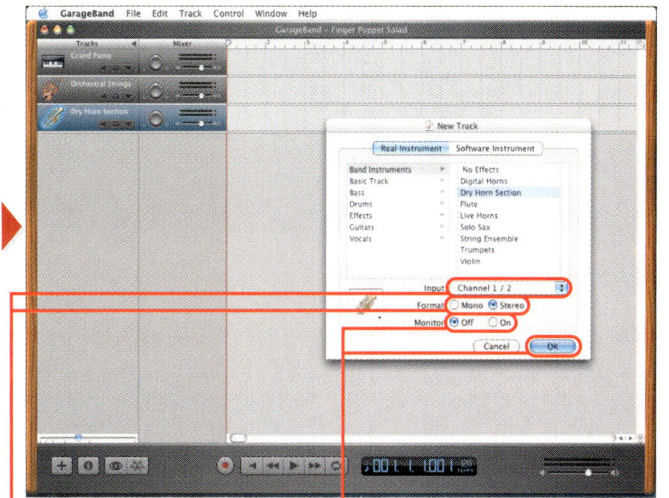

■ You can click here and select which audio input channels to record.

■ You can click an option (○ changes to ●) to make the recording mono or stereo.

Note: Changing the format may change the Input menu setting.

■ You can click an option (○ changes to ●) to select whether you can hear a recording in progress.

5 Click **OK**.

■ The New Track window closes.

307

BROWSE LOOPS

Most songs contain *loops* — sequences of notes that are repeated — that accompany their melodies. GarageBand comes with over a thousand royalty-free loops that you can use in your songs. You can use GarageBand's loop browser to quickly find and preview its collection of loops.

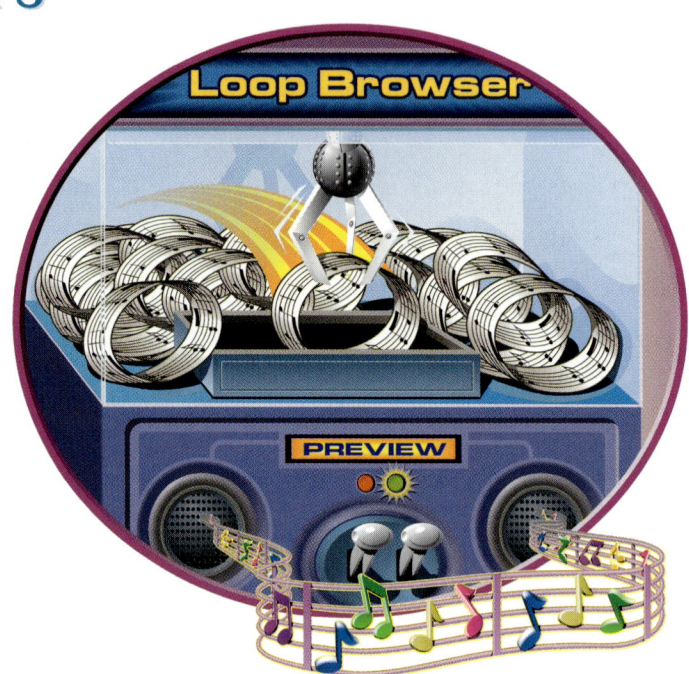

BROWSE LOOPS

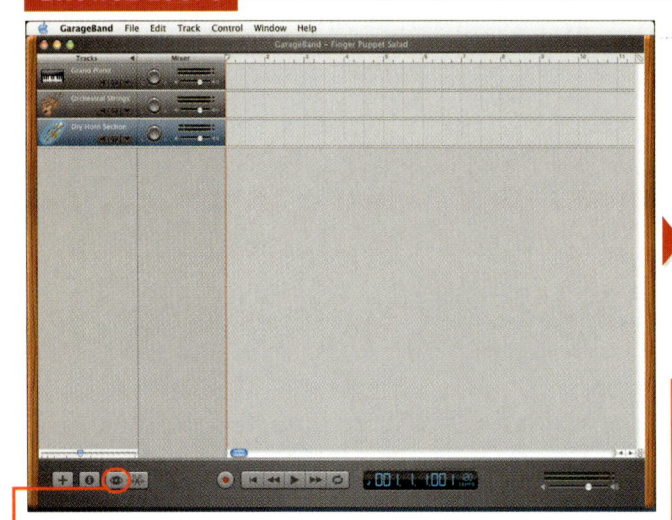

1 Click the Loop Browser button (👁).

■ The GarageBand loop browser slides up from the bottom of the song window.

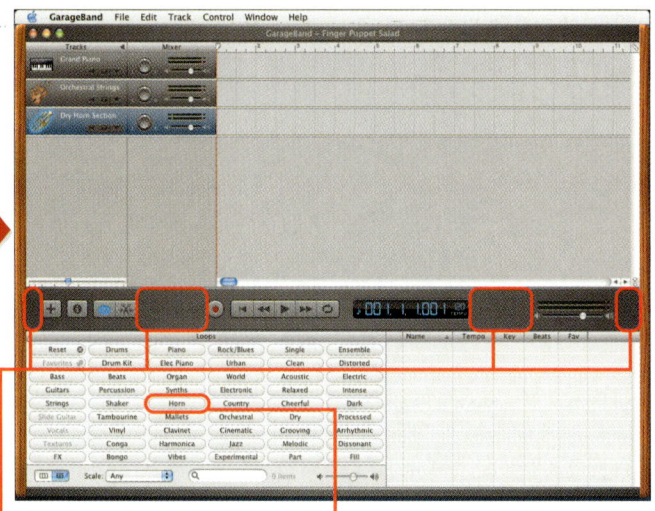

■ You can click and drag up anywhere in the gray area to show more loop buttons or drag down in the gray area to hide buttons.

■ Each button represents a collection of loops for a particular set of instruments, a mood, or a musical genre.

2 Click a loop button.

15 GarageBand Basics

WORKING WITH GARAGEBAND

How can I deselect a button in the loop browser?

Just click the button a second time to deselect it. You can also click the Reset button (Reset) in the browser's upper-left corner to deselect all the buttons at once.

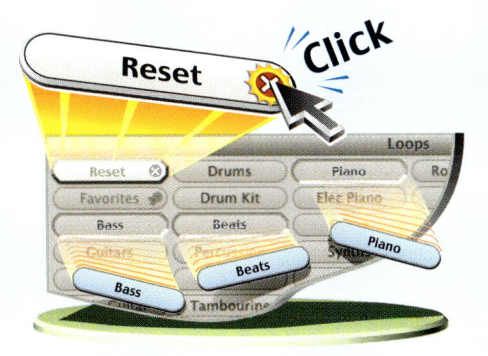

How can I arrange the loop browser's buttons so the ones I use most are together?

Click a button you want to move and drag it over another button. When you let go of the mouse, the buttons exchange positions. You can use Keyword Layout Reset button in GarageBand's General preferences to set all the buttons back to their original positions. See the section "Set Up GarageBand" for more about setting preferences.

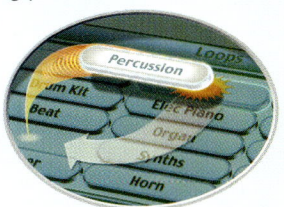

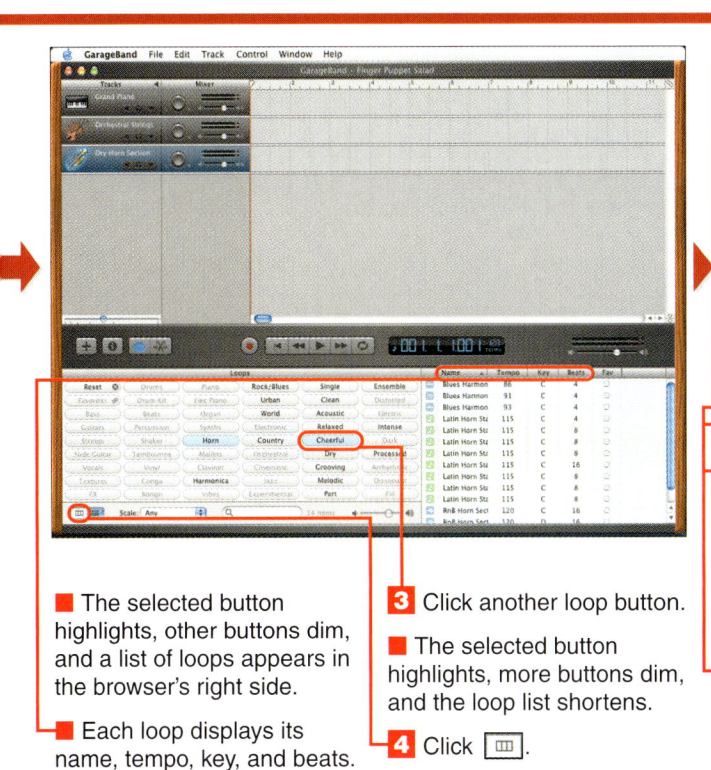

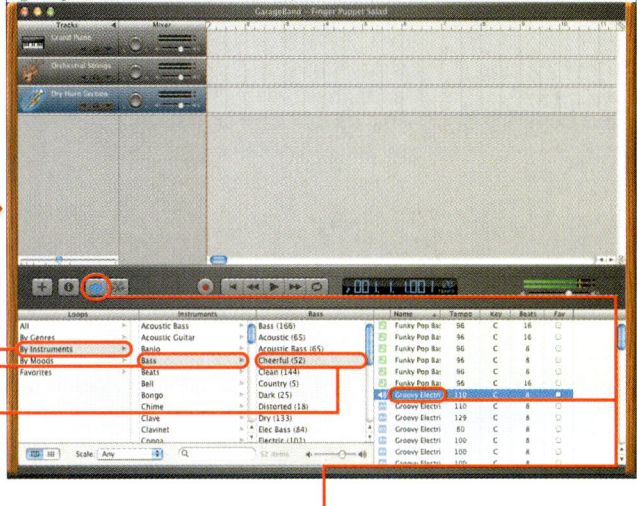

- The selected button highlights, other buttons dim, and a list of loops appears in the browser's right side.

- Each loop displays its name, tempo, key, and beats.

3 Click another loop button.

- The selected button highlights, more buttons dim, and the loop list shortens.

4 Click [icon].

- The loop browser displays a column view.

5 Click an item from each column.

- The browser displays loops that match the selected items.

- Green loops are software loops, and blue ones are real instrument loops.

- You can click a loop to hear a preview in your song's key and tempo.

6 Click [icon].

- The browser closes.

309

ADD A LOOP

You can add loops from GarageBand's collection to your song's tracks and place them anywhere you want in your song. You can also build a song entirely out of loops.

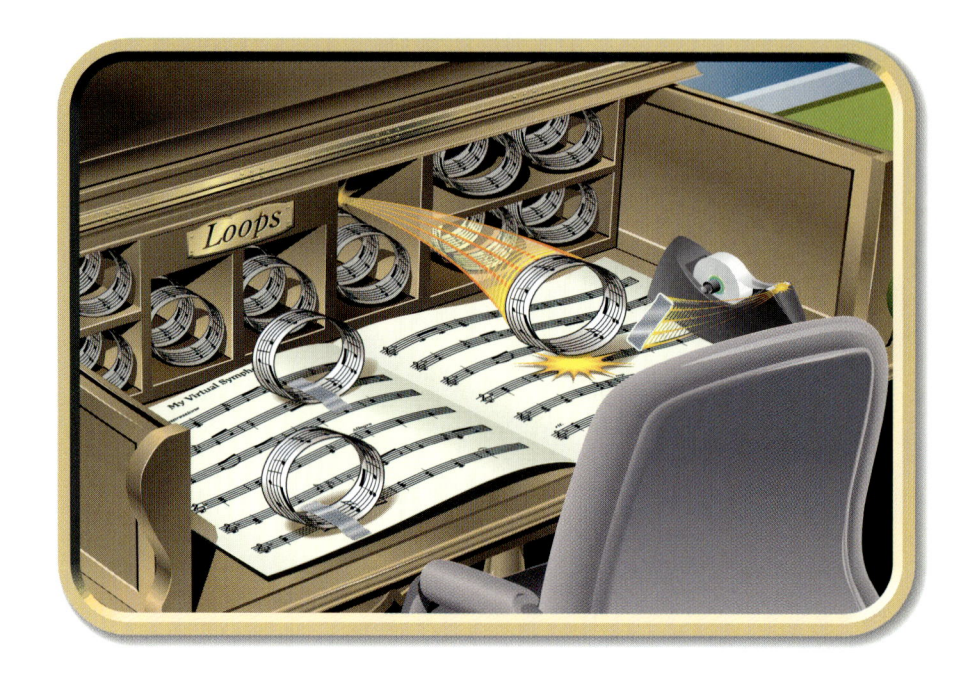

ADD A LOOP

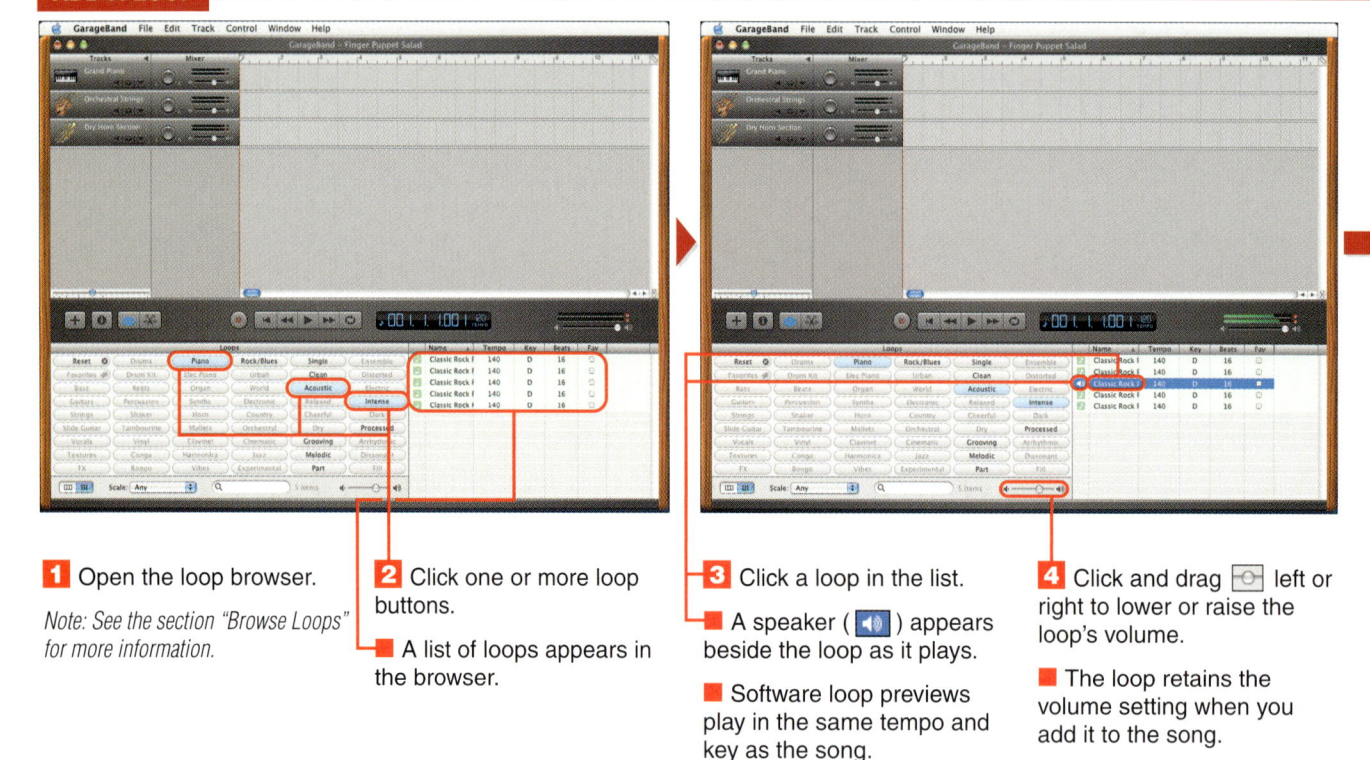

1 Open the loop browser.

Note: See the section "Browse Loops" for more information.

2 Click one or more loop buttons.

■ A list of loops appears in the browser.

3 Click a loop in the list.

■ A speaker ( ) appears beside the loop as it plays.

■ Software loop previews play in the same tempo and key as the song.

4 Click and drag left or right to lower or raise the loop's volume.

■ The loop retains the volume setting when you add it to the song.

310

15 GarageBand Basics

WORKING WITH GARAGEBAND

What happens if I drag a loop over another loop?

The loop on top replaces the portion of the loop beneath it, which becomes shorter. If the top loop completely covers the bottom loop, GarageBand deletes the bottom loop. You can click **Edit**, and then **Undo change position of region** to restore the two loops to their original positions if you make a mistake dragging.

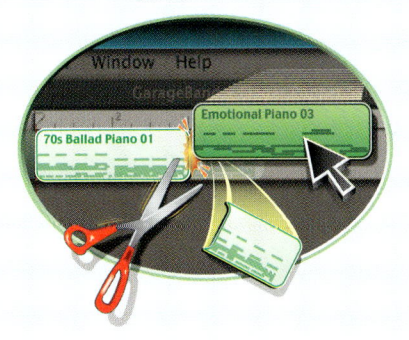

How can I quickly create a new track?

Click and drag a loop from the browser and drop it on the gray area beneath the tracks. GarageBand creates a new track to contain the loop. The new track's instrument settings and type match the instrument settings and type of the loop.

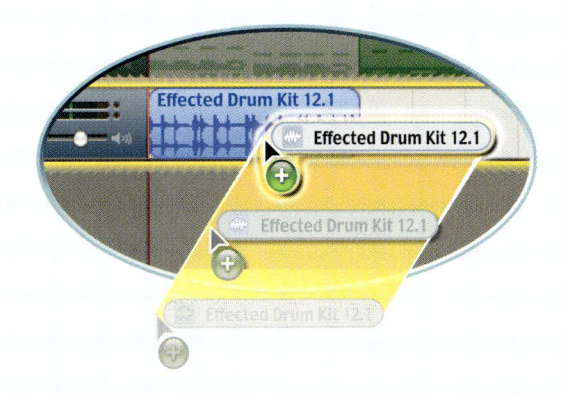

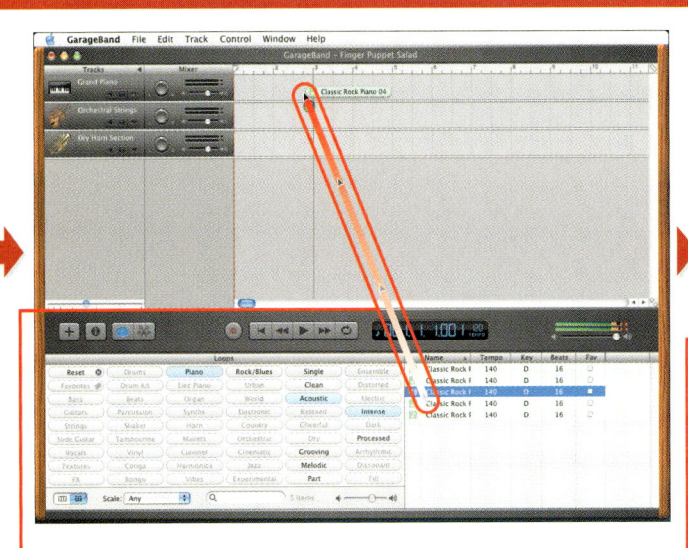

5 Click and drag a loop over one of the tracks in the timeline.

6 Release the mouse.

- A software loop ( ) that you add to a real instrument track converts to a real audio loop ( ).

Note: You cannot drag a real instrument loop ( ) to a software instrument track.

- The loop appears in the track.

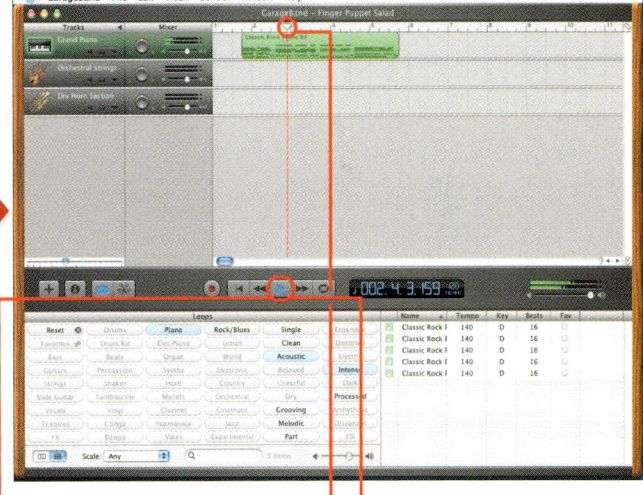

7 Click the Play button ( ) or press Spacebar.

- The playhead moves and the song plays.

Note: The loops you add to tracks take on the instrument settings assigned to the track.

8 Click or press Spacebar.

- The music stops.
- You can drag the playhead to reposition it.

311

EDIT A SOFTWARE LOOP

You can split loops, join them, and extend them so they repeat. An extended loop can form the background of your song, and the ability to combine and split loops lets you tailor your loops to fit your song's musical needs.

This section requires a software instrument track that contains a loop. See the sections "Browse Loops" and "Add a Loop" for more information.

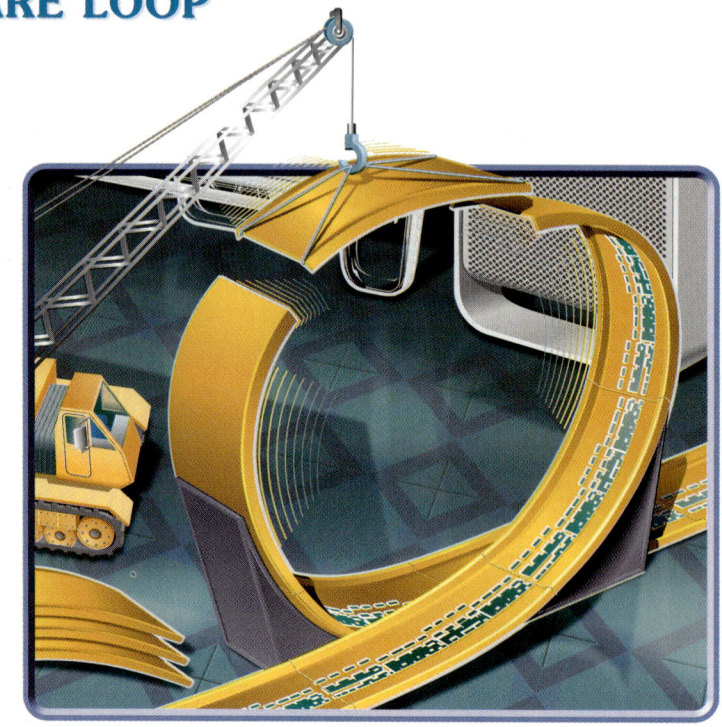

EDIT A SOFTWARE LOOP

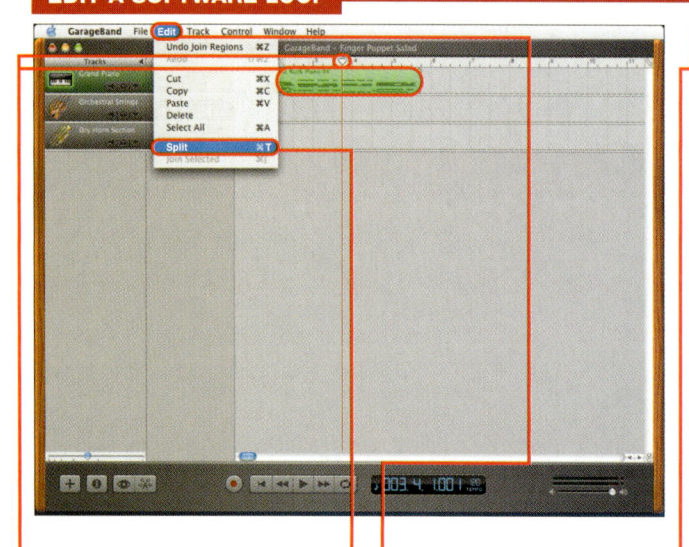

SPLIT A LOOP

1. Click to select a loop.
2. Click the beat ruler above the loop to position the playhead (▽).
3. Click **Edit**.
4. Click **Split**.

■ The loop splits at the ▽ position.

EXTEND AND REPEAT A LOOP

1. Place the cursor at the upper-right corner of a loop (the cursor changes to |↻).
2. Click and drag |↻ to the right.

■ As you drag, the loop becomes longer and notches appear, marking where the loop repeats.

3. Release the mouse.

■ The loop extends.

312

15 GarageBand Basics

WORKING WITH GARAGEBAND

How can I add silence to a software loop?

Position your cursor near the bottom-right side of a software loop (the cursor changes to ▶). Click and drag to the right and release the mouse. GarageBand extends the loop with silence. Note that you cannot extend a real instrument loop in this manner.

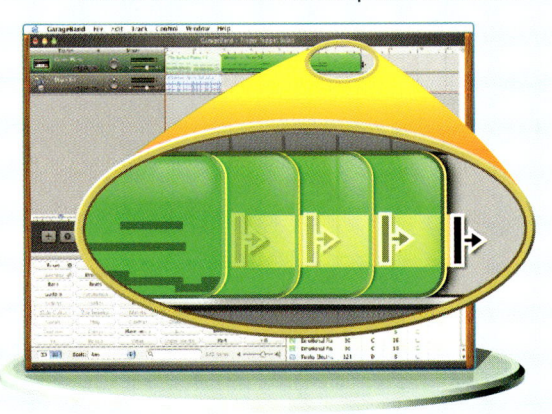

How can I duplicate a loop?

Select a loop and click **Edit**, and then **Copy**. Then position the playhead (▽) where you want the duplicate. Next, click **Edit**, and then **Paste**. You can also create a copy of a loop by holding down `option` as you drag the loop left or right.

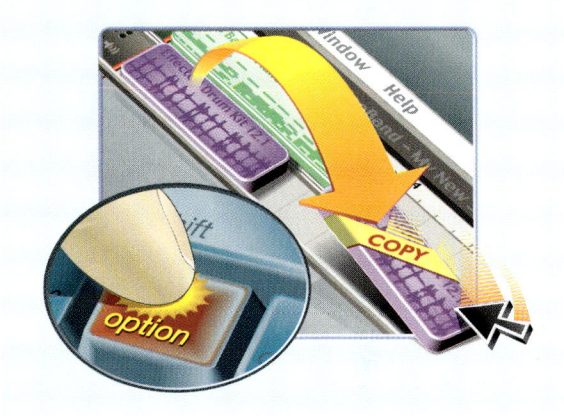

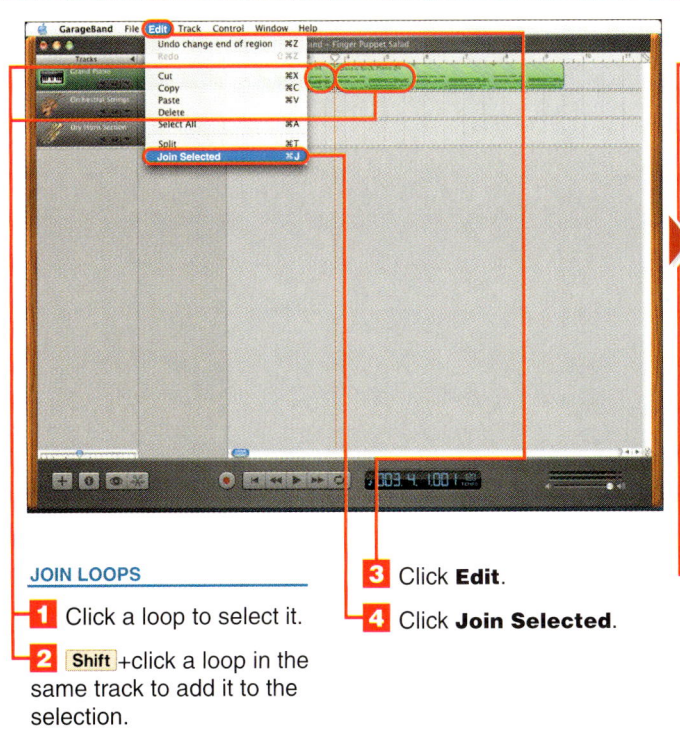

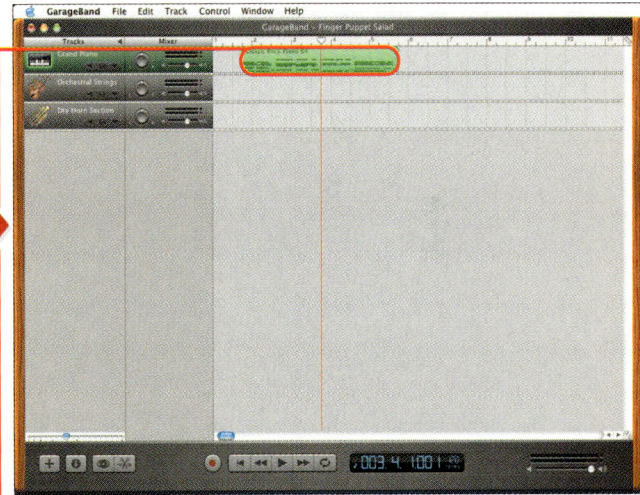

JOIN LOOPS

1. Click a loop to select it.
2. `Shift`+click a loop in the same track to add it to the selection.
3. Click **Edit**.
4. Click **Join Selected**.

- The two loops join.
- If you previously extended the rightmost loop, the joined loop only contains the first part of that loop and GarageBand deletes the repetitions.
- If the two selected loops are not adjacent, GarageBand places silence in the intervening space of the joined loop.

313

USING THE ON-SCREEN KEYBOARD

GarageBand provides an on-screen musical keyboard that you can use to try out simple melodies and to sample the sound settings of GarageBand's software instruments.

USING THE ON-SCREEN KEYBOARD

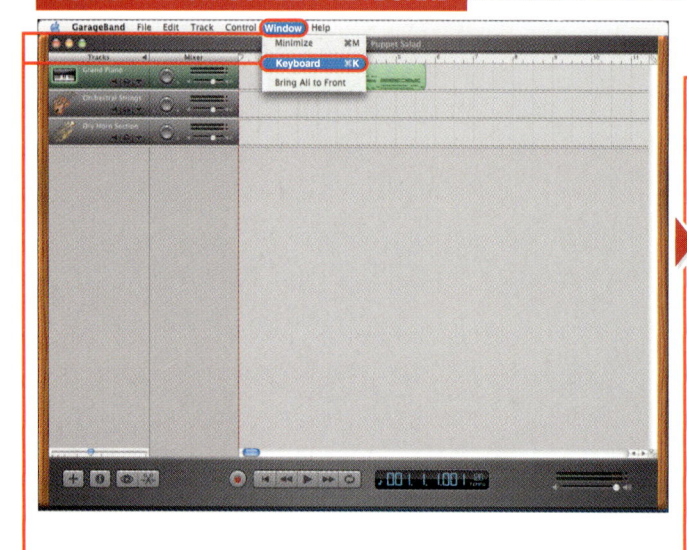

DISPLAY THE KEYBOARD

1 Click **Window**.

2 Click **Keyboard**.

■ You can also press ⌘+K to display the music keyboard.

■ The on-screen music keyboard appears.

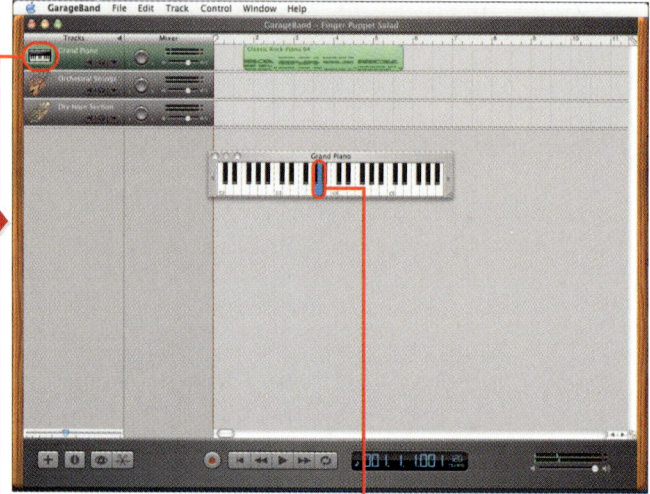

PLAY THE KEYBOARD

3 Click a software instrument track heading.

Note: For more on creating a software instrument track, see Chapter 15.

4 Click a key on the music keyboard.

■ A note plays using the selected software track's instrument settings.

■ The longer you hold down the mouse, the longer the note plays.

314

16 Make Music with GarageBand

WORKING WITH GARAGEBAND

How big can I make the keyboard?

When you click the keyboard window's grow button (🔘), the keyboard expands to display ten and a half octaves, or 128 keys. By comparison, a normal piano offers seven and a half octaves, or 88 keys.

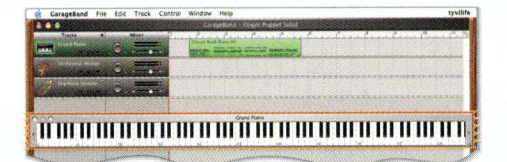

How can I play chords with the on-screen keyboard?

Unfortunately, you cannot do that with the GarageBand on-screen keyboard. There are, however, some shareware and freeware programs that provide on-screen keyboards compatible with GarageBand, and these programs let you use your Mac's keyboard as a musical keyboard. One such free program is Midi Keys, available from www.manyetas.com/creed/midikeys.html.

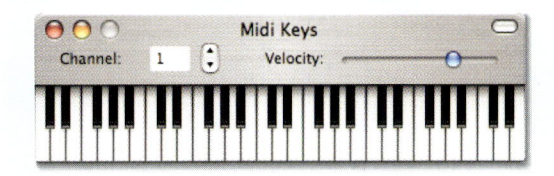

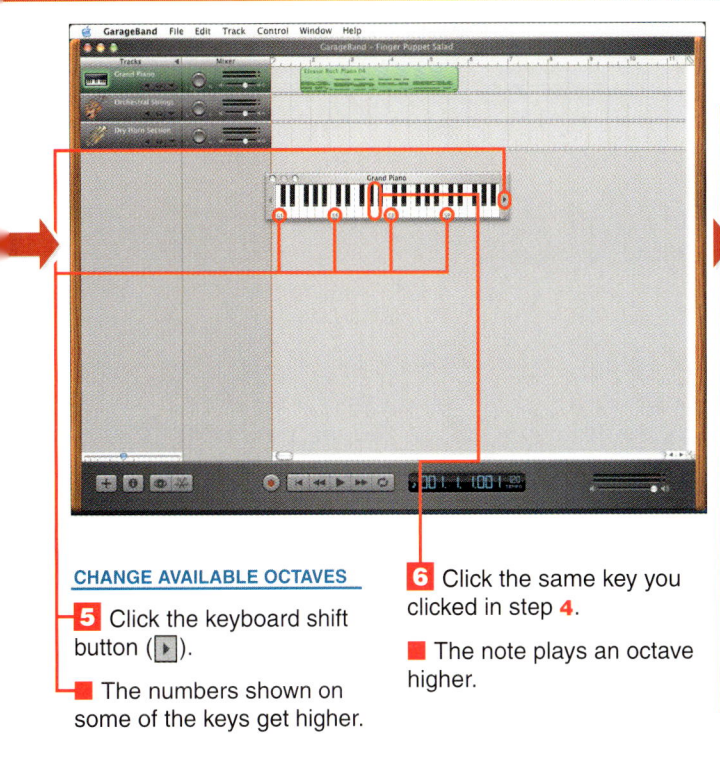

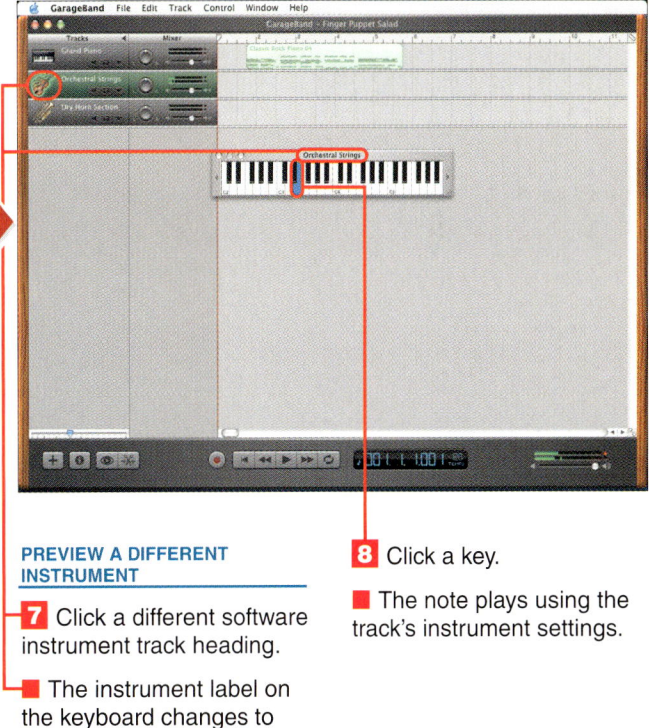

CHANGE AVAILABLE OCTAVES

5 Click the keyboard shift button (▶).

■ The numbers shown on some of the keys get higher.

6 Click the same key you clicked in step **4**.

■ The note plays an octave higher.

PREVIEW A DIFFERENT INSTRUMENT

7 Click a different software instrument track heading.

■ The instrument label on the keyboard changes to match the track's name.

8 Click a key.

■ The note plays using the track's instrument settings.

315

RECORD A SOFTWARE LOOP

You can record your own music into a software track using the on-screen keyboard. You can also set a cycle region to record notes repeatedly over the same number of beats to build up complex chords or effects.

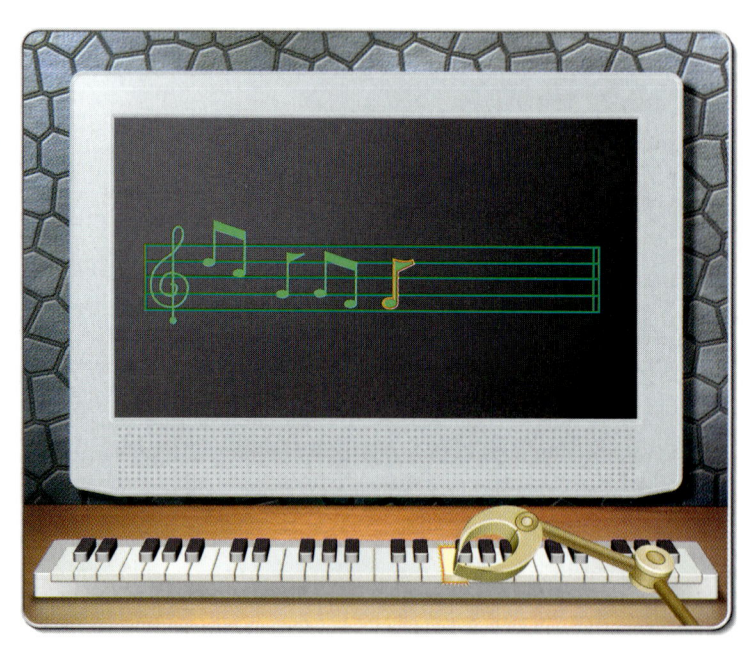

This section uses the on-screen keyboard to record a software instrument. If you have a MIDI device attached to your Mac, you can use that instead and ignore the first step of this section.

RECORD A SOFTWARE LOOP

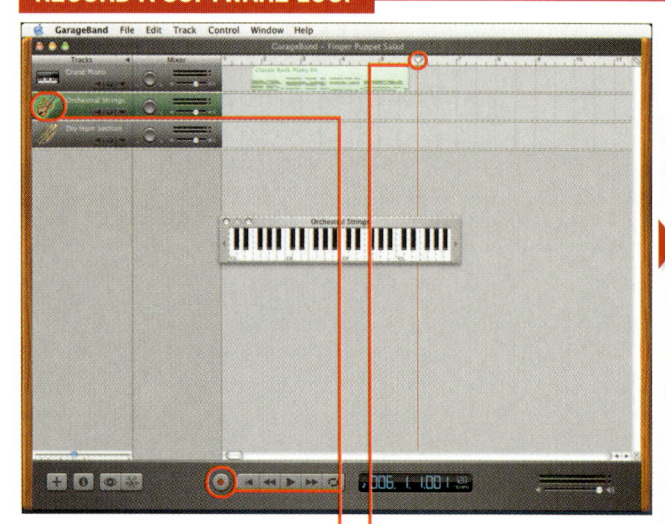

BASIC RECORDING

1 Display the on-screen musical keyboard.

Note: See the section "Using the On-Screen Keyboard" for more information.

2 Click the beat ruler to place the playhead (▽) where you want to start recording.

3 Click the heading of the track on which you want to record.

4 Click the Record button (⬤ changes to ⬤).

■ The ▽ moves and GarageBand begins recording.

5 Click the keys on the on-screen keyboard.

■ The notes appear in the track.

6 Press Spacebar (⬤ changes to ⬤).

■ The ▽ stops and the recording ends.

Note: GarageBand eliminates blank space at the end of a software recording.

316

16 Make Music with GarageBand

WORKING WITH GARAGEBAND

TEACH YOURSELF

How can I stay on the beat as I record?

Click **Control**, and then click **Metronome**. As you record you hear a metronome tick in time to the song's tempo.

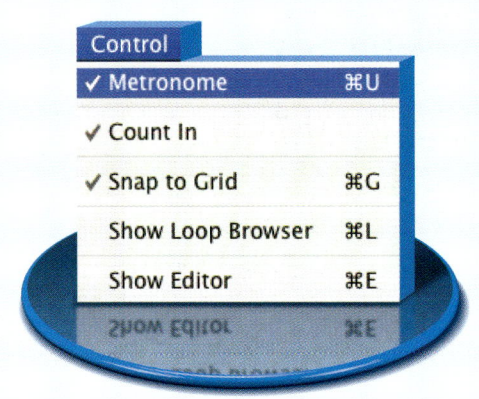

TEACH YOURSELF

How can I give myself a couple of seconds to get ready before the recording starts?

Click **Control**, and then **Count In**. When you start a recording, you get a delay of one set of beats before the recording starts. For example, you get a four-beat delay if your song is in 4/4 time. If you have turned on the metronome, it begins ticking immediately so you can count along with it as you prepare to play.

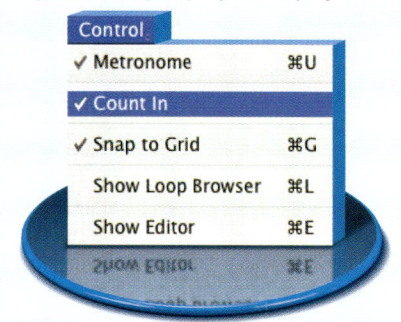

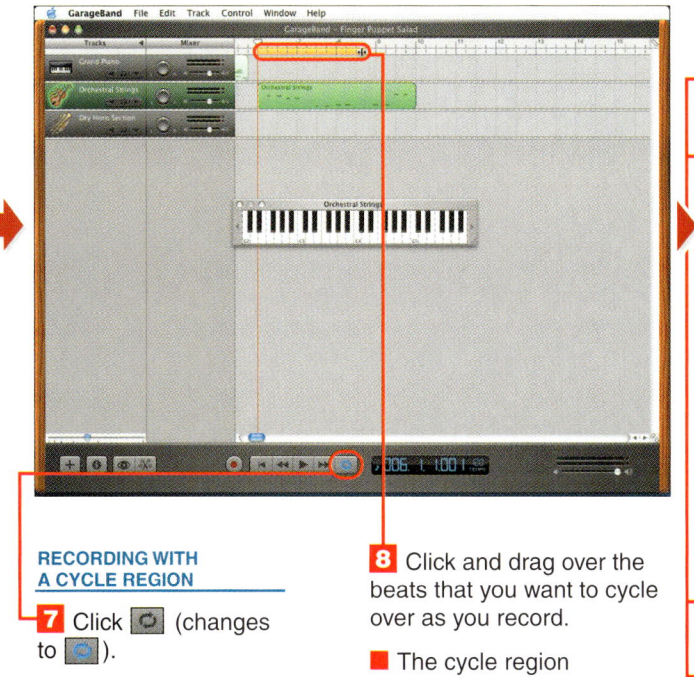

RECORDING WITH A CYCLE REGION

7 Click ⊙ (changes to ⊙).

■ The cycle region strip appears below the beat ruler.

8 Click and drag over the beats that you want to cycle over as you record.

■ The cycle region highlights.

9 Type R.

Note: R is the keyboard shortcut for recording.

■ The recording begins.

10 Click the keys on the on-screen keyboard.

■ The notes appear in the track.

■ When ▽ reaches the end of the cycle region, it jumps back to the region's beginning and the recording continues.

11 Press Spacebar (⊙ changes to ⊙).

■ The ▽ stops and the recording ends.

317

EDIT A SOFTWARE LOOP'S NOTES

You do not have to be a perfect performer when you record a software loop with GarageBand. You can easily change any badly played notes to make them sound perfect and add any notes you missed playing.

This section requires a software instrument track containing a software loop. See Chapter 15 for more on creating a software instrument track or to add a loop.

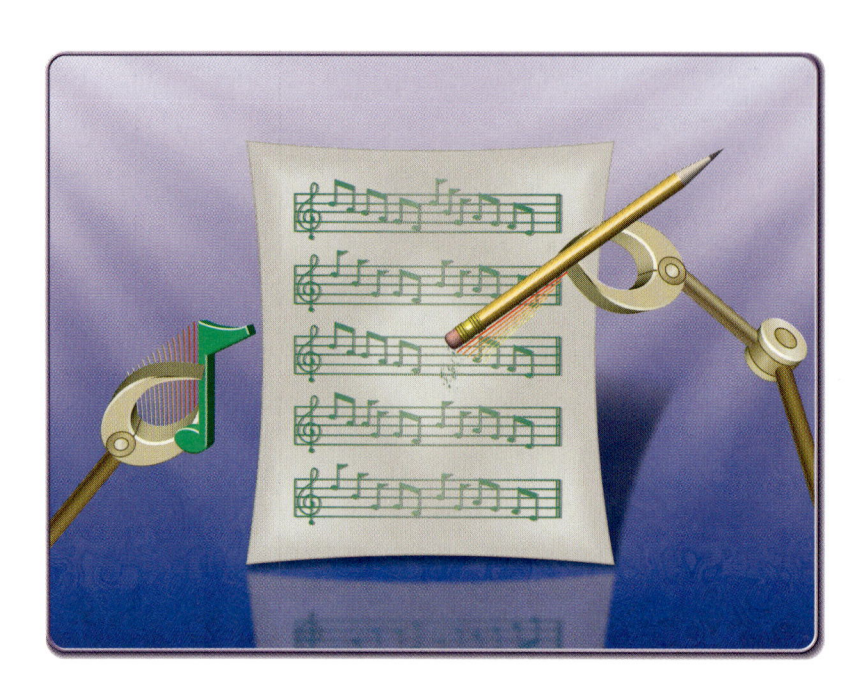

EDIT A SOFTWARE LOOP'S NOTES

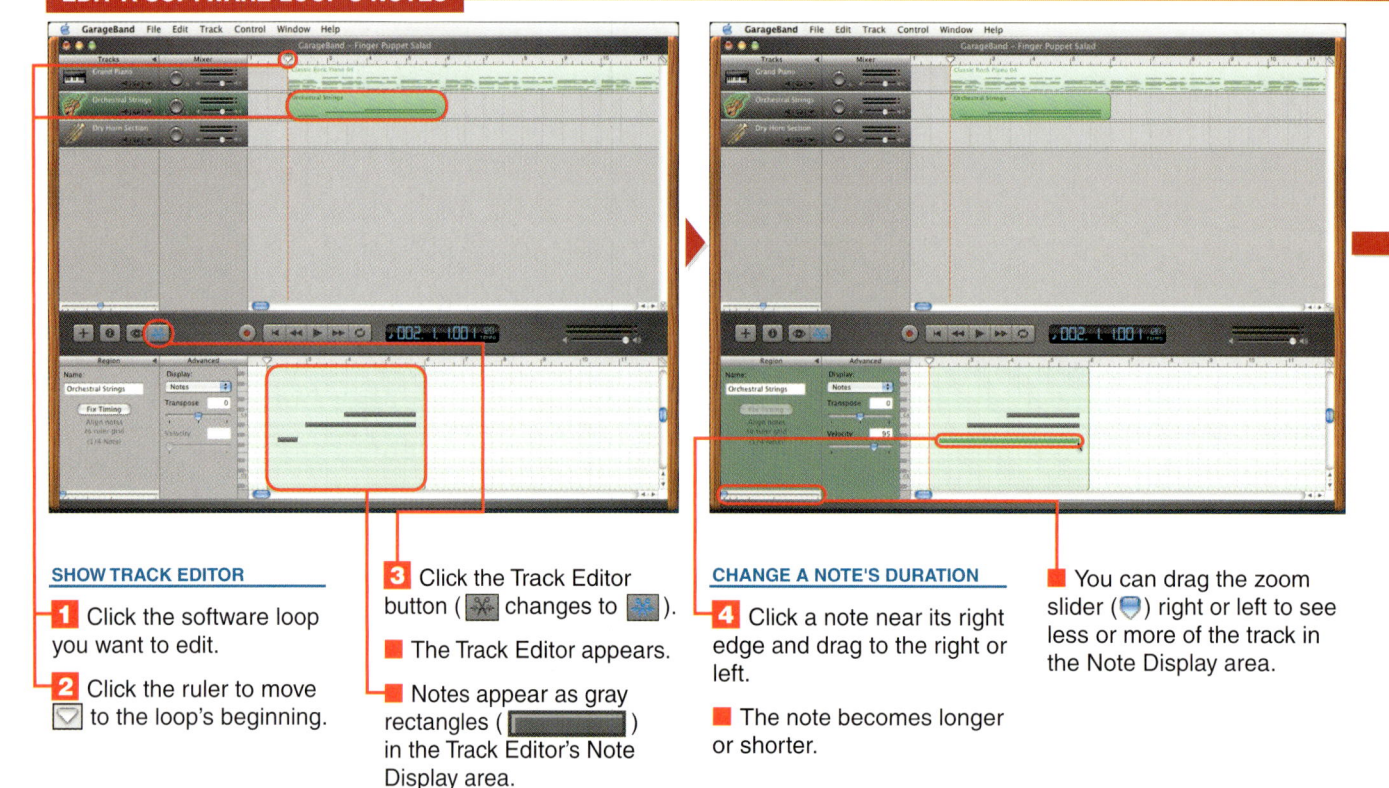

SHOW TRACK EDITOR

1 Click the software loop you want to edit.

2 Click the ruler to move to the loop's beginning.

3 Click the Track Editor button (✂ changes to ✂).

■ The Track Editor appears.

■ Notes appear as gray rectangles (▭) in the Track Editor's Note Display area.

CHANGE A NOTE'S DURATION

4 Click a note near its right edge and drag to the right or left.

■ The note becomes longer or shorter.

■ You can drag the zoom slider (⬤) right or left to see less or more of the track in the Note Display area.

318

16 Make Music with GarageBand

WORKING WITH GARAGEBAND

Why do some notes appear darker or lighter than others?

The darker notes indicate that GarageBand will play them more loudly than the lighter notes. You can control a note's loudness with the Velocity slider or by typing a number into the Velocity field — both of which you find in the Track Editor. Higher numbers are louder. The loudness control is called *Velocity* because it corresponds to how quickly and, hence, how forcefully a MIDI keyboard's keys are pressed when played.

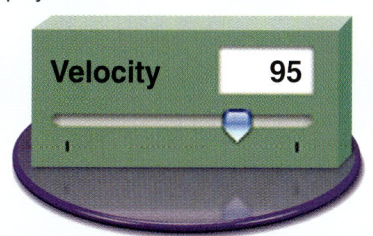

Velocity   95

What does the Transpose control do?

Located in the Track Editor, the Transpose control raises or lowers the pitch of all the notes in a software loop. Each unit represents one musical semitone — the difference between, say, C and C-sharp. For example, you can change a C-major chord — C + E + G — to a D-major chord — D + F-sharp + A — by transposing it two semitones higher. Note that the Transpose control does not affect the visible position of the notes in the Track Editor's Note Display area, just their playback pitch.

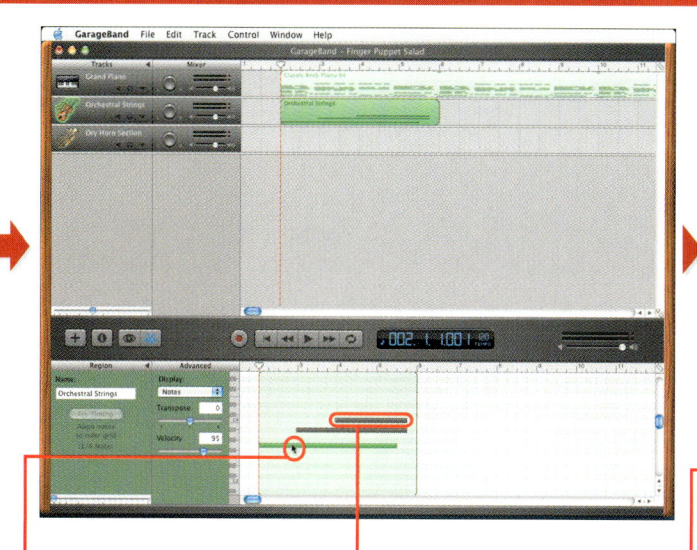

Transpose   0

MOVE OR DELETE A NOTE

5 Click near the middle of a note and drag the mouse.

■ The note moves in the Note Display and you hear the note when you click it.

Note: GarageBand does not play portions of a note that are beyond the edge of the loop region.

■ You can click a note and press Delete to remove it.

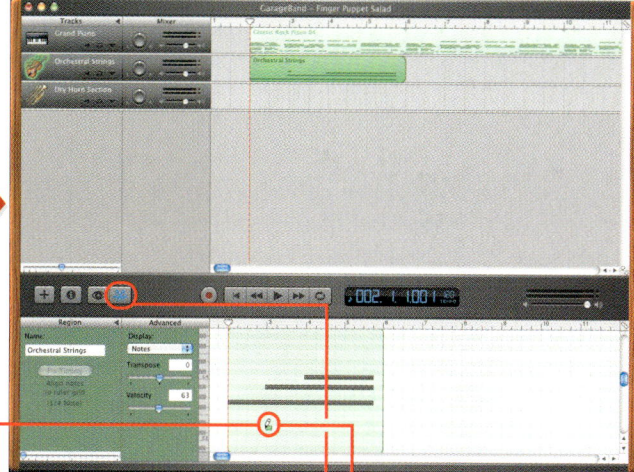

ADD A NOTE

6 Press ⌘ and click in the loop region of the Note Display.

■ A note appears where you clicked.

■ You can click and drag the note to reposition it, or click and drag the note's edge to resize it.

7 Click .

■ The Track Editor closes (changes to).

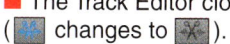

319

ADJUST TRACK VOLUME

You can control the volume of each track and add volume control points to dynamically change the track's volume as it plays.

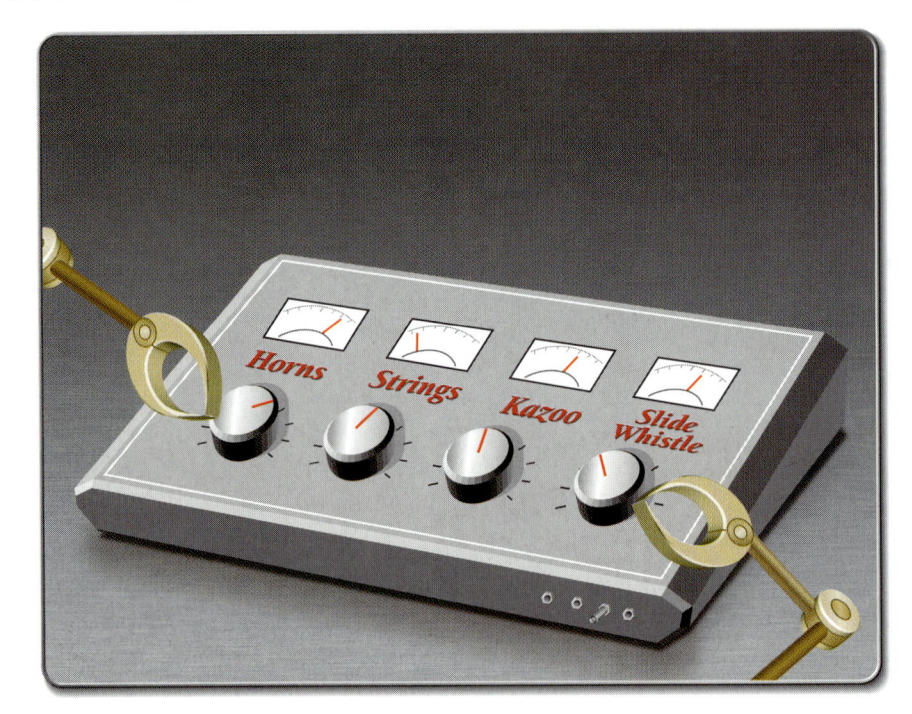

ADJUST TRACK VOLUME

SEE TRACK VOLUME

1 Click the Show Track Volume button ( ) for the track whose volume you want to adjust.

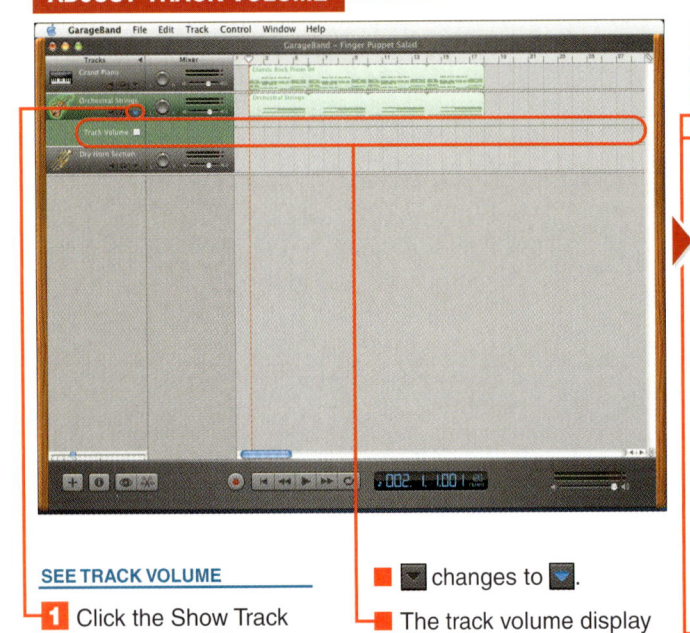

■ changes to .

■ The track volume display appears below the track.

RAISE AND LOWER TRACK VOLUME

2 Click and drag the track's volume control to the left or right.

■ The line indicating the track's volume setting moves down or up.

■ The lower the line, the lower the track's volume; the higher the line, the louder the volume.

320

16 Make Music with GarageBand

WORKING WITH GARAGEBAND

What do the other track volume do?

You can use these controls to isolate the sound of one or more tracks when editing a complex composition. Click the mute button ( ) to mute the track. Click the solo button ( ) to mute all the other tracks. If you click the solo button on several tracks, you hear only those tracks.

How can I adjust a track's stereo setting?

You can control how much of the track's sound comes from the left speaker and how much from the right by using the pan wheel control. Click the wheel and drag up to move the track's sound output to the right channel; drag down to move it to the left channel. As you drag, the white line on the wheel moves to show the current stereo setting.

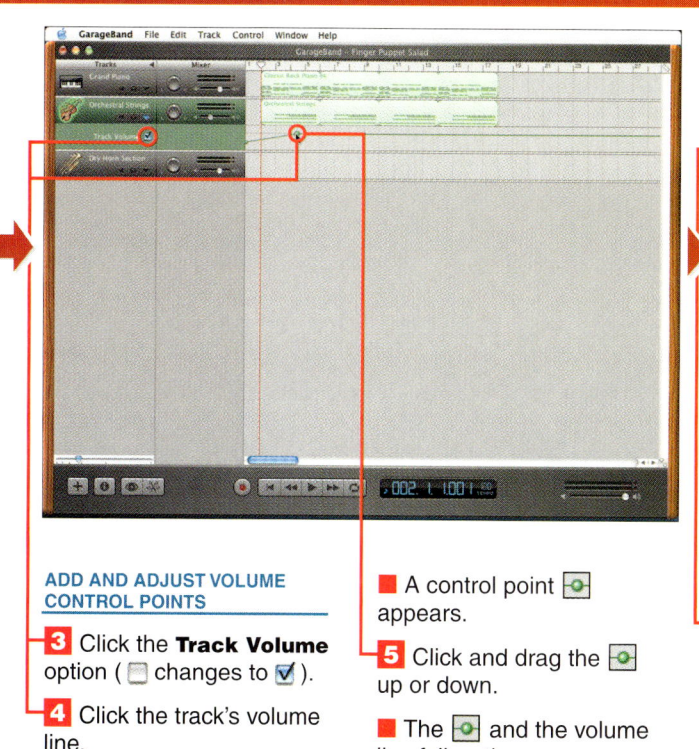

ADD AND ADJUST VOLUME CONTROL POINTS

3 Click the **Track Volume** option (changes to).

4 Click the track's volume line.

■ A control point appears.

5 Click and drag the up or down.

■ The and the volume line follow the mouse.

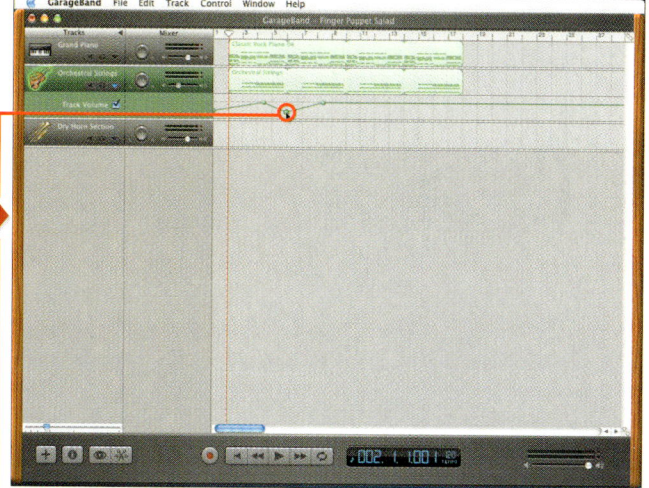

DELETE CONTROL POINTS

6 Click a control point.

■ The selected control point highlights.

7 Press Delete .

■ The control point vanishes and the volume line reshapes itself.

■ When you play a track with volume control points, the volume moves to show the current track volume.

321

CHANGE A SOFTWARE INSTRUMENT TRACK'S SETTINGS

You can use the Track Info window to change the sound of a software instrument track. You can change various effects, filters, and even the instrument generator itself if, for example, you decide the track's contents sounds better as horns rather than as strings.

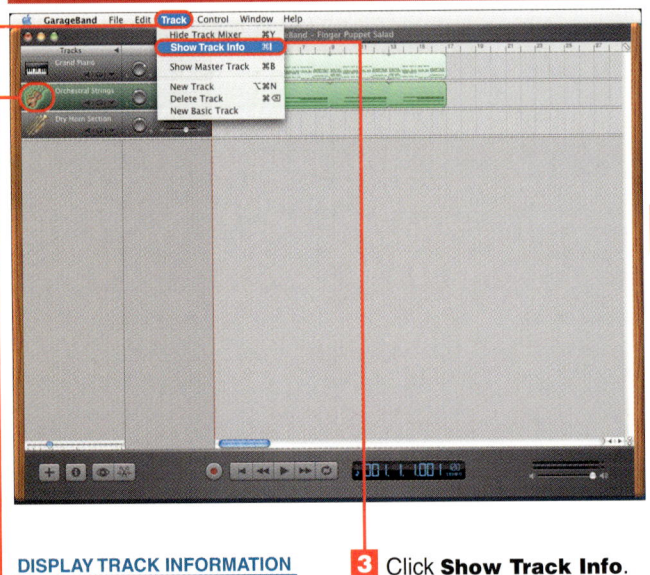

CHANGE A SOFTWARE INSTRUMENT TRACK'S SETTINGS

DISPLAY TRACK INFORMATION

1 Click the track you want to change.

2 Click **Track**.

3 Click **Show Track Info**.

■ The Track Info window for the track appears.

CHANGE SETTING DETAILS

4 Click **Details**.

■ The window expands to show controls.

■ You can click here and select an instrument generator.

■ You can click (☐ changes to ☑) to enable and disable various effects.

■ You can adjust settings for each effect.

■ You can click a details button (✎) to change a complex setting's details.

322

16 Make Music with GarageBand

WORKING WITH GARAGEBAND

Why does the playhead (▽) sometimes change color?

The color changes indicate how hard your Mac is working to produce the sounds you are hearing. The ▽ turns orange when the Mac works rather hard and becomes red when it works as hard as it can. The more notes you play at once, and the more effects and filters you use at a time, the more work the Mac has to do. If ▽ becomes red too often, try reducing the number of tracks or turning off effects.

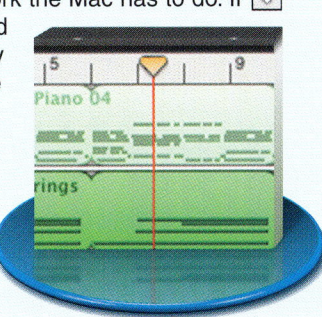

How can I figure out what all the instrument settings do?

You can use the on-screen keyboard with the Track Info window open to experiment with different settings: just press a key on the keyboard after you change a setting to hear how it sounds. Remember, however, that expert musicians created the instrument settings that GarageBand supplies, and you ordinarily do not need to change them very much...but you can if you want to.

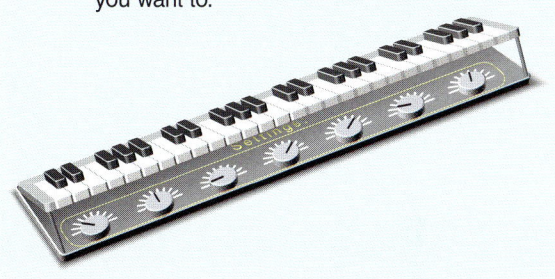

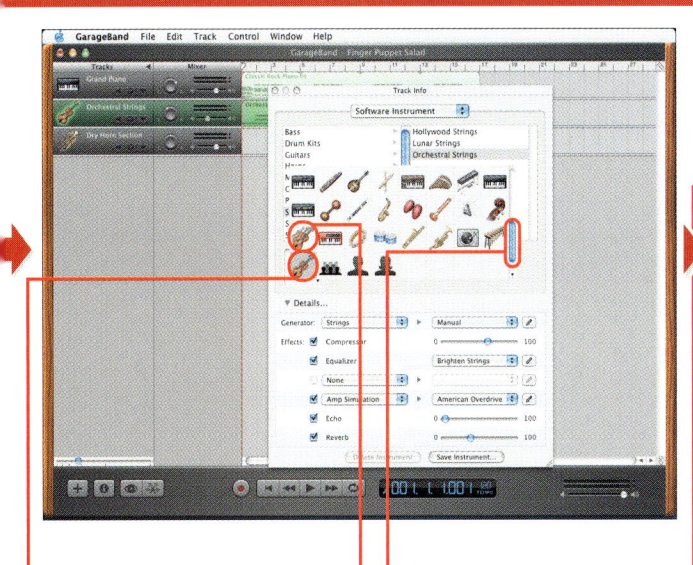

SET THE TRACK'S ICON

5 Click the icon well.

■ A palette of available track icons appears.

■ You can scroll the list to see more icons.

6 Click an icon.

■ The icon palette closes and the icon appears in the track heading.

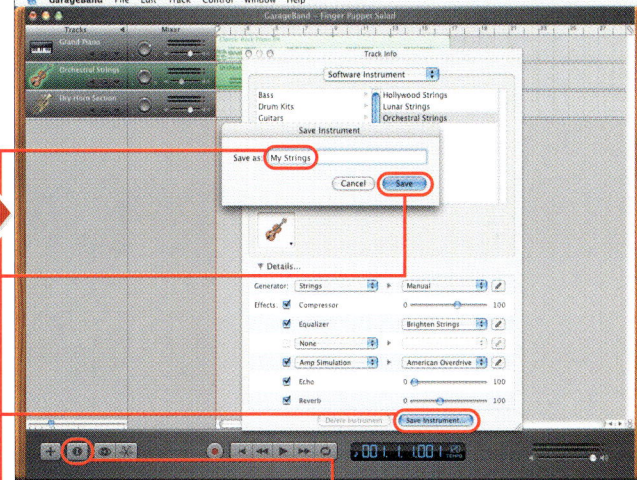

SAVE SETTINGS

7 Click **Save Instrument**.

8 In the Save Instrument dialog, type a new name for the instrument.

9 Click **Save**.

■ GarageBand saves the instrument settings, and the name appears in the Track Info window.

10 Click the Track Info button ( ).

■ The Track Info window closes.

323

RECORD A REAL INSTRUMENT

You can record your own vocals or other instruments, such as an electric guitar, into a real instrument track so that you can mix the recording with the song's other tracks.

This section requires that your song contain a real instrument track. To create a real instrument track, see Chapter 15.

RECORD A REAL INSTRUMENT

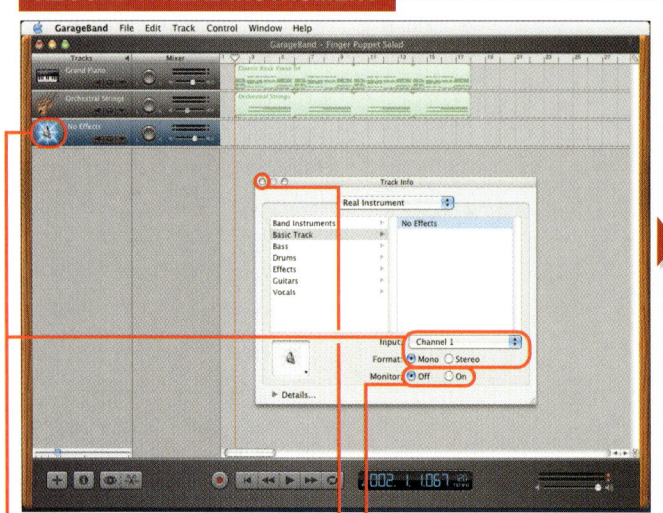

1 Double-click the real instrument track into which you want to record.

■ The Track Info window appears.

■ You can click here to set input options.

■ You can click a monitoring option (○ changes to ●).

Note: Turning monitoring off often eliminates audio feedback noise. For more information on these settings, see Chapter 15.

2 Click ●.

3 Play your instrument or sing into your microphone.

■ The sound level meter changes.

Note: If the meters consistently display red, lower the track's volume to avoid distortion.

■ You can set a cycle region to limit the length of the recording.

Note: See the section "Record a Software Loop" for more information.

324

16 Make Music with GarageBand

WORKING WITH GARAGEBAND

How can I add a recording to a song if I do not have an audio input on my Mac?

You can import any audio AIFF, WAV, or MP3 file into a GarageBand real instrument track. To import an audio file, click and drag it from a Finder window onto the timeline. GarageBand creates a new track and places the recording into it. For more on the Finder window, see Chapter 1.

Why does my recording sound out of sync with the other tracks when I play it back?

The delay is called *latency* and may be caused by several things, such as how fast your Mac is, or what kind of audio input you used. You can usually correct latency-caused timing problems by dragging the recording in the timeline. Note that to make fine-grained timing adjustments, you must click **Control**, and then deselect **Snap to Grid**.

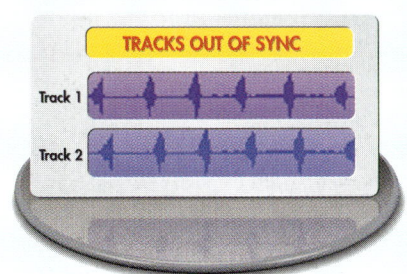

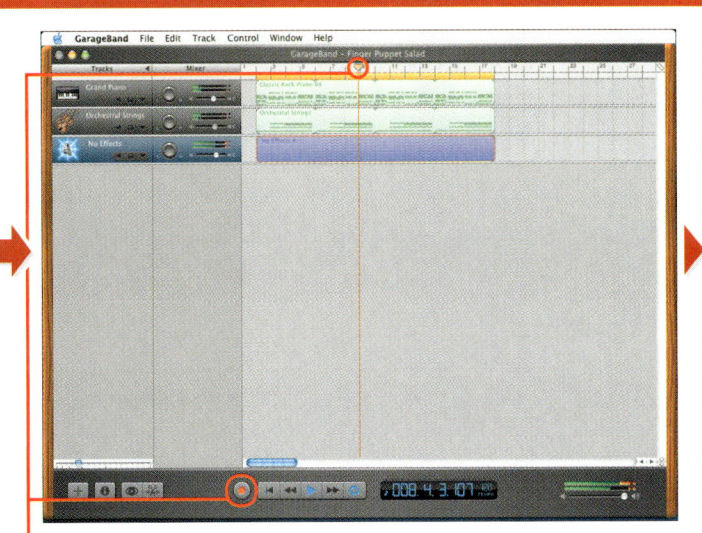

4 Click ⊙ (changes to ⊙).

■ The ▽ moves as GarageBand records your performance.

■ When ▽ reaches the cycle region's end, it moves back to the region's beginning and plays the recording.

Note: If you have no cycle region set, the recording continues until you manually stop it.

5 Press `Spacebar`.

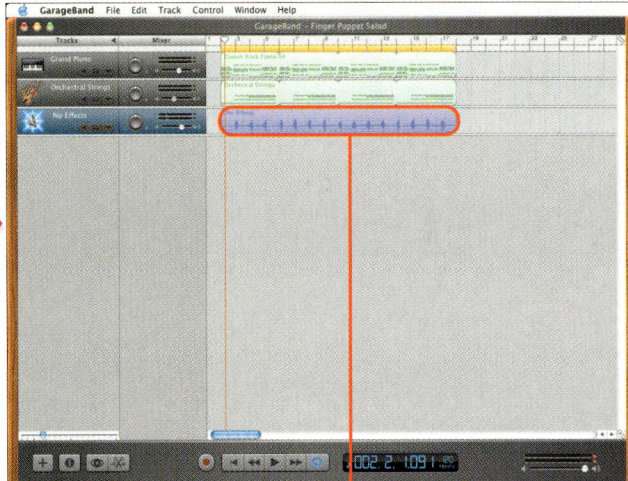

■ The playhead stops moving.

■ A graphic representation of the recording appears in the track.

325

EDIT A REAL INSTRUMENT LOOP

You can edit a real instrument loop with GarageBand's track editor to remove accidental noises or to isolate a particular sound that you want to move elsewhere. You can also transpose GarageBand's built-in real instrument loops to add harmony or dissonance.

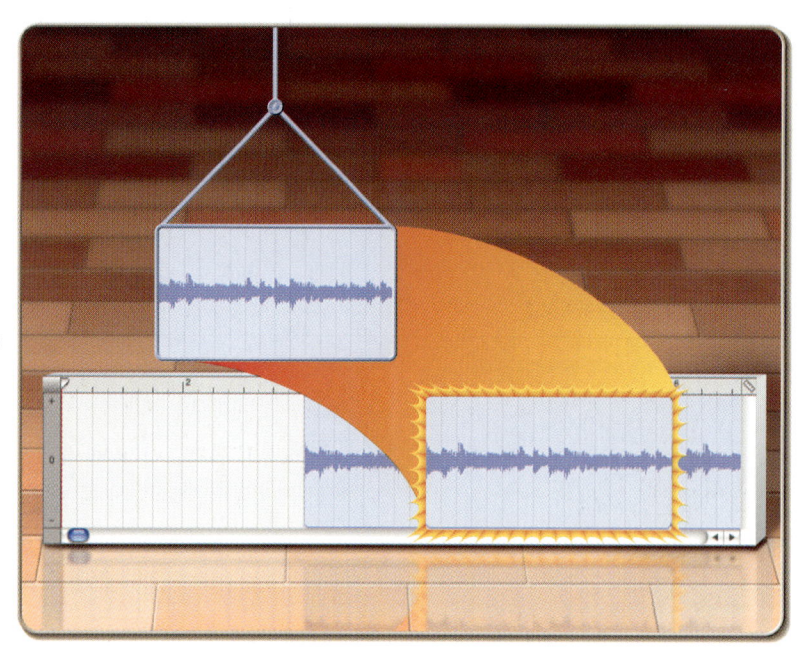

This section requires a real instrument loop containing one of GarageBand's built-in loops. To create a real instrument track or to add a loop, see Chapter 15 for more information. Note that you cannot transpose real instrument audio that you have recorded or imported.

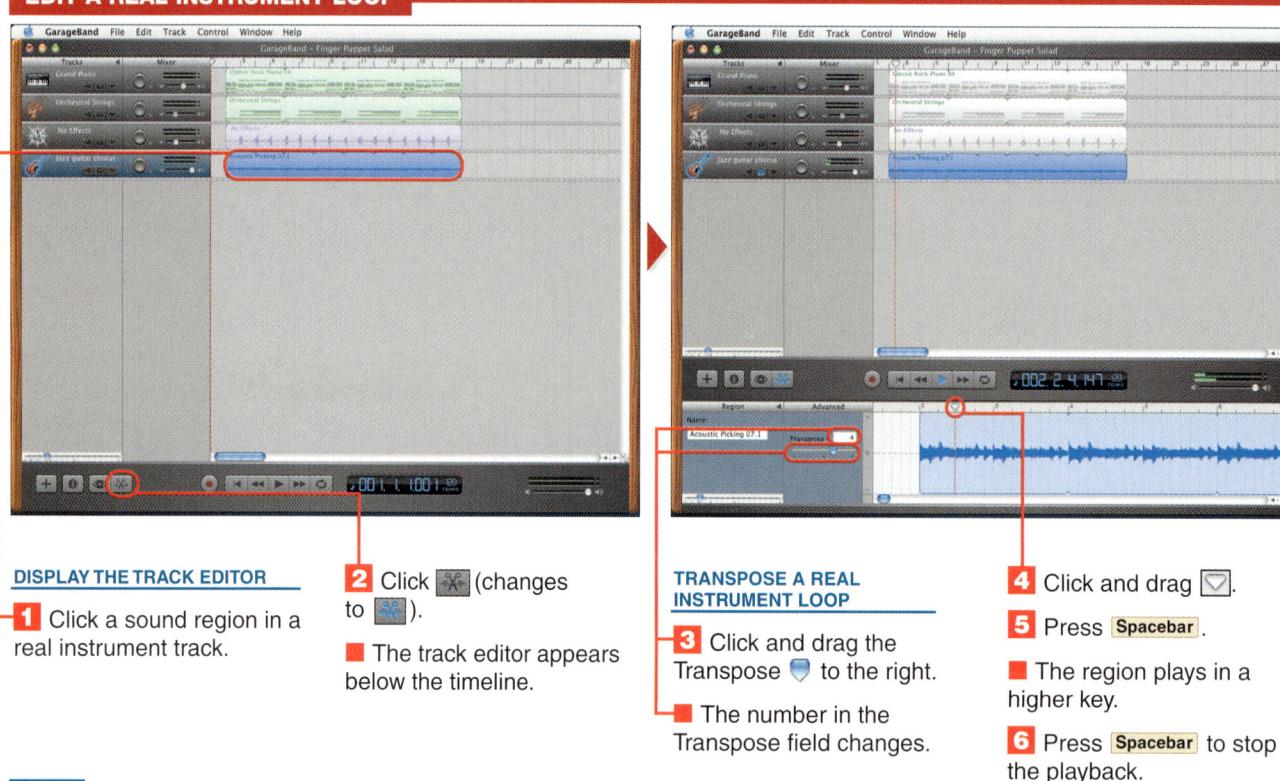

EDIT A REAL INSTRUMENT LOOP

DISPLAY THE TRACK EDITOR

1 Click a sound region in a real instrument track.

2 Click (changes to).

- The track editor appears below the timeline.

TRANSPOSE A REAL INSTRUMENT LOOP

3 Click and drag the Transpose to the right.

- The number in the Transpose field changes.

4 Click and drag .

5 Press Spacebar.

- The region plays in a higher key.

6 Press Spacebar to stop the playback.

16 Make Music with GarageBand

WORKING WITH GARAGEBAND

What happens if I place the playhead over an existing real instrument region and then paste a sound?

The sound you paste replaces the sound beneath the pasted region. You can use this technique, for example, to replace misplayed recorded notes with correctly played ones copied from elsewhere in the recording.

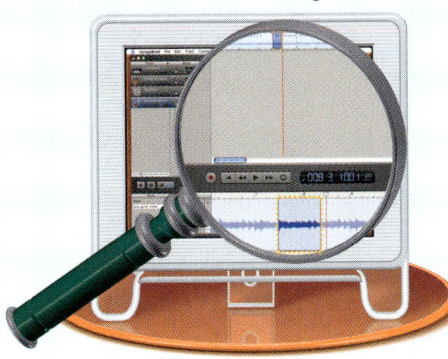

How can I rename a region?

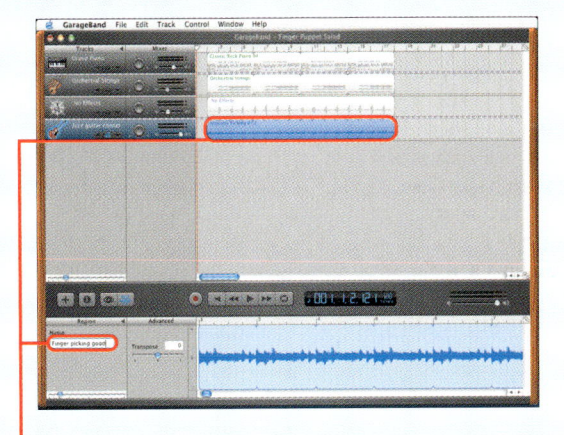

1 Click the region you want to rename in the timeline.

2 Click and type the new name in the Track Editor's Name field.

3 Press `Enter`.

■ GarageBand renames the region.

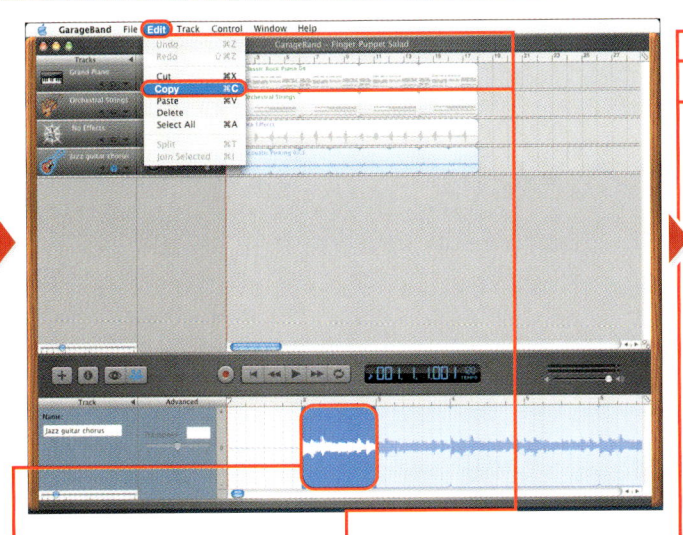

SELECT AND COPY SOUND

7 Move your mouse over the waveform (changes to ⊕).

8 Click and drag to select part of the waveform.

9 Click **Edit**.

10 Click **Copy**.

■ GarageBand copies the selected sound to its clipboard.

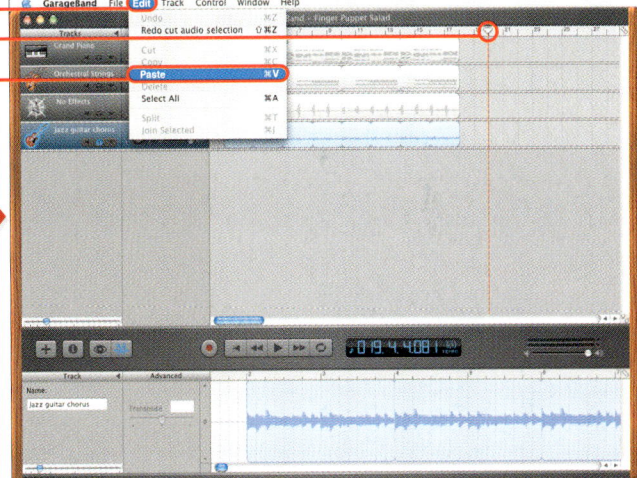

PASTE A COPIED SOUND

11 Position ▽ where you want to paste.

12 Click **Edit**.

13 Click **Paste**.

■ GarageBand pastes the sound at the ▽ position, and ▽ moves to the end of the pasted region.

327

CHANGE A REAL INSTRUMENT TRACK'S SETTINGS

You can change the filters and effects that comprise a real instrument track's settings to make it sound richer or more interesting, and you can save those settings so that you can apply them to other tracks later.

To create a real instrument track, see Chapter 15.

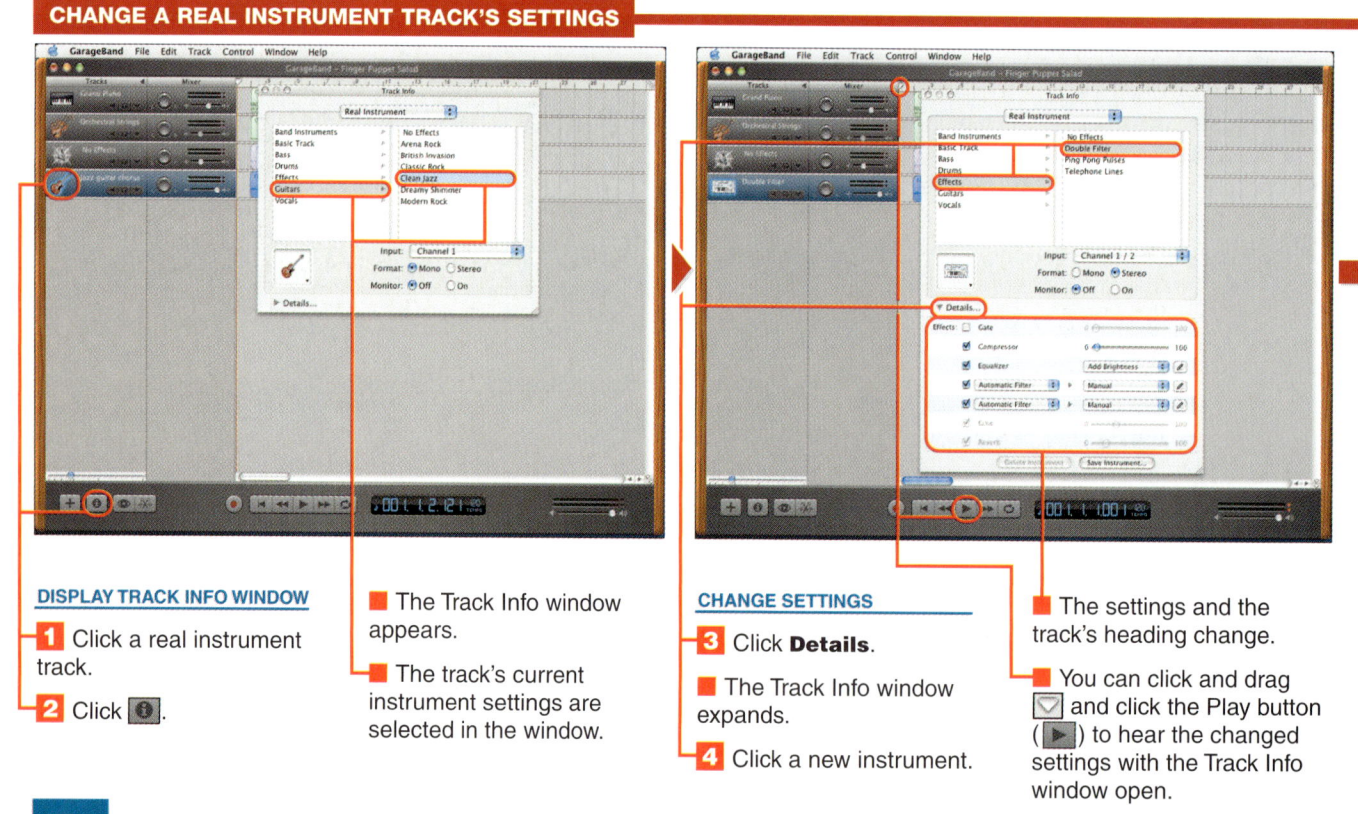

CHANGE A REAL INSTRUMENT TRACK'S SETTINGS

DISPLAY TRACK INFO WINDOW

1 Click a real instrument track.

2 Click ⓘ.

■ The Track Info window appears.

■ The track's current instrument settings are selected in the window.

CHANGE SETTINGS

3 Click **Details**.

■ The Track Info window expands.

4 Click a new instrument.

■ The settings and the track's heading change.

■ You can click and drag ▽ and click the Play button (▶) to hear the changed settings with the Track Info window open.

328

16 Make Music with GarageBand

WORKING WITH GARAGEBAND

How can other users on my Mac use my custom instrument settings?

GarageBand saves your custom instruments, both real and software, in your Mac's main Library folder, so every user on your Mac with access to GarageBand already has access to them.

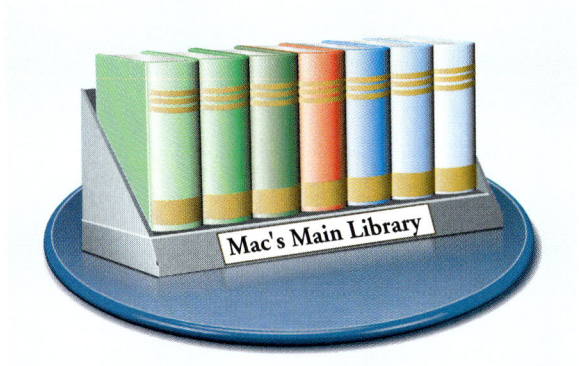

How can I remove a saved instrument?

Select the instrument in the Track Info window and click **Delete Instrument**. GarageBand asks you to confirm the deletion. Tracks that use the deleted instrument remain unaffected, however, because tracks always retain copies of the individual settings that have been assigned to them most recently. Also note that you can only remove instruments you have created.

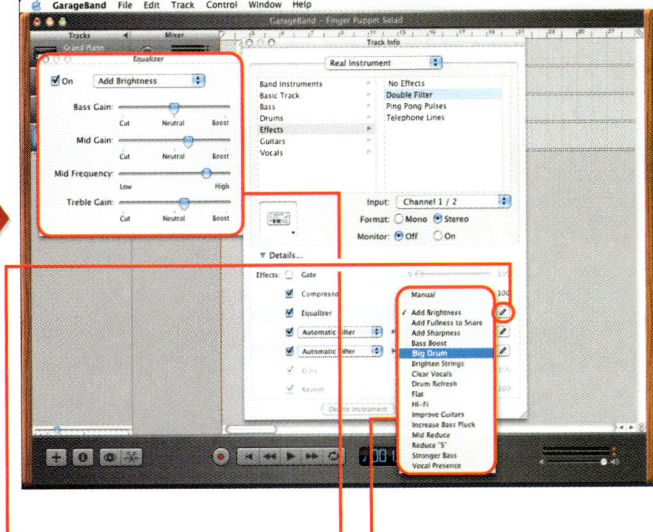

5 Click an effect's or filter's Details button ( ).

6 Click to select from an effect's or filter's menu.

■ The new settings window changes to reflect your choice.

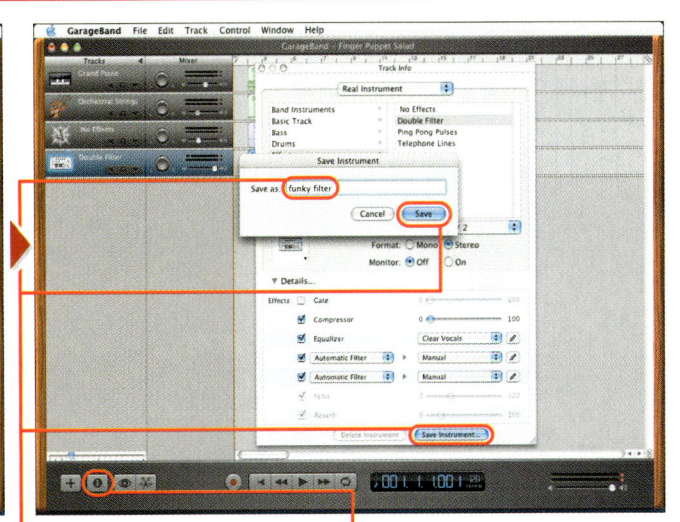

SAVE SETTINGS

7 Click **Save Instrument**.

■ A Save Instrument dialog appears.

8 Type a name for your settings.

9 Click **Save**.

■ GarageBand saves the settings, and the name appears in the Track Info window.

10 Click .

■ The Track Info window closes.

329

EXPORT A SONG TO ITUNES

When you finish composing your song, you can export it into your iTunes music library, from which you can burn it to a CD, share it over your local network, or use it with the other iLife programs. For more on iTunes, see Part II.

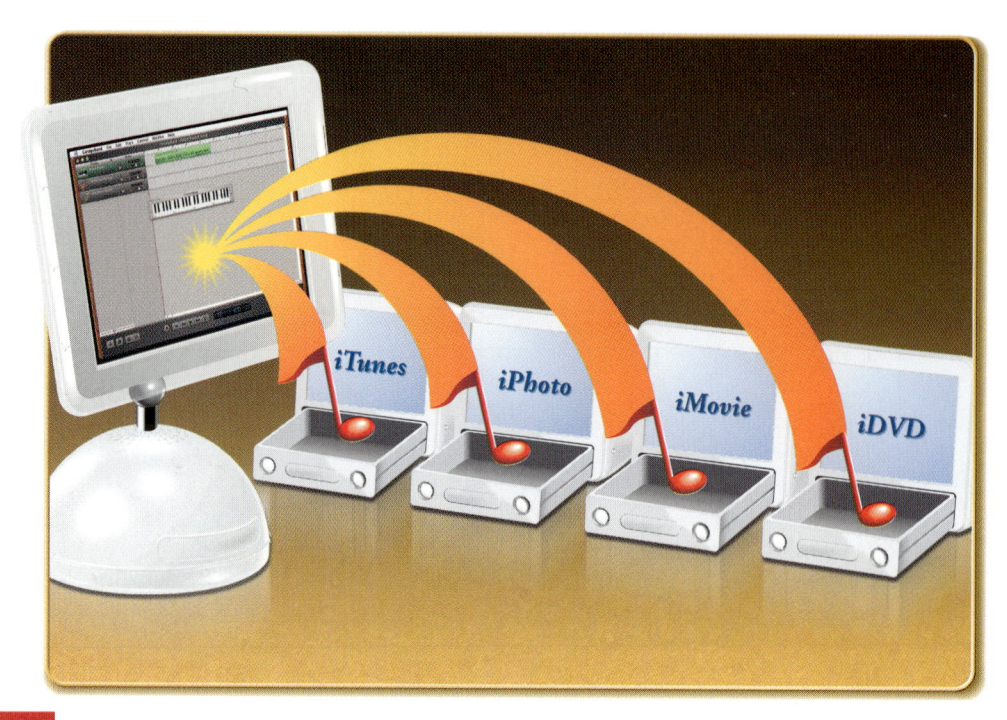

EXPORT A SONG TO ITUNES

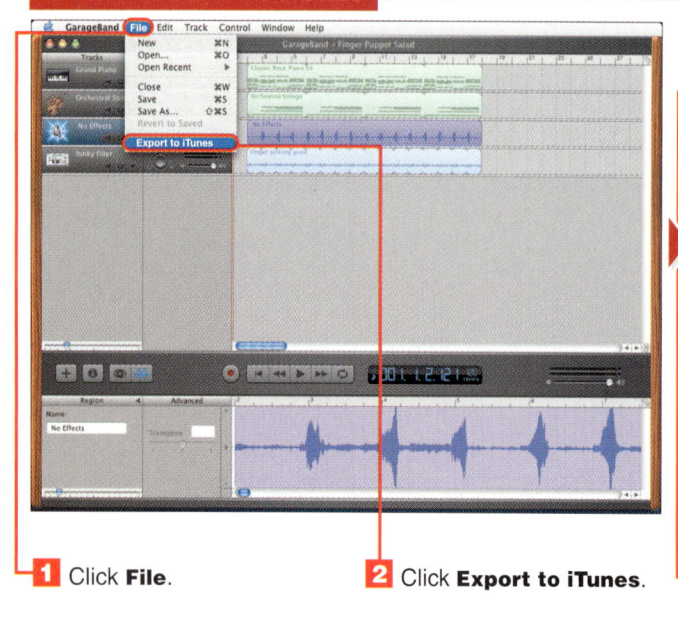

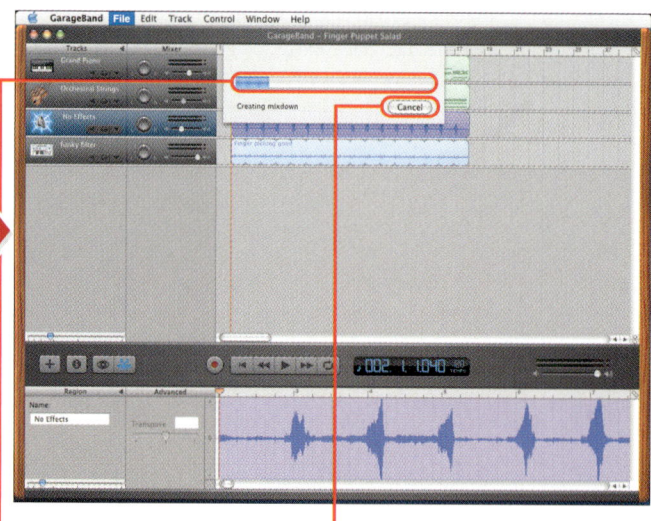

1 Click **File**.

2 Click **Export to iTunes**.

■ A progress sheet descends from the GarageBand window showing you the progress of the export.

■ The ▽ moves along the timeline to show you what part of the song GarageBand is currently exporting.

■ You can click **Cancel** to halt the export.

330

16 Make Music with GarageBand

WORKING WITH GARAGEBAND

TEACH YOURSELF

Why does GarageBand export my songs in AIFF instead of MP3 or AAC?

AIFF files, though larger than MP3 or AAC, retain the highest quality. Also, saving the file as AIFF lets you reimport the song back into GarageBand more easily because GarageBand does not import AAC format files.

TEACH YOURSELF

Why would I want to reimport a song back into GarageBand?

The more tracks in your song, the harder your Mac has to work, and you may find that your Mac is not powerful enough to handle a song with many tracks. You can reduce the number of tracks in a song by exporting the background tracks into iTunes, deleting these separate tracks in GarageBand, and then reimporting the combined track from iTunes. To learn how to record a real instrument and how to import audio, see Chapter 15.

3 Click the iTunes icon ( ) in your Dock.

Note: For more on the Dock, see Chapter 1.

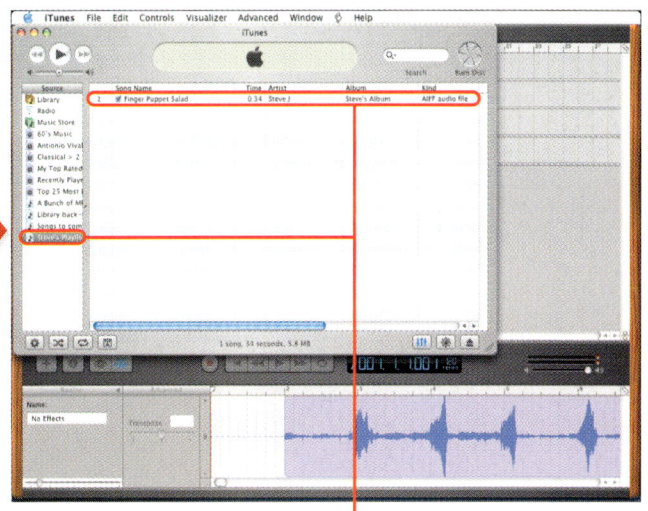

■ The iTunes window appears.

■ A playlist containing your song appears in the Source pane.

331

INDEX

A

Access CDDB display, 28
Advanced menu, 74
advanced Smart Playlists, 56–57
Album panes, 34
albums
    create, 112–113
    tag information, 78–79
    view artwork, 70–71
America Online accounts, 58, 67
Announce Slideshow button, 165
Appearance button, 91
Apple
    ID accounts, 58–59
    .Mac Web page, 160–161
    order prints, 150–151
archive CD or DVD, burn, 53
Artist panes, 34
Artwork button, 70
assemble movies, 11
audio, add to slideshow, 290–291
Audio CD option, 26
audio clips trim, 223

B

background encode, 247
Background Image set, Web pages, 163
background pictures, picture theme, 249
Batch Change command, 101
battery power, import photos, 93
black and color clips, Timeline, 218–219
blend two sounds together, 227
BMP format, 97
bookmarks, 217
borders around photos, 191
Brightness control, 130–131
browse
    library, 6
    loops, 308–309
    music library, 34–35
Browse button, 37
Browse icon, 61
burn
    archive CD or DVD, 53
    DVD, 298–299
    MP3 CD, 52
    standard audio CD, 50–51
Burn Disc icon, 51, 52
Burning icon, 26
Burning Preferences, 26, 50, 53
B&W tool, 125

C

camcorders
    connect, 180–181
    import video from, 182–183
camera images, import, 92–93
Camera mode, 183
cameras, export, 238–239
captions, 156–157
card readers, 94–95
category search, iTunes Music Store, 60

CDDB (CD database), 78
CD-RWs, 51
CDs
    archives, 170–173
    burn, 50–51
    make, 7
    play, 28–29
Changes to Edit view option, 133
chapter markers, 237
chapters for iDVD, 236–237
check
    iDVD project's status, 292
    TV Safe Area, 293
circular control, Transitions Pane, 201
clips
    change speed, 232
    reverse direction, 233
    split, 196
Clips view, 186–187
Column view, Finder window, 19
combine two tracks from same album on CD, 81
compress movies, 241
computers, deauthorize, 66–67
connect camcorder, 180–181
constrain the selection, 121
contrast, adjust, 130–131
Contrast control, 131
Convert ID3 Tags, 77
convert song format, 74–75
copy
    photos from archive, 172–173
    songs to iPod, 86–87
Copy to Play Order, 49
copyrighted material, 53
crop
    movie clips, 194–195
    photos, 122–123, 151
crop marker, 195
Crop tool, 123
cross-cut, 234
Crossfade playback option, 25
custom button image or movie, 268–269
customize iPhoto edit window, 134–135
cutaway edit, 234

D

data files to DVD, add, 296–297
date
    organize albums, 114–115
    organize iPhoto library, 104–105
Deauthorize Computer option, 66
deauthorize computer to play purchased music, 66–67
delete
    photos from iPhoto library, 110–111, 115
    songs from iPod, 87
    transition, 199
descriptions, set photo, 100–101
design photo books, 9
Desktop, Finder windows, 19
desktop photos, 166–167
Disc Format option, 26
disconnect card reader, 95
disk, import video clips from, 184–185
disk space, iMovie, 177
Display slideshow controls, 143

332

documents, Macintosh Dock, 16
drag-and-drop import, iPhoto, 97
Drop Zone theme, 256–259
DVD-Rs, 245
DVD-RWs, 245
DVDs
    archive, 170–173
    burn, 298–299
    slideshows, 146–147

E

editing preferences, 132–133
Edit Smart Album button, 119
Edit Smart Playlist option, 57
Edit view, 120–121, 132–133
Effects button, 204
Effects icon, 25
eject memory cards, 95
e-mail, 138–139
Email button, 138
Empty Trash, 111
Empty Trash dialog window, 197
Enable FireWire disk use option, iPod, 85
encode, 247
encoders, 27
Enhance tool, 124
Equalizer, 68–69
EXIF files, 107
export
    to camera, 238–239
    photos to hard disk, 168–169
    song to iTunes, 330–331
    songs, 15
    video, iMovie, 10
    Web pages, 162–163
Export Song List option, Smart Playlists, 57
Exposure tab, 107
Extract Audio, 220

F

favorites, save modified theme as, 260–261
File Export tab, 168
file formats, iPhoto, 97
file images, import, 96–97
files
    open, 20–21
    save, 20–21
film roll, organize iPhoto library by, 98–99
Film Rolls, 98
Filter audio from camera, 179
Finder windows, 16, 18–19
FireWire, 180–181
Fit button, 133
fonts, modify, 214–215
Free Position option, 271
fuzzy movies, 185

G

GarageBand
    about, 5, 14
    add loops, 14
    change score, 15
    export songs, 15
    mix sound, 15
    record performance, 15
    set up tracks, 14
    setup, 302–305
General Preferences, 24
general search, iTunes Music Store, 60
Genre column, 35
GIF format, 97

H

hard disk, export photos to, 168–169
hide page numbers, 157
High Definition video format, 177
Home directory, Finder windows, 19
HomePage button, 160

I

icon view, Finder windows, 18
icons, Macintosh Dock, 16
iDVD
    about, 5, 12
    add chapters, 236–237
    add movies, 13
    check project status, 292
    create slideshow, 13
    make DVD-ROM, 13
    pick theme, 12
    setup, 244–247
    share favorite, 12
    songs in slideshow, 13
iDVD button, 147
iDVD Slideshow Editor, 285
IEEE 1394, 180
iLife
    about, 3–5
    Macintosh Dock, 16
    obtain, 4
    quit/start, 17
iLink, 180
illegal music, 7
images, import, 92–97
iMovie
    about, 5, 10
    add effects, 11
    arrange clips, 10
    assemble movies, 11
    disk space, 177
    export/import video, 10
    preferences, 177–179
    score movies, 11
    setup, 176–179
    sound effects, 226–227
    use photos in movies, 11
import
    change format, 72–73
    with different encoders, 31
    image files, 113
    images, 92–97
    music, 6
    photos, 8, 93
    songs from CD, 225
    video, 10, 182–183, 184–185
Import Photos window, 96
Import preferences, 26
Importing settings, 26
insert movie clips, 186–187
Internet radio, 40–43

333

INDEX

iPhoto
    about, 5, 8
    account setup, 148–149
    camera drivers, 93
    create movie clips from pictures, 190–191
    delete photos from library, 110–111
    design photo books, 9
    drag-and-drop import, 97
    file formats, 97
    import photos, 8
    Internet connection, 91
    make albums, 8
    order prints, 9
    photo quantity, 91
    retouch photos, 9
    setup, 90–91
iPhoto editing window, 134–135
iPod, 84–87
iSight camera, record, 230–231
iTunes
    about, 4, 6–7, 72
    add audio to movies, 224–225
    setup, 24–27
iTunes Music Store, 58–61, 225
iTunes Preferences window, 44
iTunes Song list, 29
iTunes Status display, 40

J

Join CD Tracks, 81
JPEG format, 97

K

Ken Burns Effect option, 191–193
keyboards, CD playback, 29
keywords, 102–103

L

Last Import, 111
library, browse, 6
Library, Source list, 32
list view, Finder windows, 19
listen to songs, iTunes Music Store, 61
Live update option, Smart Playlists, 55
Lock Page option, 155
loops
    add, 14, 310–311
    browse, 308–309
low-resolution warning, 151

M

.Mac Slides button, 164
.Mac slideshow, 164–165
.Mac Web page, 160–161
Macintosh CDs, 171
Macintosh Dock, 16
Magnifying Glass, 60
Mail Photo dialog window, 138
Map, 280–281
memory cards, camera, 94–95
menu buttons, 265, 266–267, 270–271

menu titles, 262–263
menus, Macintosh Dock, 16
metadata, 71
Metronome, 317
microphones for narration, 229
MIDI (Musical Instrument Digital Interface), 305
mix sound, 15
modem connection, Internet radio, 41
modify
    keywords list, 103
    title font and color, 214–215
    visual effects, 204–205
Motion button, 251
motion menu, 272–273
motion theme, 252–255
movie clips
    arrange, 186–187
    create from iPhoto picture, 190–191
    crop, 194–195
    make from still image, 188
    play, 187
movie menu button, 264
MP3 CD, 52
MPEG-4 AAC format, 72
MPEG-1 format, 185
music CDs, rip, 30–31
music library, 32–37
muxed, 185
My Rating column, Song list, 38–39

N

narration, record, 228–229
network
    share music, 44–45
    share photos, 116–117
New Smart Album button, 119
NTSC, 179

O

on-screen keyboard, 314–315
1-Click shopping, 62–63
Open File dialog, 20
Open Stream, 42
Opens in Edit window option, 133
Options tab, 80
Order Prints button, 148
Organize view, 131
Over Black option, 213

P

page numbers, hide, 157
pages, 154–155
PAL, 179
password, Share my music option, 45
paste over clip at playhead, 234–235
Pause sliders, 209
performance, record, 15
photo books, 152–158
Photo Info window, 107
photo information view, 106–107
photos
    add to slideshow, 282–285
    assign keywords, 102–103

    change photo to black and white, 125
    color enhance, 124
    crop, 122–123
    delete from library, 110–111, 115
    descriptions, 100–101
    e-mail, 138–139
    move around photos, 121
    in movies, 11
    print, 140–141
    quantity, iPhoto, 91
    rate, 103
    retouch photos, 128–129
    rotate, 108–109
    select, 122–123
    share on network, 116–117
    titles, 100–101
pick theme, iDVD, 12
picture theme, 248–249
playhead, 194, 234–235
playlists, rearrange, 48–49
pls files, 43
PNG format, 97
Power Search, 61
Preamp option, 68
preferences, iMovie, 177–179
Preferences window, 24, 52, 64
preview
    DVDs, 294–295
    photo books, 158
print
    photos, 140–141
    song list, 57
purchase music, 62–67

Q

QT Margins checkbox, 213
QuickTime, 144–145, 241
quit iLife applications, 17

R

radio, Internet, 40–41
rate
    organize albums, 114–115
    organize iPhoto library, 104–105
    photos, 103
    songs, 38–39
reaction shot, 234
real instrument
    loop, 326–327
    record, 324–325
    track, 307, 328–329
rearrange
    playlists, 48–49
    toolbar, 135
Rebuffer message window, 41
record
    iSight camera, 230–231
    narration, 228–229
    performance, 15
    real instrument, 324–325
    software loop, 316–317
Red-Eye tool, 126–127
rename video clips, 183
resize line, Macintosh Dock, 16
Restore Clip, 205

retouch photos, 9, 128–129
Retouch tool, 128–129
reverse clip direction, 233
Revert to Original, 123
rip music CD, 30–31
Roll Credits title styles, 211
Rotate buttons, 108–109
rotate photos, 108–109

S

Sample Rate option, 73
Sampler print, 141
save
    files, 20–21
    modified theme as favorite, 260–261
    as QuickTime movie, 144–145
Save File dialog, 21
scene submenu from movie, 278–279
Scroll Block titles, 213
scrub audio, 219
search
    categories, 33
    iTunes Music Store, 60–61
    music library, 32–33
    wildcard, 33
Selected Song panel, 71
selection conditions, Smart Playlists, 55
Sepia tool, 125
Set Up Account, 148
setup
    GarageBand, 302–305
    iDVD, 244–247
    iMovie, 176–179
    iPhoto, 90–91
    iPhoto account, 148–149
    iTunes, 24–27
    tracks, 14
share
    favorite, iDVD, 12
    movies, 240–241
    music over network, 44–45
    photos, 9, 116–117
Share button, 116
Share Error message, 117
Share my music option, 44–45
sheets, 21
shop for music, 7
Shopping Cart option, 64–65
Show audio track waveforms preference, 227
Show Guides option, 156
Show Keywords, 102
Shuffle button, 48
sidebars, 21
sign in, iTunes Music Store, 58
Sign In dialog box, 58
sign out, iTunes Music Store, 59
Sign Out dialog box, 59
single clips, apply transition, 198–199
single titles, add, 206–207
slideshows
    button's image, 289
    create, 142–143
    create slideshow, 13
    duration, 288
    DVDs, 146–147
    .Mac, 164–165
    manually move slides, 143
    save as QuickTime movie, 144–145

335

INDEX

Smart Album, 118–119
Smart Playlist dialog window, 54–55
Smart Playlists, 54–57
smoothness, Visualizer, 83
snap playhead, 219
software instrument track, 306, 322–323
software loop
    edit, 312–313
    notes, 318–319
    record, 316–317
Song list, My Rating column, 38–39
songs
    end times, 80–81
    export songs, 15
    export to iTunes, 330–331
    on iPod, 84–85
    pictures in, 71
    rate, 38–39
    remove from music library, 36–37
    remove from playlist, 47
    in slideshow, 13
    start and end times, 80–81
    tag information, 76–77
sort playlists, 48
Sound Check feature, 25
Sound Enhancer option, 25
sound mix, 15
speed edit programs, 137
Speed slider, 209
split clips, 196
Split Video Clip at Playhead command, 196
start iLife applications, 17
stations, Internet radio, 42–43
Stereo Bit Rate option, 73
still frames, 189
still images, 188
stolen computers, 67
streams, MP3, 43
submenus, 274–277
subtitles, 210–211
System Preferences, 167

T

themes audio, change, 250–251
TIFF format, 97
time code numbers, 195
Timeline
    create black and color clips, 218–219
    separate audio from video, 220–221
    view, 216–217

titles
    albums, 114–115
    color, 214–215
    fonts, 214–215
    organize iPhoto library, 104–105
    set photo titles and descriptions, 100–101
Titles button, 206
tools to toolbar, add, 134
tracks
    combine, 81
    set up, 14
    volume, 320–321
Trans button, 198
transition, 198–201
Transitions Pane, circular control, 201
Transpose control, 319
Trash
    about, 197
    Macintosh Dock, 16
    photos in, 111, 115
TV Safe Area, 293

U

Undo Crop Photo command, 123
update songs on iPod, 84–85
URLs, Internet radio stations, 43
USB cable, 92
user accounts, 67

V

video clips, 183–185
Videocamera button, 238
View Keywords, 102
View Options, 27
visual effects to clips, 202–205
Visualizer, 82–83
volume, adjust, 222–223

W

Web pages export, 162–163
Web sites, Internet radio stations, 43
wildcard searches, 33
Windows CDs, 171

Z

zoom to photos, 121

The newest member of Wiley's popular Visual family brings you 100 shortcuts, tips, and tricks in every book, presented in the award-winning format Visual readers love. In no time, you'll be working smarter.

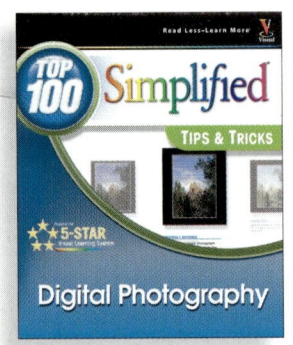

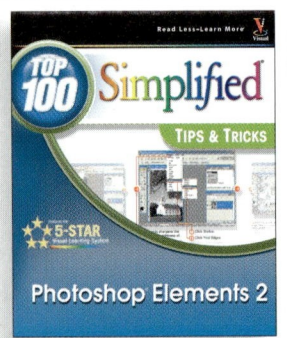

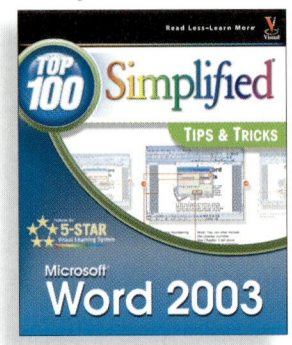

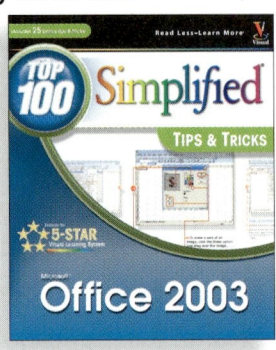

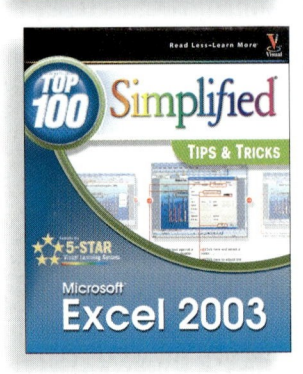

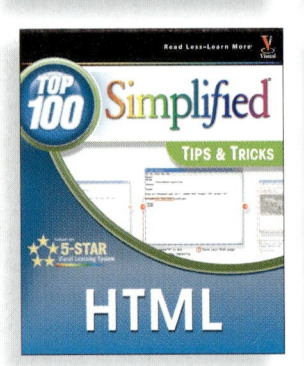

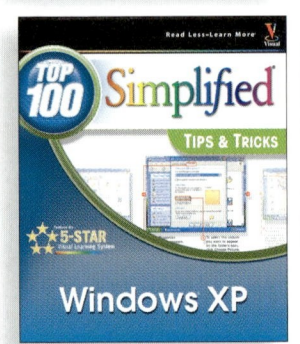

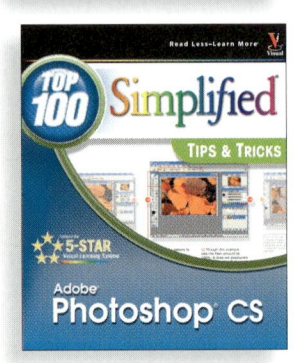

Top 100 Simplified Tips & Tricks titles:
- Digital Photography
- Photoshop Elements 2
- Microsoft Word 2003
- Microsoft Office 2003
- Microsoft Excel 2003
- HTML
- Windows XP
- Adobe Photoshop CS

More tools for visual learners

Just the essentials	Beginning computer skills for novice users	Beginning to intermediate instruction	Deeper coverage plus additional tools	Professional level instruction
Outlook 2002 in an Instant	Computers Simplified 5th Edition	Teach Yourself VISUALLY Windows XP	Master VISUALLY Office XP	Excel Data Analysis

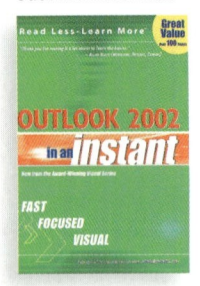

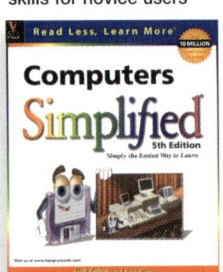

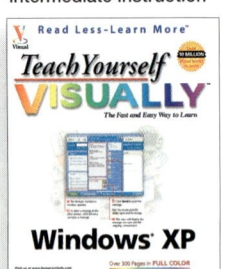

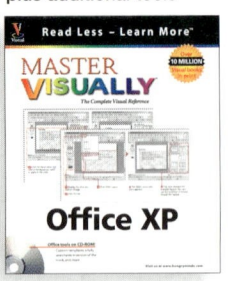

Wiley, the Wiley logo, Read Less-Learn More, Master VISUALLY, Simplified, Teach Yourself VISUALLY, Visual, the Visual logo, Visual Blueprint, and related trade dress are trademarks or registered trademarks of John Wiley & Sons, Inc. and/or its affiliates. Microsoft, Outlook, and Windows XP are trademarks of Microsoft Corporation. Photoshop and Photoshop Elements are trademarks of Adobe Systems, Inc. All other trademarks are the property of their respective owners.

Visit us at wiley.com/compbooks

WILEY
Now you know.